Human Relations
for Career
and Personal Success

SEVENTH EDITION

HUMAN RELATIONS
FOR CAREER
AND PERSONAL SUCCESS

SEVENTH EDITION

 Andrew J. DuBrin
Rochester Institute of Technology

PEARSON
Prentice
Hall

Upper Saddle River, New Jersey 07458

Library of Congress Cataloging-in-Publication Data
DuBrin, Andrew J.
  Human relations for career and personal success / Andrew J. DuBrin.—7th ed.
    p. cm.
  Includes bibliographical references and index.
  ISBN 0-13-119062-8
  1. Success in business. 2. Organizational behavior. 3. Psychology, Industrial. 4.
Interpersonal relations. I. Title.

HF5386.D768 2005
650.1'3—dc22   2004044411

Executive Editor: Elizabeth Sugg
Director of Production and Manufacturing: Bruce Johnson
Editorial Assistant: Cyrenne Bolt de Freitas
Marketing Manager: Leigh Ann Sims
Managing Editor—Production: Mary Carnis
Manufacturing Buyer: Ilene Sanford
Production Liaison: Denise Brown
Full-Service Production and Composition: Carlisle Publishers Services
Design Director: Cheryl Asherman
Senior Design Coordinator: Christopher Weigand
Cover Design: Wanda España
Cover Illustration: Jose Ortega, SIS/Images.com
Cover Printer: Lehigh Press
Printer/Binder: Courier Westford

Pearson Education LTD.   Pearson Education Australia PTY, Limited
Pearson Education Singapore, Pte. Ltd   Pearson Education North Asia Ltd
Pearson Education, Canada, Ltd   Pearson Educación de Mexico, S.A. de C.V.
Pearson Education—Japan   Pearson Education Malaysia, Pte. Ltd

10 9 8 7 6 5 4 3 2
ISBN 0-13-119062-8

To Rosie—and her sparkle
To Clare—and her spirit
To Camila—and her spontaneity

CONTENTS

▲ PART 3: DEVELOPING CAREER THRUST

PREFACE

Welcome to the seventh edition of *Human Relations for Career and Personal Success*. The purpose of this book is to show you how you can become more effective in your work and personal life through knowledge of and skill in human relations. A major theme of this text is that career and personal success are related. Success on the job often enhances personal success, and success in personal life can enhance job success. Dealing effectively with people is an enormous asset in both work and personal life.

One major audience for this book is students who will meet human relations problems on the job and in personal life. The text is designed for human relations courses taught in colleges, career schools, vocational-technical schools, and other postsecondary schools. Another major audience for this book is managerial, professional, and technical workers who are forging ahead in their careers.

▲ ORGANIZATION OF THE BOOK

The text is divided into four parts, reflecting the major issues in human relations. Part 1 covers four aspects of understanding and managing yourself: Chapter 1 focuses on self-understanding and the interrelationship of career and personal success, Chapter 2 explains how to use goal setting and other methods of self-motivation to improve your chances for success, Chapter 3 explains the basics of solving problems and making decisions with an emphasis on creativity, Chapter 4 deals with achieving wellness and managing stress, and Chapter 5 focuses on dealing with personal problems such as substance abuse, counterproductive habits, and other forms of self-defeating behavior.

Part 2 examines the heart of human relations—dealing effectively with other people. The topics in Chapters 6 through 9 are, respectively, communicating with people; handling conflict with others and being assertive; getting along with your manager, coworkers, and customers; and developing competency in working with people from other cultures.

Part 3 provides information to help career-minded people capitalize on their education, experiences, talents, and ambitions. The topics of Chapters 10 through 13 are choosing a career and developing a portfolio career, finding a suitable job, developing good work habits, and getting ahead in your career. Chapter 14 is about the related topics of developing self-confidence and becoming a leader.

Part 4 is divided into two chapters. Chapter 15 offers realistic advice on managing personal finances. Chapter 16 describes how to enhance social and family life, including how to find happiness and new friends and how to keep a personal relationship vibrant.

Human Relations for Career and Personal Success is both a text and a workbook of experiential exercises, including role plays and self-assessment quizzes. (An experiential exercise allows for learning by doing, along with guided instruction.) Each chapter contains one or more exercises and ends with a human relations case problem. All the experiential exercises can be completed during a class session. In addition, they emphasize human interaction and thinking and minimize paperwork.

▲ CHANGES IN THE SEVENTH EDITION

The seventh edition reflects an updating and selective pruning and/or expansion of concepts of previous editions. The text continues the Internet emphasis of the sixth edition, with each chapter containing an Internet Skill-Building Exercise and a Web Corner. Also, references to Web sites are mentioned throughout the text. Several more complex cases have been added, and many self-assessment exercises have been revised and many new ones added. Over 75 percent of the chapter openers, cases, and examples are new.

Chapter 1 now includes two self-evaluation traps of underestimating and overestimating our capabilities. Chapter 2 has a boxed insert about how a worker used goal setting to finally enter his dream career. Chapter 3 contains a completely revamped presentation of problem-solving styles based on the Myers-Briggs typology and also introduces *mindstorming*, a variation of brainstorming that asks questions in order to solve problems. Chapter 4 includes a table describing 10 foods that help prevent serious ailments. Chapter 5 adds information about generalized anxiety disorders and meditation as a method of stress reduction, reflecting renewed interest in these two topics.

Chapter 6 adds the topic of personal communication style. Chapter 7 now includes a table describing how accurately workers are able to identify acts of sexual harassment, the grievance procedure for resolving job conflicts, and the jury of peers for resolving job conflicts. Chapter 8 adds a description of developing a customer service orientation and service-oriented organizational citizenship behaviors. Chapter 9 now includes work orientation versus leisure orientation as a cultural value, religious values in the workplace, bicultural identities of many workers, *microinequities* (small slights) in cross-cultural relation, and role playing to forecast demands in negotiating. Chapter 10 has new information about the fastest-growing occupations through 2010 and different concepts, or models, of a career. Chapter 11 adds *extreme job hunting*—highly creative and complex methods of attracting a prospective employer.

Chapter 12 now contains information about the *inner game of work*—removing obstacles to performance, such as self-criticism. Chapter 13 includes an exhibit on networking suggestions. Chapter 14 expands on the importance of trustworthiness for leadership and adds a table of character attributes for leaders and crisis management for leaders. Chapter 15 adds the role of aversion to risk in financial investments and supplemental retirement annuities as investments. Chapter 16 now includes leading a meaningful life as a key to happiness; speed dating for finding romance, and the contribution of occasional acquiescence to resolving conflict within relationships.

▲ INSTRUCTOR'S MANUAL AND TEST BANK

The instructor's manual for this text contains 800 test questions, chapter outlines and lecture notes, answers to discussion questions and case problems, and comments about the exercises. Computerized test banks, known as the Prentice Hall Test Generator, also accompany the text. In addition, the manual includes step-by-step instruction for the use of Computer-Assisted Scenario Analysis (CASA).

CASA is a user-friendly way of using any word processing program with any computer to assist in analyzing cases. The student enters an existing case into the computer and then analyzes it by answering the case questions in the text. Next, the student makes up a new scenario or adds a new twist to the case and enters this scenario in **bold** into the case. The case questions are reanalyzed in light of this new scenario. Any changes in the answers are **printed in bold.** CASA gives the student experience in a creative application of word processing. Equally important, it helps students develop a "what-if" point of view in solving human relations problems.

▲ ONLINE AND INTERACTIVE COURSE SUPPORT

Please visit www.prenhall.com/business_studies for classroom support and distance learning materials. Students will benefit from extra practice with automatic self-assessment by accessing the free Companion Website. The book can also be packaged with the Prentice Hall Self-Assessment Library which gives students insight into their personal and professional strengths and weaknesses. Instructors can manage distance learning courses using the Blackboard course specifically developed for this text. Videos from JWA Videos are available to new adopters upon request. The JWA scenarios encourage student participation.

▲ ACKNOWLEDGMENTS

A book of this nature cannot be written and published without the co-operation of many people. My outside reviewers of this and the previous editions provided many constructive suggestions for improving the book. By name they are:

Mary D. Aun, DeVry Technical Institute

Donna Ana Branch and H. Ralph Todd, Jr., American River College

Hollis Chaleau Brown, Oakton Community College

Sheri Bryant, DeKalb Technical Institute

Win Chesney, St. Louis Community College

Joy Colwell, Purdue University

Ruth Keller, Indiana Vo-Tech College

Robert F. Pearse, Rochester Institute of Technology

Steve Quinn, Olympic College

Bernice Rose, Computer Learning Center

Pamela Simon, Baker College

Thanks also to my family members whose emotional support and encouragement assist my writing: Melanie, Will, Douglas, Gizella, Camila, Drew, Rosie, and Clare.

Andrew J. DuBrin
Rochester, New York

About the Author

An accomplished author, Andrew J. DuBrin, Ph.D., brings to his work years of research experience in human relations and business psychology. His research has been reported in *Entrepreneur, Psychology Today, the Wall Street Journal, Fortune Small Biz,* and over 100 national magazines and local newspapers. An active speaker, Dr. DuBrin has appeared as a guest on over 350 radio and television shows. He has published numerous articles, textbooks, and well-publicized professional books. Dr. DuBrin received his Ph.D. from Michigan State University and is currently teaching leadership, organizational behavior, and career management at the Rochester Institute of Technology.

Human Relations and Yourself

Learning Objectives

After studying the information and doing the exercises in this chapter, you should be able to:

◆ Explain the meaning of human relations

◆ Pinpoint how work and personal life influence each other

◆ Explain how the self-concept influences behavior

◆ Summarize the nature and consequences of self-esteem

◆ Describe how to enhance self-esteem

◆ Recognize the dangers of preoccupation with the self

*A*ngela, a data manager, is a likable person who interacts well with people both on and off the job. She is only 25 years old, while several of the people who report to her are in their 30s. As group member puts it, "Who cares if Angela is young? The woman is a natural leader." Despite Linda's commitment to her job and to a program of studies at night, she has many friends with whom she shares her free time. Her friends include those

who work during the day, those who work at night, and those who are culturally diverse. They are particularly impressed with her smooth and confident manner and her ability to be a good listener at the same time.

The person just described tells us something about the meaning of human relations. Angela is effective with people in both work and personal settings. In the context used here, **human relations** is the art of using systematic knowledge about human behavior to improve personal, job, and career effectiveness. In other words, you can accomplish more in dealing with people in both personal and work life. You can do so by relying on guidelines developed by psychologists, counselors, and other human relations specialists.

This book presents a wide variety of suggestions and guidelines for improving your personal relationships both on and off the job. Most of them are based on systematic knowledge about human behavior. Our main concern, however, will be with the suggestions and guidelines themselves, not the methods by which these ideas were discovered.

▲ HOW WORK AND PERSONAL LIFE INFLUENCE EACH OTHER

Most people reading this book will be doing so to improve their careers. Therefore, the book centers on relationships with people in a job setting. Keep in mind that human relationships in work and personal life have much in common. A study based on a nationwide sample supports the close relationship between job satisfaction and life satisfaction. The study also found that both job satisfaction and life satisfaction influence each other. Life satisfaction significantly influenced job satisfaction, and job satisfaction significantly influenced life satisfaction. The relationship between job and life satisfaction is particularly strong at a given time in a person's life.

However, being satisfied with your job today has a smaller effect on future life satisfaction.[1]

Work and personal life influence each other in a number of specific ways. First, the satisfactions you achieve on the job contribute to your general life satisfactions. Conversely, if you suffer from chronic job dissatisfaction, your life satisfaction will begin to decline. Career disappointments have been shown to cause marital relationships to suffer. Frustrated on the job, many people start feuding with their partners and other family members.

Second, an unsatisfying job can also affect physical health, primarily by creating stress and burnout. Intense job dissatisfaction may even lead to heart disease, ulcers, intestinal disorders, and skin problems. People who have high job satisfaction even tend to live longer than those who suffer from prolonged job dissatisfaction. Finding the right type of job may thus add years to a person's life.

Third, the quality of your relationships with people in work and personal life influence each other. If you experience intense conflict in your family, you might be so upset that you will be unable to form good relationships with coworkers. Conversely, if you have a healthy, rewarding personal life, it will be easier for you to form good relationships on the job. People you meet on the job will find it pleasant to relate to a seemingly positive and untroubled person.

Personal relationships on the job also influence personal relationships off the job. Interacting harmoniously with coworkers can put one in a better mood for dealing with family and friends after hours. Crossing swords with employees and customers during working hours can make it difficult for you to feel comfortable and relaxed with people off the job.

Fourth, certain skills contribute to success in both work and personal life. For example, people who know how to deal effectively with others and get things accomplished on the job can use the same skills to enhance their personal lives. Similarly, people who are effective in dealing with friends and family members and who can organize things are likely to be effective supervisors.

Can you think of any other ways in which success in work and success in personal life are related to each other?

▲ HUMAN RELATIONS BEGINS WITH SELF-UNDERSTANDING

Before you can understand other people very well, you must understand yourself. All readers of this book already know something about themselves. An important starting point in learning more about yourself is self-examination. Suppose that instead of being about human relations, this book were about dancing. The reader would obviously need to know what other dancers do right and wrong. But the basic principles of dancing cannot be fully grasped unless they are seen in relation to your own style of dancing. Watching a videotape of your dancing, for example, would be helpful. You might also ask other people for comments and suggestions about your dance movements.

Similarly, to achieve **self-understanding,** you must gather valid information about yourself. (Self-understanding refers to knowledge about yourself, particularly with respect to mental and emotional aspects.) Every time you read a self-help book, take a personality quiz, or receive an evaluation of your work from a manager or instructor, you are gaining some self-knowledge.

In achieving self-understanding, it is helpful to recognize that the **self** is a complex idea. It generally refers to a person's total being or individuality. A neuroscientist expressed wonder at the experience referred to as the self in these words:

> *It is astonishing that we have a sense of self at all, that we have—that most of us have, that some of us have—come continuity of structure and function that constitutes identity, some stable traits of behavior we call a personality. Fabulous indeed, amazing for certain, that you are you and I am me.*[2]

To help clarify the meaning of the self, a distinction is sometimes made between the self a person projects to the outside world and the inner self. The **public self** is what the person is communicating about himself or herself and what others actually perceive about the person. The **private self** is the actual person you may be.[3] A similar distinction is made between the real self and the ideal self. Many people think of themselves in terms of an ideal version of what they are really like. To avoid making continuous distinctions between the various selves throughout this text, we will use the term *self* to refer to an accurate representation of the individual.

Recent evidence suggests that the self is based on structures within the brain. According to the research of Joseph LeDoux, the self is the sum of the brain's individual components, or subsystems. Each subsystem has its own form of memory, along with its interactions with other subsystems.[4] Two examples of subsystems in the brain would be a center for speech and a center for hearing. The implication to recognize here is that the self could be an entity that is both psychological and biological.

Because an entire chapter is devoted to the self, it does not imply that the other chapters do not deal with the self. Most of this text is geared toward using human relations knowledge for self-development and self-improvement. Throughout the text you will find questionnaires designed to improve insight. The self-knowledge emphasized here deals with psychological (such as personality traits and thinking style) rather than physical characteristics (such as height and blood pressure).

Here we discuss six types of information that contribute to self-understanding, along with potential problems in self-evaluation:

1. General information about human behavior

2. Informal feedback from people

3. Feedback from superiors

4. Feedback from coworkers

5. Feedback from self-examination exercises

6. Insights gathered in psychotherapy and counseling

7. Two self-evaluation traps

GENERAL INFORMATION ABOUT HUMAN BEHAVIOR

As you learn about people in general, you should also be gaining knowledge about yourself. Therefore, most of the information in this text is presented in a form that should be useful to you personally. Whenever general information is presented, it is your responsibility to relate such information to your particular situation. Chapter 7, for example, discusses some causes of conflicts in personal relationships. One such general cause is limited resources; that is, not everyone can have what he or she wants. See how this general principle applies to you. An example involving others is, "That's why I've been so angry with Melissa lately. She was the one given the promotion, while I'm stuck in the same old job."

In relating facts and observations about people in general to yourself, be careful not to misapply the information. Feedback from other people will help you avoid the pitfalls of introspection (looking into yourself).

INFORMAL FEEDBACK FROM PEOPLE

As just implied, **feedback** is information that tells you how well you have performed. You can sometimes obtain feedback from the spontaneous comments of others or by asking them for feedback. An order-fulfillment materials-handling specialist grew one notch in self-confidence when coworkers began to call him "Net Speed." He was given this name because of the rapidity with which he processes orders. His experience illustrates that a valuable source of information for self-understanding is what the significant people in your life think of you. Although feedback of this type might make you feel uncomfortable, when it is consistent, it accurately reflects how others perceive you.

With some ingenuity you can create informal feedback. (In this sense, the term *formal* refers to not being part of a company-sponsored program.) A student enrolled in a human relations course obtained valuable information about himself from a questionnaire he sent to 15 people. His directions were as follows:

> I am hoping that you can help me with one of the most important assignments of my life. I want to obtain a candid picture of how I am seen by others—what they think are my strengths, areas for improvement, good points, and bad points. Any other observations about me as an individual would also be welcome.
>
> Write down your thoughts on the enclosed sheet of paper. The information that you provide me will help me develop a plan for personal improvement that I am writing for a course in human relations. Mail the form back to me in the enclosed envelope. It is not necessary for you to sign the form. If you are not concerned about being anonymous, just send me an e-mail with your comments. My e-mail address is _____.

A few skeptics will argue that friends never give you a true picture of yourself but, rather, say flattering things about you because they value your friendship. Experience has shown, however, that if you emphasize the importance of their opinions, most people will give you a few constructive suggestions. You also have to appear and be sincere. Since not everyone's comments will be helpful, you may have to sample many people.

Feedback from Superiors

Virtually all employers provide employees with formal and/or informal feedback on their performances. A formal method of feedback is called a *performance appraisal*. During a performance appraisal your superior will convey to you what he or she thinks you are doing well and not so well. These observations become a permanent part of your human resources record. Informal feedback occurs when a superior discusses your job performance with you but does not record these observations.

The feedback obtained from superiors in this way can help you learn about yourself. For instance, if two different bosses say that you are a creative problem solver, you might conclude that you are creative. If several bosses told you that you are too impatient with other people, you might conclude that you are impatient.

Feedback from Coworkers

A growing practice in organizations is **peer evaluations,** a system in which coworkers contribute to an evaluation of a person's job performance. Although coworkers under this system do not have total responsibility for evaluating each other, their input is taken seriously. The amount of a worker's salary increase could thus be affected by peer judgments about his or her performance. The results of peer evaluations can also be used as feedback for learning about yourself. Assume that coworkers agree on several of your strengths and needs for improvement. You can conclude that others who work closely with you generally perceive you that way.

Customer service technicians (people who service and repair photocopying machines) at Xerox Corporation use an elaborate system of peer evaluations. A group of peers indicates whether a particular aspect of job performance or behavior is a strength or a **developmental opportunity.** A developmental opportunity is a positive way of stating that a person has a weakness. The five factors rated by peers are shown in Exhibit 1–1. The initials under "Peer Evaluations" are those of the coworkers who are doing the evaluations. The person being rated thus knows who to thank (or kick) for the feedback.

In addition to indicating whether a job factor is a strength or an opportunity, raters can supply comments and developmental suggestions. For example, CJ made the following written comment about Leslie Fantasia: "Missed 50 percent of our work group meetings. Attend work group member training and review our work group meeting ground rules."

Feedback from Self-Assessment Quizzes

Many self-help books, including this one, contain questionnaires that you fill out by yourself, for yourself. The information that you pick up from

---

EXHIBIT 1-1

Peer Evaluation of Customer Service Technician

PERSON EVALUATED: Leslie Fantasia

Skill Categories and Expected Behaviors	*Peer Evaluations for Each Category and Behavior*					
	TR	JP	CK	JT	CJ	ML
Customer Care						
Takes ownership for customer problems	O	S	S	S	S	S
Follows through on customer commitments	S	S	S	S	S	S
Technical Knowledge and Skill						
Engages in continuous learning to update technical skills	O	S	S	S	S	O
Corrects problems on the first visit	O	O	S	S	S	S
Work Group Support						
Actively participates in work group meetings	S	S	S	S	O	S
Backs up other work group members by taking calls in other areas	S	O	O	S	S	S
Minimal absence	S	O	S	S	O	S
Finance Management						
Adhere to work group parts expense process	S	S	S	O	S	S
Pass truck audits	S	S	S	O	S	S

NOTE: S refers to a strength, O refers to developmental opportunity.

these questionnaires often provides valuable clues to your preferences, values, and personal traits. Such self-examination questionnaires should not be confused with the scientifically researched test you might take in a counseling center or guidance department or when applying for a job.

The amount of useful information gained from self-examination questionnaires depends on your candor. Since no outside judge is involved in these self-help quizzes, candor is usually not a problem. An exception is that we all have certain blind spots. Most people, for example, believe that they have considerably above-average skills in dealing with people.

As a starting point in conducting self-examination exercises, do Human Relations Self-Assessment Quiz 1–1. The exercise will help get you into the self-examination mode.

HUMAN RELATIONS SELF-ASSESSMENT QUIZ 1-1

The Written Self-Portrait

A good starting point in acquiring serious self-knowledge is to prepare a written self-portrait in the major life spheres (or aspects). In each of the spheres listed below, describe yourself in about 25 to 50 words. For example, under the social and interpersonal sphere, a person might write, "I'm a little timid on the surface. But those people who get to know me well understand that I'm filled with enthusiasm and joy. My relationships with people last a long time. I'm on excellent terms with all members of my family. And my significant other and I have been together for five years. We are very close emotionally and should be together for a lifetime.

A. Occupational and School: _____

_____

_____

_____

B. Social and Interpersonal: _____

_____

_____

_____

C. Beliefs, Values, and Attitudes: _____

_____

_____

_____

D. Physical Description (body type, appearance, grooming): _____

_____

_____

_____

INSIGHTS GATHERED IN PSYCHOTHERAPY AND COUNSELING

Many people seek self-understanding through discussions with a psychotherapist or other mental health counselor. **Psychotherapy** is a method of overcoming emotional problems through discussion with a mental health professional. However, many people enter into psychotherapy with the primary intention of gaining insight into themselves. A representative area of insight would be for the therapist to help the client detect patterns of self-defeating behavior. For example, some people unconsciously do something to ruin a personal relationship or perform poorly on the job just when things are going well. The therapist might point out this self-defeating pattern of behavior. Self-insight of this kind often—but not always—leads to useful changes in behavior.

TWO SELF-EVALUATION TRAPS

The theme of this section of the chapter is that self-awareness is a positive force in our lives. Yet self-awareness also has two negative extremes or traps. One of these extremes is that focusing on the self can highlight shortcomings the way staring into a mirror can dramatize every blemish and wrinkle on our face. Certain situations predictably force us to engage in self-reflection and become the object of our own attention. When we talk about ourselves, answer self-quizzes, stand before an audience or camera, or watch ourselves on videotape, we become more self-aware and make comparisons to some arbitrary standard of behavior. The comparison often results in negative self-evaluation in comparison to the standard and a decrease in self-esteem as we discover that we fall short of standards.[5] Keeping the self-awareness trap in mind will help you minimize needless underevaluation, thereby benefiting from gathering feedback about yourself.

In contrast to underevaluation, it is also true that many people tend to overestimate their competence, such as thinking we deserve a bigger raise or an A in every course. A particular area in which people overestimate their competence is in the moral domain. Many people suffer from a *"holier than thou"* syndrome. A study with college students, for example, found that they consistently overrated the likelihood that they would act in generous or selfless ways. For example, in one study 84 percent of the students initially predicted that they would cooperate with their partner, but in reality only 61 percent did.[6]

Cultural differences help explain at least some of the differences in underevaluation versus overevaluation. Several studies have shown, for example, that East Asians tend to underestimate their abilities, with an aim toward improving the self and getting along with others. North Americans are more likely to overestimate their abilities and not be so prone to look for areas of self-improvement.[7] As will be discussed further in Chapter 9, cultural differences are stereotypes that apply to the average individual from a culture.

The antidote to the twin self-evaluation traps is to search for honest and objective feedback from others to help you supplement your self-evaluation. Competing against peers, such as in school, sports, and contests on the job (such as a sales contest or creative-suggestion contest) can help you evaluate yourself more realistically.

▲ YOUR SELF-CONCEPT: WHAT *YOU* THINK OF YOU

Another aspect of self-understanding is the **self-concept,** or the way a person thinks about himself or herself in an overall sense. You might also look on the self-concept as what *you* think of you and who you think you are. The self-concept is an important part of personality development, including a person's key self-feelings and self-attitudes.[8] A successful person—one who is achieving his or her goals in work or personal life—usually has a positive self-concept. In contrast, an unsuccessful person often has a negative self-concept. Such differences in self-concept can have a profound influence on your career. If you see yourself as a successful person, you will tend to

MANY PEOPLE HAVE AN ACADEMIC SELF-CONCEPT
AND A NONACADEMIC SELF-CONCEPT

engage in activities that will help you prove yourself right. Similarly, if you have a limited view of yourself, you will tend to engage in activities that prove yourself right. For example, you may often look for convenient ways to prevent yourself from succeeding.

Self-concepts are based largely on what others have said about us. If enough people tell you that you are "terrific," after a while you will have the self-concept of a terrific person. When people tell you that you are not a worthwhile person, after a while your self-concept will become that of a not-worthwhile person. People who say "I'm OK" are expressing a positive self-concept. People who say "I'm not OK" have a negative self-concept.

Another important fact about the self-concept is that it usually has several components. Many people, for example, have an academic self-concept and a nonacademic self-concept.[9] One person might feel proud and confident in a classroom yet quite humble and shaky on the job. Another person might feel unsure and uneasy in the classroom yet proud and confident on the job. Following the same logic, a person's self-concept with respect to personal life may differ from his or her career self-concept.

Given that work life consumes so much of a working adult's time, it becomes a key component of the self-concept. Many people, in fact, establish much of their identity from their occupations. As a researcher on the topic notes, "You are the work you do," and "Work is our calling card to the rest of our world."[10] Next time you are at a social gathering, ask a person, "What do you do?" Most likely, the person will respond in terms of an occupation or a company affiliation. It is a rare person who would respond to your question, "I sleep, I eat, I watch television, I surf the Net, and I talk to friends on my cell phone."

THE SELF-CONCEPT AND SELF-CONFIDENCE

A strong self-concept leads to self-confidence, which has many important implications for job performance. People who are confident in themselves are more effective in leadership and sales positions. Self-confident workers are also more likely to set higher goals for themselves and persist in trying to reach their goals.[11] Self-confidence also contributes heavily to leadership ability. How to build self-confidence will therefore be described in Chapter 14, which deals with becoming a leader.

Why some people develop strong self-concepts and self-confidence while others have weak self-concepts and self-confidence is not entirely known. One contributing factor may be inherited talents and abilities. Assume that a person quickly learns how to perform key tasks in life, such as walking, talking, swimming, running, reading, writing, computing, and driving a car. This person is likely to be more self-confident than a person who struggled to learn these skills.

Another contributing factor to a positive self-concept and self-confidence is lifelong feedback from others (as previously mentioned). If, as a youngster, your parents, siblings, and playmates consistently told you that you were competent, you would probably develop a strong self-concept. However, some people might find you to be conceited.

YOUR BODY IMAGE AS PART OF YOUR SELF-CONCEPT

Our discussion of the self-concept so far has emphasized mental traits and characteristics. Your **body image,** or your perception of your body, also contributes to your self-concept. The current emphasis on physical fitness stems largely from a desire on the part of people to be physically fit and healthy. It is also apparent that being physically fit contributes to a positive self-concept and that being physically unfit can contribute to a negative self-concept. The relationship between the self-concept and physical fitness also works the other way: If your self-concept is positive, it may push you toward physical fitness. Conversely, if you have a negative self-concept, you may allow yourself to become physically unfit.

A distorted body image can result in such severe problems as anorexia nervosa. Anorexic people have such an intense fear of obesity that they undereat to the point of malnutrition and illness. About 5 percent of these people die from their disorder. Having a positive body image is obviously important for personal life. Some people, for example, who are dissatisfied with their bodies will not engage in sports or attend activities where too much of their bodies is revealed. Also, having a positive body image helps you be more confident in making new friends.

A positive body image can also be important on the job. Workers who have a positive body image are likely to feel confident performing jobs that require customer contact, such as sales work. Many firms expect their managers and customer-contact workers to appear physically fit and present a vigorous, healthy appearance. Managers and customer-contact workers with these qualities would generally have positive body images.

GROUP IDENTIFICATION AND THE SELF-CONCEPT

Another important source of the self-concept is the groups people join. According to research by social psychologist Marilynn Brewer, people join small groups to achieve some degree of individuality and identity.[12] People develop much of their self-concepts by comparing their own group to others. The group you identify with becomes part of your psychological self. Joining the group satisfies two conflicting needs. A person wants to retain some individuality, so being a member of a megagroup like students or a General Motors employee does not quite do the job. Yet people also yearn to have some group affiliation. So joining a small group that is distinctive from others is a happy compromise.

The smaller group the person joins becomes part of the self-image and self-concept for many people. A sampling of the groups that could become part of a person's self-concept include athletic teams, church groups, street gangs, motorcycle gangs, a musical band, and an Internet chat room. What group membership do you have that has become part of your self-concept?

▲ THE NATURE AND CONSEQUENCES OF SELF-ESTEEM

Although the various approaches to discussing the self may seem confusing and overlapping, all of them strongly influence your life. A particularly important role is played by **self-esteem,** the experience of feeling competent to cope with the basic challenges in life and of being worthy of happiness.[13] In more general terms, self-esteem refers to a positive overall evaluation of oneself.[14] People with positive self-esteem have a deep-down, inside-the-self feeling of their own worth. Consequently, they develop a positive self-concept. Before reading further, you are invited to measure your current level of self-esteem by doing Human Relations Self-Assessment Quiz 1–2. We look next at the nature of self-esteem and many of its consequences.

HUMAN RELATIONS SELF-ASSESSMENT QUIZ 1-2

The Self-Esteem Checklist

Indicate whether each of the following statements is Mostly True or Mostly False as it applies to you.

	Mostly True	Mostly False
1. I am excited about starting each day.	✓	
2. Most of any progress I have made in my work or school can be attributed to luck.		✓
3. I often ask myself, "Why can't I be more successful?"		✓
4. When my manager or team leader gives me a challenging assignment, I usually dive in with confidence.	✓	

(Continued)

5. I believe that I am working up to my potential.

6. I am able to set limits to what I will do for others without feeling anxious.

7. I regularly make excuses for my mistakes.

8. Negative feedback crushes me.

9. I care very much how much money other people make, especially when they are working in my field.

10. I feel like a failure when I do not achieve my goals.

11. Hard work gives me an emotional lift.

12. When others compliment me, I doubt their sincerity.

13. Complimenting others makes me feel uncomfortable.

14. I find it comfortable to say, "I'm sorry."

15. It is difficult for me to face up to my mistakes.

16. My coworkers think I am not worthy of promotion.

17. People who want to become my friends usually do not have much to offer.

18. If my manager praised me, I would have a difficult time believing it was deserved.

19. I'm just an ordinary person.

20. Having to face change really disturbs me.

Scoring and Interpretation: The answers in the high self-esteem direction are as follows:

1. Mostly True	8. Mostly False	15. Mostly False
2. Mostly False	9. Mostly False	16. Mostly False
3. Mostly False	10. Mostly False	17. Mostly False
4. Mostly True	11. Mostly True	18. Mostly False
5. Mostly True	12. Mostly False	19. Mostly False
6. Mostly True	13. Mostly False	20. Mostly False
7. Mostly False	14. Mostly True	

17–20 You have very high self-esteem. Yet if your score is 20, it could be that you are denying any self-doubts.

11–16 Your self-esteem is in the average range. It would probably be worthwhile for you to implement strategies to boost your self-esteem (described in this chapter) so that you can develop a greater feeling of well-being.

0–10 Your self-esteem needs bolstering. Talk over your feelings about yourself with a trusted friend or with a mental health professional. At the same time, attempt to implement several of the tactics for boosting self-esteem described in this chapter.

THE NATURE OF SELF-ESTEEM

The definition just presented tells a lot about self-esteem, yet there is much more to know about its nature. According to Nathaniel Brandon, self-esteem has two interrelated components: self-efficacy and self-respect.[15] **Self-efficacy** is confidence in your ability to carry out a specific task in contrast to generalized self-confidence. When self-efficacy is high, you believe you have the ability to do what is necessary to complete a task successfully. Being confident that you can perform a particular task well contributes to self-esteem. Hundreds of studies have shown that high self-efficacy improves performance on a variety of tasks. New evidence suggests, however, that on certain puzzle-like tasks developing high self-efficacy can lead to overconfidence and hence to making errors in logic.[16] In this way self-efficacy is like self-confidence. Watch out for feeling so good about your ability that you become careless in your thinking.

Self-respect, the second component of self-esteem, refers to how you think and feel about yourself. Self-respect fits the everyday meaning of self-esteem. Many street beggars are intelligent, able-bodied, and have a good physical appearance. You could argue that their low self-respect enables them to beg. Also, people with low self-respect and self-esteem allow themselves to stay in relationships where they are frequently verbally and physically abused. These abused people have such low self-worth that they think they deserve punishment. Another noteworthy aspect of self-respect is that when we are secure with ourselves (high self-respect), we are less likely to be self-absorbed. As a consequence, we are more likely to focus on the needs of other people.[17]

Part of understanding the nature of self-esteem is to know how it develops. As with the self-concept, self-esteem comes about from a variety of early life experiences. People who were encouraged to feel good about themselves and their accomplishments by family members, friends, and teachers are more likely to enjoy high self-esteem. A widespread explanation of self-esteem development is that compliments, praise, and hugs alone build self-esteem. Yet many developmental psychologists seriously question this perspective. Instead, they believe that self-esteem results from accomplishing worthwhile activities and then feeling proud of these accomplishments. Receiving encouragement, however, can help the person accomplish activities that build self-esteem.

Psychologist Martin Seligman argues that self-esteem is caused by a variety of successes and failures. To develop self-esteem, people need to improve their skills for dealing with the world.[18] Self-esteem therefore comes about by genuine accomplishments, followed by praise and recognition. Heaping undeserved praise and recognition on people may lead to a temporary high, but it does not produce genuine self-esteem. The child develops self-esteem not from being told he or she can score a goal in soccer but from scoring that goal.

THE CONSEQUENCES OF SELF-ESTEEM

One of the major consequences of high self-esteem is good mental health. People with high self-esteem feel good about themselves and have a positive outlook on life. One of the links between good mental health and self-esteem is that high self-esteem helps prevent many situations from being stressful. Few negative comments from others are likely to bother you when your self-esteem is high. A person with low self-esteem might crumble if somebody insulted his or her appearance. A person with high self-esteem might shrug off the insult as simply being the other person's point of view. If faced with an everyday setback, such as losing keys, the high self-esteem person might think, "I have so much going for me, why fall apart over this incident?"

Although people with high self-esteem can readily shrug off undeserved insults, they still profit well from negative feedback. Because they are secure, they can profit from the developmental opportunities suggested by negative feedback. Workers with high self-esteem develop and maintain favorable work attitudes and perform at a high level. These positive consequences take place because such attitudes and behavior are consistent with the personal belief that they are competent individuals. Mary Kay Ash, the legendary founder of a beauty-products company, put it this way: "It never occurred to me I couldn't do it. I always knew that if I worked hard enough, I could." Furthermore, research has shown that high-self-esteem individuals value reaching work goals more than do low-self-esteem individuals.[19]

The combined effect of workers having high self-esteem helps a company prosper. Long-term research by Branden, as well as more recent studies, suggests that self-esteem is a critical source of competitive advantage in an information society. Companies gain the edge when, in addition to having an educated workforce, employees have high self-esteem, as shown by such behaviors as the following:

- Being creative and innovative
- Taking personal responsibility for problems
- A feeling of independence (yet still wanting to work cooperatively with others)
- Trusting one's own capabilities
- Taking the initiative to solve problems[20]

Behaviors such as these help workers cope with the challenge of a rapidly changing workplace where products and ideas become obsolete quickly. Workers with high self-esteem are more likely to be able to cope with new challenges regularly because they are confident they can master their environment.

A major consequence of low self-esteem is poor mental health. People with low self-esteem are often depressed, and many people who appear to have "paranoid personalities" are suffering from low self-esteem. A store manager who continually accused store associates of talking behind his back finally said to a mental health counselor, "Face it, I think I'm almost worthless, so I think people have negative things to say about me."

The consequences of self-esteem are related to its source. People who evaluate their self-worth on how others perceive them and not on their value as human beings often suffer negative mental and physical consequences. In a series of studies, Jennifer Crocker found that college students who based their self-worth on external sources reported more stress, anger, academic problems, and interpersonal conflicts. In addition, these students had higher levels of drug and alcohol use and symptoms of eating disorders. (External sources of self-worth include appearance, approval from others, and grades in school.) Students who based their self-esteem (or self-worth) on internal sources generally received higher grades and were less likely to consume alcohol and drugs or develop eating disorders.[21] (An internal source would be thinking of yourself as a kind and charitable person.)

▲ HOW TO ENHANCE SELF-ESTEEM

Improving self-esteem is a lifelong process because self-esteem is related to the success of your activities and interactions with people. Following are four approaches to enhancing self-esteem that are related to how self-esteem develops.

ATTAIN LEGITIMATE ACCOMPLISHMENTS

To emphasize again, accomplishing worthwhile activities is a major contributor to self-esteem in both children and adults. Social science research suggests this sequence of events: Person establishes a goal → person pursues the goal → person achieves the goal → person develops esteem-like feelings.[22] ☺ The opposite point of view is this sequence: Person develops esteem-like feelings → person establishes a goal → person pursues the goal → person achieves the goal. ☺ Similarly, giving people large trophies for mundane accomplishments is unlikely to raise self-esteem. More likely, the person will see through the transparent attempt to build his or her self-esteem and develop negative feelings about the self. What about you? Would your self-esteem receive a bigger boost by (1) receiving an A in a course in which 10 percent of the class received an A or by (2) receiving an A in a class in which everybody received the same grade?

BE AWARE OF PERSONAL STRENGTHS

Another method of improving your self-esteem is to develop an appreciation of your strengths and accomplishments. Research with over 60 executives has shown that their self-concepts become more positive after one month of practicing this exercise for a few minutes every day.[23] A good starting point is to list your strengths and accomplishments on paper. This list is likely to be more impressive than you expected. The list of strengths and accomplishments requested in the Self-Knowledge Questionnaire presented in Human Relations Self-Assessment Quiz 1–3 can be used for building self-esteem.

You can sometimes develop an appreciation of your strengths by participating in a group exercise designed for such purposes. A group of about seven people meet to form a support group. All group members first spend about 10 minutes answering the question, "What are my three strongest points, attributes, or skills?" After each group member records his or her three strengths, the person discusses them with the other group members.

Each group member then comments on the list. Other group members sometimes add to your list of strengths or reinforce what you have to say. Sometimes you may find disagreement. One member told the group, "I'm handsome, intelligent, reliable, athletic, self-confident, and very moral. I also have a good sense of humor." Another group member retorted, "And I might add that you're unbearably conceited."

HUMAN RELATIONS SELF-ASSESSMENT QUIZ 1-3

The Self-Knowledge Questionnaire

Directions: Complete the following questionnaire for your personal use. You might wish to create a computer file for this document, enabling you to readily edit and update your answers. The answers to these questions will serve as a source document for such purposes as self-understanding, career planning, and résumé preparation.

I. Education

  1. How far have I gone in school? *through f_____*
  2. What is my major field of interest?
  3. Which are, or have been, my best subjects? *Spelling History*
  4. Which are, or have been, my poorest subjects? *math*
  5. Which extracurricular activities have I participated in?
  6. Which ones did I enjoy? Why?

II. Work and Career

  1. What jobs have I held since age 16?
  2. What aspects of these jobs did I enjoy? Why?
  3. What aspects of these jobs did I dislike? Why?
  4. What have been my three biggest job accomplishments?
  5. What compliments did I receive from managers, coworkers, or customers?
  6. What criticisms or suggestions did I receive?
  7. What would be an ideal job for me? (Give the job title and major responsibilities.)

III. Attitudes toward People

  1. What kind of people do I get along with best?
  2. What kind of people do I get along with the least?
  3. How much time do I prefer to be in contact with people versus working alone?
  4. What are my arguments with people mostly about?
  5. What characteristics of a boss would be best for me?

(Continued)

IV. Attitudes toward and Perceptions about Myself

    1. What are my strengths and good points?

    2. What are my areas for improvement or developmental opportunities?

    3. What is the biggest challenge facing me?

    4. What aspects of my life do I enjoy the most?

    5. What aspect of my life do I enjoy the least?

    6. What has been the happiest period of my life? What made it so happy?

    7. What are my key values (the things most important to me)?

    8. What do I do to defeat my own purposes?

V. How People Outside of Work See Me

    1. What is the best compliment a loved one has paid me?

    2. In what ways would any of my loved ones want me to change?

    3. What do my friends like the most about me?

    4. What do my friends like the least about me?

VI. Hobbies, Interests, and Sports

    1. What hobbies, interests, sports, or other pastimes do I pursue?

    2. Which of these do I really get excited about and why?

VII. My Future

    1. What are my plans for further education and training?

    2. What positions would I like to hold or what type of work would I like to perform in the future?

    3. What type of work would I like to be doing at the peak of my career?

    4. What hobbies, interests, and sports would I like to pursue in the future?

    5. What goals and plans do I have relating to friends, family, and marriage or partnership?

Additional Thoughts

1. What topics not covered in this questionnaire would contribute to my self-understanding?

2. To what uses can I put all this information, aside from those mentioned in the directions?

3. How did answering these questions contribute to my self-understanding?

MINIMIZE SETTINGS AND INTERACTIONS THAT DETRACT FROM YOUR FEELINGS OF COMPETENCE

Most of us have situations in work and personal life that make us feel less than our best. If you can minimize exposure to those situations, you will have fewer feelings of incompetence. The problem with feeling incompetent is that it lowers your self-esteem. An office supervisor said she detested company picnics, most of all because she was forced into playing softball. At her own admission, she had less aptitude for athletics than any able-bodied person she knew. In addition, she felt uncomfortable with the small-talk characteristic of picnics. To minimize discomfort the woman attended only those picnics she thought were absolutely necessary. Instead of playing on the softball team, she volunteered to be the equipment manager.

A problem with avoiding all situations in which you feel lowly competent is that it might prevent you from acquiring needed skills. Also, it boosts your self-confidence and self-esteem to become comfortable in a previously uncomfortable situation.

TALK AND SOCIALIZE FREQUENTLY WITH PEOPLE WHO BOOST YOUR SELF-ESTEEM

Psychologist Barbara Ilardie says that the people who can raise your self-esteem are usually those with high self-esteem themselves. They are the people who give honest feedback because they respect others and themselves. Such high-self-esteem individuals should not be confused with yes-people who agree with others just to be liked. The point is that you typically receive more from strong people than weak ones. Weak people will flatter you but will not give you the honest feedback you need to build self-esteem.[24]

Building self-esteem is a major asset in life. Yet, as with self-efficacy, a danger exists in having highly inflated self-esteem. A controversial study conducted in England found that people with high self-esteem might have an unrealistic sense of themselves: "They expect to do well at things, discount failure, and feel beyond reproach." Furthermore, people with exaggerated self-esteem are sometimes intolerant of people who are different from them.[25]

▲ POTENTIAL DISADVANTAGES OF PREOCCUPATION WITH THE SELF

We have emphasized the importance of understanding the self as a starting point in developing good human relations skills. Much of this chapter was also devoted to the importance of developing self-esteem. Despite the soundness of this advice, a person must also guard against becoming too caught up in the self. A study of the self proposes that the modern individual is burdened with a too-weighty self. For many people, the self has too many components, aspiration levels, and hard-to-meet expectations.[26]

Too much attention to the self can lead a person to be self-centered, self-conscious, and uninterested in other people and the outside world. You have met people who include in almost every conversation a statement about their health and whether they feel hot or cold. The same people are likely to inform others when they are fatigued, even when nobody asked.

Preoccupation with the self can lead to unattainable aspirations. As a consequence of not attaining these aspirations, the person develops a negative self-evaluation. According to one theory, these negative self-evaluations prompt the person to escape the self. The path chosen to escape the self is often alcoholism, drug abuse, and craze eating (bulimia).[27] The right balance is to be concerned about yourself, your self-esteem, and your personal growth yet still focus on the world outside of you. Focusing on the outside world can ultimately strengthen the self because you develop skills and interests that will enhance your self-esteem.

▲ HOW STUDYING HUMAN RELATIONS CAN HELP YOU

A person who carefully studies human relations and incorporates its suggestions into his or her work and personal life should derive the five benefits discussed next. Knowledge itself, however, is not a guarantee of success. Because people differ greatly in learning ability, personality, and life circumstances, some will get more out of studying human relations than will others. You may, for example, be getting along well with coworkers or customers so that studying this topic seems unnecessary from your viewpoint. Or you may be so shy at this stage of your life that you are unable to capitalize on some of the suggestions for being assertive with people. You might have to work doubly hard to benefit from studying that topic.

The major benefits from studying human relations are the following:

1. *Acquiring valid information about human behavior.* To feel comfortable with people and to make a favorable impression both on and off the job, you need to understand how people think and act. Studying human relations will provide you with some basic knowledge about interpersonal relationships, such as the meaning of self-esteem, why goals work, and win-win conflict resolution. You will even learn such things as effective methods of dealing with difficult people.

2. *Developing skills in dealing with people.* People who aspire toward high-level positions or an enriched social life need to be able to communicate with others, manage stress, and behave confidently. Relating well to diverse cultural groups is also an asset. Studying information about such topics, coupled with practicing what you learn, should help you develop such interpersonal skills.

3. *Coping with job problems.* Almost everyone who holds a job inevitably runs into human relations problems. Reading about these problems and suggestions for coping with them could save you considerable inner turmoil. Among the job survival skills that you will learn about in the study of human relations are how to deal with difficult people and how to overcome what seems to be an overwhelming workload.

4. *Coping with personal problems.* We all have problems. An important difference between the effective and the ineffective person is that the effective person knows how to manage them. Among the problems studying human relations will help you cope with are self-defeating behavior, finding a job when you're unemployed, overcoming low self-confidence, and working your way out of debt.

5. *Capitalizing on opportunities.* Many readers of this book will some-day spend part of their working time taking advantage of opportunities rather than solving daily problems. Every career-minded person needs a few breakthrough experiences to make life more rewarding. Toward this end, studying human relations gives you ideas for developing your career and becoming a leader.

▲ SUMMARY

Human relations is the art and practice of using systematic knowledge about human behavior to improve personal, job, and career effectiveness.

Work and personal life often influence each other in several ways. A high level of job satisfaction tends to spill over to your personal life. Conversely, an unsatisfactory personal life could lead to negative job attitudes. Another close tie between work and personal life is that your job can affect physical and mental health. Severely negative job conditions may lead to a serious stress disorder, such as heart disease.

The quality of relationships with people in work and personal life influence each other. Also, certain skills (such as the ability to listen) contribute to success in work and personal life. In recognition of the link between work and personal life, many employers conduct work/life programs, including an on-site child care center. A major rationale for these programs is that workers who have their personal lives under control can concentrate better at work. The challenge of balancing work and family demands is particularly intense for employees who are part of a two-wage-earner family.

To be effective in human relationships, you must first understand yourself. Six methods for gaining self-understanding are to (1) acquire general information about human behavior and apply it to yourself, (2) obtain informal feedback from people, (3) obtain feedback from superiors, (4) obtain feedback from coworkers, (5) obtain feedback from self-examination exercises, and (6) gather insights in psychotherapy and counseling. Be aware of the self-evaluation traps of highlighting your shortcomings and unrealistically overevaluting your competence.

An important aspect of self-understanding is the self-concept, or the way a person thinks about himself or herself in an overall sense. The self-concept is based largely on what others have said about us. The work a person performs is an important part of the self-concept. A strong self-concept leads to self-confidence, which is a basic requirement for being successful as a leader or a sales-person.

Natural abilities contribute to a person's self-concept and level of self-confidence. Your body image, or your perception of your body, also contributes to your self-concept. A positive body image can help you in both your work and your personal life because it enhances your self-concept. The relatively small-size groups to which a person belongs (such as a team or club) are other contributors to the self-concept.

Self-esteem refers to feeling competent and being worthy of happiness. People with high self-esteem develop a positive self-concept. Self-esteem has two interrelated components: self-efficacy (a task-related feeling of competence) and self-respect. People with high self-respect are more likely to focus on the needs of others. Self-esteem develops from a variety of early life experiences. People who were encouraged to feel good about themselves and their accomplishments by key people in their lives are more likely to enjoy high self-esteem. Of major significance, self-esteem also results from accomplishing worthwhile activities and then feeling proud of these accomplishments. Praise and recognition for accomplishments also help develop self-esteem.

Good mental health is one of the major consequences of high self-esteem. One of the links between good mental health and self-esteem is that high self-esteem helps prevent many situations from being stressful. Workers with high self-esteem develop and maintain favorable work attitudes and perform at a high level. A company with high-self-esteem workers has a competitive advantage.

A major consequence of low self-esteem is poor mental health. Workers with low self-esteem often develop and maintain unfavorable work attitudes and perform below expectations. A series of studies showed that students who based their self-esteem on internal sources generally received higher grades and were less likely to consume alcohol and drugs or develop eating disorders.

Self-esteem can be enhanced in many ways. Accomplishing worthwhile activities is a major contributor to self-esteem in both children and adults. Developing an appreciation of your strengths and accomplishments is another self-esteem builder. It is also important to minimize settings and interactions that detract from your feelings of competence. In addition, talk and socialize frequently with people who boost your self-esteem. Exaggerated self-esteem can sometimes lead to intolerance of people who are different than you.

Despite the importance of self-understanding, guard against becoming too caught up in the self. Too much attention to the self can lead a person to be self-centered, self-conscious, and uninterested in other people and the outside world. Another problem is that failure to attain aspirations can lead to negative self-evaluation. The negative evaluation may lead to escapist behavior, such as alcoholism.

Major benefits of studying human relations include (1) acquiring information about human behavior, (2) developing people skills, (3) coping with job problems, and (4) capitalizing on opportunities.

Questions and Activities

1. Why do you think good human relations skills are so important for supervisors who direct the work activities of entry-level workers?

2. Give an example from your own experience of how work life influences personal life and vice versa.

3. Of the six sources of information about the self described in this chapter, which one do you think is likely to be the most accurate? Why?

4. How can your self-concept affect your career?

5. How might you improve your self-efficacy for a specific job that you are performing?

6. Having workers with high self-esteem is supposed to give a company a competitive edge. If you were responsible for hiring a few new workers, how would you evaluate a given applicant's level of self-esteem?

7. What would a coworker have to do to convince you that he or she had high self-respect? Low self-respect?

8. A study mentioned in this chapter showed that people with high self-esteem are sometimes intolerant of people quite different from themselves. How would you explain these findings?

9. What can you do this week to elevate your self-esteem?

10. Interview a person whom you perceive to have a successful career. Ask that person to describe how he or she developed high self-esteem. Be prepared to discuss your findings in class.

INTERNET SKILL BUILDER: Learning More about Your Self-Esteem

The Self-Esteem Checklist in this chapter gave you one opportunity to assess your self-esteem. To gain additional insights into your self-esteem, visit www.more-selfesteem.com. Go to "quizzes" under Free Resources and take the self-esteem test. How does your score on this quiz compare to your score on *The Self-Esteem Checklist?* If your level of self-esteem as measured by the two quizzes is quite different (such as high versus low), explain why this discrepancy might occur.

HUMAN RELATIONS CASE PROBLEM

Self-Esteem Building at Pyramid Remanufacturing

Pyramid Remanufacturing opened for business 10 years ago in a cinder block building with four employees. Today Pyramid is housed in an old factory building in a low-rent district. The company has 100 full-time employees and about 50 part-timers. The nature of the company's business is to salvage parts from used or broken equipment sent to them by other companies. One of Pyramid's remanufacturing projects is to salvage the workable parts from single-use cameras and recycle the balance of the plastic parts. Another large company contract is to salvage parts from children's toys that are returned to retailers because they do not function properly. Both contracts also call for making new single-use cameras and toys, incorporating the salvaged parts.

The basic remanufacturing jobs can be learned in several hours. The work is not complex, but it is tedious. For example, a remanufacturing technician would be expected to tear down and salvage and assemble about 100 single-use cameras per day. The jobs pay about twice the minimum wage, and full-time workers receive standard benefits.

Derrick Lockett, the president and founder of Pyramid, believes that his company plays an important role in society. As he explains, "First of all, note that we

(Continued)

are *remanufacturers*. We are helping save the planet. Think of the thousands and thousands of single-use cameras that do not wind up in landfills because of our recycling efforts. The same goes for plastic toys. Consider also that we hire a lot of people who would not be working if it were not for Pyramid. A lot of our employees would be on welfare if they were not working here. We hire a lot of people from the welfare roles. We also hire a lot of troubled teenagers and seniors who can't find employment elsewhere.

"Some of our other employees have a variety of disabilities that make job finding difficult for them. Two of our highest producers are blind. They have a wonderful sense of touch, and they can visualize the parts that have to be separated and assembled. Another source of good employees for us are recently released prisoners."

Lockett was asked if all Pyramid manufacturing employees were performing up to standard. He explained that about one-fourth of the workforce were either working so slowly or doing such sloppy work that they were a poor investment for the company. "Face it," said Lockett, "some of our employees are dragging us down. After a while we have to weed out the workers who just don't earn their salary."

Next, Lockett gave his analysis of why some remanufacturing technicians are unable to perform properly. "Lots of reasons," said Lockett. "Some can't read; some have a poor work ethic; some have attention deficit disorders. But the big problem is that many of the poor performers have such rotten self-esteem. They don't believe in themselves. They think nobody wants them and that they are incapable of being valuable employees."

Lucy Winters, the director of human resources and administration, explained what Pyramid was attempting to do about the self-esteem problem: "You have to realize," she said, "that it's not easy for a company to build the self-esteem of entry-level employees. Derrick and I would both like to save the world, but we can't do everything. But we are taking a few initiatives to build the self-esteem of our employees."

"One approach is that our supervisors give out brightly colored badges, imprinted with the words, 'I'm a real remanufacturer.' The supervisors are supposed to give out the badges when a technician looks to be down in the dumps. We also have a newsletter that features stories about our remanufacturing technicians. Each month we choose somebody to be the 'Remanufacturer of the Month.' Usually it's an employee whose self-esteem appears to be hurting.

"Another approach is more informal. We ask our supervisors to remember to be cheerleaders. They're supposed to lift the spirits of employees who don't think much of themselves by saying things like, 'I know you can do it,' or 'I believe in you.'"

When asked how the self-esteem-building program was working, Winters and Lockett both said it was too early to tell with certainty. Winters did comment, however, "I see a few bright smiles out there among our technicians. And the turnover rate is down about 5 percent. So the program might be working."

Questions

1. What is your evaluation of Lockett's analysis that low self-esteem could hurt the work performance of entry-level remanufacturing technicians?

2. What is your evaluation of the self-esteem building program at Pyramid?

3. What other suggestions can you offer for building the self-esteem of the Pyramid employees who appear to be having a self-esteem problem?

WEB CORNER

Boosting self-esteem: www.innertalk.com

Integrating self-esteem into the fabric of society: www.self-esteem-nase.org

▲ REFERENCES

1. Timothy A. Judge and Schinichiro Watanabe, "Another Look at the Job Satisfaction–Life Satisfaction Relationship," *Journal of Applied Psychology,* December 1993, pp. 939–948.

2. A. R. Damasio, *The Feeling of What Happens: Body and Emotion in the Making of Consciousness* (New York: Harcourt Brace, 1999), p. 144.

3. C. R. Snyder, "So Many Selves," *Contemporary Psychology,* January 1988, p. 77.

4. Etienne Benson, "The Synaptic Self," *Monitor on Psychology,* November 2002, p. 40.

5. Saul Kassin, *Psychology,* 3rd ed. (Upper Saddle River, NJ: Prentice Hall, 2001), p. 74.

6. Research summarized in Tori DeAngelis, "Why We Overestimate Our Competence," *Monitor on Psychology,* February 2003, p. 61.

7. Ibid.

8. Dodge Fernald, *Psychology* (Upper Saddle River, NJ: Prentice Hall, 1997), p. 654.

9. John Hattie, *Self-Concept* (Hillsdale, NJ: Erlbaum, 1992).

10. Al Gini, *My Job, My Self, and the Creation of the Modern Individual* (New York: Routledge, 2000).

11. Marilyn E. Gist, "Self-Efficacy: Implications for Organizational Behavior and Human Resource Management," *Academy of Management Review,* July 1987, pp. 472–485.

12. Cited in Scott Sleek, "People Craft Their Self-Image from Groups," *The APA Monitor,* November 1993, p. 22.

13. Nathaniel Branden, *Self-Esteem at Work: How Confident People Make Powerful Companies* (San Francisco: Jossey-Bass, 1998).

14. Roy F. Baumeister and W. Keith Campbell, book review in *Contemporary Psychology,* December 1999, p. 488.

15. Cited in Wayne Weiten and Margaret Lloyd, *Psychology Applied to Modern Life* (Pacific Grove, CA: Brooks/Cole Publishing, 1994), p. 51.

16. Jeffery B. Vancouver, Charles M. Thompson, E. Casey Tischner, and Dan J. Putka, "Two Studies Examining the Negative Effect of Self-Efficacy on Performance," *Journal of Applied Psychology,* June 2002, pp. 506–516.

17. Janis Miller, "The Value of Self-Respect," www.foryou/magazine.com/summer02/selfrespect.html.

18. Cited in Randall Edwards, "Is Self-Esteem Really All That Important?" *The APA Monitor,* May 1995, p. 43.

19. Jon L. Pierce, Donald G. Gardner, Larry L. Cummings, and Randall B. Dunman, "Organization-Based Self-Esteem: Construct Definition, Measurement, and Validation," *Academy of Management Journal,* September 1989, p. 623.

20. Branden, *Self-Esteem at Work;* Timothy A. Judge and Joyce E. Bono, "Relationship of Core Self-Evaluations Traits—Self-Esteem, Generalized Self-Efficacy, Locus of Control, and Emotional Stability—with Job Satisfaction and Job Performance: A Meta-Analysis," *Journal of Applied Psychology,* February 2001, pp. 80–92.

21. Research reported in Melissa Dittmann, "Self-Esteem That's Based on External Sources Has Mental Health Consequences, Study Says," *Monitor on Psychology,* December 2002, p. 16.

22. Research mentioned in book review by E. R. Snyder in *Contemporary Psychology,* July 1998, p. 482.

23. Daniel L. Aroz, "The Manager's Self-Concept," *Human Resources Forum,* July 1989, p. 4.

24. Cited in "Self-Esteem: You'll Need It to Succeed," *Executive Strategies,* September 1993, p. 12.

25. Research reported in David Dent, "Bursting the Self-Esteem Bubble," *Psychology Today,* March/April 2002, p. 16.

26. Roy F. Baumeister, *Escaping the Self: Alcoholism, Spirituality, Masochism, and Other Flights from the Burden of Selfhood* (New York: Basic Books, 1991).

27. Ibid.

▲ ADDITIONAL READING

Branden, Nathaniel. *A Woman's Self-Esteem: Struggles and Triumphs in the Search for Identity.* San Francisco: Jossey-Bass, 2000.

Brown, Steven P., Shankar Ganesan, and Goutam Challagalla. "Self-Efficacy as a Moderator of Information-Seeking Effectiveness." *Journal of Applied Psychology,* October 2001, pp. 1043–1051.

Erez, Amir, and Timothy A. Judge. "Relationship of Core Self-Evaluations to Goal Setting, Motivation, and Performance." *Journal of Applied Psychology,* December 2001, pp. 1270–1279.

Ferrari, Michel, and Robert J. Sternberg. eds. *Self-Awareness: Its Nature and Development.* New York: Guilford Press, 1998.

Hewitt, John P. *The Myth of Self-Esteem: Finding Happiness and Solving Problems in America.* New York: St. Martin's Press, 1998.

Hoyle, Rick H., Michael H. Kernis, Mark R. Leary, and Mark W. Baldwin. *Selfhood: Identify, Esteem, Regulation.* Boulder, CO: Westview Press, 1999.

Lee, Sunhee, and Howard J. Klein. "Relationships between Conscientiousness, Self-Efficacy, Self-Deception, and Learning over Time." *Journal of Applied Psychology,* December 2002, pp. 1175–1182.

McKay, Matthew, Patrick Fanning, Carole Honeychurch, and Catharine. Sutker. *The Self-Esteem Companion.* Oakland, CA: New Harbinger, 1999.

McKay, Matthew, and Patrick Fanning. *Self-Esteem.* 3d ed. Oakland, CA: New Harbinger, 2000.

Zampelli, Sheri. *From Sabotage to Success: How to Overcome Self-Defeating Behavior and Reach Your True Potential.* Oakland, CA: New Harbinger, 2000.

CHAPTER 2

Self-Motivation and Goal Setting

Learning Objectives

After studying the information and doing the exercises in this chapter, you should be able to:

◆ Explain how needs and motives influence motivation

◆ Identify several needs and motives that could be propelling you into action

◆ Pinpoint how the hierarchy of needs could explain your behavior

◆ Explain why and how goals contribute to self-motivation

◆ Describe how to set effective goals and the problems sometimes created by goals

◆ Describe several specific techniques of self-motivation

◆ Apply the self-discipline model to achieving your goals

*G*erry enjoyed his position as an assistant branch manager at Golden Tree Savings and Loan Association. After several discussions with the branch manager, plus the branch manager's boss, Gerry was convinced that he had a good future with Golden Tree. He was told that he had the banking knowledge, ambition, and people skills to move up at the savings and loan but that he needed to be patient for promotion.

In discussing his job situation with his wife Tiffany, Gerry said, "I'm on the right track at Golden Tree, but we still need a few hundred more dollars a month to meet expenses. You can't just demand more money at a financial institution, so I've set a goal of netting $300 more per month with a side business that will not take more than about one hour per day from family life."

"You're not going to start counterfeiting money or scamming your customers are you?" joked Tiffany.

"Absolutely not," replied Gerry, "I've set a goal of earning $300 per month by having our own eBay store. My plan is simple. I'll buy interesting items from the local dollar store and other deep discounters and auction them on eBay. I'll do most of the Internet work, shopping, shipping and packing after Keith [their baby] is sleeping. And some of the shopping I can do when we are out shopping anyway."

Within two months, Gerry was earning $150 per month from T&G Specials, his eBay store. By the end of the third month, Gerry earned $301. Gerry explained his success to Tiffany and their parents in these terms- "With a goal and a little firepower, nice little dreams will come true."

Maybe selling trinkets on eBay to earn extra money is not your dream, yet Gerry's comments emphasize an important truth. You have to be motivated to achieve success in work. Strong motivation is also important for personal life. Unless you direct your energies toward specific goals, such as improving your productivity or meeting a new friend, you will accomplish very little. Knowledge of motivation and goal setting as applied to yourself can therefore pay substantial dividends in improving the quality of your life. Knowledge about motivation and goal setting is also important when attempting to influence others to get things accomplished. Motivating others, for example, is a major requirement of the manager's job.

Being well motivated is also important just to meet the demands of employers. Even when unemployment is low, most organizations insist on high productivity and quality from workers at all levels. Assuming that you have the necessary skills, training, and equipment, being well motivated will enable you to achieve high productivity. Furthermore, workers in professional-level positions are often expected to work about 55 hours per week, doing work at home included.

The general purpose of this chapter is to present information that can help you sustain a high level of motivation, centering on the importance of needs and goals.

▲ HOW NEEDS AND MOTIVES INFLUENCE MOTIVATION

According to a widely accepted explanation of human behavior, people have needs and motives that propel them toward achieving certain goals. Needs and motives are closely related. A **need** is an internal striving or urge to do something, such as a need to drink when thirsty. It can be regarded as a biological or psychological requirement. Because the person is deprived in some way (such as not having enough fluid in the body), the person is motivated to take action toward a goal. In this case the goal might be simply getting something to drink.

A **motive** is an inner drive that moves a person to do something. The motive is usually based on a need or desire and results in the intention to attain an appropriate goal. Because needs and motives are so closely related, the two terms are often used interchangeably. For example, "recognition need" and "recognition motive" refer to the same thing.

THE NEED THEORY OF MOTIVATION

The central idea behind need theory is that unsatisfied needs motivate us until they become satisfied. When people are dissatisfied or anxious about their present status or performance, they will try to reduce this anxiety. This need cycle is shown in Figure 2-1. Assume that you have a strong need or motive to achieve recognition. As a result, you experience tension that drives

Figure 2-1   The Need Cycle

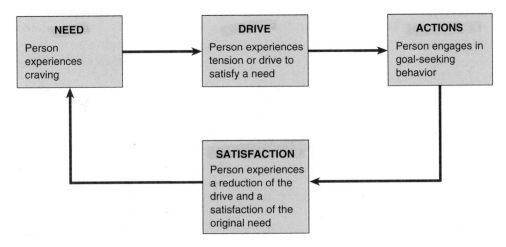

you to find some way of being recognized on the job. The action you take is to apply for a position as the team leader of your group. You reason that being appointed as team leader would provide ample recognition, particularly if the team performs well.

You are appointed to the position, and for now your need for recognition is at least partially satisfied as you receive compliments from your coworkers and friends. Once you receive this partial satisfaction, two things typically happen. Either you will soon require a stronger dose of recognition, or you will begin to concentrate on another need or motive, such as achievement.

In either case, the need cycle will repeat itself. You might seek another form of recognition or satisfaction of your need for power. For example, you might apply for a position as department manager or open your own business. Ideally, in this situation your boss would give you more responsibility. This could lead to more satisfaction of your recognition need and to some satisfaction of your need for achievement. (The needs mentioned so far, and others, are defined next.)

The need theory suggests that self-interest plays a key role in motivation. People ask, "What's in it for me?" or "WIIFM" (pronounced *wiff'em*) before engaging in any form of behavior. In one way or another people act in a way that serves their self-interest.[1] Even when people act in a way that helps others, they are doing so because helping others helps them. For example, a person may give money to poor people because this act of kindness makes him or her feel wanted and powerful.

IMPORTANT NEEDS AND MOTIVES PEOPLE ATTEMPT TO SATISFY

Work and personal life offer the opportunity to satisfy dozens of needs and motives. In this and the following section, we describe important needs that propel people into action. As you read these needs and motives, relate them to yourself. For example, ask yourself, "Am I a power-seeking person?"

Achievement

People with a strong achievement need find joy in accomplishment for its own sake. The achievement motive or need is especially important for self-employed people and employees occupying high-level managerial positions. The achievement need can be satisfied by such activities as building things from the ground up or by completing a major project.

Power

People with a high power need feel compelled to control resources, such as other people and money. Successful executives typically have a high power motive and exhibit three dominant characteristics: (1) they act with vigor and determination to exert their power; (2) they invest much time in thinking about ways to alter the behavior and thinking of others, and (3) they care about their personal standing with those around them.[2] The power need can be satisfied through occupying a high-level position or by becoming a highly influential person. Or you can name skyscrapers and hotels after yourself, following the lead of Donald Trump.

Affiliation

People with a strong affiliation need seek out close relationships with others and tend to be loyal as friends or employees. The affiliation motive is met directly through belonging to the "office gang," a term of endearment implying that your coworkers are an important part of your life. Many people prefer working in groups to individual effort because of the opportunity the former provides for socializing with others.

Recognition

People with a strong need for recognition want to be acknowledged for their contribution and efforts. The need for recognition is so pervasive that many companies have formal recognition programs in which outstanding or longtime employees receive gifts, plaques, and jewelry inscribed with the company logo. The recognition motive can be satisfied through means such as winning contests, receiving awards, and seeing your name in print.

A major reason the need for recognition is such a useful motivator is that most people think they are underappreciated (and overworked). Business school dean Gerald Graham found that out of 1,500 workers surveyed, more than 50 percent indicated they seldom or never received oral or written thanks for their efforts.[3]

Order

People with a strong need for order have the urge to put things in order. They also want to achieve arrangement, balance, neatness, and precision. The order motive can be quickly satisfied by cleaning and organizing your work or living space. Occupations offering the opportunity to satisfy the order motive almost every day include accountant, computer programmer, and paralegal.

Risk Taking and Thrill Seeking

Some people crave constant excitement on the job and are willing to risk their lives to achieve thrills. The need to take risks and pursue thrills is has grown in importance in the high-technology era. Many people work for employers, start businesses, and purchase stocks with uncertain futures. Both the search of giant payoffs and daily thrills motivate these individuals.[4] A strong craving for thrills may have some positive consequences for the organization, including willingness to perform such dangerous feats as setting explosives, capping an oil well, controlling a radiation leak, and introducing a product in a highly competitive environment. However, extreme risk takers and thrill seekers can create such problems as being involved in a disproportionate number of vehicular accidents and making imprudent investments. Take Human Relations Self-Assessment Quiz 2-1 to measure your tendency toward risk taking.

GENERATIONAL DIFFERENCES IN NEEDS

Popular opinion strongly believes that the various generations have different needs based on their values. A **value** is the importance a person attaches to something that serves as a guide to action. If you value cleanliness, you will strive to keep your work area neat. Values are also tied in with

The Risk-Taking Scale (We Dare You to Take This Quiz)

How can you size up your capacity for risk and thrills? Here's an informal quiz. Although some of the questions seem obvious, your final score reflects the range of risk that you are comfortable with, not just whether you like taking risks or not. Answer True or False:

	True	False
1. I don't like my opinions being challenged.	☐	☐
2. I would rather be an accountant than a TV anchor.	☑	☐
3. I believe that I can control my destiny.	☐	☐
4. I am a highly creative person.	☐	☑
5. I like a lot of varied romantic partners.	☐	☐
6. I don't like trying exotic foods.	☐	☑
7. I would choose bonds over growth stocks.	☑	☐
8. Friends would call be a thrill seeker.	☐	☑
9. I like to challenge authority.	☐	☑
10. I prefer familiar things to new things.	☐	☑
11. I'm known for my curiosity.	☑	☐
12. I would not like to be an entrepreneur.	☐	☐
13. I'd rather not travel abroad.	☐	☐
14. I am easily bored.	☐	☐
15. I wouldn't like to be a stand-up comedian.	☐	☐
16. I've never gotten speeding tickets.	☐	☑
17. I am extremely adventurous.	☐	☑
18. I need a lot of stimulation in my life.	☐	☑
19. I would rather work for a salary than a commission.	☐	☐
20. Making my own decisions is very important to me.	☑	☐

Give yourself 1 point each time your answer agrees with the key. If you score 16 to 20, you are probably a high risk taker; from 10 to 15; you're a moderate risk taker; from 5 to 9; you are cautious; from 0 to 4; a very low risk taker.

1. F	6. F	11. T	16. F
2. F	7. F	12. F	17. T
3. T	8. T	13. F	18. T
4. T	9. T	14. T	19. F
5. T	10. F	15. F	20. T

needs. If you value love, your needs for love and affection will be strong. Generational differences in needs and values are reflected in the stereotypes about differences among middle-age people (baby boomers) versus younger people (Generation X, Generation Y, or the Net generation). Older people will more frequently have strong needs for security. In contrast, younger people might have a stronger need for thrill seeking.[5] This is one of several reasons that middle-aged people are more likely to be hired as pilots of large commercial airplanes.

Exhibit 2-1 summarizes stereotypes about generational differences in values. The values in turn can be translated into needs, such as "appreciating hierarchy" being based on a need for order and security. Keep in mind, of course, that not everybody fits these stereotypes. Some 70-year-olds enjoy skydiving, and some 23-year-olds are looking for secure, low-risk jobs.

EXHIBIT 2-1

Value Stereotypes for Several Generations of Workers

Baby Boomers *(1946–1964)*	*Generation X* *(1965–1977)*	*Generation Y* *(1978–1984)*
Uses technology as necessary tool	Techno-savvy	Techno-savvy
Appreciates hierarchy	Teamwork very important	Teamwork very important
Tolerates teams but values independent work	Dislikes hierarchy	Dislikes hierarchy
Strong career orientation	Strives for work/life balance but will work long hours for now	Strives for work/life balance but will work long hours for now
More loyalty to organization	Loyalty to own career and profession	Belief in informality
		Wants to strike it rich quickly
Favors diplomacy	Candid in conversation	Ultracandid in conversation
Favors old economy	Appreciates old and new economy	Prefers the new economy
Expects a bonus based on performance	Would appreciate a signing bonus	Expected a signing before the dot-com crash
Believes that issues should be formally discussed	Believes that feedback can be administered informally	Believes that feedback should be given informally, even on the fly

SOURCE: Several of the ideas in this table are from Robert McGarvey, "The Coming of Gen X Bosses," *Entrepreneur,* November 1999, pp. 60–64; Joanne M. Glenn, "Teaching the Net Generation," *Business Education Forum,* February 2000, pp. 6–14; Anita Bruzzese, "There Needn't Be a Generation Gap," Gannett News Service, April 22, 2002.

Maslow's Need Hierarchy

The best-known categorization of needs is **Maslow's need hierarchy.** At the same time, it is the most widely used explanation of human motivation. According to psychologist Abraham H. Maslow, people strive to satisfy the following groups of needs in step-by-step order:

1. *Physiological needs* refer to bodily needs, such as the requirements for food, water, shelter, and sleep.

2. *Safety needs* refer to actual physical safety and to a feeling of being safe from both physical and emotional injury.

3. *Social needs* are essentially love or belonging needs. Unlike the two previous levels of needs, they center around a person's interaction with other people.

4. *Esteem needs* represent an individual's demand to be seen as a person of worth by others—and to him- or herself.

5. *Self-actualizing needs* are the highest level of needs, including the needs for self-fulfillment and personal development.[6]

A diagram of the need hierarchy is presented in Figure 2-2. Notice the distinction between higher-level and lower-level needs. With few exceptions, higher-level needs are more difficult to satisfy. A person's needs for affiliation might be satisfied by being a member of a friendly work group. Yet to satisfy self-actualization needs, such as self-fulfillment, a person might have to develop an outstanding reputation in his or her company.

The need hierarchy implies that most people think of finding a job as a way of obtaining the necessities of life. Once these are obtained, a person may think of achieving friendship, self-esteem, and self-fulfillment on the

Figure 2-2   Maslow's Need Hierarchy

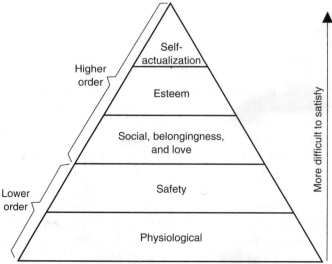

job. When a person is generally satisfied at one level, he or she looks for satisfaction at a higher level. As Maslow describes it, a person is a "perpetually wanting animal." Very few people are totally satisfied with their lot in life, even the rich and famous.

The extent of need satisfaction is influenced by a person's job. Some construction jobs, for example, involve dangerous work in severe climates, thus frustrating both physiological and safety needs. Ordinarily there is much more opportunity for approaching self-actualization when a person occupies a prominent position, such as a top executive or famous performer. However, a person with low potential could approach self-actualization by occupying a lesser position. In the current era, workers at all levels are threatened with the frustration of security needs because so many companies reduce the number of employees to save money.

How do Maslow's needs and the other needs described in this chapter relate to self-motivation? First you have to ask yourself, "Which needs do I really want to satisfy?" After answering the question honestly, concentrate your efforts on an activity that will most likely satisfy that need. For instance, if you are hungry for power, strive to become a high-level manager or a business owner. If you crave self-esteem, focus your efforts on work and social activities that are well regarded by others. The point is that you will put forth substantial effort if you think the goal you attain will satisfy an important need.

▲ GOALS AND MOTIVATION

Almost all successful people have one thing in common. At some point in their lives, they established goals, jotted them down on ordinary paper, wrote them into a hard-copy personal planner, or entered them into a computer. The goal-setting activities of successful people attests to the importance of goals. A **goal** is an event, circumstance, object, or condition a person strives to attain. A goal thus reflects your desire or intention to regulate your actions. Here we look at three topics to help you understand the nature of goals: (1) the advantages of goals, (2) the underlying reasons why they are motivational, and (3) different goal orientations.

ADVANTAGES OF GOALS

Goal setting is well accepted as a motivational tool. Substantial research indicates that setting specific, reasonably difficult goals improves performance.[7] Goals are useful for several reasons. First, when we guide our lives with goals, we tend to focus our efforts in a consistent direction. Without goals, our efforts may become scattered in many directions. We may keep trying, but we will go nowhere unless we happen to receive more than our share of luck.

Second, goal setting increases our chances for success, particularly because success can be defined as the achievement of a goal. The goals we set for accomplishing a task can serve as a standard to indicate when we have done a satisfactory job. A sales representative might set a goal of selling

$300,000 worth of merchandise for the year. By November she might close a deal that places her total sales at $310,000. With a sigh of relief she can then say, "I've done well this year."

Third, goals serve as self-motivators and energizers. People who set goals tend to be motivated because they are confident that their energy is being invested in something worthwhile. Aside from helping you become more motivated and productive, setting goals can help you achieve personal satisfaction. Most people derive a sense of satisfaction from attaining a goal that is meaningful to them. The sales representative mentioned above probably achieved this sense of satisfaction when she surpassed her quota.

Goals make an important contribution to performance by themselves, yet combined with self-efficacy, the positive effects of goals are even more pronounced.[8] Although the scientific evidence is quite complicated, the central message is straightforward. If you establish a goal and believe that you have the skills to attain that goal, your performance is likely to improve.

COGNITIVE AND NEUROLOGICAL REASONS WHY GOALS ARE EFFECTIVE

The advantages of goals just described provide some explanation of why goals help motivate people. Yet to fully understand the contribution of goals, it is important to dig further. Digging further refers here to uncovering the cognitive (or mental) and neurological reasons for the contribution of goals to motivation.

One cognitive explanation of the effectiveness of goals states that they are not motivational by themselves. Rather, the discrepancy between what individuals have and what they aspire to achieve creates dissatisfaction. (The need cycle described earlier also deals with such discrepancies between a person's ideal and actual state.) The self-dissatisfaction serves as an incentive. People respond to reduce the discrepancy. A positive self-evaluation results from achieving the goal.[9]

An example will help clarify this cognitive explanation of why goals are motivational. Bob might be working as a telemarketer (a person who sells over the phone). He sets a goal of being promoted to an outside sales position where he can call on customers and earn a bigger commission. Having set this goal, he is now dissatisfied with the discrepancy between his present job and being an outside sales representative. Bob's dissatisfaction prompts him to work extra hard to perform well as a telemarketer. Because of this, his manager might offer him a promotion.

The motivational effects of goal setting also have a neurological (nervous system) explanation. A building block for this explanation is that many of our actions are influenced by an arousal mechanism. The strength of the arousal moves along a continuum from a low point during sleep to a high point of frantic effort or excitement. (Have you ever observed a sports fan watch his or her team win the "big game" at the final buzzer?) The state of being aroused is associated with activity in the sympathetic nervous system. The sympathetic nervous system readies the body for action. It also governs the amount of energy and effort available for performing a task.[10]

Arousal is linked to goals because setting a goal often arouses the sympathetic nervous system to action. Assume that on Monday paralegal Carla establishes the goal of preparing the paperwork for 15 house closings. The goal is a stretch for Carla but not impossible. Her nervous system will be activated to gear up for the task. By having extra energy to meet these demands, Carla will in essence be well motivated. A problem, however, is that if the task is too demanding, the goal may produce overarousal. As a result, the person may be too "hyper" to perform well and will back away from getting the task accomplished.

THE LEARNING AND PROVING ORIENTATIONS TOWARD GOALS

Another useful perspective on understanding how goals influence motivation is that goals can be aimed at either learning or proving.[11] A learning-goal orientation means that an individual is focused on acquiring new skills and mastering new situations. For example, you might establish the goal of learning how to develop skill in making a computerized presentation package. You say to yourself, "My goal is to learn how to use PowerPoint [or similar software] so I know even more about how to apply information technology."

A proving-goal orientation is different. It is aimed at wanting to demonstrate and validate the adequacy of your competence by seeking favorable judgments about your competence. At the same time, the person wants to avoid seeking negative judgments. For example, your goal might be to make PowerPoint presentations that would highly impress whoever watched them. Your focus is on looking good and avoiding negative evaluations of your presentations.

A person's goal orientation usually affects his or her desire for feedback. People with a learning-goal orientation are more likely to seek feedback on how well they are performing. In contrast, people with a proving-goal orientation are less likely to seek feedback. If you focus too much on setting performance goals, you might have a tendency to overlook the value of feedback. Yet the feedback could help you improve your performance in the long run. It is also important to recognize that if you, the goal setter, seek feedback, you will create a good impression.

Goal orientation is also important because if can affect work performance. Attempting to master skills often leads to better results than does attempting to impress others. A study of the effects of the two different goal orientations was conducted with 167 salespeople working for a medical supplies distributor. The salespeople were paid mostly on the commission of the gross profits they generated. The researchers found that a learning goal orientation was associated with higher sales performance. In contrast, a

HUMANS RELATIONS SELF-ASSESSMENT QUIZ 2-2

Are You Ready for Goal Setting?

Answer each of the following questions spontaneously and candidly. As with all self-help quizzes, if you try to answer the question in a way that will put you in a favorable light, you will miss some potentially valuable diagnostic information. For each question, answer 1 for strongly disagree, 2 for disagree, 3 for a neutral attitude, 4 for agree, and 5 for strongly agree.

1. I almost always know what day of the month it is.   _____

2. I regularly prepare to-do lists.   _____

3. I make good use of my to-do lists.   _____

4. I can tell you almost precisely how many times I engaged in my favorite sport or hobby this year.   _____

5. I take my new year's resolutions seriously.   _____

6. I have a reasonably accurate idea of the different income tax brackets.   _____

7. I use a budget to control my personal expenses.   _____

8. I know how much money I want to be making in five years.   _____

9. I know what position I want to hold in five years.   _____

10. Careful planning is required to accomplish anything of value.   _____

Total   _____

Scoring and Interpretation: Add up your point score. If your score is 40 points or higher, you are probably already convinced of the value of goal setting. If your score is between 20 and 39 points, you are in the middle range of readiness to incorporate goal setting into your life. You probably need to study more about goal setting to capitalize on its value. If your score is between 10 and 19 points, you are far from ready to accept goal setting. Carefully review the information about the advantages of goal setting mentioned previously. Until you change your attitudes about the contribution of goals to your life, you will not become an active goal setter and planner.

proving-goal orientation was unrelated to sales performance. An important implication of the study for managers and workers is that a focus on skill development, even for an experienced workforce, is likely to lead to higher performance.[12]

Before studying more about goals, take Human Relations Self-Assessment Quiz 2-2. It gives you an opportunity to think through your readiness to accept goals as part of your life.

▲ GOAL SETTING ON THE JOB

If you are already well into your career, you have probably been asked to set goals or objectives on the job. Virtually all modern organizations have come to accept the value of goal setting in producing the results they want to achieve.

In most goal-setting programs, executives at the top of the organization are supposed to plan for the future by setting goals such as "Improve profits 10 percent this year." Employees at the bottom of the organization are supposed to go along with such broad goals by setting more specific goals. An example is "I will decrease damaged merchandise by 10 percent this year. I will accomplish this by making sure that our shelving is adequate for our needs."

An interesting aspect of goal-setting programs on the job is that they lead you to pursue goals set by both your employer and yourself. The firm or company establishes certain goals that are absolutely essential to staying in business. A bank, for example, might impose the following goal on the tellers: "Shortages and overages of cash must be kept within 2 percent of transactions each week." The tellers will thus work extra hard to be sure that they do not give customers too much or too little money.

You participate in the goal-setting process by designing goals to fit into the overall mission of the firm. As a teller in the bank mentioned previously, you might set a personal goal of this nature: "During rush periods, and when I feel fatigued, I will double-count all the money that I handle." In some goal-setting programs, employees are requested to set goals that will lead to their personal improvement. An auditor for the state set this goal for herself: "Within the next 12 months, I will enroll in and complete a supervisory training course in a local college." This woman aspired toward becoming a supervisor.

An important part of goal setting, both on and off the job, is priority setting. You pursue with more diligence those goals that can have the biggest impact on performance or are most important to top management. Suppose that one of a purchasing associate's goals for the month is to trim the number e-mail messages, letter files, and data files stored in his computer. He rightfully assumes that if he cleans up his computer files, he will be able to think more clearly. Yet he is also working on a goal of much more interest to top management—finding new sources of supply of a precious metal used in manufacturing a key product. The purchasing associate should set aside his need for order for a while and work on the precious metal goal.

A sample set of work goals is shown in Figure 2-3. The service and repair shop supervisor who set these objectives took into account the requirements of his boss and the automobile dealership. Even if you set goals by yourself, they must still take into account the needs of your employer. As you read through the goals listed in Figure 2-3, see if they conform to the suggestions made in the section "Guidelines for Goal Setting." The accompanying boxed insert illustrates how goal setting can improve a person's career.

Figure 2-3   Form Used in Automobile Dealership for Statement of Goals

---

JOB TITLE AND BRIEF JOB DESCRIPTION

Manager, Service Department:
Responsible for supervision of service department of automobile dealership. Responsible for staffing service department with appropriate personnel and for quality of service to customers. Work closely with owner of dealership to discuss unusual customer problems. Handle customer complaints about mechanical problems of cars purchased at dealership.

Objectives for Scott Gilley

1. By December 31 of this year, decrease by 10 percent customer demands for rework.
2. Hire two general mechanics within 45 days.
3. Hire two body specialists within 45 days.
4. Decrease by 30 percent the number of repairs returned by customers for rework.
5. Reduce by 10 percent the discrepancy between estimates and actual bills to customers.
6. Schedule at least 20 percent of our service appointments through our Web site by January 15 of next year.

Laid-Off Manufacturing Supervisor Lands His Dream Job

Jason Sauchelli worked at Precision Parts for twenty-five years starting as a tool-and die maker apprentice. After fifteen years, Jason was promoted to manufacturing supervisor, yet still spent some time doing technical work. As he explains, "Once machinery gets in your blood and your hands, you never want to give it up."

Jason, and his wife Melita, a licensed practical nurse, along with their two children live reasonably well. Jason's major hobby was restoring old cars. Said Jason, "I always have a restoration project going on in the garage. And I make decent money selling the cars I restore."

Jason's dream was to be a mechanic for luxury vehicles, but he didn't want to give up his high-paying job. However, overseas competition was taking a big chunk out of Precision's business. Soon, the owner of Precision laid off one-third of the workforce, including Jason.

Jason explained to Melita a plan that had been mulling in is head for months. "I don't see any good job prospects for me in town. I want to enroll in the automotive technology program at our community college. I would learn about the latest auto technology to supplement what I already know about auto mechanics. I would earn a degree that would make me eligible for a $70,000 per year auto technician's job at a luxury-car dealership.

(Continued)

"But how do we live on an LPN's salary in the meantime?" ask Melita. "We don't have to" replied Jason. "I'll take some money of my 401(k) plan to pay tuition and help with living expenses. Also, I'll step up my car restorations."

Two years later, Jason did get his degree. As promised by the placement office before he enrolled in the program, he would be sorting out job offers. The best one came from the local Cadillac/Hummer dealer. Said the service and parts manager, "Jason, you have every qualification we need. Cars are in your blood, you love machinery; and you are trained in repairing high-tech vehicles. We will start you at $67,500 plus full benefits per year. After a month of on-the-job training, but then you will be a certified Cadillac/Hummer automotive technician."

▲ PERSONAL GOAL SETTING

Personal goals are important in their own right. If you want to lead a rewarding personal life, your chances of doing so increase if you plan it. Personal goals heavily influence the formulation of career goals as well. For this reason, it is worthwhile to set personal goals in conjunction with career goals. Ideally they should be integrated to help achieve a balance between the demands of work and personal life. Two examples follow:

- A man might have a strong interest in watching major league professional sports, shopping at a wide variety of retail stores, visiting comedy clubs, and dining at a variety of restaurants. He might establish the personal goals of having enough money for this lifestyle and living in an area where it would be available. His career goals should then include developing skills demanded by employers in large cities. Among the general fields that he might enter would be information technology, insurance, financial services, and health services—all of which are in ample supply in large metropolitan areas.

- A woman might develop a preference early in life for the outdoors, particularly for hunting, fishing, and camping. She might also be interested in raising a large family. Part of her career goal setting should include developing skills that are in demand in rural areas where her preferences are easier to satisfy than in a large city. When she learns that many manufacturing facilities exist in rural and semirural areas, her career planning might then include the goal of developing job skills demanded in a factory or mill. She might, for example, take courses in manufacturing technology and supervision to qualify for a position as a manufacturing technician. Or she might simply seek employment in a variety of office positions found in a factory environment, such as information technology specialist or administrative assistant. Following this track, her career preparation would focus on office occupations.

TYPES OF PERSONAL GOALS

Personal goals can be subdivided into those relating to social and family life, hobbies and interests, physical and mental health, career, and finances. An example or two of each type follows:

Social and family: "By age 30 I would like to have a spouse and two children;" "have my own apartment by age 23."

Hobbies and interests: "Become a black belt in karate by age 28;" "qualify as a downhill ski instructor by age 21."

Physical and mental health: "Be able to run four miles without stopping or panting for breath by April 15 of next year;" "get my dermatitis under control within six months from now;" "maintain normal blood pressure for the indefinite future."

Career: "Become office manager by age 28;" "Conduct eBay business selling animal photos within 12 months." (See the accompanying box about a man who waited a long time to prepare himself for his dream career. Chapter 10 is mostly about career planning.)

Financial: "Within the next four years be earning $70,000 per year, adjusted for inflation;" "build my money market fund account into a total value of at least $35,000 within five years."

Human Relations Skill-Building Exercise 2-1 will give you an opportunity to set both work and personal goals. Ideally, reading this chapter and doing the exercises in it will start you on a lifelong process of using goals to help you plan your life. But before you can capitalize on the benefits of goal setting, you need a method for translating goals into action.

ACTION PLANS TO SUPPORT GOALS

An **action plan** describes how you are going to reach your goal. The major reason you need an action plan for most goals is that without a method for achieving what you want, the goal is likely to slip by. Few people ever prepare a road map or plan that will lead them to their goals. If your goal were to build your own log cabin, part of your action plan would be to learn how to operate a buzz saw, to read a handbook on log-cabin building, to learn how to operate a tractor, and so forth.

Some goals are so difficult to reach that your action plan might encompass hundreds of separate activities. You would then have to develop separate action plans for each step of the way. (A major action plan for the laid-off tooling engineer was to enroll in the Motorcyle Mechanics Institute.) If your goal is to lead a rewarding and satisfying career, the techniques presented in this book can help you formulate many of your action plans. Among these skill-building techniques are assertiveness, resolving conflict, developing good work habits, and managing your money wisely.

Some immediate goals do not really require an action plan. A mere statement of the goal may point to an obvious action plan. If your goal were

HUMAN RELATIONS SKILL-BUILDING EXERCISE 2-1

Goal-Setting and Action Plan Worksheet

Before writing down your goals, consult the section "Guidelines for Goal Setting." If you are not currently employed, set up hypothetical goals and action plans for a future job.

Long-Range Goals (beyond five years)

Work: _____

    Action plan: _____

Personal: _____

    Action plan: _____

Medium-Range Goals (two to five years)

Work: _____

    Action plan: _____

Personal: _____

    Action plan: _____

Short-Range Goals (within two years)

Work: _____

    Action plan: _____

Personal: _____

    Action plan: _____

to start painting your room, it would not be necessary to draw up a formal action plan such as: "Go to hardware store, purchase paint, brush, and rollers; borrow ladder and drop cloth from Ken; put furniture in center of room;" and so on.

▲ GUIDELINES FOR GOAL SETTING

Goal setting is an art in the sense that some people do a better job of goal setting than others. The following paragraphs provide suggestions on setting effective goals—those that lead to achieving what you hoped to achieve.

Formulate specific goals. A goal such as "to attain success" is too vague to serve as a guide to daily action. A more useful goal would be to state specifically what you mean by success and when you expect to achieve it. For

example, "I want to be the manager of customer service at a telecommunications company by January 1, 2008, and receive above-average performance appraisals."

Formulate concise goals.   A useful goal can usually be expressed in a short, punchy statement. An example: "Decrease input errors in bank statements so that customer complaints are decreased by 25 percent by September 30 of this year." People new to goal setting typically commit the error of formulating lengthy, rambling goal statements. These lengthy goals involve so many different activities that they fail to serve as specific guides to action.

Describe what you would actually be doing if you reached your goal.   An effective goal specifies the behavior that results after the goal is achieved. A nonspecific goal for a sales representative would be "to become a more effective salesperson." A more useful goal would be "to increase the percent of leads I turn into actual sales." The meaning of a "more effective salesperson" is specified in the second goal (a higher conversion rate for leads).

Describing what you will be doing implies writing down your goal statements. It is helpful to choose lively verbs to direct your efforts.[13] Instead of writing, "I will fix my Web site," your might write, "I will revitalize (or sharpen) my Web site."

Set realistic goals.   A realistic goal is one that represents the right amount of challenge for the person pursuing the goal. On the one hand, easy goals are not very motivational—they may not spring you into action. On the other hand, goals that are too far beyond your capabilities may lead to frustration and despair because there is a good chance you will fail to reach them. The extent to which a goal is realistic depends on a person's capabilities. An easy goal for an experienced person might be a realistic goal for a beginner. Self-efficacy is also a factor in deciding whether a goal is realistic. The higher your self-efficacy, the more likely you are to think that a particular goal is realistic. A person with high self-efficacy for learning Chinese might say, "I think learning two new Chinese words a day is realistic."

Set goals for different time periods.   Goals are best set for different time periods, such as daily, short range, medium range, and long range. Daily goals are essentially a to-do list. Short-range goals cover the period from approximately one week to one year into the future. Finding a new job, for example, is typically a short-range goal. Medium-range goals relate to events that will take place within approximately two to five years. They concern such things as the type of education or training you plan to undertake and the next step in your career.

Long-range goals refer to events taking place five years into the future and beyond. As such, they relate to the overall lifestyle you wish to achieve, including the type of work and family situation you hope to have. Although every person should have a general idea of a desirable lifestyle, long-range goals should be flexible. You might, for example, plan to stay single until age 40. But while on vacation next summer, you might just happen to meet the right partner for you.

Short-range goals make an important contribution to attaining goals of longer duration. If a one-year work goal is to reduce mailing and shipping costs by 12 percent for the year, a good way to motivate workers is to look for a 1 percent saving per month. Progress toward a larger goal is self-rewarding. An effective short-term goal toward living in a less cluttered office or home environment is to throw out one item every day.

Include some fantasy in your personal goal setting.   Fantasy goals can bridge the gap between personal and career goal setting. A fantasy goal would be difficult to attain at any stage in your life. Fantasy goals also reflect your vision of the ideal type of life you would like to lead. They help you dream the impossible dream. However difficult to attain, *some* people do eventually live out their wildest dreams. Here is a sampling of fantasy goals found in the career reports of students in a career development course:

> "I'd like to become a big tycoon by owning about 10 office buildings in Manhattan, along with the San Francisco Forty-Niners and the Boston Red Sox."

> "I hope to develop a personal Web site that will attract one million hits per month with at least one-half of them being repeats."

> "I hope to become a multimillionaire philanthropist and have a high school named after me in a poor neighborhood."

Aside from being exciting to pursue, fantasy goals are important for another reason. Research suggests that your fantasy life can help with personal adjustment and overcoming stress. A well-developed fantasy can result in a pleasurable state of physical and mental relaxation. Furthermore, fantasy goals can help you cope with an unpleasant current situation by giving you hope for the future.[14]

Review your goals from time to time.   A sophisticated goal setter realizes that all goals are temporary to some extent. In time, one particular goal may lose its relevance for you and therefore may no longer motivate you. At one time in your life, you may be committed to earning an income in the top 10 percent of the population. Along the way toward achieving that goal, some other more relevant goal may develop. You might decide that the satisfactions of being self-employed are more important than earning a particular amount of money. You might therefore open an antique store with the simple financial

---

HUMAN RELATIONS SKILL-BUILDING EXERCISE 2-2

Goal Sharing and Feedback

Each person selects one work and one personal goal from Skill-Building Exercise 2-1 that he or she would be willing to share with other members of the class. In turn, every class member presents those two goals to the rest of the class exactly as they are stated on the worksheet. Other class members have the opportunity of providing feedback to the person sharing his or her goals. Here are a few types of errors commonly made in goal setting that you should avoid:

1. Is the goal much too lengthy and complicated? Is it really a number of goals rather than one specific goal?

2. Is the goal so vague that the person will be hard-pressed to know if he or she has reached the goal? (Such as "I intend to become an outstanding employee.")

3. Is the action plan specific enough to serve as a useful path for reaching that goal?

4. Does the goal sound sincere? (Admittedly, this is a highly subjective judgment on your part.)

---

goal of "meeting my expenses." Human Relations Skill-Building Exercise 2-2 gives class members an opportunity to improve their goal-setting skills.

▲ PROBLEMS SOMETIMES CREATED BY GOALS

Despite the many advantages of goals, they can create problems. A major problem is that *goals can create inflexibility*. People can become so focused on reaching particular goals that they fail to react to emergencies, such as neglecting a much-needed machine repair to achieve quota. Goals can also make a person inflexible with respect to missing out on opportunities. Sales representatives sometimes neglect to invest time in cultivating a prospective customer because of the pressure to make quota. Instead, the sales rep goes for the quick sale with an established customer.

Goals can contribute to a *narrow focus, thus neglecting other worthwhile activities*. Students who have established goals for achieving a high grade sometimes face this problem. They might be tempted to concentrate their efforts on the details they think will appear on a forthcoming test and neglect to review other beneficial aspects of the course. Another problem is that *performance goals can sometimes detract from an interest in the task*. People with a proving-goal orientation (focusing on being judged as competent) will sometimes lose interest in the task. The loss of interest is most likely to occur when the task is difficult.[15] This potential problem could be stated in another way. If you focus too much on success (as defined by reaching a goal), you will become frustrated when the means to reaching the goal is difficult.

Assume that your primary reason for working as an information technology specialist is to perform well enough so that you can earn a high income. If carrying out your responsibilities encounters some hurdles, you may readily become discouraged with information technology as a field. However, if your orientation is primarily to advance your knowledge about a dynamic field, you will not be readily frustrated when you encounter problems. You might even look on it as a learning opportunity.

Consider also that *goals can interfere with relaxation.* A preoccupation with goals makes it difficult to relax. Instead of improving one's life, goals become a source of stress. In the words of one purchasing agent, "Ever since I caught on to goal setting as a way of life, I feel as if I'm a basketball player racing from one end of the court to another. Even worse, nobody ever calls a time-out." If the person is already under pressure, taking on another goal may be overwhelming.[16]

Despite the problems that can arise in goal setting, goals are valuable tools for managing your work and personal life. Used with common sense and according to the ideas presented in this chapter, they could have a major, positive impact on your life.

▲ SELF-MOTIVATION TECHNIQUES

Many people never achieve satisfying careers and never realize their potential because of low motivation. They believe they could perform better but admit that "I'm just not a go-getter" or "my motivation is low." Earlier we described how identifying your most important needs could enhance motivation. Here we describe six additional techniques for self-motivation.

1. *Set goals for yourself.* As shown throughout this chapter, goal setting is one of the most important techniques for self-motivation. If you set long-range goals and back them up with a series of smaller goals set for shorter time spans, your motivation will increase.

2. *Find intrinsically motivating work.* A major factor in self-motivation is to find work that is fun or its own reward. **Intrinsic motivation** refers to the natural tendency to seek out novelty and challenges, to extend and use one's capacities, to explore, and to learn.[17] The intrinsically motivated person is involved in the task at hand, such as a technology enthusiast surfing the Web for hours at a time. With some serious introspection, such as having completed the Self-Knowledge Questionnaire in Chapter 1, you should be able to find work you perceive to be intrinsically motivating. Next, find a job that offers your motivators in ample supply. For example, you might have good evidence from your past experience that the opportunity for close contact with people is a personal motivator. Find a job that involves working in a small, friendly department or team.

Owing to circumstances, you may have to take whatever job you can find, or you may not be in a position to change jobs. In such a situation, try to arrange your work so you have more opportunity to experience the reward(s) that you are seeking. Assume that solving difficult problems excites you but that your job is 85 percent routine. Develop better work habits so that you can take care of the routine aspects of your job more quickly. This will give you more time to enjoy the creative aspects of your job.

3. *Get feedback on your performance.* Few people can sustain a high level of motivation without receiving information about how well they are doing. Even if you find your work challenging and exciting, you will need feedback. One reason feedback is valuable is that it acts as a reward. If you learn that your efforts achieved a worthwhile purpose, you will feel encouraged. For example, if a graphics display you designed was well received by company officials, you would probably want to prepare another graphics display.

4. *Apply behavior modification to yourself.* **Behavior modification** is a system of motivation that emphasizes rewarding people for doing the right things and punishing them for doing the wrong things. Many people have used behavior modification to change their own behavior. Specific purposes include overcoming eating disorders, tobacco addiction, Internet abuse, nail biting, and procrastination.

To boost your own motivation through behavior modification, you would have to first decide what specific motivated actions you want to increase (such as working 30 minutes longer each day). Second, you would have to decide on a suitable set of rewards and punishments. You may choose to use rewards only since rewards are generally better motivators than punishments.

5. *Improve your skills relevant to your goals.* The **expectancy theory of motivation** states that people will be motivated if they believe that their efforts will lead to desired outcomes. According to this theory, people hold back effort when they are not confident that their efforts will lead to accomplishments. You should therefore seek adequate training to ensure that you have the right abilities and skills to perform your work. The training might be provided by the employer or on your own through a course or self-study. Appropriate training gives you more confidence that you can perform the work. The training also increases your feelings of self-efficacy.[18] By recognizing your ability to mobilize your own resources to succeed, your self-confidence for the task will be elevated.

6. *Raise your level of self-expectation.* Another strategy for increasing your level of motivation is to simply expect more of yourself. If you raise your level of self-expectation, you are likely to achieve more. Because you expect to succeed, you do succeed. The net effect is the same as if you had increased your level of motivation. The technical term for improving your performance through raising your own expectations is the **Galatea effect.** In one experiment, for example, the self-expectations of subjects were raised in brief interviews with an organizational psychologist. The psychologist told the subjects they had high potential to succeed in the undertaking they were about to begin (a problem-solving task). The subjects who received the positive information about their potential did better than those subjects who did not receive such encouragement.[19]

High self-expectations and a positive mental attitude take a long time to develop. However, they are critically important for becoming a well-motivated person in a variety of situations.

7. *Develop a strong work ethic.* A highly effective strategy for self-motivation is to develop a strong work ethic. If you are committed to the idea that most work is valuable and that it is joyful to work hard, you will automatically become strongly motivated. A person with a weak work ethic cannot readily develop a strong one because the change requires a profound value shift. Yet if a person gives a lot of serious thought to the importance of work and follows the right role models, a work ethic can be strengthened. The shift to a strong work ethic is much like a person who has a casual attitude toward doing fine work becoming quality conscious.

▲ DEVELOPING THE SELF-DISCIPLINE TO ACHIEVE GOALS AND STAY MOTIVATED

Another perspective on achieving goals and staying motivated is that it requires **self-discipline,** the ability to work systematically and progressively toward a goal until it is achieved. The self-disciplined person works toward achieving his or her goals without being derailed by the many distractions faced each day. Self-discipline incorporates self-motivation because it enables you to motivate yourself to achieve your goals without being nagged or prodded with deadlines. Our discussion of how to develop self-discipline follows the model shown in Figure 2-4. You will observe that the model incorporates several of the ideas about goals already discussed in this chapter. Without realizing it, you have already invested mental energy into learning the self-discipline model.

Component 1. *Formulate a mission-statement.*   Who are you? What are you trying to accomplish in life? If you understand what you are trying to accomplish in life, you have the fuel to be self-disciplined. With a mission, activities that may appear mundane to others become vital stepping-stones for you. An example would be learning Spanish grammar to help you become an international businessperson. To help formulate your mission statement, answer two questions: What are my five biggest wishes? What do I want to accomplish in my career during the next five years?

Figure 2-4   The Self-Discipline Model

Component 2.   *Develop role models.*   An excellent method of learning how to be self-disciplined is to model your behavior after successful achievers who are obviously well disciplined. To model another person does not mean you will slavishly imitate every detail of that person's life. Instead, you will follow the general pattern of how the person operates in spheres related to your mission and goals. An ideal role model is the type of person whom you would like to become, not someone you feel you could never become.

Component 3.   *Develop goals for each task.*   Your mission must be supported by a series of specific goals that collectively will enable you to achieve your mission. Successfully completing goals eventually leads to fulfilling a mission. Each small goal achieved is a building block toward larger achievements.

Component 4.   *Develop action plans to achieve goals.*   Self-disciplined people carefully follow their action plans because they make goal attainment possible. It is helpful to chart your progress against the dates established for the subactivities.

Component 5.   *Use visual and sensory stimulation.*   A self-disciplined person relentlessly focuses on a goal and persistently pursues that goal. To accomplish this consistent focus, self-disciplined people form images of reaching their goals—they actually develop a mental image of the act of accomplishing what they want. As mysterious as it sounds, visualization helps the brain convert images into reality. The more senses you can incorporate into your visual image, the stronger its power. Imagine yourself seeing, tasting, hearing, smelling, and touching your goal. Can you imagine yourself sitting in your condo overlooking the ocean, eating a great meal to celebrate the fact that the business you founded now has 10,000 employees?

Component 6.   *Search for pleasure within the task.*   A self-disciplined person finds joy, excitement, and intense involvement in the task at hand, and therefore finds intrinsic motivation. Instead of focusing on the extrinsic (or external) reward, the love of the task helps the person in pursuit of the goal. An axiom of becoming wealthy is not to focus on getting rich. Instead, focus on work. If the task at hand does not thrill you, at least focus on the pleasure from the most enjoyable element within the task. A bill collector might not find the total task intrinsically motivating, but perhaps he or she enjoys developing skill in resolving conflict.

Component 7. *Compartmentalize spheres of life.*   Self-disciplined people have a remarkable capacity to divide up (or compartmentalize) the various spheres of their lives to stay focused on what they are doing at the moment. While working, develop the knack of concentrating on work and putting aside thoughts about personal life. In the midst of social and family activities, concentrate on them rather than half-thinking about work. This approach will contribute to both self-discipline and a better integration of work and family life.

Component 8.   *Minimize excuse making.*   Self-disciplined people concentrate their energies on goal accomplishment rather than making excuses for why work is not accomplished. Instead of trying to justify why they have been diverted from a goal, high-achieving, self-disciplined people circumvent potential barriers. Undisciplined people, in contrast, seem to look for excuses. If you are an excuse maker, conduct a self-audit, writing down all the reasons blocking you from achieving any current goal. Be brutally honest in challenging each one of your excuses. Ask yourself, "Is this a valid excuse, or is it simply a rationalization for my getting sidetracked?"

▲ SUMMARY

Self-motivation is important for achieving success in work and personal life. A well-accepted explanation of human behavior is that people have needs and motives propelling them toward achieving certain goals. The central idea behind need theory is that unsatisfied needs motivate us until they become satisfied. After satisfaction of one need, the person usually pursues satisfaction of another, higher need.

Work and personal life offer the opportunity to satisfy many different needs and motives. Among the more important needs and motives are achievement, power, affiliation, recognition, and order. The need for risk taking and thrill seeking is also important for some people. Generational differences in needs have been observed, such as older people placing a higher value on security and younger people placing a higher value on risk taking.

According to Maslow's need hierarchy, people have an internal need pushing them on toward self-actualization. However, needs are arranged into a five-step ladder. Before higher-level needs are activated, certain lower-level needs must be satisfied. In ascending order, the groups of needs are physiological, safety, social, esteem, and self-actualization (such as self-fulfillment).

Need theory helps in self-motivation. First identify which needs you want to satisfy and then focus your efforts on an activity that will satisfy those needs.

Goals are valuable because they (1) focus effort in a consistent direction, (2) improve your chances for success, and (3) improve motivation and satisfaction. One explanation for the contribution of goals is that they create a discrepancy between what individuals have and what they aspire to achieve. Self-dissatisfaction with this discrepancy serves as an incentive to achieve. Goals also create a state of arousal that readies people for accomplishment.

Goals can be aimed at either learning or proving (performing). A learning-goal orientation means that an individual is focused on acquiring new skills and mastering new situations. A proving-goal orientation is aimed at wanting to demonstrate and validate the adequacy of your competence by seeking favorable judgments of competence. People with a learning-goal orientation are more likely to seek feedback on how well they are performing, and they are more likely to have higher job performance.

Goal setting is widely used on the job. Goals set by employees at lower levels in an organization are supposed to contribute to goals set at the top. Frequently, individual employees are asked to participate in goal setting by contributing ideas of their own. An important part of goal setting, both on and off the job, is priority setting. To increase the motivational impact of goals, some managers encourage workers to track their own performances.

Goal setting in personal life can contribute to life satisfaction. For maximum advantage, personal goals should be integrated with career goals. Areas of life in which personal goals may be set include (1) social and family; (2) hobbies and interests; (3) physical and mental health; (4) career; and (5) financial. To increase their effectiveness, goals should be supported with action plans.

Effective goals are specific and concise. You should describe what you would actually be doing if you reached your goal, and goals should be realistically challenging. Set goals for different time periods and include some fantasy in your personal goal setting.

Goals have some problems associated with them. They can create inflexibility and can lead you to a narrow focus, thus neglecting other worthwhile activities. Proving goals can detract from an interest in the task, and goals can interfere with relaxation.

Key techniques of self-motivation include (1) setting goals for yourself; (2) engaging in intrinsically motivating work; (3) getting feedback on your performance; (4) applying behavior modification to yourself; (5) improving your skills relevant to your job; (6) raising your level of self-expectation; and (7) developing a strong work ethic.

Achieving goals and staying motivated requires self-discipline. A model presented here for developing self-discipline consists of eight components: (1) formulate a mission statement; (2) develop role models; (3) develop goals for each task; (4) develop action plans; (5) use visual and sensory stimulation; (6) search for pleasure within the task; (7) compartmentalize spheres of life; and (8) minimize excuse making.

Questions and Activities

1. How would the need theory of motivation explain the fact that shortly after accomplishing an important goal, many people begin thinking about their next possible goal?

2. Give an example from your own life of how a lower-level need had to be satisfied first before you were able to concentrate on a higher-level need.

3. How might having a strong need for affiliation retard a person's career advancement?

4. Identify any self-actualized person you know or have heard of and explain why you think that person is self-actualized.

5. Why does a learning-goal orientation often contribute to more peace of mind than a proving-goal orientation?

6. Why is self-motivation so important during a period in which there is a surplus of workers to fill available positions?

7. Give examples of two jobs in your chosen field you think are likely to be intrinsically motivating. Explain your reasoning.

8. Explain how you might be able to use the Galatea effect to improve the success you achieve in your career and personal life.

9. What sacrifices might a highly self-disciplined person have to make in contrast to a lowly self-disciplined person?

10. Ask a person who has achieved career success how much self-discipline contributed to his or her success.

INTERNET SKILL BUILDER: What Stops Us?

At www.self-motivation.net, business and life coach Tom Hooper challenges you with questions such as "Have you ever started a diet but didn't stay on the plan?" and "Why do we procrastinate and put off the activities that would lead to such a successful conclusion?" Hooper helps you find answers about self-discipline in a sample slide show that takes about 20 minutes to download and watch. As you go through the slide show, look for similarities to the self-discipline model presented in the text.

HUMAN RELATIONS CASE PROBLEM

The Ski and Golf Seasonal Workers

Skiing and golf, two of the best amenities in the Bend, Oregon, region, are not designed just for visitors. However, most working-class locals struggle to find the time and the money to fit the costly recreational activities into their daily lives. Mount Bachelor Inc., which during the ski season hires about 450 employees, and Sunriver resort, which has 350 jobs to fill each summer, have teamed together to create a year-round recreational industry. Employees receive medical and dental benefits, free skiing and golf, and an opportunity to shift jobs each season.

Although a group within the local workforce already transfers between these two employers each season, the companies are enticing workers to return to their positions each year with added medical benefits. Pat Gerhart, human resources director at Mount Bachelor, said creating the benefits package was a natural evolution from job fair efforts and active recruitment. Benefits bridge the gap between seasons if the first job is cut short before the next one begins.

"Workforce availability shortages have prompted the human resources departments to put their heads together and find a way to being people back year after year because once a seasonal employee leaves the area, it's hard to get him or her back," Gerhart says.

Experience Wanted

Both companies would like to benefit from experienced and well-trained employees. Sunriver human resources director Joyce Luckman says the resort hopes to retain its core staffs, who will grow their customer service skills in the reciprocal employment program. "There's a need in central Oregon for year-round employment, and there's a perfect niche in this partnership."

The program benefits both sides. Although paying for the insurance for the employees adds a cost for the businesses, Luckman and Gerhart say it's worth it. Plus,

(Continued)

Luckman, adds, the employees won't file for unemployment insurance benefits when their seasons end.

The program is available to all employees but this year was limited to 25 employees on a first-come, first-served basis because the human resources directors wanted to keep the program small in its first year. "We wanted to keep it manageable to see what pitfalls we might run into," Gerhart says, adding that they are still working out details.

Program Will Grow

Gerhart hopes that eventually there will be no number limits and that anyone who wants to participate can. Gerhart says the program will grow to include Eagle Crest employees, the Inn of the Seventh Mountain, and maybe the Riverhouse or rafting companies too. But employers would have to meet some minimum coverage requirement close to the packages offered by Sunriver and Mount Bachelor. Benefits don't kick in until the employees enter their second season, so last summer's Sunriver employees working at the winter resort would now be covered.

Most Jobs Pay Low

Gerhart acknowledges that the majority of resort jobs don't pay family wages. She therefore hopes to see more people take advantage of the program who fit on the higher end of the pay scale, like groomers and golf course technicians. These workers could make a year-round family wage while bringing their families in on the recreational benefits. Besides a season pass for the whole family, Mount Bachelor employees in the program receive a company-paid medical and dental program worth $185 a month. It's a major medical program with a $250 deductible and dental insurance with a $25 deductible. Employees also receive 80 percent of most expenses paid and up to $300 worth of preventative care.

Sunriver offers employees in the program a full recreation package, including free golf at Meadows and Woodlands as well as bike and canoe rentals and other discounts at the resort.

The employees in the reciprocal program receive health insurance for the entire family. The company picks up two-thirds of the premium, which can be worth as much as $450 per family.

Managers at Mount Bachelor and Sunriver hope that their initiatives in providing year-round pay and more employee benefits will help develop a more experienced and stable workforce.

Questions

1. What needs is management attempting to satisfy with their new program of improving worker retention?

2. What other steps should managers at the golf resorts and ski resorts take to motivate experienced workers to return?

3. What is your prediction of the success of the new pay and benefits in building a stable workforce?

4. Imagine yourself as a seasonal worker in the golf and ski industries. How would you motivate yourself to (1) work year-round, and (2) return for several seasons?

SOURCE: Based on information in Anne Aurand, "Resorts Offer Benefits to Seasonal Employees," *The Bulletin* (Bend, OR), March 11, 2000.

WEB CORNER

Goal-setting software: www.goal-generator.com

Self-discipline: www.coachingwithresults.com/
FreeDisciplineReport.shtml

▲ REFERENCES

1. For a theoretical explanation of the principle of self-interest, see Dale T. Miller, "The Norm of Self-Interest," *American Psychologist,* December 1999, pp. 1053–1060.

2. David C. McClelland and Richard Boyatzis, "Leadership Motive Pattern and Long-Term Success in Management," *Journal of Applied Psychology,* December 1982, p. 737.

3. Cited in "Motivating Entry-Level Workers: Invest Your Time to Boost Their Morale," *Working Smart,* October 1998, p. 2.

4. Marvin Zuckerman, "Are You a Risk Taker?" *Psychology Today,* November/December 2000, p. 53.

5. Ron Zemke, "Generation Veneration," in *Business: The Ultimate Resource*™ (Cambridge, MA: Peresus Books Group, 2002), pp. 39–40; Scott Hays, "Generation X and the Art of the Reward," *Workforce,* November 1999, pp. 44–48.

6. The original statement is Abraham H. Maslow, "A Theory of Human Motivation," *Psychological Review,* July 1943, pp. 370–396. See also Maslow, *Motivation and Personality* (New York: Harper & Row, 1954).

7. Edwin A. Locke and Gary P. Latham, *A Theory of Goal Setting and Task Performance* (Upper Saddle River, NJ: Prentice Hall, 1990), pp. 27–62; Howard J. Klein et al., "Goal Commitment and the Goal-Setting Process: Conceptual Clarification and Empirical Synthesis," *Journal of Applied Psychology,* December 1999, p. 893.

8. The research evidence is synthesized in Albert Bandura and Edwin A. Locke, "Negative Self-Efficacy and Goal Effects Revisited," *Journal of Applied Psychology,* February 2003, p. 87.

9. P. Christopher Earley and Terri R. Lituchy, "Delineating Goals and Efficacy: A Test of Three Models," *Journal of Applied Psychology,* February 1991, pp. 81–82.

10. Ian R. Gellatly and John P. Meyer, "The Effects of Goal Difficulty on Physiological Arousal, Cognition, and Task Performance," *Journal of Applied Psychology,* October 1992, p. 695.

11. Don VandeWalle and Larry L. Cummings, "A Test of the Influence of Goal Orientation on the Feedback-Seeking Process," *Journal of Applied Psychology,* June 1997, pp. 390–400; VandeWalle, William L. Cron, and John W. Slocum Jr., "The Role of Goal Orientation Following Performance Feedback," *Journal of Applied Psychology,* August 2001, pp. 629–640.

12. Don VandeWalle, Steven P. Brown, William L. Cron, and John W. Slocum Jr., "The Influence of Goal Orientation and Self-Regulation Tactics on Sales Performance: A Longitudinal Field Test," *Journal of Applied Psychology,* April 1999, pp. 249–259.

13. Write Your Way to Goals," *WorkingSMART,* January 1999, p. 2.

14. Stephen Sprinkel, "Not Having Fantasies Can Be Hazardous to Your Health Counselor Says," Gannett News Service, April 10, 1992.

15. VandeWalle and Cummings, "A Test of the Influence of Goal Orientation," p. 392.

16. P. Christopher Earley, Terry Connolly, and Goran Ekegran, "Goals, Strategy Development, and Task Performance: Some Limits to the Efficacy of Goal Setting," *Journal of Applied Psychology,* February 1989, p. 24.

17. Richard M. Ryan and Edward L. Deci, "Self-Determination Theory and the Facilitation of Intrinsic Motivation, Social Development, and Well-Being," *American Psychologist,* January 2000, p. 70.

18. Earley and Lituchy, "Delineating Goal Effects," p. 96.

19. Taly Dvir, Dov Eden, and Michal Lang Banjo, "Self-Fulfilling Prophecy and Gender: Can Women Be Pygmalion and Galatea?" *Journal of Applied Psychology,* April 1995, p. 268.

▲ ADDITIONAL READING

Cadrain, Diane. "Cash vs. Non-Cash Rewards: In the Land of Employee Rewards, Cash Isn't Necessarily King." *HR Magazine,* April 2003, pp. 81–87.

Carnoy, David. "Rick Pitino: The Master Motivator Offers a Lesson on Consistently Beating the Odds." *Success,* October 1998, pp. 68–71.

Covey, Stephen R., with Pofeldt, Elaine. "Why Is This Man Smiling?" *Success,* January 2002, pp. 38–43.

Dannhauser, Carol Leonetti. "The Right Rewards: Make Workers Happy with More Than Money." *Working Woman,* July/August 2000, pp. 40–41.

Izzo, John B., and Pam Withers. *Value Shift: The New Work Ethic and What It Means for Business.* New York: Fairwinds Press, 2001.

Lamb, Gregory M. "How to Build Motivation in Today's Workplace." *Christian Science Monitor,* March 17, 2003, Work & Money.

Lee, Felissa K., Kennon M. Sheldon, and Daniel B. Turban. "Personality and the Goal-Setting Process: The Influence of Achievement Goal Patterns, Goal Level, and Mental Focus on Performance and Enjoyment." *Journal of Applied Psychology,* April 2003, pp. 256–265.

Sunoo, Brenda Paik. "Praise and Thanks—You Can't Give Enough." *Workforce,* April 1999, pp. 56–60.

Stajkovic, Alexander, D., and Fred. Luthans. "Social Cognitive Theory and Self-Efficacy: Going beyond Traditional Motivational and Behavioral Approaches." *Organizational Dynamics,* Spring 1998, pp. 62–74.

VandeWalle, Don, William L. Cron, and John W. Slocum. "The Role of Goal Orientation Following Performance Feedback." *Journal of Applied Psychology,* August 2001, pp. 629–640.

CHAPTER
3

Problem Solving and Creativity

Learning Objectives

After studying the information and doing the exercises in this chapter, you should be able to:

◆ Understand how personal characteristics influence the ability to solve problems and make decisions

◆ Explain problem-solving styles as defined by the Myers-Briggs Type Indicator

◆ Apply the problem-solving and decision-making steps to complex problems

◆ Summarize the characteristics of creative people

◆ Describe various ways of improving your creativity

*O*nline reverse auctions, or downward pricing auctions, stand the traditional rising price or English auction on its head. Buyers put out specifications for what they want to buy, and sellers submit bids electronically until someone wins the business. Online reverse auctions came into being about the time the Internet became popular.

Driving the boom is a desire for savings. Typical companies can expect savings of 10 to 20 percent on goods purchase through online reverse auctions, says Rob Rosenthal, e-commerce analyst. Purchasers also save time, compressing into hours price negotiations that normally take weeks. Buyers also reach new suppliers who, because of location or other reasons, never bid for their business before.

Today, large companies get the most benefit from buying through reverse auctions because they can purchase in large quantities. Sellers are charged transaction fees ranging from 1 to 3 percent. Buyers normally pay relatively nominal sums to use the services. Online auctions have some problems, such as the bother involved in switching suppliers. Yet online reverse auctions make sense for many purchases. And it is only a matter of time before small companies use them.[1]

The reverse online auction may not rival the lightbulb or the computer as creative brilliance. Yet it does illustrate a few basic facts about problem solving, decision making, and creativity. The developers of the online auction found a **problem,** a gap between what exists and what you want to exist. Companies were looking for new ways to reduce the existing prices they were paying for the products and services they needed. **Decision making** refers to choosing one alternative from the various alternative solutions that can be pursued. The developers of the reverse online auction thought through other alternatives to finding the most economical ways to purchase goods and services, such as a Web site listing prices. And thinking in a nontraditional way—reversing the approach to auction in which buyers bid on what the seller has to offer—is a major aspect of creativity, as is recognizing an opportunity to find a new way of getting buyers and sellers together.

The general purpose of this chapter is to help you become a more effective and creative problem solver when working individually or in groups. Whether you are solving problems by yourself or as part of a group, the principles apply equally well. We discuss unique problems and/or major decisions, such as developing a new product, purchasing major equipment, or weighing a job offer. Very minor decisions, such as choosing a dinner meal, do not require formal study in decision making.

▲ PERSONAL CHARACTERISTICS THAT INFLUENCE YOUR PROBLEM-SOLVING ABILITY

Many personal characteristics and traits influence the type of problem solver and decision maker you are or are capable of becoming. Fortunately, some personal characteristics that influence your decision-making ability can be improved through conscious effort. For instance, if you make bad decisions because you do not concentrate on the details of the problem, you can gradually learn to concentrate better. Most of the personal characteristics described next and outlined in Figure 3-1 can be strengthened through the appropriate education, training, and self-discipline.

COGNITIVE INTELLIGENCE, EDUCATION, AND EXPERIENCE

In general, if you are intelligent, well educated, and well experienced, you will make better decisions than people without these attributes. (The term *cognitive intelligence* refers to the intellectual, or traditional, type of intelligence that is necessary for such tasks as solving math problems and conjugating verbs.) Cognitive intelligence helps because, by definition, intelligence denotes the ability to solve problems. Education improves the problem-solving and decision-making process because it gives you a background of principles and facts to rely on.

Experience facilitates decision making because good decisions tend to be made by people who have already faced similar situations in the past. This is one of the many reasons why experienced people command higher salaries. All things being equal, would you prefer to take your computer problem to an experienced or an inexperienced specialist?

Figure 3-1   Influences on Problem-Solving Skill

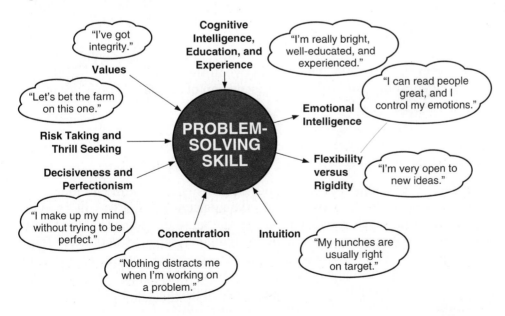

Emotional Intelligence

Being able to deal effectively with your feelings and emotions and those of others can help you make better decisions. **Emotional intelligence** refers to qualities such as understanding one's own feelings, empathy for others, and the regulation of emotion to enhance living. This type of intelligence has to do with the ability to connect with people and understand their emotions. A worker with high emotional intelligence would be able to engage in such behaviors as sizing up people, pleasing others, and influencing them.[2]

Emotional intelligence is important for decision making because how effective you are in managing your feelings and reading other people can affect the quality of your decisions. For example, if you cannot control your anger, you are likely to make decisions that are motivated by retaliation, hostility, and revenge. An example would be shouting and swearing at your team leader because of a work assignment you received. Your emotional intelligence could also influence your career decision making. If you understand your own feelings, you are more likely to enter an occupation or accept a position that matches your true attitude.

Flexibility versus Rigidity

Some people are successful problem solvers and decision makers because they approach every problem with a fresh outlook. They are able to avoid developing rigid viewpoints. Flexible thinking enables the problem solver to think of original—and therefore creative—alternative solutions to solving a problem. Another perspective on the same issue is that being open-minded helps a person solve problems well. For example, a person might face the problem of wanting to purchase a high-quality PC but lacks sufficient funds. So the person keeps searching for a high-quality PC at a bargain price. If the person were more open-minded, he or she might investigate a Net PC. Such a computer is low priced because, instead of having a hard drive of its own, it temporarily downloads programs from the Internet. The link between flexibility and creativity will be described in more detail in the discussion of the characteristics of creative people.

Intuition

Effective decision makers do not rely on careful analysis alone. Instead, they also use their **intuition,** an experience-based way of knowing or reasoning in which weighing and balancing of evidence are done automatically. Relying on intuition is like relying on your instincts when faced with a decision. Intuition takes place when the brain gathers information stored in memory and packages it as a new insight or solution. Intuitions, therefore, can be regarded as stored information that is reorganized or repackaged. Developing good intuition may take a long time because so much information has to be stored. Cognitive psychologist Gary Klein explains it this way:

> We sometimes think that experts are weighted down by information, by facts, by memories—that they make decisions slowly because they must search through so much data. But in fact, we've got it backward. The accumulation of experience does not weight people down—it lightens them up. It makes them fast.[3]

Interviews with 60 high-level professional employees emphasized the link between intuition and experience. It was found that employees who have more experience, who are older, or who hold managerial positions tend to use intuition more. The researchers claim that upper-level executives need to apply intuition more than others because of their need to see the bigger picture and to deal with the long-term.[4] Yet having good intuition helps you make better decisions in almost all professional jobs and at any stage in your career. For example, a 25-year-old credit analyst can profitably use intuition to help size up credit risks. (Watch out for those beady eyes in addition to methodically evaluating the loan applicant's credit history!)

Concentration

Mental concentration is an important contributor to making good decisions. Many people who solve problems poorly do so because they are too distracted to immerse themselves in the problem at hand. In contrast, effective problem solvers often achieve the **flow experience**—total absorption in their work. When flow occurs, things seem to go just right. The person feels alive and fully attentive to what he or she is doing. As a by-product of the flow experience, a good solution to a problem may surface. If you fail to concentrate hard enough, you may overlook an important detail that could affect the outcome of the decision. For example, a person about to purchase an automobile might be excited about the high gas mileage but forget to search the vehicle's ability to withstand a crash.

Decisiveness and Perfectionism

Some people are ill suited to solving problems and making decisions because they are fearful of committing themselves to any given course of action. "Gee, I'm not sure, what do you think?" is their typical response to a decision forced on them. If you are indecisive, this characteristic will have to be modified if you are to become successful in your field. A manager has to decide which person to hire. And a photographer has to decide which setting is best for the subject. As the old saying goes, at some point "you have to fish or cut bait."

The combination of being indecisive and a perfectionist can lead to procrastination. Also, being a procrastinator can make one indecisive. Perfectionism contributes to delayed decision making because the person keeps working on a project before deciding to submit it to somebody else. Have you noticed any students with this type of procrastination? Chapter 12, which discusses work habits, examines procrastination in depth.

Risk Taking and Thrill Seeking

The need for taking risks and seeking thrills is yet another personality characteristic that influences problem-solving skill. For some types of problems, the high risk taker and thrill seeker is at an advantage. Firefighters have to take risks to save people from burning buildings and remove people trapped in collapsed buildings. An information technology specialist might have to engage in a risky maneuver to salvage data from a crashed hard drive. Risk taking and thrill seeking can also lead to poor problem solving and decision making, such as a merchandiser buying a huge inventory of a highly original fashion. The experienced decision maker needs to know when to take high risks and seek thrills and when to be more conservative.

Values of the Decision Maker

Values influence decision making at every step. The right values for the situation will improve problem solving and decision making, whereas the wrong values will lead to poor decisions. Ultimately, all decisions are based on values. A manager who places a high value on the well-being of employees tries to avoid alternatives that create hardships for workers. Many of the financial scandals in business in recent years can be traced to executives who place a high value on greed and a low value on honesty and integrity. Another value that significantly influences problem solving and decision making is the pursuit of excellence. A worker who embraces the pursuit of excellence (and is therefore conscientious) will search for the high-quality alternative solution.

Attempting to preserve the status quo is a value that can negatively influence problem solving. Clinging to the status quo is perceived as a hidden trap in decision making that can prevent making the best decisions. People tend to cling to the status quo because by not taking action they can prevent a bad decision.[5] If you value the status quo too highly, you may fail to make a decision that could bring about major improvements. For example, an executive might not bother offering dependent-care benefits to employees because he has not received complaints. However, by not offering these benefits, the company is losing out on some talented prospective employees.

▲ PROBLEM-SOLVING (OR COGNITIVE) STYLES

People go about solving problems in various ways. You may have observed, for example, that some people are more analytical and systematic while others are more intuitive. The most widely used method of classifying problem-solving styles is the Myers-Briggs Type Indicator (MBTI).[6] Many readers of this book will have already taken the MBTI. Modes of problem solving are referred to as **cognitive styles.** According to this method of understanding problem-solving styles, your personality traits influence strongly how you approach problems, such as being introverted pointing you toward dealing with ideas. Knowledge of these cognitive styles can help you relate better to people because you can better appreciate how they make decisions.

According to the famous psychoanalyst Carl Jung, how people gather and evaluate information determines their cognitive style. Jung's analysis became the basis for the MBTI. Jung reasoned that there are four dimensions of psychological functioning:

1. *Introverted versus extroverted:* Introverts are oriented toward the inner world of ideas and feelings, whereas extroverts are oriented toward the outer world of people and objects.

2. *Thinking versus feeling:* Thinkers prefer to make decisions logically based on facts and figures, whereas feelers base decisions on subjective information.

3. *Sensing versus intuiting:* Sensing individuals prefer to concentrate on details, whereas intuitive individuals prefer to focus on broad issues (the big picture).

4. *Judging versus perceiving:* Judging types seek to resolve issues, whereas perceiving types are relatively flexible and search for additional information.

Combining the four types with each other results in 16 personality types. Exhibit 3-1 presents the personal characteristics associated with four of the total 16 types of cognitive styles. Research evidence for the MBTI is generally positive with respect to the 16 types and the fact that people with different cognitive styles prefer different occupations. For example, the ENTP cognitive type is labeled the "conceptualizer." He or she is passionate about new opportunities, dislikes routine, and is more likely to be an entrepreneur than a corporate manager. The ISTJ cognitive type is labeled the "traditionalist" and will often become an accountant or financial analyst. The INJT type is labeled the "visionary." Although a small proportion of the population, these individuals are often chief executives of business firms. One of the most common types among people in general, as well as among managers, is the ESTJ, labeled the "organizer."[7]

Many people who use the Myers-Briggs are not aware that it is an approximate measure and not a definitive scale, such as a measure of physical weight. The most reliable dimension appears to be thinking versus feeling, which is similar to reflecting about details versus jumping to a quick decision based on feel and experience or being reflective versus impulsive.

If you take the MBTI, often available in career centers, you will discover your type. You can also study these four types and make a tentative judgment as to if one of them fits your problem-solving style. Recognizing your problem-solving style can help you identify work that you are likely to perform well, such as those mentioned in Exhibit 3-1.

EXHIBIT 3-1

Four Cognitive Styles of the Myers-Briggs Typology

ENTP (Conceptualizer)	ISTJ (Traditionalist)	INTJ (Visionary)	ESTJ (Organizer)
Quick, ingenious, will argue either side of issue for fun, may neglect routine assignments (good for creative work where deadlines are not crucial)	Serious, quiet, practical, logical, dependable (good for work requiring careful attention to detail, such as accountant or auditor)	Skeptical, critical, independent, determined, original. (good for major leadership role such as CEO)	Practical, realistic, has a natural mind for business or mechanics, likes to organize and run activities (good for manufacturing supervisor)

NOTE: I = introvert, E = extrovert, T = thinking, F = feeling, S = sensing, N = intuitive, J = judging, and P = perceiving.

SOURCE: The personality descriptions are based on information from *Meyers-Briggs Type Indicator* by Katharine C. Briggs and Isabel Briggs Myers. Copyright 1983 by Consulting Psychologists Press, Inc. All rights reserved.

▲ PROBLEM-SOLVING AND DECISION-MAKING STEPS

Whatever complex problem you face, it is best to use the standard problem-solving and decision-making steps as a guide. These steps are similar to the systematic approach used in the scientific method. Figure 3-2 summarizes the steps involved in problem solving and decision making. It assumes that problem solving should take place in an orderly flow of steps. Paying attention to this model is important because deviating too far will often result in decision failure. Paul C. Hutt studied 356 decisions in medium to large organizations in the United States and Canada. He found that one-half of these decisions failed, meaning that the decision was not fully used after two years. The typical reason for failure is that the decision makers did not take a systematic approach, such as searching for many alternative solutions. The managers involved also committed the human relations error of not involving enough people in the decisions.[8]

Although the problem-solving and decision-making steps appear logical, we emphasize again that people are frequently not entirely rational when making decisions. Emotions and personality traits can cloud decision making. In fact, psychologist Daniel Kahneman won a Nobel prize in economics for his research on how people often behave irrationally in ordinary situations, such as holding on to losing mutual funds or buying insurance for inexpensive appliances.[9]

Figure 3-2   Problem-Solving and Decision-Making Steps

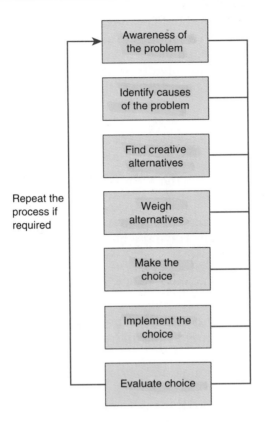

AWARENESS OF THE PROBLEM

Problem solving and decision making begin when somebody is aware that a problem exists. In most decision-making situations, problems are given to another person. At other times, people create their own problems to solve, or they find problems. Scotch Tape had its origins over 75 years ago because somebody noticed a problem. The story goes like this:

> Richard Drew, a young engineer working for the Minnesota Mining and manufacturing Co. (3M today), a small sandpaper manufacturer, noticed that car painters were having trouble masking one section while painting another in a different color. In 1925, Drew invented a masking tape using crepe paper with lines of pressure-sensitive glue running along the edges. Trouble was, the tape kept falling off. An automotive painter told a 3M representative to go back to his "Scotch" (negative stereotype that Scotch people are cheap) bosses and tell them to put adhesive all over the tape, not just on the edges. They did, the tape worked and the name stuck. Five years later Drew overcame numerous production hurdles and developed the clear, cellophane tape today that has become a worldwide staple.[10]

After you are aware that a problem exists or have identified it, recognize that it may represent an important opportunity. For example, if you are bothered enough by a problem facing your company, you might volunteer to be the person in charge of overcoming the problem.

IDENTIFY CAUSES OF THE PROBLEM

The causes of problems should be diagnosed and clarified before any action is taken because they are not always what they seem to be on the surface. Some may be more complicated than suspected or may even be the wrong problem you need to solve in a particular situation. Five key elements to ask questions about (along with some sample questions) are as follows:

- *People.*   What do the people involved contribute to the problem? Are they competent? Do they have an attitude problem?

- *Materials.*   Do we have the right materials available? Is the quality of the materials adequate?

- *Machines and facilities.*   Do we have the right machines and facilities to do the job? Have the machines and facilities changed?

- *Physical environment.*   Is anything wrong with the environment (such as toxic fumes making people sick)? Has the environment changed?

- *Methods.*   Are the processes and procedures adequate? Have new methods been introduced that workers do not understand?

The approach to analyzing causes is often place in a cause-and-effect diagram, as shown in Figure 3-3. The approach is sometimes referred to as a *fishbone diagram* because of the angles of the lines leading to the various causes. Notice that all the causes contribute to the problem at the right.

An associate in a consumer electronics shop used the above questions to quickly identify why a customer's brand-new CD player played music with such a muffled sound. In asking about the physical environment, the asso-

Figure 3-3   Basic Cause-and-Effect Diagram

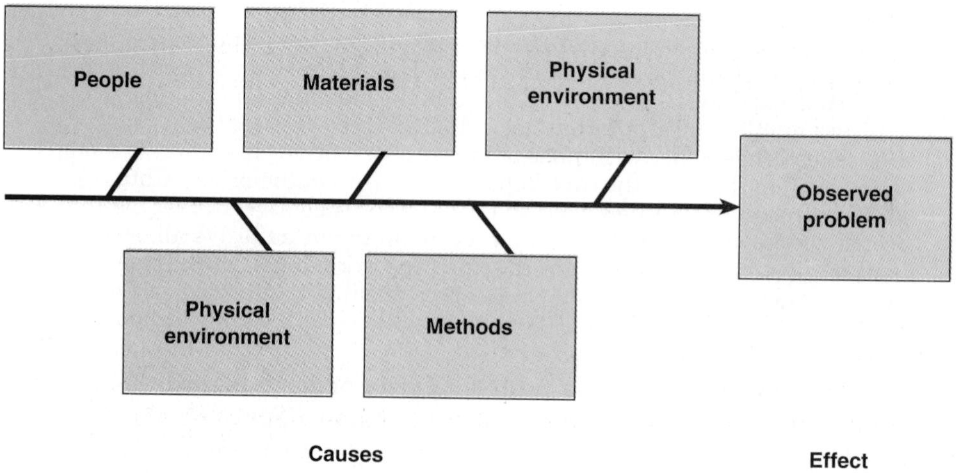

ciate identified the fact that the customer placed the CD on a thick carpet, leading to a "muffled sound."

Even when you have identified the general source of a problem, you may still need to dig further as to what, when, and where a problem *did not* occur. Suppose a friend talks about a fear of public speaking. By asking a few "but not" questions, you might be able to identify a major cause of the problem. Let's try out the method:

Your friend: I'm horribly afraid of public speaking. I hate going up in front of class.

You: But have you ever not been afraid of speaking to a group of people?

Your friend: Yes, I can remember once feeling okay speaking at a victory dinner for my high school soccer team. We came in first place in the region.

You: What did you talk about?

Your friend: I told a cute story about how my mother and father put a soccer ball in my crib. I hugged it every day like it was a teddy bear.

You: So why weren't you afraid of giving that talk?

Your friend: I knew what I was talking about. I didn't have to rehearse.

You: What else was different about the talk?

Your friend: It wasn't like talking to strangers. I was just there with my buddies and our coaches.

You: What you are really telling me is that public speaking is okay when you are well prepared and you are in a comfortable surrounding?

Your friend: Thanks for helping me understand my problem.

FIND CREATIVE ALTERNATIVES

Creativity and imagination enter into problem solving and decision making. Successful decision makers have the ability to think of different alternatives. The person who pushes to find one more alternative to a problem is often the person who finds a breakthrough solution. Creativity plays such an important role in decision making that it will be discussed again in the next two major sections of this chapter.

WEIGH ALTERNATIVES

This stage refers simply to examining the pros and cons of the various alternatives in the previous stages. In a major decision, each alternative would have to be given serious consideration. In practice, weighing alternatives often means jotting down the key good and bad points of each possible choice.

A source of error when weighing alternatives is to rely too much on the first information you receive, known as *anchoring*. The information anchors some people to their first alternatives, thereby overshadowing data and impressions that come later.[11] Anchoring can be somewhat minimized by remembering that decision making is incomplete until many alternatives have been explored.

MAKE THE CHOICE

The essence of decision making is selecting the right course of action to follow. You have to choose an alternative, even if it is not to go ahead with a new plan of action. For instance, after conducting a job campaign, you could decide *not* to change jobs. Instead of coming to a decision, some people overanalyze a problem. Do you suffer from "analysis paralysis," or do you make up your mind after a reasonable amount of thought?

In choosing an alternative, it is helpful to remember that most problems really have multiple solutions. You therefore do not have to be overly concerned with finding the only correct answer to your problem. For instance, there might be several effective ways of reducing the costs of running a department.

IMPLEMENT THE CHOICE

After you decide which course of action to take, you have to put the choice into effect. Some decisions are more difficult to implement than others. Decisions made by top management, for example, are sometimes so difficult to implement that they have to be reversed. An executive at a major online retailer announced a new policy that all customer problems would have to resolved by e-mail and that the toll-free number for customer assistance would be disbanded. Hundreds of customers complained about the new policy by e-mail, and many customer accounts became inactive. The executive reconsidered the decision in terms of its effect on customer service and goodwill and reinstated the toll-free telephone call option. The general point is that to implement many decisions, the human element must be taken into consideration.

EVALUATE THE CHOICE

The decision-making sequence is not complete until the decision has been evaluated. Evaluation may take a considerable period of time because the results of your decision are not always immediately apparent. Suppose you receive two job offers. It might take several months to a year to judge whether you are satisfied with the job you accepted. It would be necessary to look at the factors you think are most important in a job. Among them might be "Is there opportunity for advancement?" "Are the people here friendly?" "Is the work interesting?"

Evaluating your choice would be further complicated by the difficulty of determining how you might have fared in the job you didn't accept. Now and then, you might obtain some information to suggest what that alter-

native held in store for you, as did a woman who turned down a job offer with a new and promising company. She questioned that decision until she read one morning a year later that the company had gone into bankruptcy.

What happens when your evaluation of a decision is negative? You go back to the drawing board, as the line and arrow on the left-hand side of Figure 3-1 indicates. Since your first decision was not a good one, you are faced with another problem situation. A helpful decision-making aid is to visualize what you would do if the alternative you chose proved to be dreadful—the **worst-case scenario.** Suppose, for example, you choose a job that proves to be unsuited to your talents. Would you resign as soon as your mistake became apparent, or would you sweat it out for a year to show some employment stability? Or would you retain the job while starting to look around for a more suitable job? Developing a worst-case scenario helps prevent you from becoming overwhelmed by a bad decision. Closely related to the worst-case scenario is establishing an *exit strategy* that determines in advance how you will get out of a bad decision, such as having joined a failing family business.

An important point for applying the problem-solving and decision-making steps is that they can be used to tackle subparts of a larger problem. Two partners may decide that they would like to attempt self-employment. A problem of this nature is so complex that it might be resolved best by approaching various components, such as (1) what business should we enter? (2) how would be obtain financing? and (3) would it be better to start our business part time rather than quit our day jobs?

To gain practice in developing your skills in making major decisions, do Human Relations Skill-Building Exercise 3-1.

HUMAN RELATIONS SKILL-BUILDING EXERCISE 3-1

Using the Problem-Solving Process

Imagine that you have received $2 million in cash with the income taxes already paid. The only stipulation is that you will have to use the money to establish some sort of enterprise, either a business or a charitable foundation. Solve this problem, using the worksheet provided below. Describe what thoughts you have or what actions you will take for each step of problem solving and decision making.

I. *Identify causes of the problem:*   Have you found your own problem, or was it given to you?

II. *Diagnose the problem:*   What is the true decision that you are facing? What is your underlying problem?

III. *Find creative alternatives:*   Think of the many alternatives facing you. Let your imagination flow and be creative.

IV. *Weigh alternatives:*   Weigh the pros and cons of each of your sensible alternatives.

Alternatives	Advantages	Disadvantages
1.		
2.		
3.		
4.		
5.		

V. *Make the choice:*   Based on your analysis in step IV, choose the best alternative.

VI. *Implement the choice:*   Outline your action plan for converting your chosen alternative into action.

(Continued)

VII. *Evaluate the choice:* Do the best you can here by speculating how you will know if the decision you reached was a good one.

SUGGESTION: When you analyze the case about a squirrelly problem at the end of this chapter, you might want to use this same problem-solving method.

▲ CREATIVITY IN DECISION MAKING

Creativity is helpful at any stage of decision making but is essential for being aware of problems, analyzing their causes, and searching for alternative solutions. Simply put, **creativity** is the ability to develop good ideas that can be put into action. Finding a creative idea usually involves a flash of insight as to how to solve a problem, such as experienced by the person who thought of Scotch tape.

When many people see or hear the word *creativity,* they think of a rarefied talent. A more helpful perspective is to recognize that not all creativity requires wild imagination. Two types of creativity exist. *Adaptive creativity* involves improving an existing system, such as identifying what is wrong in a customer billing system and correcting the problem. *Innovative creativity* involves creating something new. Instead of trying to correct the invoicing system, the person using innovative creativity would discard it and start all over. As a result of these two types of creativity, a person might be an adaptor or an innovator with respect to creativity.

The emphasis here is on creativity applied to business and personal life rather than on creativity in science, technology, and the arts. Creativity is important for companies of all sizes, not only for large firms. According to a survey conducted by American Express Small Business Services, three-quarters of small-business owners acknowledge that creative thinking is either "very important" (54 percent) or crucial (20 percent) to the success of their firms. About three-quarters of the respondents block out time for idea generation, anywhere from less than one hour per week up to one day per week.[12]

A major theme of this chapter is that for the vast majority of people, it is possible to improve their creativity. As explained in the *Encyclopedia of Creativity,* creativity can be taught and learned, enhanced, and mastered. Enough is known about creativity that it can be integrated into every level in the educational system.[13] How to improve your creativity is described later in this chapter.

MEASURING YOUR CREATIVE POTENTIAL

One way to understand creativity is to try out exercises used to measure creative potential, such as those presented in Human Relations Self-Assessment Quizzes 3-2 and 3-3. Both exercises measure creativity based on verbal ability.

HUMAN RELATIONS SELF-ASSESSMENT QUIZ 3-2

Creative Personality Test

Answer each of the following statements as Mostly True or Mostly False. We are looking for general trends, so do not be concerned that under certain circumstances your answer might be different in response to a particular statement.

	Mostly True	Mostly False
1. I think novels are a waste of time, so I am more likely to read a nonfiction book.	____	____
2. You have to admit, some crooks are ingenious.	____	____
3. I pretty much wear the same style and colors of clothing regularly.	____	____
4. To me most issues have a clear-cut right side or wrong side.	____	____
5. I enjoy it when my boss hands me vague instructions.	____	____
6. When I'm surfing the Internet, I sometimes investigate topics I know very little about.	____	____
7. Business before leisure activities is a hard-and-fast rule in my life.	____	____
8. Taking a different route to work is fun, even if it takes longer.	____	____
9. From time to time I have made friends with people of a different sex, race, religion, or ethnic background from myself.	____	____
10. Rules and regulations should be respected, but deviating from them once in a while is acceptable.	____	____
11. People who know me say that I have an excellent sense of humor.	____	____
12. I have been known to play practical jokes or pranks on people.	____	____
13. Writers should avoid using unusual words and word combinations.	____	____
14. Detective work would have some appeal to me.	____	____
15. I am much more likely to tell a rehearsed joke than make a witty comment.	____	____
16. Almost all national advertising on television bores me.	____	____

(Continued)

17. Why write letters or send e-mail greetings to friends when there are so many clever greeting cards already available in the stores or online? ____ ____

18. For most important problems in life, there is one best solution available. ____ ____

19. Pleasing myself means more to me than pleasing others. ____ ____

20. I'm enjoying taking this test. ____ ____

Score: ____

Scoring: Give yourself a plus 1 for each answer scored in the creative direction as follows:

1. Mostly False	**8.** Mostly True	**15.** Mostly False
2. Mostly True	**9.** Mostly True	**16.** Mostly False
3. Mostly False	**10.** Mostly True	**17.** Mostly False
4. Mostly False	**11.** Mostly True	**18.** Mostly False
5. Mostly True	**12.** Mostly True	**19.** Mostly True
6. Mostly True	**13.** Mostly False	**20.** Mostly True.
7. Mostly False	**14.** Mostly True	

Interpretation: A score of 15 or more suggests that your personality and attitudes are similar to those of a creative person. A score of between 9 and 14 suggests an average similarity with the personality and attitudes of a creative person. A score of 8 or less suggests that your personality is dissimilar to that of a creative person. You are probably more of a conformist and not highly open-minded in your thinking at this point in your life. To become more creative, you may need to develop more flexibility in your thinking and a higher degree of open-mindedness.

CHARACTERISTICS OF CREATIVE WORKERS

Creative workers tend to have different intellectual and personality characteristics from their less creative counterparts. In general, creative people are more mentally flexible than others, which allows them to overcome the traditional ways of looking at problems. This flexibility often shows up in practical jokes and other forms of playfulness, such as making up a rap song about the company's product line. The characteristics of creative workers can be grouped into three broad areas: knowledge, intellectual abilities, personality.[14]

Knowledge

Creative thinking requires a broad background of information, including facts and observations. Knowledge supplies the building blocks for generating and combining ideas. This is particularly true because, according to some experts, creativity always comes down to combining things in a new

HUMAN RELATIONS SELF-ASSESSMENT QUIZ 3-2

Rhyme and Reason

A noted creativity expert says that exercises in rhyming release creative energy; they stir imagination into action. While doing the following exercises, remember that rhyme is frequently a matter of sound and does not have to involve similar or identical spelling. This exercise deals with light and frivolous emotions. After each "definition," write two rhyming words to which it refers.

Examples

1. Large hog   Big   pig
2. Television   Boob   tube
3. A computer command tool for the home   House   mouse

Now try these:

1. Happy father   _____ _____
2. False pain   _____ _____
3. Formed like a simian   _____ _____
4. Highest-ranking police worker   _____ _____
5. Voyage by a large boat   _____ _____
6. Corpulent feline   _____ _____
7. Melancholy fellow   _____ _____
8. Clever beginning   _____ _____
9. Heavy and unbroken slumber   _____ _____
10. Crazy custom   _____ _____
11. Lengthy melody   _____ _____
12. Weak man   _____ _____
13. Instruction at the seashore   _____ _____
14. Criticism lacking in effectiveness   _____ _____
15. A person who murders for pleasurable excitement   _____ _____
16. Musical stringed instrument with full, rich sounds   _____ _____
17. Courageous person who is owned as property by another.   _____ _____
18. Mature complaint   _____ _____
19. Strange hair growing on the lower part of a man's face   _____ _____

(Continued)

20. Drooping marine crustacean   _____ - _____

21. A computer whiz with a ridiculous sense of humor.   _____ - _____

22. You make one up now for the most important question of all.   _____ - _____

Answers and Interpretation: The more of these rhymes you were able to come up with, the higher your creative potential. You would also need an advanced vocabulary to score very high (for instance, what is a *simian* or a *crustacean*?). Ten or more correct rhymes would tend to show outstanding creative potential, at least in the verbal area. Here are the answers:

1. Glad dad	**9.** Deep sleep	**17.** Brave slave
2. Fake ache	**10.** Mad fad	**18.** Ripe gripe
3. Ape shape	**11.** Long song	**19.** Weird beard
4. Top cop	**12.** Frail male	**20.** Limp shrimp
5. Ship trip	**13.** Beach teach	**21.** Absurd nerd
6. Fat cat	**14.** Weak critique	**22.** Two bonus points.
7. Sad lad	**15.** Thriller killer	
8. Smart start	**16.** Mellow cello	

If you can think of a sensible substitute for any of these answers, give yourself a bonus point. For example, for number 21, how about a freak geek?

SOURCE: The current test is an updated version of Eugene Raudsepp with George P. Hough, Jr., *Creative Growth Games* (New York: Harcourt Brace Jovanovich, 1977). Reprinted with permission.

and different way. For example, the Internet-based video chats developed by Apple Computer is a combination of a video with AOL Instant Messaging. The system enables the users to send real-time videos and messages back and forth. (A digital Web camera called iSight is mounted on top of the computer.) So now you have to *look* sick when calling into the office sick.

Intellectual Abilities

In general, creative workers tend to be bright rather than brilliant. Extraordinarily high intelligence is not required to be creative, but creative people are good at generating alternative solutions to problems in a short period of time. According to Robert Sternberg, the key to creative intelligence is **insight,** an ability to know what information is relevant, to find connections between the old and the new, to combine facts that are unrelated, and to see the "big picture."[15] Creative people also maintain a youthful curiosity throughout their lives, and the curiosity is not centered on just their own field of expertise. Instead, their range of interests encompasses many areas of knowledge, and they generate enthusiasm toward almost any puzzling problem. It has also been observed that creative people are open and responsive to feelings and emotions in the world around them.

Creative people are able to think divergently. They can expand the number of alternatives to a problem, thus moving away from a single solution. Yet the creative thinker also knows when it is time to think convergently, narrowing the number of useful solutions. For example, the divergent thinker might think of 27 different names for a Web site to sell high-fashion buttons. Yet at some point, he or she will have to converge toward choose the best name, such as www.chicbutton.com.

Creativity can stem from both *fluid intelligence* and *crystallized intelligence.* Fluid intelligence depends on raw processing ability, or how quickly you learn information and solve problems. Like raw athletic ability, fluid intelligence begins to decline by age 30, particularly because our nerve conduction slows. Crystallized intelligence is accumulated knowledge that increases with age and experience.[16]

Personality

The emotional and other nonintellectual aspects of a person heavily influence creative problem solving. Creative people tend to have a positive self-image without being blindly self-confident. Because they are self-confident, creative people are able to cope with criticism of their ideas. Creative people have the ability to tolerate the isolation necessary for developing ideas. Talking to others is a good source of ideas. Yet at some point, the creative problem solver has to work alone and concentrate.

Creative people are frequently nonconformists and do not need strong approval from the group. Many creative problem solvers are thrill seekers who find developing imaginative solutions to problems to be a source of thrills. Creative people are also persistent, which is especially important for seeing that a new idea is implemented. Selling a creative idea to the right people requires considerable follow-up. Creative people enjoy dealing with uncertainty and chaos. A creative person, for example, would enjoy the challenge of taking over a customer service department that was way behind schedule and ineffective. Less creative people become frustrated quickly when their jobs are unclear and disorder exists.

The Conditions Necessary for Creativity

Creativity is not just a random occurrence. Well-known creativity researcher Teresa M. Amabile has summarized 22 years of her research about creativity in the workplace. Her findings are also supported by others.[17] Creativity takes place when three components come together: expertise, creative thinking skills, and the right type of motivation. *Expertise* refers to the necessary knowledge to put facts together. The more ideas floating around in your head, the more likely you are to combine them in some useful way. The reverse auctions mentioned in the beginning of the chapter required knowledge of business purchasing along with online auctioning.

Creative thinking refers to how flexibly and imaginatively individuals approach problems. If you know how to keep digging for alternatives and to avoid getting stuck in the status quo, your chances of being creative multiply. Along these same lines, you are much more likely to be creative if you are intentionally seeking ideas, such always being on the lookout for money-saving ideas. Persevering, or sticking with a problem to a conclusion, is essential for finding creative solutions. A few rest breaks to gain a fresh perspective may be helpful, but the creative person keeps coming back until a solution emerges.

The right type of *motivation* is the third essential ingredient for creative thought. A fascination with or passion for the task is much more important then searching for external rewards. People will be the most creative when they are motivated primarily by the satisfaction and challenge of the work itself. A Dutch psychologist attempted to analyze what separated chess masters from chess grand masters. He subjected groups of each to a variety of mental ability tests but found no difference between the two groups. The only difference was found in motivation: grand masters simply loved chess more and had more passion and commitment for the game.[18]

Passion for the task and high intrinsic motivation contribute to a total absorption in the work and intense concentration, resulting in the flow experience. (Refer back to the section in Chapter 2 about self-motivation.) Flow also means *being in the zone*. A creative businessperson, such as an entrepreneur developing a plan for worldwide distribution of a product, will often achieve the experience of flow. One analysis of creativity suggests that hard work and the love of the task can be at least as important as raw talent in ensuring creative success.[19]

In addition to the internal conditions that foster creativity, five factors outside the person are key:

1. An environmental need must stimulate the setting of a goal. This is another way of saying, "Necessity is the mother of invention." For example, several years ago independent hardware stores were faced with the challenge of large chains, such as Home Depot and Lowe's, driving them out of business. Many of these independent stores survived by forming buying alliances with each other so that they could purchase inventory in larger quantities—and therefore lower prices. The independents also emphasize doing home repairs, such as fixing ripped screens and broken windows.

2. Another condition that fosters creativity is enough conflict and tension to put people on edge. Robert Sutton advises managers to prod happy people into fighting among themselves to stimulate creativity. The fights should be about ideas, not personality conflicts and name-calling. For example, a group member should be given time to defend his or her work, and then the ideas should be sharply criticized by the other group members.[20]

3. Another external factor for creativity is encouragement, including a permissive atmosphere that welcomes new ideas. A manager or team leader who encourages imagination and original thinking does not punish people for making honest mistakes is likely to receive creative ideas from people. 3M is highly regarded as a company with many innovations in addition to Scotch tape and Post-It® notes. The company encourages creativity in many ways, such as granting people time off from regular responsibilities just to think about new ideas.

4. Humor is a key environmental condition for enhancing creativity. Humor has always been linked to creativity. Humor gets the creative juices flowing, and effective humor requires creativity. Thomas Edison started every workday with a joke-telling session. Mike Vance, chairman of the Creative Thinking Association of America, says, "Humor is unmasking the hypocritical. What makes us laugh often is seeing how things are screwed up—then sometimes seeing how we can fix them. Whenever I go into a company and don't hear much laughter, I know it's not a creative place."[21]

5. A final key environmental condition to considered here is how much time pressure the problem solver should face to trigger creativity. Conventional wisdom says that people produce the best when pressure is highest, such as thinking of ways to keep a business running after a disaster such as a fire, flood, or terrorist attack. Yet recent studies show that the more workers feel pressed for time, the less likely they are to produce creative output, such as solving a tricky problem or envisioning a new product, or to have other such "aha" experiences that result in innovation. Time pressures may diminish creativity because they limit a worker's freedom to think through different options and directions. A subtle finding, however, is that time pressures may help creativity if the worker is focused on a single task he or she considers important.[22] So if you are under heavy time pressure to arrive at a creative solution, focus on one task.

▲ IMPROVING YOUR CREATIVITY

Because of the importance of creative problem solving, many techniques have been developed to improve creativity. Let us look at both specific techniques and general strategies for becoming more creative. The goal of these experiences is to think like a creative problem solver. Such a person lets his or her imagination wander. He or she ventures beyond the constraints that limit most people. The result of thinking more creatively is to bring something new into existence. *Something new* can be a totally new creation or a combination of existing things and ideas.[23]

Concentrate Intensely on the Task at Hand

The ability to concentrate was mentioned earlier as a characteristic that contributes to effective problem solving in general. The ability to eliminate distractions also contributes mightily to generating new ideas. At times we think we are thinking intently about our problem (such as how to make an improved sport cap band), yet in reality we may be thinking about something that interferes with creativity.[24] Among the office distractions that interfere with concentration are phone calls, a computer beep informing you of an incoming message, a fax machine in the receiving mode, and a friendly hello from a work associate walking past your cubicle. All the methods that follow for creativity enhancement require concentration.

Overcome Traditional Mental Sets

An important consequence of becoming more intellectually flexible is that you can overcome a **traditional mental set,** a fixed way of thinking about objects and activities. Overcoming traditional mental sets is important because the major block to creativity is perceiving things in a traditional way. All creative examples presented so far in this chapter involved this process, and here is another one. You may be familiar with the Nalgene sports bottle for carrying water and other fluids. Aside from its decorative colors, a key feature is its durability. The bottle had its origins in chemical laboratories—the traditional use for a durable plastic bottle. However, by the 1970s, managers at Nalge noticed that scientists were using the durable bottles to hold water for camping and hiking. The company soon started a division to market its "laboratory" bottles to Boy Scouts and other hikers.[25] Today, the company is challenged to keep up with the demand for the Nalgene bottle.

An effective way of overcoming a traditional mental set (or thinking outside the box) is to challenge the status quo. If you want to develop an idea that will impress your boss or turn around an industry, you must use your imagination. Question the old standby that things have always been done in a particular way.

Human Relations Self-Assessment Quiz 3-2 gives you an opportunity to examine your tendencies toward overcoming traditional mental sets.

DISCIPLINE YOURSELF TO THINK LATERALLY

A major challenge in developing creative thinking skills is to learn how to think laterally in addition to vertically. **Vertical thinking** is an analytical, logical process that results in few answers. The vertical thinker is looking for the one best solution to a problem, much like solving an equation in algebra. In contrast, **lateral thinking** spreads out to find many different alternative solutions to a problem. In short, critical thinking is vertical, and creative thinking is lateral.

A vertical thinker might say, "I must find a part-time job to supplement my income. My income is not matching my expenses." The lateral thinker might say, "I need more money. Let me think of the various ways of earning more money. I can find a second job, get promoted where I am working, cut my expenses, run a small business out of my home. . . . "

To learn to think laterally, you have to develop the mental set that every problem has multiple alternative solutions. Do not leave the problem until you have sketched out multiple alternatives. Use a pencil or pen and paper or a computer screen, but do not walk away from your problem until you have thought of multiple alternatives.

CONDUCT BRAINSTORMING SESSIONS

The best-known method of improving creativity is **brainstorming,** a technique by which group members think of multiple solutions to a problem. Using brainstorming, a group of six people might sit around a table generating new ideas for a product. During the idea-generating part of brainstorming, potential solutions are not criticized or evaluated in any way. In this way, spontaneity is encouraged. The original device for programming

HUMAN RELATIONS SELF-ASSESSMENT QUIZ 3-3

How Well Do You Think Outside the Box?

Creativity and marketing speaker Floyd Hunt has developed a test to see whether you have been lulled into complacency and therefore are not thinking creatively.

For each statement, rank yourself on the following 10-point scale:

I can't remember	1–2 points
Not in the past year	3–4 points
Sometime in the past year	5–6 points
In the past month	7–8 points
It happens often	9–10 points

The last time I remember . . .

1. Someone saying to me, "You've never done that before!" _____

2. Changing my routine for no particular reason, other than I just wanted to _____

3. Rearranging my office, living room, or sock drawer, just for fun _____

4. Someone telling me, "It can't be done," and my trying anyway _____

5. Fighting for an idea _____

6. Feeling that I was way out on a limb _____

7. Being told, "You're wrong," because I tried something new _____

8. Being wrong _____

9. Doing something that made me nervous _____

10. Feeling afraid and exhilarated at the same time _____

Scoring

Less than 20	Get your head out of the sand.
21–50	You have potential, but your routines need more shaking up.
51–80	You've either reached or are heading for success; watch out for becoming too complacent.
81–100	Let me get out of your way!

SOURCE: "Success Quiz," *Success,* November 1998, p. 22. Reprinted with permission of *Success* Magazine.

VCRs by simply punching one number was a product of brainstorming. The product retails for about $75. It is designed for people who are unable or unwilling to learn how to program a VCR. Rules for brainstorming are presented in Exhibit 3-2. Brainstorming has many variations, including an electronic approach, brainwriting, and forced associations.

An important strategy for enhancing the outcome of brainstorming is to have intellectually and culturally diverse group members. Some group leaders purposely choose people of different problem-solving styles (such as sensation types and intuitive types) to encourage more diverse thinking. The sensation type might have more "brainstorms" based on facts, whereas the intuitive type might have more brainstorms based on hunches. Cultural diversity is likely to improve brainstorming because people with different cultural experiences often bring different viewpoints to bear on the problem. A basic example is that when developing new food products, members with different ethnic backgrounds are chosen for a brainstorming group.

EXHIBIT 3-2

Rules and Guidelines for Brainstorming

1. Use groups of about five to seven people.

2. Encourage the spontaneous expression of ideas. All suggestions are welcome, even if they are outlandish or outrageous. The least workable ideas can be edited out when the idea-generation phase is completed.

3. Quantity and variety are very important. The greater the number of ideas, the greater the likelihood of a breakthrough idea.

4. Encourage combination and improvement of ideas. This process is referred to as *piggybacking* or *hitchhiking*.

5. One person serves as the secretary and records the ideas, perhaps posting them on a chalkboard.

6. In many instances, it pays to select a moderator who helps keep the session on track. The moderator can prevent one or two members from dominating the meeting. If the moderator takes notes, a secretary is not needed.

7. Do not overstructure by following any of the above rules too rigidly. Brainstorming is a spontaneous process.

8. To broaden idea generation, think about how a characteristic of something might be if it were modified: if it were larger or more frequent, if it were smaller or less frequent, or if something else could be used instead.

Electronic Brainstorming

In electronic brainstorming, group members simultaneously enter their suggestions into a computer. The ideas are distributed to the screens of other group members. Although the group members do not talk to each other, they are still able to build on each other's ideas and combine ideas.

Electronic brainstorming helps overcome certain problems encountered in traditional brainstorming. Shyness, domination by one or two members, and participants who loaf tend to be less troublesome than in face-to-face situations. An experiment indicated that, with large groups, electronic brainstorming produces more useful ideas than the usual type.[26]

Brainwriting

In many situations, brainstorming by yourself produces as many or more useful ideas than does brainstorming in groups. **Brainwriting,** or solo brainstorming, is arriving at creative ideas by jotting them down yourself. The creativity-improvement techniques discussed so far will help you develop the mental flexibility necessary for brainstorming. After you have loosened up your mental processes, you will be ready to tackle your most vexing problems. Self-discipline is very important for brainwriting because some people have a tendency to postpone something as challenging as thinking alone.

An important requirement of brainwriting is that you set aside a regular time (and perhaps place) for generating ideas. The ideas discovered in the process of routine activities can be counted as bonus time. Even five minutes a day is much more time than most people are accustomed to spend thinking creatively about job problems. Give yourself a quota with a time deadline.

Forced Associations

A widely used method of releasing creativity is the **forced-association technique.** Using this technique, individuals or groups solve a problem by making associations between the properties of two objects. A link is found between the properties of the random object and the properties of the problem object. The forced association is supposed to help solve the problem. An individual (working alone or in a group) selects a word at random from a dictionary or textbook. If you happen to choose a preposition, try again until you find a noun to give you something more to work with. Next, the person (or group) lists many of the properties and attributes of this word. Assume you randomly chose the word *ladder.* Among its attributes are "durable," "foldable," "aluminum or wood," "moderately priced," and "easy to use." If you were trying to improve a bow tie to increase sales, for example, you might make the tie more durable and easier to use.

In the various types of brainstorming just discussed, collecting wild ideas is just the start of the process. After ideas are collected, the group or each member carefully evaluates and analyzes the various alternatives. It is usually important to also specify the implementation details. For example, how do you make a bow tie easier to use other than by adding a clip?

Human Relations Skill-Building Exercise 3-3 will give you an opportunity to practice brainstorming in an area familiar to every reader of this book. Exercise 3-4 will take you one step further in the application of brainstorming.

HUMAN RELATIONS SKILL-BUILDING EXERCISE 3-3

1-800-INSIGHT

Using conventional brainstorming or one of its variations, huddle in small groups. Your task is to develop 800, 888, or 900 telephone numbers for firms in various fields. Keep in mind that the best 800 (or 888 or 900) numbers are easy to memorize and have a logical connection to the goods or services provided. After each group makes up its list of telephone numbers (perhaps about three for each firm on the list), compare results with the other groups. Here is the list of enterprises:

- A nationwide chain of funeral homes
- A motorcycle dealer
- A software problem help line for Microsoft Corp.
- A used-car chain
- A prayer service (a 900 number)
- An introduction (dating) service (a 900 number)

HUMAN RELATIONS SKILL-BUILDING EXERCISE 3-4

Mindstorming

Mindstorming is a slight variation of brainstorming applicable to many problems facing people in work and personal life. In mindstorming you write your goal in the form of a question. After you ask the question, the group must write out 20 answers. We provide two questions, and your group provides two other questions. You then choose one of the four questions and come up with some high-quality answers.

1. As the manager of a budget hotel, how can we increase the percent of room occupancy from its present 70 percent to 85 percent for next year?

2. Having moved into a new town, how can we make new friends for the upcoming year?

3. Your original question about work or career.

4. Your other original question about personal life.

SOURCE: The idea of *mindstorming* is credited to Brian Tracy, *Victory!* (New York: AMACOM, 2002).

Borrow Creative Ideas

Copying the successful ideas of others is a legitimate form of creativity. Be careful, however, to give appropriate credit. Knowing when and which ideas to borrow from other people can help you behave as if you were an imaginative person. Creative ideas can be borrowed through such methods as the following:

Speaking to friends, relatives, classmates, and coworkers

Reading newspapers, newsmagazines, trade magazines, textbooks, nonfiction books, and novels and surfing the Internet

Watching television and listening to radio programs

Subscribing to computerized information services (expensive but worth it to many ambitious people)

Business firms borrow ideas from each other regularly as part of quality improvement. The process is referred to as *benchmarking* because another firm's product, service, or process is used as a standard of excellence. Benchmarking involves representatives from one company visiting another to observe firsthand the practices of another company. The company visited is usually not a direct competitor. It is considered unethical to visit a competitor company for the purpose of appropriating ideas. However, *competitive intelligence* involves copying the best ideas from competitors.

It is difficult to capitalize on your creative ideas unless you keep a careful record of them. A creative idea entrusted to memory may be forgotten under the pressures of everyday living. An important new idea kept on your list of daily errands or duties may become lost. Because creative ideas carry considerable weight in propelling your career forward, they deserve to be recorded in a separate notebook, such as a daily planner.

Challenge Your Ruts

A major hurdle to thinking creatively is getting locked into so many habits and routines that our thinking becomes too mechanical. According to Kathleen R. Allen, "We do the same things, the same way, every day. This is a primary barrier to creativity. Often we need to feel a little uncomfortable— we need to experience new things—to get creative sparks."[27] Challenging your ruts, or habitual way of doing things, can assist you in developing mental flexibility. Anything you do that forces you out of your normal environment will help you see things in new and different ways. Here is a sampling of challenging everyday ruts:

+ Eating lunch with the same friends at work or school

+ Watching the same television shows or reading only the same sections of the newspaper

◆ Restricting your Internet browsing to the same few bookmarks or always using the same search engine

◆ Befriending only those people in your same demographic group, such as age range, race, and ethnic background

◆ Engaging in the same pastimes exclusively

◆ Using the same form of physical exercise each time you exercise

◆ Your turn to select a rut: _____

Avoiding ruts is closely associated with overcoming traditional mental sets, as measured in Human Relations Self-Assessment Quiz 3-2. Traditional mental sets are essentially mental ruts.

ESTABLISH IDEA QUOTAS FOR YOURSELF

To enhance creativity, many companies assign idea quotas to workers. For example, workers might be instructed to bring one good idea for earning or saving money to every meeting. Establishing idea quotas is similar to brainwriting with a goal in mind. An easy way of getting started is to establish a monthly minimum quota of one creative idea to improve your personal life and one to improve your job or school performance. Although this exercise might only take about five minutes of thinking each month, it could have a tremendous impact on your life.

Using idea quotas, a rare book seller with an inventory of 150,000 rare books thought of the creative idea of putting his business online. Sales increased by $2,000 per month. A woman from Virginia who wanted to improve her social life came up with the idea of moving to Alaska, where the ratio of men to women is about seven to one. Although her golf season is now shorter, the woman has improved her social life substantially.

PLAY THE ROLES OF EXPLORER, ARTIST, JUDGE, AND LAWYER

A method for improving creativity has been proposed that incorporates many of the suggestions already made. The method calls for you to adopt four roles in your thinking.[28]

1. *Be an explorer.* Speak to people in different fields and get ideas that you can use. For example, if you are a telecommunications specialist, speak to salespeople and manufacturing specialists.

2. *Be an artist by stretching your imagination.* Strive to spend about 5 percent of your day asking "what if" questions. For example, a sales manager at a fresh-fish distributor might ask, "What if some new research suggests that eating fish causes intestinal cancer in humans?" Also, remember to challenge the commonly perceived rules in your field. For example, a bank manager challenged why customers needed their canceled checks returned each month. This questioning led to some banks not returning canceled checks unless the customer paid an additional fee for the service. (As a compromise, some banks send customers photocopies of about 10 checks on one page.)

3. *Know when to be a judge.*   After developing some wild ideas, at some point you have to evaluate them. Do not be so critical that you discourage your own imaginative thinking. However, be critical enough to prevent attempting to implement weak ideas.

4. *Achieve results by playing the role of a lawyer.*   Negotiate and find ways to implement your ideas within your field or place of work. The explorer, artist, and judge stages of creative thought might take only a short time to develop a creative idea. Yet you may spend months or even years getting your brainstorm implemented. For example, it took a long time for the developer of the electronic pager to finally get the product manufactured and distributed on a large scale.

GIVE YOURSELF A BREAK

A major challenge facing the creative thinker is to avoid frustration when a creative solution to the problem at hand does not surface. A widely recommended step for overcoming this hurdle is to reduce the tension by taking a brief break or pause of somewhere between 10 minutes and one hour and then return to the creative problem solving. Going for a walk is often effective because moderate physical exercise stimulates the brain.[29] Another break of potential value is to take a nap because a nap clears the mind and reduces tension.

▲ SUMMARY

Problem solving occurs when you try to remove an obstacle that is blocking a path you want to take or when you try to close the gap between what exists and what you want to exist. Decision making takes place after you encounter a problem. It refers to selecting one alternative from the various courses of action that can be pursued.

Many traits and characteristics influence the type of problem solver you are now or are capable of becoming. Among them are (1) cognitive intelligence, education, and experience; (2) emotional intelligence; (3) flexibility versus rigidity; (4) intuition; (5) concentration; (6) decisiveness and perfectionism; (7) risk taking and thrill seeking; and (8) values.

The Myers-Briggs Type Indicator is a widely used method of classifying problem-solving styles. Four dimensions of psychological functioning underlie the method: introverted versus extroverted; thinking versus feeling; sensing versus intuiting; and judging versus perceiving. Combining the four types with each other results in 16 personality types, such as a person being a conceptualizer, traditionalist, visionary, or organizer. For example, the organizer (ESTJ) scores high on extroversion, sensing, thinking, and judging. Recognizing your problem-solving style can help you identify work that you are likely to perform well, such as those mentioned in Exhibit 3-1.

The decision-making process outlined in this chapter uses both the scientific method and intuition for making decisions in response to problems. Decision making follows an orderly flow of events:

1. You are aware of a problem or create one of your own.

2. You identify causes of the problem.

3. You find creative alternatives.

4. You weigh the alternatives.

5. You make the choice.

6. You implement the choice.

7. You evaluate whether you have made a sound choice. If your choice was unsound, you are faced with a new problem, and the cycle repeats itself.

Creativity is the ability to look for good ideas that can be put into action. Adaptive creativity involves improving an existing system, whereas innovative creativity involves creating something new. Creative workers tend to have different intellectual and personality characteristics than their less creative counterparts. In general, creative people are more mentally flexible than others, which allows them to overcome the traditional way of looking at problems.

Creative thinking requires a broad background of information, including facts and observations. Creative workers tend to be bright rather than brilliant. The key to creative intelligence is insight. Creativity can stem from both fluid (raw) intelligence and crystallized (accumulated) intelligence. The emotional and other nonintellectual aspects of a person heavily influence creative problem solving. For example, creative people are frequently nonconformists and thrill seekers.

Creativity takes place when three components come together: expertise, creative thinking skills, and the right type of motivation. Creative thinking refers to being flexible and imaginative. The right type of motivation refers to passion for the task and intrinsic motivation. Four factors outside the person play a key role in fostering creativity. An environmental need, enough conflict and tension to put people on edge, encouragement from management, and the presence of humor. Unless a person is working on a highly focused task, time pressures are likely to diminish creativity.

Methods of improving your creativity include (1) concentrating intensely on the task at hand; (2) overcoming traditional mental sets; (3) disciplining yourself to think laterally; (4) conducting brainstorming sessions; (5) borrowing creative ideas; (6) challenging your ruts; (7) establishing idea quotas; (8) playing the roles of explorer, artist, judge, and lawyer; and (9) taking a break.

Brainstorming has several variations, including electronic brainstorming in which people enter ideas into a computer. Brainwriting is essentially solo brainstorming. The forced-association technique requires problem solving by making associations between the properties of two objects.

Questions and Activities

1. What would be some of the symptoms or signs of a "rigid thinker"?

2. How might being a perfectionist create performance problems for a team leader? For a paralegal? For a computer programmer?

3. Why does concentration improve problem solving?

4. Why is intuition often referred to as a "sixth sense"?

5. How will it help you in your career to know your problem-solving style?

6. How might you use the Internet to improve major decisions you might face on the job and in personal life?

7. How can a person still be creative in his or her work without having much talent?

8. Give an example of one work problem and one personal problem for which brainstorming might be useful.

9. Why is being passionate about the task at hand almost essential for being creative?

10. Ask an experienced manager or professional how important creative thinking has been in his or her career. Be prepared to report back to class with your findings.

INTERNET SKILL BUILDER: Creativity Training

Many Web sites offer creativity training. One such site is www.before-after.com, which mentions many reasons for improving creativity, including "Bring greater creativity to our sales process," "Infuse our meeting with creative energy," and "I'm just looking for creative inspiration." We especially recommend going to the two-minute Creative IQ test. How do the results of this test compare to the creativity test you took in this chapter? If before-after.com is no longer in operation, insert "creativity training" in your search engine to find a comparable site.

WEB CORNER

Critical thinking: www.businesspotential.com/critic_think.htm

Creative style questionnaire:
   http:etesting.modwest.com/tests.php?test=5

HUMAN RELATIONS CASE PROBLEM

Big Electricity Fights Little Squirrel

Robin Folcik was reading the newspaper at her breakfast table one Sunday when the lights blinked, smoke poured from the sockets, and a charged buzz came over the room, making the hair on her arms stand up. "I thought my house was blowing up," recalls Ms. Folcik, a waitress in Southington, Conn.

An inquiry into the matter by Connecticut Light & Power found "remnants of a squirrel" and shards of a ceramic electrical switch at the base of utility pole #85324. The conclusion: The critter had electrocuted itself and, in so doing, triggered a massive power surge that blew out appliances and television sets all over the neighborhood.

Like many other utilities around the country, Connecticut Power says it's having trouble these days with squirrels causing outages, damage and outraged customers. Utilities in recent years have stepped up the efforts to fight the acrobatic rodents—buying everything from predator urine to baffles that look like pizza pans to fend them off.

It's a war and the squirrels are winning. It's escalating as the electrical grid spreads and more wires are closer to more animals whose natural habitat has been destroyed. About a thousand miles of high-voltage transmission lines are added each year in the U.S.

Longmont Power & Communications, which serves 35,000 customers north of Denver, says that more than 90% of its significant outages are caused by squirrels, which cut the power 393 times in 2002, up from 349 two years earlier. The increase took place despite measures Longmont has taken to thwart squirrels by banding utility poles with slippery, hard plastic.

In the past two years, the municipal electricity system in Tullahoma, Tenn., spent more than $25,000 on "Varmint Shields"—dark gray plastic disks that look like barbeque grills—so squirrels can't cause trouble at various hot spots, including transformers. But the utility considers the effort a "limited" success, given than it has reduced squirrel outages to 136 in 2002, from the 148 it reported in 1997.

What customers don't understand, say exasperated utility workers, is that the cute little forager is an obsessive foe. A squirrel's teeth grow six to ten inches a year, unless the rodent has plenty to gnaw on. Squirrels follow paths that they have taken before on their way home or to an acorn stash, and have an internal navigation system for following a route over and over, using remembered objects to plot a fix with singular determination. "A squirrel thinks, 'This is the way I've gone all my life, and just because you built a substation, don't think for one minute I'm not going to go there,'" says Shelia Frazier, who advises utilities as a senior project manager for Energy Consulting Group LLC of Marietta, Ga.

Falling trees and branches obviously cause plenty of outages, too, but dealing with squirrels is "so aggravating" to utilities, Ms. Frazier says. "You've got to drive forever

(Continued)

to some place, replace the transformer—and the worst problem is you know in your heart it's a squirrel, but you don't often have a fried carcass to show anybody because predators have already snatched it, and customers are crying bloody murder."

Many utilities say trapping squirrels is too expensive. Shooting them is costly and in many places restricted. Immigration will quickly repopulate an area where squirrel numbers have reproduced drastically. Thus the development of anti-squirrel gear is surging. In one report on outages, the Electric Power Research Institute, a nonprofit analysis group in California, called the squirrel, "Public Enemy No. 1"

Entrepreneur Douglas Wulff, of Columbian, Mo. hopes for a high sale with his $50 "Critter Pole Guard." Introduced last year, it looks like a string of polypropylene bratwurst that wraps around a utility pole. When a squirrel tries to clamber over it, the bratwurst spins and tosses the animal off. In Chicago, Joe Seid, sales manager at Bird-X, Inc. is pushing products such as the $95 Transonic IXL. Based, he says, on "psycho acoustic jamming" principles, it blast high intensity sound waves that can't be heard by humans but sound like jackhammers to squirrels.

More than 100 customers have sought damages for ruined appliances, and many have already received compensation, including Ms. Folcik, who protested that she lost two TV sets, a Sony PlayStation, two video-recorders, an air conditioner, a stereo and speakers, and a treadmill.

Customers want the utility to spend more on maintenance, and have taken their case to the state's Department of Public Utility Control. The utility claims that a squirrel was responsible, and no device on the market could have prevented what happened. But some angry customers don't buy that story and have suggested, "perhaps C & P maintenance crews were responsible," DPUC records say.

"I thought, 'A squirrel? Oh yeah? Again?'" says Ms. Flocik. "It has happened before, and they always blame it on a squirrel."

Questions

1. What is the cause of the problem facing the electric companies?

2. Of the several solutions to the squirrel problem mentioned in the case, which one do you think is the most likely to ward off squirrels?

3. What creative solution can you offer to the squirrel problem facing the utilities?

4. How might the interests of the utility companies, their customers, and animal rights activists be balanced in resolving the dilemma facing the utility companies?

SOURCE: Barbara Carton, "Fried Squirrel Is Not a Favorite Dish with Public Utilities," *Wall Street Journal,* February 4, 2003, pp. A1, A15.

▲ REFERENCES

1. Mark Henricks, "Competitive Pricing: Reverse Online Auctions Will Have Suppliers Racing to Beat Each Other's Bids," *Entrepreneur,* August 2002, pp. 65–66.

2. Daniel Goleman, *Working with Emotional Intelligence* (New York: Bantam, 1998).

3. Quoted in Bill Breen, "What's Your Intuition?" *Fast Company,* September 2000, p. 300.

4. Lisa A. Burke and Monica K. Miller, "Taking the Mystery Out of Intuitive Decision Making," *Academy of Management Executive,* November 1999, p. 94.

5. John S. Hammond, Ralph L. Keeney, and Howard Rafia, "The Hidden Traps in Decision Making," *Harvard Business Review,* September–October 1998, p. 50.

6. The Myers-Briggs Type Indicator (MBTI) is published by Consulting Psychological Press, Inc., Palo Alto, CA 94306. Much of the discussion here is based on Robert P. Vecchio, *Organizational Behavior: Core Concepts,* 4th ed. (Fort Worth: Dryden Press, 2000), pp. 44–45.

7. William Woods, "Personality Tests Are Back," *Fortune,* March 30, 1987, pp. 74–82.

8. Paul C. Nutt, "Surprising but True: Half the Decision in Organizations Fail," *Academy of Management Executive,* November 1999, pp. 75–90; Nutt, *Why Decisions Fail* (San Francisco: Berrett-Koehler, 2002).

9. Peter Coy, "Laurels for an Odd Couple: A Psychologist and a Traditionalist Share This Year's Nobel," *BusinessWeek,* October 21, 2002, p. 50.

10. Carol Polsky, "This Invention Is So Useful, It Has Stuck Around for 75 Years," *Newsday* syndicated story, May 13, 2000.

11. Hammond et al., "The Hidden Traps in Decision Making," p. 50.

12. "Good Idea: Take Time to Think," *Rochester, (NY) Democrat and Chronicle,* August 7, 2000, p. 8F.

13. Mark A. Runco and Steven R. Pritzker, eds., *Encyclopedia of Creativity,* vol. 1 (San Diego: Academic Press, 1999), p. xv.

14. Richard W. Woodman, John E. Sawyer, and Ricky W. Griffin, "Toward a Theory of Organizational Creativity," *Academy of Management Review,* April 1993, pp. 293–321; Greg R. Oldham and Anne Cummings, "Employee Creativity: Personal and Contextual Factors at Work," *Academy of Management Journal,* June 1996, pp. 607–634; Mihaly Csikzentmihalyi, "If We Are So Rich, Why Aren't We Happy?" *American Psychologist,* October 1999, p. 824; Robert J. Sternberg, "Creativity as a Decision," *American Psychologist,* May 2002, p. 376.

15. Robert J. Sternberg, ed., *Handbook of Creativity* (New York: Cambridge University Press, 1999).

16. "Why Kids Beat Adults at Video Games: Two Types of Intelligence," *USA Weekend,* January 1–3, 1999, p. 5.

17. Teresa M. Amabile, "How to Kill Creativity," *Harvard Business Review,* September–October 1998, pp. 78–79.

18. Research cited in "What Happens in the Brain of an Einstein in the Throes of Creation?" *USA Weekend,* January 1–3, 1999, p. 11.

19. Robert I. Sutton, "The Weird Rules of Creativity," *Harvard Business Review,* September 2001, p. 101.

20. Teresa M. Amabile, "Beyond Talent: John Irving and the Passionate Craft of Creativity," *American Psychologist,* April 2001, p. 335.

21. Cited in Robert McGarvey, "Turn It On," *Entrepreneur,* November 1996, pp. 156–157.

22. Research cited in Bridget Murray, "A Ticking Clock Means a Creativity Drop," *Monitor on Psychology,* November 2002, p. 24.

23. Juanita Weaver, "The Mental Picture: Bringing Your Definition of Creativity into Focus," *Entrepreneur,* February 2003, p. 68.

24. Frederick D. Buggie, "Overcoming Barriers to Creativity," *Innovative Leader,* May 1997, p. 5.

25. "Sports Bottles Oh So Cool," *Rochester (NY) Democrat and Chronicle,* August 23, 2003, p. 14D.

26. R. Brente Gallupe et al., "Electronic Brainstorming and Group Size," *Academy of Management Journal,* June 1992, pp. 350–359.

27. Quoted in Mark Hendricks, "Good Thinking: Knock Down the Barrier to Creativity—and Discover a Whole World of New Ideas," *Entrepreneur,* May 1996, p. 158.

28. "Be a Creative Problem Solver," *Executive Strategies,* June 6, 1989, pp. 1–2.

29. Juanita Weaver, "Under Pressure: Ease Tension and Get the Creative Juices Flowing Again," *Entrepreneur,* August 2003, p. 69.

▲ ADDITIONAL READING

DeGraff, Jeff, and Katherine A. Lawrence. *Creativity at Work: Discovering the Right Practices to Make Innovation Happen.* San Francisco: Jossey-Bass, 2002.

Godin, Seth. "Unleash Your Ideavirus." *Fast Company,* August 2000, pp. 118–135.

Goldenbergb, Jacob, Roni Horowitz, Amnon Leavav, and David Mazursky. "Finding Your Innovation Sweet Spot." *Harvard Business Review,* March 2003, pp. 120–129.

Grossman, Robert J. "Behavior at Work." *HR Magazine,* March 2001, pp. 50–54.

Henricks, Mark. "Need Some Help Thinking More Clearly under Pressure? 'Hot-Wire' Your Brain with Meditation." *Entrepreneur,* July 2003, pp. 73–74.

Levesque, Lynn C. *Breakthrough Creativity: Achieving Top Performance Using the Eight Creative Talents.* Palo Alto, CA: Davies-Black, 2001.

Mitroff, Ian. *Smart Thinking for Crazy Times: The Art of Solving the Right Problems.* San Francisco: Berrett-Koehler Publishers, 1998.

Robertson, S. Ian. *Problem Solving.* Philadelphia: Psychology Press, 2001.

Rosenfeld, Jill. "Here's an Idea!" *Fast Company,* April 2000, pp. 97–130.

Weaver, Juanita. "Ideas on Demand: You Don't Have to Wait for Inspiration." *Entrepreneur,* April 2003, pp. 78, 79.

Achieving Wellness and Managing Stress

Learning Objectives

After studying the information and doing the exercise in this chapter, you should be able to:

◆ Explain the meaning of wellness and how it can be attained

◆ Describe the meaning of stress, its physiology, and its consequences

◆ Identify several positive and negative consequences of stress

◆ Pinpoint potential stressors in personal and work life

◆ Describe key methods for managing the potential adverse effects of stress

*S*teve Stephenson, senior manager in organization and team development at the Boeing Commercial Airplane Co. in Greenbank, Washington, conducts stress management seminars for employees. Stephenson has collected some data showing that his stress management program enhances performance. Yet he believes that anecdotal evidence is also important. For example, Stephenson tells of an engineer who attended one of

his seminars: "He was grumpy, red-faced and tense. When asked about why he came, he said, 'My supervisor sent me here.' I thought the program would be a total failure for him. Two months later, I ran by his workshop and asked him what he thought of the training. He pulled out this notebook full of numbers. 'Here's my blood pressure before I took your classes and here it is now,' he says. The improvement was amazing."[1]

The time and money Boeing Commercial Airplane invests in a training program for stress management illustrates an important workplace reality. To be successful in a competitive business world, it is not enough simply to cope with job pressures and overcome health problems. You also have to feel and be at your best. Similarly, treating and curing physical and mental health problems is still important, but considerable emphasis is now being placed on preventing illness and staying well. Well people are not simply those who are not sick. Instead, they are vibrant, relatively happy, and able to cope with life's problems.

In this chapter we describe the achievement of wellness, the nature and cause of stress, and managing personal and work stress. In the next chapter we continue with a stress-related topic: coping with personal problems.

▲ STRATEGIES FOR ACHIEVING WELLNESS

Many people believe that we can live longer, healthier lives if we choose to do so. An important principle of behavioral medicine is that the body and mind must work together for a healthy lifestyle. Consider also that lifestyle decisions contribute to 7 of the 10 principal causes of mortality and that about half the deaths resulting from these causes could be prevented by changes in behavior.[2] A person who smokes two packs of cigarettes per day, eats mostly fatty food and sweets, drinks a liter of wine per day, and leads a sedentary life has a below-average life expectancy. Note that all these life-threatening activities are under the person's control. Heart-health and lifestyle guru Dean Ornish believes that many people engage in unhealthy behaviors, such as drug abuse, alcohol abuse, overwork, and excessive television watching, just to get through the day. And these people struggle through the day at the expense of their health.[3]

Wellness is a formalized approach to preventive health care. By promoting health, company wellness programs help prevent employees from developing physical and mental problems often associated with excessive job pressures. Wellness programs focus on preventive health rather than treating problems after they have occurred. Companies with such programs usually have an atmosphere that encourages employee health. A key message about the wellness movement is that it is never too late to start getting well no matter how badly you have abused your body and mind in the past. Scientists have accumulated information indicating that the body has an astounding ability to heal itself, provided that the underlying damage is not too great, such as having destroyed your liver with alcohol. A sample positive finding is that 40-year-old women who have led a sedentary life who then begin walking briskly for 30 minutes a day, four days a week, have the same low risk of heart attack as lifelong exercising women.[4]

In this section we describe achieving wellness through exercise, appropriate rest, diet, resilience, and minimizing health and safety risks. Another key component of achieving wellness—stress management—is described later.

EXERCISING PROPERLY

The right amount and type of physical exercise contributes substantially to wellness. To achieve wellness it is important to select an exercise program that is physically challenging but that does not lead to overexertion and muscle injury. Competitive sports, if taken too seriously, can actually increase a person's stress level. The most beneficial exercises are classified as aerobic because they make you breathe faster and raise your heart rate.

Most of a person's exercise requirements can be met through everyday techniques such as walking or running upstairs, vigorous housework, yard work, or walking several miles per day. Avoid the remote control for your television; getting up to change the channel can burn off a few calories! Another exercise freebie is to park your car in a remote spot in the parking lot. The exercise you receive from walking to and from your car is an investment in your wellness. Physical exercise is particularly important for people who are seated most of the day at their jobs and who snack heavily to cope with job pressures.

The physical benefits of exercise include increased respiratory capacity, increased muscle tone, improved circulation, increased energy, increased rate of metabolism, reduced body weight and improved fat metabolism, and slowed-down aging processes. Of enormous importance, physical activity strengthens the heart and reduces harmful cholesterol, low-density lipoprotein (LDL), while increasing the level of beneficial cholesterol, high-density lipoprotein (HDL). The higher the LDL cholesterol level in the blood, the higher the risk of heart disease

The mental benefits of exercise are also plentiful. A major benefit is the euphoria that often occurs when morphinelike brain chemicals called *endorphins* are released into the body. The same experience is referred to as "runner's high." Other mental benefits of exercise include increased self-confidence; improved body image and self-esteem; improved mental functioning, alertness, and efficiency; release of accumulated tensions; and relief from mild depression.[5]

People who find intrinsic motivation in exercise are the most likely to maintain a successful program. The idea is to shift the focus from long-term, external outcomes like losing weight to positive, internal experiences you can enjoy now. Exercise, like work, is the most fun when it leads to the flow experience. When exercise is fun for its own sake, you are more likely to persist and therefore derive the many benefits mentioned above.[6] A note of caution is that exercise can become too much fun. A person might become habituated to exercise, thereby incurring frequent injuries and neglecting other important life activities.

Sleep Adequately

Getting enough sleep plays a major role in being well, yet about 80 million people in the United States and Canada suffer from sleep deprivation. Work-related problems such as increased stress, inattention, and lowered productivity are caused by workers getting too little sleep or poor-quality sleep. Adequate sleep is also important for storing both information and motor skills into the brain.[7] Also, sleep deprivation is a major contributor to vehicular accidents. The average person requires seven and one-half hours sleep per 24 hours, yet the average amount of sleep is six and one-half hours. (Some people require more sleep and others less.)

According to John Shepard, head of Sleep Disorders Center at the Mayo Clinic, you are not getting enough sleep when you rely on an alarm clock to wake you up. He defines adequate sleep as "that amount which, when you attain it on a steady basis, produces a full degree of daytime alertness and a feeling of well-being the next day."[8] Sleep deprivation appears to be cumulative, resulting in *sleep debt*. If you need eight hours of sleep per night and get only seven, by the end of the week your sleep debt is five hours.

Here are some suggestions for staying alert and getting a wellness advantage from sleep:

- At home, set a regular bedtime and observe it carefully.

- Near bedtime, avoid exercise, caffeine, and heavy food.

- Don't consume any alcohol within two hours of bedtime.

- Generally eat healthy snacks and avoid eating too much or too little.

- At work, exercise during breaks. Exercise improves mood and promotes alertness.[9]

As implied by the above bit of wisdom, exercise, diet, appropriate sleep, and wellness are linked to each other.

MAINTAINING A HEALTHY DIET

Eating nutritious foods is valuable for mental as well as physical health. To illustrate, many nutritionists and physicians believe that eating fatty foods, such as red meat, contributes to colon cancer. Improper diet, such as consuming less than 1,300 calories per day, can weaken you physically. In turn, you become more susceptible to stress.

What Is a Healthy Diet?

The subject of proper diet has been debated continually. Advice abounds on what to eat and what not to eat. Some of this information is confusing and contradictory, partly because not enough is known about nutrition to identify an ideal diet for each individual. For example, many people can point to an 85-year-old relative who has been eating the wrong food (and perhaps consuming considerable alcohol) most of his or her life. The implication is that if this person has violated sensible habits of nutrition and has lived so long, how important can good diet be?

The food requirements for wellness differ depending on age, sex, body size, physical activity, and other conditions, such as pregnancy and illness. A workable dietary strategy is to follow the guidelines for choosing and preparing food developed by the U.S. Department of Agriculture,[10] as shown in Figure 4-1. At each successive layer of the pyramid, a food group should be eaten less frequently.

At the base of the pyramid are grains (bread, cereal, rice, and pasta), which should comprise 6 to 11 servings per day. At the next level are fruits

Figure 4-1   The Food Guide Pyramid: A Guide to Daily Food Choices

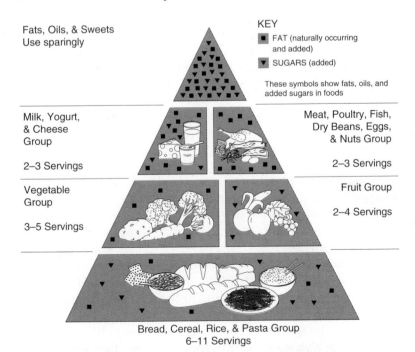

SOURCE: U.S. Department of Agriculture, 1992, 1996, 2000.

and vegetables, of which we should consume from two to five servings per day. At the next-narrower level of the pyramid are found two groups of food, of which we should eat only about two to three servings per day. One group is milk, yogurt, and cheese. The other is meat, poultry, fish, dry beans, eggs, and nuts. At the top of the pyramid are foods low in nutritional value, such as fats, oils, and sweets. It is recommended that these foods be eaten sparingly. Pizza, meat sausage, and milk shakes should therefore be an occasional treat, not a daily event.

Diet guidelines from the Department of Agriculture continue to evolve. One new suggestion is to limit your intake of beverages and foods that are high in added sugars. Another is to choose and prepare foods with less salt. Eating whole grains received new added emphasis, not just highly processed food like most breakfast cereals and pasta. In conjunction with eating well, physical activity is urged.[11] Another concern is that the meat and dairy components of the pyramid should be reduced, with a shift to whole grains, fruits, and vegetables.

The above dietary guidelines are intended only for populations with food habits similar to those of people in the United States. Also, the guidelines are for people who are already healthy and do not require special diets because of diseases or conditions that interfere with normal nutritional requirements. No guidelines can guarantee health and well-being. Health depends on many things, including heredity, lifestyle, personality traits, mental health, attitudes, and the environment in addition to diet. However, good eating habits based on moderation and variety keep you healthy and even improve your health.

Table 4-1 presents some recent evidence about how certain foods can help you in your quest to prevent ailments and stay well. Enjoy your spinach and broccoli.

In another assault against harmful fats, the Food and Drug Administration (FDA) requires as of 2006 that food makers list the amount of harmful, artery-clogging fats, known as *trans fats,* on their product labels. Trans fats are found naturally in meats and some dairy products yet also are found in large concentrations in cookies and other snack foods. Fried and baked foods contain substantial trans fats. Many nutritionists believe that trans fats offer the double danger of raising bad cholesterol and decreasing good cholesterol.[12]

The Body Mass Index

A current approach to estimating whether you are achieving the right balance of food intake and exercise is the **body mass index (BMI),** an estimation of body fat based on a person's height and weight. The National Heart, Lung and Blood Institute developed this approach to estimating body fat. People who measure high on the scale are supposedly more at risk for such ailments as heart disease, high blood pressure, and some cancers. Using this scale, about 55 percent of the U.S. population is overweight.

Exhibit 4-1 provides a chart for determining your BMI along with the actual method of calculation. According to the National Institute of Health, a normal BMI is 18.5 to 24.9, overweight is 25 to 29.9, and obesity is 30 or higher. Having a large frame and/or being muscular is likely to elevate your BMI. One reason is that muscle weighs more than fat. When interpreting

TABLE 4-1

TEN FOODS THAT HELP PREVENT SERIOUS AILMENTS

1. **Tomatoes**. Several studies have linked the cooked tomatoes in ketchup, soups, and sauces to a reduced risk of prostate cancer and other cancers of the digestive track. Tomatoes contain a powerful antioxidant called lycopene.

2. **Spinach**. Loaded with healthful ingredients, such as iron and a B vitamin, spinach can help lower amino acids that are linked to heart disease. Spinach also contains chemicals that seem to ward off macular degeneration, a leading cause of blindness.

3. **Red wine.** The skins of the grapes used to make red wine contain supercharged antioxidants including one that boosts HDL, the good kind of cholesterol. Red wine may also help prevent hardening of the arteries. Yet more than several glasses of wine per week can contribute to cirrhosis of the liver, hemorrhagic stroke, and possibly breast cancer. (However, the general rule of thumb for safe wine consumption is about two glasses per day.)

4. **Nuts**. Filled with unsaturated fats, nuts lower blood levels of LDL (bad) cholesterol while raising HDL (good) cholesterol, helping to prevent heart disease. Nuts also contain vitamin E, a powerful antioxidant that helps ward off heart disease and cancer. Yet nuts are very fattening at 150 calories per ounce.

5. **Broccoli.** Cruciferous vegetables like broccoli and Brussels sprouts may help reduce the risk of breast, colon, and stomach cancers.

6. **Oats**. Consumed daily, oats can help lower cholesterol and may lower blood pressure in hypertensive patients.

7. **Salmon**. The algae in salmon contain omega-3 fatty acids that help the heart by preventing plaque buildup in arteries and may help protect brain cells from diseases of aging like Alzheimer's. Yet some evidence suggests that the colorants in farmed salmon may contain toxic chemicals.

8. **Garlic.** The sulfides in garlic may reduce cholesterol and make the blood less sticky. Yet garlic can irritate the lining of sensitive stomachs.

9. **Green tea.** Population studies in China associate drinking green tea daily with a lowered risk of stomach, esophageal, and liver cancers.

10. **Blueberries.** Because they are loaded with antioxidants, ingredients in blueberries help prevent heart disease and cancer.

SOURCE: Based on research reported in "10 Foods That Pack a Wallop," *Time,* January 21, 2002, pp. 68–73. Katy McLaughlin, "Angling for Answers: Is Fish Healthy or Dangerous?" *The Wall Street Journal,* September 2, 2003, p. D1.

your BMI, recognize also that many factors other than body fat influence your susceptibility to disease. Among them are blood pressure, cholesterol level, and family history of disease.

DEVELOPING RESILIENCE

The ability to overcome setback is an important characteristic of successful people. It therefore follows that **resilience,** the ability to withstand pressure and emerge stronger for it, is a strategy for achieving wellness. Most people at times in their lives experience threats to their wellness. Among these threats are death of a loved one, having a fire in your home, a

---

EXHIBIT 4-1

Calculating Your Body Mass Index (BMI)

Body Mass Index: Does your weight put you at risk of health problems?

Height \ Weight	110	115	120	125	130	135	140	145	150	155	160	165	170	175	180	185	190	195	200	205	210	215	220	225	230	235	240	245	250
5'0"	21	22	23	24	25	26	27	28	29	30	31	32	33	34	35	36	37	38	39	40	41	42	43	44	45	46	47	48	49
5'1"	21	22	23	24	25	26	26	27	28	29	30	31	32	33	34	35	36	37	38	39	40	41	42	43	43	44	45	46	47
5'2"	20	21	22	23	24	25	26	27	27	28	29	30	31	32	33	34	35	36	37	37	38	39	40	41	42	43	44	45	46
5'3"	19	20	21	22	23	24	25	26	27	27	28	29	30	31	32	33	34	35	35	36	37	38	39	40	41	42	43	43	44
5'4"	19	20	21	21	22	23	24	25	26	27	27	28	29	30	31	32	33	33	34	35	36	37	38	39	39	40	41	42	43
5'5"	18	19	20	21	22	22	23	24	25	26	27	27	28	29	30	31	32	32	33	34	35	36	37	37	38	39	40	41	42
5'6"	18	19	19	20	21	22	23	23	24	25	26	27	27	28	29	30	31	31	32	33	34	35	36	36	37	38	39	40	40
5'7"	17	18	19	20	20	21	22	23	23	24	25	26	27	27	28	29	30	31	31	32	33	34	34	35	36	37	38	38	39
5'8"	17	17	18	19	20	21	21	22	23	24	24	25	26	27	27	28	29	30	30	31	32	33	33	34	35	36	36	37	38
5'9"	16	17	18	18	19	20	21	21	22	23	24	24	25	26	27	27	28	29	30	30	31	32	32	33	34	35	35	36	37
5'10"	16	17	17	18	19	19	20	21	22	22	23	24	24	25	26	27	27	28	29	29	30	31	32	32	33	34	34	35	36
5'11"	15	16	17	17	18	19	20	20	21	22	22	23	24	24	25	26	26	27	28	29	29	30	31	31	32	33	33	34	35
6'0"	15	16	16	17	18	18	19	20	20	21	22	22	23	24	24	25	26	26	27	28	28	29	30	31	31	32	33	33	34
6'1"	15	15	16	16	17	18	18	19	20	20	21	22	22	23	24	24	25	26	26	27	28	28	29	30	30	31	32	32	33
6'2"	14	15	15	16	17	17	18	19	19	20	21	21	22	22	23	24	24	25	26	26	27	28	28	29	30	30	31	31	32
6'3"	14	14	15	16	16	17	17	18	19	19	20	21	21	22	22	23	24	24	25	26	26	27	27	28	29	29	30	31	31
6'4"	13	14	15	15	16	16	17	18	18	19	19	20	21	21	22	23	23	24	24	25	26	26	27	27	28	29	29	30	30

The Actual Calculation: To calculate your BMI, follow these steps:

1. Divide your weight in pounds by your height in inches squared.
2. Multiple the result by 704.5.

For example, the BMI of a 5-foot, 11-inch, 185-pound person would be calculated as follows:

$$5 \text{ ft } 11 \text{ in} = 71 \text{ in}$$

$$71^2 = 5{,}041$$

$$185 \text{ lb} \div 5{,}041 = 0.0367$$

$$0.0367 \times 704.5 = 25.85 \text{ (rounded to 26 for the chart)} = \text{low to moderate risk}$$

SOURCE: National Institutes of Health, 1998.

NOTE: People under 5 feet or over 6 feet 4 inches will have to extrapolate the data.

family breakup, or a job loss. Recovering from such major problems helps a person retain wellness and become even more well in the long term.

Resilience also deals with being challenged and not breaking down. The ability to bounce back from setback, or resilience, is another aspect of emo-

---

HUMAN RELATIONS SELF-ASSESSMENT QUIZ 4-1

The Resiliency Quiz

From 1 to 5, rate how much each of the following applies to you (1 = very little, 5 = very much)

1	2	3	4	5	If I have a bad day at work or school it does not ruin my day.
1	2	3	4	5	After a vacation, I can usually get right back into work at my regular work pace.
1	2	3	4	5	Every "no" I encounter is one step closer to a "yes."
1	2	3	4	5	The popular saying, "Get over it" has a lot of merit in guiding your life.
1	2	3	4	5	The last time I was rejected for a job (or assignment) I wanted, it had no particular impact on me.
1	2	3	4	5	I enjoy being the underdog once in a while.
1	2	3	4	5	I enjoy taking risks because I believe that the biggest rewards stem from risk taking.
1	2	3	4	5	I rarely worry about, or keep thinking about, mistakes I have made in the past.
1	2	3	4	5	If I ran for political office and were defeated, I would be willing to run again.
1	2	3	4	5	When I encounter a major problem or setback, I will talk over the situation with a friend or confidant.
1	2	3	4	5	I am physically sick much less frequently than most people I know, including friends, coworkers, and other students.
1	2	3	4	5	The last time I lost my keys (or wallet, or handbag), I took care of the problem within a few days, and was not particularly upset.
1	2	3	4	5	I get more than my share of good breaks.

Add numbers to get your total score:

60-70 Highly resilient with an ability to bounce back from setbacks.

45-59 Average degree of resiliency when faced with problems.

30-44 Setbacks and disappointments are a struggle for you.

1-29 You may need help in dealing with setbacks.

---

tional intelligence. In the context of emotional intelligence, resilience refers to being persistent and optimistic when faced with setbacks.[13] Learning how to manage stress, as described later, is an important part of developing resilience. Being resilient also closely associated with self-confidence, as described in Chapter 14.

Human Relations Self-Assessment Quiz 4-1 gives you an opportunity to examine your tendencies toward being resilient.

MINIMIZE OBVIOUS RISKS TO HEALTH AND SAFETY

Part of staying well is staying alive. Perhaps the most effective strategy for achieving wellness is to minimize exposure to activities that can readily contribute to disease, injury, and death. The list of these environmental threats is endless, including riding in helicopters, skydiving, bungee jumping, inhaling cleaning fluid or rubber cement, playing "highway chicken," walking in a high-crime area at night, or having unprotected sex with prostitutes and intravenous drug users. Add to the list drunken driving, not wearing seat belts, and motorcycle riding or bicycle riding without a helmet. All the activities just mentioned have a common element: they are conscious behavioral acts that can, in almost all cases, be avoided.

To relate the concept of wellness and stress to yourself, take Human Relations Self-Assessment Quiz 4-2. Taking the inventory will give you many useful ideas for improving your well-being.

HUMAN RELATIONS SELF-ASSESSMENT QUIZ 4–2

The Wellness Inventory

Answer Yes or No to each question

	Yes	No
1. I rarely have trouble sleeping.	_____	_____
2. My energy level is high when I get up in the morning and it stays high until bedtime.	_____	_____
3. In the past year, I've been incapacitated by illness less than five days.	_____	_____
4. I am generally optimistic about my chances of staying well.	_____	_____
5. I do not smoke or drink alcoholic beverages habitually.	_____	_____
6. I am pain-free except for minor ailments, which heal quickly.	_____	_____
7. I am generally considered to be slim or medium, not fat.	_____	_____
8. I am careful about my diet. I restrict my intake of alcohol, sugar, salt, caffeine, and fats.	_____	_____
9. I am moderate in food and drink, and I choose fresh, whole foods over processed ones.	_____	_____
10. I strenuously exercise at least three times a week for at least 20 minutes per session.	_____	_____

(Continued)

11. I do not need any medicine (prescribed or self-prescribed) every day or most days to function. _____ _____

12. My blood pressure is 120/80 or lower. _____ _____

13. I am concerned about the future, but no one fear runs through my mind constantly. _____ _____

14. My relationships with those around me are usually easy and pleasant. _____ _____

15. I have a clear idea of my personal goals and choices. _____ _____

16. Disappointments and failures might slow me down a bit, but I try to turn them to my advantage. _____ _____

17. Taking care of myself is a high priority for me. _____ _____

18. I spend at least 20 minutes a day by myself, for myself. _____ _____

19. I know how much sleep I require, and I get it. _____ _____

20. I accept the fact that daily life can be stressful, and I am confident I can handle most problems as they arise. _____ _____

21. I have at least one hobby or form of creative expression (e.g., music, art, gardening) that is a passion for me. _____ _____

22. I can share my feelings with others and allow them to share their feelings with me. _____ _____

23. I enjoy and respect my connection to nature and the environment. _____ _____

24. I am aware of what my body feels like when I am relaxed and when I am experiencing stress. _____ _____

25. I find meaning in life and generally anticipate death with minor fear. _____ _____

Score: _____

Scoring: Give yourself four points for each Yes answer.

88–100:	Excellent health/wellness awareness. You are probably well adapted to handle stress.
76–88:	Good awareness, but there are areas where improvement is needed. Look at your No answers again.
Less than 76:	You need to evaluate your health and lifestyle habits to improve the quality of your life and your ability to handle stressful situations.

SOURCE: Anita Schambach, wellness coordinator of the Holistic Health & Wellness Center at Mercy Hospital Anderson, Cincinnati, Ohio. Reprinted with permission.

▲ THE PHYSIOLOGY AND CONSEQUENCES OF STRESS

An important part of learning about stress is to understand its meaning, underlying physiology, and consequences to the person. **Stress** is an internal reaction to any force that threatens to disturb a person's equilibrium. The internal reaction usually takes the form of emotional discomfort. A **stressor** is the external or internal force that brings about the stress. Your perception of an event or thought influences whether a given event is stressful. Your confidence in your ability to handle difficult situations also influences the amount of stress you experience. If you believe you have the resources to conquer the potentially stressful event, you are much less likely to experience stress. A computer whiz would therefore not be stressed by the prospect of having to install a new computer system. Two key aspects of understanding stress are the accompanying physiological changes and the consequences—including symptoms—of stress.

PHYSIOLOGICAL CHANGES

The physiological changes taking place within the body are almost identical for both positive and negative stressors. Riding a roller coaster, falling in love, or being fired, for example, make you feel about the same inside. The stress response begins in the brain, and a number of structures, including the pituitary gland, go on alert. The experience of stress prompts the adrenal glands to release a flood of hormones that prepare the body to fight or run when faced with a challenge. This battle against the stressor is referred to as the **fight-or-flight response.** (The "response" is really a conflict because you are forced to choose between struggling with the stressor or fleeing from the scene.) It helps you deal with emergencies.

More recent studies suggest the possibility that women, along with females of other species, react differently to major stressors. Instead of fight-or-flight response typical of males, they _tend and befriend_. When stress levels mount, women are more likely to protect and nurture their children (tend) and turn to social networks of supportive females (befriend). The researchers speculate that the tend-and-befriend behavior became prevalent over the centuries because women who tended and befriended would be more likely to have their offspring survive and pass on their mother's traits. The tend-and-befriend response could be traced to a hormone, oxytocin, produced in the brain. Although this research may not be politically correct, it has stimulated the interests of many scientists.[14]

Another useful explanation of how stress affects people is that, when faced with stress, the brain acts much like a thermostat. When outside conditions deviate from an ideal point, the thermostat sends a signal to the furnace to increase heat or air conditioning. The brain senses stress as damage to well-being and therefore sends out a signal to the body to cope. The purpose of coping is to modify the discrepancy between the ideal (low-stress) and actual (high-stress) conditions.[15] The brain is thus a self-regulating system that helps us cope with stressors.

The activation of hormones when the body has to cope with a stressor produces a short-term physiological reaction. Among the most familiar reactions are increases in heart rate, blood pressure, and blood glucose as well as blood clotting. Digestion stops during the stress episode. To help you recognize these symptoms, try to recall the internal bodily sensations the last time you were almost in an automobile accident or heard some wonderful news. Less familiar changes are a redirection of the blood flow toward the brain and large-muscle groups and a release of stored fluids from places throughout the body into the bloodstream.

CONSEQUENCES AND SYMPTOMS

If stress is continuous and accompanied by these short-term physiological changes, annoying and life-threatening conditions can occur. A stressful life event usually leads to a high cholesterol level (of the unhealthy type) and high blood pressure. Men who respond most intensely to mental stress run a higher risk of blocked blood vessels. The result is a higher risk of heart attack and stroke. One explanation of this problem is that mental stress may over time injure blood vessels and foster the buildup of arterial plaques.[16]

Other conditions associated with stress are migraine headaches, ulcers, allergies, skin disorders, and cancer. To make matters worse, stress can hamper the immune system, thus increasing the severity of many diseases and disorders. For example, people whose stress level is high recover more slowly from colds and injuries and are more susceptible to sexually transmitted diseases. Stress often results in memory problems, such as forgetting where you put your keys or not remembering an appointment.

Stress symptoms vary considerably from one person to another. A sampling of common stress symptoms is listed in Exhibit 4-2.

Despite all the problems just mentioned, stress also plays a positive role in our lives. The right amount of stress prepares us for meeting difficult challenges and spurs us on to peak intellectual and physical performance. An optimum amount of stress exists for most people and most tasks. In general, performance tends to be best under moderate amounts of stress. If stress is too great, people become temporarily ineffective because they may freeze or choke. Under too little stress, people may become lethargic and inattentive. Stress can lower job performance because the stressed person makes errors in concentration and judgment. Another problem is that distressed workers lose more time from work. A study of 323 health service workers in the United Kingdom indicated that workers who reported more distress had a greater number of days and number of times absent.[17]

Figure 4-2 depicts the relationship between stress and performance. An exception to this relationship is that certain negative forms of stress are likely to lower performance even if the stress is moderate. For example, the stress created by an intimidating boss or worrying about radiation poisoning—even in moderate amounts—will not improve performance.

The optimum amount and type of stress is a positive force that is the equivalent of finding excitement and challenge. Your ability to solve problems and deal with challenge is enhanced when the right amount of adrenaline

EXHIBIT 4-2

A Variety of Stress Symptoms

Mostly Physical

Shaking or trembling

Dizziness

Heart palpitations

Difficulty breathing

Chronic fatigue

Unexplained chest pains

Frequent teeth grinding

Frequent nausea and dizziness

Upper- and lower-back pain

Frequent headaches

Low energy and stamina

Stomach problems

Constant cravings for sweets

Increased alcohol or cigarette consumption

Frequent need to eliminate

Skin eruptions and rashes

Mostly Emotional and Behavioral

Difficulty concentrating

Nervousness

Crying

Anorexia

Declining interest in sex and romance

Anxiety or depression

Forgetfulness

Restlessness

Frequent arguments with others

Feeling high strung much of the time

Figure 4-2   The Relationship between Stress and Job Performance

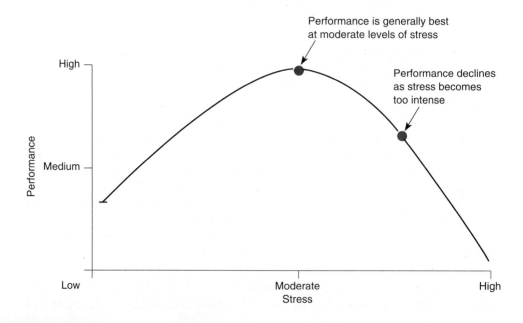

flows in your blood to guide you toward peak performance. In fact, highly productive people are sometimes said to be "hooked on adrenaline."

Where does burnout fit into the stress picture? One of the major problems of prolonged stress is that it may lead to **burnout,** a condition of emotional, mental, and physical exhaustion in response to long-term job stressors. The exhaustion aspect of burnout can be triggered by such factors as a heavy physical workload, time pressures, and shift work.[18] The burned-out person often becomes cynical. Burnout is most likely to occur among those whose jobs call for frequent and intense interactions with others, such as a social worker, teacher, or customer service representative. Yet people in other occupations also suffer from burnout, especially when not much support from others is present and the rewards are few. Also, a hostile work environment, such as being harassed by coworkers and managers, is a major contributor to burnout.[19] Students can also experience burnout because studying is hard work. Conscientiousness and perfectionism also contribute to burnout because people with these characteristics feel stressed when they do not accomplish everything they would like.

Burnout can be treated in many ways, just as with the negative effects of stress. Showing gratitude for hard work by employees is particularly helpful in preventing and treating burnout because many cases of burnout are caused by intense feelings of being unappreciated.

▲ SOURCES OF STRESS IN PERSONAL LIFE

Almost any form of frustration, disappointment, setback, inconvenience, or crisis in your personal life can cause stress. The list is dynamic because new sources of stress emerge continuously. For example, a prolonged downturn in the stock market can be a stressor for investors who previously paid little attention to how well their investments were performing. Our life stage also helps determine which events are stressors. A person close to retirement is likely to be more stressed by a stock market downturn than a career beginner. Presented next are major categories of stressful events in personal life.

1. *Significant life change.* A general stressor that encompasses both work and personal life is having to cope with significant change. According the research of Thomas Holmes and Richard Rahe, the necessity of a significant change in an individual's life pattern creates stress. The more significant the change you have to cope with in a short period of time, the greater the probability of experiencing a stress disorder.[20] As shown in Table 4-2, the maximum negative change is the death of a spouse. Twenty-four other stressors created by change are listed in the table in decreasing order of impact. The rank order shown in Table 4-2 consists of averages and do not hold true for everybody. For example, a person who could fall back into working for a family business might not find being fired from the job (item 8 in the table) to be so stressful.

2. *Low self-esteem.* A subtle cause of stress is having low self-esteem. People who do not feel good about themselves often find it difficult to feel good about anything. Low self-esteem has several links to stress. One is that being in a bad mood continually functions like a stressor. People with low self-esteem drag themselves down into a funk, which creates stress. Another link

TABLE 4-2

The Top 25 Stressors as Measured by Life-Change Units

1. Death of a spouse	14. Change in financial status
2. Divorce	15. Number of arguments with spouse
3. Marital separation	16. Major mortgage
4. Jail term/imprisonment	17. Foreclosure of a loan
5. Death of a family member	18. Change in responsibilities at work
6. Personal injury or illness	19. Son or daughter leaves home
7. Marriage	20. Trouble with in-laws
8. Fired from the job	21. Outstanding personal achievement
9. Marital reconciliation	22. Spouse begins or stops work
10. Retirement	23. Begin or end school
11. Change in health of family member	24. Change in living conditions
12. Pregnancy	25. Revision of personal habits
13. Sexual difficulties	

SOURCE: These stressors have changed over time. This version is from Thomas H. Holmes and Richard H. Rahe, "The Social Adjustment Rating Scale," *Journal of Psychosomatic Research,* 15, 1971, pp. 210–223, with an interview updating from Sue MacDonald, "Battling Stress," *Cincinnati Enquirer,* October 23, 1995, p. A

between low self-esteem and stress proneness is that people with low self-esteem get hurt more by insults. Instead of questioning the source of the criticism, the person with self-doubt will accept the opinion as valid.[21] An insult accepted as valid acts as a stressor because it is a threat to our well-being.

Low self-esteem is linked to stress in yet another way. People with low self-esteem doubt their ability to work their way out of problems. As a result, minor challenges appear to be major problems. For example, a person with low self-esteem will often doubt he or she will be successful in conducting a job search. As a result, having to conduct a job search will represent a major stressor. A person with high self-esteem might feel better prepared mentally to accept the challenge. (As you will recall, your perception of an event influences whether it is stressful.)

3. *Everyday annoyances.* Managing everyday annoyances can have a greater impact on your health than major life catastrophes. Among these everyday annoyances are losing keys or a wallet, crashing a computer file, being stuck in traffic, having your car break down, having one of your checks bounce, spilling red wine on your clothing at a social event, and being lost on the way to an important appointment. People who have the coping skills to deal with everyday annoyances are less likely to be stressed out over them. A major reason everyday annoyances act as stressors is because they are frustrating—they block your path to an important goal, such as getting your work accomplished.

4. *Social and family problems.* Friends and family are the main source of love and affection in your life. But they can also be the main source of stress. Most physical acts of violence are committed among friends and family members. One of the many reasons we encounter so much conflict with friends and family is that we are emotionally involved with them.

5. *Physical and mental health problems.* Prolonged stress produces physical and mental health problems, and the reverse is also true. Physical and mental illness can act as stressors—the fact of being ill is stressful. Furthermore, thinking that you might soon contract a life-threatening illness is stressful. If you receive a serious injury, that too can create stress. The stress from being hospitalized can be almost as severe to some patients as the stress from the illness or injury that brought them to the hospital.

6. *Financial problems.* A major life stressor is financial problems. Although you may not be obsessed with money, not having enough money to take care of what you consider the necessities of life can lead to anxiety and tension. If you do not have enough money to replace or repair a broken or faulty personal computer or automobile, the result can be stressful. A major stressor for recent graduates who move to expensive locations like New York City or Silicon Valley is being able to afford a comfortable place to live. Lack of funds can also lead to embarrassment and humiliation (both stressors), such as not being able to afford to go out to restaurants with friends.

7. *School-related problems.* The life of a student can be stressful. Among the stressors to cope with are exams in subjects you do not understand well, having to write papers on subjects unfamiliar to you, working your way through the complexities of registration, or having to deal with instructors who do not see things your way. Another source of severe stress for some students is having too many competing demands on their time. On most campuses you will find someone who works full time, goes to school full time, and has a family. This type of three-way pull often leads to marital problems.

▲ PERSONALITY FACTORS AND STRESS PRONENESS

Some people are more stress prone than others because of personality factors. Three key personality factors predisposing people to stress are type A behavior, a belief that external forces control their life, and a negative disposition.

TYPE A BEHAVIOR

People with **type A behavior** characteristics have basic personalities that lead them into stressful situations. Type A behavior has two main components. One is a tendency to try to accomplish too many things in too little time. This leads the type A individual to be impatient and demanding. The other component is free-floating hostility. Because of this combined sense of urgency and hostility, trivial things irritate these people. On the job, people with type A behavior are aggressive and hardworking. Off the job, they keep themselves preoccupied with all kinds of errands to run and things to do.

Certain features of the type A behavior pattern are related to coronary heart disease. Hostility, anger, cynicism, and suspiciousness lead to heart problems, whereas impatience, ambition, and being work driven are not associated with coronary disease. One study showed that men who received a high score on a personality test about hostility were much more likely to develop coronary heart disease several years later.[22] Many work-driven people who like what they are doing—including many business executives—are remarkably healthy and outlive less competitive people.

BELIEF IN EXTERNAL LOCUS OF CONTROL

If you believe that your fate is controlled more by external than internal forces, you are probably more susceptible to stress. People with an **external locus of control** believe that external forces control their fate. Conversely, people with an **internal locus of control** believe that fate is pretty much under their control.

The link between locus of control and stress works in this manner: If people believe they can control adverse forces, they are less prone to the stressor of worrying about them. For example, if you believed that you can always find a job, you will worry less about unemployment. At the same time, the person who believes in an internal locus of control experiences a higher level of job satisfaction. Work is less stressful and more satisfying when you perceive it to be under your control.

The everyday problem of lost computer files illustrates the importance of an internal locus of control. When a hard drive crashes or a valuable file is lost in some other way, the "external" person blames the computer or the software for the stressful event. An "internal," in contrast, would most likely have created backup files along the way. So when a crash occurs, the person is less stressed because relatively little data have been lost.

What about your locus of control? Do you believe it to be internal? Or is it external?

NEGATIVE AFFECTIVITY

A major contributor to being stress prone is **negative affectivity,** a tendency to experience aversive (intensely disliked) emotional states. In more detail, negative affectivity is a predisposition to experience emotional stress that includes feelings of nervousness, tension, and worry. Furthermore, a person with negative affectivity is likely to experience emotional states such as anger, scorn, revulsion, guilt, and self-dissatisfaction.[23] Such negative personalities seem to search for discrepancies between what they would like and what exists. Instead of attempting to solve problems, they look for them. Although negative affectivity is a relatively stable personality characteristic, the circumstances a person faces can trigger such behavior.[24] For example, a four-hour wait in an airplane parked on the tarmac might trigger a person's mild tendencies toward negative affectivity.

People with negative affectivity are often distressed even when working under conditions that coworkers perceive as interesting and challenging. In one company, a contest was announced that encouraged customer contact workers to compete against each other in terms of improving customer service. An employee with a history of negative affectivity said, "Here we go again. We're already hustling like crazy to please customers. Now we're being asked to dream up even more schemes to make sure the customer is right. It's about time the company thought of ways to please employees as well as customers."

▲ SOURCES OF WORK STRESS

No job is without potential stressors for some people. When work is lacking stressful elements, it may not have enough challenge to prompt employees to achieve high performance. Here we describe five major job stressors you might encounter or have already encountered, as listed in Figure 4-3.

WORK OVERLOAD OR UNDERLOAD

A heavy workload is a widely acknowledged source of job stress. **Role overload,** a burdensome workload, can create stress for a person in two ways. First, the person may become fatigued and thus be less able to tolerate annoyances and irritations. Think of how much easier it is to become provoked over a minor incident when you lack proper rest. Second, a person subject to unreasonable work demands may feel perpetually behind schedule, a situation that itself creates an uncomfortable, stressful feeling.

Another form of work overload is demanding higher and higher speed from workers. Consultant David Strum says that "the new corporate expectation is to do everything faster, cheaper, and it is being felt."[25] Speed is

Figure 4-3   Frequent Job Stressors

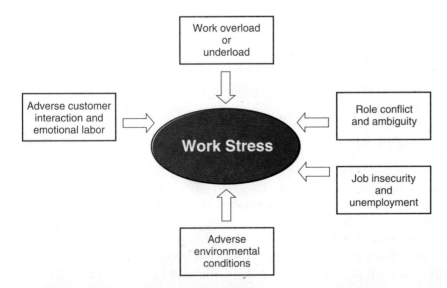

important to companies because delivering goods and services very quickly brings a competitive edge. The most stressful situation occurs when a company *downsizes* (reduces its workforce to operate more efficiently and save money) and the remaining workers are expected to carry a heavier workload at a faster pace than previously. In recent years many companies have pared down staff without reducing workloads and often expect white-collar workers to spend more than 49 hours at the office.[26] The combination of additional responsibility and high speed can be a major stressor. Among the problems are that hurried employees have very little time to ask for help or to carefully study what they are doing.

A disruptive amount of stress can also occur when people experience **role underload,** or too little to do. Some people find role underload frustrating because it is a normal human desire to want to work toward self-fulfillment. Also, making a contribution on the job is one way of gaining self-esteem. Some people, however, find it relaxing not to have much to do on the job. One direct benefit is that it preserves their energy for family and leisure activities.

ROLE CONFLICT AND ROLE AMBIGUITY

Being pulled in two directions is a classic stressor. **Role conflict** refers to having to choose between two competing demands or expectations. Many workers receive conflicting demands from two or more managers. Imagine being told by your manager to give top priority to one project. You then receive a call from your manager's manager who tells you to drop everything and work on another project. It's often up to you to resolve such a conflict. If you don't, you will experience stress. Having to choose between taking care of job responsibilities versus work responsibilities is another potent type of role conflict, such as having to work the night a good friend is getting married. Do you upset your boss or your good friend? We return to work/family conflict in Chapter 7.

Not being certain of what they should be doing is a stressor for many people. **Role ambiguity** is a condition in which the jobholder receives confusing or poorly defined expectations. A typical complaint is "I'm not really sure I know what I'm supposed to be doing around here." You will recall, however, that creative people enjoy ambiguity because they can define problems for themselves when clear directions are lacking. Role ambiguity is related to job control. If you lack a clear picture of what you should be doing, it is difficult to get your job under control.

JOB INSECURITY AND UNEMPLOYMENT

People have traditionally worried about losing their jobs because of budget cuts and automation. Two current sources of job insecurity, even during prosperity, are layoffs caused by mergers and acquisitions and downsizing. Layoffs occur for two primary reasons when one firm acquires or merges with another: (1) the merged organization will have duplicate positions, such as two managers of e-commerce, and (2) the organization

A DISRUPTIVE AMOUNT OF STRESS CAN ALSO OCCUR
WHEN PEOPLE EXPERIENCE ROLE UNDERLOAD

may have to trim the payroll in order to save money. Whatever the specific reason for the layoff, worrying about losing one's job is a potential stressor.

Many workers who survive a layoff experience elevated stress. The workplace often becomes more political and cutthroat than before the downsizing, leaving family members with even less time for family activities. Another stressor surrounding a downsizing is that many workers receive pay cuts resulting in worries about finances.[27] Unemployment itself generates more stress than job insecurity. Unemployed people have much higher rates of depression, suicide, homicide, child abuse, and partner abuse. The dramatic increase in workplace violence, such as killing company officials, is related to unemployment stress.

ADVERSE ENVIRONMENTAL CONDITIONS

A variety of adverse organizational conditions are stressors, as identified by the National Institute of Occupational Safety and Health. Among these adverse organizational conditions are unpleasant or dangerous physical conditions, such as crowding, noise, air pollution, or ergonomic problems. Enough polluted air within an office building can create a _sick building_ in which a diverse range of airborne particles, vapors, molds, and gases pollute the indoor environment. The result can be headaches, nausea, and respiratory infections as well as the stress created by being physically ill.

Working at a computer monitor for prolonged periods of time can lead to adverse physical and psychological reactions. The symptoms include headaches and fatigue, along with eye problems. Common visual problems are dry eyes and blurred or double vision. An estimated one out of five visits to vision care professionals is for computer-related problems. Another

Figure 4-4   How to Minimize Cumulative Trauma Disorder

An Ergonomic Workstation

- Keep the screen below your eye level.
- Keep your elbows on the same level with home-key row, with your wrists and lower arms parallel to floor.
- Support your back and thighs with a well-constructed chair.
- Position your feet flat on the floor.
- Use lamp to supplement inadequate room lighting.

vision-related problem is that people lean forward to scan the monitor, leading to physical problems such as back strain.

A repetitive motion disorder most frequently associated with keyboarding and the use of optical scanners is **carpal tunnel syndrome.** The syndrome occurs when repetitive flexing and extension of the wrist causes the tendons to swell, thus trapping and pinching the median nerve. Carpal tunnel syndrome creates stress because of the pain and misery. The thoughts of having to permanently leave a job requiring keyboarding is another potential stressor. Repetitive motion disorders can be prevented somewhat by computer workers taking frequent rest breaks and using a well-designed combination of the worktable, chair, and monitor. Wearing elasticized wrist bands provides enough support to the wrist tendons to prevent many cases of repetitive motion disorders. Being comfortable while working prevents much physical strain. Figure 4-4 presents the basics of a workstation designed on *ergonomic* principles. (Ergonomics has to do with making machines and equipment fit human capabilities and demands.)

ADVERSE CUSTOMER INTERACTION AND EMOTIONAL LABOR

Interactions with customers can be a major stressor, according to interviews with 93 employees. Stressful events frequently cited were customers losing control, using profanity, badgering employees, harassing employees, and lying. The employees interviewed said that these adverse interactions with customers negatively affected the quality of their work environment.[28] Part of the problem is that the sales associate often feels helpless when placed in conflict with a customer. The sales associate is told that "the customer is always right." Furthermore, the store manager usually sides with the customer in a dispute with the sales associate.

Related to adverse customer interaction is the stressor of having to control the expression of emotion to please or to avoid displeasing a customer. Imagine having to smile at a customer who belittles you or makes unwanted sexual advances. Alicia A.Grandey defines **emotional labor** as the process of regulating both feelings and expressions to meet organizational goals.[29] The process involves both surface acting and deep acting. Surface acting means faking expressions, such as smiling, whereas deep acting involves controlling feelings, such as suppressing anger toward a customer you perceive to be annoying. Sales workers and customer service representatives carry the biggest emotional labor among all workers because so often they have to fake facial expressions and feelings so as to please customers.

Engaging in emotional labor for prolonged periods of time can lead to job dissatisfaction , stress, and burnout. A contributing cause is that faking expressions and emotions takes a physiological toll, such as the intestines churning. Workers who engage in emotional labor may also develop cardiovascular problems and weakened immune systems.

▲ MANAGING STRESS

Because potentially harmful stressors surround us in work and personal life, virtually everybody needs a program of stress management to stay well. Stress management techniques are placed here into three categories: attacking the source of the stress, getting social support, and relaxation techniques. Your challenge is to select those techniques that best fit your circumstances and preferences.

DEALING WITH STRESS BY ATTACKING ITS SOURCE

Stress can be dealt with in the short range by indirect techniques such as exercise and relaxation. However, to manage stress in the long range and stay well, you must also learn to deal directly with stressors. Several of these techniques are described in the next few paragraphs.

Eliminating or Modifying the Stressor

The most potent method of managing stress is to eliminate the stressor giving you trouble. For example, if your job is your primary stressor, your stress level would be reduced if you found a more comfortable job. At other times, modifying the stressful situation can be equally helpful. Using the problem-solving method, you search for an alternative that will change the stressor. Here is a useful model to follow:

> A retailing executive repeatedly told her boss that she wanted to open a new branch of the business. He agreed with her but took no action. Feeling rejected, frustrated, and stressed, she took another approach to the problem. She drew up the plans for opening a new branch, presented them to her boss, and informed him she was ready to move ahead. To the executive's surprise, he said, "Great! I was only hesitating to ask you to do this because I thought you were overworked."
>
> Everything worked out just as she wanted after she pursued the alternative of restating her plans in writing.[30]

Placing the Stressful Situation in Perspective

Stress comes about because of our perception of the situation. If you can alter your perception of a threatening situation, you are attacking the source. A potentially stressful situation can be put into perspective by asking, "What is the worst thing that could happen to me if I fail in this activity?"

The answer to the above question is found by asking a series of questions, starting with the grimmest possibility. For instance, you are late with a report that is due this afternoon. Consider the following questions and answers:

- Will my reputation be damaged permanently? (*No.*)
- Will I get fired? (*No.*)
- Will I get reprimanded? (*Perhaps, but not for sure.*)
- Will my boss think less of me? (*Perhaps, but not for sure.*)

Only if the answer is yes to either of the first two questions is negative stress truly justified. The thought process just described allows stressful situations to be properly evaluated and kept in perspective. You therefore avoid the stress that comes from overreacting to a situation.

Gaining Control of the Situation

Feeling that a bothersome situation is out of control is almost a universal stressor. A key method of stress management is therefore to attack the stressor by gaining control of the situation. A multipurpose way of gaining control is to improve your work habits and time management, as described in Chapter 12. By being "on top of things," you can make heavy work and school demands less stressful.

A trend related to reducing stress by gaining control is to simplify your life by getting rid of unessential activities. Andrew Weill, the natural health guru, recommends that you downsize your life. He believes that significant stress stems from the complexity of our lives, a major contributor being our material possessions. Many people have to many physical objects that require attention and maintenance. Weil recommends that you get rid of what you can spare.[31] You will gain control of your life situation by having less clutter. A note of caution is that an oversimplified life can also be an impoverished life, creating stress of its own. Throw out or give to charity those physical possessions that contribute virtually nothing to your life. Yet save the sources of an enriched life. For example, why give up a digital camera, cell telephone, and MP3 player if all three are major sources of pleasure and satisfaction?

Finding the Humor in the Situation

An indirect way of gaining control of the situation to reduce stress is to find the humor in the situation. By finding humor in the potentially stressful situation, the situation becomes less threatening and therefore less likely to produce stress. Quite often, situations that were frustrating at the time become funny after time has passed. An example would be thinking back to how funny it was to have called in sick on your first day of work at your present job. Humor is a stress reliever also because it deepens breathing, lowers blood pressure, loosens tight muscles, and releases endorphins.

Receiving Social Support

An ideal way to manage stress is one that provides side benefits. Getting close to people falls into this category. You will reduce some stress symptoms and form healthy relationships with others in the process. Becka Barbatis puts it this way: "We need to view ourselves as social beings and we very much need to know that we're related to one another."[32] By getting close to others, you build a **support system,** a group of people on whom you can rely for encouragement and comfort. The trusting relationship you have with these people is critically important. People within your support network include family members, friends, coworkers, and fellow students. In addition, some people in turmoil reach out to strangers to discuss personal problems.

The usual method of reducing stress is to talk over your problems while the other person listens. Switching roles can also help reduce stress. Listening to others will make you feel better because you have helped them. Another advantage to listening to the feelings and problems of others is that it helps you to get close to them.

RELAXATION TECHNIQUES FOR HANDLING STRESS

"Relax" is the advice many people have always offered the stressed individual. Stress experts give us similar advice but also offer specific techniques. Here we describe three techniques that can help you relax and, consequently, help you reduce stress and its symptoms In addition, Exhibit 4-3 lists a variety of "stress busters," many of which are relaxation oriented. Recognize that many of these techniques contribute directly to wellness and that stress management is a major component of wellness. Pick and choose among stress management techniques until you find several that effectively reduce your stress.

Relaxation Response

A standard technique for reducing stress is to achieve the relaxation response. The **relaxation response** is a bodily reaction in which you experience a slower respiration and heart rate, lowered blood pressure, and lowered metabolism. By practicing the relaxation response, you can counteract the fight-or-flight response associated with stress.

EXHIBIT 4-3

Stress Busters

- Take a nap when facing heavy pressures. Napping is regarded as one of the most effective techniques for reducing and preventing stress.

- Give in to your emotions. If you are angry, disgusted, or confused, admit your feelings. Suppressing your emotions adds to stress.

- Take a brief break from the stressful situation and do something small and constructive, like washing your car, emptying a wastebasket, or getting a haircut.

- Get a massage because it can loosen tight muscles, improve your blood circulation, and calm you down.

- Get help with your stressful task from a coworker, boss, or friend.

- Concentrate intensely on reading, surfing the Internet, a sport, or hobby. Contrary to common sense, concentration is at the heart of stress reduction.

- Have a quiet place at home and have a brief idle period there every day.

- Take a leisurely day off from your routine.

- Finish something you have started, however small. Accomplishing almost anything reduces some stress.

- Stop to smell the flowers, make friends with a young child or elderly person, or play with a kitten or puppy.

- Strive to do a good job but not a perfect job.

- Work with your hands, doing a pleasant task.

- Hug somebody you like and who you think will hug you back.

- Become a rag doll by standing with your arms dangling loosely at your sides. Start to shake your hands, then start shaking your arms. Next, sit and repeat the same moves with you legs.

- Find something to laugh at—a cartoon, a movie, a television show, a Web site for jokes, even yourself.

- Minimize drinking caffeinated or alcoholic beverages and drink fruit juice or water instead. Grab a piece of fruit rather than a can of beer.

According to cardiologist Herbert Benson, four things are necessary to practice the relaxation response: a quiet environment, an object to focus on, a passive attitude, and a comfortable position. You are supposed to practice the relaxation response 10 to 20 minutes, twice a day. To evoke the relaxation response, Benson advises you to close your eyes. Relax. Concentrate

---

HUMAN RELATIONS SKILL-BUILDING EXERCISE 4-1

The Relaxation Response

Think of one of the most stressful moments you have experienced in recent weeks. Visualize yourself as experiencing stress. If you are currently experiencing significant stress, visualization will not be necessary. Now carry out the relaxation response. Close your eyes. Relax. Concentrate on one simple word. Repeat the word several times.

Describe to yourself in writing how effective this technique has been in reducing your stress. Share experiences with the rest of the class. Discuss what you see as the strengths and limitations of this technique.

---

on one word or prayer. If other thoughts come to mind, be passive and return to the repetition.[33] Human Relations Skill-Building Exercise 4-1 gives you an opportunity to practice the relaxation response.

Similar to any other relaxation technique, the relaxation response is harmless and works for most people. However, some very impatient people find it annoying to disrupt their busy day to meditate. Unfortunately, these may be the people who most urgently need to learn to relax.

Deep Breathing

The natural process of inhaling and exhaling slowly, filling your lungs with air and slowly letting it escape, is a powerful stress reducer for many people. Deep breathing has immediate and long-term benefits. It lowers the heart rate and blood pressure and increases your skin temperature. Deep breathing also relaxes you emotionally and helps you gain perspective. Barbatis explains how to use deep breathing for stress reduction:

1. Sit or lie down in a quiet spot. Place one hand on your waist, the other in the center of your chest. Breathe several times. The hand on your belly should move more because it indicates you are breathing from your diaphragm.

2. Now inhale slowly, filling up the lungs. As you exhale slowly, push air out from the bottom of your lungs.

3. Take long, slow breaths. If you become dizzy or lightheaded, you are breathing too fast.

4. As you inhale, elevate your shoulders and collarbone slightly to fill the lungs fully with air.

5. After you have mastered the breathing technique, with each outward breath blow out your worrisome thoughts and pains. Breathe in relaxation and calmness.[34]

HUMAN RELATIONS SKILL-BUILDING EXERCISE 4-2

The Stress-Buster Survey

Each class member thinks through carefully which techniques he or she uses to reduce work or personal stress. Class members then come to the front of the room individually to make a brief presentation of their most effective stress reduction technique. After the presentations are completed, class members analyze and interpret what they heard. Among the issues to explore are the following:

1. Which are the most popular stress reduction techniques?

2. How do the stress reduction techniques used by the class compare to those recommended by experts?

Meditation

Perhaps the oldest stress management technique of all, mediation, is back in vogue. An estimated 10 million American adults meditate regularly. **Meditation** is a systematic method of concentration, reflection, or concentrated thinking designed to suppress the activity of the sympathetic nervous system. The relaxation response is essentially a meditation technique, and napping provides some of the benefits of meditation. The meditator reaches a deep state of mental and physical calmness and relaxation, driving away accumulated stress. Meditation is also recommended as a way of preventing and slowing down and reducing the pain of chronic diseases such as heart disease, AIDS, and cancer. People who meditate learn to tolerate everyday annoyances better.

The usual approach to meditation involves four simple steps. First, find a quiet place, with a minimum of distractions. Second, close your eyes so that you can close yourself off from the outside world. Third, pick a word whose sound is soothing when repeated. Fourth, say the word repeatedly. For most people, one 15-minute session daily will accomplish the benefits of meditation.[35]

Human Relations Skill-Building Exercise 4-2 will give you and your classmates an opportunity to learn more about what stress management techniques others use.

▲ SUMMARY

Wellness is a formalized approach to preventive health care. By promoting health, company wellness programs help prevent employees from developing physical and mental problems often associated with excessive job pressures.

Five strategies for achieving wellness were described in this chapter. (1) The right amount and type of physical exercise contributes substantially to wellness. (2) Sleep adequately because getting enough sleep plays a major role in being well. (3) Maintaining a healthy diet is valuable for mental and physical health. The Food Guide Pyramid (Figure 4-1) contains many useful suggestions. (4) Being resilient is another wellness strategy. (5) Minimizing obvious risks to health and safety improves the chances of achieving wellness.

The body's battle against a stressor is the fight-or-flight response, sometimes referred to as the tend-and-befriend response in women. Another way of understanding stress is that the brain senses it as damage to well-being and therefore sends out a signal to the body to cope. The brain is a self-regulating system that helps us cope with stressors. Stress always involves physiological changes, such as an increase in heart rate, blood cholesterol, and blood pressure. Men who respond most intensely to mental stress run a higher risk of blocked blood vessels. The right amount of stress can be beneficial. Performance tends to be best under moderate amounts of stress, yet certain negative forms of stress almost always decrease performance.

Prolonged stress may lead to burnout, a condition of emotional, mental, and physical exhaustion in response to long-term job stressors, such as a heavy workload. Occupations that require frequent and intense interaction with others often lead to burnout. Yet the condition can happen whenever not much support from others is present and the rewards are few.

Almost any form of frustration, disappointment, setback, inconvenience, or crisis in your personal life can cause stress. The categories of situations that can produce stress include significant life changes, low self-esteem, everyday annoyances, social and family problems, physical and mental health problems, financial problems, and school-related problems.

Personality factors contribute to stress proneness. People with type A behavior are impatient and demanding and have free-floating hostility, all of which leads to stress. People with an external locus of control (believing that external forces control their fate) are more susceptible to stress. Negative affectivity (a predisposition to negative mental states) also contributes to stress.

Sources of job stress are quite varied. Among them are work overload or underload, role conflict and ambiguity, job insecurity and unemployment, adverse environmental control, and adverse customer interaction and emotional labor (faking expressions and feelings).

To successfully manage stress in the long range, you have to deal with the stressors directly. Four direct approaches are to eliminate or modify the stressor, to place the situation in perspective, to gain control of the situation, and to find humor in the situation. Reducing stress through emotional support by others is an effective stress management technique. Three relaxation techniques for handling stress are the relaxation response, deep breathing, and meditation (a state of deep concentration and relaxation).

Questions and Activities

1. How can a company wellness program improve profits and productivity?

2. If exercise contributes so much to wellness, why are so many athletes stressed out?

3. Claims and counterclaims abound about which particular foods are healthy. An example: "Fish is great for the brain," yet "Watch out for eating fish. It may contain pollutants found in lakes and oceans." So what is a person supposed to do to maintain a healthy diet?

4. The *body mass index* is supposed to be one way of measuring a person's healthy. So do you think it would be fair for a potential employer to take into account your body mass index when considering you for an office job?

5. What responsibility should an employer have in helping employees minimize obvious risks to health and safety?

6. Many small-business owners complain that a major job stressor is deleting spam messages every day. Yet these business owners are afraid to use spam-blocking software because they might lose a message from a legitimate customer. What advice can you offer business owners to help them cope with the spam stressor?

7. Identify several potential stressors created by cell telephones. What can be done to lessen these stressors?

8. Assume that a professional-level worker, such as a customer service representative, is convinced that napping during the workday is an excellent way of managing stress. Where should this person nap?

9. How can a person who becomes stressed from having to interact with coworkers several hours a day compete in the modern world?

10. Speak to a person you consider to be much more relaxed than most people. Ask your contact which (if any) of the relaxation or stress-busting techniques listed in this chapter he or she uses. Report your findings back to class.

INTERNET SKILL BUILDER: Achieving Wellness from Within

Noelle Noah, a peer educator at the Student Life Center at St. Olaf College, offers concise advice about achieving wellness. Identify the four aspects of the whole person Noah presents. Prepare a list of the suggestions contained within the four aspects of the whole person that you think would be practical for you to implement. Which one of the suggestions do you intend to begin implementing today?

WEB CORNER

The nature of stress: www.stress.org

Evaluation of resistance to stress:
www.pressanykey.com/stresstest.html

HUMAN RELATIONS CASE PROBLEM

Geomania Naps

Geomania is a telecommunications firm based in the information technology section of New York City. Some of the several hundred employees live in Manhattan, but many have commutes of up to two hours from other cities. Having survived the downturn in the telecommunications business during the late 1990s and early 2000s, Geomania is understaffed. Many staff members in professional, technical, support, and managerial jobs are doing work that was once performed by two people.

A case researcher asked human resources manager Stephanie Cohen what impact the heavy workload was having on employees. She replied, "We've got a bunch of great soldiers here, but the overload problem is taking its toll. Some staff members are having many more fights at home. More people are having serious medical problems like chest pains, migraine headaches, and stomach ulcers. I also think the error rate in work is going up. Manuel Gomez, the customer service manager, tells me Geomania is receiving more complaints about our systems not working."

The case researcher pointed out that Cohen's observations were to be expected when so many people are working so hard. She was asked if she noticed any other unusual behavior in the office in recent months. Cohen said that her assistant, Bonnie Boswell, had made some observations about unusual behavior and that Boswell should be asked to participate in the interview.

Boswell got right to the heart of the matter, explaining that she has observed some behavior that could be helping productivity, hurting productivity, or a combination of both. "What I've noticed," said Boswell, "is that our people are finding more and more creative ways to take naps on the job. The motto has become, 'You snooze you win,' instead of 'You snooze you lose.'

"There certainly is a positive side to napping. According to one NASA survey, 71% of corporate aviation pilots, 80% of regional pilots, and 60% of hospital workers said they took naps on the job. Another NASA study found that airline pilots who fell asleep on average for 26 minutes had a 34% improvement in performance and a 54% improvement in alertness. Of course, they were not sleeping while flying!

"But on the negative side, if you are sleeping you are not producing for the company. Besides that it looks so totally unprofessional to be sacked out in your cubicle, especially if you snore or scream because you are having a terrifying dream."

When asked where and how these workers were napping, both Boswell and Cohen had plenty of answers. Cohen said it has always been easy for executives to nap because they have private offices. Several keep their offices equipped with pillows, so they can nap comfortably on a couch, at their desk, or on the floor under the desk.

(Continued)

Cohen said that she had walked in on napping executives by mistakes, and an office assistant told her about the pillows.

Boswell said that cubicle dwellers have to be more creative about napping because other workers can readily see them. She explained, "Quite often they catch a nap during meetings. At some meetings half the audience is listing to one side or nap jerking (falling asleep, then quickly jerking the head to awake). One napper closes his eyes on his desk, and holds on to a bottle of eye drops to make it appear he is in the process of self-medication. Many nappers sleep in their car during lunch break.

"Some of the most stressed-out workers catch a few winks in the office supplies room by resting their head on a box."

Cohen said she was even wondering if Geomania should hire as a consultant psychologist Bill Anthony, who founded the Napping Company, to promote productive naps in the workplace. He contends that companies do not have to set up special sleeping rooms. Instead, they can institutionalize nap breaks the way they have the coffee break.

"My concern right now," concluded Cohen, "is what to recommend to top management. I think our CEO is opposed to napping on the job (except for his little forty winks now and then), and napping does not look professional. Yet, a formal napping program could be a real productivity booster. Maybe we could even cut down on some medical problems."

Questions

1. If you worked for Geomania and were stationed in a cubicle, explain why you would or would not nap on the job.

2. Would it be a good idea for management to just let workers decide for themselves whether to nap on the job? Explain your reasoning.

3. As the human resources director for Geomania, develop a written policy for napping on company time. (A policy is a general guideline to follow.) Include such aspects of napping as to when, where, under what circumstances, and for how long might workers nap. Mention whether Geomania should have a separate napping area.

4. How might a program of napping contribute to employee wellness at Geomania?

SOURCE: Some of the facts in this case are from Jared Sandberg, "As Bosses Power Nap, Cubicle Dwellers Doze under Clever Disguise," *Wall Street Journal*, July 23, 2003, p. B1.

▲ REFERENCES

1. Adapted from Kathryn Tyler, "Cut the Stress," *HR Magazine*, May 2003, pp. 101, 106.

2. Dot Yandle, "Staying Well May Be Up to You," *Success Workshop Folio* (a supplement to *The Pryor Report Management Newsletter*), February 1994, pp. 2–3.

3. Bridget Murray, "Getting to the Essential 'We' in Wellness," *Monitor on Psychology*, November 2002, p. 34.

4. Research summarized in Christine Gorman, "Repairing Damage," *Time*, February 5, 2001, p. 54.

5. Philip L. Rice, *Stress and Health: Principles and Practices for Coping and Wellness* (Monterey, CA: Brooks/College Publishing Company, 1987), pp. 353–354.

6. Jay Kimiecik, "Learn to Love Exercise," *Psychology Today,* January/February 2000, p. 20.

7. Research reported in "Motor-Skills Memory Works Best on Sleep," Associated Press, August 13, 2002.

8. Stephenie Overman, "Rise and Sigh," *HR Magazine,* May 1999, p. 68.

9. Overman, "Rise and Sigh," p. 70.

10. *Dietary Guidelines for Americans,* 3d ed., U.S. Department of Agriculture, U.S. Department of Health and Human Services, 1990; updated with food pyramid, May 1992, May 1996. New nutritional guidelines were released in 2000.

11. Christine Gorman, "Junk Food Takes a Hit," *Time,* June 12, 2000, p. 58.

12. Leila Abboud, "The Truth about Trans Fats: Coming to a Label Near You," *Wall Street Journal,* July 10, 2003, p. D1.

13. Daniel Goleman, "Leadership That Gets Results," *Harvard Business Review,* March–April 2000, p. 80.

14. Shelley E. Taylor et al., "Biobehavioral Responses to Stress in Females: Tend-and-Befriend, Not Fight-or-Flight," *Psychological Review,* 107, 2000, pp. 411–429.

15. Jeffrey R. Edwards, "A Cybernetic Theory of Stress, Coping, and Well-Being in Organizations," *Academy of Management Review,* April 1992, p. 248.

16. Research cited in "Mental Stress Is Linked to Blocked Blood Vessels," *Monitor on Psychology,* February 1998, p. 7.

17. Gillian E. Hardy, David Woods, and Toby D. Wall, "The Impact of Psychological Distress on Absence from Work," *Journal of Applied Psychology,* April 2003, pp. 306–314.

18. Evangelia Demerouti et al., "The Job Demands-Resources Model of Burnout," *Journal of Applied Psychology,* June 2001, p. 502.

19. Raymond T. Lee and Blake E. Ashforth, "A Meta-Analytic Examination of the Correlates of Three Dimensions of Job Burnout," *Journal of Applied Psychology,* April 1996, p. 123; Joanne Cole, "An Ounce of Prevention Beats Burnout," *HRfocus,* June 1999, pp. 1, 14–15.

20. Rabi S. Bhagat, "Effects of Stressful Life Events on Individual Performance and Work Adjustment Processes within Organizational Settings: A Research Model," *Academy of Management Review,* October 1983, pp. 660–670.

21. "Building Self-Esteem," www.ashland.com/education/self-esteem/best_shot.html.

22. Research reported in Etienne Benson, "Hostility Is among Best Predictors of Heart Disease in Men," *Monitor on Psychology,* January 2003, p. 15.

23. Peter Y. Chen and Paul E. Spector, "Negative Affectivity as the Underlying Cause of Correlations between Stressors and Strains," *Journal of Applied Psychology,* June 1991, p. 398.

24. Paul E. Spector, Peter Y. Chen, and Brian J. O'Connell, "A Longitudinal Study of Relations between Job Stressors and Job Strains while Controlling for Prior Negative Affectivity and Strains," *Journal of Applied Psychology,* April 2000, p. 216.

25. Quoted in Gail Dutton, "Cutting-Edge Stress Busters," *HRfocus,* September 1998, p. 11.

26. Michelle Conlin, "The Big Squeeze on Workers," *BusinessWeek,* May 13, 2002, pp. 97–98.

27. Michelle Conlin, "Savaged by the Slowdown," *BusinessWeek,* September 17, 2001, p. 75.

28. James D. Brodzinski, Robert P. Scherer, and Karen A. Goyer, "Workplace Stress: A Study of Internal and External Pressures Placed on Employees," *Personnel Administrator,* July 1989, pp. 77–78.

29. Alicia A. Grandey, "Emotion Regulation in the Workplace: A New Way to Conceptualize Emotional Labor," *Journal of Occupational Health Psychology,* 5, no. 1, 2000, pp. 95–110; Grandey, "When the 'Show Must Go On': Surface Acting and Deep Acting as Determinants of Emotional Exhaustion and Peer-Related Service Delivery," *Academy of Management Journal,* February 2003, pp. 86–96.

30. Making Stress Work for You," *Executive Strategies,* October 3, 1989, p. 5.

31. Andrew Weil, "Beating Stress," *USA Weekend,* December 26–28, 1997, p. 4.

32. Quoted in Sue McDonald, "Relax: Stress Can Be Managed," *Cincinnati Enquirer,* October 25, 1995, p. D6.

33. Herbert Benson (with William Proctor), *Beyond the Relaxation Response* (New York: Berkley Books, 1995), pp. 96–97.

34. Quoted in Sue McDonald, "Take a Deep Breath," *Cincinnati Enquirer,* October 24, 1995, p. D3.

35. Joel Stein, "Just Say Om," *Time,* August 4, 2003, pp. 48–56.

▲ ADDITIONAL READING

Caudron, Shari. "Meditation and Mindfulness at Sounds True." *Workforce,* June 2001, pp. 40–46.

Cropper, Carol Marie. "When the Nightmares Won't Go Away: Help for Those Still Suffering Stress from September 11." *BusinessWeek,* March 18, 2002, p. 106.

Cryer, Bruce, Rollin, McCraty, and Doc Childre. "Pull the Plug on Stress." *Harvard Business Review,* July 2003, pp. 102–107.

Franklin, Deborah. "What This CEO Didn't Know about His Cholesterol Almost Killed Him." *Fortune,* March 19, 2001, pp. 154–162.

Gale, Sarah Fister. "Selling Health to High-Risk Workers." *Workforce,* December 2002, pp. 74–76.

Gamse, Peg. "Stress for Success: Managers Can Create a 'Good Stress' Environment and Propel Employees to Success." *HR Magazine,* July 2003, pp. 101–103.

Gorell, Carin. "Fit for Life: Keeping the Weight Off." *Psychology Today,* January/February 2002, pp. 42, 44.

Nelson, Debra L., and Ronald J. Burke. *Gender, Work Stress, and Health.* Washington, DC: American Psychological Association, 2002.

Petesch, Peter. "Workplace Fitness or Workplace Fits?" *HR Magazine,* July 2001, pp. 137–140.

Weeks, Holly. "Taking the Stress Out of Stressful Conversations." *Harvard Business Review,* July–August 2001, pp. 112–119.

CHAPTER 5

Dealing with Personal Problems

Learning Objectives

After studying the information and doing the exercises in this chapter, you should be able to:

◆ Recognize how self-defeating behavior contributes to personal problems

◆ Explain the nature of addictive behavior and its link to craving for dopamine

◆ Explain how alcohol and drug abuse and online addiction interfere with career and personal success and how to deal with these problems

◆ Develop insights into dealing with the loss of a relationship

◆ Describe how depression, anxiety, and neurobiological disorders can lower job productivity

◆ Develop a strategy for dealing with anger

*B*ill Valvo knew deep down that his health was taking a turn for the worst. He had worked as a software developer for a company in Fairfax, Virginia, for a decade following a 22-year tour of duty in the Air Force. The work pressures finally got to him. "I left to start my own business," says Valvo, age 55, "but I could feel that all the stress was having physiological effects."

The negative effects were forthcoming. Valvo was diagnosed with coronary artery disease and had bypass surgery in 1999. After the operation he sunk into a deep depression, which would go into remission and then reappear with full intensity. Finally, Valvo's physician prescribed an antidepressant drug for him. The medication not only relieved the depression but also helped him convert to a new perspective about illness and health. "Did my heart operation cause the depression I'm experiencing?" he wrote in an article for a chapter of Mended Hearts, a support group for heart disease patients and their families. "Does depression cause heart disease? The answer to both these questions is probably yes."[1]

The information technology professional who made these comments about depression and health illustrates the growing awareness that a person's mental condition and attitude can affect physical health. (And poor physical health can damage the emotions.) The anecdote suggests also that untreated personal problems can force a person to change careers.

Our approach to understanding and overcoming personal problems will be to first describe self-defeating behavior in general and how to reverse the trend. We then describe various forms of self-defeating behavior, including addictions and absenteeism and tardiness. We also describe two types of personal problems that are much less under a person's control: depression, anxiety, and neurobiological disorders (such as attention-deficit disorder). Finally, we describe dealing with anger.

▲ SELF-DEFEATING BEHAVIOR

Many problems on the job and in personal life arise because of factors beyond our control. A boss may be intimidating and insensitive, an employer might lay you off, or your partner might abruptly terminate your relationship. Many personal problems, nevertheless, arise because of **self-defeating behavior.** A person with self-defeating tendencies intentionally or unintentionally engages in activities or harbors attitudes that work against his or her best interest. A person who habitually is late for important meetings is engaging in self-defeating behavior. Dropping out of school for no reason other than being bored with studying is another of many possible examples. Let's examine several leading causes of self-defeating behavior and how to reverse the pattern.

WHY PEOPLE ENGAGE IN SELF-DEFEATING BEHAVIOR

Many different forces lead people to work against their own best interests, often sabotaging their careers. The major cause of self-defeating behavior is a *loser life script.*[2] Early in life, our parents and other influential forces program our brains to act out certain life plans. These plans are known as *scripts.* People fortunate enough to have winner scripts consistently emerge victorious. When a tough assignment needs doing, they get the job done. For example, they figure out how to get a jammed computer program running again that baffles everybody else in the office.

In contrast, others have scripts that program them toward damaging their careers and falling short of their potential. Much of this damage paradoxically occurs just when things seem to be going well. A person might steal equipment from a company shortly after receiving an outstanding performance appraisal.

The simplest explanation for self-defeating behavior is that some people suffer from a personality that fosters defeat. People with a *self-defeating personality pattern* have three notable characteristics. First, they repeatedly fail at tasks they have the ability to perform. Second, they place themselves in very difficult situations and respond helplessly. Third, they typically refuse to take advantage of escape routes, such as accepting advice and counsel from a manager.[3]

Self-defeating beliefs put many people on the road to career self-sabotage. In this context, a self-defeating belief is an erroneous belief that creates the conditions for failure. For example, some people sabotage their job campaigns before even starting. They think to themselves, "I lack the right experience," "I'm not sharp enough," "I'm too old," "I'm too young," and so forth.

Fear of success is yet another contributor to career self-sabotage. People who fear success often procrastinate to the point of self-defeat. The same people worry that being successful will lead to such negative outcomes as an overwhelming workload or loss of friends. They also worry that success will bring about unrealistic expectations from others, such as winning a big suggestion award every year.

To examine your present tendencies toward self-defeating behavior, take the self-sabotage quiz presented in Human Relations Self-Assessment Quiz 5-1. Taking the quiz will help alert you to many self-imposed behaviors and attitudes that could potentially harm your career and personal life.

STRATEGIES AND TECHNIQUES FOR OVERCOMING AND PREVENTING SELF-DEFEATING BEHAVIOR

Overcoming self-defeating behavior requires hard work and patience. Here we present six widely applicable strategies for overcoming and

HUMAN RELATIONS SELF-ASSESSMENT QUIZ 5-1

The Self-Sabotage Questionnaire

Indicate how accurately each of the statements below describes or characterizes you, using a five-point scale: (0) very inaccurately, (1) inaccurately, (2) midway between inaccurately and accurately, (3) accurately, (4) very accurately. Consider discussing some of the questions with a family member, close friend, or work associate. Another person's feedback may prove helpful in providing accurate answers to some of the questions.

Answer

1. Other people have said that I am my worst enemy. _____

2. If I don't do a perfect job, I feel worthless. _____

3. I am my own harshest critic. _____

4. When engaged in a sport or other competitive activity, I find a way to blow a substantial lead right near the end. _____

5. When I make a mistake, I can usually identify another person to blame. _____

6. I have a strong tendency to procrastinate. _____

7. I have trouble focusing on what is really important to me. _____

8. I have trouble taking criticism, even from friends. _____

9. My fear of seeming stupid often prevents me from asking questions or offering my opinion. _____

10. I tend to expect the worst in most situations. _____

11. Many times I have rejected people who treat me well. _____

12. When I have an important project to complete, I usually get sidetracked, and then miss the deadline. _____

13. I choose work assignments that lead to disappointments, even when better options are clearly available. _____

14. I frequently misplace things, such as my keys, then get very angry at myself. _____

15. I am concerned that, if I take on much more responsibility, people will expect too much from me. _____

16. I avoid situations, such as competitive sports, where people can find out how good or bad I really am. _____

17. People describe me as the "office clown." _____

18. I have an insatiable demand for money and power. _____

19. When negotiating with others, I hate to grant any concessions. _____

20. I seek revenge for even the smallest hurts. _____

21. I have an overwhelming ego. _____

22. When I receive a compliment or other form of recognition, I usually feel I don't deserve it. _____

23. To be honest, I choose to suffer. _____

24. I regularly enter into conflict with people who try to help me. _____

25. I'm a loser. _____

Total score _____

Scoring and Interpretation: Add your answers to all the questions to obtain your total score.

0–25 You appear to have very few tendencies toward self-sabotage. If this interpretation is supported by your own positive feelings toward your life and yourself, you are in good shape with respect to self-defeating behavior tendencies. However, stay alert to potential self-sabotaging tendencies that could develop at later stages in your life.

26–50 You may have some mild tendencies toward self-sabotage. It could be that you do things occasionally that defeat your own purposes. Review actions you have taken during the past six months to decide if any of them have been self-sabotaging.

51–75 You show signs of engaging in self-sabotage. You probably have thoughts and carry out actions that could be blocking you from achieving important work and personal goals. People with scores in this category characteristically engage in negative self-talk that lowers their self-confidence and makes them appear weak and indecisive to others. People in this range frequently experience another problem. They sometimes sabotage their chances of succeeding on a project just to prove that their negative self-assessment is correct. If you scored in this range, carefully study the suggestions offered in this chapter.

76–100 You most likely have a strong tendency toward self-sabotage. (Sometimes it is possible to obtain a high score on a test like this because you are going through an unusually stressful period in your life.) Study this section of the chapter carefully and look for useful hints for removing self-imposed barriers to your success. Equally important, you might discuss your tendencies toward undermining your own achievements with a mental health professional.

preventing self-defeating behavior. Pick and choose among them to fit your particular circumstance and personal style.

Examine Your Script and Make the Necessary Changes

Early life programming determines whether a person is predisposed to self-defeat. A person may be predisposed to snatch defeat from the jaws of victory, but that does not mean the predisposition makes defeat inevitable. It does mean that the person will have to work harder to overcome a tendency toward self-sabotage. A good starting point is to look for patterns in your setbacks:

> Did you blow up at people who have the authority to make the administrative decisions about your future?
>
> Did you get so tense during your last few command performances that you were unable to function effectively?
>
> Did you give up in the late stages of several projects, saying "I just can't get this done"?

Stop Blaming Others for Your Problems and Cursing Fate

Blaming others for our problems contributes to self-defeating behavior and career self-sabotage.[4] Projecting blame onto others is self-defeating because doing so relieves you of most of the responsibility for your setback and failure. Consider this example: If someone blames favoritism for not receiving a promotion, he or she will not have to worry about becoming a stronger candidate for future promotions. Not to improve your suitability for promotion is self-sabotaging. If you accept most of the blame for not being promoted, you are more likely to make the changes necessary to qualify in the future.

Cursing fate or having an external locus of control is another way of placing blame outside yourself for your problems. If the cause of your problems is fate (or bum luck), you do not have to take personal responsibility for personal setbacks. Some people reason that their careers are predetermined or mysteriously out of their control. Following this logic, whatever they do or do not do is sufficient. They tell themselves, "The lucky ones are going to get the good assignments and promotions, and the rest of us won't. So why bother?" The solution here is to minimize blaming fate or chance for your problems and attempt to create your own future. When things go wrong, fight back and create your own destiny.[5]

An underlying theme to the suggestions for preventing and overcoming self-defeating behavior is that we all need to engage in thoughts and actions that increase our personal control. This is precisely why blaming others for our problems is self-sabotaging. By turning over control of your fate to forces outside yourself, you are holding them responsible for your problems. An internal locus of control helps overcome and prevent self-defeating behavior.

Solicit Feedback on Your Actions

Feedback is essential for monitoring whether you are sabotaging your career or personal life. A starting point is to listen carefully to any direct or indirect comments from your superiors, subordinates, coworkers, customers, and friends about how you are coming across to them. Consider the case of Bill, a technical writer:

> Bill heard three people in one week make comments about his appearance. It started innocently with, "Here, let me fix your collar." Next, an office assistant said, "Bill, are you coming down with something?" The third comment was, "You look pretty tired today. Have you been working

extra hard?" Bill processed this feedback carefully. He used it as a signal that his steady late-night drinking episodes were adversely affecting his image. He then cut back his drinking enough to revert to his normal healthy appearance.

An assertive and thick-skinned person might try the technique described for soliciting feedback described in Chapter 1. Approach a sampling of people both on and off the job with this line of questioning: "I'm trying to develop myself personally. Can you think of anything I do or say that creates a bad impression in any way? Do not be afraid of offending me. Only people who know me can provide me with this kind of information."

Take notes to show how serious you are about the feedback. When someone provides any feedback at all, say, "Please continue, this is very useful." Try not to react defensively when you hear something negative. You asked for it, and the person is truly doing you a favor.

Learn to Profit from Criticism

As the above example implies, learning to profit from criticism is necessary to benefit from feedback. Furthermore, to ignore valid criticism can be self-defeating. People who benefit from criticism are able to stand outside themselves while being criticized. It is as if they are watching the criticism from a distance and looking for its possible merits. People who take criticism personally experience anguish when receiving negative feedback.

Ask politely for more details about the negative behavior in question so that you can change if change is warranted. If your boss is criticizing you for being rude with customers, you might respond, "I certainly don't want to be rude. Can you give me a couple of examples of how I was rude? I need your help in working on this problem." After asking questions, you can better determine if the criticism is valid.

Stop Denying the Existence of Problems

Many people sabotage their careers because they deny the existence of a problem and therefore do not take appropriate action. Denial takes place as a defensive maneuver against a painful reality. An example of a self-sabotaging form of denial is to ignore the importance of upgrading one's credentials despite overwhelming evidence that it is necessary. Some people never quite complete a degree program that has become an informal qualification for promotion. Consequently, they sabotage their chances of receiving a promotion for which they are otherwise qualified.

Visualize Self-Enhancing Behavior

To apply visualization, program yourself to overcome self-defeating actions and thoughts. Imagine yourself engaging in self-enhancing, winning actions and thoughts. Picture yourself achieving peak performance when good results count the most. A starting point is to identify the next job situation you will be facing that is similar to ones you have flubbed in the past. You then imagine yourself mentally and physically projected into that situation. Imagine what the room looks like, who will be there, and the confident expression you will have on your face. Visualization is akin to watching a video of yourself doing something right.

▲ UNDERSTANDING AND CONTROLLING ADDICTIONS

Wellness is blocked by a variety of addictions, and addictive behavior is also a personal problem. Furthermore, people with personal problems often seek relief by lapsing into addictive behavior. An **addiction** (or **substance dependence**) is a compulsion to use substances or engage in activities that lead to psychological dependence and withdrawal symptoms when use is discontinued. A caffeine addict would suffer adverse symptoms such as headaches and tension if deprived of caffeine for an entire day. A person with a work addiction would feel ill at ease and tense if forced to stay away from work for several days.

Addictive behavior in the form of substance abuse is a major workplace problem. According to the Robert Wood Foundation, more than 20 percent of full-time workers reported binge drinking in the past month. About 12 percent report illegal drug use in the past year, and one-third are smokers.[6] (Current data suggest that smoking is down to about 22 percent of the population in the United States and Canada.)

Research about brain chemistry and behavior helps explain why addictions to substances are so widespread. The moment a person ingests a substance such as tobacco, alcohol, marijuana, or chocolate, trillions of strong molecules surge through the bloodstream and into the brain. The molecules trigger a flood of chemical and electrical events that result in a temporary state of pleasure and euphoria.

The common thread to all these mood-altering drugs is their ability to elevate levels of a chemical substance in the brain called **dopamine,** a neurotransmitter that is associated with pleasure and elation. (A neurotransmitter is a molecule in the brain that transports messages from one neuron in the brain to another. It moves across the connectors among brain cells, called synapses.) Dopamine may be responsible for the highs of infatuation, new love, joy, self-confidence, and motivation. The chemical is so effective that some scientists regard it as the master molecule of addiction.[7] Dopamine is elevated by the common addictive drugs such as heroin, amphetamines, cocaine and crack, marijuana, alcohol, nicotine, and caffeine. However, dopamine can also be elevated by a hug, sexual attraction, praise from a key person, and presumably finding an exciting new Website or book. In short, people develop addictions to get their shot of dopamine.

The balance of our study of substance abuse and addictions concentrates on alcohol abuse and a variety of other drugs, along with online addiction. Other forms of substance abuse include inhaling intoxicants such as rubber cement or cleaning fluid. Nicotine, caffeine, chocolate, and sugar could be added to the list. With the exception of nicotine, however, their symptoms are not life threatening.

ALCOHOL ABUSE

A major concern about consuming large amounts of alcohol is that health may be adversely affected. Alcohol consumption leads to marked changes in behavior. Doses even below the legal limit in most states significantly impair the judgment and coordination required to drive an automobile safely. Moderate to high doses of alcohol cause marked impairment in higher mental functions. The brain damage that results can severely alter a person's ability to learn and remember information. As alcohol takes effect, it stimulates and suppresses various areas of the brain and can result in contradictory emotions.[8] The result is often anxiety reduction, euphoria, aggression, and memory loss. Euphoria takes place because alcohol activates a pleasure center in the brain. Paradoxically, negative behavior is also stimulated. You may have noticed that some people become belligerent when drunk. Many have to be escorted out of clubs by security personnel.

Very high doses of alcohol cause respiratory depression and death. Heavy alcohol consumption over a prolonged period of time contributes to heart disease. (As mentioned in the study of diets in Chapter 4, consuming one or two alcoholic beverages a day, however, may help prevent heart disease by stimulating the heart and unclogging arteries.)

Long-term consumption of large quantities of alcohol, particularly when combined with poor nutrition, can lead to permanent damage to vital organs such as the brain and liver. Drinking large quantities of alcohol during pregnancy may result in newborns with fetal alcohol syndrome. These infants have irreversible physical abnormalities and mental retardation.

As with other drugs, including nicotine, repeated use of alcohol can lead to dependence. Abrupt cessation of alcohol consumption can produce withdrawal symptoms, including severe anxiety, tremors, hallucinations, and convulsions. Severe withdrawal symptoms can be life threatening.

Work and Personal Life Consequences of Alcohol Abuse

Heavy consumption of alcohol has many adverse consequences for a person's career and personal life. Heavy drinking will eventually interfere with work performance, resulting in some of the following behaviors:

- Low productivity and quality of work
- Erratic performance
- Erratic and unusual behavior such as swearing at coworkers during a meeting
- Excessive tardiness and absenteeism
- Increased difficulty in working cooperatively with supervisors or team leaders
- Increased difficulty in working cooperatively with coworkers
- Carelessness, negligence, or disinterest

Alcohol consumption is frequently disruptive to personal and family life. Even moderate doses of alcohol increase the incidents of a variety of aggressive acts, including partner and child abuse. Driving while intoxicated is still the major contributor to automobile accidents. Purchasing alcoholic beverages can lead to family problems because household bills may go unpaid. Many alcoholics lose friends because they are uncomfortable to be around when drinking. Sexual desire and performance often decline with heavy alcohol abuse. Many male long-term drinkers suffer from impotency. Alcohol abuse often leads to divorce and other broken relationships.

Overcoming Alcohol Abuse

A person's approach to overcoming alcohol abuse depends to some extent on whether he or she regards alcoholism as a disease or as maladaptive behavior. Regarding alcoholism as a disease is the majority viewpoint among mental health specialists and the general public. People who regard alcoholism as a disease are likely to seek medical or psychological help. To conquer alcoholism they would therefore seek help from physicians and counselors. Such help might consist of outpatient visits to mental health practitioners, often at clinics for substance abusers. People with severe alcoholism might volunteer to become inpatients at a hospital specializing in the treatment of alcoholism.

Another viewpoint is to regard alcoholism as self-defeating behavior that is somewhat under a person's control. People who accept the *bad habit* view of alcohol abuse might seek professional assistance with their problem. Yet the thrust of their efforts to overcome alcoholism will be to discipline themselves to change their counterproductive ways. Looking on alcoholism as maladaptive behavior runs contrary to groups such as Alcoholics Anonymous. Such groups label alcoholism as a sickness over which the victim has no control and therefore insist on abstinence. A person who believes that alcohol abuse is under his or her control could take the following precautions to prevent a major drinking problem:[9]

- Limit the consumption of alcoholic beverages to three on any given day but average no more than two per day. The average size male should set a maximum quota of 14 drinks per week; the average-size woman, nine drinks. Remember that in order of increasing strength, popular alcoholic beverages are ranked as follows: wine cooler, beer, wine, and whiskey. Whiskey should therefore be consumed in smaller quantities than the other three types of beverages.

- Abstain from alcoholic beverages for at least two consecutive days each week.

- Drink only standard-size beverages: one ounce of whiskey in a mixed drink, 12 ounces of beer, or five ounces of wine.

- Don't drink on an empty stomach.

- Drink slowly and intersperse alcoholic beverages with nonalcoholic beverages while at parties.

- When you have the urge for an alcoholic beverage, on occasion substitute a glass of fruit juice or water.

- Make friends with people whose social life does not revolve around drinking alcoholic beverages. Associate with responsible drinkers.

- Regard drinking before 6 P.M. as a personal taboo.

- Spend time in activities and places where alcohol consumption is forbidden or frowned on, such as in libraries, classrooms, health clubs, and events held at houses of worship.

The previous suggestions are useful because they assume that mature adults can enjoy moderate alcohol consumption without falling prey to alcohol abuse. The same suggestions can be used to convert problem drinking into relatively safe drinking. Implementing these suggestions requires considerable self-discipline, as do approaches to overcoming other forms of self-defeating behavior. However, controversy rages about whether alcoholics can ever learn to drink in moderation. The alcohol-as-disease perspective contends that an attempt at moderate drinking is doomed to failure.[10]

Many people believe that abstinence from alcohol is the only effective approach to curbing alcoholism. Twelve-step programs are widely used to treat alcoholism, and these programs follow closely the basics of Alcoholics Anonymous (see Exhibit 5-1). The 12 Steps are also used to treat a wide range of problems, including addictions to narcotics, marijuana, gambling, and sex and love.

EXHIBIT 5-1

The 12 Steps of Alcoholics Anonymous

1. To admit we are powerless over alcohol—that our lives have become unmanageable.

2. To come to believe that a Power greater than ourselves can restore us to sanity.

3. To make a decision to turn our will and our lives over to the dare of God as we understand Him.

4. To make a searching and fearless moral inventory of ourselves.

5. To admit to God, to ourselves and to another human being the exact nature of our wrongs.

6. To become entirely ready to have God remove all these defects of character.

7. To humbly asked Him to remove our shortcomings.

8. To make a list of all persons we have harmed, and to be willing to make amends to them all.

9. To make direct amends to such people wherever possible, except when to do so would injure them or others.

10. To continue to take personal inventory and when we were wrong to promptly admit it.

11. To seek through prayer and meditation to improve our conscious contact with God as we understood Him, praying only for knowledge of His will for us and the power to carry it out.

12. To have a spiritual awakening as the result of these steps, and to try to carry this message to alcoholics and to practice these principles in all our affairs.

SOURCE: www.dencities.com/12step/12step12step.html. Also found in most chapters of Alcoholics Anonymous, Narcotics Anonymous, Gamblers Anonymous, Nicotine Anonymous, Workaholics Anonymous, and so forth.

DRUG ABUSE

Another major personal problem many people face is drug abuse. The use of illegal drugs is often perceived more harshly than alcohol abuse because drinking alcoholic beverages is legal. Similarly, the abuse of prescription drugs is not considered as wrong as the abuse of illegal drugs. The health effects and personal life consequences of abusing both illegal and prescription drugs are similar to those of alcohol abuse. Human Relations Self-Assessment Quiz 5-3 will help sensitize you to the many similarities of behavioral consequences of drug and alcohol abuse.

Current studies provide clues as to why people often persist in drug use despite it many negative consequences. The challenge is that a person often begins drug use associated with a pleasant condition or surrounding, such as being among friends or attending a rave (all-night dance party). People who use alcohol and tobacco in bars to "loosen up" are rewarded with at least temporary friendships, such as buying a beer or lighting a cigarette for a stranger. Furthermore, heavy use of caffeine may be associated with better work performance at the beginning of the workday. In short, the person becomes conditioned to abusing a substance because that substance is linked to a pleasant experience.[11] Here we will summarize the effects of major categories of drugs and then describe how drug abusers can be helped.

Use and Effects of Controlled Substances

The term *drug* refers to a variety of chemicals with different chemical compositions and effects. One individual might purchase heroin for recreational use, while another person might sniff rubber cement to achieve the same effect. The U.S. government has compiled a five-way classification of frequently used drugs.[12] Each of the five categories of drugs has different possible effects and different consequences for overdoses. Each category of drug has both illegal and legitimate uses. For example, stimulants include both crack and a drug with the trade name Dexedrine.

HUMAN RELATIONS SELF-ASSESSMENT QUIZ 5-3

Symptoms of Alcohol and Drug Abuse

People with alcohol or drug abuse problems are often poor judges of the extent of their problem. Nevertheless, it is helpful to use the symptoms mentioned below as a checklist to help identify an alcohol or drug problem you might be experiencing. Review the symptoms listed below and indicate whether each one applies to you.

Alcohol Abuse	Yes	No
Sudden decreases in my job performance	____	____
Decreases in my mental alertness	____	____

(Continued)

	Yes	No
Many long lunch hours	_____	_____
Tardiness for work and social appointments	_____	_____
Wobbling instead of walking straight	_____	_____
Many absences from work or school	_____	_____
Comments by others that my speech is slurred	_____	_____
Frequent use of breath freshener	_____	_____
Frequent depressed moods	_____	_____
Trembling of my hands and body	_____	_____
Errors in judgment and concentration	_____	_____
Many financial problems because of my drinking	_____	_____
Comments by others that my eyes look sleepy	_____	_____
Much lost time due to physical illness	_____	_____
Elaborate alibis for not getting work done on the job or at home	_____	_____
Denying a drinking problem when I know I have one	_____	_____
Not showing up for many work or social appointments	_____	_____

Interpretation: If five or more of the above symptoms fit you, you may have a problem with alcohol abuse. Act on the remedial measures described previously.

Drug Abuse	Yes	No
Sudden decreases in my job performance	_____	_____
Decreases in my mental alertness	_____	_____
Hiding out on company premises	_____	_____
Many absences from work or school	_____	_____
My pupils appear dilated when I look in the mirror	_____	_____
Unusual bursts of energy and excitement	_____	_____
Prolonged and serious lethargy	_____	_____
States of apathy and elation I cannot explain	_____	_____
Errors in concentration and judgment	_____	_____
Many financial problems because of drug purchases	_____	_____
Comments by others that my eyes look sleepy	_____	_____
Frequent sniffing	_____	_____
People telling me that I look "out of it"	_____	_____
Elaborate alibis for not getting work done on the job or at home	_____	_____
Frequent dry, irritated coughing	_____	_____
Denying a drug problem when I know I have one	_____	_____
Not showing up for many work and social appointments	_____	_____

Interpretation: If five or more of the above symptoms fit you, you may have a problem with drug abuse. Act on the remedial measures described previously.

Narcotics. A **narcotic** is a drug that dulls the senses, facilitates sleep, and is addictive with long-term use. Well-known narcotics include opium, morphine, codeine, and heroin. The possible effects of narcotics include euphoria, drowsiness, and decreased breathing. A narcotic user may also experience constricted pupils and nausea. Overdosing on narcotics may lead to slow and shallow breathing, clammy skin, convulsions, and coma. Death is also possible. People who use narcotics frequently do severe damage to their careers and personal lives in the long run.

Depressants. A **depressant** is a drug that slows down vital body processes. Barbiturates are the best-known depressant (or sedative). Alcohol is also classified as a depressant. Heavy doses of depressants can lead to slurred speech and disorientation. A depressant user will show drunken behavior without the odor of alcohol. An overdose of depressants leads to shallow breathing, clammy skin, and dilated pupils. With extreme overdoses, the person may lapse into coma and then death.

Many anxious people are convinced they must take legally prescribed sedatives to calm down. The trade-off is the risk of lacking the mental alertness to perform at their peak. Frequent users of depressants make poor companions because they lack vitality.

Stimulants. The class of drugs known as **stimulants** produces feelings of optimism and high energy. Cocaine and amphetamines are the two best-known stimulants. Taking stimulants leads to increased alertness, excitation, and euphoria. The user will also experience increased pulse rate and blood pressure, insomnia, and loss of appetite. (Many diet pills are really stimulants.) Overdoses of stimulants lead to agitation, increased body temperature, hallucinations, convulsions, and possible death. Stimulant abusers are regarded by others as being "hyper" and may be too agitated to do high-quality work.

Hallucinogens. In small doses the class of drugs known as **hallucinogens** produce visual effects similar to hallucinations. Three well-known hallucinogens are LSD, mescaline, and peyote. Hallucinogens lead to illusions (misperceptions) and poor perception of time and distance. Overdoses of hallucinogens can produce "trip" episodes, psychosis (severe mental disorder), and possible death. While under the influence of a hallucinogen, a person is unfit for work. The bizarre behavior of hallucinogen abusers leads to a deterioration of their relationships with people.

Cannabis. The class of drugs known as **cannabis** are derived from the hemp plant and generally produce a state of mild euphoria. Marijuana and hashish are placed in the cannabis category. Cannabis use leads to euphoria, relaxed inhibitions, and increased appetite. The same drug may cause disorientation. Cannabis abuse may lead to fatigue, paranoia, and possible psychosis. Because marijuana is used as a cigarette, it may cause lung cancer and cardiovascular damage. Used in moderate doses, cannabis does much less damage to career and personal life than the other drugs described here.

GETTING HELP FOR DRUG ABUSE PROBLEMS

Many forms of assistance are available for drug abusers. The comments made earlier in relation to alcohol abuse also apply to drug abuse. Drug abusers can seek help from physicians and from mental health specialists (some of whom are physicians) or join a 12-Step program. At the same time, the drug abuser may view his or her problem as a form of maladaptive behavior that can be controlled through concentrated effort. Assume, for example, that a person says, "I simply cannot get through the day without an amphetamine pill. Life is too boring for me if I don't have an upper." The antidote is for the person to say something to the following effect: "This week, I won't take an amphetamine on Monday. Next week, no amphetamine on Monday or Tuesday. I'll keep adding a day until I have gone an entire week drug-free." Self-management of this type can work for many people.

INTERNET DEPENDENCE

A major modern addiction, or at least a very strong habit, is the problem of feeling compelled to spend lengthy periods of time surfing the Internet as a pastime. An **Internet dependence** (or **addiction**) is a condition whereby a person spends so much time on the Internet that other work suffers and the person experiences sleep deprivation and neglects human contact. Because the withdrawal symptoms from being deprived of the Internet are much less physiological than withdrawal from a controlled substance, the term *dependence* might be more appropriate than *addiction*. Internet abuse can be a problem for white-collar employees who typically have greater time flexibility and easier access to computers than do production employees. Because professional workers use the Internet daily, they are more likely to engage in potentially addictive behaviors, such as gambling, playing computer games, passing time in chat rooms, and watching pornography.[13] Obsessive checking of e-mail, such as every three minutes, is another symptom of Internet abuse. The negative consequence is that constant checking often detracts from other important work and personal activities.

Symptoms of pathological Internet use are presented in Human Relations Self-Assessment Quiz 5-2. A concern about the social consequences of Internet dependence is that many users, caught in maintaining contact with so many people with similar interests, seem to be substituting weak online friendships for stronger real-life relationships.[14] (This does not imply that nobody ever develops solid interpersonal relationships over the Internet. Many people find life partners and business associates online.)

About 5 to 10 percent of Internet users develop problem behaviors, about the same frequency as for people who drink alcohol or gamble. Because so many people have problems with excessive time devoted to the Internet, many Internet abuse treatment centers have evolved. Among the specific problems treated are extensive amounts of time viewing pornography, online affairs, and addictive day trading (buying and selling the same security in a single day) online. One approach to helping people overcome Internet dependence is to treat it like binge eating, where the individual frequently engages in the activity to be restricted. Clients are taught how to set limits to Internet use and schedule time without having to go cold turkey.[15] Giving up Internet use entirely would be self-defeating for both career and personal life.

HUMAN RELATIONS SELF-ASSESSMENT QUIZ 5-2

Warning Signs of Excessive Internet Use

Psychologist Kimberly Young has identified several warning signs of excessive Internet use. Behaviors that signal concern include the following:

- *Staying* online longer than you intended

- Admitting that you *can't stop* yourself from signing on

- *Neglecting* loved ones, chores, sleep, reading, television, friends, exercise, hobbies, sex, or social events because of the Internet

- Spending *38 hours* or more a week online

- Feeling *anxious,* bored, sad, lonely, angry, or *stressed* before going online but feeling happy, excited, loved, calmed, or confident while on the Internet

- Favoring *chat rooms,* games, and multiuser dungeons over other Internet activities

Although this quiz does not have a scoring key, the more of the above behaviors you have exhibited, the more severe your Internet dependence. Get help before you wind up with such outcomes as losing your job, flunking out of school, or losing an important relationship.

SOURCE: Reprinted from Carol Potera, "Trapped in the Web," *Psychology Today,* March/April 1998, p. 68.

⟩ COPING WITH THE LOSS OF A RELATIONSHIP

A major personal problem many people encounter is the loss of a valued personal relationship. The loss may take the form of separation, divorce, or a nonmarried couple splitting. A more subtle loss is when a couple stays together yet the intimacy in a relationship vanishes. Loneliness and conflict result from the lost intimacy. The loss of a close friend who is not a romantic partner may also require many of the coping behaviors presented below. Chapter 16 presents ideas on maintaining and revitalizing relationships. Our attention here is directed toward specific suggestions for dealing with the loss of an important personal relationship.

When you are emotionally and romantically involved with another person, the loss of that relationship usually has a big impact. Even if you believe strongly that splitting is in your best interests, the fact that you cared at one time about that person leads to some hurt. The major reason we need tactics for dealing with lost relationships is that many upsetting feelings surface in conjunction with the loss.

A newly unattached person might feel lonely, guilty, angry, or frightened. Your role in the disengagement will usually dictate which emotion surfaces. For instance, if you dumped your partner, you will probably experience guilt. If you were the person dumped, you would probably experience anger. If you survive a spouse, you might feel guilty about not having been nice enough to your partner during your years together.

A number of suggestions are presented below to help a person recover from a lost relationship.[16] Choose the tactics that seem to fit your personality and circumstances. As with the other personal problems described in this chapter, professional counseling may be helpful in making a recovery.

1. *Be thankful for the good in the relationship.*   An excellent starting point in recovering a broken relationship is to take stock of what went right when the two of you were together. Looking for the good in the relationship helps place the situation in proper perspective. It also helps prevent you from developing the counterproductive attitude that your time together was a total waste.

2. *Find new outlets for spare time.*   Some of the energy you were investing in your partnership can now be invested in spare-time activities. This activity provides a healthy form of the defense mechanism called *compensation* or *substitution*.

3. *Get ample rest and relaxation.*   A broken relationship is a stressor. As a result, most people need rest and relaxation to help them overcome the emotional pain associated with the departure of a partner.

4. *Pamper yourself.*   Pampering involves finding little ways of doing nice things for yourself. These could take the form of buying yourself a new outfit, taking a weekend vacation, eating pizza at midnight, or getting a body massage.

5. *Get emotional support.* A highly recommended antidote to a broken relationship is to obtain emotional support from others. Friends and relatives are often the most important source of emotional support to help you cope with postseparation blues. Be careful, however, not to let your loss of a relationship dominate conversations with friends to the point of boring them. Another source of emotional support are groups specifically designed to help people cope with recent separation or divorce. Parents without Partners is an example of such a group. A caution here is that some people stay too long with such groups rather than taking the initiative to find a new partner.

6. *Get out and go places.* The oldest suggestion about recovering from a lost relationship is perhaps the most valid—keep active. While you are doing new things, you tend to forget about your problems. Also, as you go places and do things, you increase your chances of making new friends. And new friends are the only true antidote to the loneliness of being unattached.

7. *Give yourself time to heal.* The greater the hurt, the more time it will take to recover from the broken relationship. Recognizing this fact will help curb your impatience over disentangling yourself emotionally from the former spouse or partner.

8. *Anticipate a positive outcome.* While you are on the path toward rebuilding your social life, believe that things will get better. Also believe that all the emotional energy you have invested into splitting and healing will pay dividends. Self-fulfilling prophecies work to some extent in social relationships. If you believe you will make a satisfactory recovery from a broken relationship, your chances of doing so will increase. The underlying mechanism seems to be that if you believe in yourself, you exude a level of self-confidence that others find appealing.

▲ ABSENTEEISM AND TARDINESS

Absenteeism and tardiness are the leading causes of employee discipline. Employer tolerance for absenteeism and lateness varies from industry to industry and from job level to job level. Yet as a rule of thumb, latenesses and more than five absences constitute a problem.[17] Developing a poor record of attendance and punctuality is also a form of career self-sabotage. Employees who are habitually late or absent develop a poor reputation and receive negative employment references. It becomes difficult to find a good job with another employer after establishing a poor record of attendance and punctuality. Even in a period when workers are scarce, being reliable about coming to work helps a person secure a good job.

A recent trend in absenteeism suggests that keeping lost time to a minimum enhances job security. During the sluggish economy in 2003, absentee rates were near a 12-year low. The decrease was found in taking time off from work for health, personal, or medical visits. Also, many fewer workers were asking their physicians to write sick notes, and many more workers were requesting painkillers so they could cope with their job.[18] Maintaining good attendance and punctuality is also important because the employee who is habitually absent or late detracts from productivity.

Many unexpected situations arise in which it is necessary to be absent or late. Accidents, illnesses, severe family problems, and family deaths all may require time away from the job. A serious-minded worker should therefore strive to attain near perfect attendance and punctuality when not faced with an emergency. Some suggestions follow to help a person develop the right mental set for achieving an excellent record of attendance and punctuality.

1. *Recognize that not to have excellent attendance and punctuality is self-defeating.* For reasons already described, poor attendance and punctuality can lead to a poor reputation and job loss. Why self-handicap your chances for career success?

2. *Look on your job as self-employment.* Few people operating their own business will take a day off or begin late for no valid reason. The smaller the business, the better the attendance and punctuality because so little assistance is available. You can therefore improve your attendance and punctuality by imagining that your area of responsibility is your own business.

3. *Regard your job responsibilities as being as important as those of the person in charge of opening the bank's doors in the morning.* People in charge of opening banks, department stores, movie theaters, and other retail businesses have excellent records of attendance and punctuality. To do otherwise would create panic, especially in the case of the bank. To improve your attendance and punctuality, think of your responsibilities as being as important as opening the doors in the morning.

4. *Reward yourself for good attendance and punctuality and punish yourself for the opposite.* Following the suggestions for self-motivation described in Chapter 2, modify your behavior in relation to attendance and punctuality. Treat yourself after six months of excellent attendance and punctuality—but not by taking a day off from work. Punish yourself for a poor record. For example, if you miss one day of work for a flimsy reason, punish yourself by working all day on a national holiday.

5. *Think of the consequences to coworkers if you are absent and late frequently.* Being absent or late may hurt the company. The same behavior can adversely affect your relationships with coworkers. Coworkers become annoyed and irritated quickly when they have to cover for a negligent peer. The worker who is frequently absent and late runs the risk of losing the cooperation of coworkers when he or she needs assistance.

▲ DEPRESSION, ANXIETY, AND NEUROBIOLOGICAL DISORDERS

Many employees perform poorly on the job because of reasons beyond their control. They would like to perform well, but disturbed emotions or brain malfunctioning interfere with handling some aspects of their job responsibilities well. To illustrate this problem, we describe three problems faced by many workers, depression, anxiety, and neurobiological disorders (defined later).

DEPRESSION

A widespread emotional disorder is **depression.** A depressed person has such difficulties as sadness, changes in appetite; sleeping difficulties; and a decrease in activities, interests, and energy. Depression is much more severe than simply having a mood downturn. A person cannot quickly snap out of depression, and unlike a bad mood, depression can have an adverse impact on physical health. About 10 percent will suffer depression serious enough during their lives to interfere with happiness and productivity. The diagnosis of depression is increasing in frequency, triggered by factors such as rising divorce rates, a lowered sense of community, and a greater awareness of depression. Also, with less stigma attached to mental illness, more depressed people are seeking treatment.[19]

Most cases of depression are believed to be caused primarily by a chemical imbalance in the brain whereby the functioning of the neurotransmitters is disturbed. A person's psychological makeup also contributes to susceptibility to depression. People with low self-esteem, who are pessimistic, and who manage stress poorly are prone to depression. To treat depression successfully, antidepressant medication usually needs to be accompanied by psychotherapy and counseling. One study showed that when patients were treated with both medication and psychotherapy, 85 percent improved. About 55 percent of patients improved when treated with medication alone, and 50 improved when treated only by psychotherapy.[20] Electroshock therapy, although controversial, is still used to treat heavily depressed patients who do not respond to drug treatment or psychotherapy. The treatment uses a small current of electricity to trigger a mild brain seizure that can push a depressed brain out of its slump.

New evidence indicates strongly that unless depressed people continue taking anti-depressant medication, they have a considerable risk of suffering a relapse in the year after they discontinue the drug treatment. Yet when patients complete psychotherapy—even without medication—they relapse far less frequently. The type of psychotherapy under consideration is *cognitive behavior therapy,* and affects the brain almost like a drug. The therapy quiets brain activity responsible for conceptual thought, planning, analysis, and logic.[21]

Seasonal affective disorder (SAD) is a form of depression that develops during the fall and winter months and disappears as the days lengthen in the spring. Because darkness stimulates the production of melatonin, some researchers believe that people who experience SAD may produce an excess of melatonin or may be particularly sensitive to the hormone. SAD sufferers become lethargic in the winter and fall and show other symptoms of depression. In one study of 300 patients, participants reported higher cases of depression, anxiety, hostility, anger, and irritability in winter than any other season.[22] "Winter blues" is the everyday term for this problem and SAD.

The farther north from the equator you live, the more likely you are to experience SAD. However, people who enjoy outdoor winter activities like skiing, ice skating, curling, and shoveling snow are less prone to SAD (based on this author's observations).

Being depressed on the job creates many problems. Depression drains energy and reduces productivity and quality. The reduced effectiveness triggers a cycle of failure. As effectiveness decreases, the person's thinking, acting, and feeling become more damaged. As relationships with coworkers and job performance deteriorate, the person becomes more depressed. Here is an example of how depression affects job behavior:

> A sales manager known for his exuberance and enthusiasm slowly began to withdraw from face-to-face contact with team members. During one team meeting, the manager abruptly terminated the meeting, telling the group, "I'm just too emotionally drained to continue today." Soon he rarely communicated with others in the firm except through e-mail. At times he was observed just staring out the window. Reports of his unusual behavior soon reached his manager, who in turn urged the sales manager to visit a mental health professional. A combination of antidepressant drugs and psychotherapy helped the sales manager to overcome his problems enough to function satisfactorily on the job.

Human Relations Self-Assessment Quiz 5-3 will help you better appreciate the symptoms of depression as they apply to the job. These symptoms are easier to recognize in another person than in yourself. Having more than a few of these symptoms is an indicator that treatment by a mental health professional is important. Most people who attempt or commit suicide are extremely depressed, and about 15 percent of people with severe depression eventually take their own lives.[23]

GENERALIZED ANXIETY DISORDERS

A personal problem facing an estimated 13 percent of people at some point in their life is continuous worry about real and imagined problems to the point that the person feels ill at ease and sometimes unable to function well. **Anxiety** is a feeling of distress or uneasiness caused by fear of an imagined problem. You might be anxious about being a passenger in an upcoming airplane flight, yet you do not know exactly what you are worrying

---

HUMAN RELATIONS SELF-ASSESSMENT QUIZ 5-4

Symptoms of Depression on the Job

Workers suffering from depression often experience a combination of one or more of the following symptoms. Not every depressed person will experience them all. (Most of these symptoms are also present off the job.)

- Persistent, sad, anxious, or "empty" mood
- Slow movement, drooped posture
- Decreased energy, fatigue, and frequent complaints of being tired
- Decreased ability to concentrate, remember, or make decisions
- Taking an unusually long time to complete tasks
- Speaking only when spoken to
- Crying on the job
- Attributing any personal successes to luck
- Loss of interest in activities that were once enjoyable, such as having lunch with coworkers
- Mentions of suicide, even in a joking manner
- Deterioration in grooming, such as rumpled clothing, unkempt hair, or neglected facial shaving
- Increased absenteeism
- Alcohol and drug abuse
- Appetite and/or weight loss or overeating and weight gain
- Increasing intensity and frequency of any of the above symptoms

SOURCE: Canadian Mental Health Association, 1995; *Health Guide,* America's Pharmaceutical Research Companies, 1996 (www.phrma.org); *Depression: What You Need to Know,* Office of Scientific Information, National Institute of Mental Health, undated.

---

about. Or you might be anxious about an important job interview, not knowing what to expect. A **generalized anxiety disorder** is a persistent undercurrent of "free-floating" (not linked to a specific source) anxiety. The sense of uneasiness hangs around even after a problem has passed. The person with an anxiety disorder worries more than most people about personal and work problems.

A major reason people worry so much is that so many threats to well-being exist in the world outside. Several years ago, Robert Kessler, a Harvard Medical School researcher, explained why we have so much anxiety. His analysis, as follows, is more valid than ever today:

It's a scary place and time. People are moving to strange cities, taking jobs in new industries; there's a lot of uncertainty about the future. Bad things that happen to people are on the rise. Look at the evening news: car accidents, terrorist bombs. This stuff is out there in the popular imagination and making us worried.[24]

How do you know if you are suffering from a generalized anxiety disorder? A major symptom is that you have excessive anxiety or worry the majority of the time for six months. As a result of this anxiety, your quality of life, including schoolwork and other work, is suffering. Occasional worry about a real problem—such as being unable to pay a bill or being dumped by a friend—is not a generalized anxiety disorder. The typical symptoms of this disorder are constant worry, restlessness, difficulties in concentrating or sleeping, irritability, sensitivity to criticism, fatigue, and tense muscles.[25]

As with depression, anxiety disorders are best treated with a combination of psychotherapy and drugs. A form of psychotherapy, called cognitive therapy, helps the person develop a more realistic perspective on the problem at hand. At the same time, the person might develop better problem-solving skills to cope with the anxiety-provoking problem. The person who worries about ever getting out of debt, for example, might come to realize that financial worries are inevitable in today's world. After being calmed down somewhat, the person might develop a plan for financial freedom. Both antidepressant and tranquilizing drugs are used to combat generalized anxiety disorders.

Neurobiological Disorders

Personal problems on the job are sometimes the result of **neurobiological disorders,** a quirk in the chemistry or anatomy of the brain that creates a disability. The quirk is usually inherited but could also be caused by a brain injury or poisoning, such as exposure to harmful vapors. The disability takes the form of reduced ability to control one's behavior, movements, emotions, or thoughts.[26] If you experience sudden changes in your job behavior, a thorough neurological examination is strongly recommended. The most common neurobiological disorders on the job are described below. Depression, already described, is sometimes classified as a neurobiological disorder when it stems from chemical or anatomical factors.

Attention-deficit disorder. People with this disorder have difficulty concentrating that may be accompanied by hyperactivity. The person might therefore engage in a flurry of activity on the job, yet much of the activity might be wasted effort. Many difficulties in paying attention in school are attributed to attention-deficit disorder.

Obsessive-compulsive disorder. People with this disorder have uncontrollable and recurring thoughts or behavior relating to an unreasonable fear. A job example of obsessive-compulsive disorder would be a person who becomes obsessed with cleaning his or her work area. The person could be motivated by fear of being contaminated by impurities in the ventilation system.

Narcolepsy.   People with this disorder have uncontrollable sleepiness, even after receiving adequate sleep. A person with narcolepsy may fall asleep at the desk or while driving a company vehicle or operating dangerous machinery.

Training individuals to understand their condition is an important part of the treatment. The person with narcolepsy, for example, should explain to coworkers that at times he or she may appear sleepy and unresponsive. Furthermore, coworkers can be advised not to take such behavior seriously and that the behavior is under medical control and may soon disappear entirely. Discussing a personal problem with coworkers may help reduce their fears about your problem and lead to better understanding.

▲ DEALING WITH ANGER

Limited ability to manage anger damages the career and personal life of many people. **Anger** is a feeling of extreme hostility, displeasure, or exasperation. Workplace anger is so widespread that according to a survey one in six employees surveyed was angry enough to hit a coworker.[27] The emotion of anger creates stress, including the physiological changes described in Chapter 4. One noticeable indicator of anger is enlargement of the pupils, causing the wide-eyed look of people in a rage. Blood may rush to the face, as indicated by reddening in light-skinned people. Anger often leads to aggression, which is the verbal or physical attacking of another person, animal, or object. Workplace violence, such as an ex-employee shooting a former boss who fired him, is an extreme point in expressing anger. What angry behavior have you observed on the job?

The ability to manage anger is key part of emotional intelligence. A person who cannot manage anger well cannot take good advantage of his or her regular intelligence. As an extreme example, a genius who swears at the boss regularly will probably lose his or her job despite being so talented. Our concern here is with several suggestions that will help you manage (not necessarily eliminate) anger so that it does not jeopardize your career or personal success.

A starting point is to recognize that, at its best, *anger can be an energizing force.* Instead of being destructive, channel your anger into exceptional performance. If you are angry because you did not get the raise you thought you deserved, get even by performing so well that there will be no question you deserve a raise next time. Develop the habit of *expressing your anger before it reaches a high intensity.* Tell your companion that you do not appreciate his or her using a cell phone while you are having dinner together the first time the act of rudeness occurs. If you wait too long, you may wind up grabbing the cell phone and slamming it to the floor.

As you are about to express anger, *slow down.* (The old technique of counting to 10 is still effective.) Slowing down gives you the opportunity to express your anger in a way that does not damage your relationship with the other person. Following your first impulse, you might say to another person, "You're a stupid fool." If you slow down, this might translate into, "You need training on this task." Closely related to slowing down is to say to yourself as soon as you feel angry, "Oops, I'm in the anger mode now. I had better calm

---

HUMAN RELATIONS SKILL-BUILDING EXERCISE 5-1

Learning to Manage Anger

The next few times you are really angry with somebody or something, use one or more of the good mental health statements described below. Each statement is designed to remind you that you are in charge, not your anger. For starters, visualize something that has made you angry recently. Practice making the following statements in relation to that angry episode.

- I'm in charge here, not my emotional outbursts.
- I'll breathe deeply a few times and then deal with this.
- I feel _____ when you _____.
- I can handle this.
- I'm going to take time out to cool down before I deal with this.
- Yes, I'm angry and I'll just watch what I say or do.

Now describe the effect making the above statements had on your anger.

SOURCE: Based on Lynne Namka, "A Primer on Anger: Getting a Handle on Your Mads," http://members.aol.com/AngriesOut/grown2.htm, p. 4.

---

down before I say something or do something I will regret later." To gauge how effectively you are expressing your anger, ask for *feedback*. Ask a friend, coworker, or manager, "Am I coming on too strong when I express my negative opinion?"[28]

The problem of anger has become so widespread that prosecutors across the United States are sending thousands of criminals for anger management instruction. Many companies also have been asking ill-tempered employees to attend such classes. Anger management is often included in drug treatment and couples counseling. A major part of these classes is to help clients learn self-control by such means as thinking through the consequences of unchecked anger. Another approach is to help people learn to look at the big picture and not let little things bother them. These classes are a start, but overcoming anger issues may take most people at least one year.[29]

Human Relations Skill-Building Exercise 5-1 will give you an opportunity to develop your anger management skills. However, the exercise will require some work outside of class.

▲ SUMMARY

Unless personal problems are kept under control, a person's chances of achieving career and personal success diminish. Many personal problems arise out of self-defeating behavior. The major cause of this behavior is a loser life script, a life plan of coming out a loser in important situations. Other causes of self-defeating behavior include a self-defeating personality pattern, self-defeating beliefs, and fear of success. Approaches to overcoming and preventing self-defeating behavior include the following:

1. Examine your script and make the necessary changes.
2. Stop blaming others for your problems.
3. Solicit feedback on your actions.
4. Learn to profit from criticism.
5. Stop denying the existence of problems.
6. Visualize self-enhancing behavior.

Wellness is blocked by a variety of addictions, and addictive behavior is also a personal problem. Addictive behavior toward certain substances such as alcohol and marijuana comes about because these substances elevate dopamine, a chemical substance in the brain that is associated with pleasure, elation, and infatuation. Dopamine can also be elevated by psychological events, such as a hug.

Alcohol abuse often adversely affects health. Moderate to high doses of alcohol cause marked impairment in mental functions. More than two alcoholic beverages per day would be considered a large amount. Alcohol consumption is associated with heart and liver disease and fetal alcohol syndrome. Very high doses of alcohol cause respiratory depression and death. Alcohol abuse adversely affects job performance and career success. Alcoholism can be treated as a disease or as maladaptive (counterproductive) behavior. Precautions can be taken to prevent alcohol abuse, such as limiting consumption and not drinking during the day.

The health effects and personal life consequences of abusing both illegal and prescription drugs are similar to those of alcohol abuse. The various categories of drugs have different possible effects and different consequences for overdoses. The five drug categories are (1) narcotics, (2) depressants, (3) stimulants, (4) hallucinogens, and (5) cannabis. Many forms of professional help are available for drug abusers, yet self-management of the problem is also an important form of help. Twelve-step programs and Alcoholics Anonymous insist on abstinence as the only way to control alcoholism. Internet addiction (or dependence) is becoming a widespread problem that can impair social relationships.

A major personal problem many people encounter is the loss of a valued personal relationship. Suggestions for dealing with the problem include (1) being thankful for the good in the relationship; (2) finding new outlets for spare time; (3) getting ample rest and relaxation; (4) pampering yourself; (5) getting emotional support; (6) going places; (7) giving yourself time to heal; and (8) anticipating a positive outcome.

Absenteeism and tardiness are the leading causes of employee discipline and thus can be a major problem. Keeping lost time from work to a minimum enhances job security. Workers must develop the right mental set to achieve excellent attendance and punctuality. For example, a person might look on the job as self-employment.

Many employees perform poorly on the job because they are depressed. Depression drains energy and reduces productivity and quality. As job performance deteriorates, the person becomes more depressed. Many job problems are also caused by neurobiological disorders, a quirk in the chemistry or anatomy of the brain that creates a disability. The disabilities take the form of reduced ability to control your behavior, movements, emotions, or thoughts. Seasonal affective disorder is a form of depression associated with limited sunlight during the fall and winter.

An estimated 13 percent of the population suffers from a generalized anxiety disorder whereby they have excessive anxiety or worry, leading to problems of quality of life and productivity. Generalized anxiety disorders can be treated with a combination of psychotherapy and antidpressant and tranquilizing medication.

Major neurobiological disorders are attention-deficit disorder, obsessive-compulsive disorder, and narcolepsy. These disorders can be treated with medication, but a supportive environment is also needed.

Limited ability to deal with anger damages the career and personal life of many people. The ability to manage anger is an important interpersonal skill and is now considered part of emotional intelligence. To manage anger well, recognize that it can be an energizing force. Express anger before it reaches a high intensity. As you are about to express anger, slow down and then express it constructively. Ask others for feedback on how well you are expressing anger. Anger management classes are gaining in use.

Questions and Activities

1. What is the difference between making a bad mistake once and self-defeating behavior?

2. Describe a person you know who appears to have a winner life script and justify your reasoning.

3. If it is really true that chocolate releases dopamine, do you think that eating chocolate every day will make you a more productive worker and a happier person? Explain.

4. How can looking on substance abuse as a bad habit help substance abusers overcome their problem?

5. What responsibilities should employers have to help prevent their employees from becoming online addicts?

6. An Internet abuser told an employer that he should not be fired for excessive Internet surfing because his Internet abuse amounts to a disability. What is your reaction to this worker's reasoning?

7. Find a recent magazine, journal, or Internet article about new developments in treating drug or alcohol abuse. Share this information with classmates.

8. Some companies offer awards for good attendance. Why is this necessary from a motivational standpoint?

9. Suppose a coworker of yours appeared to be depressed on most workdays. Would you approach him or her about the problem? Explain your reasoning.

10. Why is it that hockey players become so angry that they regularly physically attack their opponents, whereas tennis and golf players almost never act this way?

INTERNET SKILL BUILDER: THE VIRTUAL COUCH

Investigate the kind of mental health services a person can receive online. In other words, what type of psychotherapy and counseling can a person receive over the Internet? A good starting point would be to visit www.healthyplace.com, www.netpsych.com, and www.headworks.com. What is your opinion as to the quality of these services in comparison to visiting a mental health professional in person? What advantages might online help with personal problems offer over face-to-face help with your problems?

WEB CORNER

Center for Online and Internet Addiction: www.netaddiction.com

(But don't spend too much time visiting the site!)

Alcoholics Anonymous: www.aa.org

Narcotics Anonymous: www.wsoinc.com

HUMAN RELATIONS CASE PROBLEM

Critical Carrie of the Claims Department

Carrie Donahoe is one of five claims examiners in a regional office of a large casualty and property insurance company. The branch is still thriving despite the insurer selling many policies online and billing conducted by a centralized office. The sales group sells policies and services already-existing businesses, such as consulting with managers and business owners about upgrading their policies. The sales representatives also answer questions about policies, such as questions about whether the policy owner is covered against a terrorist attack.

Carrie works with four other examiners as well as her supervisor Michelle Pettigrew. The essential job of the claims examiner is to visit the site of a client with a demand for reimbursement for damages, such as a fire, flood, or industrial accident. The

(Continued)

claims examiner then files a report with a recommendation for payment that is reviewed by the examiner's supervisor. Also, the home office reviews estimated payments beyond $15,000. Carrie has held her position for five years. She has received satisfactory performance evaluations, particularly for the accuracy and promptness of her insurance claim reports.

Carrie lives alone with two cats in one-half of a house that she rents. Carrie dates occasionally but has not found a man to her liking in several years. She explains that most of the men she meets are "stupid," "lazy," or "creepy." Carrie went alone on two cruises in recent years but vowed that she will not take a cruise again because practically all the people she met were boring.

Carrie has frequent negative interactions with her coworkers, who resent many of her suggestions and criticisms. Jim, a senior claims analyst, says his nickname for Carrie is "Ms. Pit Bull," although he has not shared this nickname with her. Asked why he refers to Carrie as a pit bull, he replied, "It's not that Carrie physically attacks people, but it's that she's so negative about so many things. I'll give you two recent examples:

"Carrie asked me to show her a sample claims report for mud damage. I e-mailed her a report. Two days later she sent me back the report, underlining six words or phrases she said were wrong. She didn't even thank me for the report.

"I came back from a two-day trip to inspect a building damaged by a runaway truck. When I returned to the office, Carrie asked me why it took me two days to investigate a simple claim."

Sharon, a junior claims examiner, says that at her best Carrie is a charming coworker. Yet at her worst, she grates on people's nerves. "Here's what I'm talking about. Last week I came to work wearing a blue skirt and a red blouse, on a day the vice president of claims was coming to visit our office. Carrie tells me that a person should never wear a red-and-blue combination for a special event. Not only is Carrie critical, her criticisms are sometimes way off base.

"Another time she told me that I should not waste my time studying for advanced certification in claims because it's a waste of time. She said that no manager in the company really cares about certification. Either you can do your job or you can't."

A human resource specialist from the home office asked Michelle Pettigrew how she was handling Carrie's personality clashes with coworkers as well as with her personally. Michelle said that she was mildly concerned about Carrie's personality problems but that Carrie still gets her work done. Yet Michelle did mention that several clients indicated that Carrie surprised them with some of her criticisms of their operation. She told one tool-and-die shop owner that a well-managed firm never has a serious accident. That was the company's first claim in 50 years being insured by us.

"When she's snippy with me, I just shrug it off unless it gets too personal. Then I tell Carrie that she's gone too far. Like a week ago she told me that I don't do a good job of getting enough resources for our branch. That if I were a strong branch manager, we would have our offices refurbished by now. I told Carrie that our conversation was now over."

(Continued)

The human resources director said to Michelle, "I think you and I should talk about effective ways of dealing with Carrie and her problems."

Questions

1. In what way is Carrie engaging in self-defeating behavior?

2. What other types of personal problems does Carrie appear to be experiencing?

3. What kind of help would you recommend for Carrie?

4. What do you recommend that Carrie's coworkers do to develop more harmonious relationships with her?

▲ REFERENCES

1. Based on facts in Michael D. Lemonick, "The Power of Mood," *Time,* January 20, 2003, p. 64.

2. John Wareham, *Wareham's Way: Escaping the Judas Trap* (New York: Atheneum, 1983), p. 107.

3. Thomas A. Widiger and Allen J. Frances, "Controversies concerning the Self-Defeating Personality Disorder," in Rebecca C. Curtis, ed., *Self-Defeating Behaviors* (New York: Plenum Press, 1989), p. 304.

4. Seth Allcorn, "The Self-Protective Actions of Managers," *Supervisory Management,* January 1989, pp. 3–7.

5. "No More Excuses! Overcome Self-Imposed Obstacles for Career Gains," *Executive Strategies,* February 1998, p. 1.

6. Deborah Smith, "Impairment on the Job," *Monitor on Psychology,* June 2001, p. 52.

7. J. Madeleine Nash, "Addicted," *Time,* May 5, 1997, pp. 69–76.

8. Research reported in "Science News: Scanner Pinpoint's Alcohol's Effect on the Brain," *Chicago Tribune* story, September 1, 1997.

9. Harriet B. Braiker, "What All Career Women Need to Know about Drinking," *Working Women,* August 1989, p. 72; Elaine Rivera, "License to Drink," *Time,* July 31, 2000, p. 47.

10. Rivera, "License to Drink," p. 47.

11. Studies reported in Beth Azar, "Conditioned to Addiction?" *Monitor on Psychology,* July/August 2002, pp. 74–75.

12. Based on information in the Drug-Free Workplace Act of 1988 and Drug-Free Schools and Communities Act of 1989.

13. Samuel Greengard, "A White-Collar Challenge: Dealing with Addiction," *Workforce,* February 2003, p. 18.

14. Scott Sleek, "Isolation Increases with Internet Use," *APA Monitor,* September 1998, pp. 1, 30.

15. Carol Potera, "Trapped in the Web," *Psychology Today,* March/April 1998, p. 72.

16. Andrew J. DuBrin, *Bouncing Back: How to Handle Setbacks in Your Work and Personal Life* (Upper Saddle River, NJ: Prentice Hall, 1982), pp. 85–102; Melba Colgrove, Harold H. Bloomfeld, and Peter McWilliams, *How to Survive the Loss of a Love* (New York: Bantam Books, 1976).

17. Jeff Stinson, "Company Policy Attends to Chronic Absentees," *Personnel Journal,* August 1991, p. 82; "Managing Poor Attendance," *Working Smart,* July 1997, p. 6.

18. Carlos Tejada, "Working at a Fever Pitch," *Wall Street Journal,* March 20, 2003, p. D1.

19. Kathryn Tyler, "Happiness from a Bottle?" *HR Magazine,* May 2002, pp. 30–37.

20. Brown University study cited in Tyler, "Happiness from a Bottle," pp. 32–33.

21. Research reported in Sharon Begley, "New Hope for Battling Depression Relapses: Study Illuminates Why the Benefits of Therapy Are More Lasting Than Medication," *The Wall Street Journal,* January 6, 2004, p. D1.

22. Research cited in M. Waters, "Change of Season, Changes in Mood," *APA Monitor,* October 1999, p. 7.

23. "New Hope for Depression and Other Mental Illnesses," in *Health Guide* (Washington, DC: 1996). America's Pharmaceutical Research Companies.

24. Quoted in "Facing Your Fear," *USA Weekend,* September 29–October 1, 2000, p. 8.

25. Saul Kassin, *Psychology,* 3d ed. (Upper Saddle River, NJ: Prentice Hall, 2001), pp. 628–629; Christine Gorman, "The Science of Anxiety," *Time,* June 10, 2002, p. 49.

26. Peggy Stuart, "Tracing Workplace Problems to Hidden Disorder," *Personnel Journal,* June 1992, p. 84. Our discussion of neurobiological disorders is based on the Stuart article.

27. Survey cited in "It's a Mad, Mad, Corporate World," *Working Woman,* April 2000, p. 71.

28. Fred Pryor, "Is Anger Really Healthy?" *The Pryor Report Management Newsletter,* February 1996, p. 3.

29. John Cloud, "Classroom for Hotheads," *Time,* April 10, 2000, p. 53.

▲ ADDITIONAL READING

Althauser, Doug. *You Can Free Yourself from Alcohol and Drugs: Work a Program That Keeps You in Charge.* Oakland, CA: New Harbinger, 1999.

Bennett, Joel B., and Wayne E. K. Lehman, eds. *Preventing Workplace Substance Abuse: Beyond Drug Testing to Wellness.* Washington, DC: American Psychological Association, 2003.

Copeland, Mary Ellen. *The Loneliness Workbook.* Oakland, CA: New Harbinger, 2000.

Greenfield, David N. *Virtual Addiction: Help for Netheads, Cyberfreaks, and Those Who Love Them.* Oakland, CA: New Harbinger, 1999.

Jackson, Saundra, Ruhal Dooley, and Diane Lacy. "Substance Abuse, Ethics, Intermittent Leave." *HR Magazine,* July 2003, pp. 41–42.

Lee, Kibeom, and Natalie J. Allen. "Organizational Citizenship Behavior and Workplace Deviance: The Role of Affect and Cognitions." *Journal of Applied Psychology,* February 2002, pp. 131–142.

Medina, John. *Depression: How It Happens, How It's Healed.* Oakland, CA: New Harbinger, 1998.

Plutchik, Robert. *Emotions and Life: Perspectives from Psychology, Biology, and Evolution.* Washington, DC: American Psychological Association, 2003.

Truxillo, Donald M., James L. Normandy, and Talya N. Bauer. "Drug Use History, Drug Test Consequences, and the Perceived Fairness of Organizational Drug Testing Programs." *Journal of Business and Psychology,* Fall 2001, pp. 87–99.

CHAPTER 6

Communicating with People

Learning Objectives

After studying the information and doing the exercises in this chapter, you should be able to:

◆ Explain the basic communication process

◆ Describe the nature and importance of nonverbal communication in the workplace

◆ Identify the challenges to interpersonal communication created by information technology

◆ Identify and overcome many roadblocks to communication

◆ Enhance your listening skills

◆ Overcome many gender communication barriers

*L*ast year, Buck Baker came close to getting three job offers but didn't get hired. Then a friend suggested that Baker, who had been laid off as the head of marketing for a Milwaukee staffing agency, might be having trouble because of his communication style, not for any lack in his credentials. He advised Baker, then 47, to pay a few visits to Patricia Smith-Pierce, an executive coach, to hone his communication skills.

Baker did just that—and made some eye-opening discoveries. For example, Smith-Pierce showed him how his relaxed posture and habit of picking up anything within reach made him appear indecisive. So Baker practiced sitting more upright and keeping his hands at his side. After two sessions and some phone consultations on this and other issues, he landed a job as a management consultant for the Detroit office of Hewitt Associates. Baker says the cost of his training sessions were worth every penny."[1]

The story of the professional who landed the job he wanted in part because he strengthened his communication skills illustrates how these skills contribute to success at the individual level. Effective communication skills are also important for many other reasons. Communication is so vital that it has been described as the glue that holds organizations and families together. Most job foul-ups and marital disputes are considered to be communication problems. Furthermore, to be successful in work or personal life, you usually have to be an effective communicator. You can't make friends or stand up against enemies unless you can communicate with them. And you can't accomplish work through others unless you can send and receive messages effectively.

In this chapter we explain several important aspects of interpersonal communication, such as the communication process and overcoming various communication barriers. As with other chapters in this text, explanation should also lead to skill improvement. For example, if you understand the steps involved in getting a message across to another person, you may be able to prevent many communication problems.

▲ HOW COMMUNICATION TAKES PLACE

A convenient starting point in understanding how people communicate is to look at the steps involved in communicating a message. **Communication** is the sending and receiving of messages. A diagram of how the process takes place is shown in Figure 6-1. The theme of the model is that two-way

Figure 6-1 The Communication Process

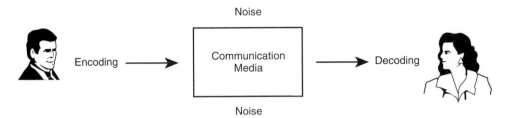

Noise

Encoding ⟶ | Communication Media | ⟶ Decoding

Noise

communication involves three major steps and that each step is subject to interference or noise. Assume that Crystal, a customer, wishes to inform Tony, a used-car sales representative, that she is willing to make an offer of $7,000 on a used car. The price tag on the car is $7,750.

Step 1. *Encoding the message.* **Encoding** is the process of organizing ideas into a series of symbols, such as words and gestures, designed to communicate with the receiver. Word choice has a strong influence on communication effectiveness. The better a person's grasp of language, the easier it is for him or her to encode. Crystal says, "Tony, this car obviously is not in excellent condition, but I am willing to give you $7,000 for it."

Step 2. *Transmission over communication media.* The message is sent via a communication medium, such as voice, telephone, paper, e-mail, or messaging. It is important to select a medium that fits the message. It would be appropriate to use the spoken word to inform a coworker that he swore under his breath at a customer. It would be less appropriate to send the same message through e-mail. Many messages on and off the job are sent nonverbally through the use of gestures and facial expressions. For example, a smile from a superior during a meeting is an effective way of communicating the message "I agree with you." Crystal has chosen the oral medium to send her message.

Step 3. *Decoding.*   In **decoding,** the receiver interprets the message and translates it into meaningful information. Decoding is the process of understanding a message. Barriers to communication are most likely to surface at the decoding step. People often interpret messages according to their psychological needs and motives. Tony wants to interpret Crystal's message that she is very eager to purchase this car. He may therefore listen attentively for more information demonstrating that she is interested in purchasing the car.

Decoding the message leads naturally to action—the receiver does something about the message. If the receiver acts in the manner the sender wants, the communication has been successful. If Tony says, "It's a deal," Crystal had a successful communication event.

Many missteps can occur between encoding and decoding a message. **Noise,** or unwanted interference, can distort or block a message. If Crystal has an indecisive tone and raises her voice at the end of her statement, it could indicate that she is not really serious about offering a maximum of $7,000 for the car.

▲ NONVERBAL COMMUNICATION (SENDING AND RECEIVING SILENT MESSAGES)

So far we have been talking mostly about spoken communication. However, much of the communication among people includes nonspoken and nonwritten messages. These nonverbal signals are a critical part of everyday communication. As a case in point, *how* you say "Thank you" makes a big difference in the extent to which your sense of appreciation registers. In **nonverbal communication,** we use our body, voice, or environment in numerous ways to help put a message across. Sometimes we are not aware how much our true feelings color our spoken message.

One problem of paying attention to nonverbal signals is that they can be taken too seriously. Just because some nonverbal signals (such as yawning or looking away from a person) might reflect a person's real feelings, not every signal can be reliably connected with a particular attitude. Jason may put his hand over his mouth because he is shocked. Lucille may put her hand over her mouth because she is trying to control her laughter about the message, and Ken may put his hand over his mouth as a signal that he is pondering the consequences of the message. Here we look at eight categories of nonverbal communication that are generally reliable indicators of a person's attitude and feelings. In addition, we describe how lying might be revealed through nonverbal communication.

ENVIRONMENT OR SETTING

Where you choose to deliver your message indicates what you think of its importance. Assume that a neighbor invites you over for dinner to discuss something with you. You will think it is a more important topic under these circumstances than if it were brought up when the two of you met in the supermarket. Other important environmental cues include room color, temperature, lighting, and furniture arrangement. A person who sits behind an uncluttered large desk, for example, appears more powerful than a person who sits behind a small, cluttered desk.

DISTANCE FROM THE OTHER PERSON

How close you place your body relative to another person's also conveys meaning when you send a message. If, for instance, you want to convey a positive attitude toward another person, get physically close to him or her. Putting your arm around someone to express interest and warmth is another obvious nonverbal signal. However, many people in a work setting abstain from all forms of touching (except for handshakes) because of concern

Figure 6-2   Four Circles of Intimacy

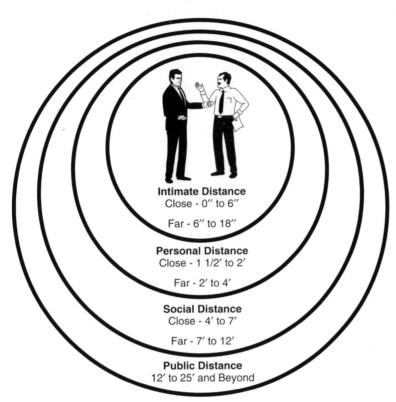

Intimate Distance
Close - 0″ to 6″

Far - 6″ to 18″

Personal Distance
Close - 1 1/2′ to 2′

Far - 2′ to 4′

Social Distance
Close - 4′ to 7′

Far - 7′ to 12′

Public Distance
12′ to 25′ and Beyond

that touching might be interpreted as sexual harassment. A compromise for expressing warmth through touching in the workplace is the sideways hug because it is less likely to be misinterpreted. Many companies discourage hugging in the workplace.

Cultural differences must be kept in mind in interpreting nonverbal cues. To illustrate, a French male is likely to stand closer to you than a British male, even if they had equally positive attitudes toward you. A set of useful guidelines has been developed for estimating how close to stand to another person (at least in many cultures).[2] They are described in the following and diagrammed in Figure 6-2.

Intimate distance covers actual physical contact to about 18 inches. Usually it is reserved for close friends and loved ones or other people you feel affectionate toward. Physical intimacy is usually not called for on the job, but there are exceptions. For one, confidential information might be whispered within the intimate distance zone.

Personal distance covers from about 1.5 to 4 feet. In this zone it is natural to carry on friendly conversation and discussions. Also, you can touch the other person if you wish to maintain a feeling of privacy (but not recommended in the workplace). When people engage in a heated argument, they sometimes enter the personal distance zone. One example is a baseball coach getting up close to an umpire and shouting in his face.

Social distance covers from 4 to 12 feet and in general is reserved for interaction that is businesslike and impersonal. We usually maintain this amount of distance between ourselves and strangers, such as retail sales associates and cab drivers.

Public distance covers from 12 feet to the outer limit of being heard. This zone is typically used in speaking to an audience at a large meeting or in a classroom, but a few insensitive individuals might send ordinary messages by shouting across a room. The unstated message suggested by such an action is that the receiver of the message does not merit the effort of walking across the room.

People sometimes manipulate personal space in order to dominate a situation. A sales representative might move into the personal or intimate circle of a customer just to intimidate him or her. Many people become upset when you move into a closer circle than the situation calls for. They consider it an invasion of their personal space, or their "territorial rights." How would you feel if, while waiting in line at the post office, a complete stranger stood within four inches of your face?

Posture

Certain aspects of your posture communicate a message. Leaning toward another individual suggests that you are favorably disposed toward his or her message. Leaning backward communicates the opposite. Openness of the arms or legs serves as an indicator of liking or caring. In general, people establish closed postures (arms folded and legs crossed) when speaking to people they dislike. Standing up straight generally indicates high self-confidence. Stooping and slouching could mean a poor self-image. In any event, there is almost no disadvantage to standing up straight.

Related to posture are the nonverbal signals sent by standing versus sitting. Sitting down during a conversation is generally considered to be more intimate and informal than standing. If you do sit down while conversing, be sure to stand up when you wish the conversation to end. Standing up sends a message to the other person that it is time to leave. It also gives you the chance to be more attentive and polite in saying good-bye.

Hand Gestures

An obvious form of body language is hand gestures. Hand gestures are universally recognized as conveying specific information to others. If you make frequent hand movements, you will generally communicate a positive attitude. If you use few gestures, you will convey dislike or disinterest. An important exception here is that some people wave their hands vigorously while arguing. Some of their hand movements reflect anger. Another example is that open-palm gestures toward the other person typically convey positive attitudes.

Facial Expressions and Eye Contact

"Here comes a potential," said one sales associate to another at a consumer electronics store. "I can tell she's interested in purchasing a television set. Just look into her eyes and at the expression on her face." The sales associate who spoke these words may have a valid point. When used in combination, the head, face, and eyes provide the clearest indications of attitudes toward other people. Lowering your head and peering over your glasses, for instance, is the nonverbal equivalent of the expression, "You're putting me on." As is well known, maintaining eye contact with another person improves communication with that person. To maintain eye contact, it is usually necessary to correspondingly move your head and face. Moving your head, face, and eyes away from another person is often interpreted as a defensive gesture or one suggesting a lack of self-confidence. Would you lend money to someone who didn't look at you directly?

The face is often used as a primary source of information about how we feel. We look for facial clues when we want to determine another person's attitude. You can often judge someone's current state of happiness by looking at his or her face. The expression "sourpuss" attests to this observation. Happiness, apprehension, anger, resentment, sadness, contempt, enthusiasm, and embarrassment are but a few of the emotions that can be expressed through the face.

Voice Quality

More significance is often attached to the *way* something is said than to *what* is said. A forceful voice, which includes a consistent tone without vocalized pauses, connotes power and control. Closely related to voice tone are volume, pitch, and rate of speaking. Anger, boredom, and joy can often be interpreted from voice quality. Anger is noted when the person speaks loudly, with a high pitch and fast rate. Boredom is indicated by a monotone. A tip-off to joy is when the person speaks loudly with a high pitch and fast rate. Joy is also indicated by loud volume.

Avoiding an annoying voice quality can make a positive impact on others. The research of voice coach Jeffrey Jacobbi provides some useful suggestions. He surveyed a nationwide sample of 1,000 men and women and asked, "Which irritating or unpleasant voice annoys you the most?" The most irritating quality was a whining, complaining, or nagging tone.

Jacobbi notes that we are judged by the way we sound. He also contends that careers can be damaged by voice problems such as those indicated in

---

HUMAN RELATIONS SELF-ASSESSMENT QUIZ 6-1

Voice Quality Checkup

Jacobbi's study of voice quality (cited in the text) ranked voice quality, in decreasing order of annoyance, as follows:

- Whining, complaining, or nagging tone—44.0 percent
- High-pitched, squeaky voice—15.9 percent
- Mumblers—11.1 percent
- Very fast talkers—4.9 percent
- Weak and wimpy voice—3.6 percent
- Flat, monotonous tone—3.5 percent
- Thick accent—2.4 percent

Ask yourself and two other people familiar with your voice if you have one or more of the above voice-quality problems. If your self-analysis and feedback from others does indicate a serious problem, get started on self-improvement. Tape your voice and attempt to modify the biggest problems. Another avenue of improvement is to consult with a speech coach or therapist.

---

the survey. Jacobbi continues, "We think about how we look and dress. And that gets most of the attention. But people judge our intelligence much more by how we sound than how we dress."[3] Human Relations Self-Assessment Quiz 6-1 provides more details about his findings.

Gesturing can be used to improve a monotonous voice quality. By raising your arms and making expansive or sweeping motions while speaking, voice volume will increase simultaneously. The act of gesturing affects the lungs, leading to a louder exhale. The vocal chords are changed to a lesser extent, yet also bringing along a variation in voice tone.[4]

PERSONAL APPEARANCE

Your external image plays an important role in communicating messages to others. Job seekers show recognition of this aspect of nonverbal communication when they carefully groom for a job interview. People pay more respect and grant more privileges to people they perceive as being well dressed and attractive. The meaning of being well dressed depends heavily on the situation. In an information technology firm, neatly pressed jeans, a stylish T-shirt, and clean sport shoes might qualify as being well dressed. The same attire worn in a financial service firm would qualify as being poorly dressed. Common sense and research indicate that a favorable personal appearance leads to higher starting salaries and, later, salary increases. One study showed that people perceived to be physically attractive tend to receive salaries 8 to 10 percent higher. A possible explanation offered for the results is that employers might attribute other positive attributes to employees they perceive as physically attractive.[5]

LYING AS REVEALED BY NONVERBAL COMMUNICATION

A person's nonverbal behavior is often used to gauge whether he or she is telling the truth. Highly practiced liars feel less anxious about lying, so their nonverbal behavior may be less revealing. Key facial clues that often reveal lying are as follows:[6]

- *Crooked smile.*   Genuine smiles are usually symmetrical, whereas phony smiles tend to be lopsided. A phony smile suggests lying about true feelings.

- *An overlong smile, frown, or look of disbelief.*   Genuine expressions last only four or five seconds, so if you smile continuously, your veracity will come into question.

- *Failure to look you in the eye.*   Avoiding eye contact is often an indicator of lying but can also reflect the desire to avoid scrutiny. Also, in some Asian cultures looking a superior in the eye is considered rude.

- *Forced eye contact.*   Trying too hard to maintain eye contact may mean the person is trying to fake a sign of truth telling. Check out potential indicators of facial tension.

- *Frequent rubbing of the nose.*   Combined with other cues, rubbing of the nose may indicate a falsehood (or itching or nervousness).

- *Facial shift.*   A facial shift is a fleeting expression, like a frown, that is quickly replaced by others, like a smile or serene face.

Computers have been applied to detecting lies. So far the most reliable observations about lying relate to facial expressions. An authentic smile is usually characterized by crinkly eyes and a generally relaxed expression. In contrast, a lying smile reveals itself in subtle ways, particularly eye wrinkles that are more crow's feet than laugh lines. Another promising development is the ability of the software to detect immediately any facial movement that indicated a conflicting emotion. An example would be the beginning of a scowl quickly covered up by a smile (a facial shift).[7]

During the next several days, use the facial expressions of others to assess whether they are lying. Look also for follow-up evidence, such as if the person who said, "I will definitely call you on Monday," ever makes the call.

EXHIBIT 6-1

Body Basics

Patricia Ball, former president of the National Speakers Association and founder of a corporate communications consulting firm, believes strongly in body language. She says that any basic body vocabulary should include the most positive body language you can muster. When you're on a sales call or in negotiations and want to say or hear an affirmative, here are the signals to look for or send:

- *Leaning Forward.*   Leaning back sends the message of aloofness or rejection.

- *No Leg Crossing.*   Keep your feet flat on the floor (both men and women).

- *A Vertical Handshake.*   Some people shake with the palm down, forcing the other person to hold his or her palm up in a submissive, uncomfortable position.

- *An Appropriate Smile.*   Smiling continuously may be interpreted as powerlessness.

- *Direct Eye Contact.*   A direct look is permissible in the United States and Canada, but in many Asian and Middle Eastern cultures, a direct look is disrespectful.

- *Mirroring the Other Person's Body Language.*   Ball warns against being an obvious mimic. However, if the other person has his or her leg crossed toward you and is leaning toward you, then crossing your leg in his or her direction and assuming that person's body language posture basically says, "I think like you. I'm with you."

SOURCE: Adapted from Mark Hennricks, "More Than Words," *Entrepreneur,* August 1995, p. 55.

Exhibit 6-1 helps integrate the information about nonverbal communication by giving you advice about using a positive basic body vocabulary.

NONVERBAL COMMUNICATION AND AIRPORT SECURITY

An advanced workplace application of nonverbal communication is to help combat drug trafficking and terrorism. The art of spotting nervous or threatening behavior has gained respect among airport security officials. Since the terrorist attacks on September 11, 2001, the Federal Bureau of Investigation started teaching nonverbal behavior analysis to all new FBI recruits. In the past, passengers were selected to be interrogated mostly on the basis of what they looked like, such as a negative ethnic stereotype. Customs agents are now trained to observe what people do and to ask pointed questions when suspicious nonverbal behavior surfaces. Among the indicators of suspicious behavior are darting eyes, hand tremors, a fleeting style, and an enlarged carotid artery (indicating the rapid blood flow associated with anxiety). Failure to make eye contact with the customs official is a strong red flag.[8]

▲ INTERPERSONAL COMMUNICATION AND INFORMATION TECHNOLOGY

Rapid advances in information technology may enable workers to communicate more easily, rapidly, and quickly than they could even a few years ago. Quite often the influence has been positive, but at other times the effectiveness of interpersonal communication has decreased. Two developments that illustrate the impact of information technology on interpersonal communication are e-mail and telecommuting.

E-MAIL AND COMMUNICATION AMONG PEOPLE

E-mail is the information technology system with the most dramatic impact on interpersonal communication in the current era. For both work and personal life, e-mail is typically less formal than a letter but more formal than a telephone conversation. The major impact of e-mail on interpersonal communication is that written messages replace many telephone and in-person exchanges. Team members often keep in regular contact with each other without having lengthy meetings or telephone conversations. E-mail continues to grow in importance and is likely to expand into a form of communication that will incorporate not only still drawings and photographs but also audio, video, and chunks of voice mail. The biggest threat to e-mail, however, is that about 40 percent of e-mails are classified as *spam,* or unwanted and uninvited messages, often of a commercial nature.

Instant messaging is a fast-growing variety of e-mail. Using instant messaging, you and the people on your buddy list can exchange messages immediately on the computer screen without having to go through the process of sending and receiving. The technology is a hybrid of e-mail and chat that enables real-time one-on-one conversations online. Instead of picking up messages at times you choose, you are exposed to them whenever at the computer.

Several potential communication problems that e-mail and instant messaging create should be kept in mind to minimize these problems.[9]

A major problem with e-mail is that it encourages indiscriminate sending of messages. Some professional workers receive an average of 300 e-mail messages per day. Some of these workers make cynical comments such as, "My job is answering e-mail" or "I answer e-mail during the day and do my work at night and on weekends." Some companywide e-mail announcements describe a battered file cabinet that is available to a "good home." Some workers conduct virtual joke-telling contests over e-mail, with some of the jokes being perceived as offensive by many other workers. The proliferation of electronic junk mail (or spam) has prompted some company officials to take corrective action, such as the installation of spam filters.

Although many people contend that they are overloaded with e-mail, a recent study suggests that e-mail is being used wisely and is under control. As revealed in a survey of close to 2,500 workers, the majority of e-mail users find that it is a manageable part of their job. The typical work user of e-mail spends approximately 30 minutes during the workday processing e-mail, receives about 10 incoming messages, and sends five messages. A subgroup of these e-mailers, labeled power e-mailers, spends two hours or more daily on e-mail. They handle between 30 and 50 messages per day, yet only 11 percent say they feel overwhelmed by processing e-mail.[10]

The informal style of many e-mail exchanges can lead a person to believe that incorrect spelling, poor grammar, and disconnected thoughts are acceptable in all forms of business communication. The opposite is true. To appear professional and intelligent, writers of business e-mail messages should use correct spelling, grammar, capitalization, and punctuation.

A major challenge in using e-mail effectively is to decide how often and when to manage your e-mail. Most senders of e-mail expect a quick response, and the message could be very important, such as responding to a customer inquiry. However, if you give e-mail constant attention, it becomes difficult to complete work that requires heavy concentration, such as analyzing data or preparing a report. For many workers, reserving two blocks of time per day for e-mail messaging will suffice.

E-mail has become a new tool for office politicians who search for ways to look good themselves and make others look bad. Many office politicians use e-mail to give credit to themselves for their contributions to a project, perhaps using a companywide distribution list. When something goes wrong, such as a failed project, the office politician will inform hundreds of people that it was not his or her fault.

Many supervisors and other workers use e-mail to reprimand others because, by sending a message over the computer, they can avoid face-to-face confrontation. E-mail is well suited for managers who would prefer to avoid face-to-face contact with group members. Harsh messages sent over e-mail create several problems. First, it is shocking to be reprimanded or insulted in writing. Second, the person cannot offer a defense except by writing back an e-mail message explaining his or her position. Third, the recipient, not knowing what to do about the harsh message, may brood and become anxious.

Exhibit 6-2 presents suggestions for good etiquette when using e-mail, including messaging. The good etiquette leads to more productive use of e-mail.

EXHIBIT 6-2

E-mail and Messaging Etiquette

Observing the following tips will enhance your e-mail etiquette and electronic communication effectiveness.

Keep it simple.   Each message should have only one piece of information or request for action so that it's easier for the executive to respond.

Include an action step.   Clearly outline what type of reply you're looking for as well as any applicable deadlines.

Use the subject line to your advantage.   Generic terms such as "details" or "reminder" do not describe the contents of your message or whether it's time

(Continued)

sensitive. So the executive may delay opening it. Do not forward a long chain of e-mails without changing the subject; otherwise, you might have a confusing subject line, such as "RE: FW: RE: FW: RE: FW."

Take care in writing e-mails.   Clearly organize your thoughts to avoid sending e-mails with confusing, incomplete, or missing information. Never use profane or harsh language (referred to as *flaming*). Use business writing style and check carefully for grammatical and typographical errors. (Also, avoid the trend to refer to spell "I" in lowercase.)

Be considerate.   Use "please" and "thank you" even in brief messages.

Don't include confidential information.   The problem is that e-mail is occasionally forwarded to unintended recipients. If your message is in any way sensitive or confidential, set up a meeting or leave a voice mail in which you request confidentially.

Do not use e-mail to blast a coworker, and send copies to others.   Criticizing another person with e-mail is equivalent to blasting him or her during a large meeting.

When in doubt, send plain text e-mail, not HTML.   Not everybody can receive e-mails with fancy formatting, and some receivers dislike nontraditional formatting.

Ask before sending huge attachments.   Do not clog e-mail systems without permission.

Avoid passing along chain letters.   Few people believe that if they pass along your e-mail letter to 10 friends, they will ultimately become rich or avoid bad luck. In a work setting, chain letters make the sender appear unprofessional.

Instant messaging requires a few additional considerations for practicing good electronic etiquette:

Don't be Big Brother.   Some bosses use instant messaging to check up on others, to make sure they are seated at their computer. Never intrude on workers unless it is urgent.

Lay down the instant messaging law.   Make sure your message has some real value to the recipient before jumping right in front of someone's face. Instant messaging is much like walking into someone's office or cubicle without an appointment or without knocking.

Take it offline.   When someone on your buddy list becomes too chatty, don't vent your frustration. By phone, in-person, or through regular e-mail, explain tactfully that you do not have time for processing so many instant messages. Suggest that the two of you might get together for lunch or coffee soon.

Set limits to avoid frustration.   To avoid constant interruptions, use a polite custom status message, such as "I will be dealing with customers today until 4:40."

SOURCE: Todd Grady, "Even via E-Mail, Courtesy Matters," *Rochester Democrat and Chronicle,* May 1, 2000, p. 1F; Carrie Patton, "Mind Your Messages," *Working Woman,* May 2000, p. 81; Andrea C. Poe, "Don't Touch That 'Send' Button!" *HR Magazine,* July 2001, pp. 76, 80; Heinz Tschabitscher, "The Ten Most Important Rules of Email Etiquette," http://email.about.com/cs/netiquettetips/tp/core_netiquette.htm (accessed September 9, 2003).

TELECOMMUTING

A **telecommuter** is an employee who works at home full time or part time and sends output electronically to a central office. An estimated 30 to 40 million people in the United States work at home as corporate employees or for self-employment.[11] Telecommuters can communicate abundantly via electronic devices, but they miss out on the face-to-face interactions so vital for dealing with complex problems. Another communication problem telecommuters face is feeling isolated from activities at the main office and missing out on the encouragement and recognition that take place in face-to-face encounters. (Of course, many telecommuters prefer to avoid such contact.) Many telecommuters have another communications problem: Because they have very little face-to-face communication with key people in the organization, they believe they are passed over for promotion. Most telecommuters spend some time in the traditional office, yet they miss the day-by-day contact.

Another communications problem with telecommuting is that it lacks a solid human connection. As one telecommuting marketing consultant put it, face time is critical for building empathy. "It's a human connection. It takes time, and human beings need visual cues, the symbols of being together and caring for one another."[12]

▲ ROADBLOCKS TO COMMUNICATION

Communication rarely proceeds as effectively as we would like. Many different factors filter out a message on its way to the intended receiver, shown as noise in Figure 6-1. In this section we look at some of the human roadblocks to communication. If you are aware of their presence, you will be better able to overcome them.

Routine or neutral messages are the easiest to communicate. Communication roadblocks are most likely to occur when a message is complex, is emotionally arousing, or clashes with the receiver's mental set. An emotionally arousing message would deal with such topics as a relationship between two people or money. A message that clashes with a receiver's mental set requires that person to change his or her familiar pattern of receiving messages. The next time you order a meal in a restaurant, order dessert first and an entrée second. The server will probably not "hear" your dessert order because it deviates from the normal ordering sequence.

LIMITED UNDERSTANDING OF PEOPLE

If you do not understand people very well, your communication effectiveness will be limited. To take a basic example, if you frame your message in terms of what can be done for you, you may be in trouble. It's much more effective to frame your message in terms of what you can do for the other person. Suppose a person in need of money wants to sell food supplements

---

EXHIBIT 6-3

A Short Course in Human Relations

The *six* most important words are "I admit I made a mistake."

The *five* most important words are "You did a good job."

The *four* most important words are "What is your opinion?"

The *three* most important words are "If you please."

The *two* most important words are "Thank you."

The *one* most important word is "We."

The one *least* important word is "I."

    Some people who first read this "short course" react to it negatively. Among their reservations are that "it is corny," "it's so obvious—anybody with common sense knows that," or "good for kindergarten students." Yet if you put these seven rules into practice, you will find they do help overcome the communication roadblock called *limited understanding of people.* As one example, if you use "I" too frequently in your conversation, you will create communication roadblocks.

---

to a friend. Mentioning financial need is a very self-centered message. It could be made less self-centered:

Very self-centered: "You've got to buy a few food supplements from me. I can't meet my credit card payments."

Less self-centered: "Would you be interested in purchasing a few food supplements that would bring you more energy and help you live longer? If your answer is yes, I can help you."

    Limited understanding of people can also take the form of making false assumptions about the receiver. The false assumption serves as a communication roadblock. A supervisor might say to a telemarketer (a person who sells over the phone), "If you increase sales by 15 percent, we will promote you to lead telemarketer." When the telmarketer does not work any harder, the supervisor thinks the message did not get across. The false assumption the supervisor made was that the telemarketer wanted a position with supervisory responsibility. What false assumptions have you made lately when trying to communicate with another person?

    Guidelines for helping a person overcome a limited understanding of people are presented in Exhibit 6-3.

ONE-WAY COMMUNICATION

Effective communication proceeds back and forth. An exchange of information or a transaction takes place between two or more people. Person

A may send messages to person B to initiate communication, but B must react to A to complete the communication loop. One reason written messages sometimes fail to achieve their purpose is that the person who writes the message cannot be sure how it will be interpreted. One written message that is subject to many interpretations is "Your idea is of some interest to me." (How much is *some*?) Face-to-face communication helps clarify meanings.

Instant messaging helps overcome the one-way barrier because the receiver reacts immediately to your message. An example: "You said ship the first batch only to good customers. What do you consider to be a *good* customer?" Ten seconds later comes the reply, "A good customer bought at least $4,000 worth of goods last year and is up to date on payments." Three seconds later, the first person writes, "Got it."

DIFFERENT INTERPRETATION OF WORDS (SEMANTICS)

Semantics is the study of the meaning and changes in the meaning of words. These different meanings can create roadblocks to communication. Often the problem is trivial and humorous; at other times, semantic problems can create substantial communication barriers. Consider first an example of trivial consequence.

Two first-time visitors to Montreal, Quebec (the French-Canadian province) entered a restaurant for dinner. After looking over the menu, the husband suggested they order the shrimp cocktail *entrées*. He said to his wife, "A whole shrimp dinner for $11.95 Canadian is quite a deal. I guess it's because Montreal is a seaport." When the entrées arrived, the visitors were sadly disappointed because they were the size of an *appetizer*.

The husband asked the server why the entrées were so small in Montreal. With a smile, the server replied, "You folks must be Americans. In French-speaking countries the entrée is the beginning of the meal, like the word *enter*. In the United States it's just the reverse—the entrée is the main meal. Are you now ready to order your main meal?"

Of greater consequence is the experience of a trainer of airplane pilots who inadvertently contributed to a crash. As a rookie pilot navigated down the runway, the trainer shouted, "Takeoff power." The pilot shut off the engine and skidded off the runway. What the trainer really meant was to *use* takeoff power—a surge of energy to lift the airplane off the ground. He was using *takeoff* as an adjective, not a verb.

CREDIBILITY OF THE SENDER AND MIXED SIGNALS

The more trustworthy the source or sender of the message, the greater the probability that the message will get through clearly. In contrast, when the sender of the message has low credibility, many times it will be ignored. Communications can also break down for a subtle variation of low credibility. The disconnect occurs from **mixed signals**—sending different messages about the same topic to different audiences. For example, company representatives might brag about the high quality of its products in its public statements. Yet on the shop floor and in the office, the company tells its employees to cut costs whenever possible to lower costs. Another type of mixed signal occurs when you send one message to a person about desired behavior yet behave in another way yourself. As a team leader, you might tell others that a tidy worker is a productive worker. However, your own cubicle contains a four-month supply of empty soft-drink cans, and old papers consume virtually every square inch of your desk.

DISTORTION OF INFORMATION

A great problem in sending messages is that people receiving them often hear what they want to hear. Without malicious intent, people modify your message to bolster their self-esteem or improve their situation. An incident that occurred between Danielle and her supervisor is fairly typical of this type of communication roadblock. Danielle asked her supervisor when she would be receiving a salary increase. Regarding the request as far-fetched and beyond the budget at the time, Danielle's supervisor replied, "Why should the company give you a raise when you are often late for work?"

Danielle *heard* her supervisor say, "If you come to work on time regularly, you will receive a salary increase." One month later Danielle said to her supervisor that she had not been late for work in a month and should now be eligible for a raise. Her supervisor replied, "I never said that. Where did you get that idea?"

DIFFERENT PERSPECTIVES AND EXPERIENCES (WHERE ARE YOU COMING FROM?)

People perceive words and concepts differently because their experiences and vantage points differ. On the basis of their perception of what they have heard, many Latino children believe that the opening line of the "Star-Spangled Banner" is "José, can you see . . . " (Note that few children have *seen* the national anthem in writing). Young people with specialized training or education often encounter communication barriers in dealing with older workers. A minority of older workers think that young people are trying to introduce impractical and theoretical ideas. It takes time to break down this type of resistance to innovation and the application of current knowledge.

EMOTIONS AND ATTITUDES

Have you ever tried to communicate a message to another person while that person is emotionally aroused? Your message was probably distorted considerably. Another problem is that people tend to say things when emotionally aroused that they would not say when calm. Similarly, a person who has strong attitudes about a particular topic may become emotional when that topic is introduced. The underlying message here is try to avoid letting strong emotions and attitudes interfere with the sending or receiving of messages. If you are angry with someone, for example, you might miss the merit in what that person has to say. Calm down before proceeding with your discussion or attempting to resolve the conflict.

COMMUNICATION OVERLOAD

A major communication barrier facing literate people is being bombarded with information. **Communication overload** occurs when people are so overloaded with information that they cannot respond effectively to messages. As a result, they experience work stress. Workers at many levels are exposed to so much printed, electronic, and spoken information that their capacity to absorb it is taxed. The problem is worsened when low-quality information is competing for your attention. An example is receiving a lengthy letter informing you that you are one of 100 select people to receive a sweepstakes prize. (All you need to do is send $29.95 to cover the shipping and handling costs for your valuable prize.) The human mind is capable of processing only a limited quantity of information at a time.

IMPROPER TIMING

Many messages do not get through to people because they are poorly timed. You have to know how to deliver a message, but you must also know *when* to deliver it. Sending a message when the receiver is distracted with other concerns or is rushing to get somewhere is a waste of time. Furthermore, the receiver may become discouraged and therefore will not repeat the message later.

The art of timing messages suggests not to ask for a raise when your boss is in a bad mood or to ask a new acquaintance for a date when he or she is preoccupied. On the other hand, do ask your boss for a raise when business has been good, and do ask someone for a date when you have just done something nice for that person and have been thanked.

POOR COMMUNICATION SKILLS

A message may fail to register because the sender lacks effective communication skills. The sender might garble a written or spoken message so severely that the receiver finds it impossible to understand. Also, the sender may deliver the message so poorly that the receiver does not take it seriously. A common deficiency in sending messages is to communicate with low conviction by using *wimpy* words, backpedaling, and qualifying. Part of the same idea is to use affirmative language, such as saying "when" instead of "if." Also, do not use phrases that call your integrity into question, such as "to be perfectly honest" (implying that you usually do not tell the truth).[13] To illustrate, here are three statements that send a message of low conviction to the receiver: "I think I might be able to finish this project by the end of the week." "It's possible that I could handle the assignment you have in mind." "I'll do what I can."

Another communication skill deficiency that can serve as a communication barrier is to have a regional accent so strong that it detracts from your message. Your regional accent is part of who you are, so you may not want to modify how you speak. Nevertheless, many public personalities and salespeople seek out speech training or speech therapy to avoid having an accent that detracts from their message.[14]

Communication barriers can result from deficiencies within the receiver. A common barrier is a receiver who is a poor listener. Improving listening skills is such a major strategy for improving communication skills that it receives separate mention later in this chapter.

▲ BUILDING BRIDGES TO COMMUNICATION

With determination and awareness that communication roadblocks and barriers do exist, you can become a more effective communicator. It would be impossible to remove all barriers, but they can be minimized. The following techniques are helpful in building better bridges to communication.

1. Appeal to human needs and time your messages.
2. Repeat your message, using more than one channel.
3. Have an empowered attitude and be persuasive.
4. Discuss differences in paradigms.
5. Check for comprehension and feelings.
6. Minimize defensive communication.
7. Combat communication overload.
8. Use mirroring to establish rapport.
9. Engage in small talk and constructive gossip.
10. Improve your telephone, voice-mail, and speakerphone communications skills.
11. Use presentation technology to your advantage.

APPEAL TO HUMAN NEEDS AND TIME YOUR MESSAGES

People are more receptive to messages that promise to do something for them. In other words, if a message promises to satisfy a need that is less than fully satisfied, you are likely to listen. The person in search of additional money who ordinarily does not hear low tones readily hears the whispered message, "How would you like to earn $400 in one weekend?"

Timing a message properly is related to appealing to human needs. If you deliver a message at the right time, you are taking into account the person's mental condition at the moment. A general principle is to deliver your message when the person might be in the right frame of mind to listen. The right frame of mind includes such factors as not being preoccupied with other thoughts, not being frustrated, being in a good mood, and not being stressed out. (Of course, all this severely limits your opportunity to send a message!)

Repeat Your Message, Using More Than One Channel

You can overcome many roadblocks to communication by repeating your message several times. It is usually advisable not to say the same thing so as to avoid annoying the listener with straight repetition. Repeating the message in a different form is effective in another way: The receiver may not have understood the message the first way in which it was delivered. Repetition, like any other means of overcoming communication roadblocks, does not work for all people. Many people who repeatedly hear the message "drinking and driving do not mix" are not moved by it. It is helpful to use several methods of overcoming roadblocks or barriers to communication.

A generally effective way of repeating a message is to use more than one communication channel. For example, follow up a face-to-face discussion with an e-mail message or telephone call or both. Your body can be another channel or medium to help impart your message. If you agree with someone about a spoken message, state your agreement and also shake hands over the agreement. Can you think of another channel by which to transmit a message?

Have an Empowered Attitude and Be Persuasive

According to Sharon Lund O'Neil, a person's communication effectiveness is directly proportional to his or her attitude. The point is that a positive attitude helps a person communicate better in speaking or writing or nonverbally. Being positive is a major factor in being persuasive, as mentioned previously in avoiding wimpy words. *Empowerment* is involved here because the person takes charge of his or her own attitude.[15] Developing a positive attitude is not always easy. A starting point is to see things from a positive perspective, including looking for the good in people and their work. If your work is intrinsically motivating, you are likely to have a positive attitude. You would then be able to communicate about your work with the enthusiasm necessary.

Discuss Differences in Paradigms

Another way of understanding differences in perspectives and experiences is to recognize that people often have different paradigms that influence how they interpret events. A **paradigm** is a model, framework, viewpoint, or perspective. When two people look at a situation with different paradigms, a communication problem may occur. For instance, one person may say, "Let's go to Las Vegas for the computer show." The other person may respond, "A ridiculous idea. It costs too much money and takes too much time. Besides, the company would never approve." These objections are based on certain unstated beliefs:

- ◆ Air travel is the most suitable mode of transportation.
- ◆ Traveling over 500 miles a day by auto is fatiguing and dangerous.
- ◆ Traveling over a weekend for business and using vacation days cannot be considered seriously.
- ◆ Paying for such a trip with personal money is out of the question.

The other person has a different set of unstated beliefs:

- ◆ It is possible, traveling on interstate highways and using two drivers, to cover 500 miles in one day.
- ◆ Traveling over a weekend and taking vacation days is sensible.
- ◆ Paying for the trip with personal money is a sound educational investment.

The solution to this communication clash is to discuss the paradigms. Both people live by different rules or guidelines (a major contributor to a paradigm). If the two people can recognize that they are operating with different paradigms, the chances for agreement are improved. Keep in mind that people can change their paradigms when the reasons are convincing.[16] For example, the first person in the preceding situation may never have thought about using personal funds for a trip as being an educational investment.

CHECK FOR COMPREHENSION AND FEELINGS

Don't be a hit-and-run communicator. Such a person drops a message and leaves the scene before he or she is sure the message has been received as intended. It is preferable to ask receivers their understanding or interpretation of what you said. For example, you might say after delivering a message, "What is your understanding of our agreement?" Also use nonverbal indicators to gauge how well you delivered your message. A blank expression on the receiver's face might indicate no comprehension. A disturbed, agitated expression might mean that the receiver's emotions are blocking the message.

In addition to looking for verbal comprehension and emotions when you have delivered a message, check for feelings after you have received a message. When a person speaks, we too often listen to the facts and ignore the feelings. If feelings are ignored, the true meaning and intent of the message is likely to be missed, thus creating a communication barrier. Your boss might say to you, "You never seem to take work home." To clarify what your boss means by this statement, you might ask, "Is that good or bad?" Your boss's response will give you feedback on his or her feelings about getting all your work done during regular working hours.

When you send a message, it is also helpful to express your feelings in addition to conveying the facts. For example, "Our defects are up by 12 percent [fact], and I'm quite disappointed about those results [feelings]." Because feelings contribute strongly to comprehension, you will help overcome a potential communication barrier.

Minimize Defensive Communication

Distortion of information was described previously as a communication barrier. Such distortion can also be regarded as **defensive communication,** the tendency to receive messages in such a way that our self-esteem is protected. Defensive communication is also responsible for people sending messages to look good. For example, when criticized for achieving below-average sales, a store manager might shift the blame to the sales associates in her store.

Overcoming the barrier of defensive communication requires two steps. First, people have to acknowledge the existence of defensive communication. Second, they have to try not to be defensive when questioned or criticized. Such behavior is not easy because of **denial,** the suppression of information we find uncomfortable. For example, the store manager just cited would find it uncomfortable to think of herself as being responsible for below-average performance.

Defensive communication sometimes takes the form of answering the wrong question. Being touchy about a particular issue, you might regard a request for information as a criticism. David's manager might say to him, "Have you collected the data yet that we need for the trade show?" Angrily defensive because he feels criticized, David might say, "You know that I'm covering for two employees who are out ill." If he had simply said no, the boss might have said, "Oh, I just wanted to offer my help."[17]

Combat Communication Overload

You will recall that a flood of information reaching a person acts as a communication barrier because people have a tendency to block out new information when their capacity to absorb information becomes taxed. You can decrease the chances of suffering from communication overload by such measures as carefully organizing and sorting information before plunging ahead with reading. Speed reading may help, provided that you stop to read carefully the most relevant information. Or you can scan through hard-copy reports, magazines, and Web sites looking for key titles and words that are important to you. Recognize, however, that many subjects have to be studied carefully to derive benefit. It is often better to read thoroughly a few topics than to skim through lots of information.

Being selective about your e-mail and Internet reading goes a long way toward preventing information overload. Suppose you see an e-mail message titled "Car Lights Left On in Parking Lot." Do not retrieve the message if you distinctly remember having turned off your lights or you did not drive to work. E-mail programs and Internet search software are available to help users sort messages according to their needs. You can help prevent others from suffering from communication overload by being merciful in the frequency and length of your messages. Also, do not join the ranks of pranksters who send loads of jokes on e-mail and who prepare bogus Web sites that look authentic but are unofficial (and unreliable) sources of information.

USE MIRRORING TO ESTABLISH RAPPORT

Another approach to overcoming communication barriers is to improve rapport with another person. A form of nonverbal communication called **mirroring** can be used to establish such rapport. To mirror someone is to subtly imitate that individual. The most successful mirroring technique for establishing rapport is to imitate the breathing pattern of another person. If you adjust your own breathing rate to someone else's, you will soon establish rapport with that person. Mirroring sometimes takes the form of imitating the boss in order to communicate better and win favor. Many job seekers now use mirroring to get in sync with the interviewer. Is this a technique you would be willing to try?

Mirroring takes practice to contribute to overcoming communication barriers. It is a subtle technique that requires a moderate skill level. If you mirror (or match) another person in a rigid, mechanical way, you will appear to be mocking that person. And mocking, of course, erects rather than tears down a communication barrier.

ENGAGE IN SMALL TALK AND CONSTRUCTIVE GOSSIP

The terms *small talk* and *gossip* have negative connotations for the career-minded person with a professional attitude. Nevertheless, the effective use of small talk and gossip can help a person melt communication barriers. Small talk is important because it contributes to conversational skills, and having good conversational skills enhances interpersonal communication. Trainer Randi Fredeig says, "Small talk helps build rapport and eventually trust. It helps people find common ground on which to build conversation."[18] A helpful technique is to collect tidbits of information to use as small talk to facilitate work-related or heavy-topic conversation in personal life. Keeping informed about current events, including sports, television, and films, provides useful content for small talk.

Being a source of positive gossip brings a person power and credibility. Workmates are eager to communicate with a person who is a source of not-yet-verified developments. Having such inside knowledge enhances your status and makes you a more interesting communicator. Positive gossip would include such tidbits as mentioning that the company will be looking for workers who would want a one-year assignment in Europe or that more employees will soon be eligible for stock options. In contrast, spreading negative gossip will often erode your attractiveness to other people.[19]

IMPROVE YOUR TELEPHONE, VOICE-MAIL, AND SPEAKERPHONE COMMUNICATION SKILLS

A direct way of overcoming communication barriers is to use effective telephone and voice-mail communication skills because these two communication media often create communication problems. Also, many businesses attract and hold on to customers because their representatives interact positively with people through the telephone and voice mail. Many other firms lose money, and nonprofit organizations irritate the public because their employees have poor communication and voice-mail skills. Furthermore, despite the widespread use of computer networks, a substantial amount of work among employees is still conducted via telephone and voice mail.

Speakerphones present some of their own communication challenges. Small noises, such as crumpling paper, eating crunchy food, and placing a handset on a hard desk, magnify when broadcast over a speakerphone. If other people are present in the office, advise the person you are telephoning at the beginning of the conversation.[20] Doing so may save a lot of embarrassment, such as the caller making negative comments about your boss or coworker.

Most of the previous comments about overcoming communication barriers apply to telephone communications including speakerphones. A number of suggestions related specifically to improving telephone and voice-mail communications are also worth considering. The general goal of the suggestions presented in Exhibit 6-4 is to help people who communicate by telephone sound courteous, cheerful, cooperative, and competent.[21]

USE PRESENTATION TECHNOLOGY TO YOUR ADVANTAGE

Speakers in all types of organizations supplement their talk with computer slides and overhead transparencies and often organize their presentation around them. Many people want presentations reduced to bulleted items and eye-catching graphics. (Have you noticed this tendency among students?) The communication challenge here is that during an oral presentation the predominant means of connection between sender and receiver is eye contact. When an audience is constantly distracted from the presenter by movement on the screen, sounds from the computer, or lavish colors, eye contact suffers, as does the message.

One of the biggest challenges is to learn how to handle equipment and maintain frequent eye and voice contact at all times. Jean Mausehund and R. Neil Dortch offer these sensible suggestions for overcoming the potential communication barrier of using presentation technology inappropriately:

- ◆ *Reveal points only as needed.* Project the overhead transparencies or computer slides only when needed and use a cursor, laser pointer, or metal pointer for emphasis.

EXHIBIT 6-4

Effective Telephone and Voice-Mail Communication Skills

1. When answering the telephone, give your name and department. Also, give the company name if the call is not a transfer from a main switching center.

2. When talking to customers or clients, address them by name, but not to the point of irritation.

3. Vary your voice tone and inflection to avoid sounding bored or uninterested in your job and the company.

4. Speak at a moderate pace of approximately 150 to 160 words per minute. A rapid pace conveys the impression of impatience, while a slow rate might suggest disinterest.

5. Smile while speaking on the phone—somehow a smile gets transmitted over the telephone wires or optic fibers!

6. If the caller does not identify himself or herself, ask, "Who is calling, please?" To overcome customer reluctance to introduce himself or herself, try "Let me put you through. Your name, please?" Knowing the caller's name gives a human touch to the conversation.

7. Use voice mail to minimize "telephone tag" rather than to increase it. If your greeting specifies when you will return, callers can choose to call again or to leave a message. When you leave a message, suggest a good time to return your call. Another way to minimize telephone tag is to assure the person you are calling that you will keep trying.

8. Place an informative and friendly greeting (outgoing message) on your voice mail or answering machine. Used effectively, a voice-mail greeting will minimize the number of people irritated by not talking to a person.

9. When you respond to a voice-mail outgoing message, leave specific, relevant information. As in the suggestions for minimizing telephone tag, be specific about why you are calling and what you want from the person called. The probability of receiving a return call increases when you leave honest and useful information. If you are selling something or asking for a favor, be honest about your intent.

10. When leaving your message, avoid the most common voice-mail error by stating your name and telephone number clearly enough to be understood. Most recipients of a message dislike intensely listening to it several times to pick up identifying information.

11. Although multitasking has become the mode, when speaking on a telephone do not conduct a conversation with another person simultaneously and do not have a television receiver or radio playing in the background. Business callers expect your undivided attention.

- *Talk to the audience and not the screen.* A major problem with computer slides is that the presenter as well as the audience is likely to focus continually on the slide. If the presenter minimizes looking at the slide and spends considerable time looking at the audience, it will be easier to maintain contact with the audience.

- *Keep the slide in view until the audience gets the point.* A presenter will often flash a slide or transparency without giving the audience enough time to comprehend the meaning of the slide. It is also important for presenters to synchronize the slides with their comments.[22]

▲ ENHANCING YOUR LISTENING SKILLS

Improving your receiving of messages is another part of developing better face-to-face and telephone communication skills. Unless you receive messages as they are intended, you cannot perform your job properly or be a good companion. Listening is a particularly important skill for anybody whose job involves solving problems for others because you need to gather information to understand the nature of the problem. Improving employee listening skills is important because insufficient listening is extraordinarily costly. Listening mistakes lead to reprocessing letters, rescheduling appointments, reshipping orders, and recalling defective products. Effective listening also improves interpersonal relationships because the people listened to feel understood and respected. Human Relations Self-Assessment Quiz 6-2 gives you the opportunity to think through possible listening traps you may have developed.

A major component of effective listening is to be an **active listener.** The active listener listens intensely, with the goal of empathizing with the speaker. **Empathy** is simply understanding another person's point of view. If you understand the other person's paradigm, you will be a better receiver and sender of messages. Empathy does not necessarily mean that you sympathize with the other person. For example, you may understand why some people are forced to beg in the streets, but you may have very little sympathy for their plight.

A useful way of showing empathy is to accept the sender's figure of speech. By so doing, the sender feels understood and accepted. Also, if you reject the person's figure of speech by rewording it, the sender may become defensive. Many people use the figure of speech "I'm stuck" when they cannot accomplish a task. You can facilitate smooth communication by a response such as, "What can I do to help you get unstuck?" If you respond with something like, "What can I do to help you think more clearly?" the person is forced to change mental channels and may become defensive.[23]

As a result of listening actively, the listener can feed back to the speaker what he or she thinks the speaker meant. Feedback of this type relies on both verbal and nonverbal communication. Feedback is also important because it facilitates two-way communication. To be an active listener, it is also important to **paraphrase,** or repeat in your own words what the sender says, feels, and means. You might feel awkward the first several times you paraphrase. Therefore, try it with a person with whom you feel comfortable.

HUMAN RELATIONS SELF-ASSESSMENT QUIZ 6-2

Listening Traps

Communication specialists have identified certain behavior patterns that interfere with effective hearing and listening. After thinking carefully about each trap, check how well the trap applies to you: Not a Problem or Need Improvement. To respond to the statements accurately, visualize how you acted when you recently were in a situation calling for listening.

	Not a Problem	Need Improvement
1. **Mind reader.** You will receive limited information if you constantly think "What is this person really thinking or feeling?"	☐	☐
2. **Rehearser.** Your mental rehearsals for "Here's what I'll say next" tune out the sender.	☐	☐
3. **Filterer.** You engage in selective listening by hearing only what you want to hear. (Could be difficult to judge because the process is often unconscious.)	☐	☐
4. **Dreamer.** You drift off during a face-to-face conversation, which often leads you to an embarrassing "What did you say?" or "Could you repeat that?"	☐	☐
5. **Identifier.** If you refer everything you hear to your experience, you probably did not really listen to what was said.	☐	☐
6. **Comparer.** When you get sidetracked sizing up the sender, you are sure to miss the message.	☐	☐
7. **Derailer.** You change the subject too quickly, giving the impression that you are not interested in anything the sender has to say.	☐	☐
8. **Sparrer.** You hear what is said but quickly belittle or discount it, putting you in the same class as the derailer.	☐	☐
9. **Placater.** You agree with everything you hear just to be nice or to avoid conflict. By behaving this way, you miss out on the opportunity for authentic dialogue.	☐	☐

Interpretation: If you checked "Need Improvement" for five or more of the above statements, you are correct—your listening needs improvement! If you checked only two or fewer of the above traps, you are probably an effective listener and a supportive person.

SOURCE: Reprinted with permission from *Messages: The Communication Skills Book* (Oakland, CA: New Harbinger Publications, 1983).

With some practice, it will become a natural part of your communication skill kit. Here is an example of how you might use paraphrasing:

Other Person: I'm getting ticked off at working so hard around here. I wish somebody else would pitch in and do a fair day's work.

You: You're saying that you do more than your fair share of the tough work in our department.

Other Person: You bet. Here's what I think we should be doing about it. . . .

To help become an active listener, consider several additional suggestions. If feasible, keep papers and your computer screen out of sight when listening to somebody else. Having distractions in sight creates the temptation to glance away from the message sender. At the start of your conversation, notice the other person's eye color to help you establish eye contact. (But don't keep staring at his or her eyes!) A major technique of active listening is to ask questions rather than making conclusive statements. Asking questions provides more useful information. Suppose a teammate is late with data you need to complete your analysis. Instead of saying, "I must have your input by Thursday afternoon," try, "When will I get your input?"

Be sure to let others speak until they have finished. Do not interrupt by talking about yourself, jumping in with advice, or offering solutions unless requested.[24] A final suggestion is not to smile continuously during your conversation. Although you may appear friendly, the smiling could also be interpreted as you not taking the other person seriously.[25]

Human Relations Skill-Building Exercise 6-1 gives you an opportunity to practice your listening skills.

▲ OVERCOMING GENDER BARRIERS TO COMMUNICATION

Another strategy for overcoming communication barriers is to deal effectively with potential cultural differences. Two types of cultural differences are those related to gender (male versus female role) and those related to geographic differences. Of course, not everybody agrees that men and women are from different cultures. Here we describe with gender differences, whereas cultural differences are described in Chapter 9.

Despite the movement toward equality of sexes in the workplace, substantial interest has arisen in identifying differences in communication style between men and women. The best-seller *Men Are from Mars, Women Are from Venus* fueled curiosity about the topic.[26] The basic difference between women and men, according to the research of Deborah Tannen, is that men emphasize and reinforce their status when they talk, whereas women downplay their status. As part of this difference, women are more concerned about building social connections.[27] People who are aware of these differences face fewer communication problems between themselves and members of the opposite sex.

HUMAN RELATIONS SKILL-BUILDING EXERCISE 6-1

Active Listening

Before conducting the following role plays, review the suggestions for active listening in this chapter. The suggestion about paraphrasing the message is particularly relevant because the role plays involve emotional topics.

The Elated Coworker.   One student plays the role of a coworker who has just been offered a promotion to supervisor of another department. She will be receiving 10 percent higher pay and be able to travel overseas twice a year for the company. She is eager to describe full details of her good fortune to a coworker. Another student plays the role of the coworker to whom the first coworker wants to describe her good fortune. The second worker decides to listen intently to the first worker. Other class members will rate the second student on his or her listening ability.

The Discouraged Coworker.   One student plays the role of a coworker who has just been placed on probation for poor performance. His boss thinks that his performance is below standard and that his attendance and punctuality are poor. He is afraid that if he tells his girlfriend, she will leave him. He is eager to tell his tale of woe to a coworker. Another student plays the role of a coworker he corners to discuss his problems. The second worker decided to listen intently to his problems but is pressed for time. Other class members will rate the second student on his or her listening ability.

As we describe these differences, recognize that they are group stereotypes. Individual differences in communication style are usually more important than group (men versus women). Furthermore, many research studies fail to show significant gender differences in communication style. A lengthy study of the topic concluded that sex and gender differences in communication are so insignificant that studying them is not worthwhile.[28] Here we will describe the major findings of gender differences in communication patterns.[29]

1. *Women prefer to use conversation for rapport building.*   For most women, the intent of conversation is to build rapport and connections with people. It has been said that men are driven by transactions, while women are driven by relations. Women are therefore more likely to emphasize similarities, to listen intently, and to be supportive.

2. *Men prefer to use talk primarily as a means to preserve independence and status by displaying knowledge and skill.*   When most men talk, they want to receive positive evaluation from others and maintain their hierarchical status within the group. Men are therefore more oriented to giving a *report,* while women are more interested in establishing *rapport.*

3. *Women want empathy, not solutions.*   When women share feelings of being stressed out, they seek empathy and understanding. If they feel they have been listened to carefully, they begin to relax. When listening to the woman, the man may feel blamed for her problems or that he has failed the woman in some way. To feel useful, the man might offer solutions to the woman's problem.

4. *Men prefer to work out their problems by themselves, whereas women prefer to talk out solutions with another person.* Women look on having and sharing problems as an opportunity to build and deepen relationships. Men are more likely to look on problems as challenges they must meet on their own. The communication consequence of these differences is that men may become uncommunicative when they have a problem.

5. *Men tend to be more directive and less apologetic in their conversation, while women are more polite and apologetic.* Women are therefore more likely to frequently use the phrases "I'm sorry" and "Thank you," even when there is no need to express apology or gratitude. Men less frequently say they are sorry for the same reason they rarely ask directions when they are lost while driving: They perceive communications as competition, and they do not want to appear vulnerable.

6. *Women tend to be more conciliatory when facing differences, while men become more intimidating.* Again, women are more interested in building relationships, while men are more concerned about coming out ahead.

7. *Men are more interested than women in calling attention to their accomplishments or hogging recognition.* One consequence of this difference is that men are more likely to dominate discussion during meetings. Another consequence is that women are more likely to help a coworker perform well. In one instance, a sales representative who had already made her sales quota for the month turned over an excellent prospect to a coworker. She reasoned, "It's somebody else's turn. I've received more than my fair share of bonuses for the month."

8. *Men and women interrupt others for different reasons.* Men are more likely to interrupt to introduce a new topic or complete a sentence for someone else. Women are more likely to interrupt to clarify the other person's thought or offer support.

9. *During casual conversation, women focus more on other people, whereas men emphasize sports and other leisure activities.* Women enjoy talking about interpersonal relationships to a greater extent than do men. Men are more likely to emphasize talk about sports, automobiles, and outdoor activities. (Although the subject of current research, this represents the oldest, most sexist stereotype about gender differences.)

10. *Women are more likely to use a gentle expletive, while men tend to be harsher.* For example, if a woman locks herself out of the car, she is likely to say, "Oh dear." In the same situation, a man is likely to say, "Oh———." (Do you think this difference really exists?)

How can this information just presented help overcome communication problems on the job? As a starting point, remember that gender differences often exist. Understanding these differences will help you interpret the communication behavior of people. For example, if a male coworker is not as polite as you would like, remember that he is simply engaging in gender-typical behavior. Do not take it personally.

A woman can remind herself to speak up more in meetings because her natural tendency might be toward holding back. She might say to herself,

"I must watch out to avoid gender-typical behavior in this situation." A man might remind himself to be more polite and supportive toward coworkers. The problem is that, although such behavior is important, his natural tendency might be to skip saying thank you.

A woman should not take it personally when a male coworker or subordinate is tight-lipped when faced with a problem. She should recognize that he needs more encouragement to talk about his problems than would a woman. If a man persists in not wanting to talk about the problem, the woman might say; "It looks like you want to work out this problem on your own. Go ahead. I'm available if you want to talk about the problem."

Men and women should recognize that when women talk over problems, they might not be seeking hard-hitting advice. Instead, they may simply be searching for a sympathetic ear so they can deal with the emotional aspects of the problem.

A general suggestion for overcoming gender-related communication barriers is for men to improve communication by listening with more empathy. Women can improve communication by becoming more direct.

In this chapter we have described many aspects of how people communicate, including gender-specific tendencies. How you combine verbal and nonverbal communication becomes part of your **personal communication style,** or your unique approach to sending and receiving information. Your personal communication style is a major component of your personality because it differentiates you from others. Hundreds of styles are possible, including the following:

- Katherine speaks loudly, smiles frequently, and moves close to people when speaking. Her communication style might be described as aggressive.

- Oscar speaks softly, partially covers his mouth with his hand while talking, and looks away from others. His communication style might be defined as passive or wimpy.

- Tim speaks rapidly, uses a colorful vocabulary, smiles frequently, and makes sweeping gestures. His communication style might be defined as flamboyant.

▲ SUMMARY

Communication is the sending and receiving of messages. Therefore, almost anything that takes place in work and personal life involves communication. The steps involved in communication are encoding, transmission over a communication medium, and decoding.

Nonverbal communication, or silent messages, are important parts of everyday communication. Nonverbal communication includes the environment or setting in which the message is sent, distance from the other person, posture, hand gestures, facial expressions and eye contact, voice quality, and personal appearance. Lying can often be detected by a person's nonverbal communication, such as a rapid shift in facial expression. An advanced application of nonverbal communication is to help combat drug trafficking and terrorism by spotting nervous or threatening behavior.

Despite its many advantages, information technology can create communication problems. The widespread use of e-mail and instant messaging creates some problems. One problem is that it encourages indiscriminate sending of messages. (Nevertheless, one study showed that managers and professionals have e-mail under control.) Many workers develop poor written communication habits because e-mail and instant messaging are so informal. E-mail is also used for such negative purposes as making yourself look good and others look bad. Some managers and other workers use e-mail to avoid direct contact with people, including discipline. Some people find it difficult to handle harsh messages sent over e-mail. Another problem with e-mail is that it can breed indecisiveness because a worker can readily ask the boss to choose an alternative decision.

Telecommuters can communicate abundantly via electronic devices, but they miss out on the face-to-face interactions so vital for dealing with complex problems. Telecommuters can also face the problem of having so little face-to-face communication with people in the office that they are passed over for promotion.

Many potential roadblocks or barriers to communication exist. These roadblocks are most likely to occur when messages are complex or emotional or clash with the receiver's mental set. Communication roadblocks include limited understanding of people, one-way communication, semantics, credibility of the sender and mixed signals, distortion of information, different perspectives and experiences, emotions and attitudes, communication overload, improper timing, and poor communication skills.

Strategies to overcome communication roadblocks include appealing to human need and timing your messages, repeating your message using more than one channel, having an empowered attitude and being persuasive, discussing differences in paradigms, checking for comprehension and feelings, minimizing defensive communication, combating communication overload, using mirroring to establish rapport, and engaging in small talk and constructive gossip. Also, a direct way of overcoming communication barriers is to use effective telephone, voice-mail, and speakerphone communication skills because these media often create communication problems. For example, vary your voice tone and inflection to avoid sounding bored or uninterested in your job and the company. When using presentation technology, it is important to maintain eye contact.

Improving your receiving of messages is another part of developing better communication skills. Unless you receive messages as intended, you cannot perform your job properly or be a good companion. A major component of effective listening is to be an active listener. The active listener uses empathy and can feed back to the speaker what he or she thinks the speaker meant. Active listening also involves paraphrasing what the speaker says, feels, and means. Another major technique of active listening is to ask questions rather than making conclusive statements.

Some opinion and evidence exists about gender differences in communication style. For example, women prefer to use conversation for rapport building, and men prefer to use talk primarily as a means to preserve independence and status by displaying knowledge and skill. Understanding gender differences will help you interpret the communication behavior of people.

How you combine verbal and nonverbal communication becomes your personal communication style.

Questions and Activities

1. How can knowing the three major steps in communication help a person communicate more effectively?

2. Many people contend they communicate much more formally when on the job and much more informally (including using a more limited vocabulary) when among family members and friends. What do you see as the potential advantages and disadvantages of using two communication styles?

3. Why is nonverbal communication so important for the effectiveness of a manager or sales representative?

4. In what way is a handshake a form of nonverbal communication?

5. What potential problems do you see in security personnel at airports and border crossings relying heavily on nonverbal communication indicators to bring people in for additional questioning?

6. In what way might an e-mail message contain nonverbal communication?

7. Based on your own observations, identify a term or phrase that creates semantic problems.

8. How does being politically correct help overcome communication barriers?

9. So what if differences in communication patterns between men and women have been identified? What impact will this information have on your communication with men and women?

10. Identify somebody on television or in person who you have good reason to believe is lying. Describe which (if any) nonverbal cues of lying the person reveals.

INTERNET SKILL BUILDER: Practicing Listening Skills

Your tax dollars are at work to help you listen. The U.S. government's Department of Veterans Affairs has prepared a Web site to help people develop their listening skills. Go to www.va.gov/adrlisten.html. The VA advises you that "hearing becomes listening only when you pay attention to what is said and follow it very closely." After studying the site, identify two responding skills and two nonverbal techniques you think will be particularly valuable for you.

HUMAN RELATIONS CASE PROBLEM

The Scrutinized Team Member Candidate

HRmanager.com is a human resources management firm that provides human resource services such as payroll, benefits administration, affirmative action programs, and technical training to other firms. By signing up with HRmanager, other firms can outsource part or all of their human resources functions. During its seven years of operation, HRmanager has grown from 3 to 50 employees and last year had total revenues of $21 million.

Teams perform most of the work, led by a rotating team leader. Each team member takes an 18-month turn at being a team leader. CEO and founder Jerry Clune regards the four-person new ventures team as vital for the future of the company. In addition to developing ideas for new services, the team members are responsible for obtaining clients for any new service they propose that Clune approves. The new ventures team thus develops and sells new services. After the service is launched and working well, the sales group is responsible for developing more clients.

As with other teams at HRmanager, the team members have a voice as to who is hired to join their team. In conjunction with Clune, the new ventures team decided it should expand to five members. The team posted the job opening for a new member on an Internet recruiting service, ran classified ads in the local newspaper, and also asked present employees for referrals. One of the finalists for the position was Gina Cleveland, a 27-year-old business graduate. In addition to interviewing with Clune and the two company vice presidents, Cleveland spent one-half day with the new ventures team, breakfast and lunch included. About two and one-half hours of the time was spent in a team interview in which Gina sat in a conference room with the four team members.

The team members agreed that Cleveland appeared to be a strong candidate on paper. Her education and experience were satisfactory, her résumé was impressive, and she presented herself well during a telephone-screening interview. After Cleveland completed her time with the new ventures team, Lauren Nielsen, the team leader, suggested that the group hold a debriefing session. The purpose of the session would be to share ideas about Cleveland's suitability for joining the team.

Nielsen commented, "It seems like we think that Gina is a strong candidate based on her credentials and what she said. But I'm a big believer in nonverbal communication. Studying Gina's body language can give us a lot of valuable information. Let's each share our observations about what Gina's body language tells us she is *really* like. I'll go first."

Lauren: I liked the way Gina looks so cool and polished when she joined us for breakfast. She's got all the superficial movements right to project self-confidence. But did anybody else notice how she looked concerned when she had to make a choice from the menu? She finally did choose a ham-and-cheese omelet, but she raised her voice at the end of the sentence when she ordered it. I got the hint that Gina is not very confident.

I also noticed Gina biting her lips a little when we asked her how creative she thought she was. I know that Gina said she was creative and gave us an example of a creative project she completed. Yet nibbling at her lips like that suggests she's not filled with firepower.

(Continued)

Michael: I didn't make any direct observations about Gina's being self-confident or not, but I did notice something that could be related. I think Gina is on a power trip, and this could indicate high or low self-confidence. Did anybody notice how Gina put her hands on her hips when she was standing up? That's a pure and clear signal of somebody who wants to be in control. Her haircut is almost the same length and style like most women who've made it to the top in Fortune 500 companies. I think she cloned her hairstyle from Carly Fiorina, the HP honcho.

Another hint I get of Gina's power trip is the way she eyed the check in the restaurant at lunch. I could see it in her eyes that she really wanted to pay for the entire team. That could mean a desire to control and show us that she is very important. Do we want someone on the team with such a strong desire to control?

Brenda: I observed a different picture of Gina based on her nonverbal communication. She dressed just right for the occasion—not too conservatively, not too far business casual. This tells me she can fit into our environment. Did you notice how well groomed her shoes were? This tells you she is well organized and good at details. Her attaché case was a soft, inviting leather. If she were really into power and control, she would carry a hard vinyl or aluminum attaché case. I see Gina as a confident and assertive person who could blend right into our team.

Larry: I hope that because I'm last, I'm not too influenced by the observations that you three have shared so far. My take is that Gina looks great on paper but that she may have a problem in being a good team player. She's too laid back and distant. Did you notice her handshake? She gave me the impression of wanting to have the least possible physical contact with me. Her handshake was so insincere. I could feel her hand and arm withdrawing from me as she shook my hand.

I also couldn't help noticing that Gina did not lean much toward us during the roundtable discussion. Do you remember how she would pull her chair back ever so slightly when we got into a heavy discussion? I interpreted that as a sign that Gina does not want to be part of a close-knit group.

Lauren: As you have probably noticed, I've been typing as fast as I can with my laptop, taking notes on what you have said. We have some mixed observations here, and I want to summarize and integrate them before we make a decision. I'll send you an e-mail with an attached file of my summary observations by tomorrow morning. Make any changes you see fit and get back to me. After we have finished evaluating Gina carefully, we will be able to make our recommendations to Jerry [Clune].

Questions

1. To what extent are new ventures team members making an appropriate use of nonverbal communication to size up Gina Cleveland?

2. Which team member do you think made the most realistic interpretation of nonverbal behavior? Why?

3. Should Lauren, the team leader, have told Gina in advance that the team would be scrutinizing her nonverbal behavior? Justify your answer.

WEB CORNER

Presentation tips: www.fastcompany.com/online/07/124present.html

Nonverbal communication:
www.shaadikaro.com/communication_skill.asp

▲ REFERENCES

1. Adapted from Anne Field, "Coach, Help Me Out with This Interview," *BusinessWeek,* October 22, 2001, p. 134E2.

2. Edward T. Hall, "Proxemics—A Study of Man's Spatial Relationships," in *Man's Image in Medicine and Anthropology* (New York: International Universities Press, 1963); Pauline E. Henderson, "Communication without Words," *Personnel Journal,* January 1989, pp. 28–29.

3. Jeffrey Jacobi, *The Vocal Advantage* (Upper Saddle River, NJ: Prentice Hall, 1996).

4. "Attention All Monotonous Speakers," *WorkingSMART,* March 1998, p. 1.

5. Genviève Coutu-Bouchard, "L'effet Pygmalion," *Montréal Campus,* April 24, 2002, p. 11.

6. *Body Language for Business Success: 77 Ways to Get Results Using Nonverbal Communication,* special report from the National Institute of Business Management, McLean, Virginia, July 1989.

7. Frederic Golden, "Lying Faces Unmasked," *Time,* April 5, 1999.

8. Ann Davis, Joseph Pereira, and William M. Bulkeley, "Silent Signals: Security Concerns Bring New Focus on Body Language," *Wall Street Journal,* August 15, 2002, pp. A1, A6.

9. "Like It or Not, You've Got Mail," *BusinessWeek,* October 4, 1999, pp. 178–184; "Using E-Mail and Voice Mail Effectively," *Business Education Forum,* October 1998, pp. 6–9, 51; Andrew Blackman, "Spam's 'Easy Target'," *Wall Street Journal,* August 19, 2003, pp. B1, B4.

10. Survey reported in Carol Monaghan, "Inbox Glutted? Maybe You're a Power E-Mailer," *Chicago Tribune,* December 15, 2002.

11. Susan J. Wells, "Two Sides to the Story," *HR Magazine,* October 2001, p. 41.

12. "Work à la Modem," *BusinessWeek,* October 4, 1999, p. 176.

13. "Weed Out Wimpy Words," *WorkingSMART,* March 2000, p. 2; George Walther cited in "Power Up Your Persuasiveness," *Executive Leadership,* July 2003, p. 1.

14. Joe Neumaier, "Sweet Sounds of Success: Dialect Coach Sam Chwat Accents Hollywood's Best," *USA Weekend,* July 12–14, 2002, p. 12.

15. Sharon Lund O'Neill, "An Empowered Attitude Can Enhance Communication Skills," *Business Education Forum,* April 1998, pp. 28–30.

16. Suzette Haden Elgin, *Genderspeak* (New York: Wiley, 1993).

17. Ibid.

18. Cited in Jacquelyn Lynn, "Small Talk, Big Results," *Entrepreneur,* August 1999, p. 30.

19. Nancy B. Kurland and Lisa Hope Pelled, "Passing the Word: Toward a Model of Gossip and Power in the Workplace," *Academy of Management Review,* April 2000, pp. 428–438; Samuel Greengard, "Gossip Poisons Business: HR Can Stop It," *Workforce,* July 2001, pp. 24–28.

20. John T. Adams III, "When You're on a Speakerphone, Don't Make Noise," *HR Magazine,* March 2001, p. 12.

21. Janice Alessandra and Tony Alessandra, "14 Telephone Tips for Ernestine," *Management Solutions,* July 1988, pp. 35–36; Donna Deeprose, "Making Voice Mail Customer Friendly," *Supervisory Management,* December 1992, pp. 7–8; "Many on Receiving End Say Call Screening Uncalled-For," Knight Ridder, September 3, 2000.

22. Jean Mausehund and R. Neil Dortch, "Presentation Skills in the Digital Age," *Business Education Forum,* April 1999, pp. 30–32.

23. Daniel Araoz, "Right-Brain Management (RBM): Part 2," *Human Resources Forum,* September 1989, p. 4.

24. Deb Koen, "Work World Needs Good Listeners," *Rochester, (NY) Democrat and Chronicle,* November 3, 2002, p. 14E.

25. "Train Yourself in the Art of Listening," *Positive Leadership,* sample issue, Summer 2000, p. 10.

26. John Gray, *Men Are from Mars, Women Are from Venus* (New York: HarperCollins, 1992).

27. Deborah Tannen, *Talking from 9 to 5* (New York: William Morrow, 1994).

28. Daniel J. Canary and Kathryn Dindia, *Sex Differences and Similarities in Communication* (Mahwah, NJ: Erlbaum, 1998).

29. Deborah Tannen, *You Just Don't Understand* (New York: Ballentine, 1990); Gray, *Men Are from Mars;* Deborah Tannen, "The Power of Talk: Who Gets Heard and Why," *Harvard Business Review,* September–October 1995, pp. 138–148.

▲ ADDITIONAL READING

Balu, Rekha. "Listen Up: It Might Be Your Customer Talking." *Fast Company,* May 2000, pp. 304–314.

Blustain, Sarah. "The New Gender Wars." *Psychology Today,* November–December 2000, pp. 42–49.

Burley-Allen, Madelyn. "Listen Up." *HR Magazine,* November 2001, pp. 115–120.

Davis, Bobbye J. "Communications—Strategies for Improving Oral Communication Skills." *Business Education Forum,* December 1999, pp. 34–36.

Digh, Patricia. "One Style Doesn't Fit All." *HR Magazine,* November 2002, p. 79.

Kiger, Patrick J. "Lessons from a Crisis: How Communication Kept a Company Together." *Workforce,* November 2001, pp. 28–36.

Lachnit, Carroll. "Tongue-Tied." *Workforce Management,* August 2003, p. 10.

McGarvey, Robert. "Get the Word Out . . . and Get Employees Communicating—Faster, Cheaper, and More Effectively." *Entrepreneur,* February 2000, pp. 131–134.

Morgan, Nick. "The Kinesthetic Speaker: Putting Action into Words." *Harvard Business Review,* April 2001, pp. 112–120.

Romaine, Suzanne. *Communicating Gender.* Mahwah, NJ: Erlbaum, 1999.

Tyler, Kathryn. "Toning Up Communications: Business Writing Courses Can Help Employees and Managers Learn to Clearly Express Organizational Messages." *HR Magazine,* March 2003, pp. 87–89.

CHAPTER 7

Handling Conflict and Being Assertive

Learning Objectives

After studying the information and doing the exercises in this chapter, you should be able to:

◆ Identify reasons why conflict between people takes place so often

◆ Pinpoint several helpful and harmful consequences of conflict

◆ Choose an effective method of resolving conflict

◆ Improve your negotiating skills

◆ Improve your assertion skills

A manager was so concerned about a problem facing her in the office that she wrote to a business columnist, "I am a manager in a small office. My problem is that one of the staff people (a man who is 12 years older than I) is verbally harassing me, telling me that I don't know what I'm doing and that I'm incompetent. A lot of times, I just avoid dealing with him. Instead of saying something I'll regret, I figure I'm better off walking away.

This man doesn't report directly to me. He reports to someone else, but I have authority over his work. What are my rights here? How should I handle this?"

The columnist, who consulted several human relations specialists, responded, "What a tense situation! And what obnoxious remarks! You're probably dreading the thought of any direct confrontation with this man. Unfortunately, however, that's exactly what the experts want you to do—talk directly with the offender about his behavior."[1]

The situation just described illustrates a reality about the workplace and personal life. Conflict takes place frequently, and being able to manage it well contributes to your feeling of well-being. **Conflict** is a condition that exists when two sets of demands, goals, or motives are incompatible. For example, if a person wants a career in retailing yet also wants to work a predictable eight-hour day with weekends off, that person faces a conflict. He or she cannot achieve both goals. When two people have differences in demands, it often leads to a hostile or antagonistic relationship between them. A conflict can also be considered a dispute, feud, or controversy. The two people described above are in conflict because the man wants to insult the woman and the woman wants a peaceful relationship.

Unless workers learn how to resolve conflict effectively, it will be difficult to achieve a workplace in which people collaborate. When the work environment is filled with collaboration and caring, the organization will be more productive, and workers will experience less negative stress. Organizational psychologist James Campbell Quick observes, "When competition and competitive behavior go to an extreme, it becomes dysfunctional and destructive. Over-the-top competition and stress can tear down individuals and organizations."[2]

A major purpose of this chapter is to describe ways of resolving conflict so that a win-win solution is reached. Both sides should leave the conflict feeling that their needs have been satisfied without having to resort to extreme behavior. Both parties get what they deserve yet preserve the dignity and self-respect of the other side. Another purpose of this chapter is to explain assertiveness because being assertive helps prevent and resolve conflict.

▲ WHY SO MUCH CONFLICT EXISTS

Many reasons exist for the widespread presence of conflict in all aspects of life. All these reasons are related to the basic nature of conflict—the fact that not every person can have what he or she wants at the same time. As with other topics in this book, understanding conflict helps you develop a better understanding of why people act as they do. Here we describe six key sources of conflict.

COMPETITION FOR LIMITED RESOURCES

A fundamental reason you might experience conflict with another person is that not everybody can get all the money, material, supplies, or human help they want. Conflict also ensues when employees are asked to compete for prizes such as bonuses based on individual effort or company-paid vacation trips. Because the number of awards is so limited, the competition becomes intense enough to be regarded as conflict. In some families, two or more children are pitted in conflict over the limited resources of money available for higher education.

Conflict stemming from limited resources has become prevalent as so many companies attempt to reduce expenses. Many units of the organization have to compete for the limited money available to hire new people or purchase new technology. An individual might be in conflict who says to the manager, "You expect higher and higher productivity, yet I am not authorized to purchase the most advanced software."

THE GENERATION GAP AND PERSONALITY CLASHES

Various value and personality differences among people contribute to workplace conflict. Differences in age, or the generation gap, can lead to conflict because members of one generation may not accept the values of another. Some observers see a clash between baby boomers and Generation X and Generation Y. (Recall the discussion in Chapter 2 about need differences among the three generations.) The baby boomers are typically considered people born between 1946 and 1964, Generation X between 1965 and 1987, and Generation Y between 1978 and 1984. Another workforce group with values of its own are veterans, born between 1922 and 1943.

According to the stereotype, baby boomers see members of Generation X and Generation Y as disrespectful of rules, not willing to pay their dues, and being disloyal to employers. Generation X and Generation Y members see baby boomers as worshiping hierarchy (layers of authority), being overcautious, and wanting to preserve the status quo. Baby boomers, however, appreciate teamwork more than the veterans, who prefer the old-fashioned, militaristic style organization. The four groups, of course, see themselves in a favorable light. Members of Generation X and Generation Y believe that employers have been disloyal to them, and baby boomers believe that the search for job security is highly sensible. Veterans believe in a centralized authority and a heroic attitude about work.[3] An example follows of a conflict based on generational differences in habits and values:

> Hosting a retirement dinner for the boss at an expensive restaurant, a senior manager was appalled when not one of the young employees bothered to dress up. Although the office dress code is casual, he had assumed employees would know enough to freshen up for the occasion, if only as a sign of respect for the leader.[4]

Many disagreements on the job stem from the fact that some people simply dislike each other. A **personality clash** is thus an antagonistic relationship between two people based on differences in personal attributes, preferences, interests, values, and styles. People involved in a personality clash often have difficulty specifying why they dislike each other. The end result, however, is that they cannot maintain an amiable work relationship. A strange fact about personality clashes is that people who get along well may begin to clash after working together for a number of years. Many business partnerships fold because the two partners eventually clash.

Aggressive Personalities Including Bullies

Coworkers naturally disagree about topics, issues, and ideas. Yet some people convert disagreement into an attack that puts down other people and damages their self-esteem. As a result, conflict surfaces. **Aggressive personalities** are people who verbally and sometimes physically attack others frequently. Verbal aggression takes the form of insults, teasing, ridicule, and profanity. The aggression may also be expressed as attacks on the victim's character, competence, background, and physical appearance.[5]

Aggressive personalities are also referred to as *workplace bullies*. Among their typical behaviors are interrupting others, ranting in a loud voice, and making threats. A typical attitude of a bullying boss is "My way or the highway," sending the message that the employee's suggestions are unwelcome. One bullying manager would frequently ask people, "Are you going to be stupid the rest of your life?" Bullied workers complain of a range of psychological and physical ailments such as the following: anxiety, sleeplessness, headache, irritable bowel syndrome, skin problems, panic attacks, and low self-esteem.[6]

Aggressiveness can also take the extreme form of the shooting or knifing of a former boss or colleague by a mentally unstable worker recently dismissed from the company. Violence has become so widespread that homicide is the second-highest cause of workplace deaths, with about 1,000 workers murdered each year in the United States.[7] Most of these deaths result from a robbery or commercial crime. Many of these killings, however, are perpetrated by a disgruntled worker or former employee harboring an unresolved conflict. As companies have continued to reduce their workforce despite being profitable, these incidents have increased in frequency. Workplace violence is sometimes referred to as *desk rage*. The problem includes such diverse behaviors as distracting rudeness, attacks on trashcans, keyboards, and even coworkers.

CULTURALLY DIVERSE TEAMS

Conflict often surfaces as people work in teams whose members vary in many ways. William L. Ury, a negotiation expert, says, "Conflict resolution is perhaps the key skill needed in a diverse work force."[8] Ethnicity, religion, and gender are three of the major factors that lead to clashes in viewpoints. Differing educational backgrounds and work specialties can also lead to conflict. Workers often shut out information that doesn't fit comfortably with their own beliefs, particularly if they do not like the person providing the information. When these conflicts are properly resolved, diversity lends strength to the organization because the various viewpoints make an important contribution to solving a problem. Groups that are reminded of the importance of effective communication and taught methods of conflict resolution can usually overcome the conflict stemming from mixed groups.[9]

COMPETING WORK AND FAMILY DEMANDS

Balancing the demands of work and family life is a major challenge facing workers at all levels. Yet achieving this balance and resolving these conflicts is essential for being successful in career and personal life. The challenge of achieving balance is particularly intense for employees who are part of a two-wage-earner family. **Work–family conflict** occurs when the individual has to perform multiple roles: worker, spouse or partner, and often parent. From the standpoint of the individual, this type of conflict can be regarded as work interfering with family life. From the standpoint of the employer, the same conflict might be regarded as family life interfering with work.

A team of researchers studying work interference with family life gathered data from approximately 501 employees in large companies. A major conclusion was that long hours at work increase work–family conflict, and that the conflict is related to depression and other stress-related health problems.[10]

Attempting to meet work and family demands is a frequent source of conflict because the demands are often incompatible. Imagine having to attend your child's championship soccer game and then being ordered at the last minute to attend a late-afternoon meeting. A survey revealed the following evidence of work–family conflict and the potential of such conflict:

- About 45 percent of students say their top consideration in selecting a first employer is the opportunity to achieve a balance between work and life outside of work.

- Approximately 80 percent of workers consider their effort to balance work and personal life as their first priority.

- More than one-third of employed Americans are working 10 or more hours a day, and 39 percent work on weekends.

- One-third of employees say that they are forced to choose between advancing in their jobs or devoting attention to their family or personal lives.[11]

The conflict over work versus family demands intensifies when the person is serious about both work and family responsibilities. The average professional working for an organization works approximately 55 hours per week, including five hours on weekends. Adhering to such a schedule almost inevitably results in some incompatible demands from work versus those from family members and friends. Conflict arises because the person wants to work sufficient hours to succeed on the job yet still have enough time for personal life.

Employers have taken major steps in recent years to help employees balance the competing demands of work and family. One reason for giving assistance in this area is that balancing work and family demands helps both the worker and the company. A survey of work and family strategies found that family-friendly business firms find big returns on their efforts. Absenteeism and turnover decrease, and productivity and profits increase.[12] Some employers have developed programs aimed directly at reducing the conflict that arises from competing work and family demands. A sampling of these programs and practices follows:

1. *Flexible work schedules.*   Many employers allow employees to work flexible hours, provided that they work the full 40-hour schedule and are present at certain core times. A related program is the compressed workweek, whereby the person works 40 hours in four days or less. Some employees prefer the compressed workweek because it gives them longer weekends with their families. Yet compressed workweeks can also be family unfriendly and create major conflicts. An example is that for some workers, having to work three 12-hour days in one week creates family problems.

2. *Dependent-care programs.*   Assistance in dealing with two categories of dependents, children and elderly parents, lies at the core of programs and policies to help employees balance the demands of work and family. At one end of child care assistance is a fully equipped nursery school on company premises. At the other end is simply a referral service that helps working parents find adequate childcare. Many companies offer financial assistance for childcare, including pretax expense accounts that allow employees to deduct dependent-care expenses.

3. *Compassionate attitudes toward individual needs.*   An informal policy that facilitates balancing work and family demands is for the manager to decide what can be done to resolve individual conflicts. Yet the manager cannot make arrangements with employees who would violate company policy. Being sensitive to individual situations could involve such arrangements as allowing a person time off to deal with a personal crisis. After the crisis is resolved, the employee makes up the lost time in small chunks of extra work time. In this way the manager helps the worker achieve success both on and off the job.

Sexual Harassment: A Special Type of Conflict

Many employees face conflict because they are sexually harassed by a supervisor, coworker, or customers. **Sexual harassment** is generally defined as unwanted sexually oriented behavior in the workplace that results in discomfort and/or interference with the job. It can include an action as violent as rape or as subdued as telling a sexually toned joke. In this way sexual harassment is defined in terms of its consequences to the victim. The harasser behaves in an aggressive and objectionable or offensive manner.

Sexual harassment creates conflict because the harassed person has to make a choice between two incompatible motives. One motive is to get ahead, keep the job, or have an unthreatening work environment. But to satisfy this motive, the person is forced to sacrifice the motive of holding on to his or her moral values or preferences. For example, a person might say, "I want to be liked by my coworkers and not be considered a prude. Yet to do this, must I listen to their raunchy jokes about the human anatomy?" Of even greater conflict, "I want a raise; but to do this, must I submit to being fondled by my boss?" Here we focus on the types and frequency of sexual harassment and guidelines for dealing with the problem.

Types and Frequency of Harassment

Two types of sexual harassment are legally recognized. Both are violations of the Civil Rights Acts of 1964 and 1991 and are therefore a violation of your rights when working in the United States. Other countries also have human rights legislation prohibiting sexual harassment. In quid pro quo sexual harassment, the individual suffers loss (or threatened loss) of a job benefit as a result of his or her response to a request for sexual favors. The demands of a harasser can be blatant or implied. An implied form of quid pro quo harassment might take this form: A manager casually comments to one of his or her employees, "I've noticed that workers who become very close to me outside of the office get recommended for bigger raises."

The other form of sexual harassment is hostile-environment harassment. Another person in the workplace creates an intimidating, hostile, or offensive working environment. No tangible loss or psychological injury has to be suffered under this form of sexual harassment.

A major problem in controlling sexual harassment in the workplace is that most workers understand the meaning and nature of quid pro quo harassment but are confused about what constitutes the hostile-environment type. For example, some people might interpret the following behaviors to be harassing, while others would regard them as friendly initiatives: (1) calling a coworker "sweetie" and (2) saying to a subordinate, "I love your suit. You look fabulous."

A group of researchers provided useful insights into the role of perception in deciding which behaviors of supervisors and coworkers constituted both types of harassment.[13] Typical harassment behaviors include physical contact, inappropriate remarks, a sexual proposition, a threat or promise associated with a job, comments on the other person's physical appearance, or a glaring stare at the person harassed. The setting for the survey was a manufacturing plant that had a strict policy against sexual harassment. Furthermore, supervisory and professional personnel had training in dealing with sexual harassment. Employee perceptions were compared to U.S. federal guidelines of sexual harassment—the basis for a "correct" response.

EXHIBIT 7-1

*Accuracy of 114 Workers In Identifying
Each Sexually Harassing Behavior*

Supervisory Behaviors	Correspondence with U.S. Federal Guidelines	
If your supervisor did this, would you consider this sexual harassment?	Inaccurate	Accurate
1. Asks you to have sex with the promise that it will help you on the job.	18	96
2. Asks you to have sex with the threat that refusing to have sex will hurt you on the job.	17	97
3. Asks you to go out on a date with the promise that it will help you on the job.	18	96
4. Asks you to go out on a date with the promise that it will hurt you if you do not go.	16	98
5. Touches you on private parts of the body; for example, breasts, buttocks, etc.	22	92
6. Touches you on parts of the body not considered private; for example, shoulder, hand, arm, etc.	77	37
7. Looks at you in a flattering way.	75	39
8. Makes gestures (signs) of a flattering nature.	51	63
9. Makes comments about your dress or appearance that are meant to be complimentary.	96	18
10. Makes comments about your appearance meant to be insulting.	91	23
11. Makes sexually offensive comments.	49	65
12. Tells sexually oriented jokes.	75	39

SOURCE: Marjorie L. Icenogle, Bruce W. Eagle, Sohel Ahman, and Lisa A. Hanks, "Assessing Perceptions of Sexual Harassment Behaviors in a Manufacturing Environment," *Journal of Business and Psychology,* Summer 2002, p. 607.

Exhibit 7-1 presents the responses of the 114 participants in the survey with regard to supervisory behavior. (The perceptions of the accuracy versus inaccuracy in classifying coworker behavior as being harassing were essentially the same.) The responses indicated that the majority of workers can accurately identify behaviors frequently associated with quid pro quo harassment. However, the same workers had difficulty identifying behaviors that are used to establish evidence of a hostile work environment. Male workers had a slight edge in the accuracy of their perceptions about what constitutes harassment, and women in white-collar jobs were more accurate than women in blue-collar jobs.

An employee who is continually subjected to sexually suggestive comments, lewd jokes, or requests for dates is a victim of hostile-environment harassment. When the offensive behavior stems from customers or vendors, it is still harassment. Although the company cannot readily control the actions of customers or vendors, the company may still be liable for such harassment. According to several legal decisions, it is a company's job to take action to remedy harassment problems involving employees.

Surveys as well as the opinions of human resource professionals suggest that somewhere between 50 and 60 percent of women are sexually harassed at least once in their career. Aside from being an illegal and immoral act, sexual harassment has negative effects on the well-being of its victims. The harassed person may experience job stress, lowered morale, severe conflict, and lowered productivity. A study with both business and university workers found that even at low levels of frequency, harassment exerts a significant impact on women's psychological well-being and productivity. High levels of harassment, however, had even more negative effects.[14]

A related study of the long-term effects of sexual harassment indicated that the negative effects remained two years after the incident. For example, 24 months after an incident of sexual harassment, many women still experienced stress, a decrease in job satisfaction, and lowered productivity.[15]

GUIDELINES FOR PREVENTING AND DEALING WITH SEXUAL HARASSMENT

A starting point in dealing with sexual harassment is to develop an awareness of the type of behaviors that are considered sexual harassment. Often the difference is subtle. Suppose, for example, you placed copies of two nudes painted by Renoir, the French painter, on a coworker's desk. Your coworker might call that harassment. Yet if you took that same coworker to a museum to see the originals of the same nude paintings, your behavior would usually not be classified as harassment. Education about the meaning of sexual harassment is therefore a basic part of any company program to prevent sexual harassment. The situation and your tone of voice, as well as other nonverbal behavior, contribute to perceptions of harassment. For example, the statement "You look wonderful" might be perceived as good natured versus harassing, depending on the sender's voice tone and facial expression.

The easiest way to deal with sexual harassment is to speak up before it becomes serious. The first time it happens, respond with statements such as, "I won't tolerate that kind of talk." "I dislike sexually oriented jokes." "Keep your hands off me." Write the harasser a stern letter shortly after the first incident. Confronting the harasser in writing dramatizes your seriousness of purpose in not wanting to be sexually harassed. If the problem persists, say something to the effect, "You're practicing sexual harassment. If you don't stop, I'm going to exercise my right to report you to management." Additional suggestions for dealing with sexual harassment are presented in Exhibit 7-2.

EXHIBIT 7-2

Tips on Harassment

Here are some tips on dealing with sexual harassment from the New York State Division of Human Rights:

- Don't leave any room for doubt that the behavior or words you heard were unwelcome.

- If the behavior continues, report your complaint to a higher authority or the person your company or organization has designated to handle such complaints.

- Put the complaint in writing to reduce the chances of confusion.

- Keep concise yet accurate notes of incidents.

- If the matter isn't resolved internally, see a lawyer promptly for advice. The person can steer you through various legal options, possibly through federal or state court.

▲ THE GOOD AND BAD SIDES OF CONFLICT

Conflict over significant issues is a source of stress. We usually do not suffer stress over minor conflicts such as having to choose between wearing one sweater or another. Since conflict is a source of stress, it can have both positive and negative consequences to the individual. Like stress in general, we need an optimum amount of conflict to keep us mentally and physically energetic.

You can probably recall an incident in your life when conflict proved to be beneficial in the long run. Perhaps you and your friend or spouse hammered out an agreement over how much freedom each one has in the relationship. Handled properly, moderate doses of conflict can be beneficial. Some of the benefits that might arise from conflict can be summarized around these key points:

1. *Talents and abilities may emerge in response to conflict.* When faced with a conflict, people often become more creative than they are in a tranquil situation. Assume that your employer told you that it would no longer pay for your advanced education unless you used the courses to improve your job performance. You would probably find ways to accomplish such an end.

2. *Conflict can help you feel better because it satisfies a number of psychological needs.* By nature, many people like a good fight. As a socially acceptable substitute for attacking others, you might be content to argue over a dispute on the job or at home.

3. *As an aftermath of conflict, the parties in conflict may become united.* Two warring supervisors may become more cooperative toward each other in the aftermath of confrontation. A possible explanation is that the shared experience of being in conflict with each other *sometimes* brings the parties closer.

4. *Conflict helps prevent people in the organization from agreeing too readily with each other, thus making some very poor decisions.*   Groupthink is the situation that occurs when group members strive so hard to get along that they fail to critically evaluate each other's ideas.

Despite the positive picture of conflict just painted, it can also have detrimental consequences to the individual, the organization, and society. These harmful consequences of conflict make it important for people to learn how to resolve conflict:

1. *Prolonged conflict can be detrimental to some people's emotional and physical well-being.*   As a type of stress, prolonged conflict can lead to such problems as heart disease and chronic intestinal disorders. President Lyndon B. Johnson suffered his first heart attack after an intense argument with a young newspaper reporter.

2. *People in conflict with each other often waste time and energy that could be put to useful purposes.*   Instead of fighting all evening with your roommate, the two of you might fix up your place. Instead of writing angry e-mail messages back and forth, two department heads might better invest that time in thinking up ideas to save the company money.

3. *The aftermath of extreme conflict may have high financial and emotional costs.*   Sabotage—such as ruining machinery—might be the financial consequence. At the same time, management may develop a permanent distrust of many people in the workforce, although only a few of them are saboteurs.

4. *Too much conflict is fatiguing, even if it does not cause symptoms of emotional illness.*   People who work in high-conflict jobs often feel spent when they return home from work. When the battle-worn individual has limited energy left over for family responsibilities, the result is more conflict. (For instance, "What do you mean you are too tired to visit friends?" or "If your job is killing your interest in having friends, find another job.")

5. *People in conflict will often be much more concerned with their own interests than with the good of the family, organization, or society.*   A married couple in conflict might disregard the welfare of their children. An employee in the shipping department who is in conflict with his supervisor might neglect to ship an order. And a gang in conflict with another might leave a park or beach strewn with broken glass.

6. *Workplace violence erupts, including the killing of managers, previous managers, coworkers, customers, as well as spouses and partners.*   The number of violent incidents at work causing death or serious injury has risen dramatically in recent years, as mentioned previously.[16] Disgruntled employees, such as those recently fired, may attempt revenge by assassinating work associates. People involved in an unresolved domestic dispute sometimes storm into the partner's workplace to physically attack him or her. Unresolved conflict and frustration from financial, marital, or other domestic problems increase the odds of a person "going ballistic" at work.

▲ TECHNIQUES FOR RESOLVING CONFLICTS

Because of the inevitability of conflict, a successful and happy person must learn effective ways of resolving conflict. An important general consideration is to face conflict rather than letting conflict slide or smoothing over it. Ignoring or smoothing over conflict does little to resolve the real causes of conflict and seldom leads to an effective long-term solution.[17] Here we concentrate on methods of conflict resolution that you can use on your own. Most of them emphasize a collaborative or win-win philosophy. Several of the negotiating and bargaining tactics to be described may be close to the competitive orientation.

CONFRONTATION AND PROBLEM SOLVING LEADING TO WIN-WIN

The most highly recommended way of resolving conflict is **confrontation and problem solving.** It is a method of identifying the true source of conflict and resolving it systematically. The confrontation in this approach is gentle and tactful rather than combative and abusive. It is best to wait until your anger cools down before confronting the other person, to avoid being unreasonable. Reasonableness is important because the person who takes the initiative in resolving the conflict wants to maintain a harmonious working relationship with the other party. Also, both parties should benefit from the resolution of the conflict.

Assume that Jason, the person working at the desk next to you, whistles loudly while he works. You find the whistling to be distracting and annoying; you think Jason is a noise polluter. If you don't bring the problem to Jason's attention, it will probably grow in proportion with time. Yet you are hesitant to enter into an argument about something a person might regard as a civil liberty (the right to whistle in a public place).

An effective alternative is for you to approach Jason directly in this manner:

> **You:** Jason, there is something bothering me that I would like to discuss with you.
>
> **Jason:** Go ahead, I don't mind listening to other people's problems.
>
> **You:** My problem concerns something you are doing that makes it difficult for me to concentrate on my work. When you whistle, it distracts me and grates on my nerves. It may be my problem, but the whistling does bother me.
>
> **Jason:** I guess I could stop whistling when you're working next to me. It's probably just a nervous habit. Maybe I can find a less disruptive habit, such as rolling my tongue inside my mouth.

An important advantage of confrontation and problem solving is that you deal directly with a sensitive problem without jeopardizing the chances of forming a constructive working relationship in the future. One reason that the method works so effectively is that the focus is on the problem at hand and not on the individual's personality.

Another approach to confrontation and problem solving is for each side to list what the other side should do. The two parties then exchange lists and select a compromise that both sides are willing to accept. Laying out each side's demands in writing is an effective confrontation technique, especially if the items on the list are laid out factually without angry comments included. Items causing a woman's conflict with her boyfriend might be as follows:

- "Please don't introduce me as 'my current girlfriend.' It makes our relationship sound temporary."

- "Turn off the television set when we talk on the phone."

- "At least once in a while, give me priority over your family when we are scheduling a social event together."

- "Please open and close the car door for me when we are driving in your car."

All these items relate to consideration and respect, so they are part of the same conflict. The partner can then point out where he can grant concessions. Of course, he will have his chance to produce a list.

The intent of confrontation and problem solving is to arrive at a collaborative solution to the conflict. The collaborative style reflects a desire to fully satisfy the desires of both parties. It is based on an underlying philosophy of **win-win,** the belief that after conflict has been resolved, both sides should gain something of value. The user of win-win approaches is genuinely concerned about arriving at a settlement that meets the needs of both parties or at least that does not badly damage the welfare of the other side. When collaborative approaches to resolving conflict are used, the relationships among the parties are built on and improved.

Here is an example of a win-win approach to resolving conflict. A manager granted an employee a few hours off on an occasional Friday afternoon because she was willing to be on call for emergency work on an occasional weekend. Both parties were satisfied with the outcome, and both accomplished their goals.

Human Relations Skill-Building Exercise 7-1 gives you an opportunity to practice the win-win approach to conflict resolution. Confrontation and problem solving typically paves the way for getting to win-win.

Disarm the Opposition

The armament your criticizer has is valid negative criticism of you. The criticizer is figuratively clobbering you with knowledge of what you did wrong. If you deny that you have made a mistake, the criticism intensifies. A simple technique has been developed to help you deal with this type of manipulative criticism. **Disarm the opposition** is a method of conflict resolution in which you disarm the criticizer by agreeing with his or her criticism of you. The technique assumes that you have done something wrong. Disarm

HUMAN RELATIONS SKILL-BUILDING EXERCISE 7-1

Win-Win Conflict Management

The class is organized into groups of six, with each group being divided into conflict resolution teams of three each. The members of the team would like to find a win-win solution to the issue separating each side. The team members are free to invent their own pressing issue or choose among the following:

◆ Management wants to control costs by not giving cost-of-living adjustments in the upcoming year. The employee group believes that a cost-of-living adjustment is absolutely necessary.

◆ The marketing team claims it could sell 250,000 units of a toaster large enough to toast bagels if the toasters could be produced at $15 per unit. The manufacturing group says it would not be feasible to get the manufacturing costs below $20 per unit.

◆ Starbucks Coffee would like to build in a new location, adjacent to a historic district in one of the oldest cities in North America. The members of the town planning board would like the tax revenue and the jobs that the Starbucks store would bring, but they still say they do not want a Starbucks store adjacent to the historic district.

After the teams have developed win-win solutions to the conflicts, the creative solutions can be shared with teammates.

the opposition generally works more effectively than counterattacking a person with whom you are in conflict.

Agreeing with criticism made of you by a manager or team leader is effective because, by so doing, you are in a position to ask that manager's help in improving your performance. Most managers and team leaders recognize that it is their responsibility to help employees to overcome problems, not merely to criticize them. Imagine that you have been chronically late in submitting reports during the last six months. It is time for a performance review and you know you will be reprimanded for your tardiness. You also hope that your boss will not downgrade all other aspects of your performance because of your tardy reports. Here is how disarming the situation would work in this situation:

Your boss:	Have a seat. It's time for your performance review, and we have a lot to talk about. I'm concerned about some things.
You:	So am I. It appears that I'm having a difficult time getting my reports in on time. I wonder if I'm being a perfectionist. Do you have any suggestions?
Your boss:	I like your attitude. I think you can improve on getting your reports in on time. Maybe you are trying to make your reports perfect before you turn them in. Try not to figure out everything to four decimal places. We need thoroughness around here, but we don't want to overdo it.

HUMAN RELATIONS SKILL-BUILDING EXERCISE 7-2

Disarming the Opposition

In each of these two scenarios, one person plays the role of the person with more power in the situation. The other person plays the role of the individual attempting to disarm the criticizer.

♦ A representative from a credit organization telephones you at work to inform you that you are 60 days behind schedule on your car payment. The agent wants a settlement as soon as possible. Unfortunately, the credit agent is correct. Run this happy scenario for about five minutes.

♦ Your manager calls you into the office to discuss the 10-page report you just submitted. The boss says in a harsh tone, "Your report is a piece of trash. I counted 25 word-use mistakes such as writing *whether* for *weather* and *seen* for *scene*. [Your spell checker couldn't catch these errors.] Besides that, I can't follow many of your sentences, and you left out the table of statistics. I'm wondering if you are qualified for this job."

Human Relations Skill-Building Exercise 7-2 gives you an opportunity to practice disarming the opposition. Also, apply the technique the next time you are being criticized for something you actually did wrong.

COGNITIVE RESTRUCTURING

An indirect way of resolving conflict between people is to lessen the conflicting elements in a situation by viewing them more positively. According to the technique of **cognitive restructuring,** you mentally convert negative aspects into positive ones by looking for the positive elements in a situation. The original purpose of cognitive restructuring was to help people overcome automatic, negative thinking about themselves or situations. An example would be recognize that a challenging situation, such as making a presentation in front of a group, is not as bad as it first seems. The idea is to overcome unhealthy thoughts. How you frame or choose your thoughts can determine the outcome of a conflict situation. Your thoughts can influence your actions. If you search for the beneficial elements in a situation, there will be less area for dispute. Although this technique might sound like a *mind game* to you, it can work effectively.

Imagine that a coworker of yours, Jennifer, has been asking you repeated questions about how to carry out a work procedure. You are about ready to tell Jennifer, "Go bother somebody else, I'm not paid to be a trainer." Instead, you look for the positive elements in the situation. You say to yourself, "Jennifer has been asking me a lot of questions. This does take time, but answering these questions is valuable experience. If I want to become a manager, I will have to help group members with problems."

After having completed this cognitive restructuring, you can then deal with the conflict more positively. You might say to Jennifer, "I welcome the opportunity to help you, but we need to find a mutually convenient time. In that way, I can better concentrate on my own work."

Appeal to a Third Party

Now and then you may be placed in a conflict situation in which the other party either holds most of the power or simply won't budge. Perhaps you have tried techniques such as confrontation and problem solving or disarming the opposition, yet you cannot resolve your conflict. In these situations you may have to enlist the help of a third party with power—more power than you or your adversary has. Among such third parties are your common boss, union stewards, or human resource managers. Taking your opponent to court is another application of the third-party technique.

In some situations, just implying that you will bring in a third party to help resolve the conflict situation is sufficient for you to gain advantage. One woman felt she was repeatedly passed over for promotion because of her sex. She hinted that if she were not given fairer consideration, she would speak to the Equal Employment Opportunity Commission (EEOC). She was given a small promotion shortly thereafter. Many conflicts about sexual harassment, as well as ethnic and racial harassment, are resolved through third-party appeal.

The Grievance Procedure

The formal process of filing a complaint and resolving a dispute within an organization is the **grievance procedure.** It can also be regarded as a formal method of resolving conflict, in which a series of third parties are brought into the picture. The third-party appeal described above skips the step-by-step approach of a formal grievance procedure. In a unionized firm, the steps in the grievance procedure are specified in the written contract between management and labor. An example of a grievance about favoritism would be, "I get the worst assignments because I'm not one of the boss's fishing buddies." An example of a grievance about discrimination would be, "I didn't get the transfer to the receptionist job because I'm 55 years old."

The steps in the grievance procedure may vary from one to six, depending on the labor agreement or company procedures. A summary of the typical steps in a grievance procedure is presented next and outlined in Exhibit 7-3. If the company does not have a labor union, a specialist from the human resources department might serve as a third party.

> **Step 1. Initiation of the formal grievance.** Suppose that an employee feels that he or she has been treated unfairly or that his or her rights have been violated in some way. The employee then files a grievance with the supervisor (or team leader). Most grievances end at step 1 by conversation among the employee,

EXHIBIT 7-3

The Grievance Procedure

Step 1: Initiation of formal grievance

> Employee files grievance, and discussion is held with employee, supervisor or team leader, and union steward.

If not settled

Step 2: Second-level manager

> Grievance now goes to next-highest level of management and must be documented in writing by both sides.

If not settled

Step 3: Higher-level manager and local union president

> Higher-level officials from both union and employer step in to settle dispute.

If not settled

Step 4: Arbitration

> Independent arbitrator is called in to settle the issue.

union steward, and the supervisor. At this stage, it makes sense to use some of the techniques for resolving conflict already described.

Step 2.   Second level of management. If the steward, supervisor or team leader, and employee cannot reach a satisfactory solution to the conflict, it goes to the next-highest level in the organization. At this point, the grievance must be documented in writing by both sides. Which people are involved at this level depends on the size of the firm. In a small firm, a high-ranking manager might be involved in step 2.

Step 3.   A higher-level manager and the local union president. If the grievance is not resolved at step 2, higher-level officials from both the union and the employer become involved in settling the dispute. A general principle is that at each higher step in the grievance process, comparable levels of management from both company and union face each other, or a higher-level representative from the human resources department might be involved.

Step 4. **Arbitration.** If the grievance cannot be settled at lower steps, an independent arbitrator may be called in to settle the issue. Only about 1 percent of grievances go all the way to arbitration. Arbitration is often used as an alternative to a strike. The arbitrator has the authority to settle the dispute and must be a person acceptable to both sides.

Mediation is often confused with arbitration. A mediator is a third party who enters a controversy but holds no power of decision. The mediator helps the two sides find a resolution to their conflict. Relatively few labor agreements allow for mediation, yet mediation might be used to settle a strike. A mediator works like a marriage counselor by helping both sides come to agreement by themselves.

A grievance procedure used in many firms without a union is the **jury of peers,** whereby unresolved grievances are submitted to a panel of coworkers. The panel chosen is similar to a jury in a criminal case. Panel members weigh evidence and, after group discussion, vote for or against the grievant. The jury-of-peers method works well when the jury members are knowledgeable about organizational justice.

The grievance processes just described are formal and legalistic. Nevertheless, to represent your interests well, it is helpful to use the informal conflict resolution techniques described above, such as confrontation and problem solving.

Engage in Metacommunication

Many conflict situations take the form of poor communications between the parties involved. In this way resolving conflict and overcoming communication barriers come together. When confronted with a conflict involving communications, one response is to work around the problem by using one of the techniques already described in this chapter or Chapter 6. A more typical response is to ignore the conflict or barrier by making no special effort to deal with it—a "take-it-or-leave-it" approach to communication. Another possibility is to **metacommunicate,** or communicate about the conflicting part of your communications to help overcome barriers or resolve a problem.

Suppose you are the team leader and one of the team members projects angry facial expressions and harsh gestures during your conversation about goals. You might say, "It looks like I'm not getting through to you. What do you dislike about our discussion?" The team member might say, "It's just that you're giving me tougher goals than the other team members. I think I'm being treated unfairly." By metacommunicating, you have laid the groundwork to resolve the conflict over goals.

You can also use metacommunication to take the initiative about aspects of your communication that might create conflict. As a team leader facing heavy deadline pressures, you might say to a team member, "I might appear brusque today and tomorrow. Please don't take it personally. It's just that I have to make heavy demands on you because the team is facing a gruesome deadline."

NEGOTIATION AND BARGAINING TACTICS

Conflicts can be considered situations calling for **negotiating and bargaining,** conferring with another person to resolve a problem. When you are trying to negotiate a fair price for an automobile, you are also trying to resolve a conflict. At first the demands of both parties seem incompatible. After haggling for a while, you will probably reach a price that is satisfactory to both sides.

Negotiation has many applications in the workplace, including buying, selling, arriving at a starting salary or raise, and deciding on a relocation allowance. Negotiation may also take place with coworkers when you need their assistance. For example, you might need to strike a bargain with a coworker to handle some of your responsibilities if you are faced with a temporary overload.

A sampling of negotiating tactics to help you resolve conflict is presented next. As with other techniques of resolving conflict already presented, choose those that best fit your style and the situation.

Create a Positive Negotiating Climate

Negotiation proceeds much more swiftly if a positive tone surrounds the session, so it is helpful to initiate a positive outlook about the negotiation meeting. A good opening line in a negotiating session is, "Thanks for fitting this meeting into your hectic schedule." Nonverbal communication such as smiling and making friendly gestures helps create a positive climate.

In negotiating with coworkers for assistance, a positive climate can often be achieved by phrasing demands as a request for help. Most people will be more accommodating if you say to them, "I have a problem that I wonder if you could help me with." The problem might be that you need the person's time and mental energy. By giving that person a choice of offering you help, you have established a much more positive climate than by demanding assistance.[18]

Allow Room for Compromise, but Be Reasonable

The basic strategy of negotiation is to begin with a demand that allows room for compromise and concession. Anyone who has ever negotiated the price of an automobile, house, or used furniture recognizes this vital strategy. If you are a buyer, begin with a low bid. (You say, "I'll give you $60 for that painting" when you are prepared to pay $90.) If you are the seller, begin with a high demand. (You say, "You can have this painting for $130" when you are ready to sell it for as low as $100.) As negotiations proceed, the two of you will

COMMON SENSE PROPELS MANY NEGOTIATORS
TO ALLOW **TOO MUCH** ROOM FOR COMPROMISE

probably arrive at a mutually satisfactory price. This negotiating strategy can also be used for such purposes as obtaining a higher starting salary or dividing property after a divorce or legal separation.

Common sense propels many negotiators to allow *too much* room for compromise. They begin negotiations by asking way beyond what they expect to receive or offering far less than they expect to give. As a result of these implausible demands, the other side may become hostile, antagonistic, or walk away from the negotiations. Assume you spotted a DVD/VCR that you really wanted in a retail store. The asking price was $298.95. In an attempt to negotiate the price, you offered the store manager $98.95 for the DVD/VCR. Most likely the store manager would move on to the next customer. However, if you began with a plausible offer such as $240, the store manager would take you seriously. Beginning with a plausible demand or offer is also important because it contributes to a positive negotiating climate.

Focus on Interests, Not Positions

Rather than clinging to specific negotiating points, keep your overall interests in mind and try to satisfy them. A negotiating point might be a certain amount of money or a concession that you must have. Remember that the true object of negotiation is to satisfy the underlying interests of both sides. Among the interests you and the other side might be trying to protect include money, lifestyle, power, or the status quo. For example, instead of negotiating for a particular starting salary, your true interests might be to afford a certain lifestyle. If the company pays all your medical and dental coverage, you can get by with a lower salary. Or your cost of living might be much lower in one city than in another. You can therefore accept a lower starting salary in the city with a lower cost of living.

Make a Last and Final Offer

In many circumstances, presenting a final offer will break a deadlock. You might frame your message something like this. "All I can possibly pay for your guitar is $250. You have my number. Call me when it is available at that price." Sometimes the strategy will be countered by a last and final offer from the other side: "Thanks for your interest. My absolute minimum price for this guitar is $300. Call us if that should seem OK to you." One of you will probably give in and accept the other person's last and final offer.

Role-Play to Predict What the Other Side Will Do

An advanced negotiating technique is to prepare in advance by forecasting what the other side will demand or offer. Two professors from New Zealand have discovered that when people role-play conflicts, their ability to predict outcomes jumps remarkably. The researchers presented 290 participants with descriptions of six actual conflicts and asked them to choose the most likely eventual decisions. The conflicts involved labor-management, commercial, and civil disputes. Five of these conflicts were chosen for role playing. Without the use of role playing, the participants did not much better than chance, with a 27 percent success ratio. Next, the researchers asked 21 international game theorists (specialist in predicting outcomes of events) to forecast the conflict outcomes. The game theorists were correct only 28 percent of the time. (Chance here would be 1/5, or 20 percent.)

Next, 352 students were instructed to role-play the conflicts in the five situations. The average correct decision was 61 percent versus 27 percent for the comparable group. The authors note that in over 40 years of studying forecasting, they have never seen a technique that led to such improvement in predictive accuracy.[19]

The implication for making you a better negotiator is to role-play with a friend in advance of the negotiating session you will be facing. The role play should help you predict what the other side and you will do so you will be better prepared. For example, if your role play suggests that the company would be willing to give you a 15 percent bonus for incredible performance, ask for a 15 percent bonus.

Allow for Face-Saving

We have saved one of the most important negotiating and conflict resolution strategies for last. Negotiating does not mean that you should try to squash the other side. You should try to create circumstances that will enable you to continue working with that person if it is necessary. People prefer to avoid looking weak, foolish, or incompetent during negotiation or when the process is completed. If you do not give your opponent an opportunity to save face, you will probably create a long-term enemy.

Face-saving could work in this way. A small-business owner winds up purchasing a network system for about twice what he originally budgeted. After the sale is completed, the sales rep says, "I know you bought a more professional networking rig than you originally intended. Yet I know you made the right decision. You will be able to do boost productivity enough with the networked PCs to pay back the cost of the networking system in two years."

▲ DEVELOPING ASSERTIVENESS

Several of the techniques for resolving conflict require assertiveness. Without being forthright, confrontation and problem solving could not be achieved. Effective negotiation would also be difficult because assertiveness is required to carefully explain your demands. Learning to express your feelings and make your demands known is also an important aspect of becoming an effective individual in general. Expressing your feelings helps you establish good relationships with people. If you aren't sharing your feelings and attitudes with other people, you will never get close to them.

Another benefit from being emotionally expressive and, therefore, assertive is that you get more of what you want in life. If you are too passive, people will neglect giving you what you want. Often it is necessary to ask someone when you want a raise, promotion, date, or better deal on a bank loan. Successful people usually make their demands known yet throw tantrums only for an occasional effect and rarely bully others. (Exceptions include flamboyant trial lawyers and athletic coaches.)

Let's examine the nature of assertiveness and then describe several techniques for building assertiveness. However, first take Human Relations Self-Assessment Quiz 7-1 to relate assertiveness to yourself.

Assertive, Nonassertive, and Aggressive Behavior

As implied above, **assertive** people state clearly what they want or how they feel in a given situation without being abusive, abrasive, or obnoxious. People who are assertive are open, honest, and "up front" because they believe that all people have an equal right to express themselves honestly. Assertive behavior can be understood more fully by comparing it to that shown by two other types of people. **Nonassertive** people let things happen to them without letting their feelings be known. **Aggressive** people are obnoxious and overbearing. They push for what they want with almost no regard for the feelings of others.

Another representative assertive behavior is to ask for clarification rather than contradicting a person with whom you disagree. The assertive person asks for clarification when another person says something irritating

HUMAN RELATIONS SELF-ASSESSMENT QUIZ 7-1

The Assertiveness Scale

Answer each question Mostly True or Mostly False as it applies to you.

		Mostly True	Mostly False
1.	It is extremely difficult for me to turn down a sales representative when that individual is a nice person.	____	____
2.	I express criticism freely.	____	____
3.	If another person were being very unfair, I would bring it to that person's attention.	____	____
4.	Work is no place to let your feelings show.	____	____
5.	No use asking for favors; people get what they deserve on the job.	____	____
6.	Business is not the place for tact; I say what I think.	____	____
7.	If a person looked as if he or she were in a hurry, I would let that person go in front of me in a supermarket line.	____	____
8.	A weakness of mine is that I'm too nice a person.	____	____
9.	I answer any e-mail message right away, even if it means that I fall behind in my other work.	____	____
10.	I have laughed out loud in public more than once.	____	____
11.	I've been described as too outspoken by several people.	____	____
12.	I have no misgivings about returning merchandise that has even the slightest defect.	____	____
13.	I dread having to express anger toward a coworker.	____	____
14.	People often say that I'm too reserved and emotionally controlled.	____	____
15.	Nice guys and gals finish last in business.	____	____
16.	I fight for my rights down to the last detail.	____	____
17.	If I disagree with a grade on a test or paper, I typically bring my disagreement to my instructor's attention.	____	____
18.	If I have had an argument with a person, I try to avoid him or her.	____	____
19.	I insist on my spouse (or roommate or partner) doing his or her fair share of undesirable chores.	____	____
20.	It is difficult for me to look directly at another person when the two of us are in disagreement.	____	____

(Continued)

21. I have cried among friends more than once. _____ _____

22. If someone near me at a movie kept up a conversation with another person, I would ask him or her to stop. _____ _____

23. I am able to turn down social engagements with people I do not particularly care for. _____ _____

24. It is in poor taste to express what you really feel about another individual. _____ _____

25. I sometimes show my anger by swearing at or belittling another person. _____ _____

26. I am reluctant to speak up in a meeting. _____ _____

27. I find it relatively easy to ask friends for small favors such as giving me a lift to work while my car is being repaired. _____ _____

28. If another person were talking very loudly in a restaurant and it bothered me, I would inform that person. _____ _____

29. I often finish other people's sentences for them. _____ _____

30. It is relatively easy for me to express love and affection toward another person. _____ _____

Scoring and Interpretation: Give yourself plus 1 for each of your answers that agrees with the scoring key. If your score is 16 or less, it is probable that you are currently a nonassertive individual. A score of 17 through 24 suggests that you are an assertive individual. A score of 25 or higher suggests that you are an aggressive individual. Retake this score about 30 days from now to give yourself some indication of the stability of your answers. You might also discuss your answers with a close friend to determine if that person has a similar perception of your assertiveness. Here is the scoring key.

1. Mostly False	11. Mostly True	21. Mostly True
2. Mostly True	12. Mostly True	22. Mostly True
3. Mostly True	13. Mostly False	23. Mostly True
4. Mostly False	14. Mostly False	24. Mostly False
5. Mostly False	15. Mostly True	25. Mostly True
6. Mostly True	16. Mostly True	26. Mostly False
7. Mostly False	17. Mostly True	27. Mostly True
8. Mostly False	18. Mostly False	28. Mostly True
9. Mostly False	19. Mostly True	29. Mostly True
10. Mostly True	20. Mostly False	30. Mostly True

EXHIBIT 7-4

Assertive, Nonassertive, and Aggressive Gestures

Assertive	*Nonassertive*	*Aggressive*
Well balanced	Covering mouth with hand	Pounding fists
Straight posture	Excessive head nodding	Stiff and rigid posture
Hand gestures, emphasizing key words	Tinkering with clothing or jewelry	Finger waving or pointing
Moderately loud voice	Constant shifting of weight	Shaking head as if other person isn't to be believed
	Scratching or rubbing head or other parts of body	Hands on hips
	Wooden body posture	Voice louder than needed, fast speech
	Voice too soft with frequent pauses	

---

rather than hurling insults or telling the other person he or she is wrong.[20] For example, assume someone says to you, "Your proposal is useless." Aggressively telling the person, "You have no right to make that judgment," shuts out any possible useful dialogue. You will probably learn more if you ask for clarification, such as "What is wrong with my proposal?"

Suppose a stranger invites you to a party and you do not wish to go with that person. Here are the three ways of responding according to the three-way classification under discussion:

Assertive: Thank you for the invitation, but I prefer not to go.
Nonassertive: I'm not sure, I might be busy. Could you call me again? Maybe I'll know for sure by then.
Aggressive: I'd like to go to a party, but not with you. Don't bother me again.

Gestures, as well as words, can communicate whether the person is being assertive, nonassertive, or aggressive. Exhibit 7-4 illustrates these differences.

BECOMING MORE ASSERTIVE AND LESS SHY

Shyness is widespread, and about 50 percent of the American population is shyer than they want to be. The personality trait of shyness has positive aspects, such as leading a person to think more deeply and become involved in ideas and things. (Where would the world be today if Bill Gates weren't shy as a youth?) However, shyness can also create discomfort and lower self-esteem.[21] There are a number of everyday actions a person can take to overcome being nonassertive or shy. Even if the actions described here do not elevate your assertiveness, they will not backfire and cause you discomfort. After reading the following six techniques, you might be able to think of others that will work for you.[22]

1. Set a goal. Clearly establish in your mind how you want to behave differently. Do you want to date more often? Speak out more in meetings? Be able to express dissatisfaction to coworkers? You can overcome shyness only by behaving differently; feeling differently is not enough.

2. Appear warm and friendly. Shy people often communicate to others through their body language that they are not interested in reaching out to others. To overcome this impression, smile, lean forward, uncross your arms and legs, and unfold your hands.

3. Make legitimate telephone calls to strangers. Telephone conversations with strangers that have a legitimate purpose can help you start expressing yourself to people you do not know well. You might call numbers listed in classified ads to inquire about articles listed for sale. Try a positive approach: "Hello, my name is _____. I'd like to know about the condition of that piano you have for sale." Call the gas and electric company to inquire about a problem with your bill. Make telephone inquiries about employment opportunities in a firm of your choice. Call the library with reference questions. Call the federal government bureau in your town with questions about laws and regulations. With practice, you will probably become more adept at speaking to strangers. You will then be ready for a more challenging self-improvement task.

4. Conduct anonymous conversations. Try starting a conversation with strangers in a safe setting such as a sporting event, the waiting room of a medical office, or a waiting line at the post office or supermarket. Begin the conversation with the common experience you are sharing at the time. Among them might be:

"How many people do you estimate are in the audience?"

"How long does it usually take before you get to see the doctor?"

"Where did you get that shopping bag? I've never seen one so sturdy before."

5. Greet strangers. For the next week or so, greet many of the people you pass. Smile and make a neutral comment such as "How ya doing?" or "Great day, isn't it." Since most people are unaccustomed to being greeted by a stranger, you may get a few quizzical looks. Many other people may smile and return your greeting. A few of these greetings may turn into conversations. A few conversations may even turn into friendships. Even if the return on your investment in greetings is only a few pleasant responses, it will boost your confidence.

HUMAN RELATIONS SKILL-BUILDING EXERCISE 7-3

Becoming More Assertive by Being Decisive

An important part of being assertive is to be decisive. To enhance your decisiveness, follow these steps:

1. Make a list of the requests people make of you that are a burden. Review the list and select one or two requests that you will refuse in the next week. Think about how you will politely but firmly inform someone of your need to say "no," then carry out your plan. What happened? Did you feel less guilty than you thought you would?

2. Review the requests you want to make of others to help you meet your own needs. Select one or two. Get clear in your mind what you specifically want. Formulate each request so that it is as reasonable as possible for the person you will ask, then make your request(s). Did you get a positive response? Are you happy with the support you obtained?

SOURCE: Adapted from Mel Silberman, with Freda Hansburg, *PeopleSmart: Developing Your Interpersonal Intelligence* (San Francisco: Berrett-Koehler Publishers, 2000), pp. 90–91.

---

6. Practice being decisive. An assertive person is usually decisive, so it is important to practice being decisive. Some nonassertive people are even indecisive when asked to make a choice from a restaurant memo. They communicate their indecisiveness by asking their friend, "What are you going to have?" or asking the server, "Could you please suggest something for me?" or "What's good?" Practice quickly sizing up the alternatives in any situation and reaching a decision. This will help you be assertive and also project an image of assertiveness. Human Relations Skill-Building Exercise 7-3 is designed to improve decisiveness.

▲ SUMMARY

Conflict occurs when two sets of demands, goals, or motives are incompatible. Such differences often lead to a hostile or antagonistic relationship between people. A conflict can also be considered a dispute, feud, or controversy.

Among the reasons for widespread conflict are (1) competition for limited resources; (2) the generation gap and personality clashes; (3) aggressive personalities including bullies; (4) culturally diverse teams; (5) competing work and family demands; and (6) sexual harassment. Many companies have programs to help their employees reduce work–family conflict including flexible work schedules and dependent care. Such programs increase productivity. Sexual harassment is of two types: quid pro quo (a demand for sexual favors in exchange for job benefits) and creating a hostile environment. It is important for workers to understand what actions and words constitute sexual harassment and how to deal with the problem.

The benefits of conflict include the emergence of talents and abilities, constructive innovation and change, and increased unity after the conflict is settled. Among the detrimental consequences of conflict are physical and mental health problems, wasted resources, the promotion of self-interest, and workplace violence.

Techniques for resolving conflicts with others include the following:

1. Confrontation and problem solving leading to win-win—get to the root of the problem and resolve it systematically. The intention of confrontation and problem solving is to arrive at a collaborative solution to the conflict.

2. Disarm the opposition—agree with the criticizer and enlist his or her help.

3. Cognitive restructuring—mentally converting negative aspects into positive ones by looking for the positive elements in a situation.

4. Appeal to a third party (such as a government agency).

5. The grievance procedure (a formal organizational procedure for dispute resolution).

6. Engage in metacommunications—talk about your conflict and differences in communication.

7. Use negotiation and bargaining tactics.

Negotiation and bargaining tactics include (1) creating a positive negotiating climate; (2) allowing room for compromise but being reasonable; (3) focusing on interests, not positions; (4) making a last and final offer; (5) role-playing to predict what the other side will do; and (6) allowing for face-saving.

Several of the techniques for resolving conflict require assertiveness, or stating clearly what you want and how you feel in a given situation. Being assertive also helps you develop good relationships with people and get more of what you want in life. People can become more assertive and less shy by using techniques such as (1) setting a goal; (2) appearing warm and friendly; (3) conducting legitimate phone conversations with strangers; (4) greeting strangers; and (5) practicing being decisive.

Questions and Activities

1. Why are conflict resolution skills considered so important in a culturally diverse workplace?

2. Give an example from your own life of how competition for limited resources can breed conflict.

3. Some conflicts go on for decades without being resolved, such as groups in North America fighting the government over the right to fish for lobsters where and when they want. Why is it so difficult to resolve such conflicts?

4. Many male managers who confer with a female worker in their offices leave the door open to avoid any charges of sexual harassment. Are these managers using good judgment, or are they being overly cautious?

5. Why is it that during a game, professional athletes touch, hug, and kiss each other yet such behavior is frowned on or forbidden in other workplaces, such as the office or factory?

6. Identify several occupations in which conflict resolution skills are particularly important.

7. How might a person use cognitive restructuring to help deal with the conflict of having received a below-average raise yet expecting an above-average raise?

8. What is your explanation of the research showing that role-playing a negotiation scenario helps people make more accurate predictions about the outcome of conflicts? (You might find some information in Chapter 6 about communications that would provide a possible clue.)

9. You are dining in an expensive restaurant with a special person in your life. A person seated at the next table starts making a series of calls, in a loud voice, on his cell telephone. You and your partner are upset about the calls interrupting your romantic dinner. Make up an assertive statement to tell the phone caller how you feel.

10. Ask a successful person how much conflict he or she experiences in balancing the demands of work and personal life. Be prepared to report your findings in class.

INTERNET SKILL BUILDER: Negotiating for a Raise or Other Benefit

To acquire several concepts that you might use to enhance your negotiating skills, visit www.negotiationskills.com/workplace.html. You will be advised to prepare for negotiation in the future by first building a good relationship with the boss and understanding your value to the organization. After reviewing the information about negotiating for a raise and negotiating a situation with a coworker, jot down two key points you have learned. How do these concepts compare to the ideas presented about negotiation in the text?

HUMAN RELATIONS CASE PROBLEM

Caught in a Squeeze

Heather Lopez is a product development specialist at a telecommunications company. For the last seven months she has worked as a member of a product development team composed of people from five different departments within the company. Heather's previously worked full time in the marketing department. Her primary responsibilities were to research the market potential of an idea for a new product. The product development team is now working on a product that will integrate a company's printers and copiers.

Heather's previous position in the marketing department was a satisfactory fit for her lifestyle. Heather thought that she was able to take care of her family responsibilities and her job without sacrificing one for the other. As Heather explains, "I worked about 45 predictable hours in my other job. My hours were essentially 8:30 A.M. to 4:30 P.M. with a little work at night and on Saturdays. But I could do the work at night and on Saturdays at home."

"Brad, my husband, and I had a smooth-working arrangement for sharing the responsibility for getting our son Christopher off to school and picking him up from the after-school child care center. Brad is a devoted accountant, so he understands the importance of giving high priority to a career yet still being a good family person."

In her new position as a member of the product-development team, Heather is encountering some unanticipated demands. Three weeks ago, at 3 P.M. on a Tuesday, Tyler Watson, Heather's team leader, announced an emergency meeting to discuss a budget problem with the new product. The meeting would start at 4 and probably end at about 6:30. "Don't worry folks," said the team leader, "if it looks like we are going past 6:30, we will order in some Chinese food."

With a look of panic on her face, Heather responded to Tyler, "I can't make the meeting. Christopher will be expecting me at about 5 at the child care center. My husband is out of town, and the center closes at 6 sharp. So count me out of today's meeting."

Tyler said, "I said that this is an emergency meeting and that we need input from all the members. You need to organize your personal life better to be a contributing member to this team. But do what you have to do, at least this once."

Heather chose to leave the office at 4:30 so she could pick up Christopher. The next day, Tyler did not comment on her absence. However, he gave her a copy of the minutes and asked for her input. The budget problem surfaced again one week later. Top-level management asked the group to reduce the cost of the new product and its initial marketing costs by 15 percent.

Tyler said to the team on a Friday morning, "We have until Monday morning to arrive at a reduced cost structure on our product development. I am dividing up the project into segments. If we meet as a team Saturday morning at 8, we should get the job done by 6 at night. Get a good night's rest so we can start fresh tomorrow morning. Breakfast and lunch will be on the company."

Heather could feel stress overwhelming her body, as she thought to herself, "Christopher is playing in the finals of his Little League soccer match tomorrow morning at 10. Brad has made dinner reservations for 6, so we can make it to the *Phantom*

(Continued)

of the Opera at 8 P.M. Should I tell Tyler he is being unreasonable? Should I quit? Should I tell Christopher and Brad that our special occasions together are less important than a Saturday business meeting?"

Questions

1. What type of conflicts is Heather facing?

2. What should Heather do to resolve her conflicts with respect to family and work responsibilities?

3. What should the company do to help deal with the type of conflict Heather is facing? Or should the company not consider Heather's dilemma to be their problem?

WEB CORNER

Cognitive restructuring:
www.garyflegal.com/cognitive_restructuring.htm

Shyness: www.shyness.com

HUMAN RELATIONS SKILL-BUILDING EXERCISE 7-4

Conflict Resolution

Imagine that Heather in the case just presented, decides that her job is taking too big a toll on her personal life. However, she still values her job and does not want to quit. She decides to discuss her problem with her team leader Tyler. From Tyler's standpoint, a professional person must stand ready to meet unusual job demands and cannot expect an entirely predictable work schedule. One person plays the role of Heather and another the role of Tyler as they attempt to resolve this incident of work–family conflict.

▲ REFERENCES

1. Kathleen Driscoll, "Manager Must Confront Disrespectful Employee, or Behavior Will Not Improve," *Rochester (NY) Democrat and Chronicle,* May 10, 1995, p. 1D.

2. Deborah Smith, "Strength in Collaboration," *Monitor on Psychology,* December 2001, p. 60.

3. Katharine Mieskowski, "Generation 8##@88##@!!, *Fast Company,* October 1999, pp. 106–108; Lynne C. Lancaster and David Stillman, *When Generations Collide: Who They Are, Why They Clash* (New York: HarperBusiness, 2002).

4. Stillman, *When Generations Collide,* as quoted in Andrea Sachs, "Generation Hex?" *Time,* March 2002, p. Y22.

5. Dominic A. Infante, *Arguing Constructively* (Prospects Heights, IL: Waveland Press, 1992).

6. Survey reported in Jessica Guynn, "Bullying Behavior Affects Morale as Well as Bottom Line," Knight-Ridder, November 2, 1998.

7. Gillian Flynn, "Employers Can't Look Away from Workplace Violence," *Workforce,* July 2000, p. 68.

8. Quoted in Sybil Evans, "Conflict Can Be Positive," *HR Magazine,* May 1992, p. 50.

9. Angela Pirisi, "Teamwork: The Downside of Diversity," *Psychology Today,* November/December 1999, p. 18.

10. Virginia Smith Major, Katherine J. Klein, and Mark G. Ehrhart, "Work Time, Work Interference with Family, and Psychological Distress," *Journal of Applied Psychology,* June 2002, pp. 427–436.

11. "When Work and Private Lives Collide," *Workforce,* February 1999, p. 27.

12. Keith H. Hammonds, "Balancing Work and Family," *BusinessWeek,* September 16, 1996, p. 75.

13. Majorie L. Icenogle, Bruce W. Eagle, Sohel Ahaman, and Lisa A. Hanks, "Assessing Perceptions of Sexual Harassment Behaviors in a Manufacturing Environment," *Journal of Business and Psychology,* Summer 2002, pp. 601–616.

14. Kimberly T. Schneider, Suzanne Swan, and Louise F. Fitzgerald, "Job-Related and Psychological Effects of Sexual Harassment in the Workplace: Empirical Evidence in Two Organizations," *Journal of Applied Psychology,* June 1997, p. 406.

15. Theresa M. Glomb, Liberty J. Munson, and Charles L. Hulin, "Structural Equation Models of Sexual Harassment: Longitudinal Explorations and Cross-Sectional Generalizations," *Journal of Applied Psychology,* February 1999, pp. 14–28.

16. Jennifer A. Sommers, Terry L. Schell, and Stephen J. Vodanovich, "Developing a Measure of Individual Differences in Organizational Revenge," *Journal of Business and Psychology,* Winter 2002, pp. 207–222.

17. "Right and Wrong Ways to Manage Conflict," *Manager's Edge,* October 2001, p. 5.

18. Joseph D'O'Brian, "Negotiating with Peers: Consensus, Not Power," *Supervisory Management,* January 1992, p. 4.

19. J. Scott Armstrong, "Forecasting in Conflicts: How to Predict What Your Opponents Will Do," *Knowledge@Wharton,* February 13, 2002.

20. "Use Assertiveness, Not Aggression," *Working Smart,* November 1998, p. 2.

21. Bernardo J. Carducci, *Shyness: A Bold Approach* (New York: HarperCollins, 1999).

22. Philip Zimbardo, *Shyness: What It Is, What␣to Do about It* (Reading, MA: Addison-Wesley, 1977), pp. 220–226; Mel Silberman with Freda Hansburg, *PeopleSmart* (San Francisco: Berrett-Koehler Publishers, 2000), pp. 75–76.

▲ ADDITIONAL READING

Blackard, Kirk, and James W. Gibson. *Capitalizing on Conflict: Strategies for Turning Conflict to Synergy in Organizations.* Palo Alto, CA: Davies-Black, 2002.

Cloke, Kenneth, and Joan Goldsmith. *Resolving Conflicts at Work: A Complete Guide for Everyone on the Job.* San Francisco: Jossey-Bass, 2000.

Fisher, Roger, Elizabeth Kopelman, and Andrea Kupfer Schneider. *Beyond Machiavelli: Tools for Coping with Conflict.* Cambridge, MA: Harvard University Press, 2000.

Janove, Jathan W. "Sexual Harassment and the Three Big Surprises." *HR Magazine,* November 2001, pp. 123–130.

Landau, Sy, Barbara Landau, and Daryl Landau. *From Conflict to Creativity: How Resolving Workplace Disagreement Can Inspire Innovation and Productivity.* San Francisco: Jossey-Bass, 2002.

Magley, Vicki J., Charles L. Hulin, Louise F. Fitzgerald, and Mary Denardo. "Outcomes of Self-Labeling Sexual Harassment." *Journal of Applied Psychology,* June 1999, pp. 390–402.

Nugent, Patrick S. "Managing Conflict: Third-Party Interventions for Managers." *Academy of Management Executive,* February 2002, pp. 139–155.

Rosa, Antonio José, and Michael G. Pratt. "Transforming Work-Family Conflict into Commitment in Network Marketing Organizations." *Academy of Management Executive,* August 2003, pp. 395–418.

Segal, Jonathan A. "The 'I Hate You' Defense." *HR Magazine,* October 2002, pp. 125–133.

Winters, Jeffrey. "The Daddy Track: Men Who Take Family Leave May Get Frowned upon at the Office." *Psychology Today,* October 2001, p. 18.

CHAPTER
8

Getting Along with Your Manager, Coworkers, and Customers

Learning Objectives

After reading the information and doing the exercises in this chapter, you should be able to:

◆ Select several tactics for developing a good relationship with your manager or team leader

◆ Deal effectively with a problem manager

◆ Describe methods of getting along with coworkers

◆ Identify tactics that help a person become a good team player

◆ Pinpoint tactics for dealing effectively with difficult people

◆ Specify approaches to building good relationships with customers

*T*he Fuller Brush man knew what he was doing. In the old days, Fuller's door-to-door salesmen learned a basic rule: After you ring the bell, take a step or two backward. That way, the woman of the house won't feel intimidated opening the door for a stranger. It wasn't just a tactic though. It was a strategy—one designed to help the company grow by treating people with respect, in contrast to rival salesmen who were taught to jam a foot in the door.

Imagine the Fuller Brush man trying to make a living today as a telemarketer, a spammer, or any of the high-pressure salespeople who jam their electronic feet in people's doors. He would last about three minutes. He's not selfish enough, not eager enough to steal the customer's time. It's a shame, but in the battle to make our businesses grow, we've forgotten how to respect the people who pay our bills.[1]

You may not agree that so many salespeople today are ruthless, yet the anecdote about the Fuller Brush salesperson of yesteryear sends an important message about having workplace relationships characterized by respect and caring. Developing effective relationships with work associates, including customers, has been framed as having good **political skills,** an interpersonal style that combines awareness of others with the ability to communicate well. People with political skill are charming and engaging, which inspires confidence, trust, and sincerity.[2]

This chapter presents information about developing productive relationships with three major groups of work associates: managers, coworkers, and customers. Along the way, we include information about coping with difficult bosses and coworkers.

▲ DEVELOPING A GOOD RELATIONSHIP WITH YOUR MANAGER OR TEAM LEADER

Getting along well with your manager is the most basic strategy of getting ahead in your career. If you cannot gain favor with the boss, it will be difficult to advance to higher positions or earn much more money. The boss might be more of a traditional boss, such as a person with the title of manager or supervisor. Or the boss might be a team leader who typically has less formal authority than a manager or supervisor. Your manager or team leader is always the person who is contacted first when someone wants to determine what kind of employee you are. Usually this information is sought when you are being considered for transfer, promotion, or a position with another firm.

Getting along with the boss is particularly important when the economy is sluggish. Workers who have good relationships with their manager have more job security than those with poor relationships. Vince Waldron, a researcher in workplace relationships, observes that employees must tend to their workplace relationships, going out of their way to communicate with managers and seek feedback on their performance.[3]

In this section we present a variety of approaches that lead to constructive relationships with an immediate superior. The goal is to be legitimately perceived as a strong contributor to your work unit.

ACHIEVE GOOD JOB PERFORMANCE

Good job performance remains the most effective strategy for impressing your manager. When any rational manager evaluates a group member's performance, the first question asked is, "Is this employee getting the job done?" And you cannot get the job done if you are not competent. Many factors contribute to whether you can become a competent performer. Among them are your education, training, personality characteristics, job experience, and special skills, such as being able to organize your work.

An advanced way of displaying good job performance is to assist your manager with a difficult problem he or she faces. Your manager, for example, might need to operate equipment outside his or her area of expertise. If you show the manager how to operate the equipment, he or she will think highly of your job performance. Another example would be helping your manager get ready for an important meeting with higher management by you preparing the PowerPoint slides.

DISPLAY A STRONG WORK ETHIC

In Chapter 2, a strong work ethic was described as a contributor to self-motivation. (A strong **work ethic** is a firm belief in the dignity and value of work.) Having a strong work ethic is also important for favorably impressing a manager. An employee with a strong work ethic will sometimes be excused if his or her performance is not yet exceptional. This is true because the manager assumes that a strong work ethic will elevate performance eventually. Six suggestions follow for demonstrating a strong work ethic.

1. *Work hard and enjoy the task.*   By definition, a person with a strong work ethic works diligently and has strong internal motivation. The person may appreciate external rewards yet appreciates the importance of any work that adds value to society.

2. *Demonstrate competence even on minor tasks.*   Attack each assignment with the recognition that each task performed well, however minor, is one more career credit. A minor task performed well paves the way for your being given more consequential tasks.

3. *Assume personal responsibility for problems.*   An employee with a problem will often approach the manager and say, "We have a tough problem to deal with." The connotation is that the manager should be helping the employee with the problem. A better impression is created when the employee says, "I have a tough problem to deal with, and I would like your advice." This statement implies that you are willing to assume responsibility for the problem and for any mistake you may have made that led to the problem.

4. *Assume responsibility for free-floating problems.*   A natural way to display a strong work ethic is to assume responsibility for free-floating (nonassigned) problems. Taking on even a minor task, such as ordering lunch for a meeting that is running late, can enhance the impression one makes on a manager.

5. *Get your projects completed promptly.*   A by-product of a strong work ethic is an eagerness to get projects completed promptly. People with a strong work ethic respect deadlines imposed by others. Furthermore, they typically set deadlines of their own more tightly than those imposed by their bosses.

6. *Accept undesirable assignments willingly.*   Another way of expressing a strong work ethic is to accept undesirable assignments willingly. Look for ways to express the attitude, "Whether this assignment is glamorous and fun is a secondary issue. What counts is that it is something that needs doing for the good of the company."

Demonstrate Good Emotional Intelligence

Dealing effectively with feelings and emotions is a big challenge in the workplace. Such behavior reflects emotional intelligence, defined in Chapter 5. Emotional intelligence can also be regarded as the use of nonverbal cues, emotions, feelings, and mood. The person with good emotional intelligence recognizes and understands his or her own feelings and those of others.

Demonstrating good emotional intelligence is impressive because it contributes to performing well in the difficult arena of dealing with feelings. A worker with good emotional intelligence would engage in such behaviors as (1) recognizing when a coworker needs help but is too embarrassed to ask for help, (2) dealing with the anger of a dissatisfied customer, (3) recognizing that the boss is facing considerable pressure also, and (4) being able to tell whether a customer's "maybe" means "yes" or "no."

Be Dependable and Honest

Dependability is a critical employee virtue. If an employee can be counted on to deliver as promised and to be at work regularly, that employee has gone a long way toward impressing the boss. A boss is uncomfortable not knowing whether an important assignment will be accomplished on time. If you are not dependable, you will probably not get your share of important assignments. Honesty is tied to dependability because a dependable employee is honest about when he or she will have an assignment completed. Dependability and honesty are important at all job levels. One of the highest compliments a manager can pay an employee is to describe the employee as dependable. Conversely, it is considered derogatory to call any employee undependable. As one company president put it when describing a subordinate, "When he's great, he's terrific; but I can't depend on him. I'd rather he be more consistent even if he delivered fewer peak successes—at least I could rely on him."[4]

BE A GOOD ORGANIZATIONAL CITIZEN

An especially meritorious approach to impressing key people is to demonstrate **organizational citizenship behavior,** the willingness to work for the good of the organization even without the promise of a specific reward. Among the characteristics of a good organizational citizen are conscientiousness, altruism (wanting to help others), courteous behavior, and sportsmanship. A good organizational citizen would do such things as assist a person with a computer problem outside his or her team or department or picking up a broken bottle on the company lawn. Organizational citizenship behavior is increasing in importance as organizations face the challenge of global competition and the need for continuous innovation. The good organizational citizen goes "above and beyond the call of duty."[5]

An effective way of being a good organizational citizen is step outside your job description. Job descriptions are characteristic of a well-organized firm. If everybody knows what he or she is supposed to be doing, there will be much less confusion, and goals will be achieved. This logic sounds impressive, but job descriptions have a major downside. If people engage only in work included in their job description, an "it's not my job" mentality pervades. An effective way to impress your manager is therefore to demonstrate that you are not constrained by a job description. If something needs doing, you will get it done whether or not it is your formal responsibility.

An impressive way of stepping outside your job description is to anticipate problems, even when the manager had not planned to work on them. Anticipating problems is characteristic of a resourceful person who exercises initiative. Instead of working exclusively on problems that have been assigned, the worker is perceptive enough to look for future problems. Anticipating problems impresses most managers because it reflects an entrepreneurial, take-charge attitude.

CREATE A STRONG PRESENCE

A comprehensive approach to impressing your manager or team leader and other key people in the workplace is to create a strong presence, keeping yourself in the forefront. Such actions impress key people and simultaneously help advance your career. Stephanie Sherman, a career consultant, offers this advice for creating a strong presence:

- Get involved in high-visibility projects, such as launching a new product or redesigning work methods. Even an entry-level position on such a project can help a worker get noticed.

- Get involved in teams because they give you an opportunity to broaden your skills and knowledge.

- Get involved in social and community activities of interest to top management, such as those sponsored by the company. Behave professionally and use your best manners.

- Create opportunities for yourself by making constructive suggestions about earning or saving money. Even if an idea is rejected, you will still be remembered for your initiative.

- Show a willingness to take on some of the tasks that your manager doesn't like to do but would be forced to do if you did not step in.[6]

Find Out What Your Manager Expects of You

You have little chance of doing a good job and impressing your manager unless you know what you are trying to accomplish. Work goals and performance standards represent the most direct ways of learning your manager's expectations. A **performance standard** is a statement of what constitutes acceptable performance. These standards can sometimes be inferred from a job description. Review your work goals and ask clarifying questions. An example would be, "You told me to visit our major customers who are 60 days or more delinquent on their accounts. Should I also visit the three of these customers who have declared bankruptcy?" In addition to having a clear statement of your goals, it is helpful to know the priorities attached to them. In this way you will know which task to execute first.

A subtle aspect of understanding the expectations of your boss is adapting to his or her preferred style of work. Managers vary in terms of wanting written versus oral briefings. Some managers prefer to receive e-mail messages from you regularly, others once a week. Some managers want to be treated informally, much like being a coworker. A minority of managers wanted to be treated as if they were royalty. Matching your work style to the work style of your boss can help build a strong relationship between the two of you.

Minimize Complaints

In the previous chapter, we extolled the virtues of being open and honest in expressing your feelings and opinions. Nevertheless, this type of behavior, when carried to excess, could earn you a reputation as a whiner. Few managers want to have a group member around who constantly complains about working conditions, coworkers, working hours, pay, and so forth. An employee who complains too loudly and frequently quickly becomes labeled a pill or a pest.

Another important reason a boss usually dislikes having a subordinate who complains too much is that listening to these complaints takes up considerable time. Most managers spend a disproportionate amount of time listening to the problems of a small number of ineffective or complaining employees. Consciously or unconsciously, a manager who has to listen to many of your complaints may find a way to seek revenge.

How, then, does an employee make valid complaints to the manager? The answer is to complain only when justified. And when you do offer a complaint, back it up with a recommended solution. Anyone can take potshots at something. The valuable employee is the person who backs up these complaints with a constructive action plan. An example follows of a complaint, backed up by action plans for its remedy:

> We have a difficult time handling emergency requests when you are away from the department. I would suggest that when you will be away for more than one or two hours, one of us can serve as the acting supervisor. It could be done on a rotating basis to give each of us some supervisory experience.

One possibility for minimizing the need for complaints is to attempt to look at decisions from the boss's point of view. The company might decide to prohibit workers from using instant messaging for personal reasons during working hours. Instead of complaining that the prohibition on instant messages is unjust, the worker might attempt to understand why company management thinks instant messages lower productivity.

AVOID BYPASSING YOUR MANAGER

A way to embarrass and sometimes infuriate your manager is to repeatedly go to his or her superior with your problems, conflicts, and complaints. Such bypasses have at least three strongly negative connotations. One is that you don't believe your boss has the power to take care of your problem. Another is that you distrust his or her judgment in the matter at hand. A third is that you are secretly launching a complaint against your manager.

The boss bypass is looked on so negatively that most experienced managers will not listen to your problem unless you have already discussed it with your immediate superior. There *are* times, however, when running around your manager is necessary, such as when you have been unable to resolve a conflict directly with him or her (see the following major section). But even under these circumstances, you should politely inform your manager that you are going to take up your problem with the next level of management.

In short, if you want to keep on the good side of your manager, bring all problems directly to him or her. If your boss is unable or unwilling to take care of the problem, you might consider contacting your boss's superior. Nonetheless, considerable tact and diplomacy are needed. Do not imply that your manager is incompetent but merely that you would like another opinion about the issues at stake. The grievance process, as described in Chapter 7, can be used to substitute for a boss bypass but should be used only when you are unable to resolve a problem with your boss.

USE DISCRETION IN SOCIALIZING WITH YOUR MANAGER

A constant dilemma facing employees is how much and what type of socializing with the manager is appropriate. Advocates of socializing contend that off-the-job friendships lead to more natural work relationships. Opponents of socializing with the boss say that it leads to **role confusion** (being uncertain about what role you are carrying out). For example, how can your manager make an objective decision about your salary increase on Monday morning when he or she had dinner with you on Sunday? To avoid cries of favoritism, you might be recommended for a below-average increase.

One guideline to consider is to have cordial social relationships with the manager of the same kind shared by most employees. "Cordial" socializing includes activities such as company-sponsored parties, group invitations to the boss's home, and business lunches. Golfing with the boss is widely accepted. Individual social activities, such as camping with the boss, double-dating, and so forth, are more likely to lead to role confusion.

Socializing should not include a casual romantic involvement. Romantic involvements between a superior and a subordinate are disruptive to work and morale. Coworkers usually suspect that the manager's special friend is getting special treatment and resent the favoritism. More will be said about office romances later in this chapter.

ENGAGE IN FAVORABLE INTERACTIONS WITH YOUR MANAGER

The many techniques described previously support the goal of engaging in favorable interactions with your manager. A study of interactions between bank employees and their supervisors showed that purposely trying to create a positive impression on the supervisor led to better performance ratings.[7] Although the finding is not surprising, it is reassuring to know that it is backed by quantitative evidence. Human Relations Self-Assessment Quiz 8-1 contains a listing of behaviors used by employees in the study to create positive interactions with their supervisors. Use these behaviors as a guide for skill building.

Although favorable interactions with a manager are valuable for relationship building, there are times when a group member has to deliver bad news. For example, you might have to inform the manager about a burst water pipe in the mainframe computer room or a bunch of customer complaints about a new product. You want to avoid being the messenger who is punished because he or she delivered bad news. Attempt to be calm and businesslike. Do not needlessly blame yourself for the problem. Mention that *we are* or *the company is* facing a serious challenge. If possible, suggest a possible solution such as, "I have already investigated a backup computer service we can use until the damage is repaired."

HUMAN RELATIONS SELF-ASSESSMENT QUIZ 8-1

Supervisor Interaction Checklist

Use the following behaviors as a checklist for achieving favorable interactions with your present manager or a future one. The more of these actions you are engaged in, the higher the probability that you are building a favorable relationship with your manager.

1. Agree with your supervisor's major opinions outwardly even when you disagree inwardly. _____

2. Take an immediate interest in your supervisor's personal life. _____

3. Praise your supervisor on his or her accomplishments. _____

4. Do personal favors for your supervisor. _____

5. Do something as a personal favor for your supervisor even though you are not required to do it. _____

6. Volunteer to help your supervisor on a task. _____

7. Compliment your supervisor on his or her dress or appearance. _____

8. Present yourself to your supervisor as being a friendly person. _____

9. Agree with your supervisor's major ideas. _____

10. Present yourself to your supervisor as being a polite person. _____

SOURCE: Adapted from Sandy J. Wayne and Gerald R. Ferris, "Influence Tactics, Affect, and Exchange Quality in Supervisor-Subordinate Interactions: A Laboratory Experiment and Field Study," *Journal of Applied Psychology,* October 1990, p. 494.

▲ COPING WITH A PROBLEM MANAGER

Up to this point we have prescribed tactics for dealing with a reasonably rational boss. At some point in their careers, many people face the situation of dealing with a problem manager—one who makes it difficult for the subordinate to get the job done. The problem is sometimes attributed to the boss's personality or incompetence. At other times, differences in values or goals could be creating the problem. Our concern here is with constructive approaches to dealing with the delicate situation of working for a problem manager.

REEVALUATE YOUR MANAGER

Some problem managers are not really a problem. Instead, one or more group members have been misperceived by them. Some employees think they have problem managers when those bosses simply have major role, goal, or value differences. (A role in this context is the expectations of the job.) The problem might also lie in conflicting personalities, such as being outgoing or shy. Another problem is conflicting perspectives, such as being detail oriented as opposed to taking an overall perspective. The differences just noted can be good or bad, depending on how they are viewed and used. For example, a combination of a detail-oriented group member with an "overall perspective" boss can be a winning combination.[8]

Another approach to being more cautious in evaluating your manager is to judge slowly and fairly. Many decisions your manager makes may prove to be worthwhile if you give the decisions time.[9] Top management at your company might issue an order that employees cannot surf the Web for personal reasons on the job. You might think this rule is unfair and treats workers like adolescents. If you wait for the result of the decisions, you might find that productivity improves. Another benefit might be that many workers no longer have to work late because they save time by not surfing.

Confront Your Manager about the Problem

A general-purpose way of dealing with a problem manager is to use confrontation and problem solving as described in Chapter 7. Because your manager has more formal authority than you, the confrontation must be executed with the highest level of tact and sensitivity. A beginning point in confronting a manager is to gently ask for an explanation of the problem. Suppose, for example, you believed strongly that your team leader snubs you because he or she dislikes you. You might inquire gently, "What might I be doing wrong that is creating a problem between us?"

Another situation calling for confrontation would be outrageous behavior by the manager, such as swearing at and belittling group members. For example, a worker reported that in meetings his manager openly belittles his peers and the people higher in the organization. The worker was concerned that this behavior fosters poor morale and unprofessional attitudes among team members and hurts productivity.[10]

Because several or all group members are involved in the example cited, a group discussion of the problem might be warranted. You and your coworkers might meet as a group to discuss the impact of the manager's style on group morale and productivity. This tactic runs the risk of backfiring if the manager becomes defensive and angry. Yet confrontation is worth the risk because the problem of abuse will not go away without discussion.

Confrontation can also be helpful in dealing with the problem of **micromanagement,** the close monitoring of most aspects of group member activities by the manager. "Looking over your shoulder constantly" is an everyday term for micromanagement. If you feel that you are being supervised so closely that it is difficult to perform well, confront the situation. Say something of this nature, "I notice that you check almost everything I do lately. Am I making so many errors that you are losing confidence in my work?"[11] As a consequence, the manager might explain why he or she is micromanaging or begin to check on your work less frequently.

LEARN FROM YOUR MANAGER'S MISTAKES

Just as you can learn from watching your manager do things right, you can also learn from watching him or her do things wrong. In the first instance, we are talking about using your manager as a positive model. "Modeling" of this type is an important source of learning on the job. Using a superior as a negative model can also be of some benefit. As an elementary example, if your manager criticized you in public and you felt humiliated, you would have learned a good lesson in effective supervision: Never criticize a subordinate publicly. By serving as a negative example, your manager has taught you a valuable lesson.

Learning from a problem manager's mistakes can also occur when a manager is fired. Should your manager be fired, analyze the situation to avoid the mistakes he or she made. Enlist the help of others in understanding what went wrong. Did the manager get along poorly with higher-level managers? Was the manager lacking in technical expertise? Did the manager work hard enough? Did the manager commit ethical or legal violations, such as sexual harassment or stealing company property? Whatever the reason, you will learn quickly what behavior the company will not tolerate. If your manager was fired simply as a way to cut costs, there is still a lesson to be learned. Attempt to prove to the company that your compensation is a good investment for the company because your work is outstanding.

▲ BUILDING GOOD COWORKER RELATIONSHIPS

Anyone with work experience is aware of the importance of getting along with coworkers. If you are unable to work cooperatively with others, it will be difficult to hold on to your job. Poor relationships with coworkers can lead to frustration, stress, and decreased productivity, whereas getting along with them makes the workplace more satisfying.[12] You need their cooperation and support, and they need yours. Furthermore, the leading reason employees are terminated is not poor technical skills but rather inability or unwillingness to form satisfactory relationships with others on the job. In this section we describe a handful of basic tactics for developing and maintaining good coworker relationships.

DEVELOP ALLIES THROUGH BEING CIVIL

People who are courteous, kind, cooperative, and cheerful develop allies and friends in the workplace. Practicing basic good manners, such as being pleasant and friendly, is also part of being civil. Being civil helps make you stand out because many people believe that crude, rude, and obnoxious behavior has become a national problem.[13] Being civil also involves not snooping, not spreading malicious gossip, and not weaseling out of group presents, such as shower or retirement gifts. In addition, it is important to be available to coworkers who want your advice as well as your help in times of crisis.

Closely related to being civil is maintaining a positive outlook. Everyone knows that you gain more allies by being optimistic and positive than by being pessimistic and negative. Nevertheless, many people ignore this simple strategy for getting along well with others. Coworkers are more likely to solicit your opinion or offer you help when you are perceived as a cheerful person.

MAKE OTHER PEOPLE FEEL IMPORTANT

A fundamental principle of fostering good relationships with coworkers and others is to make them feel important. Sheila Murray Bethela advises us to make use of the please-make-me-feel-important concept. Visualize that everyone in the workplace is wearing a small sign around the neck that says, "Please make me feel important."[14] Although the leader has primary responsibility for satisfying this recognition need, coworkers also play a key role. One approach to making a coworker feel important would be to bring a notable accomplishment of his or hers to the attention of the group. Human Relations Self-Assessment Quiz 8-2 gives you an opportunity to think through your tendencies to make others feel important.

MAINTAIN HONEST AND OPEN RELATIONSHIPS

In human relations we attach considerable importance to maintaining honest and open relationships with other people. Giving coworkers frank but tactful answers to their requests for your opinion is one useful way of devel-

HUMAN RELATIONS SELF-ASSESSMENT QUIZ 8-2

How Important Do I Make People Feel?

Indicate on a one-to-five scale how frequently you act (or would act if the situation presented itself) in the ways indicated below: very infrequently (*VI*), infrequently (*I*), sometimes (*S*), frequently (*F*), very frequently (*VF*). Circle the number underneath the column that best fits your answer.

	VI	I	S	F	VF
1. I do my best to correctly pronounce a coworker's name.	1	2	3	4	5
2. I avoid letting other people's egos get too big.	5	4	3	2	1
3. I brag to others about the accomplishments of my coworkers.	1	2	3	4	5
4. I recognize the birthdays of friends in a tangible way.	1	2	3	4	5
5. It makes me anxious to listen to others brag about their accomplishments.	5	4	3	2	1
6. After hearing that a friend has done something outstanding, I shake his or her hand.	1	2	3	4	5
7. If a friend or coworker recently received a degree or certificate, I would offer my congratulations.	1	2	3	4	5
8. If a friend or coworker finished second in a contest, I would inquire why he or she did not finish first.	5	4	3	2	1
9. If a coworker showed me how to do something, I would compliment that person's skill.	1	2	3	4	5
10. When a coworker starts bragging about a family member's accomplishments, I do not respond.	5	4	3	2	1

Scoring and Interpretation: Total the numbers corresponding to your answers. Scoring 40 to 50 points suggests that you typically make people feel important; 16 to 39 points suggests that you have a moderate tendency toward making others feel important; 10 to 15 points suggests that you need to develop skill in making others feel important. Study this chapter carefully.

oping open relationships. Assume that a coworker asks your opinion about a document he intends to send to his boss. As you read it, you find it somewhat incoherent and filled with spelling and grammatical errors. An honest response to this document might be, "I think your idea is a good one. But I think your memo needs more work before that idea comes across clearly."

As described in Chapter 7, accurately expressing your feelings also leads to constructive relationships. If you arrive at work upset over a personal problem and appearing obviously fatigued, you can expect some reaction. A peer might say, "What seems to be the problem? Is everything all right?" A dishonest reply would be, "Everything is fine. What makes you think something is wrong?" In addition to making an obviously untrue statement, you would also be perceived as rejecting the person who asked the question.

If you prefer not to discuss your problem, an honest response on your part would be, "Thanks for your interest. I am facing some problems today. But I think things will work out." Such an answer would not involve you in a discussion of your personal problems. Also, you would not be perceived as rejecting your coworker. The same principle applies equally well to personal relationships.

BE A TEAM PLAYER

An essential strategy for developing good relationships with coworkers is to be a team player. A **team player** is one who emphasizes group accomplishment and cooperation rather than individual achievement and not helping others. Team play has surged in importance because of the current emphasis on having teams of workers decide how to improve productivity and quality. You will also have to be a team player if you reach the pinnacle of power in your organization. Executives are expected to be good team players as well as individual decision makers. However, team play is even more important on the way to becoming an executive because impatience and making unilateral decisions is more tolerated in the executive suite.

Being an effective team player is important because without such capability, collaborative effort is not possible. Being an effective team player is also important because of managerial perceptions. A survey of 15 business organizations in 34 industries indicates that employers rate "team player" as the most highly ranked workplace behavior. Approximately 40 percent of the managers surveyed ranked team player as number one among seven desirable traits.[15]

Here we describe a representative group of behaviors that contribute to team play. In addition, engaging in such behavior helps you be perceived as a team player.

1. *Share credit with coworkers.*   A direct method of promoting team play is to share credit for good deeds with other team members. Instead of focusing on yourself as the person responsible for a work achievement, point out that the achievement was a team effort.

2. *Display a helpful, cooperative attitude.*   Working cooperatively with others is virtually synonymous with team play. Cooperation translates into such activities as helping another worker with a computer problem, covering for a teammate when he or she is absent, and making sure a coworker has the input required from you on time. A helpful cooperative attitude is the main component of organizational citizenship behavior.

3. *To establish trust, keep confidential information private and give honest opinions.*   Trust is important for teamwork because trust is a major contributor to cooperation.[16] Confidential information shared with you by a teammate should not be shared with others. Trust is exceedingly difficult to regain after a person has been betrayed. Giving honest opinions helps develop trust because the recipient of your honesty will regard you as a person of integrity. However, tact and diplomacy are still important. A dishonest opinion can often be detected through your nonverbal cues, such as discomfort in your voice tone. Assume that a friend of yours is starting a business selling antique toys over the Internet. She asks you if you like her proposed domain name, "WWW.OldjunkRus.com." You think the name is both ridiculous and an infringement on the Toys R Us name; yet you say, "Hey, terrific" with a sickened look on your face. You might lose some of your friend's trust.

4. *Share information and opinions with coworkers.*   Teamwork is facilitated when group members share information and opinions. This is true because one of the benefits of group effort is that members can share ideas. The result is often a better solution to problems than would have been possible if people worked alone. The group thus achieves **synergy,** a product of group effort whereby the output of the group exceeds the output possible if the members worked alone.

5. *Provide emotional support to coworkers.*   Good team players offer each other emotional support. Such support can take the form of verbal encouragement for ideas expressed, listening to a group member's concerns, or complimenting achievement. An emotionally supportive comment to a coworker who appears to be experiencing stress might be, "This doesn't look like one of your better days. What can I do to help?" According to a recent study, emotionally supporting coworkers facilitates their being able to service customers better.[17] Perhaps when workers feel emotionally supported, it is easier for them to have a positive attitude toward customers.

6. *Follow the golden rule.*   The ancient adage "Treat others the way you would like them to treat you" provides a firm foundation for effective teamwork. Although some may dismiss the golden rule as a syrupy platitude, it still works. For example, you would probably want someone to help you with a perplexing problem, so you take the initiative to help others when you have the expertise needed.

7. *Avoid actions that could sabotage or undermine the group in any way.* Frequently criticizing group members directly or complaining about them to outsiders works against the best interest of the group. Members within the group, as well as the team leader, will most likely hear that you criticized them to an outsider, thus doing severe damage to your ability to work cooperatively with them.

8. *Attend company-sponsored social events.*   A worker's reputation as a team player is often judged both on the job and in company-sponsored social events, such as parties, picnics, and athletic teams. If you attend these events and participate fully, your reputation as a team player will be enhanced. Company-sponsored social events are also important because they provide an opportunity to build rapport with coworkers. Rapport, in turn, facilitates teamwork.

9. *Share the glory.*   You will make a poor team player if you try to grab all the glory for ideas that work and distance yourself from ideas that do not work. An effective team member wants all other members to succeed. You will stand out by praising the people you work with rather than hogging any praise for the team.

10. *Avoid backstabbing.* A special category of disliked behavior is **backstabbing,** an attempt to discredit by underhanded means such as innuendo, accusation, or the like. A backstabber might drop hints to the boss, for example, that a coworker performs poorly under pressure or is looking for a new job. Sometimes the backstabber assertively gathers information to backstab a coworker. He or she might engage another worker in a derogatory discussion about the boss and then report the coworker's negative comments back to the boss. A person who develops a reputation as a backstabber will receive poor cooperation from coworkers. The person might also be considered untrustworthy by management, thus retarding his or her own career.

The 10 points just made contribute specifically to effective team play. Recognize also that all other actions directed toward good coworker relationships will enhance team play.

FOLLOW GROUP STANDARDS OF CONDUCT

The basic principle to follow in getting along with coworkers is to follow **group norms.** These refer to the unwritten set of expectations for group members—what people ought to do. Norms become a standard of what each person should do or not do within the group. Norms also provide general guidelines for reacting constructively to the behavior of coworkers. Norms are a major component of the **organizational culture,** or values and beliefs of the firm that guide people's actions. In one firm, the norms and culture may favor hard work and high quality. In another firm, the norms and culture may favor a weaker work ethic.

Group norms also influence the social aspects of behavior on the job. These aspects of behavior relate to such things as the people to have lunch with, getting together after work, joining a company team, and the type of clothing to wear to work. Sharing laughter, such as poking positive fun at coworkers, is another example of an important social behavior linked to a group norm.

Workers learn about norms through both observation and direct instruction from other group members. If you do not deviate too far from these norms, the group will accept much of your behavior. If you deviate too far, you will be subject to much rejection and the feeling of being isolated. In some instances, you might even be subjected to verbal abuse if you make the other employees look bad.

Getting along too well with coworkers has its price as well. The risk of conforming too closely to group norms is that you lose your individuality. You become viewed by your superiors as "one of the office gang" rather than a person who aspires to move up in the organization. It is important to be a good team player, but to advance in your career you must also find a way to distinguish yourself, such as through creative thinking and outstanding performance.

EXPRESS AN INTEREST IN THE WORK AND PERSONAL LIFE OF COWORKERS

Almost everyone is self-centered to some extent, as suggested by the what's-in-it-for-me (WIIFM) principle. Thus, topics that are favored are ones closely related to themselves, such as their children, friends, hobbies, work, or possessions. Sales representatives rely heavily on this fact in cultivating relationships with established customers. They routinely ask the customer about his or her hobbies, family members, and work activities. You can capitalize on this simple strategy by asking coworkers and friends questions such as these:

How is your work going? (*highly recommended*)

How are things going for you?

How did you gain the knowledge necessary for your job?

How does the company use the output from your department?

How does your present job fit in with your career plans?

How did your son enjoy computer camp?

Closely related to expressing interest in others is to investigate what you have in common, both professionally and personally, with peers. You might identify common interests, such as a focus on the company's market share, or a personal interest, such as hiking.[18]

A danger in asking questions about other people's work and personal life is that some questions may not be perceived as well intentioned. There is a fine line between honest curiosity and snooping. You must stay alert to this subtle distinction.

USE APPROPRIATE COMPLIMENTS

An effective way of developing good relationships with coworkers and friends is to compliment something with which they closely identify, such as their children, spouses, hobbies, or pets. Paying a compliment is a form of **positive reinforcement,** rewarding somebody for doing something right. The right response is therefore strengthened or reinforced. A compliment is a useful multipurpose reward.

Another way of complimenting people is through recognition. The suggestions made earlier about making people feel important are a way of recognizing people and therefore compliments. Investing a small amount of time in recognizing a coworker can pay large dividends in terms of cultivating an ally. Recognition and compliments are more likely to create a favorable relationship when they are appropriate. *Appropriate* in this context means that the compliment fits the accomplishment. Praise that is too lavish may be interpreted as belittling and patronizing.

Let's look at the difference between an appropriate and an exaggerated compliment over the same issue. An executive secretary gets a fax machine operating that was temporarily not sending messages.

> *Appropriate compliment:* Nice job, Stephanie. Fixing the fax machine took considerable skill. We can now resume sending important fax messages.

> *Exaggerated compliment:* Stephanie, I'm overwhelmed. You're a world-class fax machine specialist. Are there no limits to your talents?

Observe that the appropriate compliment is thoughtful and is proportionate to what Stephanie accomplished. The exaggerated compliment is probably wasted because it is way out of proportion to the magnitude of the accomplishment.

DEAL EFFECTIVELY WITH DIFFICULT PEOPLE

A major challenge in getting along well with coworkers is dealing constructively with difficult people. A coworker is classified as difficult if he or she is uncooperative, touchy, defensive, hostile, or even very unfriendly. Three examples of difficult people follow:

- *The lone wolf.* Can't stand being part of anything: a team, a project, or group functions. Independent to a fault—makes no attempt to hide solitary preferences.

- *Chicken Little.* No matter how sunny things seem to be, he or she will always find a cloud to cast a shadow. ("What a great Web site we have. Twenty thousand visitors in the first week." "Yeah, but are more than 1 percent buying anything?")[19]

- *The high-maintenance person.* Require so much assistance, special attention, and extra help that it wears you down. No matter what type of help you offer, they want a little more. If you bring them a high-maintenance worker a soft drink, he or she is likely to say, "Didn't they have any decaffeinated soft drinks?"

Rather than attempt to list different tactics for dealing with specific types of difficult people, here we present five widely applicable approaches for dealing with such individuals.

Take Problems Professionally, Not Personally

A key principle in dealing with difficult people is to take what they do professionally, not personally. Difficult people are not necessarily out to get you. You may just represent a stepping-stone for them to get what they want.[20] For example, if a coworker insults you because you need his help Friday afternoon, he probably has nothing against you personally. He just prefers to become mentally disengaged from work that Friday afternoon. Your request distracts him from mentally phasing out of work as early as he would like.

Give Ample Feedback

The primary technique for dealing with counterproductive behavior is to feed back to the difficult person how his or her behavior affects you. Focus on the person's behavior rather than on characteristics or values. If a *Chicken Little* type is annoying you by constantly pointing out potential disasters, say something to this effect: "I have difficulty maintaining my enthusiasm when you so often point out the possible negatives." Such a statement will engender less resentment than saying, "I find you to be a total pessimist, and it annoys me."

Listen and Respond

Closely related to giving feedback is to listen and respond. Give the difficult person ample opportunity to express his or her concerns, doubts, anger, or other feelings. Then acknowledge your awareness of the person's position.[21] An example: "Okay, you tell me that management is really against us and, therefore, we shouldn't work so hard." After listening, present your perspective in a way such as this: "Your viewpoint may be valid based on your experiences. Yet so far, I've found management here to be on my side." This exchange of viewpoints is less likely to lead to failed communication than if you are judgmental with a statement such as, "You really shouldn't think that way."

Use Tact and Diplomacy in Dealing with Annoying Behavior

Coworkers who irritate you rarely do annoying things on purpose. Tactful actions on your part can sometimes take care of these annoyances without your having to confront the problem. Close your door, for example, if noisy coworkers are gathered outside. Or try one woman's method of getting rid of office pests: She keeps a file open on her computer screen and gestures to it apologetically when someone overstays a visit.

Sometimes subtlety doesn't work, and it may be necessary to diplomatically confront the coworker who is annoying you. A useful approach is to precede a criticism with a compliment. Here is an example of this approach: "You're one of the best people I've ever worked with, but one habit of yours drives me bananas. Do you think you could let me know when you're going to be late getting back to the office after lunch?"[22]

Use Humor

Nonhostile humor can often be used to help a difficult person understand how his or her behavior is blocking others. Also, the humor will help defuse conflict between you and that person. The humor should point to the person's unacceptable behavior yet not belittle him or her. Assume that you and a coworker are working jointly on a report. For each idea that you submit, your coworker gets into the know-it-all mode and informs you of important facts that you neglected. An example of nonhostile humor that might jolt the coworker into realizing that his or her approach is annoying is at follows:

> If there is ever a contest to choose the human with a brain that can compete against a Zip file, I will nominate you. But even though my brain is limited to human capacity, I still think I can supply a few facts for our report.

Your humor may help the other person recognize that he or she is attempting to overwhelm you with facts at his or her disposal. You are being self-effacing and thereby drawing criticism away from your coworker. Self-effacement (self-criticism) is a proven humor tactic.

Avoid Creating a Dependency on You

A trap to avoid with many difficult people, and especially the high-maintenance person, is to let him or her become too dependent on you for solutions to problems. In your desire to be helpful and supportive to coworkers, you run the risk of creating a dependency. A difficult person might be pestering you to regularly help solve some of his or her most challenging work problems. The high-maintenance worker might ask to look up a number in the phone book, reboot a stalled computer, or help scrape ice from the ice of the windshield and windows of his or her auto. You may want to be a good organizational citizen, yet you also need more time for your own work, and you do not want to make the person too dependent on you.[23] As an antidote to the problem, make frequent statements such as, "You have a telephone directory," "I know you can reboot your computer," and "Perhaps you can scrape the ice yourself because I have to do the same thing with my SUV."

Reinforce Civil Behavior and Good Moods

In the spirit of positive reinforcement, when a generally difficult person is behaving acceptably, recognize the behavior in some way. Reinforcing statements would include, "It's fun working with you today" and "I appreciate your professional attitude."

The tactics for dealing with difficult people just described require practice to be effective. Also, you may have to use a combination of the seven tactics described in this section to deal effectively with a difficult person. The point of these tactics is not to out-manipulate or subdue a difficult person but to establish a cordial and productive working relationship.

FACE MATURELY THE CHALLENGE OF THE OFFICE ROMANCE

As mentioned in the discussion about socializing with the boss, office romances can be disruptive to morale and productivity. Coworker romances are a more widespread potential problem because more romances take place between coworkers on the same level than between superiors and subordinates. As more women have entered the workforce in professional positions and as professionals work longer hours, the office has become a frequent meeting place. People often work closely in teams and other joint projects, thus creating the conditions for romance to take place.

Many companies have policies against managers dating people below them in the hierarchy, but few companies attempt to restrict same-level romantic relationships. About 72 percent of companies do not have written policies about dating, yet about 14 percent have an unwritten understanding.[24] Managers widely accept the idea of employees dating each other, with nearly 68 percent of managers of all ages saying it is acceptable, according to an American Management Survey.[25] Nevertheless, sensitivity is required to conduct an office romance that does not detract from your professionalism.

Many companies are concerned about information leakage within their organization. If you date a person who has access to confidential information (such as trade secrets), management might be concerned that you are a security risk. You therefore might miss out on some opportunities for better assignments. Companies also worry about negative consequences stemming from office romances, such as sexual harassment claims, low morale of coworkers, lowered productivity from the couple involved in the romance, and an unprofessional atmosphere. Yet an important positive consequence to employers from an office romance is that while the relationship is working well, the couple may have a heightened interest in coming to work. Also, romance can trigger energy that leads to enhanced productivity.

It is important not to abuse company tolerance of the coworker romance. Do not invite the person you are dating to meals at company expense, take him or her on nonessential business trips, or create projects to work on jointly. Strive to keep the relationship confidential and restricted to after hours. Minimize talking to coworkers about the relationship. Such behavior as holding hands or kissing in public view is regarded as poor office etiquette. Disappearing acts together during working hours are taboo.

Should your coworker romance terminate, you face a special challenge. You must now work together cooperatively with a person toward whom you may have angry feelings. Few people have the emotional detachment necessary to work smoothly with a former romantic involvement. Extra effort will therefore be required on both your parts.

What should you do if you and your boss seem suited for a long-term commitment? Why walk away from Mr. or Ms. Right? My suggestion is that if you do become romantically involved, one of you should request a transfer to another department. Many office romances do lead to happy marriages and other long-term relationships. At the start of the relationship, however, use considerable discretion. Engaging in personal conversation during work time or holding hands in the company cafeteria is unprofessional and taboo.

To help deal with the complexity and the positive and negative aspects of office romance, some companies have established policies covering such relationships. To prevent charges of sexual harassment, a policy about office romance is likely to emphasize that both parties must mutually and voluntarily consent to the social relationship. Furthermore, the policy states that the social relationship must not affect job performance or negatively impact the company's business.[26]

▲ BUILDING GOOD RELATIONSHIPS WITH CUSTOMERS

Success on the job also requires building good relationships with both external and internal customers. *External customers* fit the traditional definition of customer that includes clients and guests. External customers can be classified as either retail or industrial. The latter represents one company buying from another, such as purchasing steel. *Internal customers* are the people you serve within the organization or those who use the output from your job. For example, if you design computer graphics, the other people in the company who receive your graphics are your internal customers.

The information already presented about getting along with your manager and coworkers dealt with internal customers. Here we emphasize providing good service (or delight) to external customers. An employee whose thoughts and actions are geared toward helping customers has a **customer service orientation.** Good service is the primary factor that keeps customers coming back. This is important because profits jump considerably as the customer is retained over time. Some techniques described here for serving external customers would also work well with internal customers and vice versa.

An overall approach to dealing effectively with customers is to be a good organizational citizen with respect to customer relationships. You gear a lot of your out-of-the-way effort into customer relationships. Specific behaviors of this type are presented in Exhibit 8-3. Time-tested suggestions for high-level customer service are presented next.[27] Taken together, these suggestions will help you bond with a customer, referring to a close and valued ongoing relationship.

1. *Establish customer satisfaction goals.*   Decide jointly with your manager how much you intend to help customers. Find answers to questions such as the following: Is your company attempting to satisfy every customer within 10 minutes of his or her request? Are you striving to provide the finest customer service in your field? Is your goal zero defections to competitors? Your goals will dictate how much and the type of effort you put into pleasing customers.

2. *Understand your customer's needs and place them first.*   The most basic principle of selling is to identify and satisfy customer needs. Many customers may not be able to express their needs clearly. Also, they may not be certain of their needs. To help identify customer needs, you may have to probe for more information. For example, an associate in a consumer electronics store may have to ask, "What uses do you have in mind for your television receiver aside from watching regular programs? Will you be using it to display digital photographs?" Knowing such information will help the store associate identify which television receiver will satisfy the customer's needs.

After you have identified customer needs, focus on satisfying them rather than doing what is convenient for you or the firm. Assume, for ex-

---

EXHIBIT 8-3

Service-Oriented Organizational Citizenship Behaviors

1. Tells outsiders this is a good place to work.
2. Says good things about the organization to others.
3. Generates favorable goodwill for the company.
4. Encourages friends and family to use the firm's products and services.
5. Actively promotes the firm's products and services.
6. Follows customer service guidelines with extreme care.
7. Conscientiously follows guidelines for customer promotions.
8. Follows up in a timely manner to customer requests and problems.
9. Performs duties with unusually few mistakes.
10. Always has a positive attitude at work.
11. Regardless of circumstances, exceptionally courteous and respectful to customers.
12. Encourages coworkers to contribute ideas and suggestions for service improvement.
13. Contributes many ideas for customer promotions and communications.
14. Makes constructive suggestions for service improvement.
15. Frequently presents to others creative solutions to customer problems.
16. Takes home brochures to read up on products and services.

SOURCE: Portion of a table from Lance A. Bettencourt, Kevin P. Gwinner, and Matthew L. Meuter, "A Comparison of Attitude, Personality, and Knowledge Predictors of Service-Oriented Organizational Citizenship Behaviors," *Journal of Applied Psychology,* February 2001, p. 32.

---

ample, that the customer says, "I would like to purchase nine reams of copier paper." The sales associate should not respond, "Sorry, the copying paper comes in boxes of 10, so it is not convenient to sell you nine reams." The associate might, however, offer a discount for the purchase of the full 10-ream box if such action fits company policy.

3. *Show care and concern.* During contacts with your customer, show concern for his or her welfare. Ask questions such as the following: "How have you enjoyed the television set you bought here awhile back?" "How are you feeling today?" After asking the question, project a genuine interest in the answer. A strictly business approach to showing care and concern is to follow up on requests. A telephone call or e-mail message to the requester of your service is usually sufficient follow-up. A follow-up is effective because it completes the communication loop between two people.

4. *Communicate a positive attitude.* A positive attitude is conveyed by factors such as appearance, friendly gestures, a warm voice tone, and good telephone communication skills. If a customer seems apologetic about making a heavy demand, respond, "No need to apologize. My job is to please you. I'm here to serve."

5. *Make the buyer feel good.* A fundamental way of building a customer relationship is to make the buyer feel good about himself or herself. Also, make the buyer feel good because he or she has bought from you. Offer compliments about the customer's healthy glow or a report that specified vendor requirements (for an industrial customer). An effective feel-good line is, "I enjoy doing business with you." Smiling is a useful technique for making the customer feel good. Also, smiling is a natural relationship builder and can help you bond with your customer. Smile several times during each customer contact, even if your customer is angry with your product or service. Yet guard against smiling constantly or inappropriately because your smile then becomes meaningless. (But as cautioned in Chapter 4, avoid emotional labor.)

6. *Display strong business ethics.* Ethical violations receive so much publicity that you can impress customers by being conspicuously ethical. Look for ways to show that you are so ethical that you would welcome making your sales tactics public knowledge. Also, treat the customer the same way you would treat a family member or a valued friend.

7. *Be helpful rather than defensive when a customer complains.* As described earlier, look at a complaint professionally rather than personally. Listen carefully and concentrate on being helpful. The upset customer cares primarily about having the problem resolved and does not care whether you are at fault. Use a statement such as, "I understand this mistake is a major inconvenience. I'll do what I can right now to solve the problem." Remember also that complaints that are taken care of quickly and satisfactorily will often create a more positive impression than mistake-free service. Another way of being helpful is to ask for enough details about what went wrong so that you can begin resolving the problem. Explain as soon as possible how you are going to fix the problem.

8. *Invite the customer back.* The southern U.S. expression "Y'all come back, now!" is well suited for good customer service. Specific invitations to return may help increase repeat business. The more focused and individualized the invitation, the more likely it will have an impact on customer behavior. ("Y'all come back, now!" is sometimes used too indiscriminately to be effective.) Pointing out why you enjoyed doing business with the customer and what future problems you could help with is an effective technique. Another way of encouraging the customer to return is to explain how much you value him or her.

9. *Avoid rudeness.* Although rudeness to customers is obviously a poor business practice, the problem is widespread. Rudeness by customer

---

HUMAN RELATIONS SELF-ASSESSMENT QUIZ 8-3

Am I Being Rude?

Directions: Following is a list of behaviors of customer contact workers that would be interpreted as rude by many customers. Indicate whether you have engaged in such behavior in your dealings with customers or whether you are likely to do so if your job did involve customer contact.

	Yes	No
1. I talk to a coworker while serving a customer.	____	____
2. I conduct a telephone conversation with someone else while serving a customer.	____	____
3. I address customers by their first names without having their permission.	____	____
4. I address customers as "You guys."	____	____
5. I chew gum or eat candy while dealing with a customer.	____	____
6. I laugh when customers describe an agonizing problem they are having with one of our company's products or services.	____	____
7. I minimize eye contact with customers.	____	____
8. I say the same thing to every customer, such as "Have a nice day," in a monotone.	____	____
9. I accuse customers of attempting to cheat the company before carefully investigating the situation.	____	____
10. I hurry customers when my break time approaches.	____	____
11. I comment on a customer's appearance in a flirtatious, sexually oriented way.	____	____
12. I sometimes complain about or make fun of other customers when I am serving another customer.	____	____

Interpretation: The more of these behaviors you have engaged in, the ruder you are and the more likely you are losing potential business for your company. If you have not engaged in any of these behaviors, even when faced with a rude customer, you are an asset to your employer. You are also tolerant.

contact personnel is a major problem from the employer's standpoint. Be aware of subtle forms of rudeness, such as complaining about your job or working hours in front of customers. To elevate your awareness level about rudeness among customer contact personnel, do Human Relations Self-Assessment Quiz 8-3.

HUMAN RELATIONS SKILL-BUILDING EXERCISE 8-1

Giving Good Customer Service

Role players in this exercise will demonstrate two related techniques for giving good customer service: show care and concern and make the buyer feel good.

Scenario 1: Show care and concern. A sales representative meets with two company representatives to talk about installing a new information system for employee benefits. One of the company representatives is from the human resources department and the other from the telecommunications department. The sales representative will attempt to show care and concern for both company representatives during the same meeting.

Scenario 2: Make the buyer feel good. A couple, played by two role players, enters a new-car showroom to examine a model they have seen advertised on television. Although they are not in urgent need of a new car, they are strongly interested. The sales representative is behind quota for the month and would like to close a sale today. The rep decides to use the tactic "make the buyer feel good" to help form a bond.

All the nine points just made emphasize the importance of practicing good human relations with customers and having a customer service orientation. Good customer service stems naturally from practicing good human relations. Human Relations Skill-Building Exercise 8-1 gives you an opportunity to practice two techniques for building customer relationships.

▲ SUMMARY

Adequate interpersonal skills are necessary for success in business. Developing a favorable relationship with your manager is the most basic strategy of getting ahead in your career. Specific tactics for developing a good relationship with your manager include the following:

1. Achieve good job performance.

2. Display a strong work ethic. (Use such means as demonstrating competence on even minor tasks, assuming personal responsibility for problems, and completing projects promptly.)

3. Demonstrate good emotional intelligence. (Deal effectively with the emotional responses of coworkers and customers.)

4. Be dependable and honest.

5. Be a good organizational citizen. (Be willing to work for the good of the organization even without the promise of a specific reward.)

6. Create a strong presence (keep yourself in the forefront).

7. Find out what your manager expects of you.

8. Minimize complaints.

9. Avoid bypassing your manager.

10. Use discretion in socializing with your manager.

11. Engage in favorable interactions with your manager.

Coping with a manager you perceive to be a problem is part of getting along with him or her. Reevaluate you manager to make sure you have not misperceived him or her. It is important to confront your manager about your problem. Often this problem is a case of being micromanaged. Learning from your problem manager's mistakes (even if he or she gets fired) is recommended.

Methods and tactics for building coworker relationships include the following:

1. Develop allies through being civil, including maintaining a positive outlook.

2. Make other people feel important.

3. Maintain honest and open relationships.

4. Be a team player.

5. Follow group standards of conduct.

6. Express an interest in the work and personal life of coworkers.

7. Use appropriate (nonexaggerated) compliments.

8. Deal effectively with difficult people, including taking problems professionally, giving ample feedback, listening and responding, using tact and diplomacy, using humor, avoiding creating a dependency on you, and reinforcing civil behavior and good moods.

9. Face maturely the challenge of the office romance.

Team player approaches include sharing credit, maintaining a cooperative attitude, establishing trust, sharing information and opinions, providing emotional support, practicing the golden rule, avoiding sabotaging or undermining actions, sharing the glory, and avoiding backstabbing.

Job success also requires building good relationships with both internal and external customers. Techniques for providing high-level customer service include (1) establishing customer satisfaction goals; (2) understanding your customer's needs and placing them first; (3) showing care and concern; (4) communicating a positive attitude; (5) making the buyer feel good; (6) displaying strong business ethics; (7) being helpful rather than defensive when a customer complains; (8) inviting the customer back; and (9) avoiding rudeness.

Questions and Activities

1. Many workplaces today are supposed to be more democratic, with managers having less power than in the past. Why, then, is it so important to know techniques for getting along with one's manager?

2. If team leaders don't have as much power as a regular manager, why is it still important to build a good relationship with your team leader?

3. How can a worker implement the tactic "engage in favorable interactions with your manager" without appearing to be "kissing up" to the boss?

4. Why is "creating a strong presence" considered a key strategy for getting ahead in the workplace?

5. Why study about getting along with coworkers and customers? Isn't common sense good enough to develop smooth working relationships with people?

6. Give an example of a technique you think would make a coworker feel important.

7. Many customer contact workers routinely say, "Have a nice day" when the customer's transaction has been completed. How effective is this expression in building customer relationships?

8. If rudeness is so widespread today, why bother being polite and considerate on the job?

9. How might placing too much emphasis on being a good team player and fitting in with the group hurt a person's chances of becoming an executive?

10. Ask a person who has achieved job success what he or she thinks are two important ways of getting along with coworkers and customers. Compare notes with classmates.

INTERNET SKILL BUILDER: Customer Relationship Skills at Home Depot

Visit www.npbjobs.org/HOMEDEPOT/home_depot10.asp, a Web site describing the requirements for a sales associate position at Home Depot presented by the National Business Partnership. Identify which skills mentioned relate to workplace relationships, including communication skills and self-understanding. Reflect back on any time you have visited the Home Depot or a competitor's store. How realistic is Home Depot about the interpersonal and personal skills required for a sales associate? If you happen to know a Home Depot employee, obtain his or her input in formulating your answer to the preceding question.

HUMAN RELATIONS CASE PROBLEM

What to Do about Brian?

Brian is one of 10 home mortgage refinance specialists working in his department of Cypress Finance, a substantial size financial services firm. Most of the customer contact work of the mortgage refinance department is conducted over the telephone (using a toll-free number), even when potential customers initiate their inquiry through the company Web site. Each refinance specialist does considerable individual work—including interacting with customers and potential customers and evaluating the mortgage applicant's credit worthiness. Credit checks are made with computerized databases, but occasionally clarifying information is sought.

Refinance specialists have to cooperate with each other on complex cases. The cooperation often takes the form of asking a teammate's opinion on the creditworthiness of the risk. A member of management, however, gives final approval to all but the most routine refinance applications.

At times, the supervisor of the group, Nina, makes assignments to balance the workload among the specialists. However, the work piles up so quickly that the specialists are supposed to look for ways to spread the work out evenly among themselves to prevent delays in processing refinance applications.

Nina perceives Brian to be a superior performer. His most recent performance evaluation stated that he was an outstanding refinance specialist with potential for promotion to a supervisory position in the future. Nina also rated Brian's sales performance to be outstanding. A "sale" means that an inquiry over the telephone or Web site is converted into an application to refinance that becomes approved. Despite his outstanding performance, Nina did mention that Brian could strengthen his teamwork skills. She specifically mentioned that Brian was sometimes so busy with his individual cases that he neglected to help out other team members.

During a recent team meeting, Nina told the group, "Once again I am pleased to announce that Brian has been the outstanding producer in the department. I know that we work together as a team yet still have our individual goals. Brian is great at closing applicants with good credit risks, and he still contributes his share as a team player."

Kenny, one of the other refinance specialists, gave a gentle nudge with his elbow to Cindy, a specialist seated to his right. Kenny murmured, "What a kiss-up this guy is. Nina should know what an annoyance Brian is in the office."

After the meeting, Kenny, Cindy, and Lindsay, a third specialist, were standing together near the elevator. Lindsay said while giggling, "Did you see the look on Brian's face? All smiles, like he was voted the MVP of the Super Bowl. Brian sometimes forgets that we help him with his trickiest applications, and then he grabs the glory. But ask Brian for a little help, and he will say something to the effect that he is too busy closing a major deal. You would think he was refinancing the Sears Tower in Chicago." Kenny, Cindy, and Lindsay giggled simultaneously.

The next workday at Cypress was one of the busiest ever. Newspaper and television reports throughout the country announced that mortgage rates were expected to climb by one and one-half percent the following month. The number of applicants for refinancing doubled as many home owners were eager to lock in the present low rates

(Continued)

for refinancing. The refinance specialists were asked to put in 60-hour weeks until the workload drifted back to normal.

During the lunch break on one of the peak-load days, Brian approached the three other specialists taking the break at the same time as he with this proposition. "As everyone in this office knows, I am really talented at closing deals. And the more deals we close as a group, the bigger will be the group bonus at the end of the year. So I'm suggesting that when I have a couple of big deals on the hook, I send my minnows over to you. [Minnows refer to small deals.] Also, I would like your cooperation in doing some of the detail work, such as a lengthy credit inquiry for a major deal. My time is better invested in reeling in the big deals."

One of the specialists said, "Sounds good to me." Cindy took an opposite approach, as she told Brian, "Happy fishing, but you're not my boss. Why should I volunteer to help you when you never volunteer to help me?"

Brian retorted, "Cindy, you may be a nice person, but I think you're a rotten team player. We have to divide up responsibilities for the good of the team."

Later that day, Cindy chatted with Kenny and Lindsay about the incident during the lunch break. She said, "We've got to do something about Brian, but I don't know what. It's tough when you have to do battle with the boss's pet."

Questions

1. Is Brian a *difficult person?* Explain.

2. What steps should the refinance specialists take who object to Brian's work style?

3. How might a system of peer evaluation (see Chapter 1) help Nina in her supervision of the department?

4. Do you think Cindy is being a rotten team player?

WEB CORNER

Getting along with your coworkers: www.irishjobs.ie/advice/getting_along.html

Manager relationships:
www.editorial.careers.msn.com/articles/managingup

Office romance sample contract: www.gutierrez-preciado.com/Memos/romance.htm

▲ REFERENCES

1. Seth Godin, "Contempt of Consumer: It's a Real Crime," *Fast Company,* September 2003, p. 114.

2. Gerald R. Ferris, Pamela L. Perrewé, William P. Anthony, and David C. Gilmore, "Political Skill at Work." *Organizational Dynamics,* Spring 2000, p. 25.

3. Quoted in Janie Magruder, "Getting Along with Boss Best Strategy," *Arizona Republic,* June 23, 2003.

4. William A. Cohen and Nuritt Cohen, "Get Promoted Fast," *Success,* July/August 1985, p. 6.

5. George A. Neuman and Jill R. Kickul, "Organizational Citizenship Behaviors: Achievement Orientation and Personality," *Journal of Business and Psychology,* Winter 1998, pp. 263–264.

6. Anita Bruzzese, "Get the Boss to Take Notice of You," Gannett News Service, April 21, 1997.

7. Sandy J. Wayne and Gerald R. Ferris, "Influence Tactics, Affect, and Exchange Quality in Supervisor-Subordinate Interactions: A Laboratory Experiment and Field Study," *Journal of Applied Psychology,* October 1990, pp. 487–499.

8. J. Kenneth Matejka and Richard Dunsing, "Managing the Baffling Boss," *Personnel,* February 1989, p. 50.

9. "So You're Smarter Than the Boss? Yeah, Right," *Executive Leadership,* June 2000, p. 5.

10. Cited in "Ask Annie," *Fortune,* April 1, 2002, p. 171.

11. "How's the View Back There?" *Working Smart,* December 1996, p. 1.

12. "Getting Along with Your Coworkers," www.irishjobs.ie/advice/getting_along.html.

13. Dot Yandle, "Incivility: Has It Gone Too Far to Fix?" *Success Workshop* (Supplement to *Pryor Report*), March 1997, p. 1.

14. Shelia Murray Bethel, *Making a Difference* (New York: G. P. Putnam's Sons, 1989).

15. "Team Player Gets Top Spot in Survey" (undated sample copy distributed by Dartnell Corporation), p. 3.

16. Andrew C. Wicks, Shawn L. Berman, and Thomas M. Jones, "The Structure of Optimal Trust: Moral and Strategic Implications," *Academy of Management Review,* January 1999, p. 99.

17. Alex M. Susskind, K. Michele Kacmar, and Carl P. Borchgrevink, "Customer Service Providers' Attitudes Relating to Customer Service and Customer Satisfaction in the Customer-Server Exchange," *Journal of Applied Psychology,* February 2003, pp. 179–187.

18. "Build Allies for Personal Support," *Manager's Edge,* January 2003, p. 8

19. The types are from a brochure for ETC w/Career Track, 3085 Center Green Drive, Boulder, CO 80301–5408.

20. Dru Scott, *Customer Satisfaction: The Other Half of Your Job* (Los Altos, CA: Crisp Publications, 1991), p. 16.

21. Sam Deep and Lyle Sussman, *What to Say to Get What You Want* (Reading, MA: Addison-Wesley, 1995).

22. Jane Michaels, "You Gotta Get Along to Get Ahead," *Woman's Day,* April 3, 1984, p. 58.

23. Lin Grensing-Pophal, "High-Maintenance Employees," *HR Magazine,* February 2001, p. 89.

24. Charlene Marmer Solomon, "The Secret's Out: How to Handle the Truth of Workplace Romance," *Workforce,* July 1998, p. 45.

25. Survey cited in Stephanie Armour, "Cupid Finds Work as Office Romance No Longer Taboo," *USA Today,* February 11, 2003.

26. Policy developed by law firm of Gutierrez, Preciado & House, LLP (www.gutierrez-preciado.com/Memos/romance.htm).

27. Linda Thornburg, "Companies Benefit from Emphasis on Superior Customer Service," *HR Magazine,* October 1993, pp. 46–49; "Complaints Are Good for You," *Working Smart,* June 1996, p. 1; Theodore Garrison III, "The Value of Customer Service," in Rick Crandall, ed., *Celebrate Customer Service* (Corte Madera, CA: Select Press, 1999), pp. 3–22; Hal Hardy, "Five Steps to Pleasing Difficult, Demanding Customers," *First Rate Customer Service* (sample issue distributed by Briefings Publishing Group, 2002).

▲ ADDITIONAL READING

Brown, Stephen. "Torment Your Customers (They'll Love It)." *Harvard Business Review,* October 2001, pp. 82–88.

Fram, Eugene H., and Andrew Callahan. "Viewpoint." *Journal of Services Marketing,* 16, No. 1, 2002, pp. 6–8.

Frase-Blunt, Martha. "Meeting with the Boss." *HR Magazine,* June 2003, pp. 94–98.

Goodgold, Elizabeth. "Talking Shop." *Entrepreneur,* September 2003, pp. 62–66.

Kiger, Patrick J. "Why Customer Satisfaction Starts with HR." *Workforce,* May 2002, pp. 26–32.

Lublin, Joann S. "Feeling Unappreciated? You May Find Griping Makes Things Worse." *Wall Street Journal,* June 3, 2003, p. B1.

Nicholson, Nigel. "How to Motivate Problem People." *Harvard Business Review,* January 2003, pp. 56–65.

Powers, Dennis M. *The Office Romance: Playing with Fire without Getting Burned.* New York: AMACOM, 1998.

Reinhartz, Werner, and V. Kumar. "The Mismanagement of Customer Loyalty." *Harvard Business Review,* July 2002, pp. 86–94.

Terez, Tom. "The Power of Nice." *Workforce,* January 2003, p. 22.

CHAPTER 9

Developing Cross-Cultural Competence

Learning Objectives

After studying the information and doing the exercises in this chapter, you should be able to:

◆ Explain some of the major ways in which cultures differ from one another

◆ Be sensitive to potential cultural bloopers

◆ Pinpoint barriers to cross-cultural understanding

◆ Describe techniques for improving cross-cultural relations

◆ Be prepared to overcome cross-cultural communication barriers

*T*he customer service desk for an electronic organizer was based in India. "A lot of questions came up," said Jan Wallen, an executive coach working with the company. "The company wondered, How can people who live so far away speak to our customers?"

She knew there would be hesitations, even if the people did not clearly express them. So she explained that the employees were trained in English.

Then, as an added measure, they were trained to chat a little with customers. They could ask where someone was from, quickly look it up on the Internet, and throw out a comment or two about that bad snowstorm (or heat wave) the caller must be experiencing right now.

"The training is about the American culture and what Americans are expecting," she said. Because, like it or not, we have our idiosyncratic (peculiar, unusual) ways, too.[1]

The incident just described illustrates how people from different cultures can learn to work together, sometimes by using a basic technique to overcome communication barriers. Being able to work well with people from other cultures, both outside and inside your own country, is important for career success. Being able to relate to a culturally diverse customer base is also necessary for success. Forty percent of people entering the U.S. workforce through 2008 will be members of minority groups, according to the U.S. Bureau of Labor Statistics.[2] Not only is the workforce becoming more diverse, but business has become increasingly international. Small and medium-size firms, as well as corporate giants, are increasingly dependent on trade with other countries. Furthermore, as an increasing number of jobs are sent overseas, more U.S. workers will have contact with personnel in foreign countries.

This chapter presents ideas and techniques you can use to sharpen your ability to work effectively with people from diverse backgrounds. The buzzword for this activity is to be *inclusive* in your relationships with people. To get you started thinking about your readiness to work in a culturally diverse environment, take Human Relations Self-Assessment Quiz 9-1.

▲ MAJOR DIMENSIONS OF DIFFERENCES IN CULTURAL VALUES

Everything we do in work and personal life is influenced by a combination of heredity and culture, or nature and nurture. You might be thirsty at this moment because a genetically produced mechanism in

HUMAN RELATIONS SELF-ASSESSMENT QUIZ 9-1

Cross-Cultural Skills and Attitudes

Listed below are various skills and attitudes that various employers and cross-cultural experts think are important for relating effectively to coworkers in a culturally diverse environment.

	Applies to Me Now	Not There Yet
1. I have spent some time in another country.	_____	_____
2. At least one of my friends is deaf or blind or uses a wheelchair.	_____	_____
3. Currency from other countries is as real as the currency from my own country.	_____	_____
4. I can read in a language other than my own.	_____	_____
5. I can speak in a language other than my own.	_____	_____
6. I can write in a language other than my own.	_____	_____
7. I can understand people speaking in a language other than my own.	_____	_____
8. I use my second language regularly.	_____	_____
9. My friends include people of races different than my own.	_____	_____
10. My friends include people of different ages.	_____	_____
11. I feel (or would feel) comfortable having a friends with a sexual orientation different from mine.	_____	_____
12. My attitude is that although another culture may be very different from mine, that culture is equally good.	_____	_____
13. I would be willing to (or already do) hang art from different countries in my home.	_____	_____
14. I would accept (or have already accepted) a work assignment of more than several months in another country.	_____	_____
15. I have a passport.	_____	_____

Interpretation: If you answered Applies to Me Now to 10 or more of the above questions, you most likely function well in a multicultural work environment. If you answered Not There Yet to 10 or more of the above questions, you need to develop more cross-cultural awareness and skills to work effectively in a multicultural work environment. You will notice that being bilingual gives you at least five points on this quiz.

SOURCE: Several ideas for statements on this quiz are derived from Ruthann Dirks and Janet Buzzard, "What CEOs Expect of Employees Hired for International Work," *Business Education Forum,* April 1997, pp. 3–7; Gunnar Beeth, "Multicultural Managers Wanted," *Management Review,* May 1997, pp. 17–21.

your brain tells you it is time to ingest fluid. However, if you choose to drink a Diet Pepsi or papaya juice with a coworker, you are engaging in culturally learned behavior. **Culture** is a learned and shared system of knowledge, beliefs, values, attitudes, and norms. As such, culture includes an enormous amount of behavior. Here we describe seven dimensions (or facets) of cultural values that help us understand how cultures differ from each other.[3] In other words, various cultures value different types of behavior.

1. *Individualism versus collectivism.* At one end of the continuum is individualism, a mental set in which people see themselves first as individuals and believe that their own interests take priority. Members of a society who value individualism are more concerned with their careers than with the good of the firm. Members of a society who value collectivism, in contrast, are typically more concerned with the organization or the work group than with themselves. An example of individualistic behavior would be to want to win an employee-of-the month award; an example of collectivisitic behavior would be to want to win an award for the team. Highly individualistic cultures include the Unites States, Canada, and the Netherlands. Japan and Mexico are among the countries that strongly value collectivism. However, with the increasing emphasis on teamwork in American culture, more U.S. workers are becoming collectivistic.

2. *Acceptance of power and authority.* People from some cultures accept the idea that members of an organization have different levels of power and authority. In a culture that believes in concentration of power and authority, the boss makes many decisions simply because he or she is the boss. Group members readily comply because they have a positive orientation toward authority, including high respect for elders. In a culture with less acceptance of power and authority, employees do not recognize a power hierarchy. They accept directions only when they think the boss is right or when they feel threatened. Cultures that readily accept power and authority include France, China, and India. Countries that have much less acceptance of power and authority are the United States and particularly the Scandinavian countries (e.g., Sweden).

3. *Materialism versus concern for others.* In this context, materialism refers to an emphasis on assertiveness and the acquisition of money and material objects. It also means a deemphasis on caring for others. At the other end of the continuum is concern for others, an emphasis on personal relations, and a concern for the welfare of others. Materialistic countries include Japan and Italy. The United States is considered to be moderately materialistic, as evidenced by the high participation rates in charities. Scandinavian countries all emphasize caring as a national value.

4. *Formality versus informality.* A country that values formality attaches considerable importance to tradition, ceremony, social rules, and rank. At the other extreme, informality refers to a casual attitude toward these same aspects of culture. Workers in Latin American countries highly value formality, such as lavish public receptions and processions. Americans, Canadians, and Scandinavians are much more informal. Casual observation suggests that most of the industrialized world is becoming more informal through such practices as an emphasis on using the first name only during business introductions.

5. *Urgent time orientation versus casual time orientation.* Individuals and nations attach different importance to time. People with an urgent time orientation perceive time as a scarce resource and tend to be impatient. People with a casual time orientation view time as an unlimited and unending resource and tend to be patient. Americans are noted for their urgent time orientation. They frequently impose deadlines and are eager to get started doing business. Asians and Middle Easterners, in contrast, are patient negotiators. Many corporate workers and entrepreneurs engaged in international business recognize the importance of building relationships slowly overseas.

6. *Work orientation versus leisure orientation.* A major cultural difference is the number of hours per week and weeks per year people expect to invest in work versus leisure or other nonwork activities. American corporate professionals typically work about 55 hours per week, take 45-minute lunch breaks, and take two weeks of vacation. Japanese workers share similar values with respect to time invested in work. In contrast, many European countries have steadily reduced the workweek in recent years while lengthening vacations.

7. *High-context versus low-context cultures.* Cultures differ in how much importance they attach to the surrounding circumstances, or context, of an event. High-context cultures make more extensive use of body language. Some cultures, such as the Hispanic and African American cultures, are high context. In contrast, northern European cultures are low context and make less use of body language. The Anglo-American culture is considered to be medium-low context. People in low-context cultures seldom take time in business dealings to build relationships and establish trust.

RELIGIOUS VALUES AND BICULTURAL IDENTITIES

In addition to these well-publicized dimensions of cultural values, many other cultural differences exist in the workplace that require consideration. An important example is that differences in religious practices often affect when people are willing to work or not work. One potential cultural clash is that the rights of an individual to freely practice and observe religious beliefs sometimes collide with company goals. Differences in religious practices must be recognized because the number of religions in the workplace has increased substantially.

Religious diversity can create problems as more companies move to 24/7 (around-the-clock, seven-days-per-week) schedules. Employers therefore need more flexibility from employees, yet religious beliefs often limit times at which employees are willing to work. The message for improved understanding is that employers must recognize workers' religious beliefs. At the same time, workers must understand the importance of a company meeting the demands of the marketplace, such as having 24-hour customer service support. Workers, for example, can trade off working on each others' religious holidays.

Another complexity about understanding cultural differences is that many people have **bicultural identities** because they identify with both their primary culture and another culture. As a consequence, these people may incorporate the values of two cultures. Young people develop a global identity that gives them a feeling of belonging to a worldwide culture. The feeling of belongingness enables them to communicate with people from diverse places when they travel, when others travel to where they live, and when they communicate globally through e-mail and telephone. Television and movies also help us develop a global identity

Further, according to this theory, people retain a local identity along with their global identity. Young people in India provide an apt example. The country has a rapidly growing high-tech sector, led mostly by young people. Yet most of these well-educated young people still cling to local traditions, such as a marriage arranged by the parents and the expectation that they will care for their parents in old age.[4]

APPLYING KNOWLEDGE OF CULTURAL DIFFERENCES

The key principle to recognizing cultural differences is to be alert to these differences and to be sensitive to how they could affect your dealings with people. Recognize that not everybody fits the same stereotype and adjust your assumptions accordingly. A furniture store manager who viewed the world with a *heterosexual bias* made the following mistake: A customer said he wished to return an end table because, after he brought it home, his partner said the table just didn't fit. The store manager responded, "What didn't your wife like about the table?" The customer replied angrily, "My partner is a man, and he said the design is atrocious." The customer then demanded a refund instead of a merchandise exchange.

How might you use this information about cultural differences to improve interpersonal relationships on the job? A starting point would be to recognize that a person's national values might influence his or her behavior. Assume that you wanted to establish a good working relationship with a person from a high-context culture. An effective starting point would be to emphasize body language when communicating with that individual. A related point is that people from high-context cultures are more likely to touch and kiss strangers. As Fernando, who was raised in the Dominican Republic and studying in the United States, said, "In my country I hug people I meet for the first time. When I do it here, they think I'm very rude."

▲ BARRIERS TO GOOD CROSS-CULTURAL RELATIONS

Many logical reasons exist as to why people often encounter difficulties in developing good relations and communicating with people from different cultures. The fact that cultures differ in key dimensions creates some friction in cross-cultural relations. A go-getter from Brooklyn, New York, might say to himself, "Why do I have to spend three days here in Hong Kong wining and dining customers just so I can sell them an enterprise software system?"

Here we look at several of the underlying factors that create problems in developing smooth cross-cultural relations. Toward the end of the chapter, we describe how to overcome cross-cultural communication problems. Most of the communication barriers described in Chapter 6 also apply. Not being aware of the type of barriers presented next blocks effective cross-cultural relations because such lack of awareness often leads to minunderstandings.

PERCEPTUAL EXPECTATIONS

Achieving good cross-cultural relations is hampered somewhat by people's predisposition to discriminate. They do so as a perceptual shortcut, much like stereotyping. A bank customer, for example, might be communicating with a 24-year-old man about a mortgage application. Dissatisfied with his concerns about her creditworthiness, the customer might say, "Let me speak to a mortgage officer." In reality, the man *is* a mortgage officer, but the woman expects an older person to be occupying such a position. The message in this anecdote about perceptual expectations is important. We have to overcome this form of discrimination to enhance cross-cultural relations.

Positive expectations or stereotypes can also create some barriers to cross-cultural relations. Two company representatives were entertaining Sophie, a work associate from Jamaica. They assumed that because Sophie was black and Jamaican, she enjoyed dancing, so they invited her to a dance club. Sophie was a little taken back and said, "What makes you think I like to dance? Not every Jamaican lady has natural rhythm." Similarly, on the job, we sometimes think that everybody from a certain national group has the characteristics of that group. For example, not all Chinese workers are methodical or precise or have good eye–hand coordination and exceptional math skills.

ETHNOCENTRISM

A key barrier to good cross-cultural relations is **ethnocentrism,** the assumption that the ways of one's culture are the *best* ways of doing things. Most cultures consider themselves to the center of the world, such as the French believing that any cultivated person must appreciate French painters. One consequence of ethnocentrism is that people from one culture prefer people from other cultures similar to themselves. English people would therefore have more positive attitudes toward Australians than they would toward Mexicans. Despite this generalization, some countries that appear to have similar cultures are intense rivals. Many Japanese and Korean people dislike each other, as do the French and Belgians. In what way do you feel your country's way of doing something is the best?

INTERGROUP RATHER THAN INTERPERSONAL RELATIONS

In *intergroup* relations we pay attention only to the group membership of the person, such as Sophie being Jamaican. In *interpersonal* relations we pay attention to a person's individual characteristics. An interpersonal relationship requires more effort because we have to attend to the details of the other person and listen carefully. Instead of making generalizations about a group, we search for uniqueness. For example, "Sophie, you are our guest. What would be your favorite form of entertainment for tonight?"

STEREOTYPES IN INTERGROUP RELATIONS

We described expectations as a form of stereotype that could interfere with effective cross-cultural relations. Stereotypes, in general, create some problems. As a result of stereotypes, people overestimate the probability that a given member of a group will have an attribute of his or her category. People tend to select information that fits the stereotype and reject inconsistent information. As a consequence, we readily draw conclusions about people from another cultural group without carefully listening and observing. As an Indian American business graduate reports:

> I took a job with a systems consulting company. The job was supposed to involve a lot of contact with users. But because I look and sound Indian, the managers just assumed that I'm heavy into information technology. Writing code all day gives me a headache. I try to explain my preferences, but all I get is a puzzled look from my manager. [The problem here is that being placed in the wrong job can lead to dissatisfaction and costly turnover.]

DIFFERENT NORMS AND CODES OF CONDUCT

Various cultural groups have norms of their own, such as in some countries men walking ahead of the women. Also, what is permissible conduct in one group may be frowned on and even punished in another group. In the United States it is permissible for people to publish nasty (even X-rated) cartoons about political leaders without fear of reprisal by the government. In some countries such behavior will lead to long-term imprisonment.

At times, we may make the mistake that others are similar to us and then become confused when they act differently than our expectations. We may unknowingly insult others from a different culture, or they many unknowingly insult us. If you are from a culture that highly values time, such as the Americans and the English (James Bond is always on time), you may be angry when your new Brazilian acquaintance arrives 30 minutes late for a party. Because most Brazilians do not adhere to rigid time schedules for social events, you have just experienced a clash of different cultural norms.

UNINTENTIONAL MICROINEQUITIES

Many barriers to effective cross-cultural relations surface because a person is unaware that he or she is slighting another individual. Mary Row, a researcher on gender and racial differences, defines a **microinequity** as a small, semiconscious message we send with a powerful impact on the receiver. Understanding microinequities can lead to changes in one-on-one relationships that may profoundly irritate others.[5] For example, a manager was introducing a new office assistant to the group, mentioning the name of each member one by one. However, the manager omitted mentioning the name of the one Philippine American group member.

As part of a training program in understanding microinequities, the people who are slighted are taught to confront the issue rather than let resentment build. The Philippine American worker might say tactfully to the manager, "Diane, the new assistant, was introduced to everybody but me. And I am the only Philippine in the department. Was this a coincidence?"

▲ APPROACHES TO IMPROVING CROSS-CULTURAL RELATIONS

By now you are probably already aware of how to improve cross-cultural relations by avoiding some of the mistakes already mentioned or implied, such as relying too heavily on group stereotypes. In this section, we take a systematic look at approaches you can use on your own along with training programs designed to improve cross-cultural relations.[6] The methods and techniques for such improvement are outlined in Exhibit 9-1.

DEVELOP CULTURAL SENSITIVITY

In order to relate well to someone from a foreign country, a person must be alert to possible cultural differences. When working in another country, one must be willing to acquire knowledge about local customs and learn how to speak the native language, at least passably. When working with people from different cultures, even from one's own country, the person must be patient, adaptable, flexible, and willing to listen and learn.

The characteristics just mentioned are part of **cultural sensitivity,** an awareness of and a willingness to investigate the reasons why people of

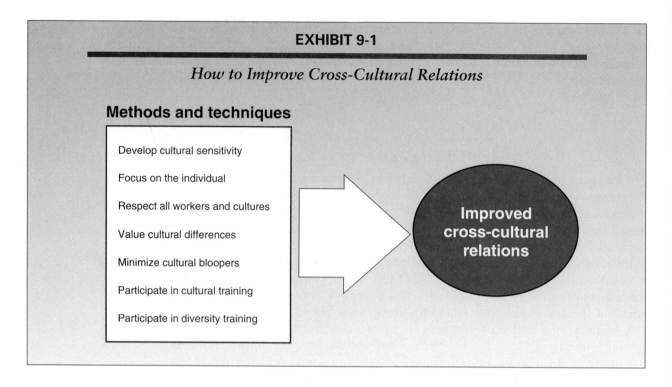

another culture act as they do.[7] A person with cultural sensitivity will recognize certain nuances in customs that will help build better relationships from cultural backgrounds other than his or her own.

One approach to enhancing cultural sensitivity is to keep in mind the types of cultural differences mentioned throughout this chapter, even down to such details as holding a fork in your left hand when dining in England and India. Another approach is to raise your antenna and observe carefully what others are doing. Suppose you are on a business trip to a different region of your country and are invited to have dinner at the plant general manager's house. You notice that she takes off her street shoes on entering the house. You do likewise to establish better rapport, even if your host says, "Oh, please don't bother." It is obvious from your host's behavior that she observes a "shoe code" in her house.

FOCUS ON INDIVIDUALS RATHER THAN GROUPS

Understanding broad cultural differences is a good starting point in building relationships with people from other cultures. Nevertheless, it is even more important to get to know the individual rather than relying exclusively on an understanding his or her cultural group. Instead of generalizing about the other person's characteristics and values (such as assuming that your Mexican American coworker chooses to be late for meetings), get to know his or her personal style. You might find that this particular Mexican American values promptness and becomes anxious when others are late for a meeting. A consultant in the area of cross-cultural relations suggests that the best way to know individuals is to build personal relationships with people and not to generalize.[8]

RESPECT ALL WORKERS AND CULTURES

An effective strategy for achieving cross-cultural understanding is to simply respect all others in the workplace, including their cultures. An important component of respect is to believe that although another person's culture is different from yours, it is equally good. Respect comes from valuing differences, such as one person speaking standard English and the other favoring American Sign Language. Respecting other people's customs can translate into specific attitudes, such as respecting one coworker for wearing a yarmulke on Friday or another for wearing an African costume to celebrate Kwanzaa. Another way of being respectful would be to listen carefully to the opinion of a senior worker who says the company should never have converted to voice mail in place of assistants answering the phone (even though you disagree).

An aspect of respecting all workers is the importance of respecting the rights of majorities, particularly white males. Gillian Flynn, a human resource professional, states the problem in this way: "These days things aren't so easy for white males. They've been under attack for a long time, en masse, for the problems of women and minorities. And some should be, certainly. But it's ironic that a movement that demands equal treatment for individuals often lumps all men into one troublesome bundle."[9] Following this logic, a true cross-cultural person would not have negative attitudes toward a person just because that person is a white male.

VALUE CULTURAL DIFFERENCES

Recognizing cultural differences is an excellent starting point in becoming a **multicultural worker,** one who can work effectively with people of different cultures. More important, however, is to *value* cultural differences. The distinction goes well beyond semantics. If you place a high value on cultural differences, you will perceive people from other cultures to be different but equally good. Gunnar Beeth, the owner of an executive placement firm in Brussels, Belgium, provides an expanded definition of a multicultural worker: "He or she who is deeply convinced that all cultures are equally good enjoys learning the rich variety of foreign cultures and mostly likely has been exposed to more than one culture in childhood."[10]

Beeth notes that you cannot motivate anyone, especially someone of another culture, until that person first accepts you. A multilingual sales representative has the ability to explain the advantages of a product in other languages. In contrast, a multicultural sales rep can motivate foreigners to make the purchase. The difference is substantial.[11]

A challenge in showing respect for other cultures is not to act revolted or shocked when a member of another culture eats something that lies outside your area of what is acceptable as food. Some westerners are shocked and repelled to find that some easterners eat insects, cats, dogs, sheep's eyeballs, chicken soup containing the feet, and rattlesnakes. Some easterners are shocked and repelled to find that westerners eat a sacred animal like a cow and are surprised about popcorn.[12]

Other cross-cultural differences in customs also represent a challenge when trying to respect another culture. An American might find it difficult to respect the Pakistani practice of having young children work in factories. In contrast, the Pakistani might find it difficult to respect the American practice of putting old relatives in nursing homes and hospices. Sometimes it takes careful reflection on one's own culture to be able to respect another culture.

Minimize Cultural Bloopers

An effective way of being culturally sensitive is to minimize actions that are likely to offend people from another culture based on their values. Cultural bloopers are most likely to take place when you are visiting another country. The same bloopers, however, can also be committed with people from a different culture within your own country. To avoid these bloopers, you must carefully observe persons from another culture. Studying another culture through reading is also helpful.

E-commerce and other forms of Internet communication have created new opportunities for creating cultural bloopers. The Web site developers and the workers responsible for adding content must have good cross-cultural literacy, including an awareness of how the information might be misinterpreted. Here is a sampling of potential problems:

- Numerical date formats can be readily interpreted. To an American, 4/9/01 would be interpreted as April 9, 2001 (or 1901!). However, many Europeans would interpret the same numerical expression as September 4, 2001.

- Colors on Web sites must be chosen carefully. For example, in some cultures purple is the color of royalty, whereas in Brazil purple is associated with death.

- Be careful of metaphors that may not make sense to a person for whom your language is a second language. Examples include "We've encountered an ethical meltdown" and "Our biggest competitor is over the hill."

International business specialist Rick Borelli recommends that being able to communicate your message directly in your customer's mother tongue provides a competitive advantage.[13] Consumers are four times more likely to purchase from a Web site written in their native language. The translator, of course, must have good knowledge of the subtleties of the language to avoid a blooper. An English-to-French translator used the verb *baiser* instead of *baisser* to describe a program of lowering prices. *Baisser* is the French verb "to lower," whereas *baiser* is the verb "to kiss." Worse, in everyday language, *baiser* is a verb that refers to having an intimate physical relationship!

Keep two key facts in mind when attempting to avoid cultural mistakes. One is that members of any cultural group show individual differences. What one member of the group might regard as an insensitive act another might welcome. Recognize also that one or two cultural mistakes will not peg you permanently as a boor. Human Relations Skill-Building Exercise 9-1 will help you minimize certain cultural bloopers.

HUMAN RELATIONS SKILL BUILDING EXERCISE 9-1

Cultural Mistakes to Avoid with Selected Cultural Groups

Western Europe

Great Britain	◆ Asking personal questions. The British protect their privacy.
	◆ Thinking that a business person from England is unenthusiastic when he or she says, "Not bad at all." English people understate positive emotion.
	◆ Gossiping about royalty.
France	◆ Expecting to complete work during the French two-hour lunch.
	◆ Attempting to conduct significant business during August—*les vacances* (vacation time)
	◆ Greeting a French person for the first time and not using a title such as "sir" or "madam" (or monsieur, madame, or mademoiselle).
Italy	◆ Eating too much pasta, as it is not the main course.
	◆ Handing out business cards freely. Italians use them infrequently.
Spain	◆ Expecting punctuality. Your appointments will usually arrive 20 to 30 minutes late.
	◆ Make the American sign for "okay" with your thumb and forefinger. In Spain (and many other countries) this is vulgar.
Scandinavia (Denmark, Sweden, Norway)	◆ Being overly rank conscious in these countries. Scandinavians pay relatively little attention to a person's place in the hierarchy.
	◆ Introducing conflict among Swedish work associates. Swedes go out of their way to avoid conflict.

Asia

All Asian countries	◆ Pressuring an Asian job applicant or employee to brag about his or her accomplishments. Asians feel self-conscious when boasting about individual accomplishments and prefer to let the record speak for itself. In addition, they prefer to talk about group rather than individual accomplishments.

(Continued)

Japan	◆ Shaking hands or hugging Japanese (as well as other Asians) in public. Japanese consider the practices to be offensive.
	◆ Not interpreting "We'll consider it" as a no when spoken by a Japanese businessperson. Japanese negotiators mean no when they say, "We'll consider it."
	◆ Not giving small gifts to Japanese when conducting business. Japanese are offended by not receiving these gifts.
	◆ Giving your business card to a Japanese businessperson more than once. Japanese prefer to give and receive business cards only once.
China	◆ Using black borders on stationary and business cards because black is associated with death.
	◆ Giving small gifts to Chinese when conducting business. Chinese are offended by these gifts.
	◆ Making cold calls on Chinese business executives. An appropriate introduction is required for a first-time meeting with a Chinese official.
Korea	◆ Saying no. Koreans feel it is important to have visitors leave with good feelings.
India	◆ Telling Indians you prefer not to eat with your hands. If the Indians are not using cutlery when eating, they expect you to do likewise.

Mexico and Latin America

Mexico	◆ Flying into a Mexican city in the morning and expecting to close a deal by lunch. Mexicans build business relationships slowly.
Brazil	◆ Attempting to impress Brazilians by speaking a few words of Spanish. Portuguese is the official language of Brazil.
Most Latin American countries	◆ Wearing elegant and expensive jewelry during a business meeting Most Latin Americans think people should appear more conservative during a business meeting.

NOTE: A cultural mistake for Americans to avoid when conducting business in most countries outside the United States and Canada is to insist on getting down to business quickly. Other stereotyped American traits to avoid are aggressiveness, impatience, and frequent interruptions to get your point across. North Americans in small towns also like to build a relationship before getting down to business.

   The preceding suggestions will lead to cross-cultural skill development if practiced in the right setting. During the next 30 days, look for an opportunity to relate to a person from another culture in the way described in these suggestions. Observe the reaction of the other person for feedback on your cross-cultural effectiveness.

PARTICIPATE IN CULTURAL TRAINING

For many years companies and government agencies have prepared their workers for overseas assignments. The method most frequently chosen is **cultural training,** a set of learning experiences designed to help employees understand the customs, traditions, and beliefs of another culture. In today's diverse business environment and international marketplace, learning about individuals raised in different cultural backgrounds has become more important. Many industries therefore train employees in cross-cultural relations. Consider also that cultural training is beneficial for rounding out our human relations skills. Here we describe one cultural training program geared to a particular industry as well as language training.

A Cross-Cultural Training Program

Cross-cultural training is taken seriously in the home-building and real estate industries. Workers in these industries are learning the Asian cultural language.[14] Such training does not necessarily involve taking crash courses in Chinese or Japanese. Instead, it means that the workers have been learning about subtle cultural differences between Eastern and Western people. (Some forms of cross-cultural training do emphasize learning another language, as described in the next section.)

One justification for this training is that Asians represent over 3 percent of the population in the United States. Also, because the fast-expanding Asian population is affluent, they are a target market for home builders and sellers. In California, for example, Asian and Asian Americans account for 30 to 40 percent of the first-time buyer's market.

Builders and Realtors hire cultural diversity specialists to help them learn how to communicate with and accommodate their customers from China, Japan, Taiwan, Korea, Vietnam, and the Philippines. (*Realtor* is a trademark name for a certified real estate broker.) Homebuilders and Realtors receive cultural training in issues such as the following:

- Negotiating styles
- Money-matter discussions
- Use of body language, such as eye contact
- Business etiquette
- Design preferences in a home, such as *feng shui* (The term refers to the ancient Chinese philosophy of creating a harmonious home environment, leading to good luck and prosperity for the inhabitant. *Feng shui* is now also popular with many other ethnic and racial groups in the United States and Canada.)

One cultural training seminar teaches participants to examine the mind-set of Asian people in order to understand their actions. Real estate personnel are taught the dynamics of an Asian family who might look at model homes as a group. A home-buying decision involves the entire family. As a trainer notes, "So when a professional couple comes in with Grandma, Grandpa, and the kids, be very respectful to everyone. Probably the older couple will be making the down payment."

Participants are also taught that carefully observing body language will help the seller determine who is the boss in the family. The trainer explains as follows: "In the United States, we always can tell who's the decision maker. It's usually the one who talks the most. But in Asian cultures, very often the one who doesn't talk is the one who has the power."

Realtors are also taught how to sell to Asian customers. Asians frown on familiarity, so sales representatives are urged not to be aggressive. Patience is a virtue in selling to Asians. Chinese, in particular, prefer to gradually develop a relationship rather than to close a deal quickly. A point established early in the seminar is that the worst error is to mistake one Asian extraction for another (such as a Vietnamese for a Japanese). The Asian continent comprises 41 countries, with 19 in the Pacific Rim.

Dozens of other small yet important details are presented in the seminar to improve relationships with Asian clients. Participants learn different types of handshakes, how to bow the correct ways, and how to exchange business cards. Participants even learn about the significance of colors and certain numbers to Asians. For example, Asians consider white, blue, and yellow to be funeral colors and might reject a house lavished with these colors. Some Asians might choose a house on the basis of whether the numbers in the address are thought to bring good or bad luck.

Cultural training is considered essential for international workers involved in negotiations with people from other cultures because negotiating styles differ across cultures.[15] For example, the Japanese prefer an exchange of information to confrontation. Russians, in contrast, enjoy combat in negotiations. (Again, we are dealing with cultural stereotypes.)

To practice improving your cross-cultural relations, do Human Relations Skill-Building Exercise 9-2. Asian and Asian American class members may have a natural advantage in playing the roles in the exercise.

Foreign Language Training

Learning a foreign language is often part of cultural training yet can also be a separate activity. Knowledge of a second language is important because it builds better connections with people from other cultures than does relying on a translator. Many workers aside from international business specialists also choose to develop skills in a target language. Speaking another language can help build rapport with customers and employees who speak that language.

Almost all language training has elements similar to taking a course in another language or self-study. Companies invest heavily in helping employees learn a target language because it facilitates conducting business in other countries. Medical specialists, police workers, and firefighters also

---

HUMAN RELATIONS SKILL-BUILDING EXERCISE 9-2

Cross-Cultural Relations Role Play

To get started applying cross-cultural sensitivity, a group of students engage in the following role play. One person plays the role of a Realtor who is showing a single-family dwelling to the Wong family (Chinese Americans). The Realtor recognizes that the family is a hot prospect because they are affluent, headed by two business professionals. Six students play the role of the Wong family: two parents, two grandparents, and two elementary school–age children. The Wong family would like to purchase this luxurious home at a fair price. The grandparents in particular think that they should buy only from a Realtor who respects their culture.

The Realtor and the Wong family engage in the selling transaction for about 10 minutes. The balance of the class will critically observe the interaction and then provide feedback.

---

find second language skills to be quite helpful. Clients under stress, like an injured person, are likely to revert to their native tongue.

As with any other skill training, the above investments can only pay off if the trainee is willing to work hard developing the new skill outside the training session. It is unlikely that almost anyone can develop conversational skills in another language by listening to foreign language cassette tapes or taking classes for 30 days. The quick training program, however, helps you develop a base for further learning. Allowing even 10 days to pass without practicing your target language will result in a sharp decline in your ability to use that language.

PARTICIPATE IN DIVERSITY TRAINING

The general purpose of cultural training is to help workers understand people from other cultures. Understanding can lead to dealing more effectively with them as work associates or customers. **Diversity training** has a slightly different purpose. It attempts to bring about workplace harmony by teaching people how to get along with diverse work associates. Quite often the program is aimed at minimizing open expressions of racism and sexism. Diversity training takes a number of forms. Nevertheless, all center on increasing awareness of and empathy for people who are different in some noticeable way from oneself.

A starting point in diversity training is to emphasize that everybody is different is some way and that all these differences should be appreciated. The subtle point here is that cultural diversity does not refer exclusively to differences in race, ethnicity, age, and sex. Diversity training emphasizes *inclusion,* or including everybody when appreciating diversity. Exhibit 9-2 presents a broad sampling of the ways in which workplace associates can

EXHIBIT 9-2

The Diversity Umbrella

Diversity has evolved into a wide range of group and individual characteristics.

- Race

- Sex or gender

- Religion

- Age (young, middle aged, and old)

- Generation differences, including attitudes (e.g., baby boomers versus the Net Generation)

- Ethnicity (country of origin)

- Education

- Abilities

- Mental disabilities (including attention deficit disorder)

- Physical disabilities (including hearing status, visual status, able-bodied, wheelchair user)

- Values and motivation

- Sexual orientation (heterosexual, homosexual, bisexual, transsexual)

- Marital status (married, single, cohabitating, widow, widower)

- Family status (children, no children, two-parent family, single parent, grandparent, opposite-sex parents, same-sex parents)

- Personality traits

- Functional background (area of specialization, such as marketing, manufacturing)

- Technology interest (high-tech, low-tech, technophobe)

- Weight status (average, obese, underweight, anorexic)

- Hair status (full head of hair, bald, wild hair, tame hair, long hair, short hair)

- Style of clothing and appearance (dress up, dress down, professional appearance, casual appearance, tattoos, body piercing including multiple earrings, nose rings, lip rings)

- Tobacco status (smoker versus nonsmoker, chewer versus nonchewer)

- Your creative suggestion _____

_____

differ from one another. All these differences are tucked under the welcoming *diversity umbrella*. Studying this list can help you anticipate the type of differences to understand and appreciate in a diverse workplace. The differences include cultural as well as individual factors. Individual factors are also important because people can be discriminated against for personal characteristics as well as group characteristics. Many people who are disfigured believe they are held back from obtaining a higher-level job because of their disfigurement, such as a facial birthmark.

Another important part of diversity training is to develop empathy for diverse viewpoints. To help training participants develop empathy, representatives of various groups explain their feelings related to workplace issues. In one segment of such a program, a minority group member was seated in the middle of a circle. The other participants sat at the periphery of the circle. First, the coworkers listened to a Vietnamese woman explain how she felt excluded from the in-group composed of whites and African Americans in her department. "I feel like you just tolerate me. You do not make me feel that I am somebody important. You make me feel that because I am Vietnamese I don't count."

The next person to sit in the middle of the circle was Muslim. He complained about people wishing him Merry Christmas. "I would much prefer that my coworkers would stop to think that I do not celebrate Christian holidays. I respect your religion, but it is not my religion."

Human Relations Skill-Building Exercise 9-3 will give you direct experience in diversity awareness training. Being nonconfrontational in nature, the exercise usually leads to harmony and other positive feelings. A criticism of many diversity training programs is that too many angry feelings are expressed and that negative stereotypes are reinforced, leading to strained relationships. Another criticism is that the program might be considered patronizing because the majority of participants are already respectful of people different from themselves and know how to work harmoniously with a wide variety of people.

HUMAN RELATIONS SKILL-BUILDING EXERCISE 9-3

Developing Empathy for Differences

Class members come up the front of the room one by one and give a brief presentation (perhaps even three minutes) of any way in which they have been perceived as different and how they felt about this perception. The difference can be of any kind, relating to characteristics such as ethnicity, race, choice of major, physical appearance, height, weight, hair color, or body piercing. After each member of the class has presented (perhaps even the instructor), class members discuss what they learned from the exercise. It is also important to discuss how this exercise can improve relationships on the job.

Support for the importance of diversity training comes from a five-year study of the impact of diversity on business results conducted by Thomas A. Kochan of the Massachusetts Institute of Technology. He concludes that a culturally diverse workforce enhances business performance only when proper training is provided to employees. An organizational culture that supports diversity, meaning that the values and atmosphere of the firm welcome inclusion, is also required.[16]

▲ OVERCOMING CROSS-CULTURAL COMMUNICATION BARRIERS

A key part of developing good cross-cultural relations is to overcome or prevent communication barriers stemming from cultural differences. Personal life, too, is often more culturally diverse today than previously, leading to culturally based communication problems. The information about avoiding cultural bloopers presented in this chapter might also be interpreted as a way to prevent communication barriers. Here we describe several additional strategies and tactics to help overcome cross-cultural communication barriers.

1. *Be alert to cultural differences in customs and behavior.* To minimize cross-cultural communication barriers, recognize that many subtle job-related differences in customs and behavior may exist (as illustrated in Human Relations Skill-Building Exercise 9-1). For example, Asians typically feel uncomfortable when asked to brag about themselves in the presence of others. From their perspective, calling attention to yourself at the expense of another person is rude and unprofessional.

2. *Use straightforward language and speak slowly and clearly.* When working with people who do not speak your language fluently, speak in an easy-to-understand manner. Minimize the use of idioms and analogies specific to your language. For example, in North America the term "over the hill" means outdated or past one's prime. A person from another culture may not understand this phrase yet be hesitant to ask for clarification. Speaking slowly is also important because even people who read and write a second language at an expert level may have difficulty catching the nuances of conversation. Facing the person from another culture directly also improves communication because your facial expressions and lips contribute to comprehension.

3. *When the situation is appropriate, speak in the language of the people from another culture.* Americans who can speak another language are at a competitive advantage when dealing with businesspeople who speak that language. The language skill, however, must be more advanced than speaking a few words and phrases. A new twist in speaking another language has surged recently: As more deaf people have been integrated into the workforce, knowing American Sign Language can be a real advantage to a worker when some of his or her coworkers or customers are deaf.

4. *Observe cultural differences in etiquette.* Violating rules of etiquette without explanation can erect immediate communication barriers. A major rule of etiquette is that in some countries older people in high-status positions expect to be treated with respect. Formality is important, unless invited to do otherwise. When visiting a company in Asia, for example, it is best to be deferent (appeal to the authority of) to company dignitaries. Visualize yourself as a company representative of a high-tech American firm that manufactures equipment for legally downloading music over the Internet. You visit Sony Corporation in Japan to speak about a joint venture. On meeting the marketing vice president, bow slightly and say something to the effect; "Mr. _____, it is my honor to discuss doing business with Sony." Do not commit the etiquette mistake of saying something to the effect, "Hi Charlie, how's the wife and kids?" (An American actually said this at a Japanese company shortly before being escorted out the door.)

5. *Be sensitive to differences in nonverbal communication.* Stay alert to the possibility that a person from another culture may misinterpret your nonverbal signal. To use positive reinforcement, some managers will give a sideways hug to an employee or will touch an employee's arm. People from some cultures resent touching from workmates and will be offended. Koreans in particular dislike being touched or touching others in a work setting. (Refer back to the discussion of cultural bloopers.)

6. *Do not be diverted by style, accent, grammar, or personal appearance.* Although all these superficial factors are related to business success, they are difficult to interpret when judging a person from another culture. It is therefore better to judge the merits of the statement or behavior.[17] A brilliant individual from another culture may still be learning your language and thus make basic mistakes in speaking your language. He or she might also not have developed a sensitivity to dress style in your culture.

7. *Listen for understanding, not agreement.* When working with diverse teammates, the differences in viewpoints can lead to conflict. To help overcome such conflict, follow the *LUNA rule:* Listen for Understanding, Not Agreement. In this way you gear yourself to consider the viewpoints of others as a first resort. For example; some older workers may express some intense loyalty to the organization, while their younger teammates may speak in more critical terms. By everyone listening to understand, they can begin to appreciate each others' paradigms and accept differences of opinion.[18] Listening is a powerful tool for overcoming cross-cultural communication barriers.

8. *Be attentive to individual differences in appearance.* A major cross-cultural insult is to confuse the identity of people because they are members of the same race or ethnic group. Psychological research suggests that people have difficulty seeing individual differences among people of another race because they code race first, such as thinking, "He has the nose of an African American." However, people can learn to search for more distinguishing features, such as a dimple or eye color.[19]

▲ SUMMARY

Being able to work well with people from other cultures, both outside and inside your own country, is important for career success. Seven dimensions of cultural values that help us understand how cultures differ from one another are as follows: (1) individualism versus collectivism; (2) acceptance of power and authority; (3) materialism versus concern for others; (4) formality versus informality; (5) urgent time orientation versus casual time orientation; (6) work orientation versus leisure orientation; and (7) high-context versus low-context cultures (with an emphasis on body language). Many other cultural differences, such as religious practices, are also noteworthy. Many people identify with more than one culture, adding to the complexity of cross-cultural relations. It is important to be alert to possible cultural differences.

Certain underlying factors create problems in developing smooth cross-cultural relations, including communication problems. Perceptual expectations are much like stereotypes that lead to misunderstandings. Ethnocentrism, or thinking that one's culture is best, leads to misunderstandings. Paying attention to intergroup (group membership) factors rather than individual (interpersonal) factors leads to problems. Misunderstandings also come about from stereotypes in intergroup relations and different norms and codes of conduct among cultures. Unintentional microinequities also create problems.

Six specific methods and techniques for improving cross cultural relations are as follows: (1) develop cultural sensitivity (being aware of differences); (2) respect all workers and cultures; (3) focus on the individual; (4) value cultural differences (this also involves showing respect); (5) minimize cultural bloopers (embarrassing mistakes); (6) participate in cultural training, including cross-cultural programs and language training; and (7) participate in diversity training, or learning to get along with diverse work associates.

Communication barriers can often be overcome by the following: being alert to cultural differences in customs and behavior; using straightforward language and speaking slowly and clearly; speaking in the language of the other group; observing cultural differences in etiquette; being sensitive to differences in nonverbal communication; not being diverted by style, accent, grammar, or personal appearance; listening for understanding, not agreement; and being attentive to individual differences in appearance.

Questions and Activities

1. How might having a culturally diverse workforce help a company earn more profits?

2. In what way might having a high acceptance for power and authority make it difficult for a person to work well on a team that has very little supervision?

3. Identify three positive stereotypes about cultural groups that are related to job behavior. (An example would be the comment made about the methodical approach of Chinese workers.)

4. When you meet someone from another culture, what can you do to demonstrate that you respect that person's culture?

5. Provide an example of cultural insensitivity of any kind that you have seen, read about, or could imagine.

6. Some companies, such as Singapore Airlines, make a deliberate effort for all customer contact personnel to be of the same ethnic group (Singapore natives). How justified is this practice in an era of cultural diversity and valuing differences?

7. All the cultural bloopers presented in Human Relations Skill-Building Exercise 9-1 dealt with errors people make in regard to people who are not American. Give an example of a cultural blooper that a person from another country might make in the United States.

8. In an era of welcoming cultural diversity, does a company have the right to exclude employees with visible body piercings from any type of positions?

9. Suppose a company wants to promote cross-cultural understanding. Should the executives then discourage students from one racial or ethnic group from forming a club or sitting together in the company cafeteria? Explain your position.

10. Many people speak loudly to deaf people, blind people, and those who speak a different language. Based on the information presented in this chapter, what mistakes are these people making?

INTERNET SKILL BUILDER: Developing Your Multicultural Skills

A useful way of developing skills in a second language and learning more about another culture is to create a cover page (the page that appears when you open a Web site) written in your target language. In this way, each time you go the Internet on your own computer, your cover page will contain fresh information in the language you want to develop.

Assume that your target language is French. Enter a phrase like "French language newspaper" or " French current events" in the search probe. Once you find a suitable choice, insert that newspaper as your cover page. The search engine might have brought you to www.france2.fr or www.cyberpresse.ca. These Web sites keep you abreast of French and French Canadian international news, sports, and cultural events—written in French. Now every time you access the Internet, you can spend a few minutes becoming multicultural. You can save lot of travel costs and time using the Internet to help you become multicultural.

A HUMAN RELATIONS CASE PROBLEM

Ralph Lauren Seeks Racial Harmony

Fashion magnate Ralph Lauren says he first became aware of racial tension within his company after an incident in 1997 at a Long Island sportswear boutique. A regional manager with Polo Ralph Lauren Corp. dropped by the new Polo Sport store in anticipation of an inspection by an important visitor: Jerome Lauren, Ralph's older brother and the executive overseeing Polo menswear. The mall where the boutique was located attracts a middle-class, racially integrated clientele. But the regional manager concluded that the store's ambiance was too "urban," meaning black, former Polo officials said.

The manager ordered two black and two Hispanic sales associates off the floor and back into the stock room so they wouldn't be visible to Mr. Lauren. The sales associates followed orders, but they later hired a lawyer and threatened to sue Polo for discrimination. The company reached confidential settlements with the four.

Ralph Lauren says he learned about the incident several weeks after it happened and "was just sick" about it. The regional manager, Greg Ladley, was ordered to undergo racial-relations training but wasn't fired. A company spokesman says that Ladley's recollection is that some sales associates working on inventory were asked to move to the stock room because they weren't "dressed appropriately."

After the episode, Ralph Lauren told subordinates, "We have to correct this. Let's make a change." But executives who worked at Polo at the time say their boss didn't make clear what changes they wanted.

Air of Exclusiveness

Polo, like some of its rivals, presents a multiracial face to the word, with black models in some of its ads and a following of young black consumers wearing its familiar logo of a horseman wielding a polo mallet. Yet internally, big fashion houses tend to exude an exclusiveness that is uninviting to many nonwhites. Few blacks or Hispanics have penetrated the upper ranks of major clothes manufacturers and retailers.

In response to complaints that have flared up at Polo, Lauren has met with lawyers, hired lieutenants to overhaul company personnel practices, and embraced diversity training. But he says he has left the details to others, as he is usually preoccupied with design work at his headquarters studio.

The Polo aura of Anglo-Saxon elitism is the elaborate creation of Polo's founder, Ralph Lauren, 62 years old, who remade himself as he rose from modest roots in the Bronx to become the chairman and Chief Executive Officer of a fashion powerhouse. Polo retail supervisors routinely tell salespeople to think Hollywood. "Ralph is the director," the instruction goes, "and you are the actors, and we are here to make a movie." But some black and Hispanic employees say the movie seems to lack parts for them.

Color Blind?

Lauren says he is color blind when it comes to hiring talent. He frequently points out the wide visibility he has given Tyson Beckford, the striking shaven-headed black fashion model who has appeared in Polo ads since 1994. "Tyson is not just in jeans," Lauren says. "We put him in a pinstripe suit, in our best Purple Label brand. Tyson is in the annual report, in our advertisements on TV."

(Continued)

Lauren says Polo "is a leader to do the right things to bring in the people who are the best in the industry." Some of his subordinates complain, however, that it is difficult to find black and Hispanic applicants with the credentials for design jobs coming out of the New York fashion schools where Polo usually recruits.

A Polo staffer recommended in 1998 that Lauren meet Lacey Moore, a 20-year-old African American from Brooklyn, who had taken some college-level communications courses and had aspirations to be in the music business. Since high school, Moore had worn Polo Oxford shirts and knit tops with flashy gold chains and a hip-hop attitude: precisely the sort of hybrid image Lauren hoped would draw younger customers. "Lacey is edgy—he gets it," Mr. Lauren recalls thinking, snapping his fingers for effect. He hired the young man as a design assistant.

The new recruit's rap-influenced personal style and lingo confounded his coworkers. Moore felt isolated. He says he understood that in any competitive workplace, "there are people who don't like you." But in Polo's cliquish and overwhelmingly white Madison Avenue headquarters, he says coworkers made it clear he wasn't welcome. "I kept getting this bad vibe," he says. He quit in 2000.

Shocked, Lauren telephoned Moore at home. "Lacey, I want you to come back," he recalls saying. After listening to Moore's complaints, Lauren says he made it clear to the young man's white coworkers, "I want you all to work this out." A couple of weeks later, Moore returned, but warily.

Advice and Pressure

Polo has received advice and pressure on the race issue from a variety of outside counselors and advocates. A civil rights authority advised Lauren that achieving a truly diverse workforce requires hiring more than a few black employees. A black activist minister met with Polo officials and helped some minority workers reach confidential settlements with the company.

Today Moore (the young design assistant) says his colleagues seem friendlier. The human resources vice president has given Moore reassurance. "You feel there is someone looking out for you," says the young assistant, who helps prepare for fashion shows and consults on clothing design.

Lauren says he is paying more attention to what he sees at work. For example, he recalls that at a company Christmas party in 2000, he was surprised that a group of blacks and Hispanics had congregated in a separate room. "Why is this happening?" he says he wondered. "What's not welcoming to those employees?"

Lauren says he didn't approach his workers to ask them, however, and is still wondering about the answers to those questions.

Questions

1. What advice can you offer Lauren to achieve fuller workplace diversity at Polo?

2. Is the Christmas holiday party incident a symptom of an organizational problem? Or were the black and Hispanic employees just behaving as they chose?

3. Does Ralph Lauren "get it" as a leader with respect to cultural diversity in the workplace?

SOURCE: Adapted from Teri Agins, "Color Line: A Fashion House with an Elite Aura Wrestles with Race," *Wall Street Journal,* August 19, 2002, pp. A1, A9.

WEB CORNER

Cultural training: www.berlitz.com and www.relowizard.com (choose a sample company profile)

Cultural diversity: www.DiversityInc.com

▲ REFERENCES

1. Amy Joyce, "Learning What to Accent on Foreign Sales Trips," *Washington Post* syndicated story, August 13, 2003.

2. Data cited in Todd Campbell, "Diversity in Depth," *HR Magazine,* March 2003, p. 152.

3. Geert Hofstede, *Culture's Consequences: International Differences in Work-Related Values* (Beverly Hills, CA: Sage, 1980; updated and expanded in "A Conversation with Geert Hofstede," *Organizational Dynamics,* Spring 1993, pp. 53–61; Jim Kennedy and Anna Everest, "Put Diversity in Context," *Personnel Journal,* September 1991, pp. 50–54.

4. Jeffrey Jensen Arnett, "The Psychology of Globalization," *American Psychologist,* October 2002, pp. 777–778.

5. Gary M. Stern, "Small Slights Bring Big Problems," *Workforce,* August 2002, p. 17.

6. Based on the contribution of Terri Geerinck in Andrew J. DuBrin and Terri Geerinck, *Human Relations for Career and Personal Success,* 2d Canadian ed. (Toronto: Prentice Hall, 2001), p. 201. Geerinck also contributed the idea of having a separate chapter on cross-cultural competency.

7. Arvind V. Phatak, *International Dimensions of Management* (Boston: Kent, 1983), p. 167.

8. Todd Raphael, "Savvy Companies Build Bonds with Hispanic Employees," *Workforce,* September 2001, p. 19.

9. Gillian Flynn, "White Males See Diversity's Other Side," *Workforce,* February 1999, p. 52.

10. Gunnar Beeth, "Multicultural Managers Wanted," *Management Review,* May 1997, p. 17.

11. Beeth, "Multicultural Managers Wanted," p. 17.

12. A few of these tasty morsels are from Lillian H. Chaney and Jeannette S. Martin, *Interpersonal Business Communication,* 3d ed. (Upper Saddle River, NJ: Pearson Prentice Hall, 2004), p. 190.

13. Rick Borelli, "A Worldwide Language Trap," *Management Review,* October 1997, pp. 52–54.

14. Marcia Forsberg, "Cultural Training Improves Relations with Asian Clients," *Personnel Journal,* May 1993, pp. 79–89. The quotes are from the same source.

15. Marc Diener, "Culture Shock," *Entrepreneur,* July 2003, p. 77.

16. Research reported in Fay Hansen, "Diversity's Business Case Doesn't Add Up," *Workforce,* April 2003, pp. 28–32.

17. David P. Tulin, "Enhance Your Multi-Cultural Communication Skills," *Managing Diversity*, 1, 1992, p. 5.

18. "Use Team's Diversity to Best Advantage, *ExecutiveSTRATEGIES*, April 2000, p. 2.

19. Siri Carpenter, "Why Do 'They All Look Alike'?" *Monitor on Psychology*, December 2000, p. 44.

▲ ADDITIONAL READING

Cohen, Sacha. "High-Tech Tools Lower Barriers for Disabled." *HR Magazine,* October 2002, pp. 60–65.

Flynn, Gillian. "Gray Areas in Controlling Employee Lifestyles." *Workforce,* February 2003, pp. 64–65.

Frase-Blunt, Martha. "Thwarting the Diversity Backlash." *HR Magazine,* June 2003, pp. 137–144.

Hirschman, Carolyn. "Off Duty, Out of Work." *HR Magazine,* February 2003, pp. 50–56.

Hobman, Elizabeth V., Prahsant Bordia, and Cynthia Gallois. "Consequences of Feeling Dissimilar from Others in a Work Team." *Journal of Business and Psychology,* Spring 2003, pp. 301–325.

Hostager, Todd J., and Kenneth P. De Meuse. "Assessing the Complexity of Diversity Perceptions: Breadth, Depth, and Balance." *Journal of Business and Psychology,* Winter 2002, pp. 189–206.

Schramm, Jennifer. "Acting Affirmatively." *HR Magazine,* September 2003, p. 192.

Stern, Gary M. "Small Slights Bring Big Problems." *Workforce,* August 2002, p. 17.

Wellner, Alison Stein. "Tapping a Silver Mine." *HR Magazine,* March 2002, pp. 26–32.

Wiscombe, Janet. "Corporate America's Scariest Opponent." *Workforce,* April 2003, pp. 34–41.

CHAPTER 10

Choosing a Career and Developing a Portfolio Career

Learning Objectives

After studying the information and doing the exercises in this chapter, you should be able to:

◆ Make a tentative career choice if you have not already selected a first career

◆ Identify skills that could serve as the basis for your career

◆ Search for useful information about occupations and careers

◆ Apply the concept of data, people, things, or ideas to yourself

◆ Explain the basics of career switching and developing a portfolio career

*P*at Connors, 55, oversees Camp Akenac, a lakeside retreat in the Pennsylvania Poconos, operated by technology company Agilent. Connors manages staff and guest reservations and maintains 26 buildings on 200 acres.

Connors says he got started in this satisfying position while he was working on the manufacturing line for Hewlett-Packard (which spun off Agilent in 1999) when he heard about the job. "I'm a naturalist at heart. As my mother said, it was a round peg in a round hole." Connors says the worst part of the job is surviving the winter. The camp is open only in the summer, but he lives there all year.

When asked where he goes next from his present position, Connors replied, "This is it. I enjoy what I do. I'm living a dream."[1]

The anecdote about the recreational site manager illustrates that some people in business-related fields do find the ideal career from their standpoint. The man in question shifted from a manufacturing position to one that was an ideal fit with his personal interests. Conners was able to apply business skills in a recreational environment. If he had not identified what he liked to do best, he would not have applied for the position as recreational site manager.

What a person does for a living is one of the key influences in his or her life. Your career is also a prime source of your self-concept and self-esteem. The purpose of this chapter is to help you choose a career by describing systematic methods of career selection. For those who have already chosen a career field in general, this chapter may help you narrow down your career choice within your field. For example, a person entering the computer field might choose to emphasize those aspects of computers dealing heavily with people, such as computer sales or information systems.

▲ SELF-KNOWLEDGE AND CHOOSING A CAREER

A **career** is a series of related job experiences that fit into a meaningful pattern. If you have a series of odd jobs all your working life, that is hardly a career. But if each job builds carefully on the previous one, we say you are "building a career." We assume that by making a sound initial choice of occupation, you will be on the first step toward building a real career. Chapters 11 through 14 provide information to help you advance in whatever career you have chosen.

A general strategy for making a sound career choice is to understand first the inner you, including what you have to offer. Above all, you must assess your skills, interests, and preferences. You then match that information with opportunities in the outside world. The Self-Knowledge Questionnaire presented in Chapter 1 asks many questions that are relevant for making a career choice. Almost any of the information provided by candid answers to those questions could help you make a sound career choice. Several specific illustrations are in order.

Question 1 asks, "How far have I gone in school?" If you answered, "Four years of high school and one years of business school," you will need additional education for many fields. Among them are management, customer service, teaching, or social work.

Question 8 asks, "What aspect of these jobs did I enjoy?" Suppose you answered, "Anytime I was left alone to do some figuring or report writing, I was happy. Thinking made me happy." Your answer could mean that you should search for a field in which working with ideas and data is more important than working with people or things. What about investigating laboratory work or financial analysis?

Question 25 asks, "What are my key values (the things most important to me)?" Suppose you answered, "Doing exciting work, having enough money for myself and my loved ones to live well, and being well respected." An answer of this nature suggests you would be motivated to perform well in an occupation that offered mentally stimulating work, that was high paying, and that was held in high regard by others. Perhaps selling financial services or commercial real estate would fit your interests. Or how about a career as an international art dealer, traveling in your private jet?

Some additional questions useful in clarifying the type of work you would prefer are presented in Human Relations Self-Assessment Quiz 10-1.

HUMAN RELATIONS SELF-ASSESSMENT QUIZ 10-1

Learning More about Yourself

By candidly answering the questions that follow, you may be able to develop some new understanding about your career preferences. Try to write at least 25 words in response to each question, even if your answer is uncertain.

1. What kind of work would make me proud?

2. What would be a horrible way for me to make a living?

3. How important is a high income to me? Why?

4. How do I really feel about what other people think of the kind of work I do?

5. What kind of work would really be fun for me to do?

6. What kind of work would I be willing to do for 10 consecutive years?

7. What kind of work would make me feel self-fulfilled?

8. What is my attitude toward doing the same thing every workday?

9. How do I really feel about being held responsible when things go wrong?

The Importance of Skills in Choosing a Career

In addition to other aspects of self-understanding, knowing which skills and abilities you possess—and enjoy performing—can be the basis for a successful career. A **skill** is a learned, specific ability, such as writing a report, developing a Web site, or conducting a job interview. A vast number of skills could be exercised in a career, including such skills as selling, calculating currency exchanges, and coaching workers. Identifying your skills is important both in choosing a career and in finding a job. Prospective employers want to know what a job candidate can actually *do,* or what skills he or she possesses.

Your best skill represents your **core competency,** or whatever you do best. But there is more to core competency than what is suggested in your job title.[2] Your core competency is the aspect of your job that you perform particularly well. As a collection agent, your core competency might be obtaining partial payments with accounts so long overdue that others consider them almost uncollectible. If you have developed a core competency early in your schooling or temporary work experience, making a sound career choice is easier. An adolescent with superior skill in explaining to others how to use electronic devices might have the necessary core competency for a career in technical writing. (A big part of a technical writer's job is preparing operating manuals for equipment.)

Julie Griffin Levitt has developed a useful way of identifying skills[3] as outlined in Human Relations Self-Assessment Quiz 10-2. As you develop several of these skills to an above-average degree, they may become your core competency.

Getting Help from a Career Counselor

In choosing a career or switching careers, a beneficial method of learning more about yourself in relation to the world of work is to obtain help from a professional **career counselor.** A counselor usually relies on a wide variety of tests plus an interview to assist you in making a sound career choice. It is untrue that any single test will tell you what occupation you should enter. Tests are designed to provide useful clues, not to give you definite answers. Nor is it true that a career counselor will tell you what occupation you should enter. Using tests and human judgment, the counselor assists you to become more aware of yourself and the alternatives that might suit your circumstances. This chapter emphasizes choosing a career by yourself. It is recommended, however, that you seek the assistance of a guidance counselor, career counselor, or counseling psychologist.

Interest Testing to Identify Careers of Interest

Career counseling emphasizes finding a career that suits a person's interests. Note that interest is not the same as ability. Some people may not have the mental aptitude and skills to do well in the occupations they would

HUMANS RELATIONS SELF-ASSESSMENT QUIZ 10-2

Skills Profile

Directions: Review the following skills areas and specific skills. In the space provided, write down each one you believe is a strong skill for you. You can also add a specific skill that was not included in the skill area listed at the left.

Skill Area	Specific Skills	A Strong Skill for Me
Communication	Writing, speaking, knowledge of foreign language, telephone skills, persuasiveness, listening	_____
Creative	Originating ideas, thinking up novel solutions, being imaginative	_____
Interpersonal relations	Ability to get along well with others, being a team player, diplomacy, conflict resolution, understanding others	_____
Management of self and others	Ability to lead, organize, plan, motivate others, make decisions, manage time	_____
Manual and mechanical	Mechanically inclined, build, operate, repair, assemble, install, drive vehicles	_____
Mathematics	Math skills, computers, analyzing data, budgeting, using statistical techniques	_____
Information technology and office	Keyboarding, word processing, spreadsheets, e-mail organizing, database management, Web design and management, business math, record keeping	_____
Sales	Persuading others, negotiating, promoting, dressing fashionably	_____
Scientific	Investigating, researching, compiling, systematizing, diagnosing, evaluating	_____
Service of customers	Serving customers, handling complaints, dealing with difficult people	_____
Service of patients	Nurturing, diagnosing, treating, guiding, counseling, consoling, dealing with emergencies	_____
Other skill area:	_____	_____

SOURCE: Abridged and adapted from Julie Griffin Levitt, *Your Career: How to Make It Happen,* 2d ed. (Cincinnati: South-Western Publishing, 1990), pp. 19–21.

enjoy. Interest is but one important factor contributing to successful performance. Being interested in your field makes its biggest contribution to keeping you motivated. The most widely used instrument for matching a person's interests with careers is the **Strong Interest Inventory (SII).** The output of the SII is a computer-generated report that provides potentially useful information about making career choices.[4]

The Strong asks 317 questions about your preferences (likes, dislikes, or indifferences) concerning occupations, school subjects, activities, amusements, and types of people. Exhibit 10-1 presents a sampling of such questions. A person's answers to these questions are used to compute three sets of scores: (1) six general occupational themes, (2) 25 basic interest scales, and (3) 211 occupational scales, involving 109 occupations.

Scores on the Strong Interest Inventory

Each of the six general occupational themes is associated with one or more basic interest scales including the following:

R Theme (realistic):   High scores on this theme tend to be rugged, robust, practical individuals who are physically strong and frequently aggressive in outlook. The basic interest scales carrying the realistic theme are Agriculture, Nature, Adventure Military Activities, and Mechanical Activities.

I Theme (investigative):   High scorers on this theme enjoy science and scientific activities and are not particularly interested in working with others. They also enjoy solving abstract problems. The basic interest scales carrying the investigative theme are Science, Mathematics, Medical Science, and Medical Service.

A Theme (artistic):   High scorers on these themes are artistically oriented and like to work in settings where self-expression is welcome. The associated interest scales are Music/Dramatics, Art, and Writing.

S Theme (social):   High scorers on this theme are sociable, responsible, humanistic, and concerned with the welfare of others. The associated interest scales are Teaching, Social Service, Athletics, Domestic Arts, and Religious Activities.

E Theme (enterprising):   High scorers on this theme are skillful with words and use this capability to sell, dominate, and lead. The associated interest scales are Public Speaking, Law/Politics, Merchandising, Sales, and Business Management.

C Theme (conventional):.   High scorers on this theme prefer the ordered activities, both verbal and numerical, that characterize office work. They are comfortable following the rules and regulations of a large firm. The associated interest scale is Office Practices.

The Strong Interest Inventory has 211 occupational scales divided among the six general occupational themes and basic interest scales. For

---

EXHIBIT 10-1

Type of Test Items Found on the Strong Interest Inventory

1. Actor	L	I	D
2. Aviator	L	I	D
3. Architect	L	I	D
4. Astronomer	L	I	D
5. Athletic director	L	I	D
6. Auctioneer	L	I	D
7. Author of novel	L	I	D
8. Author of scientific book	L	I	D
9. Auto sales representative	L	I	D
10. Auto mechanic	L	I	D

NOTE: In this section of the test, the subject indicates whether he or she would like (L), dislike (D), or be indifferent to (I) working in each occupation.

---

example, the following occupations are among those associated with the conventional theme and the office practices scales: accountant, banker, credit manager, business education teacher, food service manager, nursing home administrator, and secretary.

Interpreting the Strong Profile

With the assistance of a counselor, a person looks for patterns of high and low scores. High scores indicate interests similar to people in occupational areas and occupations, whereas low scores suggest the opposite.

Assume that a person scores very high on the Office Practices Scale and high on the occupations of banker and credit manager. The same person also scores very low on the Investigative theme, the Medical Service Interest Scale, and the medical technical and respiratory therapist Occupational Scales. We conclude that this person would be happier as an office manager than as an ambulance medic!

MATCHING YOUR CAREER TO YOUR LIFESTYLE

Another consideration in using self-knowledge to assist in choosing a career is to take into account your lifestyle preferences. Ideally, you should pursue a career that provides you with the right balance among work, leisure, and interaction with people. Some degree of compromise is usually necessary. If your preferred lifestyle is to take two-hour lunch breaks each workday, it would be difficult to attain a high level of responsibility. Executives, public relations specialists, and sales representatives who seem to spend considerable time at lunch are usually conducting business over their meals. They are not taking time out during the workday. If a cornerstone of your lifestyle is to remain in top physical and mental shape, you should probably avoid some of the high- pressure careers, such as ambulance paramedic or securities sales representative. On the other hand, you would want to avoid a career that provided too little challenge.

As just hinted, the term **lifestyle** can refer to many different key aspects of your life. In terms of making a career choice, it is helpful to regard lifestyle as the pattern by which a person invests energy into work and nonwork. Being the proverbial beach bum or ski bum is one lifestyle. So is being the 80-hour-a-week government executive.

Today, an increasing number of people at different stages in their careers are making career choices that improve their chances of leading their preferred lifestyles. The general manager of a plant in a small town makes a revealing comment about modern lifestyles: "A number of years ago we couldn't get nearly the number of skilled people we needed to work here. The people who had a choice wanted to live in an area near a big city. Now we get loads of unsolicited résumés. It seems that a lot of people want access to camping and fishing. I think they're also worried about crime and pollution in the cities."

The move toward a healthy balance between work and personal life might also be considered part of the movement toward a higher quality of life. For some people, living in a $2,800-a-month studio apartment in New York or San Francisco represents a high quality of life. Such city dwellers would, of course, have to aspire toward very high-paying occupations in order to support their preferences. How will your preferred lifestyle influence your career decision making?

Another key aspect of matching your career to your lifestyle is to choose a career that enables you to achieve the right balance between work and personal life. People vary widely in what they consider the right balance. Individuals who want to be home at regular hours and on weekends, with very little travel, will usually have to avoid industrial sales or managerial work. On the other hand, individuals who prefer the excitement of breakfast meetings, weekend meetings, and travel might choose the two occupations just mentioned.

Flexible work schedules and telecommuting are a major mechanism for matching preferred lifestyle to career choice. Many people whose preferred lifestyle does not permit full-time work seek opportunities to work part time. Others whose preferred lifestyle is to minimize commuting and working outside the home seek employment as telecommuters. If you choose to work at home, however, your job choices are more limited than a person who is willing to work in a traditional office.

An emerging trend of matching preferred lifestyle to your career takes place at a later point in a person's career. As such, it is a method of modi-

fying rather than choosing a career to fit a living pattern. **Downshifters** are workers who choose shorter hours and less demanding work to allow more time for other activities. To achieve more happiness, these people ask their employers to be even more flexible about work hours and job demands. (A job that is too stressful can interfere with the ability to enjoy leisure.) What is your evaluation of the merits of downshifting? Would you want a shorter, easier job with less pay so that you can upshift in other areas of life?

▲ FINDING OUT ABOUT OCCUPATIONS

Whether or not you have already made a career choice, you should follow a fundamental rule of plotting your career: get the facts. Few people have valid information about careers they wish to pursue. A glaring example of occupational misinformation relates to the legal field. Many young people say, "I would like to be a lawyer. I'm good at convincing people. And I know I could sway a jury." Similarly, "I want to be a paralegal. I have the mind of a detective. I know I could break most of the tough cases given me to research."

In reality, the work of a lawyer or paralegal includes the processing of much nonglamorous information. One example is figuring out how much money a bankrupt bakery owes to 27 different suppliers. Four sources of occupational information are printed and Web-based material, computer-assisted career guidance, spoken information, and firsthand experience. Without this information, it is difficult to find a good fit between yourself and career opportunities.

Printed and Web-Based Information

Most libraries, bookstores, and career centers are well supplied with information on career opportunities. The most comprehensive source document of occupational information is the *Occupational Outlook Handbook,* published every two years by the U.S. Department of Labor. Each occupation listed is described in terms of (1) nature of the work; (2) places of employment; (3) training; (4) other qualifications and advancement; and (5) employment outlook. Using the *Handbook,* you can find answers to such questions as "What do claims examiners do and how much do they earn?"

The Internet is also a useful source of career information. A starting point is www.bls.gov/oco/home.htm, the online edition of the *Occupational Outlook Handbook.* Collegeboard.com is another comprehensive source of career information. Collegeboard organizes careers into general categories, such as administrative support occupations, including clerical, marketing and sales occupations, and protective service occupations. After selecting a general career category, you are able to browse specific jobs and be informed about working conditions, job forecasts, related professions, and suggestions for attaining a goal within each occupation.

Careerbuilder.com also organizes information about careers into job categories such as banking and finance, customer service, and retail. This site is geared more toward finding employment than learning about careers, yet the information can also be used for career exploration. The information presented about opportunities in a given area can be useful in making a career choice. The Bureau of Labor Statistics Web site www.bls.gov will also provide extensive information about occupations.

The Web can also be used to find out about careers through making inferences. By poking around, you can glance through numerous job descriptions that might give you an idea for a career goal. First, explore several job-finding and employee-recruiting sights like Monster Board (www. monster.com) and America's Job Bank (www.Americas.Job Bank). For example, you might find four job openings for *robot technician.* Perhaps the field sounds fascinating yet you had not thought of it before. It could be worth exploring. A similar approach is to visit company Web sites, such as General Electric (www.ge.com), and scroll down to something like "career opportunities." Job descriptions often accompany the job titles, so you might obtain some useful ideas for a career field. You might hit on an emerging job, such as "water quality specialist," that could give you an idea for a career.

Computer-Assisted Career Guidance

Several career guidance information systems have been developed for access by computer. The information contained in these systems is designed to help users plan their careers. Guidance information systems go one step beyond printed information because you can ask questions of (interact with) the computer. For instance, when you are keyed in on a specific occupation, you can ask, "What is the promotion outlook?" and "What effect will technology have?"

A widely used career guidance information system is DISCOVER, available from the American College Testing Program (ACT). The system is intended for use by postsecondary students and by adults seeking a new career direction outside their current employment. DISCOVER enables its users to acquire self-knowledge and discover what types of careers match their interests and abilities and the recommended career path to pursue those careers. Of major utility, DISCOVER contains comprehensive databases of occupations.

SIGI Plus is another popular computerized career guidance system that allows for interaction with the computer. The program, available from the Educational Testing Service (ETS), is divided into nine sections, with each one relating to a career decision-making stage, such as having no idea which career to choose. SIGI Plus also encompasses looking at work-related values and deciding which ones are the most important. Another useful feature is a list of work activities for choosing the preferred ones. An example of a work activity would be "checking the quality of work performed by others." A key career choice feature is that SIGI Plus helps you identify occupations that might be right for you based on your values, interests, and work skills.

SPEAKING TO PEOPLE

An invaluable supplement to reading about occupations is speaking to people engaged in those occupations. No matter what occupation interests you, search out a person actually employed in that kind of work. Most people welcome the opportunity to talk about themselves and the type of work they do. If you do not know anyone engaged in the career field that interests you, do some digging. A few inquiries will usually lead to a person you can contact. It is best to interview that person in his or her actual work setting to obtain a sense of the working conditions people face in that field.

Remember, however, that many people will probably say that although they are very happy in their work, there are better ways to make a living. Ask your dentist, doctor, lawyer, or plumber about his or her field, and you will likely be told, "Don't believe all those stories about people in this field being wealthy. We work long and hard for our money. And there's always the problem of people not paying their bills. I don't recommend that you enter this field."

Suppose you want to learn about the field of insurance claims adjuster yet you do not know anyone who knows any person doing this kind of work. Try the cold-canvas method. Telephone one or two insurance companies and ask to speak to a manager in the claims adjusting department. When you reach a person in that department, indicate that you are trying to make a sound career choice and then proceed with your inquiry. The success of this approach is remarkably high. You will probably be granted an interview with an enthusiastic company representative. Or you might conduct your inquiry through e-mail at the risk of losing out on important nonverbal communication.

FIRSTHAND EXPERIENCE

If you want to explore an occupation in depth, it is important to obtain some firsthand experience in that occupation. Part-time and temporary employment is particularly useful. One man who is a self-employed landscape consultant first tried out the field by working two summers for an established business. Some schools offer cooperative, work-study, or internship programs. Internships, paid or unpaid, can be the first vital step in building a career. Above all, the internship should be a learning experience. The intern should establish clear objectives on starting the internship.[5] For example, "I want to develop the type of interpersonal skills that will enable me to deal with our most important customers" or "I want to learn how to assess risks for making loans to people of different income levels."

However modest your cooperative employment, it can provide you with much valuable information. For instance, it is surprisingly helpful to observe whether people engaged in that type of work ever smile or laugh. If not, the work might be intense and dreary.

Temporary work in a field you might wish to enter could lead to a job offer. It is standard practice for employers to use part-time and temporary jobs as a way of screening prospective employees. A woman who is now a sales representative for a well-known business corporation presents this anecdote: "I took the most menial clerical position in the marketing department. My supervisor told her boss that I was a good worker—somebody who would give a fair shake to the company. Now I'm making more money and having more fun than I thought possible at my age."

A promising approach to gaining firsthand knowledge about a potential career is through directly observing a sampling of the career. **Job shadowing** is a way of gaining information about an occupation by spending a few hours with a professional in the workplace and observing firsthand what the job entails. Closely observing a professional in action will often lead to an enhanced understanding of what the work really entails. As practiced at several schools, students get a four-hour shadowing opportunity at local business firms. Even when a student has chosen a career, the direct observation can help confirm that the choice was sound.[6]

CHOOSING A GROWTH OCCUPATION

Another important type of occupational information for career selection relates to growth opportunities within the field. An advantageous way of choosing a career is to pursue an occupation that appears to have growth potential, *provided that work in that field matches your interests*. Entering a rapidly growing field will not do a person much good if he or she does not enjoy the work because it will be difficult to perform well in the long run.

Using the growth-occupation strategy, the career seeker searches a match between his or her capabilities and a growth occupation in a growth field. For example, a person who enjoys and is good at providing support to others and working extensively with computers might choose "computer support specialist" (a growth occupation).

How do you identify growth occupations? One way is to use the sources described in the section about finding career information. Exhibit 10-2 lists

EXHIBIT 10-2

10 Fastest-Growing Occupations 2000–2010

The numbers in this table are expressed in thousands of jobs.

Occupation	Employment		Percent Change
	2000	2010	
Computer engineers, applications	380	760	100
Computer support specialists	506	996	97
Computer engineers, systems software	317	601	90
Network and computer systems administrators	229	416	82
Network systems and data communications analysts	119	211	77
Desktop publishers	38	63	67
Database administrators	106	176	66
Personal care and home health aides	414	672	62
Computer systems analysts	431	689	60
Medical assistants	329	516	57

SOURCE: U.S. Bureau of Labor Statistics (www.bis.gov/EMP).

growth occupations based on U.S. Department of Labor statistics. In addition to considering growth occupations, also consider entering a growth industry, such as the following[7]:

- *Health Care.* This industry includes everything from hospitals and clinics to pharmaceutical companies and biotechnology.

- *Government.* Many U.S. government workers are now retiring in many different specialities.

- *Primary and Secondary Education.* More than two million teachers are projected to retire by 2008.

- *Construction.* As mortgage rates remain low in the current era, the construction industry continues to boom.

- *Security.* In information technology, security is a rapidly growing specialty.

- *Insurance.* More people face more risks, so the insurance industry continues to grow.

The growth-occupation strategy is even more effective when combined with entering a growth industry (such as a desktop publishing specialist entering the health industry). The payoff from working in a growth field is that career advancement is likely to be more rapid than in a stable or declining field.

Being flexible about entering a gender-linked occupation can be helpful in choosing a growth career. For example, a man seeking a growth occupation might consider a career in personal care and home health aides or as a medical assistant. A woman might give serious thought to becoming a computer engineer.

An optimistic caution about searching for growth occupations is that an increasing number of opportunities are opening in many fields. Some economists project that the United States could be short by as many as 10 million workers by 2010.[8] As a result, for *qualified* workers, many fields will appear to contain growth occupations because so many workers will be needed.

▲ DATA, PEOPLE, THINGS, OR IDEAS

A helpful way of looking at career choices is to characterize jobs according to the amount of time devoted to data, people, or things. Ideas are often used sometimes as a fourth category. The *Dictionary of Occupational Titles,* published by the Department of Labor, uses the data, people, or things categories in describing all the occupational titles.

1. *Data* refers to working with facts, information, and ideas made from observations and interpretations. The activities involved in working with data are synthesizing, coordinating, analyzing, compiling, computing, copying, and comparing. Analyzing information by computers, for example, gives a person ample opportunity to work with data.

2. *People* refers to working with human beings and also to working with animals as if they were human. The activities involved in working with people are mentoring, negotiating, instructing, supervising, diverting, persuading, speaking/signaling, serving, and taking instructions/helping. A customer service representative would have ample opportunity to work with people, as the representative regularly handles customer complaints.

3. *Things* refers to work with inanimate objects, such as tools, equipment, and products. The activities involved in working with things are setting up, precision working, operating/controlling, driving/operating, manipulating, tending, feeding/offbearing, and handling. An office equipment repair technician would have ample opportunity to work with things while making service calls.

4. *Ideas* extends beyond the ideas contained in dealing with data to jobs that generate new ideas through the arts and sciences. "Ideas" also ties in with the idea of generating intellectual capital or thoughts that are of commercial value, such as redesigning jobs to improve efficiency.

Most jobs involve a combination of dealing with data, people, and things. Fewer jobs also involve ideas in the sense of creating intellectual capital. It is usually a question of the relative proportion of each dimension. Managers, for example, have high involvement with data and people and low involvement with things. Registered nurses have an average involvement with all three.

Understanding your preferences for working with data, people, things, and ideas sharpens a career choice. Job satisfaction is likely to increase when the individual engages in work that fits his or her relative interest in data, people, things, and ideas. A person with a balanced preference for data, people, and things would probably enjoy a position selling business equipment that also required substantial preparation of sales reports.

▲ DEVELOPING A PORTFOLIO CAREER AND CAREER SWITCHING

It is becoming increasingly common for people to either switch the emphasis of activities in their work or switch careers entirely. An example of switching the emphasis of activities would be a salesperson who is working with computers to shift to a new field in which he or she worked primarily with computers and did no selling. People modify their careers for a variety of reasons, all centering around the idea that something is missing in their present one. Here we look at two closely related approaches to changing direction in a career: developing a portfolio career and career switching.

DEVELOPING A PORTFOLIO CAREER

Many people would like to change careers yet not be confined to focusing on one major type of job activity. To accomplish this, a growing number of people are developing a **portfolio career** in which they use a variety of skills and earn money in several different ways. In addition to a desire to diversify, a portfolio career helps many people cope with the trend toward availability of fewer full-time and permanent positions. According to the Bureau of Labor Statistics, 18 percent of the U.S. workforce works part time (35 hours or less per week). To earn the equivalent of a full-time salary, many people are piecing together more than one part-time position. As more part-time positions pay benefits, working for more than one employer becomes more feasible.

Having a portfolio (or collection) of income-generating possibilities makes you more resistant to the effects of losing one job. You spread your risk by earning money in several ways. The career portfolio minimizes risks by accumulating groups of skills that can provide income. If one skill is not in demand, another might be. A benefits specialist, for example, who also sold real estate might shift to full-time real estate sales if her company discontinued an in-company benefits department. A common example of a skill portfolio is that of a person with a full-time position who has a part-time position requiring different skills. A department manager within a retail store might install satellite dishes as a part-time activity.

An important part of developing a portfolio career is keeping your occupational skills current. Suppose a person is able to translate documents from Japanese to English and English to Japanese but is currently not working as a translator. Translation skills fade rapidly, so the person should continue to practice this bilingual skill at home.

When there are more jobs available than qualified candidates to fill them, it is easy to become smug and dismiss the relevance of a portfolio career. Part of effective career management, however, is to recognize that business cycles are inevitable. Recognize also that technological change can sometimes shrink a field. Many industrial salespeople, for example, have lost their positions in recent years because so much business-to-business selling now takes place through e-commerce.

The benefits of a portfolio career include dealing with change, developing your personal skills, and risk taking. The disadvantages of such a career include lack of stability, feeling overwhelmed when the demands of more than one job peak at the same time, and the lack of a regular routine.[9] In addition, dividing your attention over several jobs may make it difficult to concentrate on one enough to attain outstanding performance.

CAREER SWITCHING

The new type of career emphasizes doing work that fits your major values in life, so many people switch careers to find work that fits their values. And these values could include earning enough money to support a family well and pursue preferred leisure activities. A major reason for switching careers is to find better opportunities after a job loss. In recent years, many people laid off from jobs in manufacturing have enrolled in school to major in nursing and education, two industries that have suffered from chronic worker shortages in recent years.[10]

A major principle of career switching is to *be thorough*. Go through the same kind of thinking and planning that is recommended for finding a first career. Everything said in this chapter about choosing a first career is also relevant for choosing a later career. We emphasize again the importance of obtaining valid career information. The advantage for the career switcher, however, is that the experienced person often has a better understanding of the type of work he or she does not want to do.

A new career should be *built gradually*. Few people are able to leave one career abruptly and step into another. For most people who switch careers successfully, the switch is more of a transition than an abrupt change. A constructive approach would be to take on a few minor assignments in the proposed new field and then search for full-time work in that field after building skill. An electronics technician, for example, might request to visit customers with sales representatives to facilitate a switch to industrial selling.

Sometimes an interim assignment can offer a person useful ideas for a complete career change or at least a different emphasis. One such possibility is to fill in for a person who is on a company-paid leave of absence, referred to as a *sabbatical*. Another possibility for an interim assignment is filling in for someone who is on family leave because of the birth or adoption of a child. Filling in for the boss, for example, can give a person a first-hand feel for managerial work.

A major reason that many employees consider a new career is that they crave more independence. As a consequence, an increasingly popular path for the career switcher is to *move from salaried employment to self-employment*. The prospective self-employed person needs to decide on which particular business to enter. For many people, self-employment means continuing to perform similar work, such as the company cafeteria manager entering the food catering business. Other formerly employed workers go into competition with their former employers, such as a print shop manager opening a print shop of her own. For those who lack specific

---

EXHIBIT 10-3

A Sampling of Opportunities for Self-Employment, as Suggested by Entrepreneur Business Start-Up Guides

Computer-Based Businesses

Computer Consulting

Computer Repair Service

Electronic Bulletin Board Service

Laser Printing Recharging and Repair

Desktop Publishing Service

Financial Services

Check Cashing Service

Financial Aid Services

Financial Broker

Real Estate Investment

Cleaning/Maintenance Businesses

Apartment Preparation Service

Damage Restoration

Garage Detailing Service

Parking Lot Striping and Maintenance

Services to Business

Collection Agency

Language Translation Service

Medical Claims Billing Service

Mobile Bookkeeping

Freight Brokerage Business

Import/Export Business

Temporary Help Service

Personal Services

Private Investigator

Event Planning Service

Image Consulting

Operating a 900 Number

Child Care Service

Home Inspection Service

Food Service Businesses

Coffeehouse

Food Court Restaurants

Mobile Frozen Yogurt

Mobile Restaurant/Sandwich Truck

Bed and Breakfast

Wholesale Businesses

Import/Export Business

Liquidated Goods Broker

Wholesale Distribution Business

Marketing a Family Recipe

Retail Businesses

Antique Sales and Restoration

Body Care Boutique

Pet Hotel and Grooming Service

Self-Storage Center

Childcare Service

Internet Entrepreneur

Automobile Detailing Service

---

plans of their own, prepackaged plans can be purchased. A sampling of these is listed in Exhibit 10-3.

Anyone contemplating self-employment should recognize that it offers potentially high rewards as well as risks. An editor of *Entrepreneur* magazine explains the downside of being a business owner in these terms:

> Any business owner knows what deep corrections in the stock market mean for young companies. Venture capital dries up. Frustrated sellers,

unable to unload shares, stop buying stock in companies like yours. Consumers resist the urge to pull the old Visas out of their wallets and buy your products. Inventories pile up, cash gets tight and pink slips appear on staffers' desks. At times like these, owning a business ranks right up there with root canals and tax audits on the list of life's undesirables.[11]

Another self-employment possibility is to purchase a _franchise_, thus lowering the risk of a start-up business. Currently, franchises account for about one-third of retail sales in the United States and Canada. Yet franchises require a substantial financial investment, ranging from about $6,000 to $600,000. Another caution is that some franchise operators may work around 70 hours per week to earn about $18,000 per year.

▲ NINE SUGGESTIONS FOR CAREER PREPARATION

Preparing for a career is closely related to choosing a career. To prepare is to be ready to meet the challenges that lie ahead in whatever career you choose. Several of the points below[12] reinforce what you have already studied in this text or will study in Chapter 12.

1. _Be flexible._   You may have one career field in mind, such as business. Do not overlook the possibilities of applying your education and skills to a rapidly expanding field such as tourism or nursing homes. Also, be flexible about the size of firm you hope to work for. Most of the job growth continues to take place in small and medium-size firms.

2. _Develop interpersonal skills._   Good interpersonal skills, especially communication skills, are a foundation for many careers. Employers seek employees who speak and write well, including sending impressive e-mail messages to customers. Most jobs require contact with coworkers and customers, or working as part of a team—meaning that people skills are essential.

3. _Think globally._   Many jobs are becoming international jobs even if they do not involve travel. An increasing amount of business is being conducted with customers and suppliers from other countries. To capitalize on the globalization of business, polish your skills in your second language. (Some people may have to learn a second language for the first time.) It is also important to study the culture associated with your second language.

4. _Develop your information technology skills._   Computers have become an integral part of most jobs, including people-oriented jobs such as sales. Have you noticed how many outside-sales representatives work with laptop computers? Lack of good computer skills, including recent informational technology tools, can be a career retardant.

5. _Get an edge._   Although we may be experiencing boom economic times, employers can still afford to be choosy. Any extra skill or knowledge can help distinguish you from other job applicants. Advanced information technology skills, foreign language skills, and another degree are assets for most fields.

6. _Keep learning after you have chosen a field._   With technologies changing so rapidly, training has become a way of life in business and industry. Be prepared to take the initiative to acquire valuable new skills before the company offers you a training program.

7. *Be less concerned about promotions; it is what you know and how you apply it that really counts.* The corporate world today places much less emphasis on promotions than on acquiring skills and applying them well. *Promotion* in the new sense of the word often means getting to work on the most exciting projects and taking turn at being a team leader. Both of these activities can lead to higher compensation even if they do not lead to a change in job title.

8. *Strive for high-quality work.* Most employers assume that workers at all levels will strive to make high-quality goods and provide high-quality service. Many companies expect employees to apply quality principles to their work, so it is important to study books and articles about quality. Apply quality principles such as "Do it right the first time." Also, think of quality as simply being conscientious and terrific at what you do.

9. *Recognize that several different concepts of a career are possible.* The same career model does not fit everyone, and careers have been classified into four concepts. For a person with a *linear career,* success means moving up the career ladder and into a corner office (or at least out of a cubicle). Success for the person with an *expert career* concept is being recognized as superior among peers. These people relish being really expert at something. For a person with a *spiral career* concept, success is defined as moving from one position to a related but bigger position every 5 to 10 years. A technician who worked up to being a project manager would be spiraling. Success to a person with a *roamer career* concept is being able to change jobs frequently, even if the job change is a demotion.[13]

▲ SUMMARY

For many people, finding the right career requires careful thinking and systematic effort. What a person does for a living is one of the key influences in his or her life. Your career is also a prime source of your self-concept and self-esteem. A general strategy for making a sound career choice is to understand first the inner you, including what you have to offer.

Knowing which skills and abilities you possess and enjoy performing can be the basis for a successful career. Your best skill is your core competency. Skill areas can be divided into communication, creative, interpersonal relations, management of self and others, manual and mechanical, mathematics, information technology and office, sales, scientific, service of customers, and service of patients.

Career counseling, including interest testing, can be helpful in making a good career choice. Ideally, a person should choose a career that meshes with his or her preferred lifestyle. A growing number of people are downshifting their careers to give them more time for leisure.

Gathering valid information about careers is useful in making a good career choice. Four sources to consult are printed and electronic information (such as Collegeboard.com) computer-assisted career guidance, speaking to knowledgeable people, and firsthand experience. The last category covers information gained from visiting places or work or from part-time or temporary employment. Choosing a career in a growth occupation is often advantageous.

A helpful way of looking at occupations is to characterize every job by the proportion of time you devote to working with data, people, things, or ideas. It is best to choose an occupation or field that fits your preferences in these four work dimensions.

It is becoming increasingly common for people to either switch the emphasis of activities in their work or switch careers entirely. A portfolio career is one in which a person has a variety of skills that can be used to earn money in different ways. The skill portfolio is particularly useful when a person holds two or more part-time positions.

Career switching is necessary for many reasons, including the pursuit of important values. Switching careers follows many of the same principles as choosing a first career. A new career should be built gradually, often by phasing into the new career part time. To satisfy a desire for independence, many people switch careers from being an employee to self-employment.

At the same time you might be choosing a career, think of preparing for a career. Suggestions along these lines include being flexible, developing interpersonal skills, thinking globally, developing information technology skills, getting an edge, continuing to learn, and focusing more on skills and knowledge than promotions and being aware of different career concepts.

Questions and Activities

1. How do you explain the fact that many students who are studying business still need to choose a career?

2. Now that you have read this chapter, what do you think you would do differently should you be choosing a career or switching careers?

3. Associations that represent professional athletes have been asking in recent years that the owners of sports teams provide career guidance for players. Why would professional athletes need career guidance?

4. Why is choosing the right career likely to have a bigger payoff in terms of personal satisfaction and income during an era when there is a labor shortage (more jobs to fill than applicants available)?

5. Which of the skills listed in Human Relations Self-Assessment Quiz 10-2 do you think will take the longest to develop? Why?

6. Suppose a person has already chosen to enter a large field such as information technology or marketing. Why would knowledge about how to choose a career still be useful?

7. How might attempting to match your career to your lifestyle block your career progress?

8. In your own words, what really is a "portfolio career"?

9. In what way might holding a second job or being self-employed on the side retard a person's career?

10. Speak to someone you think has a successful career to find out how that person made his or her career choice. Be ready to discuss your findings in class.

INTERNET SKILL BUILDER: What Job Is Best for You?

You may have already chosen a career, are in the process of career exploration or may be refining your career choice. The Career Key™, located in www.careekey.org/english, provides you the opportunity to systematically investigate the type of job that would fit your psychological makeup. The Career Key measures your skills, abilities, values, interests, and personality. In addition, the Key identifies jobs that will fit these preferences and provides in-depth information about them. After obtaining the results from the exercises in the Key, ask yourself (1) How do the results fit my perception of a good job for me, and (2) how do the results compare to the type of job I intend to have (or already have)?

HUMAN RELATIONS CASE PROBLEM

"I Know I Can Make a Contribution Somewhere"

Brad Martinez, age 43, is a senior account manager for Western Office Supply, a company that sells a wide range of products to business firms, hospitals, and schools. Western does not manufacture any products of its own but resells the products of several hundred manufacturers, much like being a department store for other firms. His company typically sells supplies in much larger quantities than sold by giant office-supply stores like Staples and OfficeMax. Western also sells office furniture and decorations, such as lamps and wall hangings.

Although Brad's job title is account manager, he is essentially an outside-sales representative who reports to the sales manager of Western Office Supply. Brad personally calls on about 50 established accounts and also solicits new business regularly. After Brad opens an account, replacement sales for smaller items are usually made by e-mail or telephone. However, he periodically makes in-person visits and telephone solicitations to sell office equipment, such as small photocopiers, desktop computers, printers, fax machines, and office telephones.

After graduating from a career school with a major in business administration with a marketing concentration, Brad thought he would explore the world before settling on a career. He joined the United States Army and worked in the medical service field as a medic in several army hospitals. Since Brad was not in service during armed combat, he assisted in training injuries and injuries to dependents of army personnel. Brad served admirably in the army and worked his way up to the rank of sergeant.

In Brad's words, "I left the Army proud of my service but looking for a more promising career. No matter how much the army liked me, they weren't going to make me the surgeon general. I thought it was time to get started in the business field."

(Continued)

After the army, Brad worked six years in the purchasing department at a machine-tool company, working his way up to a position as purchasing supervisor. After that, he joined Western as a sales trainee and progressed up to his present position.

During the last several years, Brad's sales commissions have begun to decline. One problem he has faced is that many of his customers are now purchasing their supplies directly from both distributors and manufacturers over the Internet. Another problem is Western's own e-commerce initiative. Brad and the other sales representatives receive a very small commission when a new customer makes an Internet purchase or an established customer orders more supplies.

Brad has recently become discouraged with the diminishing direct people contact in his work. As he explains, "Three times during the last month I have been turned down by purchasing agents or business owners when I asked them out to lunch. Up until a few years ago, I made some of my largest sales over lunch. I'm hearing more now that my customers just want to buy over the Internet. I guess they would rather sit at the keyboard and eat yogurt for lunch rather than talk over business in a restaurant.

"The phone has become a major headache for me also. Instead of talking to a manager or a purchasing agent, I have to conduct my business with a voice-mail message. A woman flat out told me the other day that when she wanted to order something from Western, she would use our Web site. She told me that phone conversations take up too much of her time."

During the last six-month period, Brad's commissions decline 45 percent from the previous six months. For Brad, this was the last straw. He has decided to change careers as soon as he can figure out what else he could do to earn the same kind of living he did previously. For three consecutive years, Brad had even earned a six-figure income.

One Saturday morning, Brad was looking at the job search site, Monsterboard. He murmured to himself, "Let's see Brad, the world no longer needs a good sales rep with a personal touch. You have no more talent with the computer than most 19-year-olds. Being an astronaut is out because I get motion sickness. The NFL doesn't want any 43-year-old quarterbacks without experience. My few years as an army medic doesn't qualify me to be the chief of surgery at the Mayo Clinic.

"Oops, here's an opening for a chief financial officer for a $50 million company, but they do want experience as a controller. Here's another one I like, an international marketing specialist. Except that the successful candidate must speak English, Spanish, and Italian. All I have is English, and about 20 words of Spanish I know from listening to Salsa music.

"Maybe, I should start by updating my résumé. I know I can make a contribution somewhere, but I'm not sure where to start."

Questions

1. To what extent do you think Brad really needs a career switch?

2. What approach should Brad take to finding a new career?

3. What improvements do you think Brad needs to take in his attitude before he gets down to the serious business of finding a new career?

4. What criticisms do you have of Brad's career direction so far?

WEB CORNER

Career choice using an instrument assessment: www.self-directed-search.com

Career opportunities: www.jobvault.com

(see the Industries section)

HUMAN RELATIONS SKILL-BUILDING ACTIVITY 10-1:
The Uncertain Career Seeker

The skill-building involved in the following role play is to develop skill either in thinking through career issues or in being a sympathetic listener. The previous case serves as background information for this role play. One person plays the role of Brad, who visits his career counselor to mull over his career switch dilemma. Brad has considerable emotion about making a career switch or significant job change. Another student plays the role of the career counselor who wants to both ask Brad the right questions and give him concrete advice. Run the role play for 10 to 15 minutes.

▲ REFERENCES

1. Ann Harrington and Christopher Tkaczyk, "You Get Paid to Do What?" *Fortune,* January 20, 2003, p. 146.

2. "Your Personal Core Competency," *Executive Strategies,* February 1996, p. 11.

3. Updated from Julie Griffin Levitt, *Your Career: How to Make It Happen,* 2d ed. (Cincinnati: South-Western College Publishing, 1990), pp. 11–21.

4. The description of the Strong Interest Inventory is based on James G. Clawson, John P. Kotter, Victor A. Faux, and Charles C. McArthur, *Self-Assessment and Career Development,* 3d ed. (Upper Saddle River, NJ: Prentice Hall, 1992), pp. 125–135; *Strong Interest Inventory of the Strong Vocational Interest Blanks®,* 1994.

5. Kemba J. Dunham, "The Jungle: Focus on Recruitment, Pay and Getting Ahead," *Wall Street Journal,* July 1, 2003, p. B6.

6. Carol Klieman, "'Shadowing' Offers a Few Hours of On-the-Job-Learning," *Chicago Tribune,* September 28, 1997, p. 1, Jobs Section.

7. Ann Harrington, "Make That Switch," *Fortune,* February 4, 2002, p. 160.

8. Aaron Bernstein, "Too Many Workers? Not for Long," *BusinessWeek,* May 20, 2002, p. 128.

9. "Why Have a Portfolio Career?" www.creativekeys.net/Why.htm.

10. Jon E. Hilsenrath, "Jobless Workers Switch Fields to Find Relief," *Wall Street Journal,* June 24, 2003, p. B1.

11. "The End of Entrepreneurship As We Know It?" *Entrepreneur,* September 2000, p. 18.

12. "Seven Tips for Career Preparation," *NBEA Keying In,* November 1993, p. 8; Anne Fisher, "Six Ways to Supercharge Your Career," *Fortune,* January 13, 1997, pp. 46–47.

13. Robert N. Lewellyn, "The Four Career Concepts," *HR Magazine,* September 2002, pp. 121–126.

▲ ADDITIONAL READING

Austin, Linda. *What's Holding You Back? 8 Critical Choices for Women's Success.* Boulder, CO: Basic Books/Perseus Books Group, 2000.

Bolles, Richard N. *The Three Boxes of Life and How to Get Out of Them.* Berkeley, CA: Ten Speed Press. (revised regularly)

Bolles, Richard N. *The 2004 What Color Is Your Parachute: A Practical Manual for Job Hunters and Career Changers.* Berkeley, CA: Ten Speed Press, 2004. (see the latest edition)

Butler, Timothy, and James Waldroop. *Discovering Your Career in Business.* Reading, MA: Addison-Wesley, 1997.

Holland, John L. *Making Vocational Choices: A Theory of Vocational Personalities and Work Environments.* 3rd ed. Odessa, FL: Psychological Assessment Resources, 1997.

Ibarra, Herminia. "How to Stay Stuck in the Wrong Career." *Harvard Business Review,* December 2002, pp. 40–47.

Newton, David, and Mark Henricks. "Can Entrepreneurship Be Taught?" *Entrepreneur,* April 2003, pp. 62–71.

Rubin, Harriet. *The Princessa: Machiavelli for Women.* New York: Doubleday/Currency, 1997.

CHAPTER 11

Conducting a Job Search

Learning Objectives

After studying the information and doing the exercises in this chapter, you should be able to:

◆ Improve your chances of finding a suitable job

◆ Target your job search and recognize what qualifications employers in general are seeking

◆ Identify job-finding methods and use the Internet to assist you in your job search

◆ Prepare an effective cover letter, job résumé, and follow-up letter

◆ Identify types of employment tests and physical examinations an applicant is likely to take

◆ Face the adversity sometimes found in a job search

*D*uring the lowest point of job hiring in many years, John D. Byrne thought he had to be creative to find a suitable job, so he set sail on his ambitions. In February 2002, the Clarkson University MBA student from Potsdam, New York, launched a Web site promising a four-day cruise or $500 to anyone providing him a successful lead for an upstate New York job not posted on a major job bank. He wanted a marketing or public relations (PR) position following his May graduation.

The contest drew widespread media coverage, 6,000 e-mails, 200 promising leads, two face-to-face job interviews, and one offer from an Albany financial services concern. But John Byrne spurned the marketing job offer (and withheld his prize) partly because he disliked the long hours required. The 22-year-old instead pursued an opening he discovered on the Web site of St. Lawrence University, his alma mater. In applying to be an admissions counselor, he cited his contest as evidence of "my flair for creative sales and marketing." He started work in July 2003.

Byrne said he would use extreme job-hunting tactics again. After all, he notes, "I've gotten a lot of marketing and PR experience from just doing the contest."[1]

Not every job seeker is willing to engage in "extreme job hunting," yet the job search tactics of the business student just mentioned dramatize an important point about finding a position: A systematic and creative approach is advised. With careful planning and preparation, a job search is more likely to be successful. Job searches are called for in several situations. You may be starting your career, you may be tired of your present job, you may want to boost your career, or you might lose your job involuntarily.

The purpose of this chapter is to provide the key information you need to conduct a successful job search, including sources of job leads, preparation of a cover letter and résumé, and performing well in an interview. This chapter also presents a few fine points to help give you an edge over those who do the minimum necessary to find a suitable position. Although you probably already have some job search knowledge, this chapter can be used as a refresher and a reminder to be systematic in finding a new position.

▲ TARGETING YOUR JOB SEARCH

A job search begins with a reasonably flexible description of the type of job or jobs you are looking for. Flexibility is called for because, with so many different jobs available, it is difficult to be too specific. A reasonable objective might be something of this nature: "I am searching for a job in the numerical field, with a large employer, located within 30 miles of here. I prefer accounting work. My minimum salary would be $750 per week."

Your chances of finding suitable employment are directly proportional to the number of positions that will satisfy your job objectives. One person with a degree in information technology might be interested exclusively in working in the information systems division of a major corporation. Another person with the same background is willing to work in the information technology field for a large company, a small company, a high-tech start-up, a government agency, or an educational institution. The second person has a better chance than the first of finding a job in a geographic location he or she wants.

Closely tied in with the type of work you are seeking is the type of organization in which you would prefer to work. You are much more likely to be successful in your new job and your career when you find a good **person–organization fit,** the compatibility of the individual and the organization. In other words, what type of organization culture (or atmosphere) would fit you best? Unless you have had exposure to different types of organizations, you may have only tentative answers to this question. Questioning people who work at different places can provide you with some useful clues. A vital source of input about a prospective employer is present and past employees. Further, plant tours open to the public can provide valuable tips about what it is like to work in that particular firm.

Visits to stores, restaurants, and government agencies will provide informal information about the general nature of working conditions in those places. Using the Internet to find facts about a company has become standard practice. The Internet search includes the firm's Web site as well as news stories about the company. Run your prospective company through your favorite search engines and see what you come up with. As you begin your job search, ask yourself these questions to help you identify the type of organization that *might* be right for you:

- Would I feel more comfortable working in an office with hundreds of other people? Or would I prefer just a handful of coworkers?

- Would I prefer working in a place where people went out of their way to dress in a stylish manner? Or would I prefer an informal place where not so much emphasis was placed on appearance?

- Would I prefer to work in a small town or in a busy metropolitan area?

- How important is access to stores and restaurants?

- Would it be best for me to work where I could rely on public transportation?

- Would I really prefer an easygoing atmosphere or a highly competitive, "rat race" environment?

- How important are the social aspects of work to me? Would I be happy only in a place where I could meet prospective dates and make new friends? For example, in Silicon Valley the ratio of male to female professionals is five to one. (Great for heterosexual gals, terrible for heterosexual guys!)

Not every job candidate can afford to be so selective about a prospective employer. The more your skills are in demand and the more prosperous the times, the more selective a person can be in choosing an employer.

Another important dimension of flexibility is the willingness to work off-hours jobs. Not only do these jobs offer higher pay, but they are targeted for growth because of the 24/7 global marketplace and the Internet. Another way to gain entry to good organizations is to be willing to work the night shift in service-sector jobs, such as customer service, computer support, and transportation.[2]

▲ QUALIFICATIONS SOUGHT BY EMPLOYERS

What you are looking for in an employer must be matched against what an employer is looking for in an employee. All job interviewers do not agree on the qualifications they seek in employees. Nevertheless, a number of traits, characteristics, skills, and accomplishments are important to many employers.[3] Human Relations Self-Assessment Quiz 11-1 summarizes these qualifications in a way that enables you to apply them to yourself as you think about your job search.

▲ JOB-FINDING METHODS

Two cornerstone principles of conducting a job campaign are to (1) use several different methods and (2) keep trying. These two principles should be applied because most approaches to job finding are inefficient yet effective. *Inefficient* refers to the fact that a person might have to make many contacts to find just one job. Yet the system is *effective* because it does lead to a desired outcome—finding a suitable position.

Job-finding techniques are divided here into six types: (1) networking; (2) Internet and résumé database services; (3) mail campaign; (4) telesearch; (5) placement offices, employment agencies, and career fairs; (6) help-wanted ads; and (7) extreme job hunting. Human Relations

HUMAN RELATIONS SELF-ASSESSMENT QUIZ 11-1

Qualifications Sought by Employers

Following is a list of qualifications widely sought by prospective employers. After reading each qualification, rate yourself on a 1-to-5 scale on the particular dimension. 1 = very low; 2 = low; 3 = average; 4 = high; 5 = very high.

1.	Appropriate education for the position under consideration and satisfactory grades	1	2	3	4	5
2.	Relevant work experience	1	2	3	4	5
3.	Communication and other interpersonal skills	1	2	3	4	5
4.	Motivation, tenacity, and energy	1	2	3	4	5
5.	Problem-solving ability (intelligence) and creativity	1	2	3	4	5
6.	Judgment and common sense	1	2	3	4	5
7.	Adaptability to change	1	2	3	4	5
8.	Emotional maturity (acting professionally and responsibly)	1	2	3	4	5
9.	Teamwork (ability and interest in working in a team effort)	1	2	3	4	5
10.	Positive attitude (enthusiasm about work and initiative)	1	2	3	4	5
11.	Customer service orientation	1	2	3	4	5
12.	Information technology skills	1	2	3	4	5
13.	Internet research skills	1	2	3	4	5
14.	Willingness to continue to study and learn about job, company, and industry	1	2	3	4	5
15.	Likability and sense of humor	1	2	3	4	5
16.	Dependability, responsibility, and conscientiousness (including good work habits and time management)	1	2	3	4	5
17.	Leadership ability (takes the initiative to assume responsibility for accomplishing tasks and influencing others)	1	2	3	4	5

Interpretation: Consider engaging in some serious self-development, training, and education for items that you rated yourself low or very low. If you accurately rated yourself as 4 or 5 on all the dimensions, you are an exceptional job candidate.

HUMAN RELATIONS SKILL-BUILDING EXERCISE 11-1

Creative Job-Finding Techniques

Job seekers often make the mistake of not exploring enough different methods for finding a job. After exploring a few conventional techniques, such as making a trip to the placement office or posting their résumé online, they sit back and wait for job offers to pour in. A better approach is to search for creative alternatives to finding a job. Think of every possibility, then sort out the workable from the unworkable later on. To accomplish this task, the class will be organized into brainstorming groups. The goal is to specify as large a number of job-finding techniques as possible. Follow the guidelines for brainstorming presented in Chapter 3, Exhibit 3-2.

After each group has assembled and edited its job-finding techniques, group leaders will present their findings to the rest of the class. Groups can then compare their job-finding suggestions.

Skill-Building Exercise 11-1 will help sensitize you to the many ways of finding a suitable position.

NETWORKING (CONTACTS AND REFERRALS)

The most effective method of finding a job is through personal contacts. **Networking** is the process of establishing a group of contacts who can help you in your career. Networking is particularly helpful because it taps you into the "insider system" or "internal job market." The internal job market is the large array of jobs that haven't been advertised and are usually filled by word of mouth or through friends and acquaintances of employees. Traditional wisdom states that the vast majority of job openings are found in the internal job market. However, according to recruiting specialists, the insider system is no longer so dominant. Recruiter Gerry Crispin estimates that job seekers can track down as many as 80 to 90 percent of existing job openings by sifting through the career section of an employer's Web site in addition to searching other Internet sites and print media.[4]

The best way to reach the jobs in the internal market is by getting someone to recommend you for one. When looking for a job, it is therefore important to tell every potential contact of your job search. The more influential the person, the better. Be specific about the type of job you are seeking. When workers are in short supply, some companies give cash bonuses and prizes to employees for referring job candidates to them.

To use networking effectively, it may be necessary to create contacts aside from those you already have. Networking is time consuming yet is usually well worth the effort. A study of the intensity with which unemployed people pursued networking indicated that people who are more extroverted and conscientious tried the hardest.[5] Liking people and being

diligent pay off in terms of networking. Potential sources of contacts for your network include the following:

- Friends and people you meet while traveling
- Parents and other family members
- Parents of friends
- Friends of parents
- Work associates
- Faculty and staff
- Former or present employer (if you hold a temporary job)
- Athletic team members and coaches and people you meet while participating in sports
- Religious and community groups
- Trade and professional associations
- Career and job fairs

To capitalize on these contacts, it is helpful to carry business cards. You do not have to be employed to use a business card. Simply place on your card a notation such as, "Alex Catalino, accounting specialist, Dallas, Texas." Also include your physical address, e-mail address, and telephone number. An electronic business card contained in your palm-size computer is useful in creating a favorable impression with information-technology–oriented professionals.

An important caution about networking: Too many people are consuming too much of other people's time to help them with their job searches.

Keep your request for assistance brief and pointed. Ask to reciprocate in any way you can. For example, you might prepare a chart or conduct research for a manager who gave you a job lead.

A new development in job-search networking is to join an online networking site such as LinkedIn.com or Friendster.com. The major purpose of these sites is for members to help each other find jobs. Some sites emphasize professional contacts while others focus on developing friendships. A growing number of employers recruit directly through these sites. The usefulness of online networking increases when you meet face-to-face a few of the most promising contacts.[6]

THE INTERNET AND RÉSUMÉ DATABASE SERVICES

Using the Internet, for little or no cost, the job seeker can post a résumé or scroll through hundreds of job opportunities. Web sites such as Career Mosaic and E-Span are résumé database services because they give employers access to résumés submitted by job hunters. The organizers of E-Span explain to employers that the service provides access to millions of qualified candidates through the Web, the Internet, and more than 10 online networks and bulletin boards. Exhibit 11-1 lists a handful of general job search Web sites. It is also helpful to look for job Websites for a specific field, such as information technology (e.g., www.techie.com). Also, as implied above, the employment section of company Web sites can be as effective as general job boards in finding job leads. One study showed that nearly 60 percent of all Internet hires stem from a company's own Web site.[7]

Job hunting on the Internet can lead to a false sense of security. Using the Internet, a résumé is cast over a wide net, and hundreds of job postings can be explored. As a consequence, the job seeker may think that he or she can sit back and wait for a job offer to come through the e-mail. In reality, the Internet is just one source of leads that should be used in conjunction with other job-finding methods. Thousands of other job seekers can access the same job openings, and many of the positions listed have already been filled. Many employers hire résumé screening services (much like an employment agency) to sort through the thousands of posted résumés to find qualified applicants.

A major challenge of job hunting through the Internet is find a way to speak to a company representative about your application. Telephoning the human resources department of a large company usually leads to a voice-mail system with a lengthy menu and rarely a return call. A plausible approach to making a personal contact is to call the main number of your target company and tap the operator button. Ask for the department where you hope to work, and you may be able to establish a personal contact—provided that you do not encounter another lengthy menu.[8]

UNSOLICITED LETTER OR E-MAIL CAMPAIGN

A standard method of job finding is the **unsolicited letter or e-mail campaign,** or writing directly to a company you would like to work for. The

---

EXHIBIT 11-1

Popular Job Search Web Sites

Internet Job Postings

- America's Job Bank: www.ajb.dni.us
- Best Jobs in the USA Today: www.bestjobsusa.com
- CareerMosaic: www.careermosaic.com
- CareerBuilder: www.careerbuilder.com
- 4Work: www.4work.com
- HispanData: www.HispanStar* (for employers searching for Hispanic workers and workers looking to fill such positions)
- JobHunt: Online Job Meta-List: www.jobhunt.org
- Job World: www.job.world.com
- Monster Board: www.monster.com

Online Résumé Posting Sites

- Career Web: www.cweb.com
- E-Span Résumé Bank: www.espan.com
- JobCenter: www.jobcenter.com
- Intellimatch: www.intellimatch.com
- Online Career Center: http://occ.com

---

plan is to come up with a master list of prospective employers. You make up the list according to the categories most relevant to your situation, such as by industry or geographic location. Your list can be developed through the Internet by accessing such categories as "furniture makers, South Carolina." Business directories in libraries (online databases included), such as those published by Dun and Bradstreet and Standard and Poor, provide full addresses and names of key people in the firms listed.

When writing the prospective employer, send the letter to a specific individual rather than Dear Sir, Madam, or Ms. The mailing should consist of a cover letter and résumé. A sensible approach is to scroll though company Web sites for employment information as posted by most large employers. This approach automatically creates a contact person for you. Should somebody be interested in your letter or résumé sent by e-mail, it could get you into the insider system. The person will either contact you directly or refer your letter and résumé to a hiring manager.

TELESEARCH

A related approach to the mail and e-mail campaign is the **telesearch,** obtaining job leads by making unsolicited phone calls to prospective employers. The list of prospects can be assembled in the same manner as the mail campaign. Begin your inquiry into an organization by contacting the person who would be your boss were you to land the job you really wanted. A major goal of the telesearch is to establish direct contact with as many of these decision makers as you can. It is best *not* to call an executive and ask if there are any openings. Such an inquiry invites a "no" response. Instead, use a brief presentation (about one minute) to attempt to arrange an interview:

> Mr. Caldone, my name is Jack Paradise. I have three years of experience in your area of business and would like to visit your office to discuss working for you. When would you have about 15 minutes to speak with me?

This approach is brief and direct yet ends with a choice, making it easier for the prospective employer to agree to an interview. If the person contacted has an opening or is interested in learning more about you, you will probably get the interview or be asked to send a résumé. Even if you fail to get an interview, you might be able to obtain a job lead from your contact. Inquire whether the person knows anyone who might be interested in hiring someone with your experience.

The telesearch, like the unsolicited letter or e-mail campaign, is used to make the prospective employer want to meet you. Use the interview to make him or her want to hire you. Although the prospective employer cannot see you, smile and speak with confidence and enthusiasm. Approximately 100 telephone calls will be needed to receive about 5 to 10 interviews. Some prospects will telephone you at home, so have a professional-sounding outgoing message on your answering machine. (The same holds true for any job-finding method.)

A major roadblock to a telesearch is that most telephone calls are screened through voice mail. The operator button approach described above will sometimes enable you to get around this barrier.

PLACEMENT OFFICES, EMPLOYMENT AGENCIES, AND CAREER FAIRS

Your placement office is a primary avenue for finding a job. Even if you do not find a job through the placement office, you will still gain insight into the job-finding process. If recruiters visit your campus, you can gain experience in being interviewed. Placement offices also provide information about the job search process.

Employment agencies can also lead you to the right position. Employers use employment agencies to advertise jobs and screen applicants, particularly in large cities. Agencies tend to be more valuable for people with about 5 to 10 years of work experience than for newcomers. Not to be overlooked, however, is that many employment agencies specialize in temporary help. After working for the employer for about nine months, the temporary job might become permanent. A concern expressed about employment agencies is that they sometimes encourage applicants to accept less-than-ideal positions just so the agency can earn a placement fee.

A variation of an employment agency is a *career agent,* who for a fixed fee works on behalf of his or her client (you). The career agent provides job search and career counseling and also has links with employers to help clients find positions. If a career agent finds you a position that you could not have found for free, the service can be valuable.

Career (or job) fairs function somewhat like a temporary placement office. A large number of employers may visit the fair to recruit employees. At the same time, a large number of applicants register at the fair and present their résumés. In addition to directly conducting a job search, career fairs are also useful for learning about employment trends, skills required in certain positions, or developing your network of career contacts. Job fairs offer the opportunity to make face-to-face contact with several prospective employers within a few hours.

HELP-WANTED ADS

A thorough job search includes scanning the help-wanted section of classified ads. Help-wanted ads are still a standard way of finding a suitable position. These ads are found in local and national newspapers as well as in professional and trade magazines. Because so many people respond to ads listing attractive-sounding positions, this method yields relatively few interviews—yet it can lead to finding the one job you are seeking. Four types of want ads are described next:

1. *Open ads* disclose considerable information about the position opening, including the name of the employer, phone number, nature of the job and the company's business, and qualifications sought. Starting salary is sometimes mentioned. Consequently, open ads attract the largest number of applicants.

2. *Blind ads* conceal the organization in which the advertised position is available but may contain other important information. The reader is requested to respond by sending a letter and résumé to a post office box or the newspaper. By placing a blind ad, the company does not have to deal with a large number of unqualified callers. Another reason the company uses a blind ad is to maintain secrecy with competitors and employees. One remote disadvantage of responding to a blind ad when currently employed is that the advertiser may be your employer.

3. *Employment agency ads* are placed by agencies and list one or more job openings for their employer clients. Agencies tend to advertise their more attractive openings. These positions may be filled quickly, but the agency may encourage the job hunter to examine other possibilities. One of the purposes of want ads placed by employment agencies is to enlarge their pools of qualified candidates.

4. *Catch ads* promise unusually high-paying job opportunities without requiring specific job qualifications. Frequently these jobs involve selling difficult-to-sell merchandise strictly on commission or with a modest weekly draw against commission. Respondents often find that they are required to sell home siding, food supplements, or magazine subscriptions. Furthermore, you might be asked to purchase the merchandise, which you will then attempt to sell to customers. These jobs are best suited for high-risk takers.

EXTREME JOB HUNTING

Do you recall the business student described at the outset of the chapter who used a Web site to offer a financial reward for helping him find a job? *Extreme job hunting* is any highly unusual, complicated tactic that involves a gimmick for finding a job. To attract attention to their candidacy, job applicants sometimes send a résumé in a pizza box or photos of themselves in swimsuits. A man seeking a media relations position brought to his potential supervisor a box of Krispy Kreme donuts with his résumé and cover letter attached. (At the time, this brand of donuts was not sold in the employer's region, and the man drove back and forth from Worcester, Massachusetts, to New York City to fetch the donuts.) The supervisor hired the applicant in part because the creative gesture was the kind of original thinking the supervisor wanted.[9]

Extreme job hunting techniques are likely to be rejected by some employers who would regard the applicant as a nuisance and perhaps unprofessional. Yet it is possible that a highly unusual approach will sometimes land you a job.

In addition to being aware of the various job-finding methods, it is also important to consider *when* to begin a job search. In general, the bigger the job, the longer the job campaign. Finding a position within 30 days is exceptional, whereas a total time of about six months is typical. You will usually need several months to prepare your résumé and cover letter, pursue all the methods described in this section, and wait to hear from employers. When people are in a particularly in-demand field, a position can sometimes be found in several days just by posting a résumé online. Even more quickly, some in-demand people are recruited away from their present employers without making any effort to conduct a job search.

▲ COVER LETTERS

A résumé must be accompanied by a cover letter to conduct a job campaign. The cover letter multiplies the effectiveness of the résumé because it enables you to prepare a tailor-made, individual approach to each position you pursue. The most important purpose of the cover letter is to explain why you are applying for the position in question. Simultaneously, you try to convince the prospective employer why you should be considered. Here we look at two effective types of cover letters.

ATTENTION-GETTING COVER LETTER

Most job seekers use the conventional approach of writing a letter attempting to impress the prospective employer with their backgrounds. A

EXHIBIT 11-2

Sample Attention-Getting Cover Letter

27 Buttercup Lane
Little Rock, AR 72203
Phone/fax (501) 275-5602
RMJ29@aol.com

Date of Letter
Mr. Bart Bertrand
President
South View Dodge
258 Princess Blvd.
Little Rock, AR 72201

Dear Mr. Bertrand:

Without a good service department, a new-car dealership is in big trouble. An efficiency-minded person like myself who loves autos and likes to help customers can do wonders for your service department. Give me a chance, and I will help you maintain the high quality of after-sales service demanded by your customers.

The position you advertised in the *Dispatch* and on the Internet is an ideal fit for my background. Shortly, I will be graduating from Pine Valley College with an associate's degree in automotive technology. In addition, I was an automotive mechanics major at Monroe Vocational High.

My job experience includes three years of part-time general work at Manny's Mobil Service and two years of clerical work at Brandon's Chrysler-Plymouth. Besides this relevant experience, I'm the proud owner of a mint-condition 1985 sports coupe I maintain myself.

My enclosed résumé contains additional information about me. When might I have the opportunity to be interviewed?

Sincerely yours,

Rita Mae Jenkins

more effective approach is to capture the reader's attention with a direct statement of what you might be able to do for the company. Keep this "what I can do for you" strategy paramount in mind at every stage of finding a job. It works wonders in the job interview, as it will in the rest of your career. After you have stated how you can help the employer, present a one-page summary of your education and the highlights of your work experience. A sample cover letter is presented in Exhibit 11-2. Notice that the opening line is an attention-getter: "Without a good service department, a car dealership is in big trouble." You may not want to write an outrageous or flip cover letter, but it should have enough flair to attract the reader's attention.

Consider also a five-part expanded version of the attention-getting cover letter: an attention-grabbing introduction, a paragraph selling your value to the employer, a background summary paragraph, a compelling follow-up action statement, and an appreciative close. A personal contact should be part of the attention-grabber.[10] An example: "Meg Atwood, your computer operations manager, mentioned that you are looking for a talented person to manage your Web site. I would very much like to talk to you about this position."

THE T-FORM COVER LETTER

A novel format for a cover letter is one that systematically outlines how the applicant's qualifications match up against the job requirements posted in the position announcement.[11] The T-form (or column) approach gives the reader a tabular outline of how the applicant's background fits the position description. The T-form cover letter, presented in Exhibit 11-3, is also recommended because it has an attention-getting format.

▲ PREPARING AN EFFECTIVE JOB RÉSUMÉ

The major purpose of a résumé is to help you obtain a job interview, not a job. A résumé is needed both as an outside candidate and often when seeking a transfer within a large firm. Effective résumés are straightforward, factual presentations of a person's experiences, education, skills, and accomplishments. Yet a résumé is much like art. People have different ideas about what constitutes an effective résumé. To add to the confusion, some people spell *résumé* with the acute accents (*résumé* is a French word) and some without. A challenge in preparing an effective résumé is to suit many different preferences.

Résumé length illustrates how employers hold different opinions about the best résumé format. A national survey of employers indicated that 24 percent said the résumé should be "no longer than one page," 42 percent said "no longer than two pages," and 34 percent said "determined by information."[12]

A few general guidelines will be offered here that will help you avoid serious mistakes. Done properly, a résumé can lead to an interview with a prospective employer. Done poorly, it will block you from further consideration.

THREE TYPES OF RÉSUMÉS

Three commonly used résumé formats are the chronological, functional, and targeted. You might consider using one of these types or a blend of them, depending on the information about yourself you are trying to highlight. Whichever format you choose, you must include essential information.

The **chronological résumé** presents your work experience, education, and interests, along with your accomplishments, in reverse chrono-

---

EXHIBIT 11-3

The T-Form Cover Letter

Gregory N. Colon
2127 Marketview Avenue
Atlanta, GA 30342
Phone/fax (404) 441-0761
gnc26@aol.com

Sales Manager
Southeast Supply Corporation
200 Ashford Center North, Suite 650
Atlanta, GA 30338

Dear Sales Manager:

In response to your recent advertisement in the *Atlanta Gazette* and on the Monster Board for telemarketing sales professionals, please consider the following:

REQUIREMENTS	MY QUALIFICATIONS
Prior sales experience a must	Two years of full-time and part-time selling including retail and magazine subscription renewals
Great communicator	Two different managers praised my communication skills; received an A in two communication skills courses
Self-motivated	Worked well without supervision; considered to be a self-starter
Reliable	Not one sick day in two years; never late with a class assignment

---

Your opportunity excites me, and I would be proud to represent your company. My résumé is enclosed for your consideration.

Sincerely,

Gregory N. Colon

---

logical order. A chronological résumé is basically the traditional résumé with the addition of accomplishments and achievements. Some people say the chronological résumé is too bland. However, it contains precisely the information that most employers demand, and it is easy to prepare. A chronological résumé readily displays gaps in employment and education, so it is important not to leave years unaccounted for. A year or two of unaccounted-for time might includes entries such as the following (provided that they are true):

- Spent year touring Europe to supplement formal education about understanding different cultures

- Engaged in career exploration and assistance in family business part time in both marketing and warehousing

- Variety of volunteer assignments to explore the possibility of public service as a career

The **functional résumé** organizes your skills and accomplishments into the functions or tasks that support the job you are seeking. A section of a functional résumé might read as follows:

> SUPERVISION: Organized the activities of five park employees to create a smooth-running recreation program. Trained and supervised four roofing specialists to help produce a successful roofing business.

The functional résumé is useful because it highlights the things you have accomplished and the skills you have developed. In this way, an ordinary work experience might seem more impressive. For instance, the tasks listed above under "supervision" may appear more impressive than listing the jobs "playground supervisor" and "roofing crew chief." One problem with the functional résumé is that it omits the factual information many employers demand. You might therefore appear to be hiding something about your background.

The **targeted résumé** focuses on a specific job target or position and presents only information about you that supports that target. Using a target format, an applicant for an information technology position would list only information technology jobs. Under education, the applicant would focus on information technology–related courses, such as information systems and e-commerce. A targeted résumé is helpful in dramatizing your suitability for the position you are seeking. However, this résumé format omits other relevant information about you, and a new résumé must be prepared for each target position.

Whichever résumé format you choose, it is best to place your most salable asset first. If your work experience is limited, place education before work experience. If your skills are more impressive than your education or work experience, list them first. A general-purpose résumé, following a chronological format, is presented in Exhibit 11-4. This person chose to place work experience before education. Although her résumé is chronological, it also allows room for accomplishments and skills. When listing accomplishments, look for ways to quantify them. As shown in Exhibit 11-4, the woman mentioned an 18 percent increase in sales rather than simply stating "increased sales."

Many people have achieved good results with the format recommended here. However, do not restrict yourself. Investigate other résumé formats, including exploring software that provides the user a résumé outline. For example, Microsoft Word includes job résumé templates under File | New | Other Documents. You will find there templates for contemporary, elegant,

---

EXHIBIT 11-4

General-Purpose Résumé

Rita Mae Jenkins
27 Buttercup Lane
Little Rock, AR 72203
Phone/fax (501) 275-5602
RMJ29@aol.com

Qualification Summary   Experience in administrative support activities for automobile dealership. Education in office management and automotive repairs.

Job Objective   Management position in service department of automobile dealership.

Job Experience

2004–present	◆ Senior support specialist, Brandon Chrysler-Plymouth, Little Rock. Responsible for receiving customer payments for auto services; invoice preparation; varied tasks as requested by service manager. Helped set up Web site for dealership, used to schedule some cars for servicing and also attracted customers.
2001–2004	◆ Service station attendant, Manny's Mobil Service. Performed variety of light mechanical tasks, such as assisting in brake relining, installing exhaust systems, tune-ups, independent responsibility for lubrication and oil changes.
	◆ Increased sales of tires, batteries, and accessories by 18 percent during time periods on duty.

Formal Education

2002–2004	◆ Pine Valley Vocational Technical School, associate's degree, automotive technology, May 2004. Studied all phases of auto repair, including computerized diagnostics and service department management. Attended school while working about 30 hours per week. Grade-point average, 3.35.
1998–2002	◆ Harrison Technical High School, Little Rock. Graduated 10th in class of 137. Majored in automotive repair and maintenance. Studied business education topics, including bookkeeping, computer utilization, and office systems and procedures.

Job-Related Skills	◆ Word processing, spreadsheet analysis, database development, Web site development and maintenance, and bookkeeping. Able to handle customer complaints and concerns in person or by phone. Can diagnose and repair a wide range of automotive problems for domestic and important vehicles. Can converse in Spanish with customers.
Service Activities	◆ Treasurer, Autotech Club at Pine Valley; vice president of Computer Club at Harrison Technical; participant in Big Sister Program in Little Rock.
References	◆ On file with placement office at Pine Valley Vocational Technical. Permissible to contact present or former employer.

and professional résumés plus a résumé wizard that helps you construct an individualized résumé.

The references section of the résumé is another area of varied opinion. One approach is to list several references on the résumé, giving complete identifying information so that the prospective employer can readily contact the references. A concern is that these references are often perceived as meaningless because you have identified friends. If you are a recent graduate, a slightly more objective approach is to indicate that references are on file in a placement office. References can also be provided with a cover letter or a follow-up letter. A sophisticated approach is to ask the prospective employer what type of people would be preferable for him or her and them supply them shortly by e-mail. Types of people include superiors, coworkers, and references outside of work, such as athletic coaches and community leaders.

In preparing either a print or electronic résumé, keep in mind that certain key words or references attract the attention of managers and specialists who scan résumés. The scanning is done visually, electronically, or both. In today's market, key words and phrases include the following: *foreign languages, computer, information technology, Internet, e-commerce, e-tailing, experience, hard working, overseas experience, flexible, task oriented, team player,* and *customer oriented*. A sensible tactic would be to mention those words that apply to you. Many of these words, such as *computer* and *team player,* are widely applicable.

A new emphasis in résumé construction is to incorporate your values into the presentation of yourself because of the intensified interest in ethics in business.[13] Employers are looking to hire honest people, so it is essential not to make untrue statements about your background. The personal interests section can help demonstrate your values because people engage in activities they think are important. Off-the-job activities reflecting humanistic values include reading to blind people, tutoring young children, and assisting in the Special Olympics (for youngsters with physical and mental disabilities).

How to Handle the Job Objective Section

On the résumé, a **job objective** is the position you are applying for now or intend to hold in the future. Although stating a job objective seems easy, it is a trouble spot for many résumé writers. Early in their careers, many people feel compelled to state their long-range career objectives in the job objective section. A 21-year-old might state, "To become president of an international corporation." Certainly this is a worthy objective, but it is better to be more modest at the outset.

Employers will tend to interpret the job objective as a statement of your short-term plans. If you think your long-term objective should be stated, you might divide the section into "immediate objective" and "long-term objective." Current practice is to use the position under consideration as a job objective. Longer-term objectives can then be discussed during the job interview.

Another challenge with the job objective section is that your objective will often have to be tailored to the specific job under consideration. The job objective you have printed on your résumé may not fit exactly the job you are applying for. You might be considering a sales career. You find two good leads, one for selling an industrial product and one for a consumer product. You would want your objective on one résumé to mention industrial sales and on the other consumer sales.

If you retain your computer file, you can modify the job objective section for a given job lead. Another approach is to omit the job objective section. Your cover letter can describe the link between you and the job under consideration. Notice how the cover letter in Exhibit 11-3 made this link. (The same person, however, did include a job objective on her résumé.)

Electronic Submission of the Résumé

Another consideration about the effective use of job résumés is choosing the right format for submitting to prospective employers or to job boards such as Monster or CareerBuilder. Computer consultant Kim Komando cautions that an incorrect submission can result in your résumé not being read. Do not use a program like Winzip to compress your submission because there are many people who do not have the proper equipment to, or refuse to, open a ZIP file. Saving your file as an Adobe Acrobat PDF file or Power-Point presentation can be a headache for the receiver.

The easiest approach is to submit your résumé as a Microsoft Word document or plain text file. Attach the file to your e-mail, and keyboard your cover letter as part of the e-mail. A caution, however, is that some companies will not open attachments because of concerns about computer viruses. To get around this problem, copy your résumé directly into your e-mail document, making sure that the formatting is not lost. Copying your résumé into Notepad and then copying and pasting into the e-mail will take care of the formatting problem. Using the procedure just described, e-mail your résumé to yourself to ensure that it looks fine.[14]

How Do You Write a Résumé When Your Background Does Not Fit the Position?

Job seekers sometimes lack the type of experience expected to qualify them for a position they seek. This lack of direct fit may occur when the applicant is switching fields or is entering the workforce after a long absence. In both instances, it is helpful to emphasize skills and experience that would contribute to success in the job under consideration.

Assume that a person with five years of experience as a bookkeeper applies for a sales representative position at an office equipment company. The bookkeeper is advised to make these types of entries on his or her résumé: "Five years of experience in working directly with office equipment including computers, fax machines, and high-speed copiers." "Able to size up equipment needs of accountants and bookkeepers." "Accustomed to negotiating budgets with managers."

Assume that a person has 20 years of experience managing a household but has not worked outside the home. The candidate applies for an assistant manager position in a restaurant. The person should list relevant skills such as "Able to plan and prepare holiday meals and parties for large groups of people." The candidate is also advised to describe his or her volunteer work because such experience may be job related. For example, "Coordinated church picnic for 250 people, including recruiting and supervising ten workers, and raising the necessary funds."

WHAT ABOUT THE CREATIVE-STYLE RÉSUMÉ AND GIMMICKS?

Since so many résumés are sent to employers, it is difficult to attract an employer's attention. The solution offered to this problem is a creatively prepared résumé. A **creative-style résumé** is one with a novel format and design. The creative résumé along with gimmicks is often used in extreme job hunting. One creative approach is to print your résumé in the format of a menu. One job seeker went so far as calling his education the "appetizer," his work experience the "entrée," and his hobbies and interests the "dessert." Others try to make their résumés distinctive by printing them on tinted or oversized paper. Another gimmicky approach is to place your résumé on your personal Web site and refer prospective employers and job boards to your site. (An appropriate name for your Web site for this purpose would be www.annoyingjobseeker.com.)

If done in a way to attract positive attention to yourself, creative-style résumés have merit. The generally accepted approach, however, is for résumés to be conservative. In one study, 93 percent of college recruiters surveyed preferred white or ivory color for the résumé. For the entry-level job applicant, the conservative approach is the safest bet.[15] If you are applying for a position in which creative talent is a primary factor, the creative-style résumé is helpful. Creative-style résumés work well for a variety of jobs in a cool industry such as fashion or a dot-com company. A more conventional job requires a more conventional résumé. Human resource specialists often object to oversized résumés because they are difficult to fit into standard files.

In an attempt to be different, avoid making your résumé visually distracting, such as by using more than three fonts. A useful suggestion is to print your résumé on gray paper with a half-inch white border. (Gray will probably not be disliked by people who prefer ivory.) In this way, your résumé will communicate a classy, distinctive quality while remaining easy to read.[16]

Do not confuse the *creative* résumé with the *created* résumé in which you "create" facts to make a favorable impression. Many employers verify facts presented on a résumé. Evidence of distortions of the truth or lying usually lead to immediate disqualification of the applicant. If you made the sandwiches at a sub shop, do not list your job title as "master chef" or "vice president of operations." And résumé misinformation uncovered after the applicant is hired can lead to immediate dismissal.

▲ THE SUCCESSFUL JOB INTERVIEW

A successful job campaign results in one or more employment interviews. Screening interviews are often conducted by telephone, particularly for customer service positions requiring telephone skills. More extensive interviews are usually conducted in person. Being interviewed by one person at a time is still standard practice. Many firms, however, also conduct group interviews in which the job candidates speak to several prospective work associates at the same time. Often the group interview is conducted in a casual environment, such as a restaurant or company cafeteria. The candidate may not be aware that meeting with the group is actually an interview and that he or she is being judged.

In addition to being interviewed by a group, the interviewee will often be required to go through a sequence of interviews so that abundant observations can be made about his or her qualifications. The same questions are likely to be asked by many interviewers so that multiple observations can be made about key areas, such as your ability to work well under pressure. When put through a series of interviews, it is helpful to take notes to keep track of what is said to each interviewer. Detailed notes are also a key to sending a personalized thank-you note after each interview.[17]

Another important development in employee interviewing is the **behavioral interview,** in which a candidate is asked how he or she handled a particular problem in the past. Examples of behavioral interview questions are "Describe a time when you didn't meet a deadline" and "Tell me how you dealt with an angry customer. What was the problem, and what was the outcome?"

Becoming a skillful interviewee requires practice. You can acquire this practice as you go through the job-finding process. In addition, you can rehearse simulated job interviews with friends and other students. Practice answering the questions posed in Exhibit 11-5. You might also think of several questions you would not like to be asked and develop answers for them.

Videotaping the practice interviews is especially helpful because it provides feedback on how you handled yourself. In watching the replay, pay particular attention to your spoken and nonverbal communication skills. Then make adjustments as needed.

A general guide for performing well in the job interview is to present a positive but accurate picture of yourself. Your chances of performing well in a job increase if you are suited for the job. Tricking a prospective employer into hiring you when you are not qualified is therefore self-defeating in terms of your career. Following is a list of some key points to keep in mind when being interviewed for a job you want:

1. *Prepare in advance.* Be familiar with pertinent details about your background, including your employment history. Bring to the interview your social security number, driver's license, résumé, and the names of references. Prepare a statement in your mind of your uniqueness—what differentiates you from other job candidates. Sometimes the uniqueness is not strictly job related, such as being a champion figure skater.

As described previously, it is important to know some significant facts about your prospective employer. Annual reports, company brochures, and

---

EXHIBIT 11-5

Questions Frequently Asked of Job Candidates

The following questions are of the same basic type and content encountered in most employment interviews. Practice answering them in front of a friend, camcorder, or mirror.

1. Why did you apply for this job?
2. Tell me about yourself.
3. What are your short-term and long-term goals?
4. What have you accomplished?
5. What are your strengths? Areas for improvement?
6. How do you solve problems?
7. How would other people describe you?
8. Why did you prepare for the career you did?
9. What makes you think you will be successful in business?
10. Why should we hire you?
11. Describe how well you work under pressure.
12. What has been your biggest accomplishment on the job?
13. What do you know about our firm?
14. Here's a sample job problem. How would you handle it?

---

newspaper and magazine articles should provide valuable information. Search the Internet, including www.hoover.com (for business firms), for quick access to information about the employer. A brief conversation with one or two current employees might provide some basic knowledge about the firm.

2. *Dress appropriately.*   So much emphasis is placed on dressing well for job interviews that some people overdress. Instead of looking businesslike, they appear to be dressed for a wedding or a funeral. The safest tactic is to wear moderately conservative business attire when applying for most positions. Another important principle is to gear your dress somewhat to the type of prospective employer. If you have a job interview with an employer where sports attire is worn to the office regularly, dress more casually. Dress standards are slowly moving back toward the more formal attire of years ago, yet do not turn down an invitation to dress casually for the interview. But be very cautions about wearing athletic shoes to a job interview.

3. *Focus on important job factors.*   Inexperienced job candidates often ask questions about noncontroversial topics, such as paid holidays, benefits, and company-sponsored social activities. All these topics may be important to you, but explore them after the basic issue—the nature of the job—has been discussed. In this way, you will project a more professional image.

4. *Be prepared for a frank discussion of your strengths and areas for improvement.* Almost every human resources interviewer and many hiring managers will ask you to discuss your strengths and developmental needs (or weaknesses). Everyone has room for improvement in some areas. To deny them is to appear uninsightful or defensive. However, you may not want to reveal problem areas unrelated to the job, such as recurring nightmares or fear of spiders. A mildly evasive approach is to emphasize areas for improvement that could be interpreted as strengths. An example: "I get too impatient with people who do sloppy work."

5. *Do not knock former employers.* To justify looking for a new position or having left a position in the past, job candidates often make negative statements about former employers. Employer bashing makes you appear unprofessional. Furthermore, it may suggest that you are likely to find fault with any employer. Take a positive approach by briefly explaining what went wrong, such as a change in your job that left you without the opportunity to use the skills you were hired for.

6. *Ask a few good questions.* An intelligent interviewee asks a few good questions. An employment specialist for managers said, "The best way to impress somebody on an interview is to ask intelligent questions."[18] Here are two questions worth considering:

If hired, what kind of work would I actually be doing?

What would I have to accomplish on this job to be considered an outstanding performer?

7. *Let the interviewer introduce the topic of compensation.* Often the interviewer will specify the starting salary and benefits, allowing little room for questioning. If asked what starting salary you anticipate, mention a realistic salary range—one that makes you appear neither desperate nor greedy. Careful research, such as compensation data found on the Internet (e.g., www.salary.com) or checking with the placement office, will help you identify a realistic salary range. If the interviewer does not mention salary, toward the end of the interview ask a question such as, "By the way, what is the starting salary for this position?"

8. *Smile and exhibit a positive attitude.* People who smile during job interviews are more likely to receive a job offer. It is also important to express a positive attitude in other ways, such as agreeing with the interviewer and being impressed with facts about the company. If you want the job, toward the conclusion of the interview explain why you see a good fit between your qualifications and those demanded by the job. For example, "The way I see it, this job calls for somebody who is really devoted to improving customer service. That's me. I love to take good care of customers." Smiling also helps you appear relaxed.

9. *Emphasize how your skills can benefit the employer.* An effective job-getting tactic is to explain to a prospective employer what you think you can do to help the company. Look for opportunities to make **skill-benefit statements,** brief explanations of how your skills can benefit the company.[19] Preparing these skill-benefit statements requires considerable self-examination. Practice is required to make the statements smoothly and confidently without appearing pompous or arrogant. If you were applying for a billing specialist position in a company that you knew was having trouble billing customers correctly, you might make this skill-benefit statement: "Here is how I would apply my skill and experience in setting up billing systems to help develop a billing system with as few bugs as possible: _____."

Another way to show how your skills can benefit the employer is to relate the employer problem to one you successfully resolved in the past. In the billing system example, you might state that your previous employer had a billing problem and then explain how you helped solve the problem.

10. *Avoid appearing desperate.*   A prolonged job search—particularly one lasting more than six months—makes many job seekers appear desperate. A problem with projecting desperation is that it creates a negative impression that is likely to result in being rejected once again. An executive search firm notes five signs of a desperate job seeker:

- You have considered accepting a position earning significantly less (e.g., 50 percent) than your previous job. (Or you are willing to accept a starting salary much below what other people in your field are receiving.)

- You have applied for jobs that you know will make you miserable, but you think you can cope because the pay is adequate.

- You have been asked what your job preferences are, and you responded with "I'm open."

- You have called an employment agency or placement office daily even though you have been asked to call back in two weeks.

- When an employment advertisement invites candidates to mail, fax, or e-mail their résumés, you do all three.[20]

If you recognize these signs in yourself, work hard at appearing upbeat. Role-play with a friend to learn if he or she thinks you are making a positive pitch.

11. *Ask for the job and follow through.*   If you want the job in question, be assertive. Make a statement such as, "I'm really interested. What is the next step in the process?" "Is there any other information I could submit that would help you complete your evaluation of me?" Part of asking for the job is to follow through. Mail a follow-up letter or send an e-mail message within three working days after the interview. Mention that you would like to send a follow-up note in another 10 days. Even if you decide not to take the job, a brief thank-you letter is advisable. You may conceivably have contact with that firm in the future. A sample follow-up letter is shown in Exhibit 11-6.

EXHIBIT 11-6

Sample Follow-Up Letter

Rita Mae Jenkins
27 Buttercup Lane
Little Rock, AR 72203
Phone/fax (501) 275-5602
RMJ29@aol.com

Date of Writing Letter
Mr. Bart Bertrand
President
South View Dodge
258 Princess Blvd.
Little Rock, AR 72201

Dear Mr. Bertrand:

   Thank you for my recent chance to discuss the assistant service manager position with you and Mr. Ralph Alexander. It was illuminating to see what a busy, successful operation you have.

   I was impressed with the amount of responsibility the assistant service manager would have at your dealership. The job sounds exciting, and I would like to be part of the growth of the dealership. I realize the work would be hard and the hours would be long, but that's the kind of challenge I want and can handle.

   My understanding is that my background is generally favorable for the position but that you would prefer more direct experience in managing a service operation. Since the car repair and service business is in my blood, I know I will be a fast learner. You said that about two weeks would be needed to interview additional candidates.

   Count on me to start work on July 1, should you extend me a job offer.

Sincerely yours,

Rita Mae Jenkins

▲ PSYCHOLOGICAL TESTING AND THE PHYSICAL EXAMINATION

   Psychological and physical testing are two more challenges facing job candidates who have made it through the interview. Psychological testing (sometimes referred to as employment testing) can help both the employer and the job candidate find a mutually satisfactory fit. The good fit is most likely to be found when the tests are accurate and fair and the candidate answers them accurately. It is best to take these tests with a positive, relaxed attitude. Being physically and mentally well rested is the best preparation. Specialists who develop the test profiles of successful candidates are not expecting an incredible display of human attributes. Also, psychological tests and the physical exam are but two factors in making hiring decisions.

PSYCHOLOGICAL TESTING

Five types of psychological tests are widely used: achievement, aptitude, personality, interest, and integrity (or honesty) tests. The fifth category is used particularly in the retail and financial services industries. A current trend in psychological testing is for the tests to be administered by computer, along with application forms. The computer screening is popular with candidates and with employers because of its efficiency and apparent fairness. Test results, along with recommendations for hiring or not hiring, can be sent back to a client within 10 minutes. Information about good applicants is readily transferred from one company location to another, such as between Blockbuster Video branches.

1. *Achievement tests*   sample and measure the applicant's knowledge and skills. They require applicants to demonstrate their competency on job tasks or related subjects. A person applying for a position as a paralegal might be given a test about real estate and matrimonial law. Giving an applicant a sample of work to perform, such as making a sales pitch, is based on the same idea as a paper-and-pencil or computerized achievement test.

2. *Aptitude tests*   measure an applicant's capacity or potential for performing satisfactorily on the job, given sufficient training. Mental ability tests are the best-known variety of aptitude test. They measure ability to solve problems and learn new material. Mental ability tests measure such specific aptitudes as verbal reasoning, numerical reasoning, and spatial relations (visualizing three dimensions). Scores on mental ability tests are related to success in most jobs in which problem-solving ability is important. The NFL uses mental ability testing with prospects to test their ability to learn complicated plays. Quarterbacks (the people who direct the plays on field) are expected to have the highest scores partly because they have to memorize so many different plays.

3. *Personality tests*   measure personal traits and characteristics that could be related to job performance. Among the many personal characteristics measured by these tests are conscientiousness, self-confidence, and emotional maturity. Tests are also used to measure emotional intelligence, including such factors as optimism and ability to control impulses. Personality tests have been the subject of heated controversy for many years. Critics are concerned that these tests invade privacy and are too imprecise to be useful. Nevertheless, personality factors have a profound influence on job performance. For example, conscientiousness is related to success in many different jobs.[21]

4. *Interest tests*   measure preferences for engaging in certain activities, such as mechanical, numerical, literary, or managerial work. They also measure a person's interest in specific occupations, such as accountant, social worker, or sales representative. Interest tests are designed to indicate whether a person would enjoy a particular activity or occupation. They do not attempt, however, to measure a person's aptitude for that activity or occupation. The Strong Interest Inventory described in Chapter 10 is an interest test.

5. *Honesty tests* are of two types: paper and pencil (or administered by computer) and polygraph tests (often referred to as lie-detector tests). Paper-and-pencil honesty (or integrity) tests ask people questions that directly or indirectly measure their tendency to tell the truth. A direct question would be, "Should an employee be disciplined for stealing ten dollars worth of supplies from the company?" (A dishonest person would answer no.) An indirect question would be, "Do you read the editorial page of your newspaper every day?" (Only a dishonest person would answer yes. Almost nobody can claim a perfect record in this regard.)[22] Some integrity tests measure attitudes about theft, safety regulations, company policies, and related topics.

Polygraphs record a person's internal physiological responses, such as heart rate and breathing rate, in response to questions. The level of emotional response to neutral questions is compared to responses to key questions. The federal Employee Polygraph Protection Act of 1988 severely limits the use of the polygraph for preemployment screening. Preemployment polygraphs can still be used by governments and government contractors engaged in national security activities. Applicants who will be working in security positions or those with direct access to drugs can still be administered polygraph tests. The devices also can still be used to investigate employee theft. Refusal to take the test cannot be used as the basis for dismissal.

THE PHYSICAL EXAMINATION AND DRUG TESTING

As part of the employee selection process, you will be required to take a physical examination. From the company's standpoint, this exam is important for two reasons. First, it gives some indication as to the applicant's ability to handle a particular job. A person with a back injury would have difficulty handling a job that required constant sitting. High absenteeism would be the result. Second, the physical exam provides a basis for later comparisons. This lessens the threat of an employee claiming that the job caused a particular injury or disease.

The physical examination has increased in importance since the passage of the Americans with Disabilities Act of 1991. An employer cannot deny a disabled individual a job because of increased insurance costs or the high cost of health benefits. However, the employer can deny employment to a disabled person if having the individual in the workplace poses a threat to his or her safety or the safety of others.

Approximately one-half of employers test job applicants for the use of illegal drugs. Many employers also test for overuse of prescription drugs. You may therefore have to submit to drug testing for a job you want.[23] Testing for substance abuse includes urinalysis, blood analysis, observation of eyes, and examination of the skin for punctures. Although more expensive for the employer, drug testing through hair samples is another alternative. In addition, some employers use personality tests that measure a person's tendencies toward drug use or other counterproductive behavior. As you can imagine, such drug testing is unpopular with job candidates.

Although employers have a legal right to screen applicants for illegal drug use, some people are concerned that inaccurate drug testing may unfairly deny employment to worthy candidates. A strong argument in favor of drug testing is that employees who are drug abusers may create such problems as lowered productivity, lost time from work, and misappropriation of funds.[24]

▲ MANAGING THE DOWNSIDE OF CONDUCTING A JOB SEARCH

For some people, finding a job is an easy task, particularly if they are in a field in which the number of positions available is far greater than the number of job applicants. For many other people, the job search can be a mixed experience: some joy and some frustration. Much rejection can be expected. Few people are wanted by every employer. You have to learn to accept such rejection in stride, remembering that a good deal of personal chemistry is involved in being hired. Suppose that the person doing the hiring likes you personally. You then have a much greater chance of being hired for the position than does another individual of comparable merit. If the interviewer dislikes you, the reverse is true.

Rejection and rudeness are frequently encountered in job hunting and can easily create discouragement. Keep pressure on yourself to avoid slowing down because you are discouraged. Research documents the fact that assertive behaviors are associated with success in finding a job, even when the job hunter has average job qualifications.[25] Another study showed that unemployed people who maintain good control of their motivation through such means as goal setting are more likely to keep up the intensity of their job search. Also, job seekers who maintain control over anxiety and worry are more likely to keep trying.[26]

Remember, you have to perform dozens of tasks to find a job. Many of them have already been described, such as preparing a statement of your job objective, a cover letter, and a résumé. You also have to line up your references and take care of every job lead that comes your way. When you do not have a job, almost no sensible lead should be ignored. Each lead processed takes you one step closer to finding a job. And all you are looking for is one job.

Despite the new high-tech approaches to job finding, the entire process is inefficient but effective. Although you may have to make 100 contacts to find a suitable position (inefficiency), you probably will find the position, thus making the process effective (it gets the intended results).

In case you doubt that the job search activities described here actually work, an analysis of 36 studies involving 11,010 job seekers provides positive evidence. The researchers concluded that individuals who engaged in higher levels of job search behavior were more likely to obtain employment than those who reported lower levels of such behavior. An example of a job search behavior would be visiting company Web sites looking for employment opportunities. The relationship between job search behavior and finding a job was stronger among laid-off workers than among new entrants or among employed people who were looking for a new position.[27]

▲ SUMMARY

Job search skills may be used at different stages in your career. The job search begins with a reasonably flexible statement of the type of job you are seeking (your job objective). Knowing what type of organization you would prefer to work for will help focus your job search. Qualifications frequently sought by employers are listed in Human Relations Self-Assessment Quiz 11-1 and should be kept in mind during the job search.

A systematic job search uses many job-finding methods, including networking (contacts and referrals), the Internet and résumé database services, unsolicited letter or e-mail mail campaigns, a telesearch, placement offices, employment agencies, career fairs, help-wanted ads, and extreme job hunting.

A cover letter should accompany a résumé and application form. An attention-getting cover letter should explain why you are applying for a particular position and identify your potential contribution to the employer. A T-form cover letter systematically outlines how the applicant's qualifications match up against the job requirements posted in the position announcement. The T-form approach gives the reader a tabular outline of how the applicant's background fits the position description.

The major purpose of a résumé is to help you obtain a job interview. There is no one best way to prepare a résumé. Effective résumés are straightforward, factual presentations of a person's experiences, skills, and accomplishments.

The chronological résumé presents your work experience, education, and interests, along with your accomplishments, in reverse chronological order. The functional résumé organizes your skills and accomplishments into the functions or tasks that support the job you are seeking. The targeted résumé focuses on a specific job target or position and presents only information that supports the target. A new emphasis in résumé construction is to incorporate your values into the presentation of yourself.

The job objective on your résumé should describe the position you are seeking now or in the short-term future. When your credentials do not fit closely the position description, emphasize on your résumé those skills from other experiences that would help you succeed in the position. Creative-style résumés and gimmicks bring favorable attention to your credentials but should be used with discretion. Avoid making untrue statements on your résumé.

Rehearse being interviewed and then present yourself favorably but accurately in the interview. Behavioral interviews are growing in importance. Specific interview suggestions include: (1) preparing in advance; (2) dressing appropriately; (3) focusing on important job factors; (4) being prepared to discuss your strengths and areas for improvement; (5) not knocking former employers; (6) asking a few good questions; (7) letting the interviewer introduce the topic of compensation; (8) smiling and exhibiting a positive attitude;

(9) emphasizing how your skills can benefit the employer, (10) avoiding appearing desperate, and (11) asking for the job and following through.

Psychological testing may be part of the employment process, with five types of testing being widely used: achievement, aptitude, personality, interest, and honesty (or integrity) tests. The physical exam, including possible drug testing, is another key step on the way to being hired.

Conducting a job campaign is typically inefficient but ultimately effective. The process is demanding, with some joys and many frustrations. It is therefore important to keep pressure on yourself to perform the many chores required of a successful job-hunting campaign. Follow up on every lead and try not to take rejection and rudeness personally.

Research indicates that the type of job-seeking behaviors described in this chapter actually facilitate finding a job.

Questions and Activities

1. During times when there is a shortage of skilled workers, why is it still important to study how to conduct a job campaign?

2. How realistic are the qualifications sought by employers for positions in business and related fields?

3. Despite the widespread use of the Internet for finding employment, the vast majority of executive positions are still filled by referrals or executive placement services. What might account for the limited use of the Internet for filling executive positions?

4. During a period in which there is a dire shortage of jobs available, which job-hunting tactics do you think would be the most relevant?

5. What can you do today to help you develop a contact that could someday lead to a job?

6. What special challenges do voice-mail systems present for job seekers?

7. Given that people have so many different opinions about what makes for an effective résumé, what kind of résumé should a job seeker prepare?

8. Explain whether *extreme job hunting* fits your personal style.

9. Assume that you are being interviewed for a position you really want and the interviewer asks you several questions that could be considered in violation of employment law. How would you respond to his or her questions?

10. Visit the employment section of the Web site of three large companies of interest to you. Identify several jobs you perceive to match your qualifications or for which you have a reasonable chance of being regarded as a bona fide candidate.

INTERNET SKILL BUILDER: How Much Am I in Demand?

One of the most practical applications of the Internet is for job finding. Use a job-finding site (such as those listed in Exhibit 11-2) to find at least three jobs for which you might be qualified. Assuming that you would actually apply for the position, identify what you think is your strongest qualification. Do the same for your weakest qualification.

WEB CORNER

Selection of articles about conducting the job search:
www.careerjournal.com/jobhunting strategies

Preparing for the job interview: www.jobinterview.net and
www.labmice.net/career/interview.htm

HUMAN RELATIONS CASE PROBLEM

Stacy Sings the Blues

Stacy, age 27, was proud to be an architectural technician student. She liked the idea of combining her interest in art with being part of something important. As she reasoned, "I will be helping architects erect skyscrapers, small office buildings, and houses that will last for a century. I will help provide beautiful environments for fellow human beings to work and live."

To help fund her schooling and pay her living expenses while at career school, Stacy tended bar at the Big Boar Inn, a trendy bar frequented mostly by young people. Stacy had also worked on and off as a bartender before attending career school. For several years after high school, she traveled around the world finding work at bars and resorts wherever she could. During her travels, Stacy would make note of the design of buildings and prepared many sketches of her own ideas about the building design. She knew that she wanted to someday work in the field of architecture.

Several months before graduation, Stacy's father and several friends asked her when she would be starting her job hunt. Stacy explained that she was too busy finishing her studies at school and working at the Big Boar to get seriously involved in a job hunt. "After graduation in May, I'll take a couple of months to unwind and then begin searching for a job. Besides, most architectural firms don't get serious about hiring recent graduates until after Labor Day." Stacy's dad thought she was being a little laid back in her job-hunting approach but did not think he was in a position to tell her what to do.

After graduation, Stacy continued to work at the Big Boar about 25 hours per week. She spent a lot of time at the beach and developed a deep skin tan. One day she ran into her mentor, Professor Bill Byron, at the supermarket. Byron asked Stacy how her job search was going.

Stacy replied, "I will be getting to working on my résumé soon. With the job market for architectural technicians being soft right now, I didn't see any need to rush. Would it be okay to drop by your office to get some advice on my résumé?"

Stacy met with Mr. Byron a week later. He gave Stacy a few suggestions about résumé construction and also noted that her portfolio of architectural renderings needed

(Continued)

more work before she could present the portfolio to prospective employers. Stacy then decided to sharpen her portfolio before beginning her job search.

At the urging of a friend, Stacy bought a few out-of-town newspapers to search the classified sections. She chose Washington, D.C., Atlanta, and Miami because of their warm climates. Stacy spotted a total of three openings for architectural technicians and sent a résumé and cover letter to the addresses indicated in the ads.

Two months passed, and Stacy had not heard back from any of the firms to which she sent letters. Stacy's next approach was to give a copy of her résumé to a friend who sold furniture to an architectural firm in New Jersey. The friend said he would give the résumé to a personal contact he had at the firm.

During a work break at the Big Boar, a server asked Stacy how her job hunt was proceeding. Stacy replied, "Right now, I'm just sitting back and waiting to hear. There's not much else I can do."

Questions

1. What is your evaluation of the effectiveness of Stacy's job campaign?

2. What recommendations can you make to Stacy to help her find a position as an architectural technician?

3. You be the career counselor. Does Stacy really want to leave her job as a bartender at the Big Boar Inn and become an architectural technician?

▲ REFERENCES

1. Adapted from Joann S. Lublin, "X-Treme Job Hunting: Creative Souls Make Oddball Tactics Work," *Wall Street Journal*, July 29, 2003, p. B1.

2. "Grads, Adjust Those Job Goals," *USA Weekend*, March 29–31, 2002, p. 18.

3. "CEOs Speak Out: What Is Needed to Work in Today's Ever-Changing Business World," *Keying In*, November 1996, pp. 1–2; Brien N. Smith, Carolee Jones, and Judy Lane, "Employers' Perceptions of Work Skills," *Business Education Forum*, April 1997, pp. 11–17; "Hot Commodities: How to Be the Job Candidate Everyone Wants," *Working Woman*, February 2000, pp. 40–45; Kate Berry, "Attitude and Tenacity Help in Getting an Internet Job," Knight-Ridder story, November 15, 1999.

4. Cited in Kris Maher, "The Jungle: Focus on Recruitment, Pay and Getting Ahead," *Wall Street Journal*, June 17, 2003, p. B8.

5. Connie R. Wanberg, Ruth Kanfer, and Joseph T. Banas, "Predictors and Outcomes of Networking Intensity among Unemployed Job Seekers," *Journal of Applied Psychology*, August 2000, pp. 491–503.

6. Kris Maher, "The Jungle: Focus on Recruitment, Pay and Getting Ahead," *The Wall Street Journal*, December 23, 2003, p. B6.

7. Stacy Forster, "The Best Way to Recruit New Workers," *Wall Street Journal*, September 15, 2003, p. R8.

8. Anne Fisher, "I Want to Talk to a Human Being: Is It Too Much to Ask?" *Fortune,* October 14, 2002, p. 272.

9. Lublin, "X-Treme Job Hunting," p. B1.

10. Richard H. Beatty, *The Perfect Cover Letter* (New York: John Wiley & Sons, 1997).

11. Based on form used by Garrett Associates, Alexandria, Virginia.

12. Mary Alice Griffin and Patricia Lynn Anderson, "Résumé Content," *Business Education Forum,* February 1994, p. 11.

13. Jean Sherman Chatzky, "The New World of Résumés," *USA Weekend,* March 14–16, 2003, p. 12.

14. Kim Komando, "Landing a Job: Tech Toolkit Can Help Get Your Foot in the Door," syndicated column, December 29, 2003.

15. R. Neil Dortch, "Résumé Preparation," *Business Education Forum,* April 1994, p. 47.

16. "Quick Career Booster," *Working Smart,* January 1998, p. 3.

17. Kemba J. Dunham, "The Jungle: Focus on Recruitment, Pay and Getting Ahead," *Wall Street Journal,* July 15, 2003, p. B6.

18. "Talking with Lynn Bignell about Job Hunting," *Working Smart,* November 1991, p. 7.

19. Ellen Forman, "Surviving under the Microscope," *Sun-Sentinel* syndicated story, April 21, 1997; Nancy K. Austin, "The New Job Interview: Beyond the Trick Question," *Working Woman,* March 1996, pp. 23–24.

20. Kemba J. Dunham, "The Jungle: Focus on Recruitment, Pay and Getting Ahead," *Wall Street Journal,* April 8, 2003, p. B8.

21. Orlando Behling, "Employee Selection: Will Intelligence and Conscientiousness Do the Job?" *Academy of Management Executive,* February 1998, pp. 77–88.

22. Paul R. Sackett, Laura R. Burris, and Christine Callahan, "Integrity Testing for Personnel Selection: An Update," *Personnel Psychology,* Autumn 1989, p. 493; Leonard D. Goodstein and Richard I. Lanyon, "Applications of Personality Assessment to the Workplace: A Review," *Journal of Business and Psychology,* Spring 1999, p. 317.

23. Jane Easter Bahis, "Drugs in the Workplace," *HR Magazine,* February 1998, pp. 81–87.

24. Rob Brookler, "Industry Standards in Workplace Drug Testing," *Personnel Journal,* April 1992, p. 128.

25. Mark J. Schmitt, Elise L. Amel, and Ann Marie Ryan, "Self-Reported Assertive Job-Seeking Behaviors of Minimally Educated Job Hunters," *Personnel Psychology,* Spring 1993, p. 119.

26. Connie R. Wanberg, Ruth Kanfer, and Maria Rotundo, "Unemployed Individuals: Motives, Job-Search Competencies, and Job-Search Constraints as Predictors of Job Seeking and Reemployment," *Journal of Applied Psychology,* December 1999, pp. 897–910.

27. Ruth Kanfer, Connie R. Wanberg, and Tracy M. Kantrowitz, "Job Search and Employment: A Personality-Motivational Analysis and Meta-Analytic Review," *Journal of Applied Psychology,* February 2000, pp. 86–101.

▲ ADDITIONAL READING

Bolles, Richard Nelson. *Job-Hunting Tactics on the Internet.* 2d ed. Berkeley, CA: Ten Speed Press, 1999.

Field, Anne. "The Extra-Innings Job Search." *BusinessWeek,* March 17, 2003, p. 109.

Garvey, Charlotte. "When HR Goes Job Hunting." *HR Magagine,* September 2001, pp. 58–62.

Harrington, Ann. "Can Anyone Build a Better Monster?" *Fortune,* May 13, 2002, pp. 189–192.

Huffcutt, Allen I., and Philip L. Roth. "Racial Group Differences in Employment Interview Evaluations." *Journal of Applied Psychology,* April 1998, pp. 179–189.

Merritt, Jennifer. "Improv at the Interview." *BusinessWeek,* February 3, 2003, p. 63.

Pentila, Chris. "Risky Business: Should A Prospective Employee's Credit History Determine Whether He or She Gets the Job? *Entrepreneur,* September 2003, pp. 78–79.

Thornburg, Linda. "Computer-Assisted Interviewing Shortens Hiring Cycle." *HR Magazine,* February 1998, pp. 73–79.

Useem, Jerry. "Cyberspace Is a Job Jungle: Read This before You Put a Résumé Online." *Fortune,* May 24, 1999.

CHAPTER 12

Developing Good Work Habits

Learning Objectives

After studying the information and doing the exercises in this chapter, you should be able to:

◆ Appreciate the importance of good work habits and time management

◆ Decrease any tendencies you might have toward procrastination

◆ Develop attitudes and values that will help you become more productive

◆ Develop skills and techniques that will help you become more productive

◆ Overcome time-wasting practices

*C*omputer company Gateway Inc. was hit with a $3.6 million jury verdict for a wrong number that flooded another company's toll-free telephone line with calls from thousands of angry Gateway customers. The number belongs to Mo' Money, a Pensacola, Florida, business that manufactures and distributes promotional items with company logos, including T-shirts, caps, gym bags, and jackets. A federal jury awarded the damages to Mo' Money in 2002.

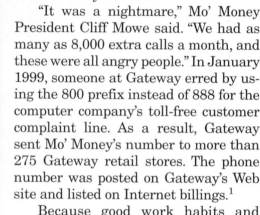

"It was a nightmare," Mo' Money President Cliff Mowe said. "We had as many as 8,000 extra calls a month, and these were all angry people." In January 1999, someone at Gateway erred by using the 800 prefix instead of 888 for the computer company's toll-free customer complaint line. As a result, Gateway sent Mo' Money's number to more than 275 Gateway retail stores. The phone number was posted on Gateway's Web site and listed on Internet billings.[1]

Because good work habits and time management (including concentrating carefully on the task at hand) improve productivity, they contribute to success in business. **Work habits** refer to a person's characteristic approach to work, including such things as organization, priority setting, and handling of paper work and e-mail. Good work habits and time management are more important than ever because of today's emphasis on **productivity,** the amount of quality work accomplished in relation to the resources consumed. Furthermore, a person is more likely to be fired from a job or flunk out of school because of poor work habits than because of poor aptitude.

People with good work habits tend to achieve higher career success and have more time to invest in their personal lives. They also enjoy their personal lives more because they are not preoccupied with unfinished tasks. Effective work habits are also beneficial because they eliminate a major stressor—the feeling of having very little or no control over your life. Being in control also leads to a relaxed, confident approach to work.

The goal of this chapter is to help you become a more productive person who is still flexible. Someone who develops good work habits is not someone who becomes so obsessed with time and so rigid that he or she makes other people feel uncomfortable. Ideally, a person should be well organized yet still flexible.

Information about becoming more productive is organized here into four related categories. One is overcoming procrastination, a problem that plagues almost everybody to some extent. The second is developing attitudes and values that foster productivity. The third category is the lengthiest: developing skills and techniques that lead to personal productivity. The fourth category is overcoming time wasters.

▲ DEALING WITH PROCRASTINATION

The leading cause of poor productivity and career self-sabotage is **procrastination,** delaying a task for an invalid or weak reason. Procrastination is also the major work habit problem for most workers and students. The presence of computers in the cubicle or office increases the risk of procrastination because it so easy to check e-mail or a favorite Web site just before starting almost any task. Unproductive people are the biggest procrastinators, but even productive people have problems with procrastination at times. A business owner who does not ordinarily procrastinate might delay preparing taxes knowing that she was behind in her taxes.

WHY PEOPLE PROCRASTINATE

People procrastinate for many different reasons. One is that we perceive the task to be done (such as quitting a job) as unpleasant. Another reason we procrastinate is that we find the job facing us to be overwhelming, such as assembling a computer console that arrives in a large box. To avoid an overwhelming or taxing task, some people flood their workday with small, easy-to-do tasks. As a result, these people do not appear to be procrastinators on the surface.[2] Another major cause of procrastination is a fear of the consequences of our actions.

One possible negative consequence is a negative evaluation of your work. For example, if you delay preparing a report for your boss or instructor, that person cannot criticize its quality. Bad news is another negative consequence that procrastination can sometimes delay. If you think your personal computer needs a new hard drive, delaying a trip to the computer store means you will not have to hear the diagnosis: "Your hard drive needs replacement. We can do the job for about $450."

Another reason some people procrastinate is the **fear of success.** People sometimes believe that if they succeed at an important task, they will be asked to take on more responsibility in the future. They dread this possibility. Some students have been known to procrastinate completing their degree requirements to avoid taking on the responsibility of a full-time position. People frequently put off tasks that do not appear to offer a meaningful reward. Suppose you decide that your computer files need a thorough updating, including deleting inactive files. Even if you know this task should be done, the accomplishment of updated files might not be a particularly meaningful reward.

Many people procrastinate as a way of rebelling against being controlled. Procrastination, used in this way, is a means of defying unwarranted authority.[3] Rather than submit to authority, a person might tell himself, "Nobody is going to tell me when I should get a report done. I'll do it when I'm good and ready." Such people might be referred to as "anticontrol freaks."

A curious reason for procrastination is to achieve the stimulation and excitement that stems from rushing to meet a deadline.[4] Some people, for example, enjoy fighting their way through traffic or running through an airline terminal so they can make an appointment or airplane flight barely on time. They appear to enjoy the rush of adrenaline, endorphins, and other hormones associated with hurrying.

Finally, some people procrastinate because they are perfectionists. They attempt to perfect a project before being willing to admit the project is completed. As a result, the person procrastinates not about beginning a project but letting go. When asked, "Have you finished that project?" the perfectionist replies, "No, there a few small details that still need to be worked out." Being a perfectionist can also block starting new projects because the perfectionist will often want to keep working on the present project. Perfectionism comes in degrees, with slight perfectionists simply being extremely conscientious and heavy-duty perfectionists almost stalled in their actions. Human Relations Self-Assessment Quiz 12-1 gives you an opportunity to measure your degree of perfectionism.

HUMAN RELATIONS SELF-ASSESSMENT QUIZ 12-1

Tendencies Toward Perfectionism

Many perfectionists hold some of the behaviors and attitudes described below. To help understand your tendencies toward perfectionism, rate how strongly you agree with each of the statements below on a scale of 0 to 4.

1. Many people have told me that I am a perfectionist.   0   1   2   3   4
2. I often correct the speech of others.   0   1   2   3   4
3. It takes me a long time to write an e-mail because I keep checking and rechecking my writing.   0   1   2   3   4
4. I often criticize the color combinations my friends are wearing.   0   1   2   3   4
5. When I purchase food at a supermarket, I usually look at the expiration date so I can purchase the freshest.   0   1   2   3   4
6. I can't stand when people use the term "remote" instead of "remote control."   0   1   2   3   4
7. If a company representative asked me "What is your *social?*" I would reply something like, "Do you mean my *social security number?*"   0   1   2   3   4
8. I hate to see dust on furniture.   0   1   2   3   4
9. I like the Martha Stewart idea of having every decoration in the home just right.   0   1   2   3   4
10. I never put a map back in the glove compartment until it is folder just right.   0   1   2   3   4

(Continued)

11. Once an eraser on a pencil of mine becomes hard and useless, I throw the pencil away. 　　　　0　1　2　3　4

12. I adjust all my watches and clocks so they show exactly the same time. 　　　　0　1　2　3　4

13. It bothers me that clocks on personal computers are usually wrong by a few minutes. 　　　　0　1　2　3　4

14. I clean the keyboard on my computer at least once a week. 　　　0　1　2　3　4

15. I organize my e-mail messages and computer documents into many different, clearly labeled files. 　　　　0　1　2　3　4

16. You won't find old coffee cups of soft-drink containers on my desk. 　　　　0　1　2　3　4

17. I rarely start a new project or assignment until I have completed my present project or assignment. 　　　　0　1　2　3　4

18. It is very difficult for me to concentrate when my work area is disorganized. 　　　　0　1　2　3　4

19. Cobwebs in chandeliers and other lighting fixtures bug me. 　　0　1　2　3　4

20. It takes me a long time to make a purchase such as a digital camera because I keep studying the features on various models. 　　　　0　1　2　3　4

21. When I balance my checkbook, it usually comes out right within a few dollars. 　　　　0　1　2　3　4

22. I carry enough small coins and dollar bills with me so when I shop I can pay the exact amount without requiring change. 　　　　0　1　2　3　4

23. I throw out any underwear or tee shirts that have even the smallest holes or tears. 　　　　0　1　2　3　4

24. I become upset with myself if I make a mistake. 　　　　0　1　2　3　4

25. When a finger nail of mine is broken or chipped, I fix it as soon as possible. 0　1　2　　　　3　4

26. I am carefully groomed whenever I leave my home. 　　　　0　1　2　3　4

27. When I notice packaged goods or cans on the floor in a supermarket, I will often place the back on the shelf. 　　　　0　1　2　3　4

28. I think that carrying around anti-bacterial cleaner for the hands is an excellent idea. 　　　　0　1　2　3　4

29. If I am with a friend, and he or she has a loose hair on the shoulder, I will remove it without asking. 　　　　0　1　2　3　4

30. I know that I am a perfectionist. 　　　　0　1　2　3　4

Scoring

91 or over: You have strong perfectionist tendencies to the point that it could interfere with your taking quick action when necessary. Also, you may annoy many people with your perfectionism.

61-90: Moderate degree of perfectionism that could lead you to produce high-quality work and be a dependable person.

31-60: Mild degree of perfectionism. You might be a perfectionist in some situations quite important to you, but not in others.

0-30: Not a perfectionist. You might be too casual about getting things done right, meeting deadlines, and being aware of details.

Techniques for Reducing Procrastination

To overcome or at least minimize procrastination, we recommend a number of specific tactics. A general approach, however, is simply to be aware that procrastination is a major drain on productivity. Being aware of the problem will remind you to take corrective action in many situations. When your accomplishment level is low, you might ask yourself, "Am I procrastinating on anything of significance?"

Calculate the cost of procrastination.   You can reduce procrastination by calculating its cost.[5] One example is that you might lose out on obtaining a high-paying job you really want by not having your résumé and cover letter ready on time. Your cost of procrastination would include the difference in salary between the job you do find and the one you really wanted. Another cost would be the loss of potential job satisfaction.

Counterattack.   Forcing yourself to do something overwhelming, frightening, or uncomfortable helps to prove that the task was not as bad as initially perceived. Assume that you have accepted a new position but have not yet resigned from your present one because resigning seems so uncomfortable. Set up a specific time to call your manager or send an e-mail to schedule an appointment. Force yourself further to show up for the resignation appointment. After you break the ice with the statement "I have something important to tell you," the task will be much easier.

Jump-start yourself.   You can often get momentum going on a project by giving yourself a tiny assignment just to get started. One way to get momentum going on an unpleasant or overwhelming task is to set aside a specific time to work on it. If you have to write a report on a subject you dislike, you might set aside Saturday from 3 P.M. to 4 P.M. as your time to first attack the project. If your procrastination problem is particularly intense, giving yourself even a five-minute task, such as starting a new file, might help you gain momentum. After five minutes, decide if you choose to continue for another five minutes. The five-minute chunks will help you focus your energy.

Peck away at an overwhelming task.   Assume that you have a major project to do that does not have to be accomplished in a hurry. A good way of minimizing procrastination is to peck away at the project in 15- to 30-minute bits of time. Bit by bit, the project will get down to manageable size and therefore not seem so overwhelming. A related way of pecking away at an overwhelming task is to subdivide it into smaller units. For instance, you might break down moving into a series of tasks, such as filing change-of-address notices, locating a mover, and packaging books. Pecking away can sometimes be achieved by setting aside as little as five minutes to work on a seemingly overwhelming task. When the five minutes are up, either work five more minutes on the task or reschedule the activity for sometime soon.

Motivate yourself with rewards and punishments.   Give yourself a pleasant reward soon after you accomplish a task you would ordinarily procrastinate about. You might, for example, jog through the woods after having completed a tough take-home exam. The second part of this tactic is to punish yourself if you have engaged in serious procrastination. How about not watching any of your favorite television shows for one week?

Follow the WIFO principle. Personal effectiveness coach Shale Paul recommends that you use the technique of *worst in, first out* for dealing with unpleasant tasks you would prefer to avoid. After you finally get the task done, Paul says, "Chances are, you'll find that you spent nearly as much time worrying and rescheduling it as you did actually doing it." If the task fits high enough on your priorities, simply get it done and out of the way.[6] A related motivational principle is that after completing the unpleasant task, moving on to a more pleasant (or less unpleasant) task functions as a reward.

Make a commitment to other people. Put pressure on yourself to get something done on time by making it a commitment to one or more other people. You might announce to coworkers that you are going to get a project of mutual concern completed by a certain date. If you fail to meet this date, you may feel embarrassed.

Express a more positive attitude about your intentions. Expressing a more positive attitude can often lead to changes in behavior. If you choose words that express a serious intention to complete an activity, you are more likely to follow through than if you choose more uncertain words. Imagine that a coworker says, "I *might* get you the information you need by next Friday." You probably will not be surprised if you do not receive the information by Friday. In contrast, if your coworker says, "I *will*. . . get you the information you need by next Friday," there is less likelihood the person will procrastinate. Psychologist Linda Sapadin believes that you are less likely to procrastinate if you change you "wish" to "will," your "like to" to "try to," and your "have to" to "want to."[7]

▲ DEVELOPING THE PROPER ATTITUDES AND VALUES

Developing good work habits and time management practices is often a matter of developing proper attitudes toward work and time. For instance, if you think that your job is important and that time is valuable, you will be on your way toward developing good work habits. In this section we describe a group of attitudes and values that can help improve your productivity through better use of time and improved work habits.

DEVELOP A MISSION, GOALS, AND A STRONG WORK ETHIC

A mission, or general purpose in life, propels you toward being productive. Assume that a person says, "My mission is to become an outstanding professional in my career, and a loving, constructive parent." The mission serves as a compass to direct your activities, such as being well organized in order to attain a favorable performance appraisal.

Goals are more specific than a mission statement. The goals support the mission statement, but the effect is the same. Being committed to a goal also propels you toward good use of time. Imagine how efficient most employees would be if they were told, "Here is five days of work facing you. If you get finished in less than five days without sacrificing quality, you can have that time to yourself." If the saved time fit your mission, such as having more quality time with family members, the impact would be even stronger.

Stephen Covey, a popularizer of time management techniques, expresses the importance of a mission of goals in his phrase, "Begin with the end in mind." He recommends you develop your mission statement by first thinking about what people who know you well would say at your funeral if you died three years from now. Also, list your various roles in life, such as spouse, child, family member, professional, and soccer player. For each role, think of one or two major lifetime goals you have in that area. Then develop a brief mission statement describing your life's purpose that incorporates these goals.[8]

A person might have the mission of becoming an outstanding professional person. Your goals to support that mission might include to achieve advanced certification in your field, become an officer in a professional organization, and make large donations to charity. When you are deciding how to spend your time each day, give goals related to your mission top priority.

Closely related to establishing a mission and goals is develop a strong work ethic, as described in Chapter 8. Developing a strong work ethic may lead to even higher productivity than goal setting alone. For example, one might set the goal of earning a high income. It might lead to some good work habits but not necessarily a high commitment to quality.

VALUE GOOD ATTENDANCE AND PUNCTUALITY

On the job, in school, or in personal life, good attendance and punctuality are essential for developing a good reputation. Also, you cannot contribute to a team effort unless you are present. Poor attendance and consistent lateness are the most frequent reasons for employee discipline. Furthermore, many managers interpret high absenteeism and lateness as signs of emotional immaturity. An important myth about attendance and punctuality should be challenged early in a person's career. The myth is that a certain number of sick days are owed an employee. Some employees who have not used up their sick days will find reasons to be sick at the end of the year.

VALUE YOUR TIME

People who place a high value on their time are propelled into making good use of time. If a person believes that his or her time is valuable, it will be difficult to engage that person in idle conversation during working hours. Valuing your time can also apply to personal life. The yield from clipping or gathering grocery coupons is an average of $9 per hour—assuming that purchasing national brands is important to you. Would a busy professional person therefore be better off clipping and gathering coupons or engaging in self-development for the same amount of time? Being committed to a mission and goals is an automatic way of making good use of time.

Value Neatness, Orderliness, and Speed

Neatness, orderliness, and speed are important contributors to workplace productivity and therefore should be valued. An orderly desk or work area does not inevitably signify an orderly mind. Yet orderliness does help most people become more productive. Less time is wasted and less energy is expended if you do not have to hunt for missing information. Knowing where information is and what information you have available is a way of being in control of your job. When your job gets out of control, you are probably working at less than peak efficiency. Being neat and orderly helps you achieve good performance. Frequently breaking your concentration for such matters as finding an e-mail message your printed a month ago inhibits high performance.

Neatness is linked to working rapidly because clutter and searching for misplaced items consume time. Employers emphasize speed today to remain competitive in such matters as serving customers promptly and bringing new products and services to the market. Speed is widely considered to be a competitive advantage. In the words of organizational consultant Price Pritchett,

> So you need to operate with a strong sense of urgency. Accelerate in all aspects of your work, even if it means living with a few more ragged edges. Emphasize *action*. Don't bog down in endless preparation trying to get things perfect before you make a move. Sure, high quality is crucial, but it must come quickly. You can't sacrifice speed. Learn to fail fast, fix it, and race on.[9]

The best approach to maintaining a neat work area and to enhance speed is to convince yourself that neatness and speed are valuable. You will then search for ways to be neat and fast, such as putting back a reference book immediately after use or making phone conversations brief. The underlying principle is that an attitude leads to a change in behavior.

Work Smarter, Not Harder

People caught up in trying to accomplish a job often wind up working hard but not in an imaginative way that leads to good results. Much time and energy are therefore wasted. A working-smart approach also requires that you spend a few minutes carefully planning how to implement your task. An example of working smarter, not harder, is to invest a few minutes of critical thinking before launching an Internet search. Think through carefully what might be the key words that will lead you to the information you need. In this way, you will minimize conducting your search with words and phrases that will lead to irrelevant information. For example, suppose you want to conduct research on backstabbing as negative office politics. If you simply use the term "back stabbing," the search engine will direct you to such topics as street crime and medical treatment for wounds. Working smarter is to try "backstabbing in the office."

An everyday application of working smarter, not harder, would be to telephone ahead to find out if a store had the merchandise you needed rather than visiting the store to search for the merchandise. Similarly, many people save time shopping by making use of e-tailing and save visits to the library by searching information over the Internet.

BECOME SELF-EMPLOYED PSYCHOLOGICALLY

A distinguishing characteristic of most self-employed people is that they care deeply about what they accomplish each day. Most of their job activities directly or indirectly affect their financial health. Additionally, many self-employed people enjoy high job satisfaction because they have chosen work that fits their interests. Because of the factors just mentioned, the self-employed person is compelled to make good use of time. Also, the high level of job satisfaction typical of many self-employed people leads them to enjoy being productive.[10]

If a person working for an employer regards his or her area of responsibility as self-employment, productivity may increase. To help regard employment by others as self-employment, keep this thought in mind. Every employee is given some assets to manage to achieve a good return on investment. If you managed the printing and copying center for your company, you would be expected to manage that asset profitably.

APPRECIATE THE IMPORTANCE OF REST AND RELAXATION

A productive attitude to maintain is that overwork can be counterproductive and lead to negative stress and burnout. Proper physical rest contributes to mental alertness and improved ability to cope with frustration. Constant attention to work or study is often inefficient. It is a normal human requirement to take enough rest breaks to allow yourself to approach work or study with a fresh perspective. Each person has to establish the right balance between work and leisure within the bounds of freedom granted by the situation.

Neglecting the normal need for rest and relaxation can lead to **workaholism,** an addiction to work in which not working is an uncomfortable experience. Some types of workaholics are perfectionists who are never satisfied with their work and therefore find it difficult to leave work behind. Career counselor Janet Salyer notes, "Workaholics put the job before family, friends, and their own health. And even if they're spending time with their families, their mind is on work."[11] In addition, the workaholic who is a perfectionist may become heavily focused on control, leading to rigid behavior.

However, some people who work long and hard are classified as happy workaholics who thrive on hard work and are usually highly productive. As executives, they encourage others to work hard to achieve company goals and also pursue what matters to them in their personal life.[12] Furthermore, many people who work long and hard to be successful in their careers also intensely enjoy other activities. Warren Buffet, the legendary investor who is one of the world's richest people, carries an enormous workload although he is in his late 70s. However, he is also a fanatic about bridge and regularly interrupts his workday to play bridge on the computer.

PLAY THE INNER GAME OF WORK

Psychologist and tennis coach Timothy Gallwey developed the *inner game of tennis* to help tennis players focus better on their game. Over time, he applied the inner game to skiing, other sports, life in general, and work. The key concept is that by removing inner obstacles, such as self-criticism, you can dramatically improve your ability to focus, learn, and perform. According to Gallwey, two selves exist inside each person. Self 1 is the critical, fearful, self-doubting voice that sends out messages like, "You have almost solved this tough problem for the customer. Don't blow it now." Intimidating comments like these hinder Self 2 from getting the job done. Self 2 encompasses all the inner resources—both actual and potential—of the individual.

Self 1 must be suppressed so that Self 2 can accomplish its task and learn effectively without being lectured. The process required to move Self 1 aside is to focus your attention on a critical variable related to performance rather than on the performance you are attempting to achieve. An example would be for a customer service representative to focus on the amount of tension in a caller's voice.[13] Or you might focus on the facial expressions of your manager as you attempt to sell him or her on an idea for improving productivity.

▲ TIME MANAGEMENT TECHNIQUES

So far we have discussed improving productivity from the standpoints of dealing with procrastination and developing the right attitudes and values. Skills and techniques are also important for becoming more productive. Here we describe some well-established methods of work habit improvement along with several new ones. For these techniques to enhance productivity, most of them need to be incorporated into and practiced regularly in our daily lives. This is particularly true because many of these techniques are habits, and habits have to be programmed into the brain through repetition.

Clean Up and Get Organized

An excellent starting point for improving work habits and time management is to clean up the work area and arrange things neatly. Eliminate clutter by throwing out unnecessary paper and deleting computer files that will probably never be used again. According to one productivity expert, 80 percent of filed paperwork is never looked at again.[14] The idea is to learn to simplify the work area so that there are fewer distractions and the brain can be more focused. In addition, finding important files becomes easier. Getting organized includes sorting out which tasks need doing, including assignments and projects not yet completed. Getting organized can also mean sorting through the many small paper notes attached to the computer and on the wall.

A major reason a cleanup campaign is needed periodically is that many people have pack-rat tendencies. It is difficult to throw out tangible items (including paper, souvenir ball pens, and supply catalogs) because possessions give us a sense of security, status, and comfort.[15] A major cleanup principle is, therefore, to discard anything that is no longer valuable. A suggestion worth considering is to throw out at least one item every day from the office and home. Since new items come into the office and home almost daily, you will always have possessions left.

Plan Your Activities

The primary principle of effective time management is **planning,** deciding what you want to accomplish and the actions needed to make it happen. The most elementary—and the most important—planning tool is a list of tasks that need doing. Almost every successful person works from a to-do list. These lists are similar to the daily goals described in Chapter 2. Before you can compose a useful list, you need to set aside a few moments each day to sort out the tasks at hand. A good starting point in using to-do lists is to prepare such a list on Sunday for the rest of the week. The list can then be modified on Monday through Saturday. A list used by a working parent is presented in Exhibit 12-1.

Where do you put your to-do lists? Many people dislike having small to-do lists stuck in different places. One reason is that these lists are readily lost among other papers. Many people therefore put lists on desk calendars or printed forms called *planners,* which are also available for desktop computers and palm-size computers. Planners give you an opportunity to record your activities in intervals as small as 15 minutes. Some planners are part of a system that enables you to link your daily activities to your mission in life.

Another useful approach for organizing your lists is to use a notebook small enough to be portable. The notebook becomes your master list to keep track of work tasks, errands, social engagements, and shopping items. Anything else requiring action might also be recorded—even a reminder to clean up the work area again.

How do you set priorities? Faced with multiple tasks to do at the same time, it is possible to feel overwhelmed and freeze as a result. The time-tested solution is to establish a priority to each item on the to-do list.

EXHIBIT 12-1

A Sample To-Do List

From the Desk of Jennifer Bartow

JOB

    Make 10 calls to prospects for new listings.
    Have "For Sale" signs put outside Hanover Blvd. house.
    Set up mortgage appointment at 1st Federal for the Calhouns.
    Update Web site listings
    Upgrade antivirus software
    Order new memo pads.
    Meet with the Guptas at 5 P.M.
    Set up time to show house to the Bowens.

HOME

    Buy new mouse for PC.
    Buy running shoes for Todd.
    Buy Jeans for Linda.
    Get defroster fixed on freezer.
    Write and send out monthly bills.
    Clip cat's nails.
    Check out problem with hot-water tank.
    Make appointment with dentist to have chipped filling replaced.

FIRST REALTY CORPORATION
Jacksonville, Florida
Jbartow@firstrealty.com

A typical system is to use *A* to signify critical or essential items, *B* to signify important items, and *C* for the least important ones. Although an item might be regarded as a *C* (for example, refilling your stapler), it still has a contribution to make to your productivity and sense of well-being. Many people obtain a sense of satisfaction from crossing an item, however trivial, off their list. Furthermore, if you are conscientious, small undone items will interfere with concentration.

    How do you schedule and follow through?   To be effective, a to-do list must be an action tool. To convert your list into action, prepare a schedule of when you are going to do each of the items on the list. Follow through by doing things according to your schedule, checking them off as you go along.

GET OFF TO A GOOD START

Get off to a good beginning, and you are more likely to have a successful, productive day. Start poorly, and you will be behind most of the day. According to Douglass Merrill, people who get going early tend to be in the right place at the right time more often, thus seeming to be lucky. "When you start early, you are lucky enough to get a good parking spot. You are lucky enough to avoid traffic jams. You are lucky enough to finish your job by the end of the day."[16] To get off to a good start regularly, it is important to start the day with the conscious intention of starting strong.

An effective way of getting off to a good start is to tackle the toughest task first because most people have their peak energy in the morning. (You will recall that a variation of this technique is useful in combating procrastination.) With a major task already completed, you are off to a running start on a busy workday.

MAKE GOOD USE OF OFFICE TECHNOLOGY

Only in recent years have companies begun to derive productivity increases from office automation. One reason that office automation was not as successful as hoped is that many office workers did not make good use of the technology available. Used properly, most high-tech devices in the office can improve productivity. Among the most productivity-enhancing devices are word processors, spreadsheets, voice mail, photocopiers, and personal information managers. How you use these ever-present devices is the key to increased productivity.

A major consideration is that the time saved using office technology must be invested in productive activity to attain a true productivity advantage. Assume that you save two hours by ordering office equipment over the Internet. If you invest those two hours in activity such as finding ways to save the company money, you are more productive.

CONCENTRATE ON ONE KEY TASK AT A TIME

Effective people have a well-developed capacity to concentrate on the problem or person facing them, however surrounded they are with potential distractions. The best results from concentration are achieved when you are so absorbed in your work that you are aware of virtually nothing else at the moment. As described in Chapter 3, this is the flow experience. Another useful by-product of concentration is that it reduces absentmindedness. If you really concentrate on what you are doing, the chances diminish that you will forget what you intended to do.

Conscious effort and self-discipline can strengthen concentration skills. An effective way to sharpen your concentration skills is to set aside 10 minutes a day and focus on something repetitive, such as your breathing pattern or a small word. This is the same approach that is used in meditation to relieve stress. After practicing concentration in the manner just described, concentrate on an aspect of your work, such as preparing a report.

Note that the suggestion here is to concentrate on one *key* task at a time. As described later in this chapter, sometimes doing two or three minor tasks at the same time can help save time. But would you want a surgeon correcting your vision with a laser device to be placing a stock order on a cell phone at the same time?

STREAMLINE YOUR WORK AND EMPHASIZE IMPORTANT TASKS

As companies continue to operate with fewer workers than in the past despite good economic times, more nonproductive work must be eliminated. Getting rid of unproductive work is part of *reengineering,* in which work processes are radically redesigned and simplified. Every employee is expected to get rid of work that does not contribute to productivity or help customers. Another intent of work streamlining is to get rid of work that does not add value for customers. Here is a sampling of work that typically does not add value:

- E-mail or paper messages that almost nobody reads
- Sending receipts and acknowledgments to people who do not need them
- Writing and mailing reports that nobody reads or needs
- Meetings that do not accomplish work, exchange important information, or improve team spirit
- Checking up frequently on the work of competent people

In general, to streamline your work, look for duplication of effort and waste. An example of duplication of effort would be to routinely send people e-mail and telephone them about the same topic. An example of waste would be to call a meeting for disseminating information that could easily be communicated by e-mail.

Important (value-contributing) tasks are those in which superior performance could have a large payoff. No matter how quickly you took care of making sure that your store paid its bills on time, for example, this effort would not make your store an outstanding success. If, however, you concentrated your efforts on bringing unique and desirable merchandise into the store, this action could greatly affect your business success.

In following the *A-B-C* system, you should devote ample time to the essential tasks. You should not pay more attention than absolutely necessary to the *C* (trivial) items. Many people respond to this suggestion by saying, "I don't think concentrating on important tasks applies to me. My job is so filled with routine, I have no chance to work on the big breakthrough ideas." True, most jobs are filled with routine requirements. What a person *can* do is spend some time, perhaps even one hour a week, concentrating on tasks of potentially major significance.

WORK AT A STEADY PACE

In most jobs, working at a steady clip pays dividends in efficiency. The spurt worker creates many problems for management. Some employees take pride in working rapidly, even when the result is a high error rate. At home, too, a steady pace is better than spurting. A spurt houseworker is one who goes into a flurry of activity every so often. An easier person to live with is someone who does his or her share of housework at an even pace through-out the year.

Another advantage of the steady-pace approach is that you accomplish much more than someone who puts out extra effort just once in a while. The completely steady worker would accomplish just as much the day before a holiday as on a given Monday. That extra hour or so of productivity adds up substantially by the end of the year. Despite the advantages of maintaining a steady pace, some peaks and valleys in your work may be inevitable. Tax accounting firms, for example, have busy seasons.

Napping may be helpful to replenish your energy supply in order to work at a steady pace. You can train yourself to take these 15-minute naps to give you short bursts of energy and stretch your stamina over a long day. A few minutes' energizing nap in the late afternoon can keep you going for an overtime assignment. Where to take these naps is left to your imagina-tion, depending on your work situation. Some workers nap in their cars when the temperature is moderate. By napping, you can boost your energy and ward off negative stress at the same time, as described in Chapter 4.

CREATE SOME QUIET, UNINTERRUPTED TIME

Many office workers find their days hectic, fragmented, and frustrating. Incessant interruptions make it difficult to get things done. The constant start-stop-restart pattern lengthens the time needed to get jobs done. Quiet time can reduce the type of productivity drain just described. To achieve quiet time, create an uninterrupted block of time enabling you to concentrate on your work. This could mean turning off the telephone, not accessing your e-mail, and blocking drop-in visitors during certain times of the workday.

Quiet time is used for such essential activities as thinking, planning, getting organized, doing analytical work, writing reports, and doing cre-ative tasks. One hour of quiet time might yield as much productive work as four hours of interrupted time.[17] Interruptions lower productivity more for mental than physical work. This is true because interruptions break the flow of thought, and it takes time to get back into a train of thought.

Quiet time is difficult to find in some jobs, such as those involving cus-tomer contact. An agreement has to be worked out with the manager about when and where quiet time can be taken. A buyer for office supplies in an insurance company worked out a sensible quiet-time arrangement. He re-ports, "I worked out a deal with my manager whereby every Thursday morning from 9 to 12, I could take my work into a vacant office adjacent to the boardroom. We agreed that I could be reached only in an emergency. It wasn't a way to goof off. Each month I had to write my boss a brief report of what I accomplished during my uninterrupted time."

Make Use of Bits of Time

A truly productive person makes good use of miscellaneous bits of time both on and off the job. While waiting in line at a post office, you might update your to-do list; while waiting for an elevator, you might be able to read a brief report; and if you have finished your day's work 10 minutes before quitting time, you can use that time to clean out a file. When traveling for business, bring as much work as you can comfortably carry. Spare time at airports because you arrive early or because of flight delays provides a good opportunity to perform routine work. By the end of the year, your productivity will have increased much more than if you had squandered these bits of time.

The practice referred to as "grazing" is a variation of making good use of bits of time. **Grazing** is eating meals on the run to make good use of time ordinarily spent on sitting down for meals. Many ambitious people today nibble at snacks rather than disrupt their work by visiting a restaurant. Grazing does have its disadvantages: You cannot network while grazing, eating while working can be bad for digestion, and it may deprive you of a needed rest break. Many office workers eat at their desk to make better use of the lunch break, often enabling them to free up more time for personal life.

Stay in Control of Paperwork, the In-Basket, and E-Mail

Despite the major shift to the use of electronic messages, the workplace is still overflowing with printed messages, including computer printouts. Paperwork essentially involves taking care of administrative details, such as correspondence, expense account forms, and completing surveys. Responding to e-mail messages has created additional administrative details that require handling, even if they are actually *electronic work* rather than paperwork.

Unless you handle paperwork and e-mail efficiently, you may lose control of your job or home life, which could lead to substantial negative stress. Ideally, a small amount of time should be invested in paperwork and routine e-mail every day. Non–prime time (when you are at less than peak efficiency but not overly fatigued) is the best time to take care of administrative routine.

The in-basket remains the center of paperwork. For many overwhelmed workers, their entire desktop becomes the in-basket. Four steps are particularly helpful in keeping an in-basket under control: (1) give some attention to the in-basket every day, (2) sort in-basket items into an action file and a reading file, (3) take care of the action items as soon as possible, and (4) read items in the reading file during bits of time on the job or at home.

Use Multitasking for Routine Tasks

Doing two or more routine chores simultaneously can sometimes enhance personal productivity. (Major tasks, however, require full concentration.) While exercising on a stationary bike, you might read work-related information; while commuting, listen to the radio for information of potential relevance for your job. Also, while reading e-mail, you might clean the outside of your computer; while waiting for a file to download, you might arrange your work area or read a brief report. Some forms of making use of bits of time, such as reviewing your to-do list as you ride the elevator, are a form of multitasking.

Despite searching for productivity gains through multitasking, it is important to avoid rude or dangerous acts or a combination of the two. A rude practice is doing paperwork while on the telephone or sitting in class. A dangerous practice is engaging in an intense conversation over the cell phone while driving. Checking out e-mail on a laptop or onboard computer is more dangerous because you are forced to lose full eye contact with the road.

▲ OVERCOMING TIME WASTERS

Another basic thrust to improved personal productivity is to minimize wasting time. Many of the techniques already described in this chapter help save time. The tactics and strategies described next, however, are directly aimed at overcoming the problem of wasted time.

MINIMIZE DAYDREAMING

Allowing the mind to drift while on the job is a major productivity drain. Daydreaming is triggered when the individual perceives the task to be boring—such as reviewing another person's work for errors. Brain research suggests that younger people are more predisposed to daydreaming than older people. Apparently, older people use neurons better to focus on tasks.[18]

Unresolved personal problems are an important source of daydreaming, thus blocking your productivity. This is especially true because effective time utilization requires good concentration. When you are preoccupied with a personal or business problem, it is difficult to give your full efforts to a task at hand.

The solution is to do something constructive about whatever problem is sapping your ability to concentrate (as discussed in Chapter 4 about wellness and stress). Sometimes a relatively minor problem, such as driving with an expired operator's license, can impair your work concentration. At other times, a major problem, such as how best to take care of a parent who has suffered a stroke, interferes with work. In either situation, your concentration will suffer until you take appropriate action.

PREPARE A TIME LOG TO EVALUATE YOUR USE OF TIME

An advanced tool for becoming a more efficient time manager is to prepare a time log of how you are currently investing your time. For five full workdays, write down everything you do, including such activities as responding to e-mail and taking rest breaks. One of the most important outputs of a time log is to uncover time leaks. A **time leak** is anything you are doing or not doing that allows time to get away from you. Among them are spending too much time for lunch by collecting people before finally leaving and walking to a coworker's cubicle rather than telephoning. The process of streamlining your work will also identify time leaks.

A major time leak for many workers is **schmoozing,** or informal socializing on the job, including small talk and telephone conversations and messaging with friends. Schmoozing is useful in relieving tension and increasing job satisfaction, and some informal socializing is necessary for building workplace relationships. Too much schmoozing, however, is a major loss of productive time.

AVOID BEING A COMPUTER GOOF-OFF OR CYBERLOAFER

An unproductive use of computers is to tinker with them to the exclusion of useful work. Many people have become intrigued with computers to the point of diversion. They become habituated to creating new reports or exquisite graphics and making endless changes. Some managers spend so much time with computers that they neglect leadership responsibilities, thus lowering their productivity.

In addition to the problems just cited, Internet surfing for purposes not strictly related to the job has become a major productivity drain. When the career Web site Vault.com surveyed more than 1,200 employees, 90.3 percent said they surfed non-work-related sites during the workday.[19] Exhibit 12-2 reports the frequency of different forms of cyberloafing. A research study suggests that many workers cyberloaf to get even with management when they feel mistreated. So, in this sense, cyberloafing is an intentionally defiant act.[20]

The message is straightforward: To plug one more potential productivity drain, avoid becoming a computer goof-off or a cyberloafer. Many companies block the use of recreational Web sites on company equipment so that the cyberloafer has to resort to authorized sites, such as study equipment and supplies catalogs!

KEEP TRACK OF IMPORTANT NAMES, PLACES, AND THINGS

How much time have you wasted lately searching for such items as a telephone number you jotted down somewhere, your keys, or an appointment book? Standard solutions to overcoming these problems are to keep a wheel file (such as Rolodex) of people's names and companies. It is difficult to misplace such a file. Many managers and professionals store such information in a database or even in a word processing file. Such files are more difficult to misplace than a pocket directory.

Two steps are recommended for remembering where you put things. First, have a parking place for everything. This would include putting your keys and appointment book back in the same place after each use. (This tactic supports the strategy of being neat and orderly to minimize time wasting.)

EXHIBIT 12-2

The 12 Most Frequent Methods of Cyberloafing*

72%	Read the news
45%	Make travel arrangements
40%	Make purchases
37%	Conduct job searches
37%	Visit special interest sites
34%	Check stocks
28%	Coordinate social events
26%	Instant message
13%	Download music
11%	Play games
9%	Chat
4%	Visit pornographic sites

At least what they admit to.

SOURCE: September 2000 Vault.com survey, adapted in Alan Cohen, "No Web for You," *Fortune Small Business,* October 2000, p. 56.

Second, make visual associations. To have something register in your mind at the moment you are doing it, make up a visual association about that act. Thus, you might say, "Here I am putting my résumé in the back section of my canvas bag."

SET A TIME LIMIT FOR CERTAIN TASKS AND PROJECTS

Spending too much time on a task or project wastes time. As a person becomes experienced with certain projects, he or she is able to make accurate estimates of how long a project will take to complete. A paralegal might say, "Getting this will drawn up for the lawyer's approval should take two hours." A good work habit to develop is to estimate how long a job should take and then proceed with strong determination to get that job completed within the estimated time period.

A productive version of this technique is to decide that some low- and medium-priority items are worth only so much of your time. Invest that much time in the project but no more. Preparing a file on advertisements that come across your desk is one example.

SCHEDULE SIMILAR TASKS TOGETHER (CLUSTERING)

An efficient method of accomplishing small tasks is to group them together and perform them in one block of time. Clustering of this type has several applications. If you are visiting an office supply store, think of whatever you need there to avoid an unnecessary repeat visit. As long as you are visiting a particular search engine, look for some other information you will need soon. A basic way of scheduling similar tasks together is to make most of your telephone calls in relation to your job from 11:00 to 11:30 each workday morning. Or you might reserve the last hour of every workday for e-mail and other correspondence. By using this method, you develop the necessary pace and mental set to knock off chores in short order. In contrast, when you flit from one task to another, your efficiency may suffer.

BOUNCE QUICKLY FROM TASK TO TASK

Much time is lost when a person takes a break between tasks. After one task is completed, you might pause for 10 minutes to clear your work area and adjust your to-do list. After the brief pause, dive into your next important task. A compliance officer at a mutual fund says that he turns over an hourglass when he needs to decompress after handling an urgent situation. When the sand runs out, he moves to the next priority.[21]

BE DECISIVE AND FINISH THINGS

A subtle way of improving your personal productivity is to be decisive. Move quickly but not impulsively through the problem-solving and decision-making steps outlined in Chapter 3 when you are faced with a nonroutine decision. Once you have evaluated the alternatives to the problem, choose and implement one of them. Set a limit to how much time you will invest in arriving at a decision to a problem. Next, set a limit to the amount of time you will spend implementing your solution. If you are in charge of this year's office party committee, you might decide to hold the party at a particular party house. Decide next on approximately how much time you should invest in the project and stick to your limit.

Another aspect of being decisive is making the decision to finish tasks you have begun. Incomplete projects lower your productivity. A point to remember is that nobody gives you credit for an unfinished project.

Now that you have studied various ways to improve your personal productivity, do Human Relations Skill-Building Exercise 12-1. Incorporating many of the ideas contained in this chapter will help you achieve peak performance or exceptional accomplishment. More will be said about this key idea in Chapter 14 about self-confidence and leadership.

The Personal Productivity Checklist

CLASS PROJECT

Each class member will use the checklist below to identify the two biggest mistakes he or she is making in work habits and time management. The mistakes could apply to work, school, or personal life. In addition to identifying the problem, each student will develop a brief action plan about how to overcome it. For instance, "One of my biggest problems is that I tend to start a lot of projects but finish very few of them. Now that I am aware of this problem, I am going to post a sign over my desk that reads, 'No one will give me credit for things I never completed.'"

Students then present their problems and action plans to the class. After each student has made his or her presentation, a class discussion is held to reach conclusions and interpretations about the problems revealed. For instance, it might be that one or two time management problems are quite frequent.

Especially Applicable to Me

Overcoming Procrastination

1. Increase awareness of the problem. _____

2. Calculate cost of procrastination. _____

3. Counterattack. _____

4. Jump-start yourself. _____

5. Peck away at an overwhelming task. _____

6. Motive yourself with rewards and punishments. _____

7. Follow the WIFO principle. _____

8. Make a commitment to other people. _____

9. Express a more positive attitude about your intentions. _____

Developing Proper Attitudes and Values

1. Develop a mission, goals, and a strong work ethic. _____

2. Value good attendance and punctuality. _____

3. Value your time. _____

4. Value neatness, orderliness, and speed. _____

5. Work smarter, not harder. _____

6. Become self-employed psychologically. _____

7. Appreciate the importance of rest and relaxation. _____

8. Play the inner game of work. _____

(Continued)

	Especially Applicable to Me

Time Management Techniques

1. Clean up and get organized. _____
2. Plan your activities (including a to-do list with priority setting). _____
3. Get off to a good start. _____
4. Make good use of office technology. _____
5. Concentrate on one key task at a time. _____
6. Streamline your work and emphasize important tasks. _____
7. Work at a steady pace. _____
8. Create some quiet, uninterrupted time. _____
9. Make use of bits of time. _____
10. Stay in control of paperwork, the in-basket, and e-mail. _____
11. Use multitasking for routine tasks. _____

Overcoming Time Wasters

1. Minimize daydreaming. _____
2. Prepare a time log to evaluate your use of time. _____
3. Avoid being a computer goof-off or cyberloafing. _____
4. Keep track of important names, places, and things. _____
5. Set a time limit for certain tasks and projects. _____
6. Schedule similar tasks together (clustering). _____
7. Bounce quickly from task to task. _____
8. Be decisive and finish things. _____

▲ SUMMARY

People with good work habits tend to be more successful in their careers than poorly organized individuals, and they tend to have more time to spend on personal life. Good work habits are more important than ever because of today's emphasis on productivity and quality.

Procrastination is the leading cause of poor productivity and career self-sabotage. People procrastinate for many reasons, including their perception that a task is unpleasant, is overwhelming, or may lead to negative consequences. Fear of success can also lead to procrastination. Awareness of procrastination can lead to its control.

Eight other techniques for reducing procrastination are (1) calculating the cost of procrastination; (2) counterattacking the burdensome task; (3) jump-starting yourself; (4) pecking away at an overwhelming task; (5) motivating yourself with rewards and punishments; (6) following the WIFO principle; (7) making a commitment to other people; and (8) expressing a more positive attitude about your intentions.

Developing good work habits and time management practices is often a matter of developing proper attitudes toward work and time. Seven such attitudes and values are (1) developing a mission, goals, and a strong work ethic; (2) valuing good attendance and punctuality; (3) valuing your time; (4) valuing neatness, orderliness, and speed; (5) working smarter, not harder; (6) becoming self-employed psychologically; (7) playing the inner game of working, and (8) appreciating the importance of rest and relaxation.

Eleven skills and techniques to help you become more productive are (1) cleaning up and getting organized; (2) planning your activities; (3) getting off to a good start; (4) making good use of office technology; (5) concentrating on one key task at a time; (6) streamlining your work and emphasizing important tasks; (7) working at a steady pace; (8) creating some quiet, uninterrupted time; (9) making use of bits of time; (10) staying in control of paperwork, the in-basket, and e-mail; and (11) using multitasking for routine tasks.

Seven suggestions for overcoming time wasting are (1) minimizing daydreaming; (2) preparing a time log and evaluating your use of time; (3) avoiding being a computer goof-off or cyberloafer; (4) keeping track of important names, places, and things; (5) setting a time limit for certain tasks and projects; (6) scheduling similar tasks together; (7) bouncing quickly from task to task, and (8) being decisive and finishing things.

Questions and Activities

1. In recent years, companies that sell desk planners and other time management devices have experienced all-time-peak demands for their products. What factors do you think are creating this boom?

2. When you meet a stranger, how can you tell if he or she is well organized?

3. Many tidy, well-organized workers never attain much in the way of career success. Which principle of work habits and time management described in this chapter might they be neglecting?

4. How can preparing a personal mission statement help a person become better organized?

5. Some students contend that because they work best when they put things off until the last moment, procrastination will probably not hurt them in their career? What is wrong with their reasoning?

6. What type of bad work habits might a person have who has very low tendencies toward perfectionism?

7. Give an example of any work you have ever performed or heard of someone else performing that could be eliminated because it is unproductive.

8. Identify five bits of time you could put to better use.

9. Identify two ways in which using a computer has increased your personal productivity.

10. Ask an experienced businessperson how he or she uses the computer (including the Internet) to improve his or her work habits and time management. Be prepared to share your findings in class.

INTERNET SKILL BUILDER: What Are You Doing with Your Time?

Go to www.getmoredone.com/tabulator.html to find the Pace Productivity Tabulator. This interactive module enables you to enter the time you spend on 11 major activities (such as employment, eating, sleeping, and television watching) and compare your profile to others. You are also able to enter your ideal profile to see where you would like to be. You just follow the straightforward instructions. After arriving at your personal pie chart, ask yourself, "What have I learned that will enhance my personal productivity?"

HUMAN RELATIONS CASE PROBLEM

The Meridian Workers Go Surfing

Charlie Yang is the director of logistics at Richardson Furnishings, a furniture manufacturer based in Durham, North Carolina. Logistics plays a major role in company operations because virtually all the furniture Richardson manufactures is packed and shipped to customers. Late deliveries are a chronic problem in the furniture industry, so Richardson's management attempts to gain a competitive edge by making shipments as promised. At times, the logistics group has to make particularly rapid deliveries to compensate for manufacturing delays.

All employees in the logistics division work at computers for such varied tasks as keeping track of deliveries and the location of trucks, e-mail, word processing, and budget preparation. In addition, logistics workers search the Internet for information such as road conditions, shipping rates for truckers and the railroad, and changes in government regulations about shipping.

In recent months, Yang has become concerned that many logistics workers at Richardson are slipping into a pattern of sometimes using the Internet for recreational purposes. For example, while walking around the office, Yang has seen several instances of travel agency and sports Web sites on computer monitors. Richardson has a written policy that is explicit about Internet use. Web access and e-mail are company resources that are to be used for business purposes only. The policy also stipulates that violators could be subject to disciplinary action. The Internet policy, however, has almost never been discussed after it was originally established.

(Continued)

Before bringing the potential problem of Internet misuse to the attention of employees, Linn decided to obtain more information. To help determine the extent of the problem, he hired a consultant who specializes in monitoring employee use of the Internet. The consultant, Carolyn Stein, studies server logs. The logs record all the Internet activity on a network, indicating who visited what Web site, how long they stayed, what they looked at, what they searched for, and which Web site they visited next. Stein also helps the company retrieve old e-mail messages so that they can be audited.

Stein dug into the server logs and also sampled e-mail messages. Her findings indicated some Internet and e-mail misuse but not an alarming pattern of substantial neglect of work. Among the activities revealed by the report were that, on average, employees were spending about 30 minutes per day surfing the Web for purposes not directly related to Richardson business. The diversionary visits to Web sites included reading the news, making travel arrangements, visiting job search sites, company recruitment ads, playing video games, and the occasional visit to sex sites. About 10 percent of e-mail messages were non–work related, including sending messages to friends and forwarding jokes to other Richardson employees.

Although not stunned by the evidence, Yang decided to confront employees about the problem. First, he held a meeting with his four supervisors to review the consultant's findings. Stein attended the meeting to present the findings in detail and answer questions. The supervisors had varied reactions to the findings. One supervisor thought the company should begin to impose strong sanctions on any employee violating the Internet policy. Another thought the recreational use of the Internet was not substantial enough to bother bringing to the attention of employees. A third supervisor thought that the company should monitor Web use regularly and punish only the severe violators. The fourth supervisor suggested that the company should hold an information-gathering session with employees to go beyond the statistical report.

Yang was impressed with the idea of an information-gathering session, so he scheduled a town hall meeting with all interested employees for 4 P.M. the following Friday. Every eligible employee attended the meeting, and most contributed input to the situation of non–work-related use of the Internet. Several employees explained why the recreational use of Web sites probably *helps* the company.

A logistics technician said, "I spend much less time on my surfing breaks than the time the smokers eat up on their smoking breaks outside the building. Since I'm not a caffeine addict either, I don't take breaks to feed my habit. Besides that, the few moments I spend surfing the Net or reading an e-mail joke give me the energy I need to dig back into work."

An office assistant contributed this input: "With all due respect to company policy, the so-called nonwork use of the Web and e-mail is a low-cost stress reducer. When I'm having a stressful day, I browse one of my favorite online stores. Five minutes of walking down the virtual isles of Abercrombie and Fitch lowers my stress level like magic. In some of those high-tech companies, you get a back rub at your desk with a real masseur if you're stressed out. That would cost Richardson a lot more, and take much more time than a few minutes of surfing the Web." (Laughter)

The most senior supervisor said, "Employees always find a way to spend a few minutes not working. It could be a trip to the water cooler, a chat at the copy machine, or watching birds outside the window. So now it's surfing. Except for a few workaholics,

(Continued)

nobody puts in 100 percent effort on the job. Even top execs have been known to take an afternoon off for golf." (More laughter)

Yang ended the meeting with these words: "Thank so much for your candor and your useful input. We're going to study our Internet policy a little further and then get back to you." As he left the meeting, Yang pondered whether some of his employees were making excuses for surfing or actually using the Internet to enhance productivity.

Questions

1. What is your opinion of the effectiveness of using Web surfing to enhance productivity?

2. What is your opinion of the effectiveness of using Web surfing to relieve stress?

3. What policy recommendations can you make to the logistics division of Meridian about the nonwork use of Web surfing and e-mail?

SOURCE: Several of the facts in this case are from Alan Cohen, "No Web for You," *Fortune Small Biz,* October 2000, pp. 44–56.

WEB CORNER

Procrastination test (must take within 48 hours):
www.queendom.com/testscareer/procrastination_access.html

National Association of Professional Organizers: www.napo.net

▲ REFERENCES

1. "Wrong Number to Cost Gateway $3.6 Million," Associated Press, July 20, 2002.

2. Research of Timothy A. Psychl, reported in Danielle Kost, "Professor Says Putting Off Chores Is a Breakable Habit," *Rochester (NY) Democrat and Chronicle,* September 22, 2002.

3. Theodore Kurtz, "10 Reasons Why People Procrastinate," *Supervisory Management,* April 1990, pp. 1–2.

4. "When to Procrastinate and When to Get Going?" *Working Smart,* March 1992, pp. 1–2.

5. Alan Lakein, *How to Gain Control of Your Time and Your Life* (New York: Wyden Books, 1973), pp. 141–151.

6. Cited and quoted in "Get with It: Nip Your Procrastination Right in the Bud," *Entrepreneur,* September 1998, p. 94.

7. Linda Sapadin, *It's About Time! The Six Styles of Procrastination and How to Overcome Them* (New York: Viking, 1996).

8. Stephen R. Covey with Elaine Pofeldt, "Why Is This Man Smiling?" *Success,* January 2000, pp. 38–40.

9. Price Pritchett, *The Employee Handbook of New Work Habits for a Radically Changing World* (Dallas: Pritchett & Associates, undated, distributed in 2003), p. 11.

10. Raymond P. Rood and Brenda L. Meneley, "Serious Play at Work," *Personnel Journal,* January 1991, p. 90.

11. Quoted in Carrie Ferguson, "The Wages of a Workaholic," Gannett News Service, May 23, 2000.

12. Stewart D. Friedman and Sharon Lobel, "The Happy Workaholic: A Role Model for Employees," *Academy of Management Executive,* August 2003, pp. 87–98.

13. Cited in "The Voices in Your Head," *Entrepreneur,* July 2000, pp. 105–107.

14. Quoted in "On-Job Disorder, Clutter Waste Time, Money; Tame It," Knight Ridder story, January 24, 2000.

15. Odette Pollar, "So, You Are Called a Packrat!" *The Pryor Report,* March 1996, p. 9.

16. Merrill Douglass, "Timely Time Tips: Ideas to Help You Manage Your Time," *Executive Management Forum,* September 1989, p. 4.

17. Douglas, "Timely Time Tips," p. 4.

18. Paul Chance, "The Wondering Mind of Youth," *Psychology Today,* December 1988, p. 22.

19. Reported in Alan Cohen, "No Web for You," *Fortune Small Business,* October 2000, p. 56.

20. Vivien K. G. Lim, "The IT Way of Loafing on the Job," *Journal of Organizational Behavior,* 2002, p. 675.

21. "Beating the Clock: Time Management When You Are under the Gun," *Working Smart,* March 1999, p. 1.

▲ ADDITIONAL READING

Burke, Michelle. *The Valuable Office Professional.* New York: AMACOM, 1997.

Drucker, Peter F. "Managing Oneself." *Harvard Business Review,* March–April 1999, pp. 64–74.

Hemphill, Barbara. *Training the Office Tiger: The Complete Guide to Getting Organized at Work.* Washington, D.C.: Kiplinger Washington Editors, 1996.

Lachnit, Carroll. "Productivity's Fine Line." *Workforce,* October 2003, p. 10.

Lublin, Joann S. "A Recruiter's Cancer Teaches Her Lessons on How to Work Better." *Wall Street Journal,* September 3, 2002, p. B1.

Oncken, William Jr., and Donald L. Wass (with commentary by Stephen R. Covey). "Management Time: Who's Got the Monkey?" *Harvard Business Review* Classic, reprinted November–December 1999, pp. 178–186.

Sittenfeld, Curtis. "She's a Paper Tiger." *Fast Company,* August 2002, p. 34.

Solomon, Charlene Marmer. "HR's Push for Productivity." *Workforce,* August 2002, p. 29.

CHAPTER
13

Getting Ahead in Your Career

Learning Objectives

After studying the information and doing the exercises in this chapter, you should be able to:

◆ Explain the alternative model of career advancement in organizations

◆ Select several strategies and tactics for getting ahead in your career by taking control of your own behavior

◆ Select several strategies and tactics for advancing your career by exerting control over your environment

◆ Understand networking techniques and be ready to implement them

◆ Recognize how to deal with the challenge of hidden barriers to career advancement

*T*he Executive Women's Golf Association (WGA), with over 100 chapters nationwide, encourages professional women to enter the game. As more women hold leadership positions, explains WGA member Polly Mohan, it is important for them to have a chance to network in a social atmosphere that their male counterparts have enjoyed at golf clubs for decades.

"I have closed so much business on the golf course," says Mohan. "Women

are at a disadvantage if they don't ask their clients, or potential clients, to golf, because their male counterparts will."

A year ahead of time, the group plans to hold golf seminars, training courses, and golf etiquette classes and to build leagues and stage competitive tournaments. At the same time the group also has a professional bent, so Mohan is planning executive networking events, business speakers, and events with local corporate sponsors. Some of the first seminars will talk about business etiquette on the golf course and how women should ask potential clients to golf.

Above all, women should not be intimidated about golfing as a way to generate new business, Mohan said. "Potential customers are not spending four or five hours with you unless they like what you have to say," she said.[1]

The story about the WGA emphasizes a basic fact of advancing your career. You need to include key people, such as customers, in your network to advance your career. And golf has been a major networking technique for at least 150 years. In this chapter we focus on strategies, tactics, and attitudes that will help you achieve promotion or hold on to a position you enjoy. The same approaches will enable you to achieve **career portability,** the ability to move from one employer to another when necessary.

We have divided the vast information about career advancement into four sections. The first section describes the new model, or concept, of career advancement. The second section deals with approaches to managing or taking control of your own behavior to advance or retain a good position. The third section deals with approaches to exerting control over your environment to improve your chances for success. The fourth section deals with the most widely accepted career advancement strategy of networking. A brief section is also included on dealing with hidden barriers to career advancement.

▲ THE ALTERNATIVE MODEL OF CAREER ADVANCEMENT

Career advancement has acquired a shift in emphasis in recent years to accommodate the new organization structures. Here we look briefly at the key components of the new model of career advancement.

1. *More emphasis on horizontal growth.*   The major shift in career advancement has been toward more emphasis on learning new skills and acquiring new knowledge in a position at the same organizational level. You advance by learning more, and therefore engage in continuous learning. Many companies even give pay raises to employees who learn new job-related skills. Despite the emphasis on horizontal growth, many workers still aspire to climb the organizational ladder. Also, many companies offer promotion to a higher-level position as a reward for good performance.

2. *More emphasis on temporary leadership assignments.*   In the traditional model of career advancement, an individual would strive to be promoted to a management or leadership position. The person would then hold on to that position unless demoted or fired. Today, many leadership positions are temporary, such as working as the head of a project to launch a new product. After the product is launched, the person might return to a group member (individual contributor) position. Or a person might be assigned as a committee head because of his or her expertise. After the committee has completed its work, the person returns to a nonleadership position.

3. *Climbing the ladder of self-fulfillment.*   For an increasing number of people, doing work that contributes to self-fulfillment is more important than a focus on promotion or earnings growth. To advance in your career would be to find work that provides more self-fulfillment. Individual preferences determine what type of work is self-fulfilling. For one person, learning more about information technology might be self-fulfilling. For another, helping career beginners grow and develop might satisfy the need for self-fulfillment.

4. *Being promoted as much for learn-how as know-how.*   According to career specialist Douglas T. Hall, demand in the labor market is shifting from those with know-how (present skills) to those with learn-how (learning capability).[2] A track record of being able to learn will give people career portability. Being able to learn rapidly makes continuous learning possible. The reason that learn-how is so important is that organizations face such rapid technological change.

The alternative model of career advancement is compatible with a modern definition of success. **Career success** as used here means attaining the twin goals of organizational rewards and personal satisfaction. Organizational rewards include such experiences as occupying a high-ranking position, more money, challenging assignments, and the opportunity for new learning. Personal satisfaction refers to enjoying what you are doing or having high intrinsic motivation. If your employer highly values your contribution and your job satisfaction is high, you are experiencing career success. However, success in general also includes accomplishment and satisfaction in personal life.

To begin relating career development to yourself, do Human Relations Self-Assessment Quiz 13-1.

HUMAN RELATIONS SELF-ASSESSMENT QUIZ 13-1

The Career Development Inventory

Career development activities inevitably include answering some penetrating questions about yourself, such as the 12 questions that follow. You may need several hours to do a competent job answering these questions. After individuals have answered these questions by themselves, it may be profitable to hold a class discussion about the relevance of the specific questions. A strongly recommended procedure is for you to date your completed inventory and put it away for safekeeping. Examine your answers in several years to see (1) how well you are doing in advancing your career and (2) how much you have changed.

Keep the following information in mind in answering this inventory: People are generous in their self-evaluations when they answer career development inventories. So you might want to discuss some of your answers with somebody else who knows you well.

1. How would you describe yourself as a person?

2. What are you best at doing? Worst?

3. What are your two biggest strengths or assets?

4. What skills and knowledge will you need to acquire to reach your goals?

5. What are your two biggest accomplishments?

6. Write your obituary as you would like it to appear.

7. What would be the ideal job for you?

8. What career advice can you give yourself?

9. Describe the two peak work-related experiences in your life.

10. What are your five most important values (the things in life most important to you)?

11. What goals in life are you trying to achieve?

12. What do you see as your niche (spot where you best fit) in the modern world?

▲ TAKING CONTROL OF YOURSELF

The unifying theme to the strategies, tactics, and attitudes described in this section is that you must attempt to control your own behavior. You can advance your career by harnessing the forces under your control. Such a perspective is important because individuals have the primary responsibility for managing their own careers. Some companies have career development programs, but the individual is still responsible for achieving his or her goals.

The following section concentrates on getting ahead by trying to control your external environment in some small way. Do not be concerned about overlap between the general categories of controlling yourself and controlling the environment. Instead, be concerned about the meaning and application of the strategies and tactics. Recognize also that the information throughout this chapter will help you take responsibility for managing your career.

DEVELOP OUTSTANDING INTERPERSONAL SKILLS

Getting ahead in business-related fields is exceedingly difficult unless you can relate effectively to other people. Workers are bypassed for promotion generally because someone thinks they cannot effectively be responsible for the work of others. Workers are more likely to be terminated for poor interpersonal skills than for poor technical skills. Effective interpersonal or human relations skills refer to many specific practices. It is particularly important to understand and cope with a wide variety of personality types. Chapters 6 through 9 of this book focus on important interpersonal skills, such as communication, resolving conflict, being assertive, and listening to customers. Interpersonal skills also include other topics in this book, such as being self-confident and exerting leadership (Chapter 14).

DEVELOP EXPERTISE, PASSION, AND PRIDE

A starting point in getting ahead is to develop a useful job skill. This tactic is obvious if you are working as a specialist, such as an insurance underwriter. Being skilled at the task performed by the group is also a requirement for being promoted to a supervisory position. After being promoted to a supervisor or another managerial job, expertise is still important for further advancement. It helps a manager's reputation to be skilled in such things as memo writing, computer applications, preparing a budget, and interviewing job candidates.

Although expertise is highly recommended, the workplace also demands that a person perform a variety of tasks as is required in working on a team. A finance specialist assigned to a product development team would also be expected to know something about marketing, such as analyzing a marketing survey. A recommended approach is to have depth in your primary field but also have breadth by having several lesser areas of expertise. A widespread example is that no matter what your specialty field, you are also expected to have information-technology skills.

Passion goes hand in hand with expertise. As explained in Chapter 4, passion contributes to creative problem solving. Passion is also a major requirement for being an effective leader, as will be explained in Chapter 14. It is difficult to sustain expertise if you are not passionate about your specialty field. A work-passionate person, for example, would regularly read printed and electronic information about his or her specialty.

Developing expertise and being passionate about your work leads naturally to being proud of what you produce. People who take pride in their work are likely to achieve higher quality and a good reputation. From the standpoint of management, proud workers are major contributors because their pride motivates them to excel.[3]

Develop a Code of Professional Ethics

Another solid foundation for developing a career is to establish a personal ethical code. An ethical code determines what behavior is right or wrong, good or bad, based on values. The values stem from cultural upbringing, religious teachings, peer influences, and professional or industry standards. A code of professional ethics helps a worker deal with such issues as accepting bribes, backstabbing coworkers, and sexually harassing a work associate. A brief guide to ethical decision making is to ask yourself three questions when faced with an ethical dilemma:

1. *Is it legal?* Will your decision violate any laws or company policies? For example, if you route a business trip over a longer distance just to pick up some more frequent-flyer miles, are you violating company policy?

2. *Is it balanced?* Is your decision fair to all parties concerned both in the short term and in the long term? In the example cited, think through whether it is fair to other employees and stockholders for you to be wasting company money by taking a longer flight.

3. *Is it right?* How does the decision make you feel about yourself? Are you proud of the decision you made or the action you took? Would you like friends, family members, and coworkers to know what you did? Is stealing more frequent-flyer miles a nice stunt?

You have passed the ethical test if you are comfortable with your answers to all three questions. Do not settle for a "yes" to only one or two of the questions.[4]

Perform Well Including Going beyond Your Job Description

Good job performance is the bedrock of a person's career. In rare instances, a person is promoted on the basis of favoritism alone. In all other situations, an employee must have received a favorable performance appraisal to be promoted. Before an employee is promoted, the prospective new boss asks, "How well did this person perform for you?"

Carly Fiorina, the top executive at Hewlett Packard, offers this advice:

> Focus 100 percent on doing the job you have better than anybody else. I've seen a lot of high-flying people fall flat because they were so focused on the next job, they didn't get the current job done. Manager sees performance as a measure of potential, not potential as a measure of performance.[5]

To be an outstanding performer, it is also necessary to go outside your job description by occasionally taking on tasks not expected of you. Going beyond your job description is part of being a good organizational citizen, as described in Chapter 8. Another way of looking at the same issue is that people tend to get promoted not because they perform their jobs well but because they take the initiative to do more than expected.[6]

Performing well on all your assignments is also important because it contributes to the **success syndrome,** a pattern in which the worker performs one assignment well and then has the confidence to take on an even more difficult assignment. Each new assignment contributes to more self-confidence and more success. As you succeed in new and more challenging assignments, your reputation grows within the firm.

CREATE GOOD FIRST IMPRESSIONS

Every time you interact with a new person inside or outside your company, you create a first impression. Fair or not, these first impressions have a big impact on your career. If your first impression is favorable, you will often be invited back by an internal or external customer. Your first impression also creates a halo that may influence perceptions about the quality of your work in the future. If your first impression is negative, you will have to work extra hard to be perceived as competent later on.

Looking successful contributes to a positive first impression. Your clothing, your desk and office, and your speech should project the image of a successful, but not necessarily flamboyant, person. Your standard of dress should be appropriate to your particular career stage and work environment. At the extreme, highly placed business executives often dress as if they were walking advertisements for the beauty and fashion industry.[7] Appropriate dress for an inventory specialist is not the same as for an outside salesperson dealing with industrial customers. Yet in the past few years, more formal business attire, such as suits for men and women, is making a comeback.

Many salespeople and managers today maintain a flexible clothing style by such means as keeping a jacket and extra jewelry in the car or office. When an unanticipated meeting with a customer or some other special occasion arises, a quick modification of clothing style is possible.[8] Appearing physically fit is also part of the success image.

Projecting a sense of control is another key factor contributing to a positive first impression. Show that you are in control of yourself and the environment and that you can handle job pressures. Avoid letting your body language betray you—fidgeting or rubbing your face sends negative nonverbal messages. Make your gestures project self-assurance and purpose. A verbal method of appearing in control is to make a positive assertion such as, "This is a demanding assignment and I welcome the challenge."

Another key contributor to first impressions is a person's communication patterns and method of self-presentation According to career coach Debra Benton, it is particularly important to avoid five self-defeating communication behaviors: (1) talking too fast, which makes what you say seem unimportant; (2) talking too much or giving more details than others want; (3) being too critical, or passing judgments about others; (4) being too self-critical or too revealing about your own inadequacies; and (5) displaying weak body language (see above) or using a weak tone of voice.[9]

Another reason first impressions are important is that, according to one theory of leadership, the leader of a group quickly sizes up new group members. Those who create a favorable impression become part of the in-group and are therefore given more favorable assignments and kept informed more regularly. Group members who do not create a favorable initial impression become part of the out-group and are treated much less favorably.[10]

DOCUMENT YOUR ACCOMPLISHMENTS

Keeping an accurate record of your job accomplishments can be valuable when you are being considered for promotion, transfer, or assignment to a team or project. Documenting your accomplishments can also be used to verify new learning. In addition, a record of accomplishments is useful when your performance is being evaluated. You can show your manager what you have done for the company lately. Many professional-level workers maintain a portfolio of their accomplishments, such as samples of work accomplished. The portfolio is much like that used by photographers, artists, and models when applying for a job. Here are two examples of documented accomplishments from different types of jobs:

1. A bank teller suggested that at least one person in the bank should be fluent in American Sign Language to facilitate serving deaf customers. After implementing the idea, the bank attracted many more deaf customers.

2. A maintenance supervisor decreased fuel costs in office by 27 percent in one year by installing ceiling fans.

After documenting your accomplishments, it pays to advertise. Let key people know in a tasteful way of your tangible accomplishments. You might request an opportunity to make a presentation to your boss to review the status of one of your successful projects. Or you could use e-mail for the same purpose if it would be presumptuous for you to request a special meeting to discuss your accomplishments.

BE CONVENTIONAL IN YOUR BEHAVIOR

Although this book does not emphasize conformity to conventional norms of behavior, they are of value in getting ahead. More precisely, by flaunting tradition, you could hurt your career. Areas in which most employers expect conventional behavior include good attendance and punctuality, careful grooming, courtesy to superiors, appropriate amount of smiling, good posture, adherence to company safety rules, and obeying authority. Employees who insist on being nonconformists in these areas do so at considerable risk to their career advancement.

Conventional behavior can also be framed as fitting in with the organizational culture or adapting to its values. In the culture of Paychex, a firm that provides payroll and human resources services for other companies, new employees are expected to gain considerable experience before making suggestions for changing work processes. Top management of Paychex believes that it has established efficient systems that best meet the needs of its customers. If you are the type of person who likes to jump in and make suggestions for change, it is best to find a company with a culture that welcomes such behavior.

TAKE A CREATIVE APPROACH TO YOUR JOB

As emphasized in Chapter 3, being creative helps you get ahead in business. Your ideas must be backed up with concrete plans for their implementation. If you are associated with an innovative idea and that idea pays dividends, your career might receive a big boost. For maximum benefit to your career, make innovative suggestions in areas that are likely to make money or save money. Here are several examples of suggestions along these lines:

- A worker at a law firm suggested that a promising new area of practice would be to challenge English-only company policies. As a result of her suggestion, the firm profitably entered this new area of litigation.

- A worker at a publisher with a large mail-order business suggested the company produce books with a smaller trim size. The yearly savings in mailing and shipping costs were enormous.

KEEP GROWING THROUGH CONTINUOUS LEARNING AND SELF-DEVELOPMENT

Given that continuous learning is part of the alternative model of career advancement, engaging in regular learning will help a person advance.

Continuous learning can take many forms, including formal schooling, attending training programs and seminars, and self-study. To engage in continuous learning, it is essential to remain open to new viewpoints on your established beliefs. A belief (or stereotype) that has been true for a long time may no longer hold true. A person might think, for example, that almost all workers over 60 are just putting in time until they reach the traditional retirement age of 65. In reality, many workers today plan to continue to work well into their 70s and 80s.

It is particularly important to engage in new learning in areas of interest to the company, such as developing proficiency in a second language if the company has customers and employees in other countries. Many companies support continuous learning, making it easier for you to implement the tactic of growth through continuous learning.

Self-development can include any type of learning but often emphasizes personal improvement and skill development. Improving your work habits or team leadership skills would be job-relevant examples of self-development.

A useful perspective on continuous learning and self-development is that it can take the form of gradual improvements that result in substantial changes. Such continuous improvement follows the Japanese philosophy of **kaizen,** the relentless quest for a better way and higher-quality work. *Kaizen* keeps you stretching to perform the same activities better than you did yesterday.

OBSERVE PROPER ETIQUETTE

Proper etiquette is important for career advancement because such behavior is considered part of acting professionally. **Business etiquette** is a special code of behavior required in work situations. Both *etiquette* and *manners* refer to behaving in an acceptable and refined way. In the digital era, etiquette is just as important as ever because of the new challenges that high-tech devices bring. For example, is it good etiquette to read the information on a coworker's computer screen when visiting his or her cubicle? The globalization of business also creates challenges, such as figuring out when visiting another country whether handshakes are acceptable.[11]

Deciphering what constitutes proper etiquette and business manners requires investigation. One approach is to use successful people as models of behavior and sources of information. Another approach is to consult a current book about business etiquette, such as the *Complete Business Etiquette Handbook*. Many of the suggestions offered in these books follow common sense, but many others are far from obvious.

The basic rules of etiquette are to make the other person feel comfortable in your presence, be considerate, and strive not to embarrass anyone. Also, be cordial to all, remembering that everyone deserves our respect.[12] Specific guidelines for practicing etiquette stem from these basic rules. Exhibit 13-1 presents examples of good business etiquette and manners.

EXHIBIT 13-1

Business Etiquette and Manners

Below are 13 specific suggestions about business etiquette and manners that should be considered in the context of a specific job situation. For example, "make appointments with high-ranking people" is not so relevant in a small, informal company when the company places less emphasis on formality.

1. *Be polite to people in person.* Say "good morning" and "good evening" to work associates at all job levels. Smile frequently. Offer to bring coffee or another beverage for a coworker if you are going outside to get some for yourself.

2. *Write polite letters.* An important occasion for practicing good etiquette is the writing of business and personal letters. Include the person's job title in the inside address and spell the person's name correctly. Use supportive rather than harsh statements. (For example, say "It would be helpful if you could" rather than "You must.") Avoid right margin justification (block writing) because it is much harsher than indented lines.

3. *Practice good table manners.* Avoid smacking your lips or sucking your fingers. If someone else is paying the bill, do not order the most expensive item on the menu (such as a $175 bottle of Dom Pérignon champagne). Offer to cut bread for the other person and do not look at the check if the other person is paying.

4. *Names should be remembered.* It is good manners and good etiquette to remember the names of work associates, even if you see them only occasionally. If you forget the name of a person, it is better to admit this rather than guessing and coming up with the wrong name. Just say, "I apologize, but I have forgotten your name. Tell me once more, and I will not forget your name again."

5. *Males and females should receive equal treatment.* Amenities extended to females by males in a social setting are minimized in business settings. During a meeting, a male is not expected to hold a chair or a door for a woman, nor does he jump to walk on the outside when the two of them are walking down the street. Many women resent being treated differently from males with respect to minor social customs. In general, common courtesies should be extended by both sexes to one another. A handshake and a smile are a better greeting than a kiss on the cheek of the opposite-sex person. Yet if a client or customer initiates the light kiss, it is acceptable to follow suit.

6. *Shouting is out.* Emotional control is an important way of impressing superiors. Following the same principle, shouting in most work situations is said to detract from your image.

7. *The host or hostess pays the bill.* An area of considerable confusion about etiquette surrounds business lunches and who should pay the check—the man or the woman. The rule of etiquette is that the person who extends the invitation pays the bill.

8. *Introduce the higher-ranking person to the lower-ranking person.* Your boss's name will be mentioned before a coworker's, you introduce the older person to the younger person, and a client is introduced first to coworkers. ("Ms. CEO I would like you to meet our new custodial assistant.")

9. *Address superiors and visitors in their preferred way.* As the modern business world has become more informal, a natural tendency has developed to address people at all levels by their first names. It is safer to first address people by a title and their last names and then wait for them to correct you if they desire.

10. *Make appointments with high-ranking people rather than dropping in.* Related to the preceding principle, it is taboo in most firms for lower-ranking employees to casually drop in to the office of an executive.

11. *When another person is opening a door to exit a room or building, do not jump in ahead of him or her.* In recent years, many people have developed the curious habit of quickly jumping in past another person (moving in the opposite direction) who is exiting. Not only is this practice rude, but it can also lead to an uncomfortable collision.

12. *Be courteous about the copy machine.* If you are using the copy machine for a large run and someone approaches the machine wanting to copy one or two pages, allow that person to interrupt. When two people arrive at the copy machine simultaneously, the person with the smaller job goes first. Refill the machine with paper and reset the machine to "1 copy."

13. *Be sensitive to cross-cultural differences in etiquette.* When dealing with people from different cultures, regularly investigate possible major differences in etiquette. For example, using the index finger to point is considered rude in most Asian and Eastern countries. The American sign for okay (thumb and index finger forming a circle) is considered a vulgarity in most other countries. Another example is that Finns are very private people, so don't ask questions about their private life unless they bring up the topic first. Instead, talk about the safe topic of sports. Don't blow your nose in public in Belgium where it is considered an offensive gesture. (It's not too cool elsewhere, either.)

Caution: Although all the above points could have some bearing on the image you project, violation of any one of them would not necessarily have a negative impact on your career. It is the overall image you project that counts the most. Therefore, the general principle of being considerate of work associates is much more important than any one act of etiquette or manners.

SOURCE: Jim Rucker and Jean Anna Sellers, "Changes in Business Etiquette," *Business Education Forum,* February 1998, p. 45; "Business Etiquette: Teaching Students the Unwritten Rules," *Keying In,* January 1996, pp. 1–2; "Meeting and Greeting," *Keying In,* January 1996, p. 3; compilation from other sources in Andrea Sachs, "Corporate Ps and Qs," *Time,* November 1, 1999, p. 23; Letitia Baldrige, *The Executive Advantage* (Washington, DC: Georgetown Publishing House, 1999); Chad Graham and Dawn Sagario, "Business Etiquette Doesn't Bow as Much to Chivalry," syndicated column from the *Des Moines Register,* February 9, 2003.

DEVELOP A PROACTIVE PERSONALITY

If you are an active agent in taking control of the forces around you, you stand a better chance of capitalizing on opportunities. Also, you will seek out opportunities such as seeing problems that need fixing. A **proactive personality** is a person relatively unconstrained by forces in the situation and who brings about environmental change. People who are highly proactive identify opportunities and act on them show initiative and keep trying until they bring about meaningful change. A health and safety specialist with a proactive personality, for example, might identify a health hazard others had missed. She would identify the nature of the problem and urge management for funding to control the problem. Ultimately, her efforts in preventing major health problems would be recognized.

Managers prefer workers with a proactive personality because these workers become proactive employees, or those who take the initiative to take care of problems. The modern employee is supposed to be enterprising. Instead of relying solely on the manager to figure out what work needs to be accomplished, he or she looks for projects to undertake.[13] The proactive employee, however, may clash with an old-fashioned manager who believes that an employee's job is strictly to follow orders. A study conducted with close to 500 men and women workers in diverse occupations examined the relationship between career success and a proactive personality. Proactive personality, as measured by a test, was related to salary, promotions, and career satisfaction.[14]

It may not be easy to develop a proactive personality, but a person can get started by taking more initiative to fix problems and attempt to be more self-starting.

TAKE SENSIBLE RISKS

An element of risk taking is necessary to advance very far in your career. Almost all successful people, including proactive personalities, have taken at least one moderate risk in their careers. These risks include starting a new business with mostly borrowed money, joining a fledgling firm, or submitting a groundbreaking idea to management. Terrie M. Williams, the founder of a public relations firm, believes that risk taking is the most essential ingredient in advancing a career. Not risking anything can mean risking even more, including inhibiting your career. Williams offers this explanation:

> When I'm approaching an important meeting, I sometimes find myself thinking, "I'm scared. I don't know if I can carry this off." Whenever I feel that way, I make a conscious effort to remind myself that being scared is good. It means I'm embarking on something new and different, and I can only go to the next level.[15]

LEARN TO MANAGE ADVERSITY

Some adversity is almost inevitable in an ambitious person's career. It is difficult to get through a career without at least once being laid off, fired, demoted, or transferred to an undesirable assignment or making a bad investment. Company mergers and takeovers also contribute to adversity because so many people are laid off in the process or assigned to lesser jobs.

Personal resilience—the capacity to bounce back from setback—is necessary to overcome adversity. A general-purpose way of handling adversity is to first get emotional support from a friend or family member and then solve the problem systematically. Follow the decision-making steps described in Chapter 3.

Two other points about managing adversity are particularly relevant here. First, attempt not to be bitter and cynical about your problem. Bitterness and cynicism can freeze a person into inaction. Second, look to minimize the self-doubt that grows from a mental script called the *fear narrative*. According to Kenneth Ruge, this is a narrative in which you tell yourself that if you try again, something terrible will happen. "The word *can't* becomes the operative word and you become its prisoner." The best antidote is to create an opposite narrative whereby you think, "How can I use my imagination and creativity to move beyond this *can't* to achieve my goals?"[16]

A current method of managing career adversity is to do a career *boomerang*. The scenario works like this: An employee quits a comfortable job to find employment that seems more promising, such as joining a high-tech start-up. The new job fails, and the person overcomes this adversity by boomeranging to the original employer. Some career counselors do not recommend the boomerang because your old firm will forever regard you as disloyal.

Develop the Brand Called You

Well-known consultant Tom Peters urges career-minded people to develop their credentials and their reputation to the extent that they stand out so much that they become a brand name. Although the analogy of each person becoming a recognizable brand name like Nike is far-fetched, the idea of becoming a trusted person with value is sound. As Peters sees it, you don't belong to any company for life, and your chief affiliation isn't any particular function or department (such as accounting). You are not defined by your job title or your job description. "Starting today you are a brand."[17]

You begin developing brand You by identifying the qualities or characteristics that distinguish you from coworkers. What have you done recently to make you stand out? What benefit do you offer? Do you deliver high-quality work on time? Are you a creative problem solver? Next, you would make yourself visible so you can cash in your uniqueness (your brand). Almost all the ideas in this chapter will help you develop brand You!

▲ EXERTING CONTROL OVER THE OUTSIDE WORLD

In this section we emphasize approaches that require you to exert some control over the outside environment. If you do not control it, at least you can try to juggle it to your advantage. For example, the "Find a Mentor" section suggests that you search out a friendly and supportive person in your field who can help you advance in your career.

DEVELOP A FLEXIBLE CAREER PATH

Planning your career inevitably involves some form of goal setting. If your goals are laid out systematically to lead to your ultimate career goal, you have established a **career path,** a sequence of positions necessary to achieve a goal. Here we describe two types of career paths. One type emphasizes climbing up the ladder in a traditional organization. The other emphasizes the horizontal movements that fit better the new model of career advancement.

The Traditional Career Path

A traditional career path is based on the assumption that a person will occupy a series of positions, each at a higher level of responsibility than the previous one. A person thus climbs the organizational ladder or hierarchy. If a career path is laid out in one firm, it must be related to the present and future demands of that firm. If you aspire toward a high-level manufacturing position, you would need to know the future of manufacturing in that company. Many U.S. firms, for example, continue to conduct more of their manufacturing in China. If you were really determined, you might study the appropriate language and ready yourself for a global position.

Before establishing the goals on the career path, it is helpful to clarify your values. These are probably the same values that enabled you to choose a career in the first place. Questions to think about are, "Can you name the three things most important to your job satisfaction? What do you really look for in a job? Do you want to be part of a team? To think creatively? Are you passionate about helping people and improving the world? Do you want to carefully follow directions, or do you want to decide which tasks are important?"[18]

While sketching out a career path, you should list your personal goals. They should mesh with your work plans to help avoid major conflicts in your life. Some lifestyles, for example, are incompatible with some career paths. You might find it difficult to develop a stable home life (spouse, children, friends, community activities, garden) if you aspired toward holding field positions in international marketing.

Your career path is a living document and may need to be modified as your circumstances change. Keep in mind changes in your company and industry. If becoming a branch manager is an important step in your career path, check to see if your company or industry still has branch managers. The changing preferences of your family can also influence your career path. A family that wanted to stay put may now be willing to relocate, which could open up new possibilities on your career path.

Contingency (what-if?) plans should also be incorporated into a well-designed career path. For instance, "If I don't become an agency supervisor by age 35, I will seek employment in the private sector." Or, "If I am not promoted within two years, I will enroll in a business school program."

Lisa Irving, an ambitious 20-year-old, formulated the following career path prior to receiving an associate's degree in business administration. Lisa's career goals are high, but she has established contingency plans. Presented as an example, not as an ideal model, is Lisa's career plan path:

Work

1. Purchasing trainee for two years
2. Assistant purchasing agent for three years administration
3. Purchasing agent for five years (will join Purchasing Managers Association and obtain certification in enterprise software)
4. Purchasing supervisor for five years
5. Purchasing manager for six years
6. Manager, materials handling, for five years
7. Vice president, procurement, until retirement

Personal Life

1. Rent own apartment after one year of working
2. Attend college evenings until receive B.S. in business administration
3. Marriage by age 27 (plan only one marriage)
4. One child by age 30
5. Live in private home with husband and child by age 33
6. Volunteer work for Down syndrome children
7. Travel to India before age 50

Contingency Plans

1. I will seek new employment by stage 3 if not promoted to purchasing agent.
2. If not promoted to vice president by stage 6, I will consider opening small retail business.
3. If I do not receive certification in enterprise planning software, I will develop competence without outside certification
4. If I encounter sex discrimination at any stage, I will look for employment with firm that has large government contracts (where discrimination is much less likely).
5. If I develop stress disorder at any point, I will seek nonsupervisory position in purchasing field.

Career paths can also be laid out graphically, as shown in Figure 13-1. One benefit of a career path laid out in chart form is that it gives a clear

Figure 13-1 A Vertical Career Path

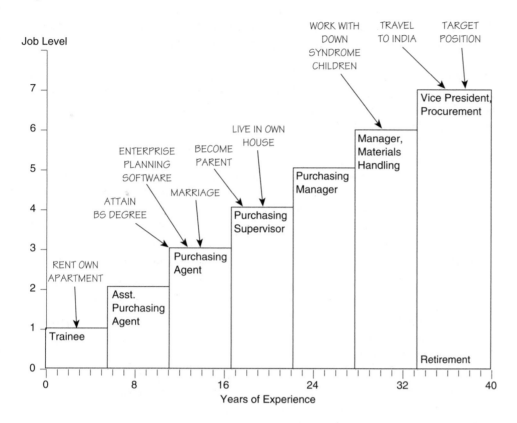

perception of climbing steps toward your target position. As each position is attained, the corresponding step can be shaded in color or crosshatched.

Most of the goals just mentioned include a time element, which is crucial to sound career management. Your long-range goal might be clearly established in your mind (such as owner and operator of a health spa). At the same time you must establish short-range goals (get any kind of job in health spa) and intermediate-range goals (manager of a health spa by age 30). Goals set too far in the future that are not supported with more immediate goals may lose their motivational value.

The career path under discussion features a steady progression of promotions yet a reasonable number of years in each position. Such planning is realistic because promotions often take a long time to achieve.

The Horizontal Career Path
Many organizations today have no fixed career paths. Instead of plotting a series of moves over a long time period, many individuals can only make predictions about the type of work they would like to be doing rather than target specific positions. A significant feature of the horizontal career path is that people are more likely to advance by moving sideways than moving up. Or, at least, people who get ahead will spend a considerable part of their

career working in different positions at or near the same level. In addition, they may occasionally move to a lower-level position to gain valuable experience. With a horizontal career path, the major reward is no longer promotion but the opportunity to gain more experience and increase job skills.

A horizontal career path, as well as a traditional (or vertical) career path, does not necessarily mean the person stays with the same firm. For example, a worker might spend three years in one company as an electronics technician, three years in another as an e-commerce coordinator, and then three years as a customer service specialist in a third company. All three positions would be approximately at the same level. The third company then promotes the individual to a much-deserved position as the marketing team leader. Following is a horizontal career path for Michael Wang, a career school graduate who did attempt to make long-range predictions about his career.

Career

1. Electronics technician at office equipment company for three years
2. Computer repair technician for three years for computer company
3. Customer service representative for two years
4. Sales support specialist at computer company for three years
5. Marketing research specialist for two years
6. Outside sales representative for digital copying machine company for four years
7. Sales manager in small office equipment company for five years
8. Owner of electronic equipment servicing company for rest of career

Personal Life

1. Rent own apartment after one year of working
2. Attend seminars to upgrade marketing and computer knowledge
3. Study Spanish with goal of becoming bilingual
4. Purchase condo
5. Marriage by age 29
6. Start raising family by age 31
7. Run for county legislature by age 34
8. Spend one month in Taiwan visiting relatives by age 36
9. Begin investment program for children's education

Contingency Plans

1. If cannot obtain experience as market research analyst, customer service rep, or sales rep, will continue to develop as electronic technician

Contingency Plans

1. Will purchase double or triple house if purchasing condo is not feasible

Figure 13-2 A Career Path

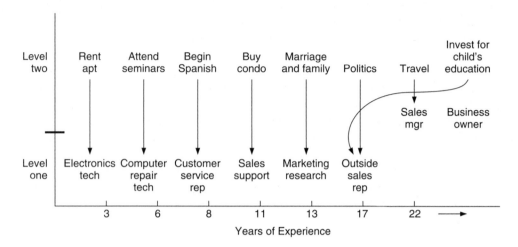

2. If cannot find employment as sales manager, will attempt to become supervisor of electronic technicians

3. If do not raise sufficient funds for starting own business, will continue in corporate job until retirement

2. If cannot raise funds for running for office, will do volunteer work for youths

3. If not married by age 29, will continue to search for life partner beyond that age

Figure 13-2 presents a horizontal career path. After having studied the two types of career paths, do Human Relations Skill-Building Exercise 13-1.

HAVE AN ACTION PLAN TO REACH YOUR GOALS

As described in Chapter 2, a useful goal is backed up by a logical plan for its attainment. A recommended practice is to supplement your career path with a description of your action plans. Lisa Irving, the woman who wants to succeed in the purchasing field, might include an action plan of this nature:

> To become manager of materials handling, I will need to (1) perform in an outstanding manner as purchasing manager by such means as coordinating the billing system with the sales department, (2) engage in continuous self-study about the entire materials-handling field, (3) be active in the local purchasing association group, and (4) make sure that top management is aware of my talent and ambition.

Action plans can be drawn up in minute detail. As with any other aspect of career planning, however, avoid becoming too rigid in your thinking. Career paths and career plans are only tentative. A different path to your goal might fall right in your lap. Ten years from now, for instance, Lisa might receive a telephone call from an executive employment agency. The caller

---

HUMAN RELATIONS SKILL-BUILDING EXERCISE 13-1

Career Pathing

1. Each class member will develop a tentative career path, perhaps as an outside assignment. About six volunteers will then share their paths with the rest of the class. Feedback of any type will be welcomed. Class members studying the career paths of others should keep in mind such issues as the following:

   a. How logical does it appear?

   b. Is this something the person really wants, or is it simply an exercise in putting down on paper what the ambitious person is supposed to want?

   c. How well do the individual's work plans mesh with personal plans?

2. Each class member will interview an experienced working person outside of class about his or her career path. Most of the people interviewed will have already completed a portion of their path. They will therefore have less flexibility (and perhaps less idealism) than people just getting started in their careers. The conclusions reached about these interviews will make a fruitful class discussion. Among the issues raised might be the following:

   a. How familiar were these people with the idea of a career path?

   b. How willing were they to talk about themselves?

   c. Were many actual "paths" discovered, or did a series of jobs simply come about by luck or "fate"?

---

might say, "My client has engaged me to find a materials manager who is a high performer. Your name was given to us. Could we possibly meet for lunch to discuss this exciting career opportunity?"

ACHIEVE BROAD EXPERIENCE

Most people who land high-ranking positions usually have broad experience. Therefore, a widely accepted strategy for advancing in responsibility is to strengthen your credentials by broadening your experience. Workers who follow the alternative model of career advancement, as illustrated by the horizontal career path, are automatically achieving broad experience. It is best to achieve breadth early in your career because it is easier to transfer when an individual's compensation is not too high. Broadening can come about by performing a variety of jobs or sometimes by performing essentially the same job in different organizations. You can also achieve breadth by working on committees and special assignments.

Breadth can also be attained through self-nomination. Have the courage and assertiveness to ask for a promotion or a transfer. Your manager or team leader may not know that you are actually seeking more responsibility. An effective method of convincing him or her is to volunteer for specific job openings or for challenging assignments. A boss may need convincing because many more people will be seeking advancement than are actually willing to handle more responsibility.

A major benefit of broad experience is that you achieve more career portability, allowing you to move to another employer should the need exist. The employability derives from being a more flexible person with a broader perspective. A person, for example, who has worked in both the underwriting (setting rates for risks) and the claims aspects of insurance would be well regarded by insurance companies.

BE VISIBLE

A big career booster for many people is to call favorable attention to themselves and their accomplishments. You will recall that to develop the brand called You, a person must be visible to key people. Ways of gaining visibility include performing well on committee assignments, winning a suggestion award, performing well in a company-sponsored athletic event, getting an article published in a trade magazine, establishing a personal Web site that attracts attention, getting your name in the firm's newspaper, or distinguishing yourself in a community activity. Once you achieve visibility, you have a better chance of being noticed by an important person in the firm.

FIND A MENTOR

Most successful career people have had one or more mentors during their careers. A **mentor** is a more experienced person who guides, teaches, and coaches another individual. In years past, mentors were almost always higher-ranking people. Today mentors can be peers and even lower-ranking individuals. A lower-ranking individual, for example, can educate you on how other parts of the organization work—something you may need to know to advance. Sometimes you are able to develop a mentor from the contacts you make on the Internet. After the person becomes your mentor, much of the mentoring can take place through e-mail and messaging. (Busier mentors may prefer e-mail because they can respond at their leisure.) E-mentoring will sometimes increase the pool of potential mentors and allow relationships to develop without social bias, such as people being suspicious of the nature of a mentoring relationship between a middle-age man and a young woman.[19]

Mentorship is an important development process in many occupations: master-apprentice, physician-intern, teacher-student, and executive–junior executive. An emotional tie exists between the less experienced person (the protégé) and the mentor. The mentor serves as a positive model and a trusted friend. In return, the person being mentored expresses appreciation, gives positive feedback to the mentor, and shares victories. It is also important to offer a concrete service in return for the mentor's advice. Possibilities include offering to collect information, prepare computer graphics, or run a few errands.

Finding a mentor is the same process as networking (described later in this chapter). One possibility to mention for now is that you can ask people you already know if they could think of a possible mentor for you. With e-mentoring, geographic distance does not create a substantial barrier. With any prospective mentor, it is best to begin gradually by asking for some advice and then see how the relationship develops.

Manage Luck

Few people do well in their careers without a good break along the way. Lucky events include your company suddenly expanding and therefore needing people to promote into key jobs, your boss quitting on short notice and you being asked to take over his or her job, or the business field in which you are working suddenly experiencing a boom, similar to the biotechnology business today.

To be lucky, you first have to clarify what you want. Otherwise, you may not recognize an opportunity when it comes your way. Assume that you know you want to become an officer in your trade association. Consequently, you will seize the opportunity when you hear that the group is looking for a new treasurer.

The strategy is not to simply wait for luck to come your way. In the words of Ray Kroc, founder of McDonald's, "Luck is a dividend of sweat. The more you sweat, the luckier you get."[20] Manage luck to some extent by recognizing opportunities and taking advantage of them. The unlucky person is often the individual who, out of timidity, lets a good opportunity slip by. A good way of capitalizing on luck is to be ready to take advantage of opportunities when they come along. If you maintain a record of excellent work performance and strive to complete your program of studies, you will position yourself to take advantage of opportunities. And, of course, have an updated résumé immediately available.

Balance Your Life

Balancing your life among the competing demands of work, social life, and personal interests can help you advance your career. As mentioned several places in this book, having balance gives you additional energy and vitality that will help you in your career. Without balance, a career person runs the risk of burnout and feeling that work is not worthwhile. Stephen Covey writes, "Always being the last to leave the office does not make you an indispensable employee. In fact, those who work long hours for extended periods are prone to burnout. The trick is to have your priorities clear, honor your commitments and keep a balance in life."[21]

▲ DEVELOPING YOUR NETWORKING SKILLS

Developing a network of contacts is important for finding a job. As a career advancement tactic, **networking** has several purposes. The contacts you establish can help you find a better position, offer you a new position, become a customer, become a valuable supplier, help you solve difficult problems, or find a mentor. People in your network can also offer you emotional support during periods of adversity.

A recommended approach to networking is to keep a list of at least 25 people whom you contact at least once a month. The contact can be as extensive as a luncheon meeting or as brief as an e-mail message. The starting point in networking is to obtain an ample supply of business cards. You then give a card to any person you meet who might be able to help you now or in the future. While first developing your network, be inclusive. Later, as your network develops, you can strive to include a greater number of influential and successful people. People in your network can include relatives; people you meet while traveling, vacationing, or attending trade shows; and classmates.

Community activities and religious organizations can also be a source of contacts. As mentioned at the outset of the chapter, golf is still considered the number-one sport for networking because of the high-level contacts the sports generate. A substantial amount of social networking also takes place on the Internet. The range of potential people in your network is much greater over the Internet than if networking is done locally and in person. The people in these groups can become valuable business contacts. Cybernetworking includes newsgroups, mailing lists, chat rooms, and e-mail. Corporate Web sites usually have a listing of contact people for a company, and it is possible that some of these people will become part of your network.

Human Relations Skill-Building Exercise 13-2 recommends a systematic approach to networking to help you capitalize on its potential advantages. Exhibit 13-2 offers some additional networking suggestions.

Now that you have studied many methods for advancing your career, do Human Relations Skill-Building Exercise 13-3 to help you analyze the strategies and tactics you might choose to fit your personality and work situation.

HUMAN RELATIONS SKILL-BUILDING EXERCISE 13-2

Building Your Network

Networking can be regarded as the process of building a team that works with you to achieve success. You can start the following exercise now, but it will probably take your entire career to implement completely. To start networking or make your present networking more systematic, take the following steps:

Step 1. Jot down your top three goals or objectives for the following three months, such as obtaining a new job or promotion, starting a small business, or doing a field research study.

1. _____

2. _____

3. _____

(Continued)

Step 2. List family members, friends, or acquaintances who could assist you in meeting your goals or objectives. Prepare a contact card or database entry for each person on your list, including as many details as you can about the person and the person's family, friends, employers, and contacts.

Step 3. Identify what assistance you will request of your contact or contacts. Be realistic in light of your prior investment in the relationship. Remember, you have to be a friend to have a friend.

Step 4. Identify how you will meet your contact or contacts during the next month. Could it be for lunch or at an athletic field, nightclub, sports club, recreational facility on campus, cafeteria, and so forth? Learn more about your contacts during your face-to-face meetings. In some cases you may have to use the telephone or e-mail to substitute for an in-person meeting. Look for ways to mutually benefit from the relationship. At the beginning of each week, verify that you have made a small investment in building these relationships.

Step 5. Ask for the help you need. A network must benefit you. Thank the contact for any help given. Jot down on your planner a reminder to make a follow-up call, letter, or e-mail message to your contacts. In this way, you will have less work to do before you make another request for help.

Step 6. For each person in your network, think of a favor, however small, that you can return to him or her. Without reciprocity, a network fades rapidly.

SOURCE: Adapted and expanded from Cheryl Kitter, "Taking the Work Out of Networking," Success Workshop, supplement to *The Pryor Report,* March 1998, pp. 1–2.

EXHIBIT 13-2

Networking Suggestions

The following networking suggestions are gathered from a number of career counselors and business writers. Select and choose from among the list those ideas that appear to best fit your personality and circumstances.

- Expand and diversify your network. Everyone you come in contact with is a potential resource to help you in your career. Even someone whose sole purpose is to cheer you on during downturns can be a valuable ally. Keep filling your network with new contacts because older contacts may fade away. Retired people who have had successful careers can be a valuable source of contacts. Also, retired people typically enjoy assisting people at earlier stages in their careers.

- Add value as well as ask for assistance. Consider how you can help the other person and listen as much as talk.

(Continued)

- When networking by e-mail, include your telephone number and address. The other person may want to contact you by means other than an e-mail. Also, be persistent because e-mail messages may get deleted by accident or just disappear because of technical problems.

- When approaching someone to be part of your network, explain how you received his or her name or refresh the person's mind as to how you met previously.

- If you attend a formal networking event (such as a professional meeting), "work the room." Engage in professional conversations with as many people as feasible.

- Create good relationships with your peers and fellow students. Some of them will occupy influential positions in the future. Stay in touch with your more promising classmates.

- Strive to develop a personal relationship with at least two people at higher levels in your place of work. Keep these people informed of what you are doing and ask for their advice.

- Be memorable for positive reasons. Making a lasting positive impression is a promising way of keeping a network alive.

- When you have a change of status, such as accepting a new position, let this be an opportunity to notify network members. Let everyone know should you change your e-mail address or telephone number.

SOURCE: Anita Bruzzese, "Restrain Yourself and Think When Networking by E-Mail," Gannett News Service, June 30, 2003; "Networking Isn't for Spectators: Meeting People, Discovering Trends, and Arriving Early Can Pay Dividends," Knight Ridder, February 24, 2003; Deb Koehn, "Networking Vital in Ever-Evolving Workplaces," *Rochester (NY) Democrat and Chronicle*, July 14, 2002, p. 4E; Deb Koehn, "Know Etiquette of Networking," *Rochester (N.Y.) Democrat and Chronicle*, October 27, 2002, p. 4E; " '85 Broads' Shares Networking Tips," *Executive Leadership*, February 2002, p. 3; Anne Fisher, "How Do I Network When I Don't Even Know Anyone?" *Fortune*, July 22, 2002, p. 226.

HUMAN RELATIONS SKILL-BUILDING EXERCISE 13-2

Selecting a Suitable Career Advancement Strategy

As with most suggestions for self-improvement, some of the suggestions in this chapter will have more relevance for you than others. Among the factors influencing which strategy is best suited to you are your personality, the stage of your career, and the place you work.

Each class member will write down the two strategies described in this chapter that he or she will most probably put into action (or is already using) and provide a brief explanation of why this strategy is particularly relevant. Once these analyses are completed, each person will share his or her answers with the rest of the class.

It will be interesting to note if virtually all class members mention any strategy or tactic for getting ahead.

▲ DEALING WITH HIDDEN BARRIERS TO ADVANCEMENT

Concern exists that many white women as well as people of color of both sexes are held back from high-level promotions by a glass ceiling. A **glass ceiling** is an invisible but difficult-to-penetrate barrier to promotion based on subtle attitudes and prejudices. White women, women of color, and men of color face few barriers to advancement for one or two promotions. Women appear to be making a breakthrough at middle-management levels. Yet after that point, with many notable exceptions, their promotional opportunities are often limited.

A study conducted in a financial services firm compared the career progress of 69 women and 69 men executives. Career success was measured by the person's organizational level (such as department head or vice president) and compensation. Consistent with the idea of a glass ceiling, women reported greater barriers, such as not fitting in with the culture and being excluded from informal networks. In terms of career advancement, the women attached greater importance to a good track record and developing relationships than did men. In other words, the women in this study had to try harder to advance equally.[22]

One strategy for overcoming the glass ceiling is to be patient. Barriers are lifting gradually in some companies and rapidly in others. As the workforce continues to be more diverse, additional promotional opportunities are opening up to women and minorities. Within five years, the glass ceiling may be shattered, particularly as women and minorities gain middle-management experience.

Individuals who have strong evidence that they are discrimination victims can lodge a formal complaint with the company and then with an outside agency. Filing discrimination charges is more effective if a person is denied a first promotion. It is more difficult to prove that discrimination took place when a person is not offered an executive position. The reason is that executives are chosen by difficult-to-pin-down factors, such as broad thinking ability and personal appeal.

A subtle barrier to advancement many hardworking, talented people face is that they are considered too good to transfer or promote by their bosses. Rather than recommend a star performer for promotion, the manager wants to keep that key player in his or her department. One antidote to this problem is to be so effective in your networking that higher-ups in the company know of your potential and will request that you be promoted. Another approach is to patiently discuss your desire for promotion or transfer with your boss and explain that you will be available to help your boss somewhat after you have been transferred.[23]

Another strategy for overcoming barriers to advancement is to enthusiastically apply all the other approaches described in this chapter. For example, African Americans are using networking more extensively today to help them land influential positions in industry. A glass ceiling may exist for most people but not for every woman and every member of selected minority groups. An outstanding performer who is also perceived as having superior leadership characteristics will often break though barriers to advancement.

▲ SUMMARY

Career advancement has acquired a shift in emphasis in recent years to accommodate the new organization structures. The major shift has been from less emphasis on vertical mobility to more emphasis on lateral growth, or advancing by learning more. The alternative model also shows more emphasis on temporary leadership assignments, more self-fulfillment, continuous learning, and being promoted for the ability to learn.

One set of strategies and tactics for getting ahead can be classified as taking control of your own behavior. Included are (1) developing outstanding interpersonal skills; (2) developing expertise, passion, and pride; (3) developing a code of professional ethics; (4) performing well, including going beyond your job description; (5) creating good first impressions; (6) documenting your accomplishments; (7) being conventional in your behavior; (8) taking a creative approach to your job; (9) keeping growing through continuous learning and self-development; (10) observing proper etiquette; (11) developing a proactive personality; (12) taking sensible risks; (13) learning to manage adversity; and (14) developing the brand called You.

Another set of strategies and tactics for career advancement center around taking control of your environment, or at least adapting it to your advantage. Included are following: (1) developing a flexible career path, including the traditional and lateral types; (2) having an action plan to reach your goals; (3) achieving broad experience; (4) being visible; (5) finding a mentor; (6) managing luck; and (7) balancing your life.

Developing networking skills is a major career advancement tactic that can help you find a new position, become a customer, become a valuable supplier, solve difficult problems, find a mentor, and receive emotional support. Keep a list of at least 25 people whom you contact monthly and add value as well as ask for assistance.

For some people, another part of managing their careers is dealing with hidden barriers to advancement. These barriers take the form of a glass ceiling, an invisible but difficult-to-penetrate barrier to promotion based on subtle attitudes and prejudices. Diligently applying career advancement strategies and tactics, including outstanding performance, can help you overcome these barriers.

Questions and Activities

1. Explain in your own words the modern model of career advancement in organizations.

2. What are some of the organizational rewards that a successful person can hope to attain?

3. Many adults, even in their 50s, repeat the cliché, "I still don't know what I want to be when I grow up." What does their statement imply about career planning?

4. With the upcoming labor shortage, graduates in almost all business-related specialties looks bright for at least the next 10 years. So why be concerned with strategies for career advancement?

5. People seeking jobs early in their careers often comment that employers are looking for specialists, not generalists. Which career advancement tactic does this comment support?

6. Identify several jobs for which observing good business etiquette would be particularly important.

7. What similarities do you see between a person with a *proactive personality* and one who displays good *organizational citizenship behavior?*

8. If you had to find a mentor right now, whom would you ask to be your mentor?

9. Identify several tactics you would be willing to use to become more visible in a large company.

10. Use the Internet to search for a good career advancement suggestion. Be prepared to share your findings in class.

INTERNET SKILL BUILDER: Career Paths at a Major Business Corporation

The General Electric Company (GE) has been one of the world's major business corporations for many years, stemming back to the days of Thomas Edison. Whether or not you aspire to work for GE, the company has a Web site (www.gecareers.com/GECareers/paths.jsp) that provides useful insights into career paths in a large business firm. Profiles are presented of people from different functional areas, such as human resources and information systems. Each person profiled tells you something about his or her career path at GE. After reading a few of the profiles of most interest to you, think through what you learned that would be useful in planning your career.

HUMAN RELATIONS CASE PROBLEM

San Deep Wants the Fast Track

At age 25, San Deep already had impressive leadership experience. She was the head of her Girl Scout troop at age 11, the president of the Asian Student Association in high school, and the captain of her soccer team in both high school and college. She also organized a food drive for homeless people in her hometown for three consecutive summers. Deep believed that these experiences, in addition to her formal education, were preparing her to be a corporate leader. At college, Deep majored in information systems and business administration.

Deep's first position in industry was a business analyst at a medium-size consulting firm that helped clients implement large-scale systems such as enterprise software. She explained to her team leader at the outset that she wanted to be placed on

(Continued)

a management track rather than a technical track because she aspired to becoming a corporate executive. Deep's team leader explained, "San, I know you are in a hurry to get ahead. Lots of capable people are looking to climb the ladder. But you first have to build your career by proving that you are an outstanding analyst."

Deep thought, "It looks like the company may need a little convincing that I'm leadership material, so I'm going to dig in and perform like a star." And Deep did dig in, much to the pleasure of her clients, her team leader, and her coworkers. Her first few performance appraisals were outstanding, yet the company was still not ready to promote San to a team leader position. Deep's team leader explained, "Bob [the team leader's manager] and I both agree that you are doing an outstanding job, but promotions are hard to come by in our company these days. The company is shrinking more than expanding, so talks about promotion are a little futile right now."

Deep decided that it would take a long time to be promoted to team leader or manager in her present company, so she began to quietly look for a new position in her field. Her job hunt proceeded more swiftly than she anticipated. Through a sports club contact, Deep was granted a job interview with a partner in a larger consulting firm offering similar services. After a series of four interviews, Deep was hired as a senior business analyst performing work on a system similar to the one she had been working with for two years. During her interviews, Deep emphasized her goals of occupying a leadership position as soon as the company believed that she was ready for such a role. Her first client assignment would be helping a team of consultants install a state income tax call center.

After a one-month-long orientation and training program, Deep was performing billable work at her new employer. At the outset, she reminded her new manager and team leader again that she preferred the managerial route to remaining in a technical position. After six months of hard work, Deep looked forward to her first formal performance evaluation. Deep's team leader informed her that her performance was better than average but short of outstanding. Deep asked for an explanation of why her performance was not considered outstanding. She informed her team leader and manager, "I need an outstanding rating to help me achieve my goals of becoming a leader in our company."

The manager replied, "Our performance evaluations are based on your contribution to the company. We care much less about writing performance evaluations to help a senior business analyst reach her career goals. Besides, San, you've made your point enough about wanting to be a leader in our firm. Let your performance speak for itself."

That evening, Deep met with her fiancé, Ryan, to discuss her dilemma. "The problem, Ryan, is that they don't get it. I'm leadership material, and they don't see it yet. I'm performing well and letting my intentions be known, but my strategy isn't working. The company is missing out on a golden opportunity by not putting me on a fast leadership track. I have to convince them of their error in judgment."

Ryan, a human resources specialist, replied, "I'm listening to you, and I want to give you good advice. Let me be objective here despite the fact that I love you. What have you done lately to prove to the company that you are leadership material?"

Questions

1. Who has the problem here, San or the consulting firm in question?

2. What advice can you offer San to help her increase her chances of being promoted to a formal leadership position in the company?

3. What is your evaluation of the validity of the advice Ryan offered San?

WEB CORNER

Association of image consultants: www.aici.org

Career adviser: www.thelabrat.com/jobs/advice.shtml

Career advice: www.vault.com

(go to "Career Topics")

Career tips along with job finding: www.123- jobs.com

▲ REFERENCES

1. Richard Mullins, "A Women's Drive for Par," *Rochester (NY) Democrat and Chronicle,* December 10, 2002, pp. 10D, 6D.

2. Douglas T. Hall, "The New Protean Career Track," *Organizational Dynamics,* Winter 1998, p. 10.

3. Jon Katzenbach, *Why Pride Matters More Than Money* (San Francisco: Jossey-Bass, 2003).

4. Based on the work of Ken Blanchard and Normal Vicente Peale, as reported in "How Big a Part Do Ethics Play in How You Lead?" *Executive Leadership,* April 2003, p. 4.

5. Free-standing quote in *Executive Strategies,* June 1999, p. 2.

6. Suzanne Koudski, "You're Stuck," *Fortune,* December 2001, p. 272.

7. Carol Hymowitz, "Female Executives Use Fashion to Send a Business Message," *The Wall Street Journal,* September 16, 2003, p. B1.

8. Jacquelyn Lynn, "Apparel Perils: 'Dress for Success' Isn't So Cut and Dried Anymore," *Entrepreneur,* June 1999, p. 36.

9. Quoted in "Career Breakers," *Rochester (NY) Democrat and Chronicle,* March 29, 1999, p.1F.

10. Randall P. Settoon, Nathan Bennett, and Robert C. Liden, "Social Exchange in Organizations: Perceived Organizational Support, Leader-Member Exchange, and Employee Reciprocity," *Journal of Applied Psychology,* June 1996, pp. 219–227.

11. Andrea Sachs, "Corporate Ps and Qs," *Time,* (Select Business Section), November 1, 1999, p. 23.

12. "Business Etiquette: Teaching Students the Unwritten Rules," *Keying In,* January 1996, p. 2.

13. Donald J. Campbell, "The Proactive Employee: Measuring Workplace Initiative," *Academy of Management Executive,* August 2000, pp. 52–66.

14. Scott E. Seibert, J. Michael Crant, and Maria L. Kraimer, "Proactive Personality and Career Success," *Journal of Applied Psychology,* June 1999, pp. 416–427.

15. "When the Knot in Your Stomach Is a *Good* Thing," *Executive Strategies,* July 1996, p. 5.

16. "The Bounce-Back Factor: Regain Lost Confidence and Charge Ahead," *Executive Strategies,* June 1997, p. 6.

17. Tom Peters, "The Brand Called You: You Can't Move Up if You Don't Stand Out," *Fast Company,* August–September 1997, pp. 83–94. The quote is from p. 86.

18. Deb Koen, "Identifying Values Clarifies Career Goals," *Rochester (NY) Democrat and Chronicle,* June 4, 2000.

19. Betti A. Hamilton and Terri A. Scandura, "E-Mentoring: Implications for Organizational Learning and Development in a Wired World," *Organizational Dynamics,* 32, no. 4, p. 388.

20. Quoted in "The Secret to Being Lucky," *Success Workshop* (supplement to *The Pryor Report*), March 1996, p. 1.

21. Stephen Covey, "How to Succeed in Today's Workplace," *USA Weekend,* August 29–31, 1997, pp. 4–5.

22. Karen S. Lyness and Donna E. Thompson, "Climbing the Corporate Ladder: Do Female and Male Executives Follow the Same Route?" *Journal of Applied Psychology,* February 2000, pp. 86–101.

23. Joann S. Lublin, "When Your Boss Thinks You're Just Too Good to Let Go," *The Wall Street Journal,* September 30, 2003, p. B1.

▲ ADDITIONAL READING

Bolles, Richard Nelson. *The 2005 What Color Is Your Parachute?* Berkeley, CA: Ten Speed Press, 2005.

D'Allesandro, David F. *Career Warfare: 10 Rules for Building a Successful Personal Brand and Fighting to Keep It.* New York: McGraw-Hill, 2004.

DeLong, Thomas J., and Vineeta, Vijayaraghavan. "Let's Hear It for B Players." *Harvard Business Review,* June 2003, pp. 96–102.

Feldman, Daniel C. *Work Careers: A Developmental Perspective.* San Francisco: Jossey-Bass, 2002.

Hosada, Meghumi, Eugene F., Stone-Romero, and Gwen, Coats. "The Effects of Physical Attractiveness on Job-Related Outcomes: A Meta-Analysis of Experimental Studies." *Personnel Psychology,* Summer 2003, pp. 431–462.

Loehr, Jim, and Tony Schwartz. "The Making of a Corporate Athlete." *Harvard Business Review,* January 2001, pp. 120–128.

Moses, Barbara. *Career Intelligence: The 12 Rules for Work and Life Success.* San Francisco: Berrett-Koehler, 1998.

Robinson, Joe. *Work to Live.* New York: Dimensions, 2003.

Ryan, John J. "Work Values and Organizational Citizenship Behaviors: Values That Work for Employees and Organizations." *Journal of Business and Psychology,* Fall 2002, pp. 123–132.

Thomas, David A. "The Truth about Mentoring Minorities: Race Matters." *Harvard Business Review,* April 2001, pp. 98–107.

CHAPTER 14

Developing Self-Confidence and Becoming a Leader

Learning Objectives

After studying the information and doing the exercises in this chapter, you should be able to:

◆ Develop a strategy for increasing your self-confidence if you think it is desirable to do so

◆ Understand the relationship of self-confidence to leadership

◆ Identify a number of personal traits and characteristics of effective leaders

◆ Identify a number of behaviors of effective leaders

◆ Map out a tentative program for developing your leadership potential and skills

When a new management team took charge of Rite Aid Corp. several years back, it was clear the drugstore chain would flounder unless it reduced debt, closed a few hundred stores, and laid off a few thousand workers. What was less evident in early 2000 was how Rite Aid president Mary Sammons would use a warm-and-fuzzy relationship with the remaining 73,000 employees as one of the pillars of the company's financial recovery.

Now that Rite Aid has completed its cost cutting and debt restructuring without resorting to bankruptcy court, revenue is rising, it is building new stores, and it was on track to be profitable in 2004. While Rite Aid's troubles were making the headlines, Sammons and a team of executives began asking employees—from cashiers, to pharmacists, to store managers, and to headquarters staff—how to solve alls sorts of problems.

"In the end, it's the people who are going to make you successful," said Sammons, who was promoted from chief operating officer to chief executive officer in June 2003. "I think that's why our company has been able to achieve a turnaround under very adverse circumstances. . . . People get you to the cause of problems, not just reports and numbers."[1]

The story about Mary Sammons illustrates one of many characteristics of effective leaders: They have excellent interpersonal skills, including being trusted enough to receive honest suggestions from employees. If your efforts at developing career thrust are successful, you will eventually become a leader. Rising to leadership can happen when people come to respect your opinion and personal characteristics and are thus influenced by you. Another way of becoming a leader is to be appointed a formal position, such as a supervisor or team leader, in which it is natural to exert leadership. As a result, an individual with appealing personal characteristics who is placed in a position of authority will find it relatively easy to exert leadership.

The study of leadership warrants your attention because today people at all levels in the organization are expected to exert some leadership. Organizations seek people to exert leadership at all levels by giving many people an opportunity to engage in such tasks as motivating others and setting goals.[2] Even if your job title does not include the mention of management responsibility, you will often be called on to be a temporary leader, such as being appointed the head of a committee or project.

Our study of leadership will first focus on self-confidence because of its close relationship to leadership. We then focus on the characteristics of leaders—their actions and attitudes—followed by an overview of how to develop your leadership potential.

▲ THE IMPORTANCE OF SELF-CONFIDENCE AND SELF-EFFICACY

Self-confidence is necessary for leadership because it helps assure group members that things are under control. Assume you are a manager in a company that is rumored to be facing bankruptcy. At a meeting you attend, the chief executive officer sobs, "I'm sorry, I'm just no good in a crisis. I don't know what's going to happen to the company. I don't think I can get us out of this mess. Maybe one of you would like to try your hand at turning around a troubled company."

In this situation, company employees would feel insecure. Many would be so preoccupied with finding new employment that they couldn't concentrate on their work. You would want the president to behave in a confident, assured manner. Yet if the president were too arrogant about things, if he or she dismissed the problem too lightly, you might not feel secure, either.

In other leadership situations as well, the leader who functions best is self-confident enough to reassure others and to appear in control. But if the leader is so self-confident that he or she will not admit errors, listen to criticism, or ask for advice, that too creates a problem as well. Being too self-confident can lead the person to ignore potential problems, thinking that "I can handle whatever comes my way." Human Relations Self-Assessment Exercise 14-1 provides some insight into your level of self-confidence.

An appropriate amount of self-confidence is also important because it contributes to self-efficacy. Various studies have shown that people with a high sense of self-efficacy tend to have good job performance. They also set relatively high goals for themselves.[3] Self-efficacy is thus related to self-confidence but is tied more directly into performing a task. A straightforward implication of self-efficacy is that people who think they can perform well on a task do better than those who think they will do poorly.

An encouraging note is that self-efficacy can be boosted through training. In an experiment, 66 unemployed people participated in a self-efficacy workshop. The group included bookkeepers, clerks, teachers, skilled mechanics, and technicians. The workshop featured watching video clips of successfully performing job search behaviors, followed by encouragement from the trainer and peers. In contrast to unemployed people who did not attend the workshop, the people who were trained in self-efficacy became more involved in job searches.[4] Being involved in job searches included telephoning about a job and obtaining an interview.

Self-efficacy contributes to leadership effectiveness because a leader with high self-efficacy will usually believe that a task is doable. As a result, the leader can inspire others to carry out a difficult mission, such as correcting a serious customer problem.

HUMAN RELATIONS SELF-ASSESSMENT QUIZ 14-1

How Self-Confident Are You?

Indicate the extent to which you agree with each of the following statements. Use a 1-to-5 scale: (1) disagree strongly; (2) disagree; (3) neutral; (4) agree; (5) agree strongly.

	DS	D	N	A	AS
1. I frequently say to people, "I'm not sure."	5	4	3	2	1
2. I perform well in most situations in life.	1	2	3	4	5
3. I willingly offer advice to others.	1	2	3	4	5
4. Before making even a minor decision, I usually consult with several people.	5	4	3	2	1
5. I am generally willing to attempt new activities for which I have very little related skill or experience.	1	2	3	4	5
6. Speaking in front of the class or other group is a frightening experience for me.	5	4	3	2	1
7. I experience stress when people challenge me or put me on the spot.	5	4	3	2	1
8. I feel comfortable attending a social event by myself.	1	2	3	4	5
9. I'm much more of a winner than a loser.	1	2	3	4	5
10. I am cautious about making any substantial change in my life.	5	4	3	2	1

Total score: _____

Scoring and Interpretation: Calculate your total score by adding the numbers circled. A tentative interpretation of the scoring is as follows:

45–50	Very high self-confidence with perhaps a tendency toward arrogance
38–44	A high, desirable level of self-confidence
30–37	Moderate, or average, self-confidence
10–29	Self-confidence needs strengthening

▲ DEVELOPING SELF-CONFIDENCE

Self-confidence is generally achieved by succeeding in a variety of situations. A confident civil engineering technician may not be generally self-confident unless he or she also achieves success in activities such as forming good personal relationships, navigating complex software, writing a letter, learning a second language, and displaying athletic skills.

Although this general approach to self-confidence building makes sense, it does not work for everyone. Some people who seem to succeed at everything still have lingering self-doubt. Low self-confidence is so deeply ingrained in this type of personality that success in later life is not sufficient to change things. Following are some specific strategies and tactics for building and elevating self-confidence. They will generally work unless the person has deep-rooted feelings of inferiority. The tactics and strategies are arranged approximately in the order in which they should be tried to achieve best results.

TAKE AN INVENTORY OF PERSONAL ASSETS AND ACCOMPLISHMENTS

Many people suffer from low self-confidence because they do not appreciate their own good points. Therefore, a starting point in increasing your self-confidence is to take an inventory of personal assets and accomplishments. This same activity was offered in Chapter 1 as a method of developing self-esteem. Personal assets should be related to characteristics and behaviors rather than tangible assets, such as an inheritance or an antique car.

Accomplishments can be anything significant in which you played a key role in achieving the results. Try not to be modest in preparing your list of assets and accomplishments. You are looking for any confidence booster you can find. Two lists prepared by different people will suffice to give you an idea of the kinds of assets and accomplishments that might be included.

Lillian

Good listener; most people like me; good handwriting; good posture; inquisitive mind; good at solving problems; above-average Internet search skills; good sense of humor; patient with people who make mistakes; better-than-average appearance. Organized successful fund drive that raised $40,000 for church; graduated tenth in high school class of 500; achieved first place in industrial bowling league; daughter has an excellent career.

Angelo

Good mechanical skills including automotive repair and computer repair; work well under pressure; good dancer; friendly with strangers; great physical health (drug and disease free); good cook; can laugh at my own mistakes; favorable personal appearance; respectful of authority. Made award-winning suggestion that saved company $35,000; scored winning goal in college basketball tournament; dragged child out of burning building.

The value of these asset lists is that they add to your self-appreciation. Most people who lay out their good points on paper come away from the activity with at least a temporary boost in self-confidence. The temporary boost, combined with a few success experiences, may lead to a long-term gain in self-confidence.

An important supplement to listing your own assets is hearing the opinion of others on your good points. This tactic has to be used sparingly, however, and mainly with people who are personal growth minded. A good ice-breaker is to tell your source of feedback that you have to prepare a list of your assets for a human relations exercise. Since that person knows of your work on your capabilities, you hope that he or she can spare a few minutes for this important exercise.

For many people, positive feedback from others does more for building self-confidence than does feedback from you. The reason is that self-esteem depends to a large extent on what we think others think about us. Consequently, if other people—whose judgment you trust—think highly of you, your self-image will be positive.

Develop a Solid Knowledge Base

A bedrock for projecting self-confidence is to develop a base of knowledge that enables you to provide sensible alternative solutions to problems. Intuition is very important, but working from a base of facts helps you project a confident image. Formal education is an obvious and important source of information for your knowledge base. Day-by-day absorption of information directly and indirectly related to your career is equally important. A major purpose of formal education is to get you in the right frame of mind to continue your quest for knowledge.

In your quest for developing a solid knowledge base to project self-confidence, be sensitive to abusing this technique. If you bombard people with quotes, facts, and figures, you are likely to be perceived as an annoying know-it-all.

Use Positive Self-Talk

A basic method of building self-confidence is to engage in **positive self-talk,** saying positive things about yourself to yourself. The first step in using positive self-talk is to objectively state the incident that is casting doubt about self-worth.[5] The key word here is *objectively*. Terry, who is fearful of poorly executing a report-writing assignment, might say, "I've been asked to write a report for the company, and I'm not a good writer."

The next step is to objectively interpret what the incident *does not* mean. Terry might say, "Not being a skilled writer doesn't mean that I can't figure out a way to write a good report or that I'm an ineffective employee."

Next, the person should objectively state what the incident *does* mean. In doing this, the person should avoid put-down labels such as "incompetent," "stupid," "dumb," "jerk," or "airhead." All these terms are forms of negative self-talk. Terry should state what the incident does mean: "I have a problem with one small aspect of this job."

The fourth step is to objectively account for the cause of the incident. Terry would say, "I'm really worried about writing a good report because I have very little experience in writing along these lines."

The fifth step is to identify some positive ways to prevent the incident from happening again. Terry might say, "I'll get out my textbook on business communications and review the chapter on report writing" or "I'll enroll in a course or seminar on business report writing."

The final step is to use positive self-talk. Terry imagines his boss saying, "This report is really good. I'm proud of my decision to select you to prepare this important report."

Positive self-talk builds self-confidence and self-esteem because it programs the mind with positive messages. Making frequent positive statements or affirmations about the self creates a more confident person. An example would be, "I know I can learn this new equipment rapidly enough to increase my productivity within five days."

Business coach Gary Lockwood emphasizes that positive self-talk is also useful for getting people past difficult times. "It's all in your head," he said. "Remember you are in charge of your feelings. You are in control of your attitude." Instead of berating yourself after making a mistake, learn from the experience and move on. Say to yourself, "Everyone makes mistakes," "Tomorrow is another day," or "What can I learn from this?"[6]

AVOID NEGATIVE SELF-TALK

As implied, you should minimize negative statements about yourself to bolster self-confidence. A lack of self-confidence is reflected in statements such as, "I may be stupid but . . . ," "Nobody asked my opinion," "I know I'm usually wrong, but . . . ," "I know I don't have as much education as some people, but . . . " Self-effacing statements like these serve to reinforce low self-confidence.

It is also important not to attribute to yourself negative, irreversible traits, such as "idiotic," "ugly," "dull," "loser," and "hopeless." Instead, look on your weak points as areas for possible self-improvement. Negative self-labeling can do long-term damage to your self-confidence. If a person stops that practice today, his or her self-confidence may begin to increase.

USE POSITIVE VISUAL IMAGERY

Assume you have a situation in mind in which you would like to appear confident and in control. An example would be a meeting with a major customer who has told you by e-mail that he is considering switching suppliers. Your intuitive reaction is that if you cannot handle his concerns without fumbling or appearing desperate, you will lose the account. An important technique is this situation is **positive visual imagery,** or picturing a positive outcome in your mind. To apply this technique in this situation, imagine yourself engaging in a convincing argument about why your customer should retain your company as the primary supplier. Imagine yourself talking in positive terms about the good service your company offers and how you can rectify any problems.

Visualize yourself listening patiently to your customer's concerns and then talking confidently about how your company can handle these concerns. As you rehearse this moment of truth, create a mental picture of you and the customer shaking hands over the fact that the account is still yours.

Positive visual imagery helps you appear self-confident because your mental rehearsal of the situation has helped you prepare for battle. If imagery works for you once, you will be even more effective in subsequent uses of the technique.

Strive for Peak Performance

A key strategy for projecting self-confidence is to display **peak performance,** or exceptional accomplishment in a given task. The experience is transient but exceptionally meaningful. Peak performance refers to much more than attempting to do your best. Experiencing peak performance in various tasks over a long time period would move a person toward self-actualization.[7] To achieve peak performance, you must be totally focused on what you are doing. When you are in the state of peak performance, you are mentally calm and physically at ease. Intense concentration is required to achieve this state. You are so focused on the task at hand that you are not distracted by extraneous events or thoughts. To use an athletic analogy, you are *in the zone* while you are performing the task. In fact, many sport psychologists and other sports trainers work with athletes to help them attain peak performance.

The mental state achieved during peak performance is akin to a person's sense of deep concentration when immersed in a sport or hobby. On days tennis players perform way above their usual game, they typically comment, "The ball looked so large today, I could read the label as I hit it." On the job, focus and concentration allow the person to sense and respond to relevant information coming both from within the mind and from outside stimuli. When you are at your peak, you impress others by responding intelligently to their input. While turning in peak performance, you are experiencing flow (see Chapter 3).

Although you are concentrating on an object or sometimes on another person during peak performance, you still have an awareness of the self. You develop a strong sense of the self, similar to self-confidence and self-efficacy, while you are concentrating the task. Peak performance is related to self-confidence in another important way. Achieving peak performance in many situations helps you develop self-confidence.

Based on his study of more than 1,500 successful people, Charles Garfield concludes that peak performers have a mission in their work and lives. They have something they deeply care about to which they are fully committed.[8]

Bounce Back from Setbacks and Embarrassments

Resilience has been mentioned several times in this book as a contributor to personal effectiveness. Overcoming setbacks also builds self-confidence. An effective self-confidence builder is to convince yourself that you can conquer adversity such as setbacks and embarrassments, thus being resilient. The vast majority of successful leaders have dealt successfully with at least one significant setback in their careers, such as being fired or demoted. In contrast, crumbling after a setback or series of setbacks will usually lower self-confidence. Two major suggestions for bouncing back from setbacks and embarrassments are presented next.

Get Past the Emotional Turmoil

Adversity has enormous emotional consequences. The emotional impact of severe job adversity can rival the loss of a personal relationship. The stress from adversity leads to a cycle of adversity followed by stress, followed by more adversity. A starting point in dealing with the emotional aspects of adversity is to *accept the reality of your problem*. Admit that your problems are real and that you are hurting inside. A second step is *not to take the setback personally*. Remember that setbacks are inevitable so long as you are taking some risks in your career. Not personalizing setbacks helps reduce some of the emotional sting. If possible, *do not panic*. Recognize that you are in difficult circumstances under which many others panic. Convince yourself to remain calm enough to deal with the severe problem or crisis. Also, *get help from your support network*. Getting emotional support from family members and friends helps overcome the emotional turmoil associated with adversity.

Find a Creative Solution to Your Problem

An inescapable part of planning a comeback is to solve your problem. You often need to search for creative solutions, using the problem-solving and decision-making steps described in Chapter 3. Suppose a person faced the adversity of not having enough money for educational expenses. The person might search through standard alternatives such as applying for financial aid, looking for more lucrative part-time work, and borrowing from family members. Several students have solved their problem more creatively by asking strangers to lend them money as intermediate-term investments. An option the investors have is to receive a payback based on the future earnings of the students.

▲ LEADERSHIP AND BEING A LEADER

So far we have emphasized the importance of developing self-confidence so that you are able to provide leadership to others. **Leadership** is the process of bringing about positive changes and influencing others to achieve worthwhile goals. (In a work setting, the worthwhile goals would relate to what the company wanted to accomplish.) Self-confidence makes a contribution to leadership because people tend to be influenced by a person of high—but not unreasonable—self-confidence. The key words in understanding leadership are *change* and *influence*. A leader often challenges the status quo and brings about improvements. A leader also influences people to do things, such as achieve higher performance, that they would not do otherwise.

Effective leadership at the top of organizations is necessary for their prosperity and even survival. Effective leadership is also important throughout the organization, particularly in working with entry-level workers. Good supervision is needed to help employees deal with customer problems, carry out their usual tasks, and maintain high quality. The most rapidly growing leadership position in the workplace is the team leader. A **team leader** is a person who facilitates and guides the efforts of a small group that is given some authority to govern itself. Many firms use work teams instead of traditional departments to accomplish work. For example, a work team might take care of various aspects of issuing an insurance policy. Instead of having power over the group, the team leader works with teammates to help them achieve their goals.

Before studying the personal qualities and behaviors of effective leaders, do Human Relations Self-Assessment Quiz 14-2. The exercise will help you understand how ready you are to assume a leadership role. Taking the quiz will also give you insight into the type of thinking that is characteristic of leaders.

TRAITS AND CHARACTERISTICS OF EFFECTIVE LEADERS

A major thrust to understanding leaders and leadership is to recognize that effective leaders have the "right stuff." In other words, certain inner qualities contribute to leadership effectiveness in a wide variety of situations. **Effectiveness** in this situation means that the leader helps the group accomplish its objectives without neglecting satisfaction and morale. The characteristics that contribute to effectiveness depend somewhat on the situation. A supervisor in a meatpacking plant and one in an information-technology department will need different sets of personal characteristics. The situation includes such factors as the people being supervised, the job being performed, the company, and the cultural background of employees.

HUMAN RELATIONS SELF-ASSESSMENT QUIZ 14-2

Readiness for the Leadership Role

Indicate the extent to which you agree with each of the following statements. Use a 1-to-5 scale: (1) disagree strongly; (2) disagree; (3) neutral; (4) agree; (5) agree strongly. If you do not have leadership experience, imagine how you might react to the questions if you were a leader.

1. It is enjoyable having people count on me for ideas and suggestions.   1   2   3   4   5

2. It would be accurate to say that I have inspired other people.   1   2   3   4   5

3. It's a good practice to ask people provocative questions about their work.   1   2   3   4   5

4. It's easy for me to compliment others.   1   2   3   4   5

5. I like to cheer up people even when my own spirits are down.   1   2   3   4   5

(Continued)

6. What my team accomplishes is more important than my personal glory.   1 2 3 4 5

7. Many people imitate my ideas.   1 2 3 4 5

8. Building team spirit is important to me.   1 2 3 4 5

9. I would enjoy coaching other members of the team.   1 2 3 4 5

10. It is important to me to recognize others for their accomplishments.   1 2 3 4 5

11. I would enjoy entertaining visitors to my firm even if it interfered with my completing a report.   1 2 3 4 5

12. It would be fun for me to represent my team at gatherings outside our department.   1 2 3 4 5

13. The problems of my teammates are my problems, too.   1 2 3 4 5

14. Resolving conflict is an activity I enjoy.   1 2 3 4 5

15. I would cooperate with another unit in the organization even if I disagreed with the position taken by its members.   1 2 3 4 5

16. I am an idea generator on the job.   1 2 3 4 5

17. It's fun for me to bargain whenever I have the opportunity.   1 2 3 4 5

18. Team members listen to me when I speak.   1 2 3 4 5

19. People have asked to me to assume the leadership of an activity several times in my life.   1 2 3 4 5

20. I've always been a convincing person.   1 2 3 4 5

Total score: _____

Scoring and Interpretation: Calculate your total score by adding the numbers circled. A tentative interpretation of the scoring is as follows:

90–100	High readiness for the leadership role
60–89	Moderate readiness for the leadership role
40–59	Some uneasiness with the leadership role
39 or less	Low readiness for carrying out the leadership role

If you are already a successful leader and you scored low on this questionnaire, ignore your score. If you scored surprisingly low and you are not yet a leader or are currently performing poorly as a leader, study the statements carefully. Consider changing your attitude or your behavior so that you can legitimately answer more of the statements with 4s or 5s. Studying the rest of this chapter will give you additional insights into the leader's role that may be helpful in your development as a leader.

Figure 14-1 Seven Key Leadership Traits

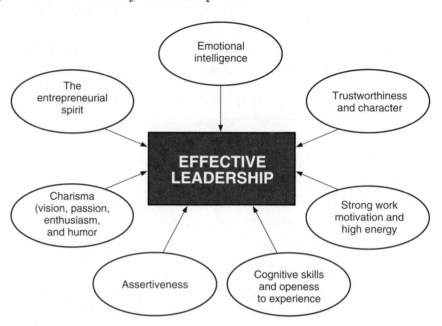

In the next several pages, we describe some of the more important traits and characteristics of leaders. Many of these traits and characteristics are capable of development and refinement. Figure 14-1 outlines the seven key traits.

Emotional Intelligence

Emotional intelligence is considered a major contributor to leadership effectiveness. As described in Chapter 3 and 8, the concept refers to managing ourselves and our relationships effectively with an emphasis on dealing with emotion. A current conception of emotional intelligence is so broad that it encompasses many traits and behaviors related to leadership effectiveness, including self-awareness, self-management, social awareness, and relationship management.[9]

1. *Self-awareness.* The ability to understand your own emotions is the most essential of the four emotional intelligence competencies. Having high self-awareness allows people to know their strengths and limitations and have high self-esteem. Being self-aware also helps leaders capitalize on their strengths and overcome their developmental needs.

2. *Self-management.* The ability to control one's emotions and act with honesty and integrity in a consistent and adaptable manner is another key component of emotional intelligence. The right degree of self-management helps prevent a person from throwing temper tantrums when things go wrong. Self-management would also help a person from going out of control with laughter during a meeting.

3. *Social awareness.* This includes having empathy for others and having intuition into company problems. Socially aware leaders go

beyond sensing the emotions of others by showing that they care. In addition, they accurately size up what kind of politics are being played in the office.

4. *Relationship management.*   Managing relations includes the interpersonal skills of being able to communicate clearly and convincingly, disarm conflicts, and build strong personal bonds. Relationship management ability also helps the leader continue to build his or her network.

Emotional intelligence can be developed through working on some of its components, such as learning to control your temper and developing empathy by listening to people carefully. It is also important to develop the habit of looking to understand the feelings and emotions of people around you. Also, ask yourself, "How do I feel about what's going on here?" When you have a hunch about people's motives, look for feedback in the future to see if you were right. Here is an example of applying emotional intelligence:

> Visualize yourself as a team leader. Vanessa, one of the team members, says to you, "I'm worried about Rick. I think he needs help. He looks like he has a drinking problem." If you have good emotional intelligence, you might think to yourself, "I wonder why Vanessa is telling me this. Is she simply being helpful? Or is she out to backstab Rick?" So you seek some tangible evidence about Rick's alleged problem before acting. You would also seek to spend more time with Vanessa so you can better understand her motives. Your investigation might reveal that Vanessa and Rick are rivals and have a personality clash.
>
> With much less emotional intelligence, you would immediately get in touch with Rick, accuse him of having a drinking problem, and tell him to get help or get fired.

TRUSTWORTHINESS

Considerable evidence exists that being trustworthy and/or honest contributes to being an effective leader. Group members consistently believe that leaders must display honesty, integrity, and credibility. Leaders themselves believe that honesty and integrity make a difference in their effectiveness.[10] An effective leader is supposed to *walk the talk,* thereby showing a consistency between deeds (walk) and words (talk). In this context, **trust** is defined as a person's confidence in another individual's intentions and motives and in the sincerity of that individual's words. Leaders must be trustworthy, and they must also trust the group members.

It takes a leader a long time to build trust, yet one brief incident of being untrustworthy behavior can destroy it. An example of untrustworthy behavior would be using company money for private purposes or sexually harassing a team member. Leaders are usually allowed a fair share of honest mistake. In contrast, dishonest mistakes quickly erode leadership effectiveness.

Having certain character traits contributes to being trustworthy and being perceived as a trustworthy person. **Character** in this context refers to doing the right things despite outside pressures to do the opposite. Being of good character also includes leaving enduring marks that set one apart from another.[11] To be of good character is to be moral. The United States Air Force has developed a list of 12 attributes that are part of its character program. Air Force leaders are expected to have many of these attributes, and leaders in other organizations will benefit as well. Exhibit 14-1 lists and defines these twelve traits.

EXHIBIT 14-1

Character Attributes of Leaders

1. *Integrity.* Consistently adhering to a moral or ethical code or standard. A person who consistently chooses to do the "right thing" when faced with alternate choices.

2. *Honesty.* Consistently being truthful with others.

3. *Loyalty.* Being devoted and committed to one's organization, supervisors, coworkers, and subordinates.

4. *Selflessness.* Genuinely concerned about the welfare of others and willing to sacrifice one's personal interest for others and their organization.

5. *Compassion.* Concern for the suffering or welfare of others and their organization.

6. *Competency.* Capable of performing tasks assigned in a superior fashion and excels in all task assignments. Is effective and efficient.

7. *Respectfulness.* Shows esteem for and consideration and appreciation of other people.

8. *Fairness.* Treats people in an equitable, impartial, and just manner.

9. *Responsibility and self-discipline.* Can be depended on to make rational and logical decisions and to do tasks assigned. Can perform tasks assigned without supervision.

10. *Decisiveness.* Capable of making logical and effective decisions in a timely manner. Does not "shoot from the hip" but does promptly make a good decision after considering data appropriate to the decision.

11. *Spiritual appreciation.* Values the spiritual diversity among individuals with different backgrounds and cultures and respects all individuals rights to differ from others in their beliefs.

12. *Cooperativeness.* Willingness to work or act together with others in accomplishing a task or some common end or purpose.

What is your standing on the above character dimensions? Do you have enough self-awareness to find some room for improvement?

Copyright © 2000 by William H. Hendrix

Strong Work Motivation and High Energy

Leadership positions tend to be both physically and mentally demanding. A successful leader must be willing to work hard and long to achieve success. Many leaders appear to be driven by a need for self-fulfillment. Another fundamental reason strong work motivation is required for effectiveness is that a person has to be willing to accept the heavy responsibility that being a supervisor entails. As one department manager said, "Whoever thought being a manager would mean that I would have to fire a single parent who has three children to feed and clothe?"

Cognitive Skills and Openness to Experience

Cognitive skills, as well as personality, are important for leadership success. Problem-solving and intellectual skills are referred to collectively as **cognitive skills.** The term *cognition* refers to the mental process of faculty by which knowledge is gathered. To inspire people, bring about constructive changes, and solve problems creatively, leaders need to be mentally sharp.

A cognitive skill of major importance is *knowledge of the business,* or technical competence. An effective leader has to be technically or professionally competent in some discipline, particularly when leading a group of specialists. It is difficult for the leader to establish rapport with group members when he or she does not know what they are doing. A related damper on leadership effectiveness is when the group does not respect the leader's technical skill. Having good practical intelligence (*street smarts*) is also part of an effective leader's intellectual makeup. A leader with high practical intelligence could size up a good opportunity without spending an extensive amount of time analyzing what could possibly go wrong.

Closely related to cognitive skills is the personality characteristic of **openness to experience,** a positive orientation toward learning. People who have considerable openness to experience have well-developed intellects. Traits commonly associated with this dimension of the intellect include being imaginative, cultured, curious, original, broad-minded, intelligent, and artistically sensitive.

Assertiveness

In Chapter 7, assertiveness was described in relation to resolving conflict. Assertiveness is also a widely recognized leadership trait. If you are self-confident, it is easier to be assertive with people. An assertive leader might say, "I know that the ice storm put us out of business for four days, but we can make up the time by working smart and pulling together. Within 30 days, we will have met or surpassed our goals for the quarter." This statement reflects self-confidence in his leadership capabilities and assertiveness in expressing what he thinks.

Assertiveness helps leaders perform many tasks and achieve goals. Among them are confronting group members about their mistakes, demanding higher performance, and setting high expectations. An assertive leader will also make demands on higher management, such as asking for equipment needed by the group.

CHARISMA

An important quality for leaders at all levels is **charisma,** a type of charm and magnetism that inspires others. Not every leader has to be charismatic, yet to be an effective leader you need some degree of this personality quality. A leader's charisma is determined by the subjective perception of him or her by other people. It is therefore impossible for even the most effective leaders to inspire and motivate everyone. Even popular business leaders are disliked by some of their employees. Charisma encompasses many traits and characteristics. The quality has also been referred to as *it,* or executive presence. *It* refers to the ability to take hold of a room by making a smooth entrance, shaking people's hands, and forging connections with others.[12] Here we focus on vision, enthusiasm and excitement, and humor.

Vision

Top-level leaders need a visual image of where the organization is headed and how it can get there. The person with vision can help the organization or group establish a vision. The progress of the organization is dependent on the executive having a vision, or an optimistic version of the future. Effective leaders project ideas and images that excite people and therefore inspire employees to do their best. Leadership positions of lesser responsibility also call for some vision. Each work group in a progressive company might be expected to form its own vision, such as "We will become the best accounts receivable group in the entire auto replacement parts industry."

Passion, Enthusiasm, and Excitement

Charismatic leaders are passionate about their work and their group members. Andrea Jung, the stylish and inspirational chief executive officer of Avon Products, tells Avon ladies (and a few Avon gentlemen) at company meetings that she loves them. The charismatic business owner is likely to think about the company's product or service day and night. Because of their

KEEP UP YOUR SPIRITS. I SEE A DAY IN THE NOT-TOO-DISTANT FUTURE WHEN OUR FLY SWATTERS WILL BE RANKED NUMBER ONE IN THE WORLD.

contagious excitement, charismatic leaders stimulate group members. Workers respond positively to enthusiasm, especially because enthusiasm may be perceived as a reward for good performance. Enthusiasm is also effective because it helps build good relationships with group members. Spoken expressions of enthusiasm include such statements as "great job" and "I love it." The leader can express enthusiasm nonverbally through gestures, nonsexual touching, and so forth.

Sense of Humor

Humor is a component of charisma and a contributor to leadership effectiveness. Humor helps leaders influence people by reducing tension, relieving boredom, and defusing anger. The most effective form of humor by a leader is tied to the leadership situation. It is much less effective for the leader to tell rehearsed jokes. A key advantage of a witty, work-related comment is that it indicates mental alertness. A canned joke is much more likely to fall flat.

A sales manager was conducting a meeting about declining sales. He opened the meeting by saying, "Ladies and gentlemen, just yesterday I completed a spreadsheet analysis of our declining sales. According to my spreadsheet analysis, if we continue our current trend, by the year 2010 we will have sales of negative $3,750,000. No company can support those figures. We've got to reverse the trend." The manager's humor helped dramatize the importance of reversing the sales decline.

Although inherited characteristics, such as energy, contribute to charisma, most people can develop some charismatic qualities. Exhibit 14-2 presents suggestions for becoming more charismatic.

EXHIBIT 14-2

Suggestions for Becoming More Charismatic

Following are a number of suggestions for behaving charismatically, all based on characteristics and behaviors often found among charismatic leaders and other charismatic persons as well.

1. *Communicate a vision.* A charismatic leader offers an exciting image of where the organization is headed and how to get there. A vision is more than a forecast because it describes an ideal version of the future of an entire organization or an organizational unit, such as a department. The supervisor of paralegal services might communicate a vision such as, "Our paralegal group will become known as the most professional and helpful paralegal group in Arizona."

2. *Make frequent use of metaphors and analogies.* To inspire people, the charismatic leader uses colorful language and exciting metaphors and analogies. Develop metaphors to inspire people around you. To pick up the spirits of her maintenance group, a maintenance supervisor told the group, "We're a lot like the heating and cooling system in a house. A lot of people don't give us much thought, but without us their lives would be very uncomfortable."

(Continued)

3. *Inspire trust and confidence.* Make your deeds consistent with your promises. As mentioned earlier in this chapter, being trustworthy is a key leadership trait. Get people to believe in your competence by making your accomplishments known in a polite, tactful way.

4. *Be highly energetic and goal oriented.* Impress others with your energy and resourcefulness. To increase your energy supply, exercise frequently, eat well, and get ample rest. You can also add to an image of energy by raising and lowering your voice frequently and avoiding a slow pace.

5. *Be emotionally expressive and warm.* A key characteristic of charismatic leaders is the ability to express feelings openly. In dealing with team members, refer to your feelings at the time, such as "I'm excited because I know we are going to hit our year-end target by mid-October." Nonverbal emotional expressiveness, such as warm gestures and frequent touching (nonsexual) of group members, also exhibits charisma.

6. *Make ample use of true stories.* An excellent way of building rapport is to tell stories that deliver a message.[13] Storytelling adds a touch of warmth to the teller and helps build connections among people who become familiar with the same story.

7. *Smile frequently, even if you are not in a happy mood.* A warm smile seems to indicate a confident, caring person, which contributes to a perception of charisma.

8. *Be candid.* Practice saying directly what you want rather than being indirect and evasive. If you want someone to help you, don't ask, "Are you busy?" Instead, ask, "Can you help me with a problem I'm having right now?"

9. *Make everybody you meet feel that he or she is quite important.* For example, at a company social gathering, shake the hand of every person you meet. Also, thank people frequently both orally and by written notes.

10. *Multiply the effectiveness of your handshake.* Shake firmly without creating pain and make enough eye contact to notice the color of the other person's eyes. When you take that much trouble, you project care and concern.

11. *Stand up straight and also use other nonverbal signals of self-confidence.* Practice having good posture. Minimize fidgeting, scratching, foot tapping, and speaking in a monotone. Walk at a rapid pace without appearing to be panicked. Dress fashionably without going to the extreme that people notice your clothes more than they notice you.

12. *Be willing to take personal risks.* Charismatic leaders are typically risk takers, and risk taking adds to their charisma. Risks you might take include suggesting a bright but costly idea and recommending that a former felon be given a chance in your firm.

13. *Be self-promotional.* Charismatic leaders are not shy. Instead, they toot their own horns and allow others to know how important they are. Without appearing self-absorbed, you too might let others know of your tangible accomplishments. Explain to others the key role that you played on your team or how you achieved a few tough goals.

THE ENTREPRENEURIAL SPIRIT

An entrepreneurial leader assumes the risk of starting an innovative business. We ordinarily think of an entrepreneur as being self-employed because the person is a business owner. Yet the same entrepreneurial spirit can be applied as an employee. (This is much like the work habit technique of being self-employed psychologically.) A group leader with an entrepreneurial spirit would search for new activities for the group. The head of a manufacturing unit might say to the group, "Let's ask top management if we can take a shot at making this part that we now buy from a supplier."

The entrepreneurial spirit can also be expressed by reading trade publications, newspapers, and Internet source to keep up with what is happening in the industry. Talking with customers or others in the organization to keep aware of changing needs and requirements shows a spark of entrepreneurial thinking. The leader with an entrepreneurial spirit also visits other firms, attends professional meetings, and participates in educational programs. All the activities just mentioned help the leader think of new activities for the group.

BEHAVIORS AND SKILLS OF EFFECTIVE LEADERS

The personal traits, skills, and characteristics just discussed help create the potential for effective leadership. A leader also has to *do* things that influence group members to achieve good performance. The behaviors or skills of leaders described next contribute to productivity and morale in most situations.

Practice Strong Ethics

Being trustworthy facilitates a leader practicing strong (or good) **ethics,** the study of moral obligation, or separating right from wrong. Ethics deals with doing the right thing by employees, customers, the environment, and the law.[14] Practicing good ethics contributes to effective leadership for several reasons. Workers are more likely to trust an ethical than an unethical leader, which helps the leader gain the support of the group. Good ethics serves as a positive model for group members, thus strengthening the organization. Also, ethical leaders help group members avoid common ethical pitfalls in the workplace. Many of these unethical practices, as listed next, can lead to lawsuits against the company:

- Lying or misrepresenting facts
- Blaming others for your mistakes
- Divulging personal or confidential information to others in the company to promote yourself
- Permitting or failing to report violations of legal requirements
- Protecting substandard performers from proper discipline

- Condoning or failing to report theft or misuse of company property

- Suppressing grievances and complaints

- Covering up accidents and failing to report health and safety hazards

- Ignoring or violating higher management's commitments to employees

- Taking credit for the ideas of others[15]

To simplify a complex issue, an effective leader practices the Golden Rule: *Do unto others as you would have others do unto you.* Similarly, Steven Covey encourages leaders to follow natural principles, such as doing only good things.[16] He urges corporate executives, for example, to establish only those goals that will benefit people.

Direction Setting

Given that leaders are supposed to bring about change, they must point people in the right direction. Setting a direction includes the idea of establishing a vision for the organization or a smaller group. An example of direction setting by a top-level manager would be for the chief executive officer of a toy company to decide that the company should now diversify into the bicycle business. Direction setting by a team leader would include encouraging the group to strive toward error-free work from this point forward or to collaborate more with each other to form a true team.

Develop Partnerships with People

Leadership is now regarded as a long-term relationship, or partnership, between leaders and group members. According to Peter Block, in a **partnership** the leader and group members are connected in such a way that the power between them is approximately balanced. To form a partnership, the leader has to allow the group members to share in decision making. Four conditions are necessary to form a true partnership between the leader and group members:

1. *Exchange of purpose.* The leader and team member should work together to build a vision.

2. *A right to say no.* In a partnership, each side has the right to say no without fear of being punished.

3. *Joint accountability.* Each person takes responsibility for the success and failure of the group.

4. *Absolute honesty.* In a partnership, not telling the truth to each other is an act of betrayal. When group members recognize that they have power, they are more likely to tell the truth because they feel less vulnerable to punishment.[17]

Help Group Members Reach Goals and Achieve Satisfaction

Effective leaders help group members in their efforts to achieve goals.[18] In a sense, they smooth out the path to reaching goals. One important way to do this is to provide the necessary resources to group members. An important aspect of a leader's job is to ensure that subordinates have the proper tools, equipment, and human resources to accomplish their objectives.

Another way of helping group members achieve goals is to reduce frustrating barriers to getting work accomplished. A leader who helps group members cut through minor rules and regulations would be engaging in such behavior. In a factory, a supervisory leader has a responsibility to replace faulty equipment, make sure unsafe conditions are corrected, and see that troublesome employees are either rehabilitated or replaced.

Another important general set of actions characteristic of an effective leader is looking out for the satisfaction of the group. Small things sometimes mean a lot in terms of personal satisfaction. One office manager fought for better coffee facilities for her subordinates. Her thoughtfulness contributed immensely to job satisfaction among them. Giving group members emotional support is another effective way of improving worker satisfaction. An emotionally supportive leader would engage in activities such as listening to group members' problems and offering them encouragement and praise. Again, basic human relations skills contribute to leadership effectiveness.

Set High Expectations

In addition to making expectations clear, it is important for leaders to set high expectations for group members. If you as a leader expect others to succeed, they are likely to live up to your expectations. This mysterious phenomenon has been labeled the **Pygmalion effect.** According to Greek mythology, Pygmalion was a sculptor and king of Cyprus who carved an ivory statue of a maiden and fell in love with the statue. The statue was soon brought to life in response to his prayer.

The point of the Pygmalion effect is that the leader can elevate performance by the simple method of expecting others to perform well. The manager's high expectations become a self-fulfilling prophecy. Why high expectations lead to high performance could be linked to self-confidence. As the leader expresses faith in the group members' abilities to perform well, they become more confident of their skills.

Give Frequent Feedback on Performance

Effective leaders inform employees how they can improve and praise them for things done right. Less effective leaders, in contrast, often avoid confrontation and give limited positive feedback. An exception is that some ineffective leaders become involved in many confrontations—they are masters at reprimanding people!

Manage a Crisis Effectively

When a crisis strikes, that's the time to have an effective leader around. When things are running very smoothly, you may not always notice whether your leader is present. Effectively managing a crisis means giving reassurance to the group that problems will soon be under control, specifying the alternative paths for getting out of the crisis, and choosing one of the paths.

Ask the Right Questions

Leaders do not need to know all the answers. Instead, a major contribution can be to ask the right questions. Although being knowledgeable about the group task is important, there are many times when asking group members penetrating questions is more important. In today's complex and rapidly changing business environment, the collective intelligence of group members is needed to solve problems.[19] Asking questions rather than giving answers is the natural method of helping group members become better problem solvers. Here are sample questions a leader might ask group members to help them meet their challenges:

- What are you going to do differently to reduce by 50 percent the time it takes to fill a customer order?

- Top management is thinking of getting rid of our group and subcontracting the work we do to outside vendors. What do you propose we do to make us more valuable to the company?

- Can you figure out why the competition is outperforming us?

- How can you justify the salary and benefits we are paying you?

Be a Servant Leader

A humanitarian approach to leadership is to be a **servant leader,** one who serves group members by working on their behalf to help them achieve their goals, not the leader's goals. The idea behind servant leadership, as developed by Robert K. Greenleaf, is that leadership stems naturally from a commitment to service. Serving others, including employees, customers, and the community, is the primary motivation for the servant leader.[20] Servant leadership encompasses many different acts, all designed to make life easier or better for group members. Several acts of servant leadership are mentioned next.

A good starting point is for the leader to see himself or herself as a humble servant. ("I'm here to serve you.") Servant leaders also look for the opportunity to lend assistance directly to employees, such as a supermarket manager bagging groceries during an unanticipated rush of business. A servant leader would also provide the tools people needed to accomplish their work, such as fighting for enough budget to purchase expensive new equipment.

Although a servant leader is idealistic, he or she recognizes that one individual cannot accomplish everything. So the leader listens carefully to the array of problems facing group members and then concentrates on a few. As the head of a nurses' union told the group, "I know you are hurting in many ways. Yet I think that the work overload issue is the biggest one, so we will head into negotiations working on obtaining sensible workloads. After that we will work on job security."

▲ DEVELOPING YOUR LEADERSHIP POTENTIAL

How to improve your potential for becoming a leader is a topic without limits. Almost anything you do to improve your individual effectiveness will have some impact on your ability to lead others. If you strengthen your self-confidence, improve your memory for names, study this book carefully, read studies about leadership, or improve your physical fitness, you stand a good chance of improving your leadership potential. Eight strategies might be kept in mind if you are seeking to improve your leadership potential:

1. *General education and specific training.* Almost any program of career training or education can be considered a program of leadership development. Courses in human relations, management, or applied psychology have obvious relevance for someone currently occupying or aspiring toward a leadership position. Many of today's leaders in profit and nonprofit organizations hold formal degrees in business. Specific training programs will also help you improve your leadership potential. Among them might be skill development programs in interviewing, employee selection, listening, assertiveness training, budgeting, planning, improving work habits, resolving conflict, and communication skills. After acquiring knowledge through study, you then put the knowledge into practice as a leader.

2. *Leadership development programs.* A focused way of improving your leadership potential is to attend development programs designed specifically to improve your ability to lead others and develop self-confidence. A popular type of leadership development program called *outdoor training* places people in a challenging outdoor environment for a weekend or up to 10 days. Participants are required to accomplish physical feats, such as climbing a mountain, white-water canoeing, building a wall, or swinging between trees on a rope. Participants in these outdoor programs learn such important leadership skills and attitudes as teamwork and trusting others and gain confidence in their ability to accomplish the seemingly impossible.

3. *Acquire broad experience.* Because leadership varies somewhat with the situation, a sound approach to improving leadership effectiveness is to attempt to gain supervisory experience in different settings. A person who wants to become an executive is well advised to gain supervisory experience in at least two different organizational functions, such as customer service and finance.

First-level supervisory jobs are an invaluable starting point for developing your leadership potential. It takes considerable skill to manage a fast-food restaurant effectively or to direct a public playground during the summer. First-level supervisors frequently face situations in which subordinates are poorly trained, poorly paid, and not well motivated to achieve company objectives. Taking a turn as a team leader is also valuable experience for developing leadership skills.

4. *Modeling effective leaders.* Are you committed to improving your leadership skill and potential? If so, carefully observe a capable leader in action and incorporate some of his or her approaches into your own behavior. You may not be able to or want to become that person's clone, but you can model (imitate) what the person does. For instance, most inexperienced leaders have a difficult time confronting others with bad news. Observe a good confronter handle the situation and try his or her approach the next time you have some unfavorable news to deliver to another person.

5. *Self-development of leadership characteristics and behavior.*   Study the leadership characteristics and behaviors described in this chapter. As a starting point, identify several attributes you think you could strengthen within yourself given some self-determination. For example, you might decide that with effort you could improve your passion and enthusiasm. You might also believe that you could be more emotionally supportive of others. It is also helpful to obtain feedback from reliable sources, such as a trusted manager, about which traits and behaviors you particularly need to develop.

6. *Practice a little leadership.*   An effective way to develop your leadership skills is to look for opportunities to exert a small amount of helpful leadership in contrast to waiting for opportunities to accomplish extraordinary deeds.[21] A "little leadership" might involve such behaviors as mentoring a struggling team member, coaching somebody about how to use a new high-tech device, or making a suggestion about improving a product.

7. *Help your leader lead.*   According to Michael Useem, leaders need your assistance so they can do a good job. "If people are afraid to help their leaders lead, their leaders will fail."[22] A group member is often closer to the market and closer to how the product is used. So he or she can provide useful information to the person in the formal leadership position. When you help the people who are above you avoid a mistake or capitalize on an opportunity, you help the entire company. At the same time, you are developing your ability to take the initiative and lead.

8. *Become an integrated human being.*   A philosophical approach to leadership suggests that the model leader is first and foremost a fully functioning person. According to William D. Hitt, mastering the art of leadership comes with self-mastery. Leadership development is the process of self-development. As a result, the process of becoming a leader is similar to the process of becoming an integrated human being. For example, you need to develop values that guide your behavior before you can adequately guide the behavior of others.

The model (or ideal) leader, according to Hitt, must possess six character traits: identity (know thyself), independence, authenticity, responsibility, courage, and integrity.[23] All these traits have everyday meanings, but they can also have personal meanings. Part of becoming an integrated person is to answer such questions as, "What do I mean when I say I have integrity?"

▲ SUMMARY

Before most people can exert leadership, they need to develop an appropriate amount of self-confidence. Self-confidence is necessary for leadership because it helps assure group members that things are under control. A leader who is too self-confident, however, may not admit to errors, listen to criticism, or ask for advice. Also, you may appear insecure if you are too self-confident. Self-confidence is also important because it contributes to self-efficacy.

A general principle of boosting your self-confidence is to experience success (goal accomplishment) in a variety of situations. As you achieve one set of goals, you establish slightly more difficult goals, thus entering a success cycle. The specific strategies for building self-confidence described here are (1) taking an inventory of personal assets and accomplishments; (2) developing a solid knowledge base; (3) using positive self-talk; (4) avoiding negative self-talk; (5) using positive visual imagery; (6) striving for peak performance; and (7) bouncing back from setbacks and embarrassments.

Leadership is the process of bringing about positive changes and influencing others to achieve worthwhile goals. Effective leadership is needed at the top of organizations, but supervisors and team leaders also need to provide effective leadership. Effective leaders have the "right stuff." Certain traits and characteristics contribute to leadership effectiveness in many situations. Among them are emotional intelligence, trustworthiness and character, strong work motivation and high energy, cognitive skills and openness to experience, assertiveness, charisma (including vision, passion, enthusiasm, and a sense of humor), and an entrepreneurial spirit.

Behaviors and skills of an effective leader (one who maintains high productivity and morale) include (1) practicing strong ethics; (2) setting directions for others; (3) developing partnerships with people (emphasizing power sharing); (4) helping group members reach goals and achieve satisfaction; (5) setting high expectations (the Pygmalion effect); (6) giving frequent feedback on performance; (7) managing a crisis effectively; (8) asking the right questions; and (9) being a servant leader.

Many activities in life can in some way contribute to the development of a person's leadership potential. Eight recommended strategies for improving your leadership potential or leadership skills are (1) general education and specific training; (2) participating in leadership development programs; (3) acquiring broad experience; (4) modeling effective leaders; (5) developing leadership characteristics and behavior; (6) practicing a little leadership; (7) helping your leader lead; and (8) becoming an integrated human being.

Questions and Activities

1. When you meet another person, on what basis do you conclude that he or she is self-confident?

2. What positive self-talk can you use after you have failed on a major assignment?

3. Which work habits and time management practices (see Chapter 12) are well suited to helping a person achieve peak performance?

4. Provide an example of something a leader motivated or inspired you to do that you would not have done without his or her presence.

5. Why is the "ability to perform the group task" essential for a team leader?

6. What is the relationship between a vision and a goal?

7. Identify three areas in life in which being charismatic would help a person achieve his or her goals.

8. Suppose a person who wanted to be an effective leader was convinced that a sense of humor would contribute to his or her effectiveness. How might that person develop his or her sense or humor?

9. How can a leader be both charismatic and evil at the same time? Do any business or political leaders fit into the "evil charismatic" category?

10. How might your current program of study contribute to your development as a leader?

INTERNET SKILL BUILDER: Developing Your Self-Confidence Online

As described in this chapter, self-confidence is a major contributor to leadership effectiveness in a variety of situations. www.self-confidence.co.uk offers a free self-confidence course online. After you sign up for the course, you will receive your first installment immediately. After that, you will receive one tutorial a week for six weeks. The lessons include self-confidence-boosting stories, information and quotes, and skill development exercises. Sponsors of the site will invite you to take related courses for a fee.

HUMAN RELATIONS CASE PROBLEM

Charismatically Challenged Colleen

Twenty-seven-year-old Colleen McFerguson worked as a merchandising specialist for ValuMart, one of the largest international retail chains. Based in the United States, ValuMart also has a strong presence in Canada, Europe, Japan, and Hong Kong. Colleen began her employment with ValuMart as a cashier and two years later was invited into the training program for merchandising specialists.

Colleen performed well as a merchandising trainee in the soft-goods line. Her specialty areas included men's, women's, and children's clothing; linens and bedding; men's and women's jewelry; and home decorations. For several years in a row, Colleen received performance evaluation ratings of above average or outstanding. Among the write-in comments made by her supervisors were "diligent worker," "knows the tricks of merchandising," "good flair for buying the right products at the right price," and "fits right into the team."

Despite the positive performance appraisals supported with positive comments, Colleen had a gnawing discontent about her career at ValuMart. Despite five years of good performance, she was still not invited to become a member of the group called "ValuTrackers." The ValuTrackers are a group of merchandising and operations specialists who are regarded as being on the fast track to become future ValuMart leaders. The leaders hold high-level positions, such as head merchandiser, regional vice president, and store manager.

(Continued)

Several times when Colleen inquired as to why she was not invited to join the ValuTrackers, she was told something to the effect that she was not quite ready to be included in this elite group. She was also told not to be discouraged because the company still valued her contribution.

One day, Colleen thought to herself, "I'm headed toward age 30, and I want a great future in the retail business now." So she convinced her boss, the merchandising supervisor (Evan Tyler), to set up a career conference with three people: Colleen, the boss, and her boss's boss (Heather Bridges), the area merchandising manager. She let Evan know in advance that she wanted to talk about her potential for promotion.

Evan started the meeting by saying, "Colleen, perhaps you can tell Heather and me again why you requested this meeting."

Colleen responded, "Thanks for asking Evan. As I mentioned before, I'm wondering what you think is wrong with me. I receive a lot of positive feedback about my performance, but I'm not a ValuTracker. Also, you seem to change the subject when I talk about wanting to become a merchandising supervisor and eventually a merchandising executive. What am I doing wrong?"

Heather responded, "Evan and I frequently talk about the performance and potential of all our merchandising specialists. You're a good performer, Colleen, but you lack that little spark that makes a person a leader. You go about your job efficiently and quietly, but that's not enough. We want future leaders of ValuMart to make an impact."

Evan added, "I go along with Heather's comments. Another point, Colleen, is that you rarely take the initiative to suggest ideas. I was a little shocked by your request for a three-way career interview because it's one of the few initiatives you have taken. You're generally pretty laid back."

"Then what do I have to do to convince you two that I should be a ValuTracker?" asked Colleen.

Heather replied, "Start acting more like a leader. Be more charismatic." Evan nodded in agreement.

Questions

1. What career advice can you offer Colleen McFerguson?

2. What might Colleen do to develop more charisma?

3. What is your opinion of the fairness of the ValuTracker program?

WEB CORNER

Overview of leadership: www.ccl.org

Leadership development programs:
    www.academyleadership.com/exec.htm

Peak performance training: www.inner-act.com

Servant leadership: http://greenleaf.org

▲ REFERENCES

1. Tom Belden, "Healing from the Ground Up," *Philadelphia Inquirer,* August 25, 2003.

2. Josepah A. Raelin, *Creating Leaderful Organizations: How to Bring Out Leadership in Everyone* (San Francisco: Berrett-Koehler Publishers, 2003).

3. Marilyn E. Gist and Terence R. Mitchell, "Self-Efficacy: A Theoretical Analysis of Its Determinants and Malleability," *Academy of Management Review,* April 1992, pp. 183–211.

4. Dov Eden and Arie Aviram, "Self-Efficacy Training to Speed Reemployment: Helping People to Help Themselves," *Journal of Applied Psychology,* June 1993, pp. 352–360.

5. Jay T. Knippen and Thad B. Green, "Building Self-Confidence," *Supervisory Management,* August 1989, pp. 22–27.

6. "Entrepreneurs Need Attitude: Power of Being Positive Can Help You to Succeed in Spite of Setbacks," Knight Ridder, September 16, 2002.

7. Frances Thornton, Gayle Privette, and Charles M. Bundrick, "Peak Performance of Business Leaders: An Experience Parallel to Self-Actualization Theory," *Journal of Business and Psychology,* Winter 1999, pp. 253–264.

8. Work cited in Michael Rozek, "Can You Spot a Peak Performer?" *Personnel Journal,* June 1991, p. 77.

9. Daniel Goleman, Richard Boyatsis, and Annie McKee, "Primal Leadership: The Hidden Driver of Great Performance," *Harvard Business Review,* December 2001, pp. 42–51.

10. Gareth R. Jones and Jennifer M. George, "The Experience and Evolution of Trust: Implications for Cooperation and Teamwork," *Academy of Management Review,* July 1998, pp. 531–546; Jenny C. McCune, "That Elusive Thing Called Trust," *Management Review,* August 1998, pp. 10–16.

11. Cassie R. Barlow, Mark Jordan, and William H. Hendrix, "Character Assessment: An Examination of Leadership Levels," *Journal of Business and Psychology,* Summer 2003, p. 563.

12. Michelle Conlin, "She's Gotta Have 'It,'" *BusinessWeek,* July 22, 2002, p. 88.

13. Elizabeth Weil, "Every Leader Tells a Story," www.fastcompany.com/online/15/rftf.html (accessed May 6, 1999.)

14. "Ethics—Business Educators Teach Students to . . . Do the Right Thing!" *Keying In,* January 1997, p. 1.

15. Robert B. Maddux and Dorothy Maddux, *Ethics in Business: A Guide for Managers* (Los Altos, CA: Crisp Publications, 1994).

16. George W. Fotis, "Interactive Personal Ethics," *Management Review,* December 1996, p. 46, and "Covey Proposes Principle-Based Leadership," *Management Review,* September 1995, pp. 20–21.

17. Peter Block, *Stewardship: Choosing Service Over Self-Interest* (San Francisco: Berrett-Koehler Publishers, 1993), pp. 27–32.

18. Robert T. Keller, "A Test of the Path-Goal Theory of Leadership with Need for Clarity as a Moderator in Research and Development Organizations," *Journal of Applied Psychology,* April 1989, pp. 208–212.

19. Ronald A. Heifetz and Donald L. Laurie, "The Work of Leadership," *Harvard Business Review,* January–February 1997, p. 124.

20. Robert K. Greenleaf, *The Power of Servant Leadership: A Journey into the Nature of Legitimate Power and Greatness* (San Francisco: Berrett-Koehler Publishers, 1998).

21. Michael E. McGill and John W. Slocum Jr., "A Little Leadership Please?" *Organizational Dynamics,* Winter 1998, p. 48.

22. Cited in Bill Breen, "Trickle-Up Leadership," *Fast Company,* November 2001, pp. 70–72.

23. William D. Hitt, *The Model Leader: A Fully Functioning Person* (Columbus, OH: Battelle Press, 1993).

▲ ADDITIONAL READING

Bennis, Warren G., and Robert J. Thomas. "Crucibles of Leadership." *Harvard Business Review,* September 2002, pp. 39–45.

Carless, Sally A., Alexander J. Wearing, and Leon Mann. "A Short Measure of Transformational Leadership." *Journal of Business and Psychology,* Spring 2000, pp. 389–405.

Covey, Stephen R. *First Things First.* New York: Simon & Schuster, 1994.

Frese, Michael, Sisanne Beimel, and Sandra Schoenborn. "Action Training for Charismatic Leadership: Two Evaluations of Studies of a Commercial Training Module on Inspirational Communication of a Vision." *Personnel Psychology,* Autumn 2003, pp. 671–697.

Galford, Robert, and Anne Seibold Drapeau. *The Trusted Leader: Bringing Out the Best in Your People and Your Company.* New York: Free Press, 2003.

Kim, W. Chan, and Renée Mauborgne. "Tipping Point Leadership." *Harvard Business Review,* April 2003, pp. 60–69.

Quirk, M. P., and P. M. Fandt. *The Second Language of Leadership.* Mahwah, NJ: Lawrence Erlbaum, 2000.

Schaeffer, Leonard D. "The Leadership Journey." *Harvard Business Review,* October 2002, pp. 42–47.

Teerlink, Rich, and Lee Ozley. *More Than a Motorcycle: The Leadership Journey of Harely-Davidson.* Boston: Harvard Business School Publishing, 2000.

Useem, Michael. "The Leadership Lessons of Mount Everest." *Harvard Business Review,* October 2001, pp. 51–58.

CHAPTER 15

Managing Your Personal Finances

Learning Objectives

After studying the information and doing the exercises in this chapter, you should be able to:

- ◆ Do a better job of managing your personal finances

- ◆ Establish a tentative financial plan for yourself and your family

- ◆ Pinpoint basic investment principles

- ◆ Identify several major forms of investments

- ◆ Develop a plan for managing your creditworthiness

- ◆ Give yourself a yearly financial checkup

*F*or more than a year, Rachel Hulin paid $90 a month for a gym membership. She used it maybe four times in all—for a per-visit rate of approximately $315. "I sort of felt like an idiot," says the 24-year-old photographer. "I think I signed up for it to try to make myself go." Ms. Hulin later dropped her expensive membership and joined another, less expensive gym at $55 a month. But she admits she hasn't "gone in a while" there, either.

Hulin is not alone in her casual control of her expenses. Research suggests that consumers often pay too much for services, ranging from gym memberships to movie rental clubs, because the overestimate how often they will use them.[1]

The brief mention of the woman who underuses her gym membership and the supporting research illustrate the importance of managing personal finances well. People who do scrutinize their spending will often be able to squeeze some money out of expenses and invest that money into other sources of pleasure. Equally important, they will have more money available for savings and investments.

It is important to manage personal finances in such a way that money becomes a source of satisfaction rather than a major worry. Financial problems can lead to other problems. Poor concentration stemming from financial worries may lead to low job performance. Many relationship problems stem from conflict about finances. Worry about money can also drain energy that could be used to advance your career or enrich your personal life.

The purpose of this chapter is to present information that should enable you to start on the road to financial comfort and escape financial discomfort. Our approach is to cover the basics of personal financial planning, investment principles, choosing investments, managing and preventing debt, giving yourself a yearly financial checkup, and retiring rich.

▲ YOUR PERSONAL FINANCIAL PLAN

A highly recommended starting point in improving your present financial condition and enhancing your future is to develop a personal financial plan. Two key elements of a personal financial plan are financial goals and a budget. The spending plan, or **budget,** helps you set aside the money for investments that you need to accomplish your goals. The subject of how to invest the money your investment plan provides is described at later points in this chapter.

ESTABLISHING FINANCIAL GOALS

Personal finance is yet another area in which goal setting generally improves performance. A common approach to financial goal setting is to specify amounts of money you would like to earn at certain points in time. An individual might set yearly financial goals, adjusted for inflation. Another might set goals for five-year intervals. Another common financial goal is to obtain enough money to cover a specific expense, such as making a down payment on a new car. These goals should include a target date, such as shown in Exhibit 15-1. An important supplement to establishing these goals is an investment table that specifies the amount of money needed to achieve the goal (see Table 15-1). Financial goals are sometimes expressed in terms of the allocation of money. Among these goals would be the following:

- Putting pay raises into savings or reducing debt
- Participating in an automatic savings or retirement plan whereby a financial institution deducts money from each paycheck
- Investing 10 percent of each net paycheck into a mutual fund

Financial goals are sometimes more motivational when they point to the lifestyle you hope to achieve with specific amounts of money. In this way, money becomes the means to the ends that bring satisfaction and happiness. Here are two examples of financial goals expressed in terms of what money can accomplish:

- By 2009 I want to earn enough money to have my own apartment and car and buy nice gifts for my family and relatives.
- By 2033, I want to earn enough money to have paid for my house, own a vacation home near a lake, and take a winter vacation each year.

EXHIBIT 15-1

Financial Goal Setting

Goal	Target Date	Years to Goal	Dollars Needed
1. Pay off credit cards	June 2005	1½	$5,675
2. Pay for son's college	September 2025	18	$175,000
3. Down payment on home	June 2009	4½	$28,000

			TABLE 15-1		

MONTHLY SAVINGS NEEDED TO REACH GOAL
(5% AFTER-TAX RATE OF RETURN)

Dollar Goals

Years	$5,000	$10,000	$20,000	$50,000	$100,000
2	198	395	791	1,977	3,954
4	94	188	376	939	1,878
6	59	119	238	594	1,189
8	42	85	169	423	846
10	32	64	128	321	641
20	12	24	48	121	242
30	6	12	24	60	120

NOTE: This chart assumes that deposits are made at the beginning of each month and that interest is compounded monthly.

DEVELOPING A BUDGET (SPENDING PLAN)

When most people hear the word *budget,* they think of a low-priced item or miserly spending habits. Their perception is only partially correct. A budget is a plan for spending money to improve your chances of using your money wisely and not spending more than your net income. John Gilligan, the executive director of a consumer credit counseling service, reminds us of the important of following a budget. He says that 90 percent of clients do not have a budget in place or do not know how to develop one when they first seek his agency's services.[2] Developing a budget can be divided into a series of logical steps. Exhibit 15-2 presents a worksheet helpful for carrying out the plan. Many people today use software that helps you lay out a budget. For most people, a monthly budget makes the most sense because so many expenses are once-a-month items.

Step 1. *Establishing goals.* Decide what you or your family really need and want. If you are establishing a family budget, it is best to involve the entire family. For the sake of simplicity, we will assume here that the reader is preparing an individual budget. Individual budgets can be combined to form the family budget. Goal setting should be done for the short, intermediate, and long term. A short-term goal might be "replace hot water heater this February." A long-term goal might be "accumulate enough money for a recreational vehicle within 10 years."

Step 2. *Estimating income.* People whose entire income is derived from salary can readily estimate their income. Commissions, bonuses, and investment income are more variable. So is income from part-time work, inheritance, and prizes.

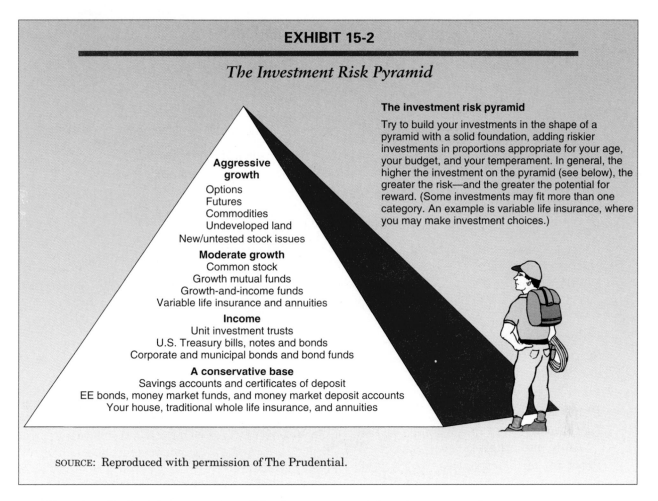

EXHIBIT 15-2

The Investment Risk Pyramid

Aggressive growth
Options
Futures
Commodities
Undeveloped land
New/untested stock issues

Moderate growth
Common stock
Growth mutual funds
Growth-and-income funds
Variable life insurance and annuities

Income
Unit investment trusts
U.S. Treasury bills, notes and bonds
Corporate and municipal bonds and bond funds

A conservative base
Savings accounts and certificates of deposit
EE bonds, money market funds, and money market deposit accounts
Your house, traditional whole life insurance, and annuities

The investment risk pyramid

Try to build your investments in the shape of a pyramid with a solid foundation, adding riskier investments in proportions appropriate for your age, your budget, and your temperament. In general, the higher the investment on the pyramid (see below), the greater the risk—and the greater the potential for reward. (Some investments may fit more than one category. An example is variable life insurance, where you may make investment choices.)

SOURCE: Reproduced with permission of The Prudential.

Step 3. *Estimating expenses.* The best way to estimate expenses is to keep close track of what you are actually spending now. After listing all your expenses, perhaps for two weeks, break the expenses down into meaningful categories such as those shown in Exhibit 15-3. Modify the specific items to suit your particular spending patterns. For instance, computer supplies and Internet service might be such a big item in your spending plan that it deserves a separate category. It is possible that an expense you have now will soon decrease (such as paying off a loan) or increase (such as joining a health club).

Try to plan for large expenses so that they are spaced at intervals over several years. If you plan to purchase a car one year, plan to remodel your kitchen another. If you buy an overcoat one season, you might have to delay buying a suit until the next year.

Use your records and recollections to help you decide whether to continue your present pattern of spending or to make changes. For instance, estimating your expenses might reveal that you are spending far too much on gas for the car. An antidote might be to consolidate errand-running trips or make some trips by foot or bicycle.

EXHIBIT 15-3

Your Monthly Spending Plan

Monthly Expenses

Fixed:

Mortgage or rent _____

Property insurance _____

Health insurance _____

Auto insurance _____

Other insurance _____

Educational expenses _____

Child support payments _____

Local telephone and Internet
   service provider _____

Cable or satellite TV _____

Taxes:

Federal _____

State or provincial _____

Social Security _____

Local _____

Property _____

Installment loans
   (auto and others) _____

Set-aside for emergencies _____

Variable:

Food _____

Household supplies _____

Home maintenance _____

Medical and dental _____

Toll calls and cell phone _____

Clothing _____

Hair care and cosmetics _____

Transportation _____

Car maintenance _____

Entertainment including
   pay-for-view TV _____

Travel and vacation _____

Clubs/organizations _____

Hobbies _____

Other _____

Total expenses _____

Monthly Income

Salary _____

Tips _____

Bonuses and commissions _____

Interest and dividends _____

Insurance benefits _____

Child support received _____

Other _____

Total income _____

Summary:

Total income

Less total expenses _____

Balance for savings
   and investment _____

Step 4.   *Comparing expenses and income.*   Add the figures in your spending plan. Now compare the total with your estimate of income for the planning period. If the two figures balance, at least you are in neutral financial condition. If your income exceeds your estimate of expenses, you may decide to satisfy more of your immediate wants, set aside more money for future goals, or put the balance into savings or investment.

Remember that the true profit from your labor is the difference between your net income and your total expenses. Set-asides are considered an expense since you will inevitably use up that money to meet future goals or pay for seasonal expenses. Without a miscellaneous category, many budgets will project a profit that never materializes. Any household budget has some miscellaneous or unpredictable items each month. After working with your budget several months, you should be able to make an accurate estimate of miscellaneous expenses.

If your income is below your estimated expenses, you will have to embark on a cost-cutting campaign in your household. If you brainstorm the problem by yourself or with friends, you will come up with dozens of valid expense-reducing suggestions.

Step 5.   *Carrying out the budget.*   After you have done your best job of putting your spending plan on paper or hard drive, try it out for one, two, or three months. See how close it comes to reality. Keep accurate records to find out where your money is being spent. It is helpful to make a notation of expenditures at the end of every day. Did you forget about that $29 you spent on party snacks Sunday afternoon? It is a good idea to keep all financial records together. You may find it helpful to set aside a desk drawer, a large box, or other convenient place to put your record book, bills, receipts, and other financial papers. Converting paper records into computerized files is strongly recommended for maintaining a spending plan.

Step 6.   *Evaluating the budget.*   Compare what you spent with what you planned to spend for three consecutive months. If your spending was quite different from your plan, find out why. If your plan did not provide for your needs, it must be revised. You cannot live with a spending plan that allows for no food the last four days of the month. If the plan fitted your needs but you had trouble sticking to it, the solution to your problem may be to practice more self-discipline. Each succeeding budget should work better. As circumstances change, your budget will need revision. A budget is a changing, living document that serves as a guide to the proper management of your personal finances.

▲ BASIC INVESTMENT PRINCIPLES

After you have developed a spending plan that results in money left over for savings and investment, you can begin investing. To start developing an investment strategy or refining your present one, consider the eight investment principles presented next. They are based on the collected wisdom of many financial planners and financially successful people.

1. *Spend less money than you earn.* The key to lifelong financial security and peace of mind is to spend less money than you earn. By so doing, you will avoid the stresses of being in debt and worrying about money. A widely accepted rule of thumb is to set aside 10 percent of your net income for savings and investments. For many people struggling to make ends meet, the 10 percent rule is unrealistic. These people may choose to implement the 10 percent rule later in their careers. A growing practice is to have savings and investments deducted automatically from your paycheck or bank account. The automatic plans ensures that you will set aside some money each month for investments.

2. *Invest early and steadily to capitalize on the benefits of compounding.* Investments made early in life grow substantially more than those made later. You will slowly and steadily accumulate wealth if you begin investing early in life and continue to invest regularly. Let's look at a straightforward example. Assume that you invest $1,000 at the start of each year for five years. It earns 8 percent a year, and the earnings are compounded (interest is paid on the accumulated principal plus the accumulated interest). You would have $6,123 at the end of five years. If you invested $1,000 at the start of each year for 25 years, you would have $79, 252. To achieve these full results, you would have to make tax-free, or tax-deferred, investments.

3. *Keep reinvesting dividends.* As implied in the second principle, dividends and interest payments must be reinvested to fully benefit from early and regular investments. Here is an illustration based on stock dividends. Assume that a person had invested $5,000 in a representative group of common stocks 35 years ago. The amount accumulated *with* reinvesting dividends is four times as great as that *without* reinvesting. The person who did not reinvest the dividends would have accumulated approximately $60,000, while the person who reinvested the dividends would have stocks worth approximately $240,000.

4. *Diversify your investments (use asset allocation).* A bedrock principle of successful investing is to diversify your investments. This approach is referred to as *asset allocation* because you allocate your assets to different types of investments. Money is typically apportioned among stocks, bonds, short-term instruments like money market funds, and real estate (including home ownership). A starting point in diversifying your investments is to accumulate enough money in cash or its equivalent to tide you over for three months in case you are without employment. Your specific allocation of assets will depend on your tolerance for risk and your time frame. At the conclusion of the section on choosing your investments, we will describe several different investment allocations.

5. *Maintain a disciplined, long-term approach.* If you have an investment plan suited to your needs, stick with it over time. The patient, long-term investor is likely to achieve substantial success. Investors who make investments based on hunches and hot tips and sell in panic when the value of their investments drop generally achieve poorer returns. A representative study showed that investors held their shares in mutual funds for an average of 30 months from 1984 through 2002. Along the way, they achieved a yearly gain of 2.6 percent. The Standard & Poor's 500 stock index showed a gain of 12.2 percent during the same time period.[3] Investing regularly often lowers the average cost of your investment purchases. (This technique is referred to as *dollar-cost averaging* and is described later.)

6. *Practice contrary investing.*   If your purpose in making investments is to become wealthy, follow the principle of **contrary investing**— buy investments when the demand for them is very low and sell when the demand is very high. When others are discouraged about purchasing real estate and there are very few buyers around, invest heavily in real estate. When others are excited about real estate investing, sell quickly before prices fall again. In the words of the late billionaire J. Paul Getty, "Buy when everybody else is selling, and hold until everyone else is buying." This is not merely a catchy slogan. It is the very essence of successful investing.[4] For example, the Nasdaq index of stocks sunk to 1,114 on October 9, 2002. By March 6, 2004 the index had jumped to 2048, an upturn of 84 percent. The person who bought a portfolio of stocks in the Nasdaq index in October and sold in June would have profited substantially.

Contrary investing may conflict somewhat with the disciplined long-term approach. However, you might stay with contrary investing as a consistent, long-term strategy.

7. *Invest globally as well as domestically.*   Diversifying your investments among different countries is another contributor to financial success. Financial advisers regularly suggest international stocks and bonds as a diversification possibility. Overseas markets may offer investors values more promising than those provided domestically. One way to invest internationally is to purchase mutual funds geared to this purpose. It is also possible to invest in savings accounts known as *certificates of deposit (CDs)* that might pay a higher rate of interest than domestically.

Be aware, however, that overseas investments have two substantial risks. The value of the overseas currency may go down rapidly, thus lowering your return should you sell your stocks or bonds. Another problem is that a politically unstable government can create havoc in the investment markets. One example is that a government might take over a private company and declare its stocks and bonds invalid.

8. *Pay off debt.*   One of the best investment principles of all is the most straightforward. Paying off debt gives you an outstanding return on investment. A common scenario is a person paying about 13 percent on credit card debt while earning 2 percent from an investment. Paying off the 13 percent debt with money from savings would thus yield an 11 percent profit. (We are excluding home equity loans from consideration because they carry tax-deductible interest.)

Another major strategy for paying off debt is to work toward reducing a home mortgage. Making extra payments on a mortgage substantially reduces the time it takes to pay off the mortgage. Suppose a person has a $100,000 mortgage at 8 percent for 30 years. By increasing the mortgage payment just 4 percent each year, the loan will be retired in 15 years and would save $82,845 in interest. At the same time, the additional payments build equity in your house, thus increasing your net worth. A concern, however, is that as you pay down the interest on the mortgage, your tax deduction dwindles.

▲ CHOOSING YOUR INVESTMENTS

After understanding some basic principles of investing, you are ready to make choices among different investments. We describe investments here because they are an integral part of managing your personal finances. Investments can be categorized into two basic types: lending money or owning assets. Lending money is referred to as a *fixed-income investment,* while owning an asset is an *equity investment.* For example, when you purchase a corporate bond, you are lending money that will pay a fixed rate of return. When you purchase stocks, you become an owner of an asset. Our discussion of choosing investments includes their relative risks, relative returns, different types, and selecting the right mix.

TOLERANCE FOR INVESTMENT RISKS

To be a successful investor, you must be able to tolerate some risk. As illustrated in Exhibit 15-2, investments vary in the risk of losing the money you invested. Yet not even so-called *safe* investments are without risk. As an investor, you must decide how much and what kind of risk you can tolerate. One person might not be able to tolerate watching the values of his or her mutual funds fluctuate from month to month. Another person might not be able to tolerate the risk of missing out on big profits in the stock market by putting money in a savings bank. A third person might worry about inflation eroding the value of money in a low-interest savings account (or stored in a safe deposit box). And yet another person might not want to contend with the risk of having too little money for retirement. The longer the time period for investment, the more risk of loss of principal most people are willing to accept. A person with a 30-year horizon might be more willing to invest in a technology stock than would a person approaching retirement.

A major factor in tolerating investment risks is that most people are loss averse, as described in Chapter 3 about problem solving. People feel the pain of an investment loss about two to two and one-half times as strongly as they feel pleasure from good performance.[5] People who are strongly risk averse might prefer to choose investments where the risk of severe downward swings in value are less probable, such as real estate.

Understanding how much and what kind of risk you can tolerate will then help you map the best investment strategy for yourself. To explore your attitude toward investment risks, you are invited to do Human Relations Self-Assessment Quiz 15-1 and visit the associated Web site.

DIFFERENT TYPES OF INVESTMENTS

Dozens of different savings plans and investments are available. They include everyday methods of savings as well as exotic investments, such as

HUMAN RELATIONS SELF-ASSESSMENT QUIZ 15-1

Your Money Personality

Below is a two-part quiz that addresses you willingness to take risks and your desire to be involved with the investment decision-making process. Take it, and perhaps you'll find out something you didn't know about yourself.

Risk versus Safety

1. If I found a secure job which I thoroughly enjoyed, I would
   _____ a. probably stay in it indefinitely.
   _____ b. stay unless a better opportunity came along.
   _____ c. be on the lookout for a better opportunity or investigate ways to start a business of my own.

2. I would become involved with a new business
   _____ a. only as a customer.
   _____ b. as an employee if I've checked it out and it seems as if it's a good opportunity.
   _____ c. as an investor if there's the chance of a big payoff.

3. Buying a car, I prefer
   _____ a. an economy model with good performance ratings and an extended warranty.
   _____ b. an exciting model, still unrated, with a standard warranty.
   _____ c. a sleek and prestigious vintage car that would increase in value but may be costly to maintain.

4. Visiting a casino, I
   _____ a. generally feel uncomfortable.
   _____ b. enjoy some games but budget how much I can afford to lose and stop after that.
   _____ c. get caught up in the games and sometimes have big losses.

5. I've discovered that I'm most nervous around someone who
   _____ a. spends frivolously and/or takes big risks with money.
   _____ b. misses opportunities because of risk or fear.
   _____ c. never takes a chance in hopes of a big payoff.

High Involvement versus Lack of Involvement

1. At any given time, I know
   _____ a. my total assets and liabilities, down to the last $200.
   _____ b. more or less what my assets and liabilities are.
   _____ c. which bills I have to pay from my latest paycheck.

2. If the interest on my credit card were raised, I would

_____ a. shop until I found a lower rate.

_____ b. look into a few other cards.

_____ c. go on paying as before because it's convenient.

3. My personal checkbook is

_____ a. always balanced.

_____ b. balanced every few checks of every week.

_____ c. only balanced when I receive a statement and sometimes not even then.

4. If suddenly I had a much larger income, I would

_____ a. manage all of it myself and enjoy doing it.

_____ b. work with my partner as well as with financial experts.

_____ c. hire financial experts as well as someone to manage my day-to-day expense money.

5. I'd prefer an investment that

_____ a. would make money for me if I kept an eye on it constantly.

_____ b. I need to evaluate only every few months.

_____ c. I never have to worry about.

Interpretation of Results

Risk Versus Safety

- If you scored three or more a's—you tend to be safety oriented.
- Three or more b's—you tend to be more at ease with some risk.
- Three or more c's—you tend to be a risk taker.

If you are making inappropriate money decisions because you're miscalculating your willingness for risk taking, Kathleen Gurney, chief executive officer of Financial Psychology Corporation, says you might counter those reactions by taking the time to carefully consider any decisions about money before you make them. For those who are overly cautious, her suggestion is to take small, calculated risks to build up your confidence and risk tolerance.

High Involvement versus Lack of Involvement

- Three or more a's—you tend to like being in charge of money.
- Three or more b's—you tend to be responsible, but can share control.
- Three or more c's—you tend to easily relinquish control over money.

According to Gurney, those who score high in involvement need control over their money to have peace of mind. To learn more about your attitudes toward money, visit her Web site at www.finpsych.com. The site contains a 28-question quiz dealing with money habits.

SOURCE: © 1999, Kathleen Gurney, Ph.D. Reprinted in "Your Money Personality Quiz," *Fidelity Focus,* Summer 1999, pp. 13, 15.

betting on the fluctuations in the future prices of commodities, such as "pork futures." Here we summarize a variety of popular investments ranging from the most conservative to the more speculative.

Certificates of Deposit

Banks and savings-and-loan associations offering certificates of deposit (CDs) require that you deposit a reasonably large sum of money for a specified time period. The time period can be anywhere from 30 days to 10 years. CDs come in denominations such as $500, $5,000, and $10,000, paying a rate of return in excess of the rate of inflation. If you have a considerable amount of cash and are not worried about having your money tied up for a fixed time period, CDs are ideal. Also, like other bank deposits, CDs are government insured. If you close one of these accounts before its due date, the amount of penalty lowers the interest rate to approximately that of an interest-bearing checking account.

Money Market Funds

Many people use these high-yielding but uninsured funds as an alternative to an ordinary bank deposit. Paying above the inflation rate, many money market funds can be used almost like checking accounts. Usually you need to invest an initial $2,500 in these funds. An important feature is that you have easy access to your money. Most funds allow you to write checks for amounts of $500 or more. The funds themselves charge a small, almost unnoticed management fee. They invest your money in high-yield, short-term investments, such as loans to the federal government or to top-quality business corporations.

U.S. Treasury Securities

The U.S. government offers five types of secure investments to the public: Treasury bills, Treasury notes, Treasury bonds, U.S. savings bonds, and Treasury inflation-indexed securities (also known as inflation-indexed Treasury bonds). Two notable advantages of Treasuries are (1) that they are exempt from state and local taxes and (2) that they always pay their face value when they mature. You may lose out considerably if you cash in your government bonds early, particularly with the inflation-indexed bonds. A general disadvantage of investing in Treasuries is that their yield is usually less than money market funds or corporate bonds. Long-term government bonds (such as 30 years), however, have returns quite competitive with corporate bonds.

Corporate Bonds

Large corporations sell bonds to the public to raise money to further invest in their business. Many of these bonds are 20- to 30-year loans. They pay a fixed rate of return, such as 5 or 7 percent. If you want to cash in your bond early, you may not be able to sell it for the original value, especially if interest rates rise. You would thus take a loss. You can, however, purchase a bond for less than its face value. You might be able to buy a $1,000 bond for $920, collect interest on it, and eventually redeem it for its face value. *Junk bonds* are bonds offering a high yield because they are rated as having a high risk. One reason could be that the firm offering them is facing financial trouble.

Junk bonds are best suited to big investors, but some mutual funds invest in them, making them accessible to smaller investors. High-yield bonds are best for people with a high tolerance for risk and a long-term time horizon.

Bonds can also be purchased through *bond funds* that diversify into many different bonds and are essentially a portfolio of bonds. Bond funds pay income every month, and they soften the risk of investing a large amount of money in the bonds of a company that defaults on its bonds. When the general stock market climbs, bond funds tend to decrease in value. The reverse is also true: When the stock market climbs, bond funds tend to increase in value. The reasoning is that when stocks increase in value, investors are less interested in bonds and vice versa.

Municipal Bonds

Similar in design to corporate bonds, municipal bonds are issued by governments of cities, states, and U.S. territories. "Munis" have strong appeal to many investors because of their tax-free status. Interest income from most municipal bonds is not taxed at the federal level and, in many cases, at state and local levels. Residents of the state in which a municipal bond is issued are also exempt from paying state income tax on the interest. Because of their tax-exempt status, munis pay lower interest rates than comparable taxable bonds. The higher your tax bracket, the more appealing a municipal bond. The formula to determine the tax-equivalent yields (what interest a taxable bond would have to pay to bring the same return) is

$$\frac{\text{tax - free yield}}{(1 - \text{tax rate})} = \text{tax-equivalent yield}$$

If the tax-free yield of a muni is 3 percent, a taxable bond would have to pay 4.17 percent, assuming you are fortunate enough to be in the 28 percent federal income tax bracket. Here is the basic math:

$$\frac{3\%}{1 - .28} = \frac{.03}{.72} = 0.417 = 4.17\%$$

If you also figure in state or provincial tax exemption, the tax-equivalent yield would be even higher. Paying state and local taxes lowers your effective federal tax rate because state and local taxes are deductible from federal taxes.

Common Stocks

Every reader of this book has heard of the stock market, a place where you can purchase shares of public corporations. On a given business day, it is not unusual for over one billion shares of stocks to be bought and sold on the American and Canadian stock exchanges. Common stocks are actually shares of ownership in the corporations issuing them. Stocks pay dividends, but the hope of most investors is that the stock will rise in value. The majority of buying and selling of stocks today is done by institutions rather than by small investors. These institutions include pension funds, banks, and mutual funds (described later).

Stock prices rise and fall over such tangible factors as a company's present and potential earnings, the price of oil, and fluctuations in interest rates. Yet good news in general, such as progress in peace talks, elevates stock prices. An example of the volatility in the stock market took place in 2000, when the stocks of many well-known high-technology companies dropped as much as 85 percent in value. The stock market, in general, dropped about 40 percent in value between the years 2000 and 2003.

To cope with these price fluctuations, investors are advised to use dollar-cost averaging. Using **dollar-cost averaging,** you invest the same amount of money in a stock or mutual fund at regular intervals over a long period of time. This eliminates the need for the difficult task of trying to time the highs and lows. Since you are investing a constant amount, you buy less when the price is high and more when the price is low. Over a long period of time, you pay a satisfactory price for your stock or mutual fund. One disadvantage of dollar-cost averaging is that if the value of the stock continues to rise, you would have been better off financially by making a lump-sum investment at the outset.

Table 15-2 illustrates dollar-cost averaging.

Mutual Funds

Since most people lack the time, energy, and knowledge to manage their own stock portfolios, mutual funds are increasingly relied on. The concept of mutual funds is straightforward. For a modest management fee, a small group of professional money managers invest your money, along with that of thousands of other people, into a broad group of common stocks. Numerous mutual funds exist to suit many different purposes and risk-taking attitudes. You can find mutual funds that invest in conservative, low-risk stocks or flashy, high-risk stocks. The latter tend to have a larger payoff if the company succeeds. Some funds specialize in particular industries, such as telecommunications or energy. Mutual funding is no longer restricted to stocks. Some mutual funds invest only in corporate bonds, government securities, or municipal bonds.

TABLE 15-2
HOW DOLLAR-COST AVERAGING WORKS

Month	Investment	Share Price	Shares Purchased
1	$200	$20	10
2	200	18	11.1
3	200	16	12.5
4	200	18	11.1
5	200	20	10
	$1,000	average = $18.4	54.7

NOTE: Your average cost per share is $18.28 (the total invested divided by the number of shares purchased). This figure is lower than if you had invested $1,000 in the first month at $20.

A type of mutual fund called an *index fund* has grown in favor in recent years. The idea behind an index fund is that it uses passive management. The fund automatically purchases the investments that make up a particular market index. Two such indexes are the Standard & Poor's 500 index of big-company stocks and the Russell 2000, representing small-company stocks. The objective is to meet but not surpass the performance of the fund's benchmark index. If the S&P index gains 15 percent in one month, so would the index fund minus a management fee of about .03 percent. Many investment specialists argue that it is difficult to beat the benefits of a good index fund, particularly because its fees are lower than other mutual funds. Many managers of mutual funds, however, present evidence that their active management results in better investment gains.

The image of mutual funds has been tarnished in recent years because of scandal associated with giving preferential treatment to big customers over ordinary investors. An example would be letting these people purchase funds after hours at prices that would guarantee profits for trading the next day if the value of the fund increased that day. Such "late trading" is illegal.

Real Estate

A natural starting point in making money in real estate is to purchase a single-family dwelling, maintain it carefully, and live in it for many years. Temporary downturns in the housing market should not deter the patient investor. In the long run, most homes increase in value equal to or faster than inflation. A subtle advantage of home ownership (condos included) is that you are likely to hold on the investment for longer than a stock, bond, or mutual fund. Home owners receive many tax benefits, such as income tax deductions on mortgage interest and interest paid for home equity loans (loans using your house as collateral). Real estate taxes are fully tax deductible. As with any other form of real estate investment, the long-term trend has been for homes to increase in value beyond the rate of inflation. In recent years, however, many home owners throughout the United States have had to sell homes at a loss because real estate values declined. Another concern about home ownership as an investment is that houses can become "money pits" that require spending on repairs, insurance, and taxes.

An investment that is really a form of business ownership is income property—real estate that you rent to tenants. The activities required of a landlord include collecting rent, resolving conflicts among tenants, and maintenance, such as fixing broken water pipes and painting rooms. The highest returns from income property are derived from rehabilitating dilapidated property—if the owner does most of the physical work. Many people who own income property receive almost no operating profit from their work and investment in the early years. However, in the long run, the property increases in value. Also, because the mortgage payments remain stable and rents keep increasing, monthly profits gradually appear.

An indirect way to invest in real estate is through a real estate investment trust, or **REIT,** a pooling of many people's money to invest in real estate or mortgages. REITs must distribute at least 90 percent of taxable income to shareholders, but they avoid corporate taxes. REITs invest in properties such as apartment buildings, office buildings, shopping malls, and even real estate companies. The value of REITs as investments rises and falls with the overall real estate market. Real estate mutual funds are another way to invest in real estate without owning physical property because they invest in REITs as well a real estate operating companies.

Gold Bullion

Gold has long been considered a sound long-term investment despite declining prices in recent years. In January 1980, gold sold for $875 an ounce, in early 2001 it sold for $535, and in March 2004 it sold for $399. For many years, hoarding gold coins or bars was considered an intelligent hedge against inflation and global unrest. Gold still has its fans who think that it is a solid investment in an unstable world. Even when the price of gold is rising, it still has two key disadvantages. Gold has to be stored safely, and it pays no dividends or interest. Another way to invest in gold is to purchase gold funds, which tend to perform well during uncertain economic times. For example, in 2002, when most investments plunged in value, gold funds increased an average of 62.9 percent. A caution is that gold jewelry is not likely to increase substantially in value when gold or gold funds increase because much of the value in gold jewelry stems from the handcrafting.

Coins, Antiques, Paintings, and Other Collectibles

An enjoyable way of investing is to purchase coins and objects of art that you think will escalate in value. Almost anything could become a collectible, including stamps, old advertising items, or even today's combination of cell telephone and camera. You have to be both patient and lucky to cash in on collectibles. You should have a sound, diversified investment program before you invest your money in collectibles. If you are looking for an expensive hobby that might pay off financially, however, collectibles are ideal. As an investment, collectibles are high risk

Life Insurance and Variable Annuities

An investment plan should include life insurance for two reasons. First, the proceeds from life insurance protect dependents against the complete loss of income from the deceased provider. Second, most forms of life insurance accumulate cash, thus making such insurance a profitable investment. The exception is term life insurance, which is much like insurance on a house or car. To figure out how much life insurance is necessary, calculate what would be required to support your family members until they can take care of themselves without your income. Take into account all assets in addition to life insurance. If you are single, consider the financial help you are providing loved ones.

Variable annuities are related to life insurance because they offer a death benefit and are geared toward retirement. The beneficiary receives either the initial investment or the plan's current value, whichever is greater. A variable annuity allows the investor to make regular contributions without having to pay taxes on any gains until retirement. The investment, whether it be money market funds, stocks, or mutual funds, compounds tax free until withdrawn. In the past, variable annuities carried high commissions, but now many are being offered online at a much lower cost.

Choosing the Right Mix of Investments (Asset Allocation)

A major investment decision is how to allocate your investments among short-term interest-bearing accounts (including cash), stocks, and bonds, and real estate. The best answer depends on such factors as your career stage, age, and tolerance for risk. In general, younger people are in a better position to take investment risks than those nearing retirement. Yet young people who need money for major items such as education or a down payment on a house or apartment may want to avoid high-risk investments. (In many large cities, apartments are sold just like houses.)

A starting point in choosing the right mix of investments is to use the following rule of thumb: If you invest in stocks, subtract your age from 100, giving you about the percentage that should be in stocks. If you are 25, about 75 percent of your portfolio should be in stocks. About two-thirds of the balance should be in bonds, the rest in cash. The 25-year-old would therefore invest about 17 percent in bonds and 8 percent in cash (or cash equivalents, such as money market funds). If you are 100 years old, take all your money out of the stock market and put it in bonds and cash. A default position for people who are uncertain about what mix of investments is best is to invest 60 percent in equities and 40 percent in fixed-income instruments. In selecting the right mix of investments, choose among five diversification strategies with respect to risk:

1. *Capital preservation*—you want to preserve you capital without taking too much risk

2. *Income*—you want your investments to generate income

3. *Income and growth*—you want to generate income from your investments but you also want growth

4. *Growth*—you want your investments to grow

5. *Aggressive growth*—you are willing to take high risks to win big

No matter which one of these five strategies you choose, it is sound to have first invested in real estate, not including REITs, or real estate mutual funds. The rest of your investments can then be placed in the five categories. Remember that real estate is so named because it is *real*. These five investment strategies are the basis for the broad guidelines presented in Exhibit 15-4. The stocks in your portfolio should be mixed among stocks of large company stocks, midcompany stocks, small company stocks, and international stocks.

As implied by the five different investment strategies, selecting the right portfolio of investments for you depends somewhat on emotional factors. For example, if you are a risk taker and thrill seeker, you would feel comfortable with an aggressive growth strategy. A field of study called *behavioral economics* deals with some of the emotional factors in investing. As mentioned earlier, one such factor is the enormous dislike many people have for losing money. People hate losses much more than they enjoy gains. This is why most investors in stocks demand much higher returns from them to compensate for the dread of losses.

EXHIBIT 15-4

Selecting the Right Mix of Investments

Investor Profile	Stocks	Bonds	Cash
Capital preservation	10%	55%	35%
Income	30%	60%	10%
Income and growth	40%	50%	10%
Growth	70%	25%	5%
Aggressive growth	80%	10%	10%

SOURCE: "Tired of Stock Market Volatility: Bonds May Offer Relief," *Merrill Lynch & You,* June 2000, p. 2.

Another key behavioral is that people procrastinate. Many people who are well aware of the importance of financial planning early in life keep procrastinating even when they have some discretionary money to get started investing. The chore of planning seems such a burden, and the loss of delaying planning for a few days seems insignificant. In reality, every day without a financial plan can result in lost opportunity in the long run.[6]

RELATIVE RETURNS OF STOCKS AND BONDS

Another key factor in choosing among investments is their relative returns in the past. The past may not guarantee future performance, but it serves as a reliable predictor. Between 1972 and 2003, large-company stocks have returned about 10.7 percent annually and corporate bonds about 5 percent. Intermediate Treasury bonds have paid about 5.1 percent and three-month Treasury bills about 3.6 percent. The inflation rate over the same periods has been about 3 percent. Throughout the period 1990–2000, investment yields improved over the long-term historical pattern. During this period, the annual return averaged about 17.5 percent for stocks, 12 percent for corporate bonds, and 6 percent for long-term Treasury bills. During the period 2000–2003, investment yields turned sharply down. Stocks returned a negative 9 percent, corporate bonds about 6 percent, and long-term Treasury bills about 4 percent.

The attractive return on investment from stocks over the years is forthcoming only to those who invest in a portfolio of stocks or mutual funds that match or exceed average returns. A person could easily invest in stocks that become worthless or have substantially below-average returns. A person could also invest in bonds of a company that defaulted on the bonds. Mutual funds, including index funds that invest in a portfolio of stocks, are less likely to be poor investments.

Another caution is that investing in stocks, bonds, and mutual funds with taxable returns can be expensive to continue. For example, you must pay income taxes on part of the returns from mutual funds annually, even if you did not cash in the investments. Some people wind up selling off portions of their portfolios or borrowing money just to pay taxes on a profit that exists only on paper.

▲ MANAGING AND PREVENTING DEBT

Debt is inevitable for most people. Few people are wealthy enough or have sufficient self-discipline to avoid debt entirely. Major purchases, such as a house, cooperative apartment, postsecondary education, or automobile, usually require borrowing. Dealing with debt is therefore an important component of managing your personal finances. Here we describe three major aspects of managing and preventing debt: credit management, getting out of debt, and staying out of debt.

MANAGING CREDIT WISELY

Credit management is a problem for many people of all career stages. The number of people filing for bankruptcy in the United States has been climbing steadily, with over 1.8 million people filing annually. Millions of other working people struggle with making car payments, installment loans, and insurance premiums. Borrowing money, of course, is not inherently evil. Imagine what would happen to the banking industry and the economy if nobody borrowed money. Some borrowing in your early career is desirable because without a credit record, it is difficult to obtain automobile loans and home mortgages. Good credit is also important because prospective landlords and employers carefully consider an applicant's creditworthiness. Consider the following guidelines for the wise use of credit.[7]

1. Recognize the difference between good debt and bad debt. Good debt finances something that will benefit you in the future, such as a house, education, or self-development. Bad debt typically finances something that you consume almost immediately or that provides little real benefit. Borrowing for a trip to a gambling casino, including money for betting, might fall into this category.

2. Prepare a monthly budget to determine how much debt (if any) you can afford to assume. As a general rule, limit your total borrowing to 15 to 20 percent of monthly take-home pay, not including a house mortgage payment.

3. Stick to one major credit card and perhaps your favorite department store's charge card. At the same time, avoid lending your credit card to friends. Cards on loan to friends can be lost, stolen, or misused. When you own multiple credit cards, there is more temptation to lend one.

4. Before accepting any new extension of credit, review your budget to see if you can handle it easily. You will have less need for a credit extension if you wait two weeks before making purchases

that seem desirable at the time. After the two-week cooling-off period, many of the purchases will seem unimportant.

5. A home owner with substantial equity accumulated should consider a home equity loan for financing a major purchase, such as an automobile or educational expenses. The interest on home equity loans is fully tax deductible. However, resist the temptation to pay for a $750 refrigerator for 15 years.

6. Make monthly payments on your debts large enough to reduce the principal on your credit cards and other loans. Otherwise, you may be paying almost all interest and making small progress toward paying off the loan.

7. Even as you are paying off debts, set aside some savings each month. Attempt to increase your savings as little as $15 per month. Within two years, you will be saving a substantial amount of money.

8. If you are unable to pay your bills, talk to your creditors immediately. Explain your situation and let them know you plan to somehow meet your debt obligations. Agree to a payment schedule you can meet. Never ignore bills. Many employers will not hire a job applicant with a bad credit record.

9. Choose personal bankruptcy only as a last, desperate option. A bankruptcy filing will remain on your credit record for 7 to 10 years. Creditors may look on you as a bad risk even 10 years after filing bankruptcy. Future employers may be wary of hiring a person who was such a poor money manager. Of even greater significance, bankruptcy may result in a substantial blow to your self-esteem.

WORKING YOUR WAY OUT OF DEBT

Working your way out of debt is a major component of debt management. Heavy debt that forces you to postpone savings and investments can also create adverse amounts of stress. You must therefore assertively attack your debts to improve your general well-being. How do you know if you are too far in debt? Human Relations Self-Assessment Quiz 15-1 provides an answer.[8]

A recommended strategy of reducing debt is to **concentrate on one bill at a time.** According to this technique, you first pay off your smallest debt with a variable payment and then concentrate on your next-smallest variable-payment debt. You keep concentrating on one bill at a time until the last debt is eliminated. The technique is illustrated and described in Exhibit 15-5.

A financial specialist might rightfully contend that some loans are un-economic to discharge more quickly than required. The interest rate you pay on such loans might be less than the return you would earn by investing your extra payments elsewhere, such as in growth stocks. Although this is true from a financial standpoint, the biggest return on your investment from a mental health standpoint is getting out of debt.

A more conventional approach to reducing debt is to apply any money available for debt repayment to the loan bearing the highest interest. Ordinarily this would be credit card debt or unsecured loans. (The latter are

---

HUMAN RELATIONS SELF-ASSESSMENT QUIZ 15-1

Are You Too Far in Debt?

1. Is an increasing percentage of your income being spent to pay debts?

2. Do you use credit to buy many of the things you bought in the past for cash?

3. Are you paying bills with money targeted for something else?

4. Have you taken out loans to consolidate your debts or asked for extensions on existing loans to reduce monthly payments?

5. Does your checkbook balance get lower by the month?

6. Do you pay the minimum amount due on your charge accounts each month?

7. Do you get repeated dunning notices (letters demanding payments) from your creditors?

8. Are you threatened with repossession of your car or cancellation of your credit cards or with other legal action?

9. Have you been drawing on your savings to pay regular bills that you used to pay out of your paycheck?

10. Do you depend on extra income, such as overtime and part-time work, to get to the end of the month?

11. Do you take out new installment loans before old ones are paid off?

12. Is your total savings less than three months' take-home pay?

13. Is your total installment credit (not counting mortgage) more than 20 percent of your take-home pay?

14. Do you become horrorstruck when you look at your credit card bills?

15. Has a credit card company *rejected* your application in the past two years?

If your answer is yes to two or more of the above questions, financial counselors would advise you to declare war on some of your debts.

---

lent by finance companies and often carry charges up to 24 percent.) By paying off loans carrying the highest interest, you pay less in debt. Another debt reduction tactic is to pay more than the minimum on all loans that allow for variable payment. If you pay only the minimum demanded by most credit card issuers, it might take 12 years to pay off the balance. In the interim, you would pay far more in interest than the purchase price of the goods and services being bought on time.

Switching to a credit card with lower interest is another way of reducing interest payments. You pay off the old credit card debt by borrowing

EXHIBIT 15-5

Heath and Judy Concentrate on One Bill at a Time

After 17 years of marriage, Heath and Judy had acquired an upsetting level of debt. Part of their problem was the debt they had accumulated in the process of acquiring two two-family houses that they used as income property. At the urging of a financial counselor, Heath and Judy scrutinized both their debts and their spending habits. Their debt picture looked like this:

Type of Loan	Approximate Balance on Loan	Monthly Payment
Auto	$2,850	$215
Home improvement	1,975	149
Visa	1,828	85
MasterCard	1,859	95
Furnaces for income properties	2,562	185
Tuition	800	90
Orthodontist	750	75
	$12,624	$894

An indebtedness of $12,624 may not seem extreme. Nevertheless, in terms of their living expenses, including the support of three children, $894 a month of debt was creating stress for Heath and Judy. The couple might have tried the traditional debt reduction program of spreading out their monthly debt reduction fund over all their bills. In so doing, they would have tried to make approximately equal payments to all creditors. Instead, Heath and Judy chose to reduce their debts by concentrating first on the variable-payment debt with the smallest balance. In other words, they concentrated first on the debt that they were capable of eliminating first.

Following this strategy, Heath and Judy began their debt reduction program by first working down the Visa debt. Each month they would put as much money as they could spare into their Visa payment, even though they had previously paid only $85 monthly for that particular bill. The couple kept making minimum payments to MasterCard until their Visa balance was reduced to zero. Then came big progress when they were able to make two double payments. (The general principle is to eliminate, one by one, each of the loans for which variable—rather than fixed—payments are possible. In addition, take on new debts for emergency purposes only.)

The preceding case history indicates that an effective program of debt reduction involves both financial and emotional issues. Getting rid of debts one by one provides an important emotional boost to the debtor. As the debts are peeled off, tension is reduced. The one-debt-at-a-time strategy is also tied in with goal theory. You experience a feeling of accomplishment as each debt is eliminated. Simultaneously, you are motivated to tackle the next variable debt.

money from the new credit card. Begin payments the first month to avoid incurring extra interest charges.

If you are having problems getting out of debt despite using the tactics just described, the problem could be that you are spending too much. To remedy the situation, you can either earn more income or reduce discretionary spending. Look for even minor savings. Many people, for example, are surprised to learn how much they are spending on soft drinks. Purchasing store-brand soft drinks in bulk or drinking water instead of soft drinks can result in more money for debt reduction.

Debt consolidation loans are widely used by people whose expenses exceed their income. The consolidation loan means that you pay off all your debts with one large loan and then proceed to tackle the one big loan. The emotional relief can be substantial, but you will be extending your indebtedness well into the future, often at a higher interest rate than the average rate of your existing loans. Suppose you borrowed $10,000 for 60 months at 8.99 percent to consolidate your loans. Your monthly payments would be $210, for total payments of $12,600. You would be paying 26 percent of the $10,000 loan in finance charges.

STAYING OUT OF DEBT

No one who bought things for cash only ever went bankrupt. Cash also refers to money orders, checks drawn against funds that you legitimately have on hand, and debit cards. If you buy only things that you can actually pay for at the moment of purchase, you may suffer some hardships. It would be agonizing if you needed dental treatment but had to wait until payday to have a broken tooth repaired. On balance, these are small miseries to endure in comparison with the misery of being overburdened with debt. For many people, preoccupation with debt interferes with work concentration and sleep.

Staying out of debt is often difficult because the debtor has deep-rooted problems that prompt him or her to use credit. Among these problems are the following:

- Perceiving material objects as a way of gaining status

- Purchasing goods and services to relieve depression

- Incurring heavy charges to get even with a spouse or family member

- Believing that the world owes him or her a higher standard of living

Having problems of this nature may require both debt counseling and personal counseling. Unless the person understands his or her emotional problems surrounding borrowing money, the cycle of going into debt and then struggling to get out of debt will continue.

PREPARING AN ANNUAL NET WORTH ANALYSIS

A potentially uplifting strategy of managing your finances is to chart your yearly financial status. You can accomplish this by annually evaluating your **net worth,** the difference between your assets and liabilities. Net worth is considered a much better barometer of your financial stability than the amount of money you earn or the value of your investment portfolio.[9]

Your asset list should begin with **liquid assets,** those that can be converted into cash relatively quickly. Personal belongings should be valued only at what they could be sold for now, not the purchase price. A house or condominium contributes to your net worth if you have accumulated equity. (Equity is the net price you could receive for a house minus the mortgage balance, real estate commissions, and closing costs.)

Net worth analyses for two years are presented in Exhibit 15-6. The person who prepared both reports was in financial difficulty when the first report was prepared. Notice the progress this individual has made over the

---

EXHIBIT 15-6

Net Worth Comparison Between Two Years

Assets	December 31, Year 1	December 31, Year 4
House equity (based on market value)	$28,000	$38,000
Cash in checking account	141	392
Cash on hand	75	315
Savings account	118	792
Mutual fund	—	896
Car resale value	3,600	1,800
Jewelry resale value	850	2,000
	$32,784	$44,195
Liabilities		
Auto payments	$3,500	—
Visa	1,215	$350
MasterCard	2,150	1400
American Express	850	80
Sears charge	1550	1128
Home improvement loan	3,975	—
Loan from uncle	895	—
Property tax due	850	350
School tax due	650	350
Plumber	275	400
	$15,910	$4,058

four-year period. In the first year, his liquid assets aside from his home equity and car resale value totaled $1,184. Including house and car, his assets were $32,784. Thanks in part to both self-discipline and modest inflation, his assets jumped to $44,195 four years later. Without the house equity and car resale value, his liquid assets were $4,395.

The liability picture is even more impressive. In the first year, the man had outstanding debts of $15,910. Four years later, his debts had shrunk to $4,058. His liability position had improved an enviable $11,852. Over the same period, his asset picture had improved $11,411. Adding both improvements together, we are able to give the individual a financial improvement score of $23,263 for the four-year period. Recognize, however, that the $10,000 growth in house equity was a major contributing factor to his financial improvement.

▲ HOW TO RETIRE RICH

Many people do not prepare adequately for the financial aspects of retirement. According to the Employee Benefit Research Institute, 29 percent of American workers say that have not yet begun to save for retirement. Furthermore, 61 percent have not calculated how much they will need to invest to attain their retirement goal.[10] If you start investing early in your career, you can retire rich even without earning exceptional compensation or winning a lottery. The basic idea is to start a systematic savings and investment plan set aside for retirement only. The dividends and interest paid on these investments are not taxed until retirement, and they keep compounding. As a result, you wind up with an extraordinary amount of money at the end of your career. Details about several of these retirement investment plans are presented next.

Whichever retirement plan you enter, remember to follow the key investment principle of asset allocation. Your retirement funds should be divided among stocks, bonds, short-term notes and cash, and real estate. In addition to these personal investments, many workers receive retirement income from Social Security, company pension plans or 401(k) plans, and individual retirement accounts. Financial planners often recommend that people will need about 75 percent of their preretirement incomes to live comfortably during retirement. The following paragraphs describe several of the most popular retirement programs.

Social Security Benefits

Citizens who qualify in terms of employment experience received security benefits. The Social Security Administration makes available a Personal Earnings and Benefit Statement that estimates how much retirement income a person can anticipate at ages 62, 65, 67, or older. In addition, the statement estimates survivor and disability benefits. Social Security pays approximately an entry-level office worker salary to individuals who were middle-class wage earners. For example, the average monthly benefit for Social Security recipients in 2004 was $922 for individuals and $1,523 for couples. The maximum benefit was $1,825 per month.

Social Security payments are adjusted for inflation periodically, as measured by Consumer Price Index. Social Security retirement benefits are subject to income tax. For example, a couple with a combined income of more than $44,000 must pay tax on up to 85 percent of their benefits.

Employee Pensions and 401(k) Plans

Many employers in both the private and the public sector offer pensions to long-term employees. Some of these pensions pay around 60 percent of the employee's salary at the time of retirement in addition to medical insurance. However, not everybody stays with one employer for many years, and some companies go bankrupt or misuse pension funds, thus putting your retirement pay at risk. The most widely used company-related retirement programs are 401(k) plans in which the employer and employee both contribute. An employer, for example, might contribute 35 percent as much as the employee contributes. However, the employee essentially owns the money in the plan and can move it from one employer to another. A major advantage of a 401(k) plan is that a person can take the money in a lump sum in retirement rather than receiving a guaranteed monthly payout as with an annuity.

Your 401(k) plan can be invested in stocks, bonds, and many other types of investments. Each plan sets a limit on the percentage of your current salary that you can contribute to the plan. The Internal Revenue Service also sets limits, which were 15 percent of your salary up to a maximum of $10,500 in 2000. Some employers contribute 50 cents or more for every dollar you contribute. Provided that you stay with the employer for a specified period of time, such as three to five years, you can keep the matching contribution. A 401(k) plan held for many years goes a long way toward paying for most people's retirement. A problem noted with 401(k) plans is that the employee has too much discretion in making allocations and might therefore make imprudent investment decisions.

Supplemental Retirement Annuities

Another way of investing your own money in a company-sponsored plan is to purchase **supplemental retirement annuities (SRAs).** These fixed and variable tax-deferred annuities enable you to invest money through your employer's payroll retirement system on a pretax basis. You make investments beyond the regular retirement plan offered by your employer, and these investments are deducted automatically from your pay. The key advantages of an SRA are that you have a tax-deferred investment and at the same time you lower your tax liability for the current year. The lower tax occurs because contributions are made before you pay taxes, leading to a lower tax bill. A potential disadvantage of an SRA is that your take-home pay may shrink too much to meet current expenses. You might prefer to make variable investments, depending on monthly expenses.

Individual Retirement Accounts and Simplified Employee Plans

Retirement accounts held by individuals rather than offered by employers can be used to invest in most of the types of savings and investments described earlier. Both **individual retirement accounts (IRAs)** and **simplified employee plans (SEPs)** are popular because they offer generous tax savings. An IRA is a supplemental retirement account, fully funded by the individual, that qualifies for certain tax advantages. Anyone, including government employees with earned income, may open an IRA. Single workers may contribute up to $2,000 per year. One-paycheck couples may invest up to $2,250 annually. Two-paycheck couples may contribute up to $4,000 a year if both work and each earns at least $2,000. Distributions from your IRA may begin as early as 591/2 but must begin by 701/2. Early withdrawal incurs a 10 percent penalty plus the payment of taxes on the amount withdrawn.

IRA contributions are tax deductible only for individuals who are not active participants in an employer-sponsored retirement plan. Also, employees with moderate incomes are eligible for some tax deductions from an IRA. Dividends and interest from an IRA are not taxed as long as they are not withdrawn. When you begin withdrawals, IRA distributions are taxed as ordinary income. Roth IRAs, designed for families earning less than $150,000 annually ($100,000 for individuals), offer several advantages over traditional IRAs. Although you cannot deduct Roth contributions, your money grows tax free, permanently. As long as you leave your savings in a Roth IRA for a minimum of five years and you wait until you are 591/2 to withdraw the money, the IRA earnings will never be taxed. All the money can be withdrawn when you reach age 60, and you can even leave the entire some in your estate.

SEPs are retirement plans for individuals who are self-employed or for those who earn part of their income from self-employment. SEPs and IRAs follow many of the same rules, with several exceptions. First, to qualify, you must earn some self-employment income. Second, you can invest up to 15 percent of your self-employment income in a SEP tax free. An individual can hold an IRA and a SEP.

The dramatic financial returns from an IRA or SEP are shown in Table 15-3, which assumes that a person invested $2,000 each year. Much of the growth in funds is attributable to compound interest and no withdrawals on which to pay taxes. Even though you pay taxes on your IRA and SEP accounts when you make withdrawals, you profit because you had more money working for the length of your investment. For example, your yearly contribution of $2,000 is invested instead of the $2,000 minus tax you could invest if you did not place the money in an IRA or SEP.

Despite all we have said in this chapter about saving and investing for the long term, all retirement investments must be balanced against the importance of having a joyful present life. You might want to invest in the pleasure of mountain climbing now even though that same amount of money might be worth 10 times as much when you are 85. Yet at 85 you might not be able to climb mountains. Some people contend they want to run

TABLE 15-3
How IRAs Can Grow

Years of Contribution	Rate of Return		
	8%	10%	12%
5	$ 11,733	$ 12,210	$ 12,705
10	$ 12,973	$ 31,875	$ 35,097
15	$ 54,304	$ 63,544	$ 74,559
20	$ 91,524	$114,550	$144,104
25	$146,212	$196,694	$266,667
30	$226,566	$328,998	$482,554
35	$344,634	$542,048	$863,326

NOTE: This chart assumes a $2,000 yearly contribution at year end, compound interest, and no tax payments.

out of retirement money exactly on the last day of their life. Few people can plan with such precision, so a good bet is to invest in both the long term and present happiness.

▲ SUMMARY

An important part of managing your personal life is to manage your personal finances in such a way that money is not a major source of worry and concern in your life. Financial problems often lead to marital problems, for example.

Setting financial goals is an important starting point in managing your personal finances. Such goals can be expressed in dollars, the type of things you would like to accomplish with money, or the type of lifestyle you would like to lead.

A vital aspect of financial management is to establish a budget or spending plan, which can be divided into six steps: (1) establishing goals; (2) estimating income; (3) estimating expenses; (4) comparing expenses and income; (5) carrying out the budget; and (6) evaluating the budget.

An effective spending plan allows room for investing. Basic investment principles include (1) spending less money than you earn; (2) investing early and steadily to capitalize on the benefits of compounding; (3) keeping reinvesting dividends; (4) diversifying your investments (use asset allocation); (5) maintaining a disciplined, long-term approach; (6) practicing contrary investing; (7) investing globally as well as domestically; and (8) paying off debt.

The two basic types of investments are fixed-income investments and equity investments. All investments carry some risk, and you must decide how much and what types of risk you can tolerate.

Among the many ways of investing or saving money are the following: certificates of deposit; money-market funds; U.S. Treasury securities; corporate bonds; municipal bonds; common stocks; mutual funds; real estate; gold bullion; coins, antiques, paintings, and other collectibles; and life insurance and variable annuities.

A major investment decision is how to allocate your investments among short-term interest-bearing accounts, stocks, and bonds. Younger people should typically hold more stocks. In selecting the right mix of investments, choose among diversification strategies with respect to risk. Emotional factors, particularly risk toleration, influence the choice of investments.

Common stocks pay higher rates of return than corporate or government bonds. However, the return on a given stock or mutual fund is less predictable than bonds held to maturity. Yearly taxes must be paid on some of the profits from mutual funds, stocks, and corporate bonds.

Managing and preventing debt is an important component of managing personal finances. To use credit wisely, recognize the difference between good debt and bad debt. Limit your total borrowing to 15 to 20 percent of monthly take-home pay, not including a house mortgage payment. Using credit cards wisely includes such factors as restricting their use, selectively using a home equity loan, and making more than the minimum monthly payments on loans.

One way of working your way out of debt is to concentrate on one bill at a time—try to pay off first your variable payment with the smallest balance. To stay out of debt, pay for goods and services with cash or check and therefore stop borrowing money. We recommend a yearly financial checkup by preparing a list of your liquid assets and liabilities. Progress is measured in terms of the difference between assets and liabilities. The bigger the positive difference, the better your financial health.

People who start a retirement savings or investment program early in their careers may accumulate large sums of money by retirement. Asset allocation is a major strategy for accumulating retirement funds. Social security benefits contributed modestly to retirement. Employee pensions and 401(k) plans (a portable self-directed pension) are major contributors to funding retirement. An SRA is another vehicle for tax-deferred retirement investing. In addition, consider an individual IRA or SEP.

Question and Activities

1. What types of human relations problems might people avoid by carefully managing their finances?

2. Assume that after preparing a budget, you conclude that your expenses must be reduced by 10 percent. What cuts would you make?

3. It has often been observed that the majority of people who file for bankruptcy have incomes that are well above average. How can this be?

4. How might good work habits and time management help a person make good use of a budget?

5. How can a person resolve the conflict between investing money for the long range and buying things he or she wants right now?

6. What is the difference between having a high income and being wealthy? How can this difference in meaning provide people an important lesson?

7. During the stock market downturn during 2000 through 2003, some people heavily invested in technology stocks lost 95 percent of the value of their investments. How does this event influence your attitudes toward investing for the future?

8. If you think you will live at least 100 years, how will this affect your investment strategy?

9. How can you use the Internet to reduce your cost of living?

10. Talk to a retired person and inquire what, if anything, he or she would do differently to plan financially for retirement. Be prepared to discuss your findings in class.

INTERNET SKILL BUILDER: What's Your FICO (Credit) Score?

A necessary part of building a good financial future is to be aware of your credit rating. One of the widely accepted methods of rating people's creditworthiness is FICO, the credit score system offered by Fair Issac Corporation. Your credit score is obviously important when you need to borrow money and is also used by some prospective employers to help judge your dependability. FICO scores range from a low of 300 to a high of 850. Each person has three FICO scores, each based on one of the three national credit reporting agencies, TransUnion, Equifax, and Experian. You are able to purchase your FICO scores and the accompanying credit report and view them online at www.myfico.com for $13 each. Even if you are not ready to invest in obtaining your credit score, you might profit from studying the Score Power® Sample at www.equifax.com. Score Power divides your credit history into different categories and offers suggestions for improving your score over time. After your receive your credit score, compare it to your self-evaluation of your creditworthiness.

A HUMAN RELATIONS CASE PROBLEM

The Problem Budget

The spending plan presented below was submitted by Greg Walters, a 28-year-old man with a good job. He says that owning a home and entertaining his friends are important parts of his lifestyle. Yet he also contends, "I'm committing slow-motion financial

(Continued)

suicide. Each month I go further into debt. Right now I don't see a good way out unless I give up a lot of things that are important to me. You've got to have fun in life, don't you?"

Review Greg's budget and make some specific recommendations to him for improving his financial health. Also, what flaws do you find in his logic?

Budget for Greg Walters

Monthly Expenses		Monthly Income	
Fixed:		Salary	$4,375
Mortgage or rent	$ 825	Tips	
Property insurance	55	Bonuses and commissions	
Health insurance	45	Interest and dividends	1
Auto insurance	55	Insurance benefits	
Other insurance	40	Child support received	
Educational expenses	125	Other	
Internet Service Provider	22		
Satellite TV	45	Total income	$4,376
Taxes:			
Federal	765		
State or provincial	225		
Social security	218	*Summary:*	
Local		Total income	$4,376
Property	190	Less total expenses	4,560
Installment loans (auto		Balance for savings	
and others)	330	and investment	(184)
Set aside for emergencies	0		
Variable:			
Food and beverage	275		
Household supplies	55		
Home maintenance	85		
Medical and dental	50		
Telephone	75		
Clothing	140		
Hair care and cosmetics	65		
Transportation	110		
Car maintenance	135		
Entertainment including			
pay-per-view TV	175		
Travel and vacation	275		
Clubs/organizations	145		
Hobbies	35		
Total expenses	$ 4,560		

WEB CORNER

Cost-of-living comparisons between cities: www.cityrating.com/costofliving.asp

Mutual fund profiles: http://biz.yahoo.com/i

Personal finance: www.financecenter.com

Social Security retirement planner: www.ssa.gov/retirecharted.htm

Treatment of money disorders related to other addictive behavior: www.themeadows.org

▲ REFERENCES

1. Rachel Emma Silverman, "Why You Waste So Much Money," *Wall Street Journal,* July 16, 2003, p. D1.

2. Frank Bilovsky, "Budgets Can Help Down the Road," *Rochester (NY) Democrat and Chronicle,* January 26, 2003, p. 3E.

3. Dalbar Inc. study cited in Ian McDonald, "Study Shows Investors Lack Timing," The *Wall Street Journal,* July 16, 2003, p. D7.

4. Quoted in "The $3 Billion Man Shares His Secret," *Invest,* September 1993, p. 10.

5. Research by Daniel Kahneman and Mark W. Riepe cited in *HandSignals,* OppenheimerFunds Shareholder Newsletter, November 2002, p. 1.

6. Charles J. Whalen, "Putting a Human Face on Economics," *BusinessWeek,* July 31, 2000, pp. 76–77.

7. "Taking Control of Debt," *Aide Magazine,* December 1993, pp. 17–28; "Credit Card Pitfalls: How to Help Your College Student Avoid the Credit Trap," *USAA Magazine,* August/September 1996, pp. 27–29; Jean Sherman Chatzy, "He Spends, She Spends," *USA Weekend,* June 2–4, 2000, p. 4; David Grainger, "The Suzie Orman Show," *Fortune,* June 16, 2003, pp. 82–88.

8. "Debt-Danger Signal Quiz," *Aide Magazine,* December 1992, p. 26; Jane Bryant Quinn, "More People Facing Personal Credit Crisis," syndicated column, September 10, 1991.

9. "How to Figure Out Your Net Worth," *Women's Consumer Network Straight Talk,* March/April 2000, p. 1.

10. Survey cited in T. Shawn Taylor, "Retirement Saving Put on Hold," *Chicago Tribune,* October 5, 2003.

▲ ADDITIONAL READING

Anuff, Joey, and Gary Wolf. *Dumb Money: Adventures of a Day Trader.* New York: Random House, 2000.

Graham, Benjamin. *The Intelligent Investor—Revised Edition.* New York: Harper-Business, 1973. New material, copyright © 2003 by Jason Sweig.

Grainger, David. "The Suzie Orman Show." *Fortune,* June 16, 2003, pp. 82–88.

Kiyosaki, Robert T, with Sharon Lechter. *Rich Dad, Poor Dad: A Tale of Two Fathers—One Rich, One Poor.* Niles, IL: Nightingale Conant, undated.

Morse, Walena C. "Risk Taking In Personal Investments." *Journal of Business and Psychology,* Winter 1998, pp. 281–288.

Pentila, Chris. "Risky Business: Should a Prospective Employee's Credit History Determine whether He or She Gets the Job?" *Entrepreneur,* September 2003, pp. 78–79.

CHAPTER
16

Finding Happiness and Enhancing Your Personal Life

Learning Objectives

After studying the information and doing the exercises in this chapter, you should be able to:

◆ Explain how happiness is contingent on keeping the various spheres of life in balance

◆ Specify factors that contribute to personal happiness

◆ Describe a plan for meeting a romantic partner

◆ Explain how partners can meet the challenge of being a two-income couple

◆ Choose among techniques for keeping a relationship of yours vibrant

When it comes to finding that special someone, Steve Lee waxes analytic: In 16 months, the Manhattan hedge-fund manager sped through 2,500 three-minute HurryDates, at about $1.45 per day, not to mention 100 "real dates" that lasted at least the length of a cup of coffee.

"I take a very practical approach to finding the right person," says Lee, a Wharton Business School graduate who likens the dating market to the stock market, tossing around terms such as "liquidity" and "market value." In fact, if he had his druthers, those minidates would last a minute, just enough time to gauge someone's personality and whether "they have bad breath."

Last September, 495 days into this, his "second full-time job," Lee found social worker Elyse Hart, 30, "by far the most amazing person I've met in my life." They've made it past date number 10. The marriage proposal? That's scheduled for "around February 7."[1]

Some people would criticize Steve Lee for being too planned and business-like in his approach to finding romance. Yet the point he illustrates is profoundly important. A meaningful romantic relationship is so important for a person's well-being that finding such a relationship merits extensive effort and attention. In this final chapter, we look at some of the major issues involved in leading an enriched personal life: the components of happiness, finding a partner, managing a two-income relationship, and keeping a relationship vibrant.

▲ ACHIEVING HAPPINESS

When asked what is the most important thing in life, most people respond, "Happiness." Research and opinion on the topic indicate that people can take concrete steps to achieve happiness. Planning for happiness is possible because it appears to be somewhat under people's control. Another factor to consider is that many researchers consider happiness to be a natural human condition. David T. Lyken observes that those genes that combine to produce a happy person were favored by natural selection. Given that happier people were more likely to survive, the survivors tend to be a happy breed.[2]

Our approach to the unlimited topic of understanding how to achieve happiness involves a model of happiness, a listing of keys to happiness, and the five principles of psychological functioning.

THE SPHERES OF LIFE AND HAPPINESS

A practical way of understanding happiness is that it is a by-product of having the various components of life working in harmony and synchrony. To understand this approach, visualize about six gears with teeth, spinning in unison. As long as all gears are moving properly (and no teeth are broken), a state of equilibrium and fluid motion is achieved. Similarly, imagine that life has six major components. The exact components will differ among people. For most people, the components would be approximately as follows:

1. Work and career

2. Interpersonal life, including loved ones and romantic life

3. Physical and mental health

4. Financial health

5. Interests and pastimes, including reading, surfing the Internet, and sports

6. A spiritual life or belief system, including religion, science, or astrology

When a person has ample satisfactions in all six spheres, he or she achieves happiness. However, when a deficiency occurs in any of these six factors, the person's spheres are no longer in harmony, and dissatisfaction or unhappiness occurs. Yet sometimes if a person is having problems in one sphere, satisfaction in the other spheres can compensate temporarily for a deficiency in one. For the long range, a state of happiness is dependent on all six spheres working in harmony. In short, the theme of this book surfaces again: Work and personal life are mutually supportive. Figure 16-1 presents the spheres-of-life model of happiness.

People vary as to how much importance they attach to each sphere of life. A person with intense career ambitions, for example, might place less weight on the interests sphere than would a more leisure-oriented person. However, if any of these spheres are grossly deficient, total happiness will not be forthcoming. Another source of variation is that the importance people attach to each sphere may vary according to the stage of life. A full-time student, for example, might need just enough money to avoid worrying about finances. However, after about 10 years of full-time career experience, a person's expenses might peak. The person would then attach more importance to the financial sphere.

THE KEYS TO HAPPINESS

Much research has been conducted about the ingredients of happiness. If you are aware of these contributors to happiness, you might be able to enhance your happiness. The spheres-of-life model of happiness also furnishes

Figure 16-1 The Spheres-of-Life Model of Happiness

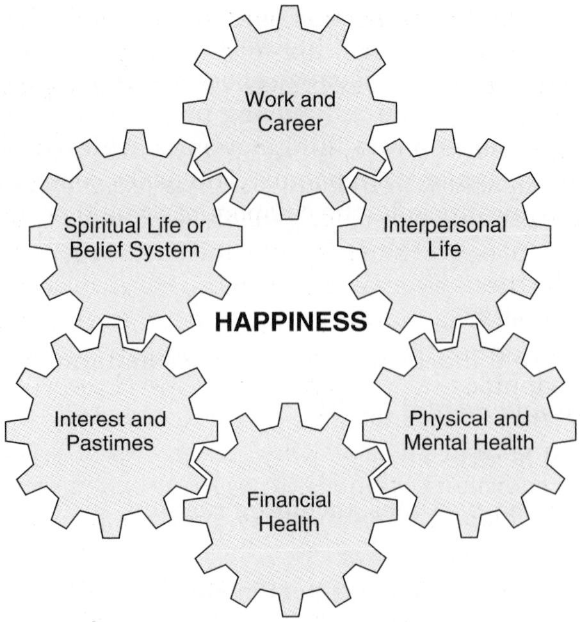

direction for the person seeking happiness: Strive for acceptable levels of achievement in all six spheres. Here we summarize and synthesize a wide range of research and opinion on the keys to happiness.[3]

1. *Give high priority to the pursuit of happiness.* Having the intention or goal of being happy will enhance your chances of being happy. A key principle is to discover what makes you happy and make the time to pursue those activities. Spending time doing what you enjoy contributes directly to happiness.

2. *Experience love and friendship and find a life partner.* A happy person is one who is successful in personal relationships and who exchanges care and concern with loved ones. Happy people are able to love and be loved. Hugging people you like or being hugged by them is an important part of having enjoyable personal relationships. Married adults, in general, are happier than unmarried, and the results are similar for men and women. According to the Men's Health Network, married men take fewer health risks, eat better, and are involved in more health-enhancing behaviors. Furthermore, married men also earn an average of 10 to 40 percent more than those never married, even with comparable education and work experience.[4] (Good health and high income make some contribution to happiness.) Despite the consistency of this finding about marriage, it must be interpreted cautiously. It takes a satisfying marriage to bring happiness, and unmarried partners who have a long-term, caring relationship are also likely to be happy.

3. *Develop a sense of self-esteem.* Self-love must precede love for others. High self-esteem enables one to love and be loved. Developing a good self-image leads to the self-esteem required for loving relationships. A feeling of self-worth is important because it helps prevent being overwhelmed by criticism. An important part of developing self-esteem is to not want financial success more than other things. Insecure people seek society's approval in the form of purchasing consumer goods and accumulating investments.

4. *Work hard at what you enjoy and achieve the flow experience.*   Love may be the most important contributor to happiness, with staying involved in work you enjoy coming in second. To achieve happiness, it is necessary to find a career that fits your most intense interests. In addition, it helps to achieve regularly the flow experience mentioned in Chapters 2 and 12. Happiness stemming from flow is powerful because it is not dependent on favorable external circumstances, such as recognition or love. The individual creates the happiness that follows from flow. Hard work contributes to happiness in another important way. A fundamental secret of happiness is accomplishing things and savoring what you have accomplished. Lyken, the happiness researcher mentioned above, argues that happiness is available to anyone who develops skills, interests, and goals that he or she finds meaningful and enjoyable.[5] A log cabin dweller who lived off the land and whose goal was to be close to nature would therefore be happier than a wealthy person in a luxurious house who was not leading the lifestyle he or she wanted.

5. *Appreciate the joys of day-to-day living.*   Another key to happiness is the ability to live in the present without undue worrying about the future or dwelling on past mistakes. Be on guard against becoming so preoccupied with planning your life that you neglect to enjoy the happiness of the moment. The essence of being a happy person is to savor what you have right now.

6. *Be fair, kind, helpful, and trusting of others.*   The Golden Rule is a true contributor to happiness. It is also important to practice charity and forgiveness. Helping others brings personal happiness. Knowing that you are able to make a contribution to the welfare of others gives you a continuing sense of satisfaction and happiness. Related to fairness and kindness is trust of others. Happy people have open, warm, and friendly attitudes.

7. *Have recreational fun in your life.*   A happy life is characterized by fun, zest, joy, and delight. When you create time for fun (in addition to the fun in many kinds of work), you add an important element to your personal happiness. However, if you devote too much time to play, you will lose on the fun of work accomplishments. In choosing fun activities, avoid overplanning. Because novelty contributes to happiness, be ready to pursue an unexpected opportunity or to try something different.

8. *Learn to cope with grief, disappointment, setbacks, and stress.*   To be happy, you must learn how to face problems that occur in life without being overwhelmed or running away. It is also important to persevere in attempting to overcome problems rather than to whine or engage in self-pity. Once you have had to cope with problems, you will be more able to appreciate the day-to-day joys of life.

9. *Live with what you cannot change.*   Happiness researcher Martin Seligman says that attempting to change conditions unlikely to change sets us up for feeling depressed about failing. Weight loss is a prime example. Nineteen out of 20 people gain the weight they lost. It is therefore better to worry less about weight loss and concentrate on staying in good physical condition by engaging in moderate exercise. Good condition contributes much more to health than does achieving a weight standard set primarily to achieve an aesthetic standard.[6] You can then concentrate on being happy about your good physical condition instead of being unhappy about your weight.

10. *Energize yourself through physical fitness.*   Engage in regular physical activity, such as dancing or sports, that makes you aerobically fit. Whether it is the endorphins released by exercise, dopamine released by the excitement, or just the relaxed muscles, physical fitness fosters happiness.

11. *Satisfy your most important values.*   Based on a survey of over 6,000 individuals, Steven Reiss concluded that people cannot find lasting happiness by aiming to have more fun or seeking pleasure. Instead, you have to satisfy your basic values or desires and take happiness in passing. To increase your value-based happiness, you have to first identify your most important desires and then gear you life toward satisfying these values. Among these key values are curiosity, physical activity, honor, power, family, status, and romance.[7] For example, if power and romance are two of your basic values, you can achieve happiness only if your life is amply provided with power and romance. Religion also fits into the realm of values, and religious people tend to be happier than nonreligious people.[8]

12. *Lead a meaningful life.*   Most of the 11 principles just stated, as well as the spheres-of-life happiness model, all point toward the conclusion that having a meaningful life is a major contributor to happiness. A meaning or an important purpose helps a person get through periodic annoyances that temporarily lower happiness. Seligman says that the ultimate level of happiness is the meaningful life. It consists of identifying your core strengths and then using them in the services of something you perceive to be bigger than you are.[9] For example, if you are a greeting card designer and you perceive that you are contributing to improved personal relationships, you are likely to be happy.

THE FIVE PRINCIPLES OF PSYCHOLOGICAL FUNCTIONING

According to Richard Carlson, the best way to achieve inner serenity (or happiness) is to follow the five principles of psychological functioning.[10] These principles act as guides toward achieving a feeling of inner happiness. The first is *thinking,* which creates the psychological experience of life. Feelings come about only after you thought about something or somebody. If you think of another person as attractive, it will lead to a warm feeling toward that person. People who learn to direct their thinking in positive directions will contribute to their own happiness. Remember that you produce your own thoughts.

The second principle is *moods,* meaning that the positive or negative content of your thinking fluctuates from moment to moment and day to day.

Practice ignoring your low (bad) moods rather than analyzing them, and you will see how quickly they vanish. Developing this skill will contribute substantially to healthy psychological functioning. The third principle is *separate psychological realities*. Because each person thinks in a unique way, everyone lives in a separate psychological reality. Accept the idea that others think differently than you, and you will have much more compassion and fewer quarrels. As a result, you will be happier. Also, if you accept the principle of separate realities, you will waste less time attempting to change people. At the same time, others will like you more, thus contributing to your happiness.

The fourth principle of psychological functioning is *feelings*. Combined with emotions, feelings are a built-in feedback mechanism that tells us how we are doing psychologically. If your feelings turn negative suddenly, you know that your thinking is dysfunctional. It is then time to make a mental readjustment. If you feel discontented, for example, it is necessary to clear the head and start thinking positively. As a consequence, you will experience contentment and happiness. A key point is that the person will maintain a sense of well-being as long as he or she does not focus on personal concerns.

The fifth principle is *the present moment*. Learning to pay attention to the present moment and to your feelings enables people to live at peak efficiency without the distraction of negative thinking. Much like the flow experience, the present moment is where people find happiness and inner peace. Carlson advises, "The only way to experience genuine and lasting contentment, satisfaction, and happiness is to learn to live your life in the present moment."[11](This supports happiness key number 5.)

Now that you have studied attitudes and activities that contribute to happiness, you are invited to do Human Relations Skill-Building Exercise 16-1. It is designed to bring about a state of happiness.

HUMAN RELATIONS SKILL-BUILDING EXERCISE 16-1

Achieving Happiness

The following exercises will help you develop attitudes that contribute mightily to happiness.

1. *Start the day off right.* Begin each day with five minutes of positive thought and visualization. Commit to this for one week. When and how do you plan to fit this into your schedule?

   _____

   _____

   _____

(Continued)

2. *Make a list of five virtues you believe in.* Examples would include patience, compassion, and helping the less fortunate.

_____

_____

_____

3. *Each week, for the next five weeks, incorporate a different virtue into your life.* On a simple index card, write this week's virtue in bold letters, such as "helping the less fortunate." Post the card in a prominent place. After you have completed one incident of helping the less fortunate, describe in about 10 to 25 words what you did. Also record the date and time.

_____

_____

_____

4. *Look for good things about new acquaintances.* List three students, customers, or coworkers you have just met. List three *positive* qualities about each.

_____

_____

_____

5. *List the* positive *qualities of fellow students or coworkers you dislike or have trouble working with.* Remember, keep looking for the good.

_____

_____

_____

6. *Think of school assignments or job tasks you* dislike *and write down the* merits *of these tasks.* Identify the benefits they bring you.

_____

_____

_____

7. *Look at problems as opportunities.* What challenges are you now facing? In what way might you view them that would inspire and motivate you?

_____

_____

_____

SOURCE: Adapted from Stu Kamen, "Turn Negatives into Positives," *Pryor Report Success Workshop,* May 1995, pp. 1–2.

▲ A PLANNED APPROACH TO FINDING A RELATIONSHIP

How many people have you heard complain about a poor social life because of circumstances beyond their control? Such complaints take various forms: "The women in this school are all unappreciative," "The men at my school don't really respect women," "There's absolutely nobody to meet at work," or "This is the worst town for meeting people."

Some of the people expressing these attitudes are systematic when it comes to handling business or technology problems. Under those circumstances, they use the problem-solving method. But when it comes to their social lives, they rely heavily on fate or chance.

The approach recommended here is to use your problem-solving skills to improve your personal life. Whatever the problem, try to attack it in a logical, step-by-step manner. The businessperson described in the chapter opener exemplifies the application of problem-solving skills to finding romance. We are not ruling out the influence of emotion and feeling in personal life. We are simply stating that personal life is too important to be left to fate alone. With good fortune you might form a relationship with a stranger you meet at a rapid-oil-change-and-lubrication center. Unfortunately, such good fortune is infrequent.

Too many people leave finding a new relationship to chance or to a few relatively ineffective alternatives. Too many unattached adults lament, "Either you go to a bar or you sit at home." In reality, both men and women can find dates in dozens of constructive ways. It is a matter of identifying some of these alternatives and trying out a few that fit your personality and preferences. See Exhibit 16-1 for more details.

No matter which environment you choose for conducting your date or mate search, you will usually need to reach out and make contact with the other person. A subtle method of making contact is through flirting, described by etiquette consultant Letitia Baldrige as being understated, subtle, witty, teasing, and sophisticated. Flirting involves getting close to another person and making that person aware of you in the best possible way.[13] Being charismatic helps substantially in flirting because charismatic people are charming and feel so comfortable complimenting others. An effective flirt extends a suggestion that is positive but not too explicitly romantic. You might flirt with a photographer by saying, "I would be very interested in seeing a few of your favorite photos. I have a lot of respect for photographers." What have you found to be an effective method of flirting?

Body language is another key part of flirting. According to Dee Ann Stiles, some of the best signals for flirting include the simple touch, leaning toward the person, tilting your head with interest, winking, mirroring the other person, and teasingly twirling something, like straws or pens.[14]

A key principle of finding romantic companionship is to be realistic in terms of the type of person you are likely to attract—one who will be interested in you. It is necessary to take a candid look at yourself and decide what category of people are most likely to be seeking a person of your general type. For example, a person in poor physical shape who smokes

EXHIBIT 16-1

In Search of a Date?

Every relationship begins with one person meeting another. In order to find one good relationship, you may need to date more than a dozen people. Next is a sampling of potentially effective methods for making a social contact.

Highly Recommended

1. Participate in an activity that you do well and enjoy. For example, if you are a good racquetball player, use racquetball playing as a vehicle for meeting people.

2. Get involved in your work, studies, or another activity not logically related to dating. People naturally gravitate toward a busy, serious-minded person. Besides, the workplace has now become the number one, natural meeting place for singles. However, beware of some of the potential problems with an office romance, as described in Chapter 8.

3. Take courses in which the male-to-female ratio is in your favor, such as automotive technology for women and cooking for men.

4. Ask your friends for introductions and describe the type of person you are trying to meet—but don't be too restrictive.

5. Get involved in a community or political activity in which many single people participate. A good example is to become a political party worker.

6. For men who like older women, go on a singles cruise. Most of these cruises attract many more women than men.

7. For women, join a National Guard reserve unit. The membership of these units is overwhelmingly male.

8. Take advantage of every social invitation to a party, picnic, breakfast, or brunch. Social occasions are natural meeting places.

9. Use an Internet dating service. Finding romance through an online dating service is growing rapidly in popularity and is much more in vogue than print ads. In a recent year, about 16 million people in the United States visited an online dating service.[12] Internet dating services have so many members that it is often possible to restrict your choices to the geographic area you desire. Several dating services attempt to match people by compatible personality types, as measured by a personality test administered online. Most Internet dating services encourage members to post photographs. As with most forms of meeting people, you do not know if the facts presented about the prospective date are true. Some members of online dating services have been know to post photos of people other than themselves.

10. Participate in Internet chat rooms (*cyberdating*). Many people rely on the Internet as their exclusive method of finding romance. Chat rooms can be selected according to interests, including movie fans, gays and lesbians, and astrology believers. After exchanging a series of e-mail messages or instant messages, the two people

(Continued)

arrange for an in-person meeting. Many of the people you meet might live in a faraway location. Another problem is that many chat room participants badly misrepresent themselves, and a few have proved to be deranged sex criminals.

11. Place a personal ad in a local newspaper or magazine, stating the qualifications you are seeking in a companion and how you can be reached. Personal ads have achieved such popularity that several national magazines now accept them. Personal ads are frequently integrated with voice mail. (You leave a voice message for the person who placed the ad.) Under many systems, your personal ad consists of a voice message to which people respond. Furthermore, some personal ads are strictly phone based, and no print ad appears. With some personals, your phone ad is also posted online. Be creative when composing an ad so that it stands out from others.

12. Join special-promotion singles groups, such as indoor tennis for singles or a singles ski weekend. Similarly, join singles groups associated with churches, temples, or mosques. Singles groups outside of religious institutions are also worth exploring.

At Least Worth a Try

1. While networking for career purposes, also prospect for social companions.

2. Join an introduction (dating) service, particularly one that has an established membership. Introduction services are usually best for those seeking to meet people over age 30 and are much more costly than other methods mentioned in this exhibit. Speed dating is a new trend in introduction services. A group of unattached people meets at a café or bar (or a section thereof) that has been rented out for the evening. The café is filled with tables for two, and each table is numbered. You will have a set amount of time of 3 to 10 minutes to interview a number of opposite-sexed members of the group. After the interviews, each member lists the people he or she would like to pursue. If the other person also wants to meet you, you are given the person's telephone number and/or e-mail address.

3. Shop at supermarkets around dinnertime and from 11 P.M. to 2 A.M. You will frequently find other single people shopping at that time. Some women claim that you are the most likely to find an unattached male in the frozen food department around 6:30 P.M. because they are planning their evening meal.

4. Strike up a conversation while waiting in line for tickets at the movies, concerts, or athletic events.

5. Congregate or float around in large gatherings, such as rallies for causes, registration for courses, or orientation programs.

6. Organize a singles party and require each person invited to bring along an unattached person of the opposite sex—no regular couples allowed.

7. Find valid reasons for visiting other departments at your place of work. Chance meetings at photocopying machines and centralized printers, for example, have allegedly spawned thousands of romances.

heavily and does not participate in sports will have difficulty attracting an Olympic athlete. Besides, there are relatively few Olympic athletes, and most of them may already be attached.

An important consideration in searching for a relationship is to recognize when you experiencing **quest fatigue.** This is the feeling of demoralization and disappointment that takes place when all your efforts at finding a date or mate fail.[15] When quest fatigue sets in, give yourself some time off from the search. Enjoy your activities without a partner and revitalize yourself before resuming the quest.

▲ WHY PEOPLE ARE ATTRACTED TO ONE ANOTHER

As part of enriching social life, it is helpful to understand why people are attracted to each other. Understanding these forces may help in choosing a compatible person for a long-term relationship. Three different psychological explanations of why people develop a strong attraction to each other are balance theory, exchange theory, and the need for intimacy. Attraction can also be attributed to chemical or hormonal reasons. All four of these explanations, to be described next, can apply in a given situation.

BALANCE THEORY OF ATTRACTION

According to **balance theory,** people prefer relationships that are consistent or balanced. If we are very similar to another person, it makes sense (it is consistent or balanced) to like that person. We are also attracted to similar people because they reinforce our opinions and values. It is usually reassuring and rewarding to discover that another person agrees with you or has similar values.[16]

Balance theory explains why we are eager to stay in a relationship with some people, but it does not explain why opposites often attract each other. People sometimes get along best with those who possess complementary characteristics. A talkative and domineering person may prefer a partner who enjoys listening. The explanation is that a dominant person needs someone to dominate and therefore might be favorably disposed toward submissive people.

SOCIAL EXCHANGE THEORY OF ATTRACTION

A long-standing explanation of why two people become a couple is **social exchange theory,** the idea that human relationships are based mainly on self-interest. This research shows that people measure their social, physical, and other assets against a potential partner's. The closer the match, the more likely they are to develop a long-term relationship.

Exchange theory has been able to predict the permanence of a relationship based on the way each partner feels he or she stacks up against the other. One study of 537 dating men and women found that partners who thought they were getting far more in exchange for what they were giving felt guilty and insecure. In comparison, those who believed they gave more than they got were angry.

The giving was mostly psychological. It included such things as being more physically attractive than the partner, kinder, or more flexible. The greater the imbalance, the more likely the couple was to split up; the more equitable the partners believed the exchange to be, the more likely they were to remain partners. One explanation of these findings is that the feeling of being taken advantage of corrodes a relationship. It is also disturbing to feel that you are taking advantage of your partner.[17]

NEED FOR INTIMACY

For some, the balance and exchange theories of mutual attraction are too mechanical and logical. The late psychologist David McClelland proposed instead that love is an experience seated in the nonrational part of the brain (the right side). People who believe that they are in love have a strong **need for intimacy.** This craving for intimacy is revealed in the thoughts of people in love who are asked to make up stories about fictitious situations. Their stories reveal a preoccupation with harmony, responsibility, and commitment and a preference for a relationship that includes warmth and intimacy.

McClelland and his associates say that these themes show up repeatedly in many guises in the stories told by people who say they are in love. The same stories are told by people in situations where love feelings run high, such as just having seen a romantic movie.[18]

The concept of love is part of the need for intimacy as well as a key part of understanding personal relationships. Every reader has an idea of what love means to him or her. Harry Stack Sullivan, the famous psychiatrist, developed a particularly useful description of love, as follows:

> When the satisfaction or the security of another person becomes as significant to one as is one's own satisfaction or security, then the state of love exists. So far as I know, under no other circumstance is a state of love present, regardless of the popular usage of the word.

A Biochemical Explanation of Attractiveness

Another explanation of why certain people are attracted to one another is based on chemicals and specifically hormones. According to this theory, our hormones direct us to sense or screen potential mates. After the initial biochemical attraction, our conscious, psychological preferences, (e.g., Does he enjoy action movies and golfing?) come into play. The interests and lifestyle preferences of the potential mate carry more weight after the initial attraction. While the biochemical factors are at work, the brain is processing the external clues people use to measure sex appeal. Among these personality factors are appearance, clothing, makeup, scent, body language, and voice.[19]

A more specific explanation of attraction between people is based on the presence of pheromones. These are chemical substances released by a person (or animal) to influence the behavior of another member of the same species. A person who emits high doses of pheromones will therefore attract more partners. Conversely, we are physically attracted to people with high doses of pheromones.

The pheromone theory is particularly geared toward explaining why one person is strongly attracted to another person on first sight. After the initial physical attraction, however, other, more rational factors (e.g., Is this person employed?) enter into the picture. Several companies sell cologne for men and perfume for women that allegedly contains pheromones, thus making it easier to attract Prince or Princess Charming and also to be noted by others. Because these "attractant" substances are considered cosmetics and not drugs, they are free from government regulation. Buyer beware.

The Importance of Choosing a Partner Carefully

Having a plan for meeting a partner and understanding why people are attracted to each other should be regarded as helpful information for making the right choice. A principal problem in many poor relationships is that the couple used faulty judgment in choosing each other. Of course, it is difficult to be objective when choosing a partner. Your needs at the time may cloud your judgment. Many people have made drastic mistakes in choosing a spouse because they were lonely and depressed when they met the person they married. Being on the rebound from a relationship that went bad makes you particularly vulnerable.

The problem of mate selection is indeed complicated. Do you marry for love, companionship, infatuation, or all three? It has been pointed out that the success rate of the arranged marriages still practiced in a few countries is about as good as that of nonarranged marriages. Since most people have only a limited amount of time to invest in finding the ideal mate, they are content to marry a good fit.

An in-depth study of 300 happy marriages provides a practical clue about mate selection. The most frequently mentioned reason for an enduring and happy marriage was having a generally positive attitude toward each other.[20] If you view your partner as your best friend and like him or her "as a person," you will probably be happy together. As obvious as it sounds, choose only a life partner whom you genuinely like. Some people deviate from this guideline by placing too much emphasis on infatuation.

A unique approach to mate selection would be to ask your family and close friends what they thought of your potential for happiness with your prospective mate. Research supports the wisdom of this approach. Tara K. McDonald and Michael Ross studied 74 college students who had been dating approximately six months. The couples were asked how serious they thought they were, how satisfied they were in the relationship, and how in love they were. The researchers also asked the couples' roommates and parents the same questions.

Follow-ups were conducted at 6 and 12 months to see which couples were still together and who made the most accurate predictions. The couples themselves were much more optimistic about the prospects for the relationship. Parents were more accurate than the couples in predicting the length of the relationship. The roommates, however, made the most accurate predictions.[21]

The message here is to recognize that when you are contemplating choosing a life partner, you are facing one of life's major decisions. Put all your creative resources into making a sound decision.

▲ WORKING OUT ISSUES WITHIN RELATIONSHIPS

People emotionally involved with each other often find themselves in conflict over a variety of issues, especially when they are emotionally dependent on each other. Without conflict, relationships would be artificial. Human relations specialists have formulated some ground rules for resolving the many types of conflicts that frequently occur in relationships. These rules supplement the techniques for conflict resolution presented in Chapter 9.

1. *Listen carefully and give feedback.*   Many conflicts intensify because the people involved never stop to listen carefully to what the other side is trying to say. After listening to your partner's point of view, express your feelings about the issue. Expressing your feelings leads to more understanding than expressing your judgments. It is preferable to say "I feel left out when you visit your mother" than to say "You're insensitive to my needs. Look at the way you visit your mother all the time."

To help improve understanding, provide mutual feedback. Although you may disagree with your partner, communicate your understanding: "From your point of view, it's frivolous of me to spend so much money on bowling. You would prefer that I invest money in home improvements."

2. *Use more positive behaviors than negative behaviors during arguments.* A 10-year study of arguments between partners in relationships, involving hundreds of couples, supported several basic ideas about good human relations. Some negative emotions used in arguments are more toxic than others. At the top of the corrosive list are criticism, contempt, defensiveness, and stonewalling (withdrawing from a discussion). On the positive side, the team of researchers found that happy couples use five times more positive behaviors in their arguments than negative behaviors. One way to be positive is to use humor to ease the tension in an argument. The humor is considered an effort to mend the conflict.[22] To illustrate, Jennifer might be upset that her husband Larry spent most of his time at an office party they attended together talking to other women. On their way home, Jennifer said, "I don't know whether to be angry at you for flirting all evening or to compliment you for networking with every women at the party sharp enough to have a future in business."

3. *Define the real problem.* What your partner or you grumble about at first may not be the real issue in the conflict. It will require mutual understanding combined with careful listening and sympathy to uncover the real problem. A man might be verbally attacking a woman's dress when he really means that she has gained more weight than he would like. Or a woman might verbally attack a man's beer drinking when her real complaint is that he should be out in the yard raking leaves instead of sitting inside playing video games.

4. *Don't hit below the belt.* The expression "below the belt" refers to something that is unfair. Some issues are just plain unfair to bring up in a marital dispute. When you are intimate with another person, you are bound to know one or two vulnerable areas. Here are two below-the-belt comments:

> "You're lucky I married you. What other woman would have married a man who was so much of a loser that he had to declare bankruptcy?"

> "Don't complain so much about being abused verbally. Remember that your father went to jail for battering your mother."

Is anyone really as cruel as the preceding quotes would suggest? Yes, in the heat of a tiff between partners, many cruel, harsh things are said. If two people want to live harmoniously after the conflict, they should avoid below-the-belt comments. Another problem is that these comments reflect negative rather than positive behaviors.

5. *Be prepared to compromise.* For many issues compromise is possible. The compromise you reach should represent a willingness to meet the other person halfway, not just a temporary concession. On some issues the only compromise can be letting the other person have his or her way now and waiting to have your turn later. Among such issues that cannot be split down the middle are whether to have children, whether to live in an apartment or a house, whether to go to Miami or London for a vacation, or whether to run a kosher or nonkosher household. Several of these issues should be settled before marriage or living together since no real compromise on the basic issue is possible in these instances.

6. *Minimize an accusatory tone.*   You lessen the accusatory tone when you make "I" statements instead of "you" statements. The door to dialogue is opened when you make a statement such as, "I felt really disappointed when you did not call me to ask about how my promotion interview went." You shut off dialogue when you say, "You don't care about my happiness. You didn't even call to ask about how my promotion interview went."

7. *Use e-mail as a substitute for face-to-face confrontations.*   At times a couple may be so emotionally charged that resolving conflicts face to face is not possible. To back off temporarily from the difficulty of in-person conflict resolution, it may be worthwhile to correspond through e-mail, messaging, or hard-copy letters. According to Andrew Christensen and Neil Jacobsen, the written message can help the couple avoid raising their voices and escalating the conflict.[23] While sending notes to each other, it is valuable to put down in writing what you think the other side is angry about. For instance, "You are ticked off at me because I think your family is intolerant of people who are not like themselves." After dealing with the conflict in writing, the couple may be calm enough to move on to a face-to-face discussion.

8. *Be acquiescent when appropriate.*   A practical, although controversial, approach to dealing with relationship conflict is to surrender to the wishes of your partner from time to time.[24] You submit to your partner's wishes rather than combating every small demand with which you disagree. The idea is not to lose your self-respect but to minimize conflict over issues that are not terribly important. Suppose the wife says to the husband, "Lets paint the kitchen the color of sand." The husband would prefer a sky blue kitchen, but he thinks to himself, "If I disagree on the kitchen color, this will be the fourth time I've disagreed with one of Jennifer's suggestions this week. So, I'll live with a sand-colored kitchen." Or take this scenario: The wife objects to attending a hockey game instead of going dancing. She says to herself, "I'll go along with the hockey game, even though I would prefer a romantic evening. I've already nagged John enough this week."

The strategy of being acquiescent may appear to suppress conflict. However, by submitting to a small demand today, you help establish a climate in which your small demands may be met the next time a disagreement surfaces.

▲ MEETING THE CHALLENGES OF BEING A TWO-INCOME COUPLE

The number of couples in which both partners have full-time jobs has now reached 75 percent, as estimated by the U.S. Bureau of Labor Statistics. Two critical factors influencing this steady growth are women's career aspirations and the need for two incomes to meet living expenses. It is a challenge to run a two-income household in a way that will enhance the couple's personal life. In Chapter 7 we presented information about using organizational support systems to help reduce work–family conflicts. Following are suggestions that couples themselves can implement to increase the chances of a two-income household running more smoothly.

1. *Establish priorities and manage time carefully.*   A major contributor to the success of a working couple relationship is careful time management. Each partner must establish priorities, such as ranking quality time together ahead of adding a community activity to the schedule. Or both partners might inform their employer of a certain date they would be taking as a vacation day to celebrate their wedding anniversary. Another aspect of priority setting and time management is to schedule time for romance. Many working couples fall into the trap of neglecting romantic time together because the job and household tasks consume most of their energy. As a consequence, joyful time together diminishes rapidly.

2. *Deal with feelings of competitiveness.*   Feelings of competitiveness between husband and wife about each other's career often exist even when both have a modern outlook. Competitive feelings are all the more likely to surface when both parties are engaged in approximately the same kind of work. One man became infuriated with his wife when she was offered a promotion before he was. They had both entered the same big company at the same time in almost identical jobs. In contrast, the working couple with traditional views is unlikely to have a problem when the husband outdistances his wife in career advancement.

The familiar remedy of discussing problems before they get out of hand is offered again here. One partner might confess to the other, "Everybody is making such a fuss over you since you won that outstanding employee award. It makes me feel somewhat left out and unimportant." A sympathetic spouse might reply, "I can understand your feelings. But don't take all this fuss too seriously. It doesn't take away from my feelings for you. Besides, two months from now maybe people will be making a fuss over you for something."

3. *Share big decisions equally.*   A distinguishing characteristic of today's two-income families is that both partners share equally in making important decisions about the domestic side of life. Under such an arrangement, neither has exclusive decision-making prerogatives in any particular area. He may make a decision without consulting her over some minor matter (such as the selection of a plant for the living room). She may make the decision the next time a plant is to be selected for inside the house. But on major decisions—such as relocating to another town, starting a family, or investing in the stock market or real estate—husband and wife collaborate.

4. *Divide the household tasks equitably.*   Many women who work outside the home rightfully complain that they are responsible for too much of the housework and household errands. When household chores are divided unequally, conflict in the home is probable. The recommended solution is for the working couple to divide household tasks in some equitable manner. Equity could mean that tasks are divided according to preference or the amount of effort required. In one family, the husband might enjoy food shopping while the wife enjoys cleaning. Assignments could be made accordingly. Each couple should negotiate for themselves what constitutes an equitable division of household tasks. To participate equitably in household chores and child rearing, one or both partners might have to reduce the amount of time invested in the career. (Do you recall the term *downshifting?*)

5. *Take turns being inconvenienced.*   In a highly traditional family, the woman assumes the responsibility for managing inconvenient household tasks even if she, too, has a job outside the home. The underlying assumption may be that her work is less important than his work. For more modern couples, a more equitable solution is to take turns being inconvenienced. If Sue has to go to work late one day to be around for the plumber, Ted can go to work late when the dog has to be taken to the veterinarian. A working couple with children will frequently have to miss work because of a child's illness or accident, parent-teacher conferences, or school plays.

6. *Develop adequate systems for child care.*   Any working couple with a young child or children will attest to the challenge of adequately balancing work and child demands. Imagine this scenario: Your spouse has already left for work, and you discover that your four-year-old child has a fever of 102 degrees. The child care center will not accept a sick child, nor will your neighbor, who helps out occasionally. She fears contaminating her children. The logical solution is to stay home from work, but you have a crucial work meeting scheduled for 11 A.M.

One solution to dilemmas of this nature and less serious problems is to have a diverse support system. Make arrangements with at least three people, including relatives, who could help you out in an emergency. Retired people, for example, often welcome the challenge of helping out in an emergency.

7. *Decide who pays for what.*   The problem of negotiating who pays for what arises for many two-income families. Many couples find that the additional expenses of a working couple prevent them from getting ahead financially. Child care expenses are often involved; restaurant meals become more frequent; and a second car is usually a necessity outside of large metropolitan areas. The "big pool" arrangement of dividing expenses works well for many couples. Under this arrangement, the couple pools its money into a joint account for household expenses and savings. Each partner receives personal spending money out of the common pot or from additional income such as second jobs.

When the two partners trust each other, a joint account might be maintained with one partner taking responsibility for bill paying. Another approach is for the couples to maintain separate accounts and divide bills on the basis of how much each partner earns. A third approach is for one partner to hand over a paycheck to the other, who has complete charge of bill paying, budgeting, savings, and investments. The person who hands over the paycheck would need to trust his or her partner completely.

▲ KEEPING YOUR RELATIONSHIP VIBRANT

One of the major challenges in personal life is to keep a relationship with a partner vibrant. For many people, relationships that begin with enthusiasm, rapport, and compatibility end in a dull routine and splitting up. A gruesome statistic is that nearly two-thirds of all first marriages end in permanent separation or divorce.[25] Understanding how to maintain a vibrant relationship is thus exceptionally important. For a relationship to succeed, the absence of misery is not sufficient. Instead, joy and delight must also be present.[26] Human Relations Self-Assessment Quiz 16-1 pinpoints some of the symptoms of a relationship gone bad. Here we describe major factors in achieving a mutually rewarding long-term relationship.

Keep Romantic Love in Proper Perspective

A speaker told an audience that you can tell you are infatuated with your partner if your heart begins pounding at a chance meeting with him or her. An 80-year-old in the audience responded, "I know just what you mean. The Mrs. and I have been married for 55 years, and that's exactly how I feel whenever I run into her downtown." This happy husband is an exception; although infatuation or romantic love is vital in getting a relationship started, it usually cools down within several years. When infatuation declines, instead of being disappointed, the couple should realize that the relationship has grown more mature and lasting.

A relationship counselor observes that as full of rapture and delight as the first phase of a relationship is, it is essentially a trick of nature designed to bring us together. Nature knows that without the illusion of perfection, we might not choose each other. After the emotional bond is secure, nature lifts the veil.[27] To avoid discouragement and disillusionment, it is important to keep romantic love in proper perspective. It helps launch a relationship but does not have to be kept at its initial high intensity for a relationship to endure. However, the spark should not be *extinguished*.

Another significant key to keeping romantic love in perspective is to review your expectations in the relationship. Over the years, the expectations for relationships have increased: People want more from marriage than in times past. Fifty years ago, for example, more people thought of a marriage as an institution primarily to raise a family and gain economic security. Many more people today want marriages to be gratifying and satisfying and intimate. So when these expectations are not met, one or both partners may become discouraged.[28] In reviewing your expectations, you might decide that you have set the bar too high and are therefore creating the opportunity for disappointment.

HUMAN RELATIONS SELF-ASSESSMENT QUIZ 16-2

Early Warning Signs of a Relationship in Trouble

You know your relationship is in trouble and in need of revitalization when several or more of the indicators below are present. The term "partner" refers to a spouse, boyfriend, girlfriend, or significant other.

- You observe that you partner has terrible table manners.

- You perceive that your partner is not as attractive or cute as you thought previously.

- The sound your partner makes with his or her teeth annoys you.

- Your conversation is confined to routine matters such as "Did you put gas in the car?" or "Why are you 15 minutes late?"

- A significant change in routine takes place, such as the partner calling every other day instead of at least once a day.

- You rarely plan ahead for social occasions, such as parties, dinner, or movies, but decide to go out at the last moment—such as making plans for Saturday night at 4 P.M. that day.

- You spend progressively less time together.

- You nitpick each other frequently, and all your partner's quirks begin to bother you.

- You touch each other less and less, including holding hands while walking or driving the car.

- Your fights are more frequent and last longer.

- Small tokens of affection, such as sending love notes, almost disappear.

- You rarely mention your partner favorably to a third party.

- You notice frequent criticisms, including backhanded compliments, such as, "You look nice today for a person with so little taste in clothing."

- You jump into binding commitments with little planning, such as having a baby, moving, or buying a house. (Quite often partners think that such major joint activities will save a sinking relationship.)

- You look for an opportunity to spend time with your friends, watching television, or surfing the Internet rather than with your partner.

- You rarely look forward to spending time alone with your partner.

- Neither partner ever says, "I love you" any longer.

SOURCE: Several of the signs were collected from relationship experts by Elaine Gross, "Love On the Edge," Gannett News Service story, March 12, 1996, and from "The Relationship Quiz" used by Worldwide Marriage Encounter (undated).

Hold Communication Sessions

Good communication is vital for creating and maintaining a loving relationship. Therefore, one way to keep a relationship alive is to hold formal communication sessions in which you tell each other almost anything on your mind. The topics can be both positive and negative. A man may want to tell his partner of something she did that he appreciated very much. Or a woman may want to talk about the way her partner offended her in public. Or a couple may want to discuss concerns about finances, a child, in-law relations, or anything else. One of many reasons that communication sessions are important is that many couples have different perceptions about what is good and bad in their relationship. The communication sessions help clear up misperceptions. A vital aspect of these sessions is that both facts and feelings are expressed. The statement "I am really afraid we are drifting apart" communicates much more than "You and I haven't been talking too much lately." The role play at the end of this chapter explores the type of communication that can keep a relationship thriving.

Communication sessions are also important because they can sometimes revive a failing relationship. This is true because communication breakdowns often lead to failed relationships. Typically, in the early stages of a relationship, the couple is keenly attuned to each other's thoughts and feelings. The partners look for small verbal and nonverbal signals of contentment and discontent in each other.

After the relationship seems secure, couples often replace the intense monitoring of the early stages with a nonrevealing style of communication. For example, the man and woman may mechanically say to each other, "How was your day?" or "Love ya." This shorthand style of communication obstructs the sending and receiving of messages that could indicate the relationship is in trouble. Introducing communication sessions can make it possible for the couple to deal with subtle problems in the relationship.

Brief communication sessions are particularly needed when a couple travels together because so many relationships take a turn for the worse while traveling. Many couples, for example, are surprised by the conflict that emerges during their honeymoon. One of the problems is that such continuous contact with another person requires considerable adjustment. While driving in a car or seated next to each other in an airplane for a long period of time, the other person's eccentricities become more evident. Have you ever heard of a couple fighting over the *correct way* to fold a road map?

Strive for Novelty in Your Relationship

An unfortunate aspect of many relationships is that they drift toward a routine. A married couple might go to the same place for vacation, meeting the same family and friends for years on end. A man dating a woman might call her every night at the same time. Or a couple's sex life may turn into a routine. Many people have suggested that you try pleasant surprises to keep your relationship vibrant and fun. Make up a list of your own, but here are a few ideas to jog your thinking:

Ask your mate out for dinner on a *Monday* evening.

Write your partner a poem instead of sending a commercial greeting card.

Take up a new activity together in which you are both beginners (such as swing dancing or scuba diving) and learn with each other.

TAKE AN OPTIMISTIC VIEW OF THE RELATIONSHIP

Earlier we described the importance of being positive when working out differences in a relationship. Viewing your partner positively will often help the relationship stay romantic and endure. A 10-year study was conducted to identify what saves marriages, with the initial interviews accomplished within six months of marriage. Ninety-five Seattle-area couples were traced for seven to nine years. Couples who will endure see each other through rose-colored glasses and show positive behavior toward each other. Those who will divorce within six months see each other through fogged lenses, seeming cynical and unable to say good things about each other.

The researchers noted that more important than what was actually said was "if they expressed fondness and admiration for their partner, if they talked about themselves as a unit, if they finished each other's sentences, reference each other when they told a story, and whether what came to mind was pleasant."[29]

Additional support for the link between positive behavior and a lasting relationship stems from research by John Gottman. He has videotaped thousand of couples with the aim of coding positive and negative facial expressions, body language, and comments. For instance, eye rolling in reaction to a spouse's comment is a strong predictor of divorce. The data of Gottman and his colleagues reveal that strong marriages have at least a five-to-one ratio of positive to negative interactions. As the ratio begins to drop, the marriage is at high risk for divorce. Four negative qualities are the most characteristics of couples that split: contempt, criticism, defensiveness, and stonewalling. Negative facial expressions also dampen a relationship.[30]

MAINTAIN A NONPOSSESSIVE RELATIONSHIP

A **nonpossessive relationship** is one in which both partners maintain separate identities and strive for personal fulfillment yet are still committed to each other. Such a relationship is based on interdependent love—love involving commitment with self-expression and personal growth.[31] A nonpossessive relationship does not mean that the partners have sexual relationships with other people.

HUMAN RELATIONS SKILL-BUILDING EXERCISE 16-1

Keeping Your Relationship Vibrant

The role-playing exercise described here will help you experience the type of communication and interaction required for keeping a relationship vibrant. As with any other role play visualize yourself in the role briefly described. Try to develop the feel and the flavor of the person depicted.

The man in this relationship is becoming concerned that his wife does not enthusiastically participate in activities involving his family. He prefers that he and his wife spend their Sunday afternoons with his parents and other relatives. He thinks they are all loads of fun and cannot imagine why his wife is beginning to drag her heels about spending time with them. Twice in the last month she has come up with excuses for not going along with him to visit his folks on Sunday.

The woman in this relationship still loves her husband but thinks his preference for Sunday afternoons with his folks is unreasonable. She thinks that it is time for her to pursue her own interests on Sunday afternoons. She plans to confront her husband about the situation this evening.

Two people act out this role play for about 10 to 15 minutes. Other members of the class can act as observers. Among the observation points will be the following: (1) How well did the couple get to the key issues? (2) How much feeling was expressed? (3) Do they appear headed toward a resolution of this problem?

A nonpossessive relationship is helpful because some people find the traditional form of marriage stifling. For example, many married people feel compelled to give up a hobby or interest because the partner does not share the interest. In a nonpossessive relationship, the couple can take many separate paths and pursue different interests and have friends of their own. Unfortunately, if couples pursue nonpossessive relationships too far, they wind up drifting away from each other. The reason is that happy partners spend considerable time with each other enjoying shared activities. Each couple must find the right balance between maintaining separate identities and spending sufficient time together to remain close.

To further develop your sensitivity to keeping a relationship vibrant, do Human Relations Skill-Building Exercise 16-1.

▲ SUMMARY

A satisfying and rewarding personal life can help a person absorb a career setback and also contributes to a satisfying and rewarding career. Planning for happiness is somewhat under a person's control. A practical way of understanding happiness is that it is a by-product of having the spheres of life working in harmony and synchrony. For most people, these spheres would be work and career; interpersonal life, including romance; physical and mental health; financial health; interests and pastimes; and spiritual life or belief system.

Contributors or keys to happiness include the following: (1) giving priority to happiness; (2) love and friendship; (3) self-esteem; (4) working hard at things enjoyed; (5) appreciation of the joys of day-to-day living; (6) fairness, kindness, helpfulness, and trust; (7) recreational fun; (8) coping with grief, disappointment, setbacks, and stress; (9) living with what you cannot change; (10) energizing yourself through physical fitness; and (11) developing a philosophy or system of belief.

According to Richard Carlson, the best way to achieve inner serenity (or happiness) is to follow the five principles of psychological functioning. First is *thinking,* which brings about feelings. Second is *moods,* including the idea that you can ignore bad moods. Third is *separate psychological realities,* meaning that each person thinks in a unique way. Fourth is *feelings,* which can be turned from negative to positive. Fifth is the *present moment,* which is where people find happiness and inner peace.

A good social life begins with finding people you want to date. Such an important activity in life should not be left to chance or fate alone. Instead, use a planned approach that includes exploring many sensible alternatives. Be realistic about the type of person you are likely to attract. However, when you experience quest fatigue, back off and enjoy activities without a partner.

Understanding why people are attracted to one another helps in choosing a compatible partner. The balance theory of attraction contends that people prefer relationships that are consistent or balanced, and therefore they are comfortable with people similar to themselves. According to social exchange theory, people seek relationships in which there is an even match of personal assets. A third explanation is that people are attracted to each other because their need for intimacy prompts them to fall in love. A fourth explanation of attraction is based on biochemistry, suggesting that our hormones direct us to sense or screen potential mates. After the initial biochemical attraction, our conscious, psychological preferences come into play.

Whatever the basis for attraction, a partner must be chosen carefully to help prevent a split based on a poor fit. One suggestion would be to ask your family and close friends what they thought of your potential for happiness with your prospective mate.

To keep an intimate relationship healthy, you should resolve issues as they arise. Suggestions for accomplishing this include (1) listening carefully and giving feedback, (2) being more positive than negative during arguments, (3) defining the real problem, (4) avoiding opening old wounds, (5) not hitting below the belt, (6) being prepared to compromise, (7) minimizing an accusatory tone, (8) communicating by e-mail when emotions are high, and (9) being alert to gender differences in communication.

Two-income couples are subject to unique pressures. To sustain a good relationship, a two-income (or dual-career) couple should consider these approaches: (1) establishing priorities and managing time carefully, (2) dealing with feelings of competitiveness, (3) sharing big decisions equally, (4) dividing the household tasks equitably, (5) taking turns being inconvenienced, (6) developing adequate systems for child care, and (7) decideing who pays for what.

Keeping a relationship vibrant is a major challenge. Among the approaches proposed to meet this goal are (1) keeping romantic love in perspective; (2) holding communication sessions, including while traveling;

(3) striving for novelty in your relationship; (4) taking an optimistic view of the relationship; (5) maintaining a nonpossessive relationship; and (6) maintaining a differentiation of self.

Questions and Activities

1. What are some of the skills a person needs to acquire to become happy?

2. How do your "spheres of life" compare with those in Figure 16-1?

3. Identify several positive and at least one negative consequence of being happy.

4. In this chapter you were told that the office has become the most frequent place for meeting a mate. In Chapter 9 you were cautioned about the hazards of an office romance. How do you integrate these two opinions?

5. What is your reaction to the practice of having a third party conduct a background investigation of a prospective mate? Also, should the prospective mate be informed of the investigation after it is completed?

6. What do you perceive to be the advantages and disadvantages of finding a romantic relationship over the Internet?

7. In what way is speed dating much like a job fair?

8. In Chapter 6 about communications, you were told that a problem with e-mail is that it may not be well suited to conveying feelings. In this chapter e-mail is recommended as a way of dealing with some of the emotional issues in a relationship. How do you reconcile this apparent contradiction?

9. When one person in a dual-income couple loses a job, should that person be responsible for all the household chores? Explain your reasoning.

10. Find a couple that has been together for 30 years or more. Find out what they perceive to be the secret of their successful relationship. Share your findings with class members.

INTERNET SKILL BUILDER: Daily Doses of Happiness on the Web

Visit www.thehappyguy.com to receive your "daily dose of happiness." The Daily Dose of Happiness offers you happiness quotes and suggestions for self-actualization. Happyguy promises to help you achieve such ends as becoming inspired about life, discovering the meaning of happiness, and achieving personal growth. After trying out this program of happiness and personal growth, you be the judge. Have you made strides toward becoming happier? Do you feel any better emotionally? What impact do the Daily Happiness mugs have on your personal well being? Be happy!

HUMAN RELATIONS CASE PROBLEM

The Love Lab

Psychologist John Gottman began his research on the quality of marital relationships 30 years ago. Since then, his University of Washington laboratory, called the Love Lab, has focused on determining exactly what makes marriages thrive or fail. The conversation that follows is a taken from the records of the Love Lab. Valerie, 24, and Mark, 25, have a young baby. They have recently moved, and both have new jobs.

Valerie: (Laughter) We don't go that long without talking.

Mark: I know, I just start going stir-crazy.

Valerie: The problem...

M: Huh?

V: ...is, you told me that when you took the job as manager at Commonwealth that you'd come home in the afternoons and spend some time with us.

M: That's right, but I did not say that it would start in the first week when I'm trying to do two different jobs. I gotta get myself replaced. Right now, I'm not just a manager.

V: It's been three weeks.

M: Well, I just don't go out on the street and say, "Hey you. Want to sell insurance?" It's not that easy. There are two people in the program. One of them is probably gonna be hired within the next couple of weeks. But in the meantime it's tough. It's just the way it's gotta be.

V: I realize that.

M: Okay.

V: But.

M: At midnight when you get off work and you're all keyed up, I'm all worn out.

V: I realize that. That doesn't bother me that much, you going to sleep at night.

M: I'll just be starting to go to sleep and you'll go, "Are you listening to me?" I'll be trying to stay awake . . .

V: I'm laughing about it usually. I'm not upset about it.

M: I don't know by then. I'm half out.

V: But now with me having a car, you'll be able to go to sleep early and get up with Stephanie a little bit. That's one of my big problems. I'm not getting any sleep. I don't get to sleep until two.

M: I've been getting up with her.

V: You've been real good about that.

M: Okay.

V: I guess I just wish that you didn't have to go in early.

M: Yeah, we don't get a whole lot of time together.

V: When I have the car, I can get out and get stuff then. I feel like I'm stuck at home, and here you are...

M: I'll be able to meet you for lunch and stuff. I guess that wasn't any big problem.

V: It is a problem. It seems like we talk about it every day.

M: Yeah, we do.

V: That's about the only thing we really complain about.

(Continued)

M: Yeah. The last couple of nights I tried to take you out to the lake and look at the stars and stuff, so . . .

V: I know.

M: We just need to get used to our schedules.

V: That first week I was so, I was real upset, cause it seemed like all I did was stay home with Stephanie all morning till three and just work all evening. I wasn't doing anything. It didn't seem like we had family gatherings every weekend. We never had time to go out, just the two of us.

M: I got a little surprise for ya next weekend.

V: Yeah, it's always next weekend. It's never this weekend.

M: Eight weekends in a row.

V: I just went from not working at all and being home. We've both been through major job changes and all.

M: And I can't breathe.

V: But we're getting used to it, and I feel so much better about going to work at three, three-thirty now than I did that first week.

M: Um.

V: I just wish I had more time to do what I wanted to do. I, it's just being. . .

M: I'll be able to stay. . .

V: . . . a wife and mother.

M: . . . to stay at home during the days a little bit more or I'll have to go in early, but then I can take a couple of hours off in the afternoons.

V: Do you have to go in early every day?

M: 'Cause there are things I need to do every morning.

V: I think you just like going in to your office.

M: You don't know a thing about it then. Randy was in there early every day, tell me why?

V: Yeah, but he was home at a decent hour, too.

M: He stays out late.

V: Eight to eight or eight to nine every day.

M: Every day.

V: Now, then, I don't want you taking that job. You forget it.

M: No.

Questions

1. What evidence do you find in this transcript that Valerie and Mark have conflict and low levels of marital satisfaction?

2. What evidence do you find that Valerie and Mark have reasonably good marital satisfaction?

3. What recommendations can you offer Valerie and Mark to improve their relationship?

SOURCE: John Gottman and Sybil Carrere, "Welcome to the Love Lab," *Psychology Today,* September/October 2000, pp. 44–45. Reprinted with permission.

WEB CORNER

Dual career couples: www.bigcat.com/dual-career-couples.html

Enhancing the relationship of couples: www.couplebiz.com

Finding love: www.findinglove.com

Free dating service: www.dating.com

Speed dating: www.SpeedDatingSites.Com

▲ REFERENCES

1. Olivia Barker, "No Time for Dating? You're Not Alone," *USA Today,* November 13, 2003, p. 1.

2. David T. Lyken, *Happiness: What Studies on Twins Show Us about Nature, Nurture, and the Happiness Set Point* (New York: Golden Books, 1999), p. 12.

3. The major sources of information for this list are Mihaly Csikzentmihalyi, "Finding Flow," *Psychology Today,* July/August 1997, pp. 46–48, 70–71; Martin Seligman, *What You Can Change and What You Can't* (New York: Knopf, 1994); Richard Corliss, "Is There a Formula for Joy?" *Time,* January 20, 2003, pp. 72–74; Dennis McCafferty, "The Happiest Guy," *USA Weekend,* March 7–9, 2003, pp. 6–8.

4. Survey reported in Jennifer Wirth, "Hubbies Earn More, Study Says," Gannett New Service, October 24, 2003.

5. Lyken, *Happiness,* p. 67.

6. Martin Seligman, "Don't Diet, Be Happy," *USA Weekend,* February 4–6, 1994, p. 12.

7. Steven Reiss, "Secrets of Happiness," *Psychology Today,* January/February 2001, pp. 50–52, 55–56.

8. Corliss, "Is There a Formula for Joy?" p. 74.

9. Quoted in Corliss, "Is There a Formula for Joy?" p. 74.

10. Richard Carlson, *You Can Be Happy No Matter What: Five Principles Your Therapist Never Told You,* rev. ed. (Novato, CA: New World Library, 1997).

11. Ibid., p. 71

12. Jennifer Mulrean, "Can You Find True Love for $25 a Month?" *MSN Money,* syndicated story, May 26, 2003.

13. Cited in Roxanne Roberts, "The Fine Art of Flirting Is Badly in Need of a Renaissance," *Washington Post,* syndicated story, July 18, 2000.

14. Dee Anne Stiles, "8 Secrets to Flirt Effectively," www.match.com, November 22, 2002.

15. Howard Halpern, "Single or Married People Share Same Joys and Problems," syndicated column, November 12, 1988.

16. Dodge Fernald, *Psychology* (Upper Saddle River, NJ: Prentice Hall, 1997), p. 564.

17. Daniel Goleman, "Making a Science of Why We Love Isn't Easy," *New York Times,* syndicated story, July 23, 1986.

18. Ibid.

19. Pam Janis, "The Science of Sex," *USA Weekend,* March 29–31, 1996, pp. 16–17; Theresa Crenshaw, *Guide to the Ingredients in Our Sex Soup* (New York: Putnam, 1996).

20. Jeannette Lauer and Robert Lauer, "Marriages Made to Last," *Psychology Today,* June 1985, p. 24.

21. Psychologists Explore Why Relationships Last," *American Psychological Association Monitor,* October 1997, p. 9.

22. John Gottman and Sybil Carrere, "Welcome to the Love Lab," *Psychology Today,* September/October 2000, pp. 42–43.

23. Andrew Christensen and Neil Jacobensen, *Reconcilable Differences* (New York: Guilford Press, 2000).

24. Laura Doyle, *The Surrendered Wife* (New York: Simon & Schuster, 2001).

25. Data cited in book review by Elaine Hatfield in *Contemporary Psychology,* August 2003, p. 437.

26. Ibid.

27. Harville Hendrix, "Love and Marriage," *Family Circle,* syndicated story, March 17, 1990.

28. Cited in Murray Dubin, "The Knack of Marriage: You Can Learn the Skills, Say Those Rooting for Coupledom," *Philadelphia Inquirer,* syndicated story, August 20, 2000.

29. Research cited in Karen Peterson, "Rose-Colored Glasses Might Help Marriages," Gannett News Service, March 30, 2000.

30. Research cited in Tara Parker-Pope, "Can Eye-Rolling Destroy a Marriage? Researchers Try to Predict Divorce Risk." *Wall Street Journal,* August 6, 2002, p. D1; www.gottman.com.

31. Francesca M. Cancian, *Love in America: Gender and Self-Development* (Cambridge: Cambridge University Press, 1987).

▲ ADDITIONAL READING

Ackerman, Diane. *A Natural History of Love.* New York: Random House, 1994.
Bing, Stanley. *You Look Nice Today.* New York: Bloomsbury, 2003.
Botting, Douglas and Kate Botting. *Sex Appeal: Who Has It, and How to Get It.* New York: St. Martin's Press, 1996.
Csikzentmihalyi, Mihaly. *Finding Flow.* New York: Basic Books/HarperCollins, 1997.
Harvey, John, and Amy Wenzel. *Close Romantic Relationship: Maintenance and Enhancement.* Mahwah, NJ: Erlbaum, 2001.
Kirchler, Erich, Christa, Rodler, Erick, Holzl, and Katja Meier. *Conflict and Decision-Making in Close Relationships: Love, Money, and Daily Routine.* Philadelphia: Psychology Press, 2001.
McBride, James Dabbs with Mary Godwin Dabbs. *Heroes, Rogues, and Lovers: Testosterone and Behavior.* New York: McGraw-Hill, 2000.
Opdyke. Jeff D. *Love & Money.* New York: John Wiley, 2004.
Schenebly, Lee. *Nurturing Yourself and Others: Learn How to Fill Your Life with Happiness.* Cambridge, MA: Fisher, 2000.
Stone, Douglas, Bruce Patton, and Shelia Heen. *Difficult Conversations: How to Talk about What Matters Most.* New York: Viking, 1999.

GLOSSARY

Achievement need   The need to accomplish something difficult, to win over others.

Action plan   A description of how a person is going to reach a goal.

Active listener   A person who listens intensely, with the goal of empathizing with the speaker.

Addiction (substance dependence)   A compulsion to use substances or engage in activities that lead to psychological dependence and withdrawal symptoms when use is discontinued.

Aggressive   Being obnoxious and overbearing.

Aggressive personality   A person who verbally and sometimes physically attacks others frequently.

Anger   A feeling of extreme hostility, indignation, or exasperation.

Anxiety   A feeling of distress or uneasiness caused by fear of an imagined problem.

Assertive   To state clearly what you want or how you feel in a given situation without being abusive, abrasive, or obnoxious.

Backstabbing   An attempt to discredit by underhanded means, such as innuendo, accusation, or the like.

Balance theory   An explanation of attraction stating that people prefer relationships that are consistent or balanced.

Behavior   The tangible acts or decisions of people, including both their actions and their words.

Behavior modification   A system of motivating people that emphasizes rewarding them for doing the right things and punishing them for doing the wrong things.

Behavioral interview   A job interview in which the candidate is asked how he or she handled a particular problem in the past.

Bicultural identities   The fact that many people identify with their primary culture and another culture.

Body image   Your perception of your body.

Body mass index   An estimation of body fat based on a person's height and weight.

Brainstorming   A technique by which group members think of multiple solutions to a problem.

Brainwriting (solo brainstorming)   Arriving at creative ideas by jotting them down yourself.

Budget   A plan for spending money to improve your chances of using your money wisely and not spending more than your net income.

Burnout   A condition of emotional, mental, and physical exhaustion along with cynicism in response to long-term job stressors.

Business etiquette   A special code of behavior required in work settings.

Cannabis   A class of drugs derived from the hemp plant that generally produce a state of mild euphoria.

Career   A series of related job experiences that fit into a meaningful pattern.

Career counselor   A specialist whose professional role is to provide counseling and guidance to individuals about their careers.

Career path   A sequence of positions necessary to achieve a goal.

Career portability   The ability to move from one employer to another when necessary.

Career success   Attaining the twin goals of organizational rewards and personal satisfaction.

Carpal tunnel syndrome   A condition that occurs when repetitive flexing and extension of the wrist causes the tendons to swell, thus trapping and pinching the median nerve.

Character   Doing the right things despite outside pressures to do the opposite.

Charisma   A type of charm and magnetism that inspires others.

Chronological résumé   A job résumé that presents work experience, education, and interests, along with accomplishments, in reverse chronological order.

Cognitive restructuring   A way of dealing with conflict in which you mentally convert negative aspects into positive ones by looking for the positive elements in a situation.

Cognitive skills   Problem-solving and intellectual skills.

Cognitive styles   Modes of problem solving.

Communication   The sending and receiving of messages.

Communication overload   A condition that occurs when people are so overloaded with information that they cannot respond effectively to messages.

Concentrate on one bill at a time   A technique of debt reduction by which you pay off your smallest debt with a variable payment and then concentrate successively on your next-smallest debts.

Conflict   A condition that exists when two sets of demands, goals, or motives are incompatible.

Confrontation and problem solving   A method of identifying the true source of conflict and resolving it systematically.

Contrary investing   The principle of buying investments when the demand for them is very low and selling when the demand is very high.

Core competency   With respect to a person, whatever he or she does best.

Creative-style résumé   A job résumé with a novel format and design.

Creativity   The ability to develop good ideas that can be put into practice.

Cultural sensitivity   An awareness of and a willingness to investigate the reasons people of another culture act as they do.

Cultural training   A set of learning experiences designed to help employees understand the customs, traditions, and beliefs of another culture.

Culture   A learned and shared system of knowledge, beliefs, values, attitudes, and norms.

Customer service orientation   Thoughts and actions geared toward helping customers.

Debit card   A bank card that instantly transfers money from your bank account to the account of a merchant.

Decision making   Choosing one alternative from the various alternative solutions that can be pursued.

Decoding   The process of the receiver interpreting the message and translating it into meaningful information.

Defensive communication   The tendency to receive messages in such a way that our self-esteem is protected.

Denial   The suppression of information we find uncomfortable.

Depressant   A drug that slows down vital body processes.

Depression   A widespread emotional disorder in which the person has such difficulties as sadness, changes in appetite, sleeping difficulties, and a decrease in activities, interests, and energy.

Developmental opportunity   A positive way of stating that a person has a weakness (or a need for improvement).

Disarm the opposition   A method of conflict resolution in which you disarm the criticizer by agreeing with a valid criticism directed toward you.

Diversity training   A program that attempts to bring about workplace harmony by teaching people how to get along with diverse work associates.

Dollar-cost averaging   An investment technique in which you spend the same amount of money to purchase shares in a stock or mutual fund at regular intervals over a long period of time.

Dopamine   A neurotransmitter that is associated with pleasure and elation. (A neurotransmitter is a molecule that transports messages from one neuron in the brain to another over a synapse.)

Downshifter   A worker who chooses shorter hours and less demanding work to allow more time for other activities.

Downsizing (rightsizing)   A method of reducing the number of employees to save money and improve efficiency.

Effectiveness   In relation to leadership, helping group members accomplish their objectives without neglecting satisfaction and morale.

Effectiveness ethic   A focus on the need for excellent work and doing work the best way.

Emotional intelligence   Qualities such as understanding your feelings, empathy for others, and the regulation of emotion to enhance living.

Emotional labor   The process of regulating both feelings and expressions to meet organizational goals.

Empathy   Understanding another person's point of view.

Encoding   The process of organizing ideas into a series of symbols, such as words and gestures, designed to communicate with the receiver.

Ethics   The study of moral obligation or separating right from wrong.

Ethnocentrism   The assumption that the ways of one's culture are the *best* ways of doing things.

Expectancy theory of motivation   An explanation of motivation stating that people will be motivated if they believe that their efforts will lead to desired outcomes.

External locus of control   A belief that external forces control your fate.

Fear of success   The belief that if you succeed at an important task, you will be asked to take on more responsibility in the future.

Feedback   Information that tells you how well you have performed.

Fight-or-flight response   The body's battle against a stressor that helps you deal with emergencies.

Flow experience   Total absorption in your work.

Forced-association technique   The process of individuals or groups solving a problem by making associations between the properties of two objects.

Functional résumé   A job résumé that organizes your skills and accomplishments into the functions or tasks that support the job you are seeking.

Galeta effect   Improving your performance through raising your own expectations.

Generalized anxiety disorder   A persistent undercurrent of "free-floating" (not linked to a specific source) anxiety.

Glass ceiling   An invisible but difficult-to-penetrate barrier to promotion based on subtle attitudes and prejudices.

Goal   An event, circumstance, object, condition, or purpose for which a person strives. Also, a conscious intention to do something.

Grazing   Popular term for eating meals on the run to make use of time ordinarily spent sitting down for meals.

Grievance procedure   The formal process of filing a complaint and resolving a dispute within an organization.

Group norms   The unwritten set of expectations for group members—what people ought to do.

Hallucinogens   A class of drugs that in small doses produce visual effects similar to hallucinations.

Human relations   The art of using systematic knowledge about human behavior to improve personal, job, and career effectiveness.

Individual retirement account (IRA)   A supplemental retirement account, fully funded by the individual, that qualifies for certain tax advantages.

Information (communication) overload   A condition in which the individual is confronted with so much information to process that he or she becomes overwhelmed and therefore does a poor job of processing information.

Insight   An ability to know what information is relevant, find connections between the old and the new, combine facts that are unrelated, and see "the big picture."

Internal locus of control   A belief that fate is pretty much under your control.

Internet dependence (addiction)   A condition in which a person spends so much time on the Internet that other work suffers and the person experiences sleep deprivation and neglects human contact.

Interpersonal   Anything relating to the interactions between and among people.

Intrinsic motivation   The natural tendency to seek out novelty and challenges, to extend one's capacities, to explore, and to learn.

Intuition   An experienced-based way of knowing or reasoning in which weighing and balancing of evidence are done automatically.

Job objective   The position you are applying for now or a job you intend to hold in the future.

Job shadowing   A way of gaining information about an occupation by spending a few hours with a professional in the workplace and observing firsthand what the job entails.

Jury of peers   A grievance procedure whereby unresolved grievances are submitted to a panel of coworkers.

Kaizen   The relentless quest for a better way of working and higher-quality work.

Lateral move   Transferring to a job at the same level and approximate salary as your present one.

Lateral thinking   Thought process whereby an individual seeks out many alternative solutions to a problem.

Leadership   The process of bringing about positive changes and influencing others to achieve worthwhile goals.

Lifestyle   In terms of making a career choice, the pattern by which a person invests energy into work and nonwork.

Liquid assets   Assets that can be converted into cash relatively quickly.

Maslow's need hierarchy   A widely accepted theory of motivation emphasizing that people strive to fulfill needs. These needs are arranged in a hierarchy of importance—physiological, safety, belongingness, esteem, and self-actualization. People tend to strive for need satisfaction at one level only after satisfaction has been achieved at the previous one.

Meditation   A systematic method of concentration, reflection, or concentrated thinking designed to suppress the activity of the sympathetic nervous system.

Mentor   A more experienced person who guides, teaches, and coaches another individual.

Metacommunicate   Communicating about the conflicting part of your communications to help overcome barriers or resolve a problem.

Microinequity   A small, semiconscious message we send with a powerful impact on the receiver.

Micromanagement   The close monitoring of most aspects of group member activities by the manager.

Mirroring   A form of nonverbal communication in which one person subtly imitates another, such as following the other person's breathing pattern.

Mixed signals   Sending different messages about the same topic to different audiences.

Motive   An inner drive that moves a person to do something.

Multicultural worker   One who can work effectively with people of different cultures.

Narcotic   A drug that dulls the senses, facilitates sleep, and is addictive with long-term use.

Need   An internal striving or urge to do something. (Or a deficit within an individual that creates a craving for its satisfaction.)

Need for intimacy   An explanation of love centering on the idea that people crave intimacy.

Negative affectivity   A tendency to experience aversive (intensely disliked) emotional states.

Negotiation and bargaining   Conferring with another person to resolve a problem.

Networking   The process of establishing a group of contacts who can help you in your career.

Net worth   The difference between your assets and liabilities.

Neurobiological disorders   A quirk in the chemistry or anatomy of the brain that creates a disability.

Noise   An unwanted interference that can distort or block a message.

Nonassertive   A passive type of behavior in which people let things happen to them without letting their feelings be known.

Nonpossessive relationship   A relationship in which both people maintain separate identities and strive for personal fulfillment.

Nonverbal communication   Sending messages other than by direct use of words, such as in writing and speaking with gestures.

Nonverbal feedback   The signs other than words that indicate whether the sender's message has been delivered.

Openness to experience   A positive orientation toward learning.

Organizational citizenship behavior   The willingness to work for the good of the organization even without the promise of a specific reward.

Organizational culture   The values and beliefs of the firm that guide people's actions.

Paradigm   A model, framework, viewpoint, or perspective.

Paraphrase   In listening, to repeat in your own words what the sender says, feels, and means.

Participative leader   A person in charge who shares power and decision making with the group.

Partnership   In leadership, when the leader and group members are connected in such a way the power between them is approximately balanced.

Peak performance   The mental state necessary for achieving maximum results from minimum effort.

Peer evaluations   A system in which coworkers contribute to an evaluation of a group member's job performance.

Perfectionism   A pattern of behavior in which the individual strives to accomplish almost unattainable standards of flawless work.

Performance standard   A statement of what constitutes acceptable performance.

Personal communication style   Your unique approach to sending and receiving information.

Personality clash   An antagonistic relationship between two people based on differences in personal attributes, preferences, interests, values, and styles.

Planning   Deciding what needs to be accomplished and the actions needed to make it happen.

Political skills   An interpersonal style that combines awareness of others with the ability to communicate well.

Portfolio career   A career in which people use a variety of skills to earn money in several different ways.

Positive mental attitude   A strong belief that things will work in your favor.

Positive reinforcement   Rewarding somebody for doing something right.

Positive self-talk   Saying positive things about yourself to yourself to build self-confidence.

Positive visual imagery   Picturing a positive outcome in your mind.

Private self   The actual person that you may be.

Proactive personality   A person relatively unconstrained by forces in the situation and who brings about environmental change.

Problem   A gap between what exists and what you want to exist.

Procrastination   Putting off a task for no valid reason.

Productivity   The amount of quality work accomplished in relation to the resources consumed.

Psychotherapy   A method of overcoming emotional problems through discussion with a mental health professional.

Public self   What the person is communicating about himself or herself and what others actually perceive about the person.

Pygmalion effect   The mysterious phenomenon that occurs when group members succeed because their leader expects them to (i.e., a group tends to live up to the leader's expectations).

Quest fatigue   The demoralization and disappointment that takes place when all your efforts at finding a date or mate fail.

Realistic goal   One that represents the right amount of challenge for the person pursuing the goal.

REIT (real estate investment trust)   A pooling of many people's money to invest in real estate or mortgages.

Relaxation response   A bodily reaction in which the person experiences a slower respiration and heart rate, lowered blood pressure, and lowered metabolism.

Resilience   The ability to withstand pressure and emerge stronger for it.

Role ambiguity   A condition in which a jobholder receives confusing or poorly defined expectations.

Role conflict   The state that occurs when a person has to choose between two competing demands or expectations.

Role confusion   Uncertainty about the role you are carrying out. For example, socializing with your boss may create fuzzy demarcation lines at work.

Role overload   A burdensome workload that can lead to stress.

Role underload   Having too little to do.

Seasonal affective disorder (SAD)   A form of depression that develops during the fall and winter months and disappears as the days lengthen in the spring.

Schmoozing   Informal socializing on the job.

Self   A person's total being or individuality.

Self-concept   The way a person thinks about himself or herself in an overall sense.

Self-defeating behavior   A behavior pattern in which the person intentionally or unintentionally engages in activities or harbors attitudes that work against his or her best interests.

Self-discipline   The ability to work systematically and progressively toward a goal until it is achieved.

Self-disclosure   The process of revealing your inner self to others.

Self-efficacy   Confidence in your ability to carry out a specific task in contrast to generalized self-confidence.

Self-esteem   The experience of feeling competent to cope with the basic challenges in life and of being worthy of happiness.

Self-respect   How you think and feel about yourself.

Self-understanding   Knowledge about yourself, particularly with respect to mental and emotional aspects.

Sensitivity   Taking people's needs and feelings into account when dealing with them.

Servant leader   One who serves group members by working on their behalf to help them achieve goals, not the leader's goals.

Sexual harassment   Unwanted sexually oriented behavior in the workplace that results in discomfort and/or interference with the job.

Simplified employee plan (SEP)   Retirement plans for individuals who are self-employed or for those who earn part of their income from self-employment.

Skill   A learned, specific ability to perform a task competently, such as writing a report.

Skill-benefit statement   A brief explanation of how your skills can benefit the company.

Social exchange theory   The idea that human relationships are based mainly on self-interest; therefore, people measure their social, physical, and other assets against a potential partner's.

Stimulants   A class of drugs that produce feelings of optimism and high energy.

Stress   An internal reaction to any force that threatens to disturb a person's equilibrium.

Stressor   The external or internal force that brings about the stress.

Strong Interest Inventory (SII)   The most widely used instrument for matching a person's interests with careers.

Style   A person's characteristic way of doing things.

Success syndrom   A pattern in which the worker performs one assignment well and then has the confidence to take on even more difficult assignments.

Supplemental retirement annuities (SRAs)   Fixed and variable tax-deferred annuities that enable you to invest money through your employer's payroll retirement system on a pretax basis.

Support system   A group of people a person can rely on for encouragement and comfort.

Targeted résumé   A job résumé that focuses on a specific job target or position and presents only information about you that supports the target.

Team leader   A person who facilitates and guides the efforts of a small group that is given some authority to govern itself.

Team player   A person who emphasizes group accomplishment and cooperation rather than individual achievement and not helping others.

Telecommuter   An employee who works at home full time or part time and sends output electronically to a central office.

Telesearch   Obtaining job leads by making unsolicited phone calls to prospective employers.

Time leak   Anything you are doing or not doing that allows time to get away from you.

Traditional mental set   A fixed way of thinking about objects and activities.

Trust   A person's confidence in another individual's intentions and motives.

Type A behavior   A demanding, impatient, and overstriving pattern of behavior also characterized by free-floating hostility.

Unsolicited-letter or e-mail campaign   Writing directly to a company that you would like to work for.

Value   The importance a person attaches to something that serves as a guide to action.

Vertical thinking   An analytical, logical thought process that results in few answers.

Wellness   A formalized approach to preventive health care.

Win-win   The belief that, after conflict has been resolved, both sides should gain something of value.

Workaholicism   An addiction to work in which not working is an uncomfortable experience.

Work ethic   A firm belief in the dignity and value of work.

Work–family conflict   A situation that occurs when the individual has to perform multiple roles: worker, spouse or partner, and often parent.

Work habits   A person's characteristic approach to work, including such things as organization, priority setting, and handling of paperwork and e-mail.

Worst-case scenario   The dreadful alternative in a decision-making situation.

INDEX